Lecture Notes in Computer Science 3531

Commenced Publication in 1973
Founding and Former Series Editors:
Gerhard Goos, Juris Hartmanis, and Jan van Leeuwen

John Ioannidis   Angelos Keromytis
Moti Yung (Eds.)

Applied Cryptography and Network Security

Third International Conference, ACNS 2005
New York, NY, USA, June 7-10, 2005
Proceedings

 Springer

Volume Editors

John Ioannidis
Columbia University
Center for Computational Learning Systems
NY, USA
E-mail: ji@cs.columbia.edu

Angelos Keromytis
Moti Yung
Columbia University
Department of Computer Science
NY, USA
E-mail: {angelos,moti}@cs.columbia.edu

Library of Congress Control Number: 2005926829

CR Subject Classification (1998): E.3, C.2, D.4.6, H.3-4, K.4.4, K.6.5

ISSN   0302-9743
ISBN-10   3-540-26223-7 Springer Berlin Heidelberg New York
ISBN-13   978-3-540-26223-7 Springer Berlin Heidelberg New York

Springer is a part of Springer Science+Business Media

springeronline.com

© Springer-Verlag Berlin Heidelberg 2005
Printed in Germany

Typesetting: Camera-ready by author, data conversion by Olgun Computergrafik
Printed on acid-free paper   SPIN: 11496137   06/3142   5 4 3 2 1 0

Preface

The 3rd International Conference on Applied Cryptography and Network Security (ACNS 2005) was sponsored and organized by ICISA (the International Communications and Information Security Association). It was held at Columbia University in New York, USA, June 7–10, 2005. This conference proceedings volume contains papers presented in the academic/research track.

ACNS covers a large number of research areas that have been gaining importance in recent years due to the development of the Internet, wireless communication and the increased global exposure of computing resources. The papers in this volume are representative of the state of the art in security and cryptography research, worldwide.

The Program Committee of the conference received a total of 158 submissions from all over the world, of which 35 submissions were selected for presentation at the academic track. In addition to this track, the conference also hosted a technical/ industrial/ short papers track whose presentations were also carefully selected from among the submissions. All submissions were reviewed by experts in the relevant areas.

Many people and organizations helped in making the conference a reality. We would like to take this opportunity to thank the Program Committee members and the external experts for their invaluable help in producing the conference's program. We also wish to thank Michael E. Locasto for his help in all technical and technological aspects of running the conference and Sophie Majewski for the administrative support in organizing the conference. We wish to thank the graduate students at Columbia University's Computer Science Department who helped us as well.

We wish to acknowledge the financial support of our sponsors, and their employees who were instrumental in the sponsorship process: Morgan Stanley (Ben Fried) and Gemplus (David Naccache).

Finally, we would like to thank all the authors who submitted papers to the conference; the continued support of the security and cryptography research community worldwide is what really enabled us to have this conference.

May 2005

John Ioannidis
Angelos Keromytis
Moti Yung

ACNS 2005

3rd International Conference on Applied Cryptography and Network Security

New York, USA
June 7–10, 2005

Sponsored and organized by the
International Communications and Information Security Association (ICISA)

In coöperation with
Columbia University, USA

General Chair

John Ioannidis .... Columbia University

Program Chairs

Moti Yung .... Columbia University and RSA Labs
Angelos Keromytis .... Columbia University

Program Committee

Scott Alexander .... Telcordia, USA
Tuomas Aura .... Microsoft Research, UK
David Brumley .... CMU, USA
Ran Canetti .... IBM Research, USA
Marc Dacier .... Eurecom, France
Ed Dawson .... Queensland University of Technology, Australia
Glenn Durfee .... PARC, USA
Virgil Gligor .... University of Maryland, USA
Peter Gutman .... University of Auckland, New Zealand
Goichiro Hanaoka .... National Institute of Advanced Industrial Science
                                                    and Technology (AIST), Japan
Amir Herzberg .... Bar Ilan University, Israel
Russ Housley .... Vigilsec, USA
John Ioannidis .... Columbia University, USA
Sotiris Ioannidis .... University of Pennsylvania, USA

External Reviewers

Table of Contents

Two-Server Password-Only Authenticated Key Exchange

Jonathan Katz[1,*], Philip MacKenzie[2], Gelareh Taban[3], and Virgil Gligor[3]

[1] Dept. of Computer Science, University of Maryland
jkatz@cs.umd.edu
[2] DoCoMo USA Labs, USA
philmac@docomolabs-usa.com
[3] Dept. of Electrical and Computer Engineering, University of Maryland
{gelareh,gligor}@eng.umd.edu

Abstract. Typical protocols for password-based authentication assume a single server which stores all the information (e.g., the password) necessary to authenticate a user. Unfortunately, an inherent limitation of this approach (assuming low-entropy passwords are used) is that the user's password is exposed if this server is ever compromised. To address this issue, a number of schemes have been proposed in which a user's password information is shared among multiple servers, and these servers cooperate in a threshold manner when the user wants to authenticate. We show here a two-server protocol for this task assuming public parameters available to everyone in the system (as well as the adversary). Ours is the first provably-secure two-server protocol for the important *password-only* setting (in which the user need remember only a password, and not the servers' public keys), and is the first two-server protocol (in any setting) with a proof of security in the standard model.

1 Introduction

A well-known fact in the context of designing authentication systems is that human users/clients typically choose "weak", low-entropy passwords from a relatively small space of possibilities. Unfortunately, protocols designed and proven secure for the case when clients use *cryptographic* (i.e., high-entropy) secrets are generally insecure when passwords (i.e., low-entropy secrets) are used instead; this is so because these protocols are typically not resistant to *off-line dictionary attacks* in which an eavesdropping adversary derives information about the password from observed transcripts of login sessions. In recent years, much attention has focused on designing password-based authenticated key-exchange protocols resistant to such attacks. (We remark that *on-line dictionary attacks* – in which an adversary simply attempts to log-in repeatedly, trying each possible password – cannot be prevented by cryptographic means but can be dealt with using other methods outside the scope of this work.)

---

* Supported by NSF CAREER award 0447075 and Trusted Computing grant 0310751.

J. Ioannidis, A. Keromytis, and M.Yung (Eds.): ACNS 2005, LNCS 3531, pp. 1–16, 2005.
© Springer-Verlag Berlin Heidelberg 2005

Means of protecting against off-line dictionary attacks in a single-server setting were first suggested by Gong, et al. [23] in a "hybrid", PKI-based model in which users are assumed to know the server's public key in addition to a password. Bellovin and Merritt [5] were the first to suggest protocols for what we term *password-only authenticated key exchange* (PAKE), where the clients are required to "store" (i.e., remember) *only* a short password and no additional information. These initial works (and others [6, 25, 30, 38]) were relatively informal and did not provide definitions or proofs of security. More recently, formal definitions and provably-secure protocols for the "hybrid" model have been given [7, 24], followed soon thereafter by formal models for the password-only setting [1, 8, 22] and associated protocols with proofs of security in the random oracle/ideal cipher models[1] [1, 8, 31] and in the standard model [20, 22, 27, 28]. (The protocols of [20, 27, 28] assume some public information which is available to all parties. Note, however, that since this information can be hard-coded into implementations of the protocol, clients do not need to memorize or store any high-entropy, cryptographic information as they are required to do in the PKI-based setting.)

Although the above protocols protect against off-line dictionary attacks, they do nothing to mitigate the concern that an adversary might obtain users' passwords via *server compromise*. Such attacks represent a serious threat since they are potentially cost-effective (in that an adversary might be able to obtain thousands of users' passwords by corrupting a single, poorly-protected server) and users frequently utilize the same password at multiple sites. Unfortunately, it is easy to show the *impossibility* of protecting against server compromise when a single server holds the necessary information to authenticate a user (assuming the only secret information held by the user is a low-entropy password). To protect against server compromise, Ford and Kaliski [19] thus proposed a *threshold* protocol in the PKI-based model, in which the authentication functionality is distributed across n servers who must all cooperate to authenticate a user. Their protocol remains secure (and, in particular, an adversary learns nothing about users' passwords other than what it learns from its on-line password guesses) as long as $n - 1$ or fewer servers are compromised. Jablon [26] subsequently suggested a protocol with similar functionality in the password-only setting. Neither of these works, however, include rigorous definitions or proofs of security.

A number of provably-secure protocols for threshold password-based authentication have recently appeared. We summarize what is known:

○ MacKenzie, et al. [35] showed a protocol in the "hybrid", PKI-based setting which requires only t (out of n) servers to cooperate in order to authenticate a user, for any values of t, n (of course, security is only obtained as long as $t - 1$ or fewer servers are compromised). They prove security for their protocol in the random oracle model.

---

[1] In the random oracle model [2], parties are assumed to have "black-box" access to a random function. (The ideal cipher model assumes that parties have "black-box" access to a random keyed permutation, an even stronger assumption.) In practice, the random oracle is instantiated with a cryptographic hash function. It is known [10], however, that protocols secure in the random oracle model may not be secure for *any* choice of hash function.

○ Di Raimondo and Gennaro [16] proposed a protocol in the password-only setting with a proof of security in the standard model. (A second protocol given
in their paper, which we will not discuss further, achieves the weaker functionality in which the same session key is computed by all servers.) However,
their protocol requires less than $1/3$ of the servers to be compromised (i.e.,
they require $n > 3t$) and thus does not give a solution for the two-server case[2].
We remark that, in general, threshold cryptosystems for the two-party case
do not follow immediately from threshold solutions for the case of general n;
see, e.g., the work of [17, 21, 32–34] in this regard.

○ Brainard, et al. [9] have developed a two-server protocol (called "Nightingale"
and being shipped by RSA Security), a variant of which has been proven secure in the random oracle model [37]. These protocols assume the PKI-based
setting: as stated in the papers, the protocols assume a "secure channel" between the client and the server(s) which would in practice be implemented
using public-key techniques such as SSL.

1.1 Our Contributions

We show here a two-server protocol for password-only authenticated key exchange, with proof of security in the standard model. Ours is the first *provably-
secure* two-server protocol in the password-only setting, and is the first two-server
protocol (in any setting) with a proof of security in the standard model.

Our protocol extends and builds upon the (non-threshold) protocol of Katz-
Ostrovsky-Yung [28] and a more efficient variant of this protocol – called, for
brevity, KOY* – described by Canetti, *et al.* [11] (we also introduce an additional modification that makes the protocol even more efficient). In Section 3
we describe a "basic" two-server protocol which is secure against a passive (i.e.,
"honest-but-curious") adversary who has access to the entire state of one of the
servers throughout its execution of the protocol, but cannot cause this server to
deviate from its prescribed behavior. We believe this protocol is interesting in
its own right (when the assumption on adversarial behavior is warranted), and
anyway the basic protocol and its proof of security serve as a useful prelude to
our second result. In Section 4 we show how to modify the basic protocol so as to
achieve security against an *active* adversary who may arbitrarily deviate from the
protocol. The changes we make consist of having the servers (efficiently) prove
to each other that their computations were performed according to the protocol.
Here, we make use of techniques developed by MacKenzie [32] for performing
these proofs efficiently even in a concurrent setting.

The protocols we construct are relatively efficient. Each party in the basic
two-server protocol performs roughly twice the amount of work as in the KOY*
protocol. For the protocol secure against active adversaries, the work of the client
stays the same but the work of the servers increases by a factor of roughly 2–4.

---

[2] The approach in their paper does not extend to the case $t \geq n/3$. The authors
mention (without details) that "[i]t is possible to improve the fault-tolerance to
$t < n/2 \ldots$", but even this would not imply a two-server solution.

2   Definitions and Preliminaries

We assume the reader is familiar with the model of [1] (building on [3, 4])
for password-based key exchange in the single-server case. Here, we generalize
their model and present formal definitions for the case of two-server protocols.
While the model presented here is largely equivalent to the model proposed
by MacKenzie, et al. [35] (with the main difference that we do not assume a
PKI), we can simplify matters a bit since we focus on the two-server setting
exclusively. For convenience we describe the model for the case of a "passive"
adversary first and then discuss briefly the modifications needed in the case
of "active" adversaries. (As discussed below, in both the "passive" and "active"
cases the adversary is free to interfere with all communication between the client
and the servers. These cases only differ in the power of the adversary to control
the actions of the corrupted servers: specifically, a "passive" adversary is unable
to control the actions of corrupted servers, whereas a "active" adversary can.)

   We first present a general overview of the system as we imagine it. For simplicity only, we assume that every client C in the system shares its password pw
with exactly two servers A and B. In this case we say that servers A and B are
associated with C. (Note that a single server may be associated with multiple
clients.) In addition to holding password shares, these servers may also be provisioned with arbitrary other information which is *not* stored by C. Any such
information is assumed to be provisioned by some incorruptible, central mechanism (a system administrator, say) at the outset of the protocol. Note that
this does *not* represent an additional assumption or restriction in practice: the
servers *must* minimally be provisioned with correct password shares anyway, and
there is no reason why additional information cannot be provided to the servers
at that time (in particular, the servers' password shares are already high-entropy
values, and the servers have no restriction – as the client does – on the amount
of information they can store). An (honest) execution of a password-based key-
exchange protocol between client C and associated servers A and B should result
in the client holding independent session keys $\mathsf{sk}_{C,A}, \mathsf{sk}_{C,B}$, and servers A and B
holding $\mathsf{sk}_{A,C}$ and $\mathsf{sk}_{B,C}$, respectively, with $\mathsf{sk}_{C,A} = \mathsf{sk}_{A,C}$ and $\mathsf{sk}_{C,B} = \mathsf{sk}_{B,C}$.

2.1   Passive Adversaries

We first describe the adversarial model under consideration. We assume an adversary who corrupts some servers at the outset of the protocol, such that for any
client C at most one of the servers associated with C is corrupted. In the case
of a passive adversary, a corrupted server continues to operate according to the
protocol, but the adversary may monitor its internal state. Following [16, 35],
we make the (largely conceptual) assumption that there exists a single *gateway*
which is the only entity that *directly* communicates with the clients. This gateway essentially acts as a "router", splitting messages from the clients to each of
the two associated servers and aggregating messages from these servers to the
client; we also allow the gateway to perform some simple, publicly-computable
operations. Introduction of this gateway is not strictly necessary; however, it

enables a simplification of the formal model and also provides a straightforward way to quantify the number of on-line attacks made by an adversary.

During the course of the protocol, then, there may potentially be three types of communication: between the clients and the gateway, between the servers and the gateway, and between the servers themselves. We assume the adversary has the ability to eavesdrop on all of these. We further assume that the client-gateway communication is under the full control of the adversary, and thus the adversary can send messages of its choice to either of these entities, or may tamper with, delay, refuse to deliver, etc. any messages sent between clients and the gateway. On the other hand, in the case of a passive adversary we assume that the server-gateway and server-server communication is determined entirely by the protocol itself (i.e., a corrupted server follows the protocol exactly as specified)[3]. In addition, the adversary is assumed to see the entire internal state of any corrupted servers throughout their execution of the protocol. With the above in mind, we proceed to the formal definitions.

Participants, passwords, and initialization. We assume a fixed set of protocol participants (also called principals) each of which is either a client $C \in$ Client or a server $S \in$ Server, where Client and Server are disjoint. Each $C \in$ Client is assumed to have a password pw_C chosen uniformly and independently from a "dictionary" of size N [4]. (In fact, we further simplify matters and assume that passwords are chosen from the set $\{1, \ldots, N\}$.) As noted earlier, we make the simplifying assumption that each client shares his password with exactly two other servers (and no more). If client C shares his password with the distinct servers A, B, then A (resp., B) holds a *password share* $pw_{C,A}$ (resp., $pw_{C,B}$); the mechanism for generating these shares depends on the protocol itself. We also allow each server to hold information in addition to these password shares. For example, as described in footnote 3, two servers associated with a particular client may be provisioned with a shared, symmetric key. As we have already discussed, the initialization phase during which this information is provisioned is assumed to be carried out by some trusted authority. Any information stored by a corrupted server is available to the adversary.

In general, additional information can be generated during the initialization phase. For example, in the "hybrid" password/PKI model [7, 24] public/secret key pairs are generated for each server and the secret key is given as input to the appropriate server, while the public key is provided to the appropriate client(s). For the protocol presented here, we require only the weaker requirement of a single set of public parameters which is provided to all parties.

---

[3] For the case of a passive adversary, the assumption that the adversary cannot tamper with the server-server communication is easy to realize via standard use of message authentication codes or signatures (as the servers can store long-term keys for this purpose). The assumption that the adversary cannot tamper with the server-gateway communication is essentially for convenience/definitional purposes only, as the adversary can anyway tamper with client-gateway communication (and the gateway processes messages in a well-defined and predictable way).

[4] As in other work, though, our proof of security may be adapted to handle arbitrary dictionaries and arbitrary distributions over these dictionaries.

Execution of the protocol. In the real world, a protocol determines how principals behave in response to input from their environment. In the formal model, these inputs are provided by the adversary. Each principal is assumed to be able to execute the protocol multiple times (possibly concurrently) with different partners; this is modeled by allowing each principal to have an unlimited number of *instances* [1, 4] with which to execute the protocol. We denote instance i of principal U as Π_U^i. A given instance may be used only once. The adversary is given oracle access to these different instances; furthermore, each instance maintains (local) state which is updated during the course of the experiment. In particular, each instance Π_U^i has associated with it the following variables, initialized as NULL or FALSE (as appropriate) during the initialization phase:

- sid_U^i, pid_U^i, and sk_U^i are variables containing the *session id*, *partner id*, and *session key(s)* for an instance, respectively. A client's partner id will be a set of two servers; a server's partner id will be a single client (viewed as a set for notational convenience). For C a client, sk_C^i consists of a pair $\mathsf{sk}_{C,A}^i, \mathsf{sk}_{C,B}^i$, where these are the keys shared with servers A and B, respectively. A server instance Π_S^i with partner C has only a single session key $\mathsf{sk}_{S,C}^i$.
- term_U^i and acc_U^i are boolean variables denoting whether a given instance has terminated or accepted, respectively. state_U^i records any state necessary for execution of the protocol by Π_U^i.

As highlighted earlier, the adversary is assumed to have complete control over all communication between the client and the gateway. This is modeled via access to *oracles* which are essentially as in [1] and are described formally in the full version of this paper. Briefly, these include various Send oracles modeling "active" attacks in which the adversary tampers with communication between the client and the servers; an Execute oracle modeling passive eavesdropping attacks; a Reveal oracle which models possible leakage of session keys; and a Test oracle used to define security.

Sessions ids, partnering, correctness, and freshness. Session ids in our protocol are defined in a natural way, which then allows us to define notions of partnering, correctness, and freshness. Due to lack of space the details appear in the full version.

Advantage of the adversary. Informally, the adversary succeeds if it can guess the bit b used by the Test oracle on a "fresh" instance associated with a non-corrupted participant. Formally, we say an adversary A *succeeds* if it makes a single query $\mathsf{Test}(U, U', i)$ regarding a fresh key $\mathsf{sk}_{U,U'}^i$, and outputs a single bit b' with $b' = b$ (recall that b is the bit chosen by the Test oracle). We denote this event by Succ. Note that restricting the adversary to making its Test query regarding a fresh key is necessary for a meaningful definition of security. The advantage of adversary A in attacking protocol P is then given by:

$$\mathsf{Adv}_{A,P}(k) \stackrel{\text{def}}{=} 2 \cdot \Pr[\mathsf{Succ}] - 1,$$

where the probability is taken over the random coins used by the adversary as well as the random coins used during the course of the experiment.

It remains to define a secure protocol, as a PPT adversary can always succeed by trying all passwords one-by-one in an on-line impersonation attack. Informally, a protocol is secure if this is the best an adversary can do. Formally, we define in the full version what it means for an instance to represent an *on-line attack* (which, in particular, will not include instances used in Execute queries). The number of on-line attacks bounds the number of passwords the adversary could have tried in an on-line fashion, motivating the following definition:

Definition 1. *Protocol P is a* secure two-server protocol for password-only authenticated key-exchange *if there exists a constant c such that, for all dictionary sizes N and for all* PPT *adversaries A making at most $Q(k)$ on-line attacks and corrupting at most one server associated with each client, there exists a negligible function $\varepsilon(\cdot)$ such that $\mathsf{Adv}_{A,P}(k) \leq c \cdot Q(k)/N + \varepsilon(k)$.*

Of course, we would optimally like to achieve $c = 1$; however, as in previous definitions and protocols [1, 22, 38] we will allow $c \neq 1$ as well. The proof of security for our protocol shows that we achieve $c = 2$, indicating that the adversary can (essentially) do no better than guess *two* passwords during each on-line attack.

Explicit mutual authentication. The above definition captures the requirement of *implicit* authentication only (and the protocol we present here achieves only implicit authentication). Using standard techniques, however, it is easy to add explicit authentication to any protocol achieving implicit authentication.

2.2   Active Adversaries

The key difference in the active case is that the adversary may now cause any corrupted servers to deviate in an arbitrary way from the actions prescribed by the protocol. Thus, if a server is corrupted the adversary controls all messages sent from this server to the gateway as well as messages sent from this server to any other server. As in the passive case, however, we continue to assume that communication between the gateway and any non-corrupted servers (as well as communication between two non-corrupted servers) is *not* under adversarial control. See footnote 3 for the rationale behind these conventions.

3   A Protocol Secure Against Passive Adversaries

3.1   Description of the Protocol

We assume the reader is familiar with the decisional Diffie-Hellman (DDH) assumption [15], strong one-time signature schemes, and the Cramer-Shoup encryption scheme [14] with labels. A high-level depiction of the protocol is given in Figures 1–3, and a more detailed description, as well as some informal discussion about the protocol, follows.

Initialization. During the initialization phase, we assume the generation of public parameters (i.e., a common reference string) which are then made available to all parties. For a given security parameter k, the public parameters will contain a group $\mathbb{G}$ (written multiplicatively) having prime order q with $|q| = k$; we assume the hardness of the DDH problem in $\mathbb{G}$. Additionally, the parameters include random generators $g_1, g_2, g_3, h, c, d \in \mathbb{G}^\times$ and a hash function $H : \{0,1\}^* \to \mathbb{Z}_q$ chosen at random from a collision-resistant hash family.

As part of the initialization, each server S is provisioned with an El Gamal [18] public-/secret-key pair (pk_S, sk_S), where $pk_S = g_1^{sk_S}$. If A and B are associated with the same client C, then A (resp., B) is given pk_B (resp., pk_A). We stress that, in contrast to the PKI-based model, the client is not assumed or required to know the public keys of any of the servers.

Passwords and password shares are provisioned in the following way: a password pw_C is chosen randomly for each client C and we assume that this password can be mapped in a one-to-one fashion to $\mathbb{Z}_q$. If A and B are the servers associated with a client C, then password shares $pw_{A,C}, pw_{B,C} \in \mathbb{Z}_q$ are chosen uniformly at random subject to $pw_{A,C} + pw_{B,C} = pw_C \bmod q$, with $pw_{A,C}$ given to server A and $pw_{B,C}$ given to server B. In addition, both A and B are given $\mathsf{Com}_{A,C}, \mathsf{Com}'_{A,C}, \mathsf{Com}_{B,C}$, and $\mathsf{Com}'_{B,C}$, where:

$$\mathsf{Com}_{A,C} \stackrel{\text{def}}{=} \mathsf{EIG}_{g_3}(g_1^{pw_{A,C}}) = \left(g_1^{r_a},\ g_3^{r_a} g_1^{pw_{A,C}}\right)$$

$$\mathsf{Com}'_{A,C} \stackrel{\text{def}}{=} \mathsf{EIG}_{pk_A}(g_1^{pw_{A,C}})$$

$$\mathsf{Com}_{B,C} \stackrel{\text{def}}{=} \mathsf{EIG}_{g_3}(g_1^{pw_{B,C}}) = \left(g_1^{r_b},\ g_3^{r_b} g_1^{pw_{B,C}}\right)$$

$$\mathsf{Com}'_{B,C} \stackrel{\text{def}}{=} \mathsf{EIG}_{pk_B}(g_1^{pw_{B,C}}).$$

Note that different public keys are used. Server A (resp., server B) is additionally given the randomness r_a (resp., r_b) used to construct $\mathsf{Com}_{A,C}$ (resp., $\mathsf{Com}_{B,C}$).

Protocol execution. At a high level one can view our protocol as two executions of the KOY* protocol, one between the client and server A (using server B to assist with the authentication), and one between the client and server B (using server A to assist with the authentication). Note that the assistance of the other server is necessary since the password information is split between the two servers. For efficiency, the signature and verification for the two executions are combined, and shares of the El Gamal encryption of the password sent by the servers (i.e., (F, G) in Figure 1) are fixed and stored by the servers.

When a client with password pw_C wants to initiate an execution of the protocol, this client computes Cramer-Shoup "encryptions" of pw_C for each of the two servers. In more detail (cf. Figure 1), the client begins by running a key-generation algorithm for a one-time signature scheme, yielding VK and SK. The client next chooses random $r_1 \in \mathbb{Z}_q$ and computes $A_a = g_1^{r_1}$, $B_a = g_2^{r_1}$, and $C_a = h^{r_1} \cdot pw_C$. The client then computes $\alpha_a = H(Client|\mathsf{VK}|A_a|B_a|C_a)$ and sets $D = (cd^{\alpha_a})^{r_1}$. This exact procedure is then carried out again, using an independent random value $r_2 \in \mathbb{Z}_q$. The client sends

$$\mathsf{msg}_1 \stackrel{\text{def}}{=} \langle Client, \mathsf{VK}, A_a, B_a, C_a, D_a, A_b, B_b, C_b, D_b \rangle$$

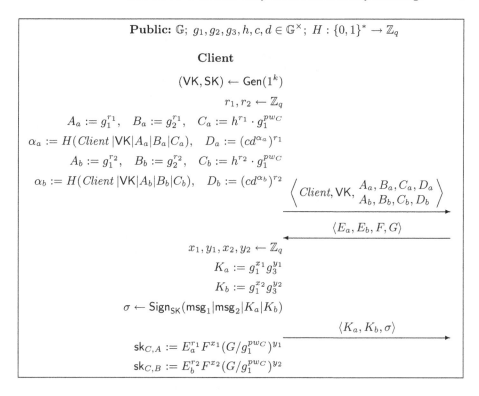

Public: $\mathbb{G}$; $g_1, g_2, g_3, h, c, d \in \mathbb{G}^{\times}$; $H : \{0,1\}^* \to \mathbb{Z}_q$

Client

$$(\mathsf{VK}, \mathsf{SK}) \leftarrow \mathsf{Gen}(1^k)$$

$$r_1, r_2 \leftarrow \mathbb{Z}_q$$

$$A_a := g_1^{r_1}, \quad B_a := g_2^{r_1}, \quad C_a := h^{r_1} \cdot g_1^{pw_C}$$

$$\alpha_a := H(\mathit{Client}\,|\mathsf{VK}|A_a|B_a|C_a), \quad D_a := (cd^{\alpha_a})^{r_1}$$

$$A_b := g_1^{r_2}, \quad B_b := g_2^{r_2}, \quad C_b := h^{r_2} \cdot g_1^{pw_C}$$

$$\alpha_b := H(\mathit{Client}\,|\mathsf{VK}|A_b|B_b|C_b), \quad D_b := (cd^{\alpha_b})^{r_2}$$

$$\left\langle \mathit{Client}, \mathsf{VK}, \begin{array}{l} A_a, B_a, C_a, D_a \\ A_b, B_b, C_b, D_b \end{array} \right\rangle \longrightarrow$$

$$\longleftarrow \langle E_a, E_b, F, G \rangle$$

$$x_1, y_1, x_2, y_2 \leftarrow \mathbb{Z}_q$$

$$K_a := g_1^{x_1} g_3^{y_1}$$

$$K_b := g_1^{x_2} g_3^{y_2}$$

$$\sigma \leftarrow \mathsf{Sign}_{\mathsf{SK}}(\mathsf{msg}_1|\mathsf{msg}_2|K_a|K_b)$$

$$\langle K_a, K_b, \sigma \rangle \longrightarrow$$

$$\mathsf{sk}_{C,A} := E_a^{r_1} F^{x_1} (G/g_1^{pw_C})^{y_1}$$

$$\mathsf{sk}_{C,B} := E_b^{r_2} F^{x_2} (G/g_1^{pw_C})^{y_2}$$

Fig. 1. An execution of the protocol from the client's point of view.

to the gateway as the first message of the protocol. Note that this corresponds to two independent "encryptions" of pw_C using the label $\mathit{Client}\,|\mathsf{VK}$.

When the gateway receives msg_1 from a client, the gateway simply forwards this message to the appropriate servers. The servers act symmetrically, so for simplicity we simply describe the actions of server A (cf. Figure 2). Upon receiving msg_1, server A sends "shares" of (1) two values of the form $g_1^x g_2^y h^z (cd^\alpha)^w$ (for $\alpha \in \{\alpha_a, \alpha_b\}$), one for server A and one for server B, and (2) an El Gamal encryption of pw_C. In more detail, server A chooses random $x_a, y_a, z_a, w_a \in \mathbb{Z}_q$ and computes $E_{a,1} = g_1^{x_a} g_2^{y_a} h^{z_a} (cd^{\alpha_a})^{w_a}$. It also chooses random $x_a', y_a', z_a', w_a' \in \mathbb{Z}_q$ and computes $E_{b,1} = g_1^{x_a'} g_2^{y_a'} h^{z_a'} (cd^{\alpha_b})^{w_a'}$. Finally, it sets (F_a, G_a) equal to $\mathsf{Com}_{A,C}$ (which, recall, is an El Gamal encryption of $g_1^{pw_{A,C}}$ using "public key" g_3 and randomness r_a). The message $\langle E_{a,1}, E_{b,1}, F_a, G_a \rangle$ is sent to the gateway.

The gateway combines the values it receives from the servers by multiplying them component-wise. This results in a message $\mathsf{msg}_2 = \langle E_a, E_b, F, G \rangle$ which is sent to the client, and for which (1) neither server knows the representation of E_a with respect to $g_1, g_2, h, (cd^{\alpha_a})$ (and similarly for E_b with respect to $g_1, g_2, h, (cd^{\alpha_b})$), and (2) the values (F, G) form an El Gamal encryption of the client's password pw_C (with respect to public key g_3).

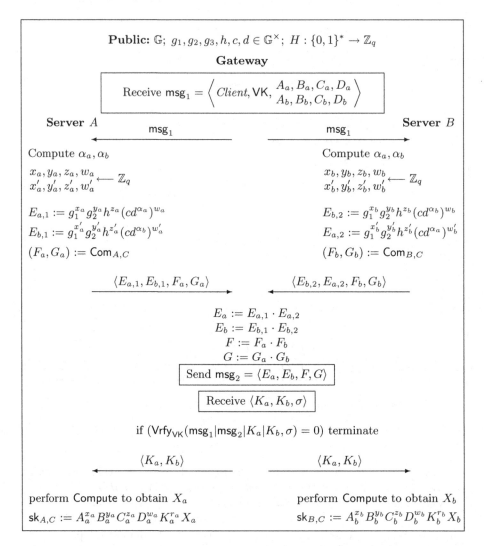

Fig. 2. Execution of the protocol from the servers' points of view (client-gateway messages are boxed). The Compute protocol is depicted in Figure 3.

Upon receiving msg_2, the client proceeds as follows (cf. Figure 1): it chooses random values $x_1, y_1, x_2, y_2 \in \mathbb{Z}_q$ and computes $K_a = g_1^{x_1} g_3^{y_1}$ and $K_b = g_1^{x_2} g_3^{y_2}$. It then computes a signature σ on the "message" $\mathsf{msg}_1|\mathsf{msg}_2|K_a|K_b$ using the secret key SK that it had previously generated. It sends the message $\langle K_a, K_b, \sigma \rangle$ to the gateway and computes session keys

$$\mathsf{sk}_{C,A} := E_a^{r_1} F^{x_1} (G/g_1^{pw_C})^{y_1}$$
$$\mathsf{sk}_{C,B} := E_b^{r_2} F^{x_2} (G/g_1^{pw_C})^{y_2}.$$

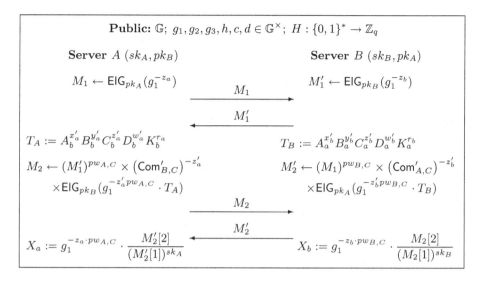

Fig. 3. The Compute protocol. See text for a description of the notation used.

Upon receiving $\langle K_a, K_b, \sigma \rangle$ from the client, the gateway first verifies that σ is a valid signature on the "message" $\mathsf{msg}_1|\mathsf{msg}_2|K_a|K_b$ with respect to the key VK [5]. If verification fails, the gateway terminates this instance of this protocol and send a special message to the servers indicating this fact. Otherwise, it sends K_a, K_b to each of the servers. The servers then execute the Compute protocol (cf. Figure 3 and described next) in order to compute their session keys.

Before describing the Compute protocol, we introduce some notation for manipulation of El Gamal ciphertexts. Given a message $m \in \mathbb{G}$ and a public key (i.e., group element) pk, we let $M \leftarrow \mathsf{EIG}_{pk}(m)$ denote the act of choosing a random $r \in \mathbb{Z}_q$ and setting $M = (g_1^r, pk^r m)$. We let $M[1]$ refer to the first component of this ciphertext, and let $M[2]$ refer to the second. Note that if sk is the corresponding secret key (i.e., $pk = g_1^{sk}$), then we have $m = \frac{M[2]}{M[1]^{sk}}$.

If M, M' are two El Gamal ciphertexts (encrypted with respect to the same public key pk), then we let $M \times M'$ denote $(M[1]\cdot M'[1],\ M[2]\cdot M'[2])$. Note that if M is an encryption of m and M' is an encryption of m', then $M \times M'$ is an encryption of $m \cdot m'$. For $x \in \mathbb{Z}_q$, we let M^x denote the ciphertext $(M[1]^x, M[2]^x)$. Here, the resulting ciphertext is an encryption of m^x.

With this in mind, we now describe the Compute protocol. Since the protocol is symmetric, we simply describe it from the point of view of server A. This server sets M_1 to be an El Gamal encryption (with respect to pk_A) of $g_1^{-z_a}$. It then sends M_1 to server B, who computes

$$M_2' \leftarrow M_1^{pw_{B,C}} \times \left(\mathsf{Com}_{A,C}'\right)^{-z_b'} \times \mathsf{EIG}_{pk_A}(g_1^{-z_b' pw_{B,C}} A_a^{x_b'} B_a^{y_b'} C_a^{z_b'} D_a^{w_b'} K_a^{r_b'})$$

---

[5] We remark that this can just as easily be done by the servers; allowing the gateway to perform this check, however, simplifies things slightly.

and sends this value back to server A (recall that r_b is the randomness used to construct $\mathsf{Com}_{B,C}$). Finally, server A decrypts M_2' and multiplies the result by $g_1^{-z_a \cdot pw_{A,C}}$ to obtain X_a. Note that

$$X_a = g_1^{-(z_a + z_b') \cdot pw_C} \cdot \left(A_a^{x_b'} B_a^{y_b'} C_a^{z_b'} D_a^{w_b'} K_a^{r_b} \right), \tag{1}$$

using the fact that $pw_C = pw_{A,C} + pw_{B,C} \bmod q$.

Although omitted in the above description, we assume that the client and the gateway always verify that incoming messages are well-formed, and in particular that all appropriate components of the various messages indeed lie in $\mathbb{G}$ (we assume that membership in $\mathbb{G}$ can be efficiently verified).

Correctness. One can easily verify correctness of the above protocol. Due to space limitations, we omit the detailed computations.

Security against passive adversaries. A proof of the following theorem appears in the full version of this paper.

Theorem 1. *Assuming (1) the DDH problem is hard for* $\mathbb{G}$*; (2)* (Gen, Sign, Vrfy) *is a secure one-time signature scheme; and (3) H is collision-resistant, the protocol of Figures 1–3 is a secure two-server protocol for password-only authenticated key exchange in the presence of a passive adversary (in particular, it satisfies Definition 1 with* $c = 2$*).*

4   Handling Active Adversaries

Here, we describe the necessary changes to the protocol in order to handle active adversaries. At a high level, these changes can be summarized as follows:

Proofs of correctness. We require servers to give *proofs of correctness* for their actions during the Compute protocol. We stress that we use only the fact that these are *proofs* (and not *proofs of knowledge*) and therefore we do not require any rewinding in our proof of security. This is crucial, as it enables us to handle concurrent executions of the protocol. Nevertheless, as part of the proofs of correctness we will have the servers encrypt certain values with respect to (additional) per-server public keys provisioned during protocol initialization. This will, in fact, enable extraction of certain values from the adversary during the security proof.

Commitments to password shares. The protocol as described in the previous section already assumes that each server is provisioned with appropriate El Gamal encryptions of the password share of the other server. We will use these shares (along with the proofs of correctness discussed earlier) to "force" a corrupted server to use the appropriate password share in its computations.

Simulating proofs for non-corrupted servers. During the course of the proof of security it will be necessary for non-corrupted servers to deviate from the prescribed actions of the protocol, yet these servers must give "valid" proofs of correctness to possibly corrupted servers. We cannot rely on "standard" use of zero-knowledge proofs in our setting, since (1) this would require rewinding which we explicitly want to avoid, and (2) potential malleability issues arise due to the fact that a corrupted server may be giving its proof of correctness at the same time a non-corrupted server is giving such a proof (this is so even if we force sequential executions of the proofs of correctness within any particular instance, since multiple instances may be simultaneously active). To enable simulatability we rely on techniques of MacKenzie [32] described in greater detail below.

4.1 Detailed Description of Changes to the Protocol

We first discuss the necessary modifications to the initialization phase (this is all in addition to the provisioned values already discussed in Section 3.1): (1) each server S is given a random triple $\mathsf{triple}_S = (U_{S,1}, U_{S,2}, U_{S,3})$ of elements chosen uniformly at random from $\mathbb{G}$. Furthermore, (2) each server S is given $\mathsf{triple}_{S'}$ for any server S' for which there is a client with associated servers S, S'.

We will next describe the necessary changes to the protocol itself. In what follows, we will use witness-indistinguishable Σ-protocols (with negligible soundness error[6]) [12] of various predicates and it will be useful to develop some notation. If Ψ represents a predicate (defined over some public values), we let $\Sigma[\Psi]$ denote a Σ-protocol for this predicate. If Ψ_1, Ψ_2 are two predicates, then we let $\Sigma[\Psi_1 \vee \Psi_2]$ denote a Σ-protocol for the "or" of these predicates. We remark that given Σ-protocols for Ψ_1 and Ψ_2, it is easy to combine these so as to obtain a Σ-protocol for $\Psi_1 \vee \Psi_2$ [13]. We define the predicate DDH_S, for any server S with $\mathsf{triple}_S = (U_1, U_2, U_3)$, as follows:

$$\mathsf{DDH}_S(U_1, U_2, U_3) \stackrel{\text{def}}{=} [\exists x, y \text{ s.t. } U_1 = g_1^x \wedge U_2 = g_1^y \wedge U_3 = g_1^{xy}];$$

i.e., DDH_S denotes the predicate asserting that triple_S is a Diffie-Hellman triple.

Given the above, the protocol is modified in the following ways:

Initial server message. To construct the second message of the protocol (i.e., msg_2), the servers first construct $E_{a,1}, E_{b,1}, E_{b,2}$, and $E_{a,2}$ as in Figure 2. The servers also choose random $\mathsf{nonce}_A, \mathsf{nonce}_B \in \{0,1\}^k$. Server A sends to the gateway the message $\langle \mathsf{nonce}_A, E_{a,1}, E_{b,1}, \mathsf{Com}_{A,C}, \mathsf{Com}_{B,C} \rangle$. Similarly, server B sends to the gateway the message $\langle \mathsf{nonce}_B, E_{b,2}, E_{a,2}, \mathsf{Com}_{A,C}, \mathsf{Com}_{B,C} \rangle$. The gateway verifies that $\mathsf{Com}_{A,C}$ and $\mathsf{Com}_{B,C}$ (as sent by the two servers) are identical: if so, it constructs the outgoing message as in Figure 2 but also including $\mathsf{nonce}_A, \mathsf{nonce}_B$; if not, the gateway sends a special abort message to each of the servers. (The client will sign all of msg_2 – including the nonces – exactly as in Figure 1, and this signature will be verified by the gateway as in Figure 2.)

The Compute protocol. After the gateway receives msg_3 and verifies the signature as in Figure 2, it forwards the values $E_{a,1}, E_{b,1}$ (resp., $E_{b,2}, E_{a,2}$) to

---

[6] From now on, "Σ-protocol" means a witness-indistinguishable Σ-protocol with negligible soundness error.

server B (resp., server A) in addition to forwarding (K_a, K_b) as before. The Compute protocol is then modified as follows (we describe the changes from the point of view of server A, but they are applied symmetrically to server B): In the first phase, in addition to computing $M_1 \leftarrow \mathsf{EIG}_{pk_A}(g_1^{-z_a})$, server A computes

$$v_{x_a, y_a, z_a, w_a} := A_a^{x_a} B_a^{y_a} C_a^{z_a} D_a^{w_a} \quad \text{and} \quad V_{x_a, y_a, z_a, w_a} \leftarrow \mathsf{EIG}_{pk_A}(v_{x_a, y_a, z_a, w_a})$$

and sends these values to B. Define the predicate Ψ_1 as follows:

$$\Psi_1 \stackrel{\text{def}}{=} \left[\exists x_a, y_a, z_a, w_a, r, \tilde{r} \text{ s.t. } : \begin{array}{l} E_{a,1} = g_1^{x_a} g_2^{y_a} h^{z_a} (cd^{\alpha_a})^{w_a} \\ M_1 = \left(g_1^r, \ pk_A^r \cdot g_1^{-z_a} \right) \\ V_{x_a, y_a, z_a, w_a} = \left(g_1^{\tilde{r}}, \ pk_A^{\tilde{r}} \cdot A_a^{x_a} B_a^{y_a} C_a^{z_a} D_a^{w_a} \right) \end{array} \right].$$

Server A then acts as a prover in the protocol $\Sigma[\Psi_1 \vee \mathsf{DDH}_A]$. Meanwhile, A acts as a verifier in the symmetric Σ-protocol being given (possibly concurrently) by server B. If B's proof fails, then A aborts immediately.

In the second phase of the Compute protocol, in addition to computing M_2 as in Figure 3, server A also computes

$$v_{z_a'} := g_1^{z_a'} \qquad v_{x_a', y_a', z_a', w_a'} := A_b^{x_a'} B_b^{y_a'} C_b^{z_a'} D_b^{w_a'}$$
$$V_{z_a'} \leftarrow \mathsf{EIG}_{pk_A}(v_{z_a'}) \qquad V_{x_a', y_a', z_a', w_a'} \leftarrow \mathsf{EIG}_{pk_A}(v_{x_a', y_a', z_a', w_a'})$$

and sends these values to B. Define the predicate Ψ_2 as follows:

$$\Psi_2 \stackrel{\text{def}}{=}$$

$$\left[\begin{array}{l} \exists x_a', y_a', z_a', w_a', \\ r_a, pw_{A,C}, r, \tilde{r}, \hat{r} \text{ s.t. } \end{array} : \begin{array}{l} E_{b,1} = g_1^{x_a'} g_2^{y_a'} h^{z_a'} (cd^{\alpha_b})^{w_a'} \\ V_{z_a'} = \left(g_1^r, \ pk_A^r \cdot g_1^{z_a'} \right) \\ V_{x_a', y_a', z_a', w_a'} = \left(g_1^{\tilde{r}}, \ pk_A^{\tilde{r}} \cdot A_b^{x_a'} B_b^{y_a'} C_b^{z_a'} D_b^{w_a'} \right) \\ M_2 = (M_1')^{pw_{A,C}} \times (\mathsf{Com}_{B,C}')^{-z_a'} \\ \quad \times \left(g_1^{\hat{r}}, \ pk_B^{\hat{r}} \cdot g_1^{-z_a' \cdot pw_{A,C}} A_b^{x_a'} B_b^{y_a'} C_b^{z_a'} D_b^{w_a'} K_b^{r_a} \right) \\ \mathsf{Com}_{A,C} = \left(g_1^{r_a}, \ g_3^{r_a} g_1^{pw_{A,C}} \right) \end{array} \right].$$

Server A then acts as a prover in the protocol $\Sigma[\Psi_2 \vee \mathsf{DDH}_A]$. Meanwhile, A acts as a verifier in the symmetric Σ-protocol being given (possibly concurrently) by server B. If B's proof fails, then A aborts without computing a session key.

Relatively efficient Σ-protocols for the above predicates can be constructed using standard techniques, and we omit further details.

Security against active adversaries. A proof of the following theorem appears in the full version of this paper.

Theorem 2. *With the modifications described above and under the same assumptions as in Theorem 1, we obtain a secure two-server protocol for password-only authenticated key exchange in the presence of an active adversary.*

References

1. M. Bellare, D. Pointcheval, and P. Rogaway. Authenticated Key Exchange Secure Against Dictionary Attacks. *Adv. in Cryptology – Eurocrypt 2000*, LNCS vol. 1807, Springer-Verlag, pp. 139–155, 2000.
2. M. Bellare and P. Rogaway. Random Oracles are Practical: A Paradigm for Designing Efficient Protocols. *Proc. 1st ACM Conference on Computer and Communications Security*, ACM, pp. 62–73, 1993.
3. M. Bellare and P. Rogaway. Entity Authentication and Key Distribution. *Adv. in Cryptology – Crypto 1993*, LNCS vol. 773, Springer-Verlag, pp. 232–249, 1994.
4. M. Bellare and P. Rogaway. Provably-Secure Session Key Distribution: the Three Party Case. *27th ACM Symposium on Theory of Computing (STOC)*, ACM, pp. 57–66, 1995.
5. S.M. Bellovin and M. Merritt. Encrypted Key Exchange: Password-Based Protocols Secure Against Dictionary Attacks. *IEEE Symposium on Research in Security and Privacy*, IEEE, pp. 72–84, 1992.
6. S.M. Bellovin and M. Merritt. Augmented Encrypted Key Exchange: a Password-Based Protocol Secure Against Dictionary Attacks and Password File Compromise. *1st ACM Conf. on Computer and Comm. Security*, ACM, pp. 244–250, 1993.
7. M. Boyarsky. Public-Key Cryptography and Password Protocols: The Multi-User Case. *7th Ann. Conf. on Computer and Comm. Security*, ACM, pp. 63–72, 1999.
8. V. Boyko, P. MacKenzie, and S. Patel. Provably-Secure Password-Authenticated Key Exchange Using Diffie-Hellman. *Adv. in Cryptology – Eurocrypt 2000*, LNCS vol. 1807, Springer-Verlag, pp. 156–171, 2000.
9. J. Brainard, A. Juels, B. Kaliski, and M. Szydlo. Nightingale: A New Two-Server Approach for Authentication with Short Secrets. *12th USENIX Security Symp.*, pp. 201–213, 2003.
10. R. Canetti, O. Goldreich, and S. Halevi. The Random Oracle Methodology, Revisited. *J. ACM* 51(4): 557–594, 2004.
11. R. Canetti, S. Halevi, J. Katz, Y. Lindell, and P. MacKenzie. Universally-Composable Password Authenticated Key Exchange. Eurocrypt 2005, to appear.
12. R. Cramer. Modular Design of Secure Yet Practical Cryptographic Protocols. PhD Thesis, CWI and University of Amsterdam, 1996.
13. R. Cramer, I. Damgård, and B. Schoenmakers. Proofs of Partial Knowledge and Simplified Design of Witness Hiding Protocols. *Adv. in Cryptology – Crypto 1994*, LNCS vol. 839, Springer-Verlag, pp. 174–187, 1994.
14. R. Cramer and V. Shoup. A Practical Public Key Cryptosystem Provably Secure Against Chosen Ciphertext Attack. *Adv. in Cryptology – Crypto 1998*, LNCS vol. 1462, Springer-Verlag, pp. 13–25, 1998.
15. W. Diffie and M. Hellman. New Directions in Cryptography. *IEEE Transactions on Information Theory* 22(6): 644–654, 1976.
16. M. Di Raimondo and R. Gennaro. Provably Secure Threshold Password-Authenticated Key Exchange. *Adv. in Cryptology – Eurocrypt 2003*, LNCS vol. 2656, Springer-Verlag, pp. 507–523, 2003.
17. Y. Dodis, M. Krohn, D. Mazieres, and A. Nicolosi. Proactive Two-Party Signatures for User Authentication. NDSS 2003.
18. T. El Gamal. A Public Key Cryptosystem and a Signature Scheme Based on Discrete Logarithms. *IEEE Transactions on Information Theory* 31: 469–472, 1985.
19. W. Ford and B.S. Kaliski. Server-Assisted Generation of a Strong Secret from a Password. *Proc. 5th IEEE Intl. Workshop on Enterprise Security*, 2000.

20. R. Gennaro and Y. Lindell. A Framework for Password-Based Authenticated Key Exchange. *Adv. in Cryptology – Eurocrypt 2003*, LNCS vol. 2656, Springer-Verlag, pp. 524–543, 2003.
21. N. Gilboa. Two-Party RSA Key Generation. *Adv. in Cryptology – Crypto 1999*, LNCS vol. 1666, Springer-Verlag, pp. 116–129, 1999.
22. O. Goldreich and Y. Lindell. Session-Key Generation Using Human Passwords Only. *Adv. in Cryptology – Crypto 2001*, LNCS vol. 2139, Springer-Verlag, pp. 408–432, 2001.
23. L. Gong, T.M.A. Lomas, R.M. Needham, and J.H. Saltzer. Protecting Poorly-Chosen Secrets from Guessing Attacks. *IEEE J. on Selected Areas in Communications* 11(5): 648–656, 1993.
24. S. Halevi and H. Krawczyk. Public-Key Cryptography and Password Protocols. *ACM Trans. Information and System Security* 2(3): 230–268, 1999.
25. D. Jablon. Strong Password-Only Authenticated Key Exchange. *ACM Computer Communications Review* 26(5): 5–20, 1996.
26. D. Jablon. Password Authentication Using Multiple Servers. *RSA Cryptographers' Track 2001*, LNCS vol. 2020, Springer-Verlag, pp. 344–360, 2001.
27. S. Jiang and G. Gong. Password Based Key Exchange With Mutual Authentication. *Workshop on Selected Areas of Cryptography (SAC)*, 2004.
28. J. Katz, R. Ostrovsky, and M. Yung. Efficient Password-Authenticated Key Exchange Using Human-Memorable Passwords. *Adv. in Cryptology – Eurocrypt 2001*, LNCS vol. 2045, Springer-Verlag, pp. 475–494, 2001.
29. T.M.A. Lomas, L. Gong, J.H. Saltzer, and R.M. Needham. Reducing Risks from Poorly-Chosen Keys. *ACM Operating Systems Review* 23(5): 14–18, 1989.
30. S. Lucks. Open Key Exchange: How to Defeat Dictionary Attacks Without Encrypting Public Keys. *Proc. of the Security Protocols Workshop*, LNCS 1361, Springer-Verlag, pp. 79–90, 1997.
31. P. MacKenzie, S. Patel, and R. Swaminathan. Password-Authenticated Key Exchange Based on RSA. *Adv. in Cryptology – Asiacrypt 2000*, LNCS 1976, Springer-Verlag, pp. 599–613, 2000.
32. P. MacKenzie. An Efficient Two-Party Public-Key Cryptosystem Secure against Adaptive Chosen-Ciphertext Attack. *Public Key Cryptography (PKC) 2003*, LNCS vol. 2567, Springer-Verlag, pp. 47–61, 2003.
33. P. MacKenzie and M. Reiter. Networked Cryptographic Devices Resilient to Capture. *IEEE Security and Privacy*, 2001.
34. P. MacKenzie and M. Reiter. Two-Party Generation of DSA Signatures. *Adv. in Cryptology – Crypto 2001*, LNCS vol. 2139, Springer-Verlag, pp. 137–154, 2001.
35. P. MacKenzie, T. Shrimpton, and M. Jakobsson. Threshold Password-Authenticated Key Exchange. *Adv. in Cryptology – Crypto 2002*, LNCS vol. 2442, Springer-Verlag, pp. 385–400, 2002.
36. V. Shoup. A Proposal for an ISO Standard for Public-Key Encryption, version 2.1. Draft, 2001. Available at http://eprint.iacr.org/2001/112.
37. M. Szydlo and B. Kaliski. Proofs for Two-Server Password Authentication. *RSA Cryptographers' Track 2005*, LNCS vol. 3376, Springer-Verlag, pp. 227–244, 2005.
38. T. Wu. The Secure Remote Password Protocol. *Proc. Internet Society Symp. on Network and Distributed System Security*, pp. 97–111, 1998.

Strengthening Password-Based Authentication Protocols Against Online Dictionary Attacks*

Peng Wang[1], Yongdae Kim[1], Vishal Kher[1], and Taekyoung Kwon[2]

[1] Computer Science and Engineering,
University of Minnesota - Twin Cities, Minnesota, USA
{pwang,kyd,vkher}@cs.umn.edu
[2] School of Computer Engineering, Sejong University, Seoul, Korea
tkwon@sejong.ac.kr

Abstract. Passwords are one of the most common cause of system break-ins, because the low entropy of passwords makes systems vulnerable to brute force guessing attacks (dictionary attacks). Existing Strong Password-based Authentication and Key Agreement (SPAKA) protocols protect passwords from passive (eavesdropping-offline dictionary) attacks, but not from active online dictionary attacks. This paper presents a simple scheme that strengthens password-based authentication protocols and helps prevent online dictionary attacks as well as many-to-many attacks common to 3-pass SPAKA protocols. The proposed scheme significantly increases the computational burden of an attacker trying to launch online dictionary attacks, while imposing negligible load on the legitimate clients as well as on the authentication server.

1 Introduction

Password-based authentication protocols cannot rely on persistent stored information on the client side. Instead, they rely on users' ability of *precise recall* of a secret information. It is mainly due to this precise recall requirement that users typically choose simple and low entropy passwords that are easy to remember [7, 15, 16, 21, 24]. The weakness of passwords becomes the weak link of the system, which attackers exploit by launching *offline* or *online* dictionary attacks. In online dictionary attacks, the attacker tries to guess the correct password by interacting with the login server. In offline dictionary attacks, the attacker first collects messages between the users and the server or finds a copy of the password file. Then, the attacker tries to guess correct passwords by matching the passwords in her dictionary with the collected information without requiring any feedback from the login server.

Typically, online dictionary attacks are prevented by using *account locking* or *delayed response* techniques. In account locking a server locks accounts after few unsuccessful attempts. However, account locking enables denial of service attacks against users' accounts and may increase administrators' load if the locks have

---

* This research is supported in part by the Intelligent Storage Consortium at Digital Technology Center (DISC), University of Minnesota.

J. Ioannidis, A. Keromytis, and M.Yung (Eds.): ACNS 2005, LNCS 3531, pp. 17–32, 2005.

to be opened manually. Delayed response aims to reduce the number of passwords attackers can check in a period of time. However, if the attacker wants to compromise any account in the target system, she can initiate many sessions simultaneously (parallel attacks) and can still check (using different usernames) a large number of passwords in her dictionary. For example, attacker can marshal the muscle of a few thousand computers and perform online dictionary attacks. Recent trends indicate that hackers are renting out vast networks of infected home computers (zombies) without their owner's knowledge [30, 31]. An attacker can rent a network of 20,000 computers for less than a few thousand dollars ($2,000). If the attacker aims to perform online dictionary attacks against highly sensitive networks, such as the military networks, the attacker has enough incentives to buy such network of zombies. Using these networks the attacker can launch parallel online dictionary attacks and verify large number of guesses within a short period of time. We stress that employing account locking and delayed response techniques in such scenarios does not help.

In general, strong password-based authentication protocols should not reveal any useful information about the users' passwords to the login server (which can be malicious) and should not be susceptible to online dictionary attacks and eavesdropping attacks. The goal of the proposed work is to strengthen existing password based authentication protocols against online dictionary attacks. *Strong Password-based Authentication and Key Agreement (SPAKA) protocols* [1, 12] are remote password only protocols that can provide authentication and key agreement over insecure channel without the support of previously shared cryptographic keys or a Public Key Infrastructure (PKI). Other authentication protocols, such as SSH [29] and protocols running on SSL [25] are vulnerable to man-in-the-middle attacks (since public key certificates are rarely checked) and these protocols forward the password (or some simple function of the password such as hash) to the server. SPAKA protocols are vulnerable to online dictionary attacks, but they do not reveal any secret information to the login server. Further, they are not susceptible to eavesdropping and man-in-the-middle attacks. Therefore, we choose to strengthen SPAKA protocols against online dictionary attacks, and, as a result, complete the general set of security requirements of a strong password based authentication protocols. However, the scheme presented in this paper is generic enough to be integrated with other password based authentication protocols.

In addition to online dictionary attacks, the 3-pass SPAKA protocols are vulnerable to a more powerful many-to-many guessing attack [18]. In 3-pass SPAKA protocols, when the client initiates the login protocol, the server sends out only one message (during the second pass) that contains both the server's challenge and its proof of the knowledge of the verifier. In many-to-many guessing attacks, an attacker can collect these values and terminate the protocol at the end of the second pass. The attacker can then use these values to mount guessing attacks offline. She can initiate multiple of such half-open sessions and gather a lot of information before the server detects the attack. Thus, the attacker can verify more number of guesses than that allowed by the server's policy. In this paper we present a scheme that strengthens existing authentication protocols against online dictionary attacks. We integrate our scheme with SPAKA protocols to strengthen SPAKA protocols against online dictionary attacks as well as many-to-many guessing attacks. We call the modified SPAKA protocols as SPAKA+.

Overview of Our approach There is a fundamental difference between the login attempts performed by the legitimate users and the login attempts performed by the attackers trying to launch online dictionary attacks. A user who knows the password can successfully login within a couple of trials, while an attacker is expected to perform several magnitudes more trials than legitimate users do. In general, one of the main factors that limit the success of an attacker attempting to launch dictionary attacks is the amount of time required by a program (password cracker) to guess a user's password. The threat of parallel attacks can be eliminated by requiring the client to send a "proof of work" with an aim to keep the attacker busy and reduce the number of sessions that an attacker can initiate.

SPAKA+ strengthens SPAKA protocols against online dictionary attacks and many-to-many attacks by asking clients to solve a cryptographic puzzle (proof of work). The scheme is designed to distinguish between legitimate users and attackers and puts negligible computational burden on the legitimate users. Attackers are forced to solve puzzles, which increases the complexity of online dictionary attack approximately by the hardness of puzzles. If under attack, the authentication server can self-adjust the hardness of the puzzle. Therefore, our protocol will impose significant computation burden on sophisticated attackers using rented zombies, and, thus, greatly increase the amount of time required to break passwords. The computational burden on the authentication server is negligible and the server has to maintain only one long term state information (near-stateless) if users' computers are assumed to be secure. In case users' computers are not secure, we suggest a way to minimize the success of the attacker by maintaining some state information on the server. Our generic puzzle-based scheme can be generalized to non-SPAKA protocols, such as the authentication protocols used with SSL or SSH as long as the basic protocols generate shared secrets (e.g., session keys) between the client and the server. We use these secrets to "mark" the computers used by legitimate users.

Organization The rest of the paper is organized as follows. Section 2 introduces SPAKA. We present our protocols in section 3. Section 4 discusses security and performance issues. Section 5 reviews related work, and section 6 concludes the paper and outlines future work.

2   SPAKA Protocols

Since Lomas *et al.* introduced LGSN in 1989 [19], there have been considerable research efforts on Strong Password-based Authentication and Key Agreement (SPAKA) protocols, such as EKE [5], SPEKE [13], SRP [27], AMP [17], AuthA [4], PAK[6], etc, (refer [1] and [12] for a complete list of papers). SPAKA protocols are remote password-only protocols. They can provide authentication and key agreement over insecure channel without the support of previously shared cryptographic keys or a Public Key Infrastructure (PKI). In a SPAKA protocol, a party only commits high entropy information to the other party and never shows any information except the fact of knowing the password or the verifier of the password. Since messages transferred over the network do not leak information about passwords, attackers cannot launch offline dictionary attacks based on the eavesdropped massages.

SPAKA protocols typically have two stages: a key agreement phase that ends with two parties sharing a common secret that can be used to generate the shared session key, and a key confirmation phase in which two parties verify that they share the common key so that they can believe they are talking to the right party. At the end of a successful run of this protocol, each party holds a session key for subsequent secure communications. We list security properties of SPAKA protocols below.

- SPAKA protocols provide mutual authentication.
- They are secure against offline dictionary attacks.
- They are secure against *Denning-Sacco attack* [10]. Learning already distributed session keys will not help the attacker to discover passwords, verifiers or new session keys.
- They provide *perfect forward secrecy*. Learning the password and (or) the verifier will not help the attacker to discover previous session keys.
- They do not require clock synchronization between the client and the server.

3   SPAKA+

SPAKA Protocols protect passwords from eavesdropping-offline dictionary attacks. However, online dictionary attacks are still possible. Delayed response also failed because attackers can initiate parallel attacks. We eliminate the threat by requiring the client to solve a puzzle with an aim to keep the attacker busy and reduce the number of sessions that an attacker can initiate. Ideally, only attackers should be asked to solve puzzles. Since a user typically uses a limited set of computers that are not accessible to attackers, legitimate users can be distinguished from attackers based on the origin of the login request. SPAKA+ uses successful authentication sessions (old session keys) to "mark" computers of legitimate users. The following table lists the notations we will use in the rest of this paper.

Symbol	Meaning	Symbol	Meaning
C	Client's ID	S	Server's ID
π	Client's password	q	System parameter of SPAKA protocols
v	Client's verifier	$f_i(\cdot)$	Functions used in SPAKA protocols, $i \in [1,6]$
IP_c	Client's IP address	$h^{-1}(\cdot)$	Procedure used to solve the puzzle
$h(\cdot)$	Hash function	k_1, k_2, k_1', k_2'	Temporary values of SPAKA protocols
N	Output size of $h(\cdot)$	k_p, k_q, k_p', k_q'	Temporary values of SPAKA+
x, y	Random numbers	$E_k(\cdot)$	Encryption function with key k
X, Y	Challenges	k_s	Server's symmetric encryption key
sk	Session key	sk_{old}	Previous session key
z	Random number	a, a'	Hash values of previous session keys
z'	Solution of puzzle	l	Lifetime of cookies and tickets
n	Length of z	t, t'	Timestamps on the tickets and cookies

3.1   Overview

Similar to private-public key pairs in public key systems, in SPAKA protocols, Alice (the client) generates a **password** π and a **verifier** v that is the public part (trapdoor one-way function) of her password. The verifier is only revealed to Bob (login server) via a secure channel. During a successful execution of a SPAKA protocol, Alice and Bob authenticate each other and agree on a session key. At this time, in our proposed protocols, Bob issues a $cookie = E_{k_s}(C,\ a',\ t',\ l)$ to Alice.

The $cookie$ contains the client ID (C), the hash value of the session key $(a' = h(sk_{old}))$, a timestamp (t'), and the lifetime (l) of the cookie. (The session key will be called sk_{old} when the $cookie$ is used next time.) The $cookie$ is encrypted using Authenticated Encryption [3] with a key k_s known only to Bob. Note that both the encryption and the decryption of the $cookie$ are done by Bob himself. Also note that the timestamp records Bob's local time. Only Bob will check the timestamp when the $cookie$ is used.

Alice generates a $ticket = \{C,\ a,\ t,\ l\}$, which contains the same fields as in the $cookie$ except the timestamp (t) of the $ticket$ records Alice's local time. For the sake of clarity, we denote the hash value $(h(sk_{old}))$ generated by Alice as a to distinguish it from the hash value (a') generated by Bob. Only Alice will check t before using the $(cookie, ticket)$ pair. Hence, Alice and Bob do not need clock synchronization for using $cookie$ and $ticket$. Alice stores both the $cookie$ and the unencrypted $ticket$ in her local computer. Bob does not store any of them.

When Alice tries to login again, she sends the $cookie$ to Bob and finds a in her corresponding $ticket$. Then they run the SPAKA protocol. In the proposed protocols, in order to proceed, Alice must prove that she knows a. If Alice tries to login from a computer without a valid $(cookie, ticket)$ pair, Bob makes a $puzzle$ as described in section 3.2. In order to proceed, Alice must solve the puzzle first.

The proposed protocols achieve following properties:

1. If a user tries to login from a computer without a valid $(cookie, ticket)$ pair, the client must solve a $puzzle$. In other words, an attacker cannot verify her guesses without solving a $puzzle$, even if she launch many-to-many guessing attacks to 3-pass protocols.
2. A client with a valid $(cookie, ticket)$ pair does not have to solve a puzzle. In this case, our protocol adds negligible computation on the legitimate client side.
3. They add negligible computation on the server side.
4. They do not increase the number of messages exchanged between the clients and the servers.
5. Servers can easily self-adjust the hardness of puzzles as well as the lifetime of $(cookie, ticket)$ pairs.
6. If an attacker can somehow get access to one of the user's computers, she may steal a $(cookie, ticket)$ pair. Only this user will be affected. Her account still has the strength of the original SPAKA protocols. In addition, in section 4 we present a scheme to counter the stolen tickets problem.

3.2   A Puzzle Tailored for SPAKA Protocols

For our purpose, a puzzle shall satisfy the following requirements.

- Creating a puzzle and verifying a solution shall be inexpensive.
- The cost of solving the puzzle shall be easy to adjust.
- It shall not be possible to precompute solutions to the puzzles.
- An attacker shall not be able to relay the puzzles to a third party.
- It shall not require clock synchronization between the client and the server.
- It shall not use encryption.

The first four requirements are common to most cryptographic puzzle schemes. Clock synchronization and encryption are not used because they are not used in the most of SPAKA protocols. Since we integrate our puzzle to SPAKA protocols and aim to use the new protocols in any environment where the original SPAKA protocols are used, we do not ask for more cryptographic primitives or system services than those already used in the original SPAKA protocols. Note that statelessness, which is a common requirement of a client puzzle system aiming to prevent TCP SYN flood attack [8] is not a concern in our scheme, because our puzzle is integrated to SPAKA protocols that are not stateless.

The solution to our puzzle is the brute-force reversal of a cryptographically strong hash function, such as SHA-1 [20]. Suppose a server requires a client to solve a puzzle, the server computes $puzzle = h(z, Y, IP_c)$, where $z \in_R \mathbb{Z}_{2^n}$ is a n-bit random number ($0 \leq n \ll N$), n controls the hardness of the $puzzle$. Y is a random (long and unpredictable) challenge sent by Bob to Alice in the SPAKA protocols. IP_c is the IP address of the client. If IP_c is not included then a relaying attack is possible where the attacker also runs his own SPAKA+ server. The attacker acquires puzzles from the legitimate SPAKA+ server and relays these puzzles to her clients through her SPAKA+ server; thus, forcing her clients to solve puzzles on her behalf. The server sends $puzzle$, Y, and n to the client. Since Y is long and changes per session, it is not possible for the client to precompute solutions to the puzzles. Creating a puzzle that requires one random number generation and one hash computation is inexpensive. The server can adjust the cost of solving the puzzle by simply tuning n.

Even if the client knows Y and IP_c, due to the one-way property of the cryptographic hash function $h(\cdot)$, the client has no efficient way to solve the puzzle than trying different numbers $z' \in \mathbb{Z}_{2^n}$ until $puzzle = h(z', Y, IP_c)$. We denote $h^{-1}(\cdot)$ as the procedure used to solve the puzzle. On average, it takes 2^{n-1} trials to solve this puzzle. Next, the client proves to the server that a solution of the puzzle is found. The verification of the solution requires one hash computation on the server side. This step is integrated into SPAKA protocols (see sections 3.3 and 3.4 for detail).

Since above computations only use functions already used in SPAKA protocols, the puzzle can be used in any type of client platform running SPAKA protocols. It is easy to see that the simple puzzle satisfies all requirements listed above.

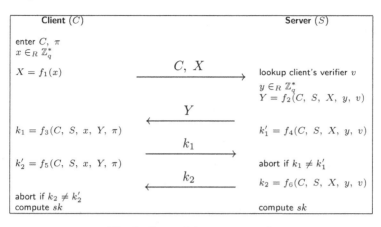

Fig. 1. General 4-pass protocol.

3.3 Strengthening 4-Pass Protocols

Figure 1 depicts the general structure of 4-pass SPAKA protocols described below.

- Alice enters her username C and password π.
- Alice generates a random number x and composes a challenge X based on x. She sends C and the challenge X to Bob.
- Bob looks up Alice's entry in the password file and finds her verifier v. He generates a random number y and composes his challenge Y based on y and other information such as v. Y is sent to Alice.
- Alice computes k_1 and sends it to Bob. The value k_1 serves as her response to Bob's challenge, the proof of her knowledge of π, and the key confirmation.
- Bob computes k_1' that should be the same as k_1 if Alice entered the correct password. If k_1' is equal to k_1, then Bob computes k_2 and sends it to Alice. Similarly, the value k_2 serves as his response to Alice's challenge, the proof of his knowledge of v, and the key confirmation.
- Alice computes k_2' and checks if k_2 and k_2' match.
- Both Alice and Bob believe they are talking to the right party. They then compute the session key sk.

When Alice (or Eve who is an attacker) tries to login from a machine **without** a valid (*cookie, ticket*) pair, she must solve a puzzle. The situation is depicted in Figure 2. Bob creates a *puzzle* and sends *puzzle*, Y and n to Alice together in the second message. Alice solves the puzzle by brute-force reversing $h(\cdot)$. Instead of sending k_1 to Bob, she sends $k_p = h(k_1, z')$. Bob computes k_1' and $k_p' = h(k_1', z)$. He proceeds only if k_p is equal to k_p'. To keep the protocol to be 4-pass, Bob computes sk before sending out the 4th message. Finally, he sends *cookie*$_{new}$ and the lifetime of *cookie*$_{new}$ in the 4th message.

Assume the output of $h(\cdot)$ is random. Then the probability that $\exists z' \in_R \mathbb{Z}_{2^n}$, s.t. $z' \neq z$ and $h(z', Y, IP_c) = h(z, Y, IP_c)$ is $\frac{1}{2^{N-n}}$. Since $n \ll N$, with

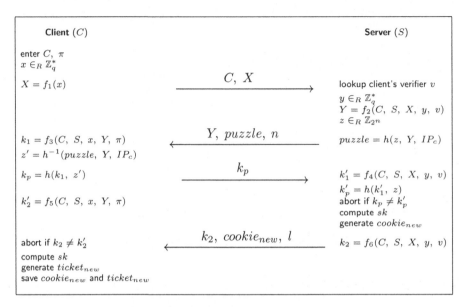

Fig. 2. 4-pass protocol without *cookie* and *ticket*.

high probability z' is equal to z. If k_1 is equal to k_1', i.e., the password and the verifier match, then k_p is equal to k_p'. In this case, mutual authentication between Alice and Bob is successful. On the other hand, suppose Eve is running an online dictionary attack. She has to solve the puzzle. Without correct z', with the probability $1 - \frac{1}{2^n}$, $k_p \neq k_p'$ even if k_1 is equal to k_1', (i.e., even if she guessed the correct password). So checking if k_p is equal to k_p' implicitly verifies if k_1 is equal to k_1' as well as if z is equal to z'. In other words, it verifies if Alice (or Eve) entered the correct password and has solved the puzzle.

Figure 3 represents the scenario when Alice tries to login **with** a valid (*cookie*, *ticket*) pair. Alice sends the cookie to Bob in the first message. Bob decrypts the cookie and verifies if it is expired. If not, he saves a'. Instead of sending k_1 to Bob in the third message, Alice sends $k_p = h(k_1, a)$. Bob computes k_1' and $k_p' = h(k_1', a')$. He proceeds only if k_p is equal to k_p'. Similar to the above protocol, this step implicitly verifies if k_1 is equal to k_1' as well as if a is equal to a'. Finally, Bob sends *cookie*$_{new}$ and l in the 4th message. In this case, Alice is not asked to solve a puzzle, but she must have a valid (*cookie*, *ticket*) pair.

3.4   Strengthening 3-Pass Protocols

In a 3-pass protocol, Bob computes k_1 and sends it to Alice in the second message with Bob's challenge. Alice verifies it, then sends k_2 in the third message. Figure 4 represents the general structure of 3-pass SPAKA protocols.

As depicted in figure 5, when a Alice (or Eve) tries to login from a machine **without** a valid (*cookie*, *ticket*) pair, she must solve a puzzle. Similar to 4-pass protocol, Bob creates a *puzzle*. He also computes $k_p = h(k_1, z)$ and sends them

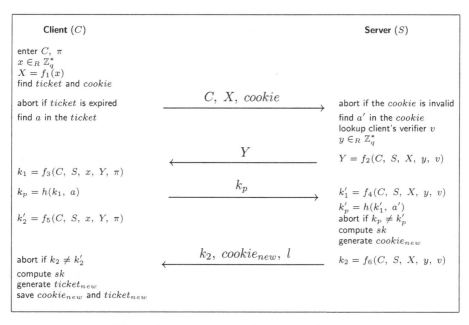

Fig. 3. 4-pass protocol with *cookie* and *ticket*.

to Alice in the second message. To keep the protocol to be 3-pass, Bob computes sk earlier and sends $cookie_{new}$ and l in the second message since that is the only message Bob sends to Alice. After receiving the second message, Alice solves the *puzzle* by brute-force reversing $h(\cdot)$ and computes k_1' and $k_p = h(k_1, z')$. If k_p is equal to k_p', she concludes that the solution of the puzzle is correct and the verifier matches the password. Following the general 3-pass protocol she first computes k_2 and then computes $k_q = h(k_2, z')$ and sends k_q to Bob instead of sending k_2.

The value k_1 sent in the second message must be replaced with k_p. Otherwise Eve can disconnect after receiving the second message. Since k_1 serves as key confirmation, it gives Eve enough information to check if her guessing is correct or not. On the other hand, the value k_p is the hash value of (k_1, z). To verify k_1, Eve has to first solve the *puzzle*. The solution of the *puzzle* is also sent back to Bob in the third message implicitly. Suppose only k_2 is sent to Bob, Eve can bypass the *puzzle* and wait to see if Bob aborts or not. If not, she knows her guess is correct. Note z and k_2 can be sent in clear. We use k_q to keep the protocol consistent with the 3-pass with cookie case since a cannot be sent in clear. To keep the new protocol to be 3-pass, Bob must send $cookie_{new}$ in the second message. If Eve gets $cookie_{new}$, but it is not useful to her as she cannot decrypt $cookie_{new}$.

Similar to 4-pass protocol, when Alice tries to login **with** a valid (*cookie*, *ticket*) pair, she is not asked to solve a *puzzle*. Figure 6 depicts this scenario. As in the 3-pass without cookie case, we use k_p and k_q instead of k_1 and k_2. Again, Bob sends $cookie_{new}$ and l in the second message.

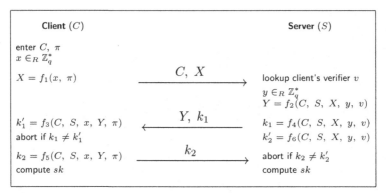

Fig. 4. General 3-pass protocol.

3.5   Adjusting Hardness of Puzzles

We modified a test program of the SRP implementation [28] to test the performance of generating a puzzle, solving the puzzle, and verifying the solution. We run the test program on a Pentium-4 2.4GHz computer running Linux with kernel version 2.4.20. As expected, generating a puzzle and verifying the solution takes negligible amount of time. The time required to solve a puzzle is roughly doubled, when we increase the hardness by one. Bob can self-adjust the hardness of puzzles by keeping a global counter to count the number of failed attempts to all accounts in the system within an interval. He adjusts the hardness of puzzles when the counter reaches predefined threshold values.

4   Discussion

In this section we highlight the various aspects of our scheme. Especially, we present a mechanism that does not give Eve significant advantage even if Eve successfully steals Alice's (*cookie, ticket*) pairs by exploiting vulnerabilities in the underlying system.

Usability. Given a computationally intensive cryptographic puzzle, different machines may spend different amount of time to solve it. If a legitimate user is using a slower machine, she has to spend more time solving a puzzle. However, after a successful login she will have a (*cookie, ticket*) pair, and, therefore, she does not need to solve puzzles as long as she keeps using the same set of machines. The usability of the system is not sacrificed.

Client-side cookies. In our approach, *cookies* are stored in users' computers. Once the client receives a new *cookie* (after successful login), the client can simply delete the stale *cookies* for that account; therefore, the maximum number of *cookie* stored on a user's computer is equal to the the number of accounts the user has. If *cookies* are stored in the server, then the server has to store all *cookies* that have not expired. If the authentication service is heavily used and if the lifetime of *cookies* is long, then the server has to store a large number of *cookies*.

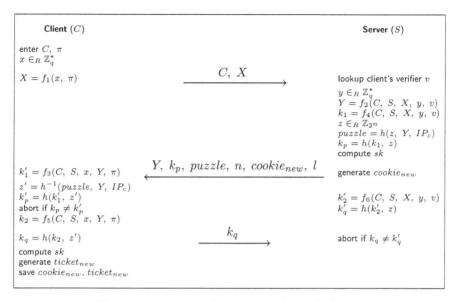

Fig. 5. 3-pass protocol without *cookie* and *ticket*.

No information leakage. Comparing to the 3-pass or 4-pass general protocols, more information is sent in our new protocols, namely *puzzle*, k_p, k_q, *cookie*, *cookie*$_{new}$. These pieces of information do not help Eve to find valuable information, such as the password, the verifier, previous session keys, or the new session key. The *cookie*$_{new}$ (or *cookie*) contains the hash of (previous) session key and is encrypted with a key known only to the server; therefore, Eve cannot find the (previous) session key. In the case when Alice attempts to login without a valid (*cookie*, *ticket*) pair, k_p (or k_q) is the hash value of (k_1, z) (or (k_2, z)). Since we assume that the general protocols are secure, k_1 (k_2) that can be easily eavesdropped in SPAKA protocols does not leak valuable information, neither does k_p (k_q) as a result. In the case when Alice attempts to login using a valid (*cookie*, *ticket*) pair, the same argument applies, k_p (k_q) does not leak valuable information including a.

Combatting many-to-many attacks. 3-pass SPAKA protocols are vulnerable to the many-to-many guessing attack [18]. This attack is common to 3-pass SPAKA protocols because Bob must send his challenge and the key confirmation that also helps Alice to authenticate Bob in one message. This enables Eve to disconnect an ongoing session earlier (right after receiving Bob's message) and verify her guess later offline. She can also run multiple sessions simultaneously and collect more useful values. With SPAKA+, Eve can still disconnect earlier. However, she cannot verify her guesses without solving puzzles. The amount of work Eve can save is one message per guess. The cost of sending one message is several magnitudes lower than the cost of solving a puzzle. Hence, Eve's cost of running online dictionary attacks and her cost of running many-to-many attacks

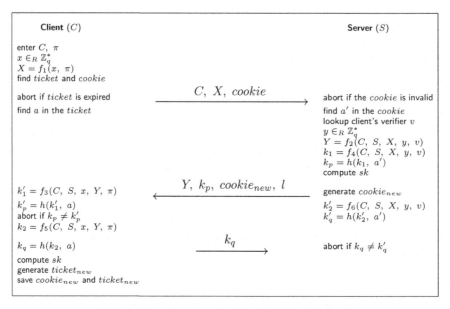

Fig. 6. 3-pass protocol with *cookie* and *ticket*.

is about the same. Therefore, the vulnerability of 3-pass SPAKA protocols is significantly reduced.

Analyzing the possibility of ticket theft. If an attacker is able to steal a ticket, then she may be able to bypass our puzzle. We now analyze the scenarios in which a client's ticket can be stolen. If a user is always using her home (or personal) computer or a well administered lab computer with appropriate user accounts, then the chances of stealing the client's ticket are slim, since the ticket is protected with a strong access control mechanism. Even in the case where a user is using a well administered lab computer, which is using a network file system, the chances that an attacker successfully steals a client's ticket are low as the attacker will have to run a sniffer on the local network to eavesdrop the ticket stored on the remote file server, which typically is difficult (or to some extent easy to detect) in a well administered lab. In the aforementioned scenarios, an attacker will have to hack into the user's account to get the ticket. If a client is travelling and uses for a short time a computer that is not well administered, then an attacker can steal the client's ticket, but just stealing one ticket does not give substantial advantage to the attacker. The threat of ticket theft is high only when a lot of users are frequently using computers in a public lab that does not have any notion of user accounts. In this scenario, an attacker can simply read the tickets stored on these computers and bypass the puzzle. Below, we explain in detail how SPAKA+ minimizes the threat of stolen tickets. The mechanism described is quite light weight if the number of stolen tickets is small as compared to the number of users in the system, which is true for most of the cases discussed above.

Resisting stolen tickets. To minimize the threat of stolen tickets, Bob maintains two lists, namely *Cookie Cache* and *Black List*, to store *cookies*. Both of the lists are initially empty. He also maintains a counter (initialized to 0) for each *cookie* stored in the *Cookie Cache* and a small threshold value (*thresh*), say 5. When a user C tries to login with a (*cookie, ticket*) pair and his password π, Bob first checks if C is been served by one of his instances. If so, Bob aborts this session, because it is likely that C is Eve exploiting many-to-many attack [18]. Bob does not allow parallel SPAKA+ sessions for one user account. If not, Bob searches the *cookie* in the *Black List*. If found, Bob runs the SPAKA+ and asks C to solve a puzzle. If Bob does not find the *cookie* in the *Black List*, he runs the SPAKA+ protocol without asking C to solve a puzzle. If Bob cannot authenticate C, he checks the *Cookie Cache*. If the *Cookie* is not in the *Cookie Cache*, then he inserts the *Cookie* is the *Cookie Cache*. If the *cookie* is already in the *Cookie Cache*, then he increase the counter of this *Cookie*. If the counter is larger than *thresh*, then he adds the *Cookie* in the *Black list*. On the other hand, if C entered the correct password, then Bob allows C to login and delete the *Cookie* from the *Cookie Cache* if it is there. Bob will also delete expired *cookies* from the *Cookie Cache* and the *Black List* periodically.

Following above scheme, when Alice tries to login with a valid (*cookie, ticket*) pair but entered a wrong password, the login attempt will fail. At this time, Bob temporarily caches the *cookie*. Since Alice knows the correct password, she is very likely to try again and enters the correct password within a couple of trails. Bob sees that Alice entered the correct password, then deletes the cached *cookie* and the corresponding counter. In this case, Bob only maintains a short term state.

If Eve runs online dictionary attacks with one of Alice's valid (*cookie, ticket*) pairs, she gets at most (*thresh* − 1) + *thresh* chances without being asked to solve a puzzle. She tries (*thresh* − 1) times then waits for Alice to login with the same (*cookie, ticket*) pair. Bob deletes the *cookie* from *Cookie Cache*, and, therefore, Eve gets *thresh* more chances. Note that Alice will delete this (*cookie, ticket*) pair from her computer since she gets a new pair on the next successful login. Therefore, she will not use the pair that Eve has again. It is very unlikely that Eve can guess the correct password within (*thresh* − 1) + *thresh* trials. Now Bob considers that this *cookie* and its corresponding *ticket* are stolen and puts Alice's ID and the *cookie* in his *Black List*. In this case, Bob maintains a long term state. The more insecure the computer is, the more (*cookie, ticket*) pairs Eve can steal, as a result bigger the Bob's *Black List*. As a side effect, the system employing above scheme benefits from the *Black List*. By periodically analyzing the *Black List*, Bob can estimate if Alice's computer is secure by counting the number of Alice's *cookies* in the *Black List* and notifying Alice if he believes Alice's computer is not secure.

5   Related Work

Pinkas and Sander proposed a well crafted scheme that attempts to slow down online dictionary attacks on web applications with Reverse Turing Test (RTT)

[22]. To increase the usability, servers issue *cookies* to clients. The *cookies* must be protected against eavesdropping and *cookie* theft. Hence, it requires that the server keeps a counter for every *cookie* stored in a user's machine. First of all, these schemes are mainly restricted to GUI based applications and cannot be applied to non-GUI based applications. The scheme presented in this paper can be easily integrated with GUI based as well as non-GUI based authentication systems. In addition, if under attack, the hardness of the puzzle can be increased to further slow down the attacker. Cookies used in Pinkas and Sander scheme are vulnerable to web based cookie stealing attacks. We use tickets and encrypted cookies to avoid puzzles. Clients prove that they have tickets without revealing the tickets (sending the tickets on the network). The only way an attacker can steal a ticket is by breaking into a user's account. Hence, our cookie-ticket pair approach is more secure than the cookie only approach used in Pinkas and Sander's approach. Further, our scheme requires less server storage than that required in [22]. In their approach, a server keeps a counter for every cookie stored on users' computers. In our approach, on one hand, if we assume that users' computers are secure, then the server does not cache cookies, it only stores one global counter. On the other hand, if users' computers are not assumed to be secure and the "resisting stolen tickets" protocol (explained at the end of section 4) is used, then the number of cookies and the corresponding counters maintained by the server is equal to the number tickets stolen by an attacker, which is still less than their approach.

Cryptographic puzzles have been used in the literature for several related tasks. Rivest *et al.* used puzzles to create digital time capsules [23]. Juels and Brainard introduced the first proposal for using a client puzzle approach to defend against connection depletion attacks [14]. Aura *et al.* [2] proposed an approach to protect authentication protocols against denial-of-service. [9] reported a implementation of client puzzles in the context of TLS. Wang and Reiter's [26] approach enables each client to "bid" for resources by tuning the difficulty of the puzzles it solves, and to adapt its bidding strategy in response to apparent attacks. The sever allocates resources first to the client that solved the most difficult puzzle when the server is busy. Dwork and Naor introduced the *pricing via processing* paradigm and designed puzzles for combatting spam [11]. One interesting property of their puzzle is the *short cut*. The short cut information is only known by trusted agents and "pricing authority". Normal legitimate users do not know the short cut. For the various purposes of their applications, the above approaches are not required to distinguish between legitimate users and attackers. Every one is required to solve a puzzle.

6   Conclusion and Future Work

We introduced SPAKA+ that strengthens SPAKA protocols against online dictionary attacks using cryptographic puzzles. SPAKA+ significantly increases the complexity of online dictionary attacks as well as many-to-many guessing attacks. The server can self-adjust the computational burden of an attacker by tuning the hardness of the puzzles in real-time based on the server's estimate of ongoing online dictionary attacks. SPAKA+ is secure and adds negligible load on the legitimate clients. We designed a simple cryptographic puzzle that utilizes the nice structure of the SPAKA protocols for generating puzzles, transferring puzzles and solutions, and verifying solutions. The puzzle is designed such that attackers cannot relay it to others. The puzzle does not require any function other than those used in the SPAKA protocols. As a result, the new scheme can be used without requiring additional support from the underlying system and is easy to implement. If the users' computers are secure, the server's load in our scheme is low. Whereas if the users' computers are assumed to be insecure we have presented an approach that resists stolen tickets by maintaining state information on the server.

Future work includes integrating the new scheme into available SPAKA implementations, such as SRP and PAK. We plan to implement an experimental system to perform online dictionary attacks and many-to-many guessing attacks in order to evaluate the success of our scheme. A detailed evaluation both from performance perspective as well as usability perspective will be performed. We also plan to apply our idea to SSH.

References

1. Research papers on password-based cryptography. http://www.jablon.org/passwordlinks.html.
2. T. Aura, P. Nikander, and J. Leiwo. DOS-resistant authentication with client puzzles. In *the 8th International Workshop on Security Protocols*, 2001.
3. M. Bellare and C. Namprempre. Authenticated encryption: Relations among notions and analysis of the generic composition paradigm. In *ASIACRYPT*, 2000.
4. M. Bellare and P. Rogaway. The AuthA protocol for password-based authenticated key exchange, 2000. Submission to IEEE P1363.2.
5. S. M. Bellovin and M. Merritt. Encrypted key exchange: Password-based protocols secure against dictionary attacks. In *IEEE Symposium on Security and Privacy*, 1992.
6. V. Boyko, p. MacKenzie, and S. Patel. Provably secure password authentication and key exchange using diffie-hellman. In *EUROCRYPT*, 2000.
7. P. Buxton. Egg rails at password security. Netimperative, June, 24, 2002.
8. CERT. TCP syn flooding and ip spoofing attack. CERT Advisory CA-96.21, November 1996.
9. D. Dean and A. Stubblefield. Using client puzzles to protect TLS. In *the 10th Annual USENIX Security Symposium*, 2001.
10. D. Denning and G. Sacco. Timestamps in key distribution systems. *Communications of the ACM*, August 1981.
11. C. Dwork and M. Naor. Pricing via processing or combatting junk mail. In *CRYPTO*, 1993.
12. IEEE P1363 Working Group. IEEE P1363-2: Standard specifications for password-based public key cryptographic techniques. http://grouper.ieee.org/groups/1363.
13. D. P. Jablon. Strong password-only authenticated key exchange. *Computer Communication Review*, 26(5):5–26, 1996.

14. A. Juels and J. Brainard. Client puzzles: A cryptographic defense against connection depletion attacks. In *Network and Distributed System Security Symposium*, 1999.
15. D. V. Klein. "foiling the cracker" – A survey of, and improvements to, password security. In *the second USENIX Workshop on Security*, 1990.
16. E. Knight and C. Hartley. The password paradox. Business Security Advisor magazine, December 1998.
17. T. Kwon. Authentication and key agreement via memorable password. In *Network and Distributed System Security Symposium*, 2001.
18. T. Kwon. Practical authenticated key agreement using passwords. the 7th Information Security Conference (ISC), 2004.
19. T. Lomas, L. Gong, J. Saltzer, and R. Needhamn. Reducing risks from poorly chosen keys. In *the twelfth ACM symposium on Operating systems principles (SOSP)*, 1989.
20. A. J. Menezes, P. C. van Oorschot, and S. A. Vanstone. *Handbook of Applied Cryptography*. CRC Press, October 1996.
21. R. T. Morris and K. Thompson. Password security: A case history. *Communications of the ACM*, 22(11):594–597, Nov 1979.
22. B. Pinkas and T. Sander. Securing passwords against dictionary attacks. In *the 9th ACM conference on Computer and communications security*, 2002.
23. R. L. Rivest, A. Shamir, and D. A. Wagner. Time-lock puzzles and timed-release crypto. Technical Report LCS/TR-684, MIT, 1996.
24. E. Spafford. Observing reusable password choices. In *the 3rd UNIX Security Symposium*, 1992.
25. Transport Layer Security Working Group. SSL 3.0 specification. `http://wp.netscape.com/eng/ssl3/`.
26. X. Wang and M. K. Reiter. Defend against denial-of-service attacks with puzzle auctions. In *the IEEE Symposium on Security and Privacy*, 2003.
27. T. Wu. The secure remote password protocol. In *Network and Distributed System Security Symposium*, 1998.
28. T. Wu. The stanford SRP authentication project, February 2004. `http://srp.stanford.edu`.
29. T. Ylonen. SSH - secure login connections over the internet. volume the 6th USENIX Security Symposium, 1996.
30. Scotland Yard and the case of the rent-a-zombies. `http://news.zdnet.com/2100-1009_22-5260154.html`, July 2004.
31. Zombie PCs for Rent. `http://securitynews.weburb.dk/show.php3?item=InformationSecurity&p%5Bne%wsletterId%5D=609`, September 2004.

Cryptanalysis of an Improved Client-to-Client Password-Authenticated Key Exchange (C2C-PAKE) Scheme

Raphael C.-W. Phan[1] and Bok-Min Goi[2,*]

[1] Information Security Research (iSECURES) Lab,
Swinburne University of Technology (Sarawak Campus), 93576 Kuching, Malaysia
rphan@swinburne.edu.my
[2] Faculty of Engineering,
Multimedia University, 63100 Cyberjaya, Malaysia
bmgoi@mmu.edu.my

Abstract. Password-Authenticated Key Establishment (PAKE) protocols allow two parties, to share common secret keys in an authentic
manner based on an easily memorizable password. At ICCSA 2004, an
improved PAKE protocol between two clients of different realms was
proposed that was claimed to be secure against attacks including the
replay attack. In this paper, we cryptanalyze this protocol by showing
two replay attacks that allow an attacker to falsely share a secret key
with a legal client.

Keywords: Password-authenticated key exchange, client-to-client, cryptanalysis, replay attack, unknown key-share.

1 Introduction

Authenticated key exchange (AKE) protocols allow two parties, say a client and
a server, to share a common secret key for subsequent communication sessions
between them. Further, password-authenticated key exchange (PAKE) protocols allow for the use of a password for authentication, and is desirable since a
password is easier to memorize compared to a secret value.

Due to diverse communication environments where clients from one environment (realm) wish to communicate with clients from other realms, Byun *et
al.* presented at ICICS '02 [2] a PAKE protocol allowing two clients with different passwords and who are in different realms to securely establish a secret
key between them. This was called the C2C-PAKE protocol. However, Chen
[3] showed that the C2C-PAKE protocol is insecure against a dictionary attack
by a malicious server in a different realm. Similarly, Wang *et al.* at ACNS '04
[9] presented three different dictionary attacks on the same protocol. Further,
at ICCSA '04 [4], Kim *et al.* showed that the C2C-PAKE scheme is vulnerable
to a Denning-Sacco-style attack where the attacker is an insider with knowledge of the password of a client in a different realm. Kim *et al.* also proposed

---

* The second author acknowledges the Malaysia IRPA grant (04-99-01-00003-EAR).

J. Ioannidis, A. Keromytis, and M.Yung (Eds.): ACNS 2005, LNCS 3531, pp. 33–39, 2005.
© Springer-Verlag Berlin Heidelberg 2005

an improved C2C-PAKE protocol that was claimed to be secure against their Denning-Sacco-style attack, Chen's attack, and replay attacks in general.

In this paper, we present two attacks on Kim *et al.*'s improved C2C-PAKE protocol. Our attacks do not require any knowledge of passwords, and therefore does not require the attacker to be an insider, hence they can be mounted by any attacker. Surprisingly, the original C2C-PAKE protocol as proposed by Byun *et al.* is not vulnerable to our attacks. In "improving" the original C2C-PAKE protocol, Kim *et al.* have caused the protocol to be even more insecure. This suggests that simply fixing protocols for resistance against known attacks does not always guarantee a more secure variant.

Note that our attacks on Kim *et al.*'s improved protocol are different from previous ones [3, 4, 9] on Byun *et al.*'s original protocol, in that we mount unknown key-share attacks such that an authorized party is falsely led to believe that he is sharing a key with another authorized party when in fact he is sharing it with the attacker. Meanwhile, the previous attacks mount dictionary attacks to recover the passwords.

Designing efficient and secure key exchange protocols need extra care due to the stringent security requirements. Over the past years, many protocols have been proposed and many have been easily broken and re-designed time and again. Among others, some recent cryptanalyses of PAKE protocols include [1, 5–8].

1.1   Some Common Attacks

We list some common attacks that PAKE protocols should generally be resistant to, and security requirements that they should have.

Dictionary attack: Originally, a dictionary attack is a password guessing technique in which the adversary attempts to determine a user's password by successively trying words from a dictionary (a compiled list of likely passwords) in the hope that one of these password guesses will be the user's actual password. This attack can be performed in *online mode* (trying successive passwords until a login is successful) or *off-line mode* (hashing or encrypting a dictionary of words and looking for any matches in a copied system file of hashed or encrypted user passwords). Informally, in the scenario of PAKE protocols, we say that a protocol is secure against *off-line dictionary attacks* if an adversary who obtains all the communication data between the client and the server is unable to carry out the dictionary attack to obtain the client's password. This can be achieved if and only if there is no verifiable ciphertext based on a human-memorizable password in the protocol run.

Unknown key-share attack: This is a type of replay attack where a party A believes that she shares a key with another party B upon completion of a protocol run (this is in fact the case), but B falsely believes that the key is instead shared with a party $E \neq A$.

Man-in-the-middle (MITM) attack: An attack where the adversary is able to read, and possibly modify at will, messages between two parties without letting either party know that they have been attacked.

Forward secrecy: If long-term private keys of one or more parties are compromised, the secrecy of previously established session keys should not be affected.

Key-compromise impersonation resilience: The compromise of any party's (client or server) secret should not enable the adversary to impersonate any other parties.

2   The C2C-PAKE Protocols Due to Kim *et al.* [4]

Throughout this paper, we will use the following notations:

A, B	The clients
ID_i	Client i's identity
pw_i	Client i's human-memorizable password
KDC_i	The key distribution center which stores the client i's identity (ID_i) and password (pw_i)
K	The symmetric secret key shared between different KDCs
$E_i(\cdot)$	Symmetric encryption using the secret key, i
p, q	Sufficiently large primes such that $q|p-1$
g	The generator of a finite subgroup, G of Z_p^* of order q
H_i	A cryptographic hash function

Henceforth, all the operations are done under modulo p, except operations in the exponents, and all protocols are based on the Diffie-Hellman (DH) assumption.

For simplicity, we depict in Figure 1 the improved C2C-PAKE protocol proposed by Kim *et al.* in [4]. Basically, this protocol involves nine steps as follows:

1. A, who wishes to initiate a secret communication session by generating a new session key with B in different realm, selects a random number $x \in Z_p^*$ and computes $M_1 = E_{pw_A}(g^x)$. Then, A sends $\langle M_1, ID_A, ID_B \rangle$ to KDC_A.
2. Based on ID_A from the received message, KDC_A can retrieve pw_A from the database. Hence, only KDC_A can decrypt M_1 to recover g^x. KDC_A selects $r \in Z_p^*$ at random and computes $Ticket_B = E_K(g^{x\cdot r}, g^r, ID_A, ID_B, L)$ where L is $Ticket_B$'s lifetime. Then, KDC_A replies $\langle ID_A, ID_B, Ticket_B, L \rangle$ to A.
3. Upon receiving the message, A forwards $\langle ID_A, Ticket_B \rangle$ to B.
4. B chooses a random number $y \in Z_p^*$ and computes $M_2 = E_{pw_B}(g^y)$. Then, B sends $\langle ID_A, ID_B, Ticket_B, M_2 \rangle$ to KDC_B.
5. KDC_B decrypts $Ticket_B$ to verify the received message (i.e., ID_A, ID_B and L). KDC_B also computes and sends $\langle g^{x\cdot r\cdot r'}, g^{r\cdot r'} \rangle$ back to B, where $r' \in Z_p^*$ is randomly selected.
6. B computes $cs = H_1(g^{x\cdot y\cdot r\cdot r'})$, $g^{r\cdot r'\cdot y}$ and $M_3 = E_{cs}(g^a)$. Next, B sends $\langle M_3, g^{r\cdot r'\cdot y} \rangle$ to A.

7. A can also compute cs with the knowledge of x and the received $g^{r \cdot r' \cdot y}$. Hence, he can obtain g^a by decrypting M_3 with cs. Then, A chooses a random $b \in Z_p^*$, and computes the session key, $sk = H_2(g^{a \cdot b})$, as well as $M_4 = E_{sk}(g^a)$ and $M_5 = E_{cs}(g^b)$. A then sends $\langle M_4, M_5 \rangle$ to B for session key confirmation.

8. B decrypts M_5 with cs to obtain g^b. Then, he computes $sk = H_2(g^{a \cdot b})$ with g^b and a, and uses this to verify M_4. B further computes and sends $M_6 = E_{sk}(g^b)$ to A for session key confirmation.

9. Finally, A verifies g^b by decrypting M_6 with sk. This completes the protocol.

The authors claimed that, besides sk, cs can also be directly used as a session key in their improved C2C-PAKE protocol.

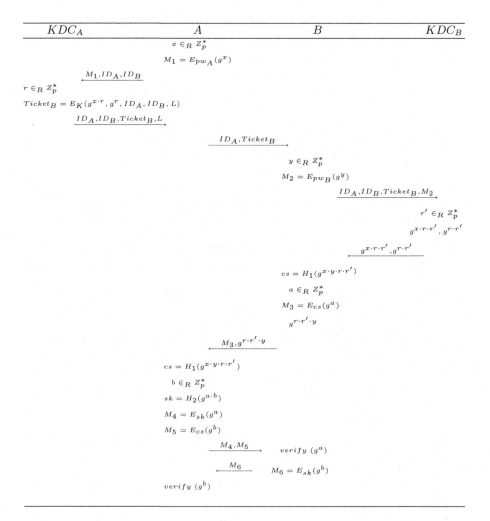

Fig. 1. The improved C2C-PAKE Protocols due to Kim *et al.* [4].

3   Cryptanalysis of the Improved C2C-PAKE

Kim *et al.* [4] claimed that their improved C2C-PAKE protocol is secure against all basic types of attacks considered in [2] including the replay attack. However, we show that this is not true.

3.1   By Any Attacker

Our first attack exploits the fact that $g^{x \cdot r \cdot r'}$ and $g^{r \cdot r'}$ are sent in the clear from KDC_B to B in Step(5). An attacker, B' can perform an unknown key-share attack as follows:

1. Firstly, B' uses $g^{r \cdot r'}$ to compute $g^{r \cdot r' \cdot y'}$, and further uses $g^{x \cdot r \cdot r'}$ to compute the values of $cs' = g^{x \cdot r \cdot r' \cdot y'}$ and $M'_3 = E_{cs'}(g^{a'})$, where $y', a' \in Z_p^*$ are any values of his choice.
2. B' then replaces $\langle M_3, g^{r \cdot r' \cdot y} \rangle$ with $\langle M'_3, g^{r \cdot r' \cdot y'} \rangle$ that is sent by B to A in Step(6). Upon receiving the message, A will compute $cs' = g^{x \cdot r \cdot r' \cdot y'}$ and the session key, $sk' = H_2(g^{a' \cdot b})$. Note that the value of cs' computed by A would then be identical as B''s one. A sends $M'_4 = E_{sk'}(g^{a'})$ and $M'_5 = E_{cs'}(g^b)$ back to B as in Step(7).
3. B' intercepts this and easily decrypts M'_5 to obtain g^b and further computes $sk' = H_2(g^{a' \cdot b})$. Therefore, B' can compute $M'_6 = E_{sk'}(g^b)$ to be sent back to A for session key confirmation in Step(8). This completes the protocol with A thinking it has successfully authenticated B's identity and that it is sharing a secret session key with B, but in fact it is sharing the secret session key, sk' with the attacker, B'.

Note that our attack on Kim *et al.*'s protocol is more severe than both Kim *et al.*'s Denning-Sacco-style and Chen's attack on Byun *et al.*'s original C2C-PAKE protocol, because our attack does not need knowledge of any secrets such as the password.

3.2   By a Malicious Client

Our second attack exploits the fact that the identities, ID_A and ID_B of A and B are sent in the clear, and that an initiating client, A authenticates another client, B based only on the fact that B's corresponding KDC_B can view $Ticket_B$ generated by KDC_A for KDC_B. It works as follows:

1. An innocent client, B and a malicious client, I are in the same realm with corresponding key distribution center, KDC_{BI}. I replaces the ID_B that is sent by A to KDC_A with ID_I in Step(1). This leads KDC_A into thinking that A wishes to establish a session key with I. KDC_A then generates $Ticket'_B$ in Step(2) which should in fact be considered $Ticket_I$ since it contains ID_I as the party that A wishes to establish a session key with. Obviously, A would not know this, since A has no idea what is in $Ticket'_B$; it has been encrypted with a key, K shared between KDC_A and KDC_{BI}. However, A simply forwards this to B in Step(3).

2. I intercepts this and performs Step(4); namely, I communicates with KDC_{BI}. Hence, KDC_{BI} will forward back the values $g^{x \cdot r \cdot r'}$ and $g^{r \cdot r'}$ to I in Step(5). Note that in this case I is using KDC_{BI} as a decrypting oracle, and KDC_{BI} would comply since I is one of its clients and further it believes A really wants to communicate with I.

3. I can therefore compute cs, and masquerade as B to complete the rest of the protocol with A. In the end, I would successfully authenticate itself to A as B, and also share a secret session key with A, but all the while with A thinking it is sharing a key with B.

Note that this attack does not require B to be present at all. Further, the original C2C-PAKE protocol resists this since the identities of both clients A and B are encrypted with R known only by A and KDC_A hence there's no way for the identities to be modified.

4   Conclusion

We have presented two attacks on the improved C2C-PAKE protocol proposed by Kim *et al.* Our attacks on this improved version are more severe than previous attacks on the original C2C-PAKE protocol proposed by Byun *et al.* since we do not require knowledge of any secrets nor passwords. Surprisingly, the original version is not vulnerable to our attacks. This is mainly because in order to counter the Denning-Sacco-style attack and Chen's attack, Kim *et al.* [4] simply eliminated all verifiable ciphertexts and plaintexts based on the clients' passwords. As a result, there is no more mutual authentication between A and KDC_A (also B and KDC_B), and so it is easier for an attacker to access to messages between party i and its KDC_i. In contrast, all these had been taken into consideration in the design of original C2C-PAKE [2] .

As an intuition to counter our attacks, we reiterate that the original version's encryption of $\langle ID_A, ID_B \rangle$ in Step(2) and similarly of $g^{x \cdot r \cdot r'}$ and $g^{r \cdot r'}$ in Step(5) makes it resistant to our attacks, and the very fact that they were removed caused the "improved" version to fall. Since our attacks on the "improved" version are more severe than previous attacks on the original version, this suggests that the "improved" version is less secure than the original.

Acknowledgement

We thank God for His many blessings and our wives for their understanding that at times working at night is inevitable when it comes to meeting strict deadlines ⌣

References

1. F. Bao. Security Analysis of a Password Authenticated Key Exchange Protocol. In *Proc. ISC 2003*, LNCS 2851, pp. 208-217, 2000.

2. J.W. Byun, I.R. Jeong, D.H. Lee, and C.S. Park. Password-Authenticated Key Exchange between Clients with Different Passwords. In *Proc. ICICS 2002*, LNCS 2513, pp. 134-146, 2002.

3. L. Chen. A Weakness of the Password-Authenticated Key Agreement between Clients with Different Passwords Scheme. *Circulated for consideration at the 27th SC27/WG2 meeting in Paris, France*, 2003-10-20.24, 2003.

4. J. Kim, S. Kim, J. Kwak, and D. Won. Cryptanalysis and Improvement of Password-Authenticated Key Exchange Scheme between Clients with Different Passwords. In *Proc. ICCSA 2004*, LNCS 3043, pp. 895-902, 2004.

5. C.-L. Lin, H.-M. Sun and T. Hwang. Three-Party Encrypted Key Exchange: Attacks and a Solution. In *ACM Operating Systems Review*, Vol. 34, No. 4, pp.12-20, 2000.

6. C.-L. Lin, H.-M. Sun and T. Hwang. Three-Party Encrypted Key Exchange Without Server Public-Keys. In *IEEE Communication Letters*, Vol. 5, No. 12, pp.497-499, 2001.

7. P. MacKenzie, S. Patel, and R. Swaminathan. Password-Authenticated Key Exchange based on RSA. In *Proc. Asiacrypt 2000*, LNCS 1976, pp. 599-613, 2000.

8. S. Patel. Number Theoretic Attacks on Secure Password Schemes. In *Proc. IEEE Symposium on Research in Security and Privacy*, pp. 236-247, 1997.

9. S. Wang, J. Wang, and M. Xu. Weaknesses of a Password-Authenticated Key Exchange Protocol between Clients with Different Passwords. In *Proc. ACNS 2004*, LNCS 3089, pp. 414-425, 2004.

Efficient Security Mechanisms
for Overlay Multicast-Based Content Distribution

Sencun Zhu[1], Chao Yao[2], Donggang Liu[3], Sanjeev Setia[2], and Sushil Jajodia[2]

[1] Department of Computer Science and Engineering and School of Information Sciences and Technology, The Pennsylvania State University, University Park, PA 16801
szhu@cse.psu.edu
[2] Center for Secure Information Systems, George Mason University, Fairfax, VA 22030
{cyao,setia,jajodia}@gmu.edu
[3] Department of Computer Science, North Carolina State University, Raleigh, NC27695
dliu@unity.ncsu.edu

Abstract. This paper studies the security issues that arise in an overlay multi-cast architecture where service providers distribute content such as web pages, static and streaming multimedia data, realtime stock quotes, or security updates to a large number of users. In particular, two major security problems of overlay multicast, *network access control* and *group key management*, are addressed. We first present a bandwidth-efficient scheme, called CRBR, that seamlessly integrates network access control and group key management. Next we propose a DoS-resilient key distribution scheme, called k-RIP, that delivers updated keys to a large fraction of nodes with high probability even if an attacker can *selectively* compromise nodes in the multicast data delivery hierarchy and command these compromised nodes to drop keying packets. The proposed schemes do not rely on knowledge of overlay topology, and can scale up to very large overlay networks.

1 Introduction

We consider the security issues that arise in an overlay multicast architecture where service providers distribute content such as web pages, static and streaming multimedia data, realtime stock quotes, or security updates (e.g., new virus signatures, certificate revocation lists) [14].

Overlay multicast, also called end system multicast or application-level multicast [8], was proposed as a new group communication paradigm in place of IP multicast whose deployment has been very slow due to both technical and operational concerns. Recently several studies [7, 8, 12, 24] have investigated research problems in overlay multicast such as algorithms for tree or mesh construction, routing, reliability, and resource allocation. However, security issues in overlay multicast have received relatively little attention so far. Previous work on overlay network security either investigates the impact of selfish cheating nodes on the performance of overlay multicast trees [15], or investigates schemes that improve the fault-tolerance or denial-of-service(DoS) resilience of overlay networks by introducing path redundancy [3, 19, 21, 22].

Contributions: We concentrate on two major security problems of overlay multicast: *network access control* and *group key management*. In IP multicast, network access

J. Ioannidis, A. Keromytis, and M.Yung (Eds.): ACNS 2005, LNCS 3531, pp. 40–55, 2005.

control and group key management were considered as two *independent* issues and they were studied *separately*, one in the network layer [11] and the other in the application layer [5, 16, 17, 20]. In this paper, we propose a bandwidth-efficient scheme called CRBR that seamlessly integrates network access control with group key management. CRBR exploits the special property of overlay multicast that a node is both a group member and a router. We show through analysis and simulation that CRBR greatly outperforms other two representative group rekeying schemes: LKH [20] and SDR [16] when they are applied in overlay multicast. Moreover, using a queueing model, we show the impact of node presence dynamics (i.e.,coming online/going offline) on the performance of group rekeying protocols.

We also propose a simple but effective DoS-resilient key distribution scheme, called k-RIP (stands for k Random Injection Points), that delivers updated keys to a large fraction of nodes via an overlay network. Specifically, in addition to propagating one copy of updated keys using a multicast tree rooted at the source node, our scheme injects k additional copies of updated keys into the multicast tree through k randomly selected nodes in the network. These selected nodes propagate the message to both their child nodes (if any) and parent nodes, thereby spreading the message over the multicast tree. Our simulation and analysis results show that k-RIP can greatly increase the probability that nodes receive messages even if an attacker can *selectively* compromise nodes in the multicast tree, compared to a scheme in which only one copy of the message is injected via the root node. Unlike previously proposed schemes [3, 19, 21, 22], k-RIP does not rely on the knowledge of the overlay topology. Thus, it is scalable to very large overlay networks.

Organization: The remainder of this paper is organized as follows. Section 2 discusses some related work on group key management, network attacks and countermeasures. Section 3 describes the system model and our design goal. In Section 4, we present our scheme CRBR for providing both network access control and group key management, followed by its security and performance analysis. In Section 5 we describe our k-RIP key distribution scheme. Finally, Section 6 concludes this paper.

2   Related Work

We introduce the related work in four categories: *group key management*, *network attacks and countermeasures*, and *resilient overlay multicast*.

Group key management. Group key management has been extensively studied in the context of secure multicast in IP multicast. The previous group rekeying schemes can be categorized into stateful and stateless protocols. The stateful class of protocols includes several protocols based upon the use of logical key trees, e.g., LKH [20], OFT [5]. In these protocols, the key server uses key encryption keys that were transmitted to members during previous rekeying operations to encrypt the keys that are transmitted in the current rekeying operation. Thus, a member must have received all the key encryption keys of interest in all the previous rekey operations to decipher the current group key. Adding redundancy in key distribution [18, 23] does not fully address the issue in the case of burst packet loss or nodes going offline frequently. *Stateless* group rekeying protocols [13, 16] form the second class of rekey protocols. In these protocols, a legitimate user only needs to receive the keys of interest in the current rekey operation to decode the current group key. The stateless feature makes these protocol very attractive for applications in which members go offline very frequently. However, these protocols usually have much higher communication overhead than the stateful protocols. Our scheme also provides the stateless property, but it incurs significantly smaller communication overhead than the other schemes in the context of overlay multicast. Moreover, it also provides network access control.

Network attacks and countermeasures. Mathy et al [15] studied the impact of selfish nodes cheating about their distance measurements in application-level multicast overlay tree. Badishi et al [4] proposed a gossip-based multicast protocol called Drum, which combines multiple techniques such as push, pull, random port selections, and resource bounds, for mitigating DoS attacks in secure gossip-based multicast. Wright et al [21] presented k-redundant depender graphs for distributing public-key certificate revocation lists (CRLs), which provides every node in the graph with k disjoint paths to the root of the graph, thus guaranteeing delivery even when up to $k - 1$ paths between them have failed. Song et al [19] improved the scalability of the above scheme by presenting expander graphs for constructing robust overlay networks that have constant degree. Yang et al [22] proposed to augment tree-like hierarchy with hierarchical overlay networks, which is actually also a type of graphs, to achieve DoS resilience.

All these schemes provide stronger fault-tolerance or DoS resilience at the cost of higher (re)construction complexity to maintain their security property, especially when nodes join or leave the tree frequently. Moreover, these schemes are subject to selective attacks in which an attacker can prevent a large number of nodes from receiving messages by compromising (or becoming) the nodes close to the root. Our random injection points scheme directly works with the existing overlay multicast schemes without changing trees into graphs, and it is especially suitable for distributing small-size but critical messages. Our scheme is robust to selective attacks; therefore, we believe that the combination of our scheme with the other DoS-resilient schemes will make a distribution system more robust to DoS attacks.

Resilient overlay multicast. Banerjee et al [3] introduced a probabilistic forwarding scheme for overlay multicast. In their scheme, every node forwards received packets to a randomly selected set of nodes, assuming that every node has global knowledge of overlay topology or it can discover other nodes on the fly. Our k-RIP scheme also uses randomness, but the randomness is used by the key server to inject packets into the overlay network, not used by the regular nodes to forward packets. The main reason we do not employ their scheme directly is because of scalability consideration. For large-scale and dynamic overlay networks, the overhead for discovering other nodes on the fly or maintaining global topological knowledge would be very large. In k-RIP neither the key server nor the nodes need knowledge on overlay topology. This allows k-RIP to scale up to arbitrarily large overlay networks.

3   System Model and Design Goal

This section describes our system model and design goal. For ease of presentation, we use the terms "join" and "leave" to denote the actions of a subscriber coming online and going offline, respectively, whereas use "add" and "revoke" to denote the actions of becoming a member and cancelling the membership status of a subscriber, respectively.

3.1   System Model

There are potentially a large number of application scenarios of overlay multicast, which are characterized by different parameters (e.g., group size, membership dynamics, number of data sources). It seems unlikely that a single system model can cover all these scenarios. Therefore, we focus on a specific application scenario, which we believe is (or will be) very representative. We consider a commercial application of overlay multicast, in which a service provider distributes data (e.g., live content or streaming media) to a large number of subscribers (also called member nodes hereafter). For simplicity, we assume that online nodes are self-organized into an overlay multicast delivery tree rooted at the distribution server of a service provider, although our security schemes work for various distribution infrastructures, such as trees, meshes, or other types of graphs. The algorithms for constructing and maintaining overlay multicast trees [2, 8, 12] are out of the scope of our work.

The population of the system could be up to hundreds of thousands or even millions of nodes. We assume that a node may join or leave a multicast group very frequently and at any time. For example, a user may subscribe to multiple service providers for different programs. She may switch between multiple channels to find an interesting program to join. A user may also leave a channel immediately after she has received the data of interest to her.

In this model, the service provider has three types of servers playing different roles. A key server (or many key servers for scalability) provides subscription services to users. Before a user is able to join the group for the first time, it needs to subscribe to the key server (e.g., through a website). After successful subscription based on certain policies or rules (e.g., agreeing to pay service fee), a user is provided with a service credential that allows it to join the multicast delivery tree later. A user must also contact the key server to cancel its membership later if it wants. The key server also manages the update of data encryption keys (DEKs). When it changes its DEK, it sends a new DEK to the data server, which encrypts the future messages with the new key. The key server also sends to the distribution server its (updated) network access control policy or access control list indicating which nodes are currently authorized to join the group. The data server is mainly engaged in processing the data to be distributed, e.g., computing encryptions and digital signatures. It transmits the prepared data to the distribution server for distribution.

3.2   Design Goal

Security requirements of overlay multicast are similar to those of other networks. Some of the general security properties are *authentication*, *confidentiality*, *network access control*, *availability*, *anonymity*, and *fairness*.

In this paper, however, we focus on two of these security issues in the context of overlay multicast. First, we want to provide data confidentiality and network access control. Data confidentiality ensures that only authorized nodes can understand the multicast data. It must be provided because an unauthorized user may attempt to receive multicast data by eavesdropping on the communication links of authorized nodes or even of Internet routers. Network access control is also critical because it ensures that

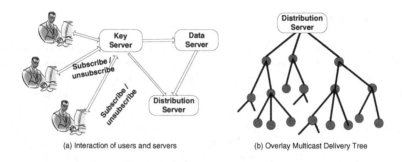

(a) Interaction of users and servers   (b) Overlay Multicast Delivery Tree

Fig. 1. The system model.

only authorized nodes can join the overlay multicast tree; otherwise, the resources of a legitimate node are consumed for forwarding data to unauthorized nodes. Second, we want to provide a DoS-resilient key distribution scheme that delivers keys to existing member nodes with high probability even if some selectively compromised nodes *drop* the keys they are supposed to forward. Note that We do not address another type of DoS attack in which an attacker floods the network with junk data. Instead, we assume the existence of an appropriate multicast source authentication scheme by which member nodes can immediately verify the data from the data server and the key server and drop false data.

4   A Certificate Revocation Based Group Rekeying Scheme (CRBR)

An important, while challenging, issue for providing multicast data confidentiality is group key management. To enforce both backward confidentiality (i.e., a new user should not be able to decipher the data distributed before its subscription) and forward confidentiality (i.e., a revoked user should not be able to decipher the future data), it is required to distribute a new group data encryption key (DEK) to all authorized members in a *secure*, *reliable*, and *timely* fashion when group membership changes. This is referred to as *group rekeying*.

Unicast-based group rekeying, in which the key server sends a new DEK to every individual node, has the communication complexity of $O(N)$ keys. Recently proposed group rekeying schemes [5, 16, 20] use logical key trees to reduce the complexity of a group rekeying operation from $O(N)$ to $O(logN)$. Further, it has been proposed that groups be re-keyed periodically instead of on the basis of every membership change [17, 23]. Periodic or batched rekeying can reduce both the processing and communication overhead at the key server, and improve the scalability and performance of key management protocols. Note that in all these schemes, the key server includes keys for *all* the member nodes when distributing its rekeying message, and every member receives the entire message although it is only interested in a small fraction of the content.

Network access control, which is another critical security service, was studied *independently* with group key management in IP multicast. It is usually enforced by Internet edge routers [11]. Specifically, each router maintains inclusion or exclusion access control lists (ACLs) for all supported multicast groups, and every member presents its authorization certificate or token to its edge router to join a group. Network access control is hard to implement in IP multicast because routers are required to authenticate packets, to establish trust relationship with individual group controllers, and to keep their ACLs up-to-date.

4.1 Scheme Overview

We exploit the property of an overlay network that nodes are both hosts and routers when designing group rekeying and network access control schemes. In IP Multicast, all group members are end hosts, and they have no responsibility for forwarding keying materials to other group members. In contrast, for group communication in an overlay network, the nodes in the delivery tree also act as routers. As such, the key server only has to deliver a new DEK securely to a small number of nodes, which are its immediate children, and these children then forward the new DEK securely to their own child nodes. In this way, a group key is propagated to all the online member nodes in a hop-by-hop fashion. The amortized transmission cost per node is one key, independent of the group size.

For the above scheme to work, a basic requirement is the existence of a secure channel between every pair of neighboring nodes. We employ conventional public key techniques for establishing pairwise keys between two nodes. The use of public key techniques can additionally provide network access control because public key techniques such as digital signatures support strong source authentication. In overlay multicast, because nodes are both routers and hosts, network access control will be achieved as long as every node authenticates every other node that contacts it for joining the network.

In our system model, it is very natural that data access control (through encryption) and network access control (through authentication) be integrated. A node should have both privileges if it is authorized, and it should not have either of them if it is revoked. This motivates us to update group keys and invalidate the public keys (or certificates) of revoked nodes simultaneously. Moreover, since periodic group rekeying is much more scalable than individual rekeying [17] and certificate revocation information is also distributed periodically [6], group rekeying and the distribution of certificate revocation information can be performed with the same time interval. An appropriate rekeying interval is application dependent and requires a trade-off between security and performance. The selection of rekeying interval is out of the scope of this paper.

4.2 Scheme Specifications

This subsection describes the details in CRBR.

- **Node registration:** The key server issues every member a public-key certificate when a member subscribes to the group.

- **Security update generation:** The key server generates a new certificate revocation list (CRL) and a new DEK K_g for every group rekeying. It further computes a digital signature over the CRL, K_g, and a timestamp. Denote SU as a *security update* that includes the CRL, the timestamp, and the above digital signature (note that K_g is not included in SU). The key server sends SU and K_g to the distribution server.
- **Security update distribution:** For the ease of presentation, here we use a traditional, non-DOS-resilient scheme for the distribution of security updates. This is referred to as base scheme (a DOS-resilient scheme will be presented in Section 5). In the base scheme, the distribution server forwards SU and K_g to each of its child nodes. SU is sent in cleartext, whereas K_g is encrypted with a pairwise key shared between two nodes in every link. A node establishes a pairwise key with another node and then propagates K_g to it only if the CRL indicates that node is still a legitimate member. Also note that every node can verify the authenticity of the received group key K_g by verifying the signature. After successfully verifying the message, these child nodes forward the message to their own child nodes. Recursively, the security update and K_g are propagated to all on-line nodes in a hop-by-hop fashion.
- **Local recovery:** A node that has missed one or several security update information because it was off-line can authenticate itself to any one of the online nodes to obtain the up-to-date security update and the group key when it joins the network, because that node knows if the joining node is legitimate or not based on the CRL it possesses.

Certificate management. The key server issues every node a unique public-key certificate if the node is authorized. The node is also given the public key of the key server, which allows the node to verify the certificates (hence their public keys) presented by other nodes.

The key issue in using digital certificate is certificate management. In general, there are mainly two challenges. The first challenge is for a node to verify a received certificate in an efficient and timely fashion in the presence of complex CA hierarchy. In our applications, fortunately, there is no CA hierarchy since every user receives a certificate from the same key server. The second challenge is certificate revocation because users may unsubscribe from the group at any time. We adopt a push-based approach in which the key server distributes its certificate revocation lists (CRLs) periodically. To minimize the communication overhead, we employ the following techniques.

- The key server assigns a unique integer to every node as the identifier of the certificate of the node. The integer starts from '0' and is incremented by one for a new node. Note that the key server does not assign the ids of revoked nodes to any new nodes. Also, the certificate of a user does not contain any personal information about the user. Instead, the key server has a database that records the personal information of a user and its certificate.
- The CRL is a bit string of size Z, where Z is the number of nodes that have so far subscribed to the system. Every certificate is mapped to a bit in the bit string and the id of the certificate is the index of the bit in the bit string. A bit value of '0' indicates that a corresponding certificate is invalid and '1' indicates valid. When a node is revoked from the system, its corresponding bit in the bit string is set '0'.

Node joining. When a node u joins the multicast delivery tree after its subscription process, it follows the existing overlay multicast routing protocol, except that it authenticates to all the nodes it contacts with and also verifies any messages from those nodes. For example, nodes u and its parent node v can authenticate to each other and establish a pairwise key K_{uv} based on their certificates and their public/private keys. Node v also checks if the bit indexed by node u's id in its CRL is '1'. Then node v sends node u the current K_g encrypted by K_{uv} and SU. Node u can verify the authenticity of K_g based on SU. Note that a pairwise key is not merely for delivering K_g. In all the overlay multicast routing protocols [2, 7, 8, 12, 24], two neighboring nodes in the multicast tree exchange KEEPALIVE messages periodically. They can use their pairwise key for authenticating these KEEPALIVE messages to each other.

4.3 Security Analysis

In our scheme, no unauthorized nodes can get the group key K_g because a member node only forwards K_g to other member nodes. Nor can a compromised node inject a false group key into the network because the group key is signed by the key server. In addition, an unauthorized node cannot join the multicast tree. Our scheme also provides weak anonymity in the sense that the certificate of a user only has an integer field to uniquely identify the user. A node cannot figure out the identities of other users in the system; however, it may know the IP addresses of other nodes it is communicating with.

4.4 Performance Evaluation

This subsection compares the performance of our scheme CRBR with two well-known group rekeying schemes: LKH [20] and SDR [16], assuming that they are employed in overlay multicast. The purpose of this comparison is to show that it is more desirable to design a specific group rekeying scheme like CRBR than to directly apply other schemes that were not designed for overlay multicast.

The metric of interest is key server bandwidth overhead. Because security updates are propagated in the entire multicast tree, the more the key server distributes, the more network and node resources are consumed. Hence, key server bandwidth overhead is also an indication of the total network bandwidth overhead and an individual user's bandwidth overhead, which we may care the most in practice.

Two scenarios are studied. The first scenario considers the bandwidth overhead of the key server for multicasting keys to online nodes. The second scenario considers the bandwidth overhead of the key server for unicasting the current keys to individual nodes that have missed one or several previous group rekeying operations because they were offline. To study the performance of these schemes quantitatively, below we first present an analytical model for node presence dynamics.

The analysis of node presence dynamics. A member node can be in either of two statuses: presence (online) or absence (offline), and it can switch its status between these two statuses until its membership duration is expired and is then revoked from the group. We use the term "presence duration" and "absence duration" to denote a continuous time period a node stays in a group and stays outside a group, respectively.

Previous study [1] based on multiple sessions in MBone showed that presence durations in a multicast session follow either an exponential distribution or a Zipf distribution. For simplicity, in this study we assume that the durations of node membership follow an exponential distribution with mean $1/\theta$. We also assume that presence durations of nodes follow another exponential distribution with mean $1/\mu$, and further assume that the absence durations of nodes are exponentially distributed with mean R/μ. Thus R is the ratio of the average time for which a node is absent to the average time for which it is present.

Figure 2 depicts our analytic model. Let the group rekeying interval be T. When the system is in its steady status, during T the number of new subscribers J is equal to the number of revoked subscribers L. Based on queueing theory, the revocation rate of the system is $N \cdot \theta$ where N is the population of the system. Thus, $L = N \cdot \theta \cdot T$.

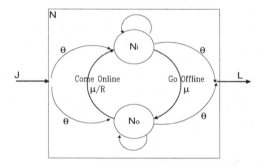

Fig. 2. An analytical model.

In this model, the rate of an online user going offline is μ and the rate for an offline user coming online is μ/R. Let N_i and N_o be the populations of online and offline users just after a rekeying operation, respectively, then $N_i + N_o = N$. Denote S as the number of nodes switching from offline status to online status in T. In the steady status, S is also the number of nodes switching from online to offline in T. For periodic batched rekeying, both node additions and revocations are processed at the end of a group rekeying. Thus, $S = N_i \cdot \mu \cdot T = N_o \cdot \mu/R \cdot T$. We have $N_i = \frac{N}{R+1}$ and

$$S = \frac{N \cdot \mu \cdot T}{R + 1}. \tag{1}$$

We will use S in our evaluation study shortly.

The impact of presence dynamics on group rekeying

Scenario I: Multicast Cost. For LKH, we adopt the analytic result in [23] to compute the communication cost of the LKH-based group rekeying scheme. For SDR, the upper bound of group rekeying cost is $2r$, where r is the accumulated number of nodes that have been revoked from the system so far. We use simulations to show its average cost in different rekeying periods.

The setting for the comparison is as follows. We assume that in the steady status, $N = 65536$. Let the average membership duration be $1/\theta = 30$ days and the group rekeying interval be $T = 1$ day. Let the size of a key be 20 bytes (128-bit AES encryption, with a key version field and encoding overhead). Figure 3 depicts the bandwidth overhead of LKH, SDR, and CRBR in the first thirty rekeying events. We can observe that LKH has the same bandwidth overhead during different rekeying operations, whereas in SDR the bandwidth overhead starts at a small value and eventually exceeds that in LKH. The bandwidth overhead in CRBR increases slightly with time, but it is still far smaller than that in the other two schemes.

Note that although in this simulation setting the bandwidth overhead seems not a big concern even for individual users in any one of these three schemes, the bandwidth saving of our scheme over the other two schemes is very meaningful for a very large group. For example, when N reaches one million, under the same setting every rekeying cost in LKH is 8.3 MB, in SDR it becomes several megabytes when r reaches hundreds of thousands, whereas in CRBR it is upper bounded by 128 KB. Because of its small size, the rekeying message in CRBR can be distributed using our DoS-resilient k-RIP scheme introduced in Section 5.

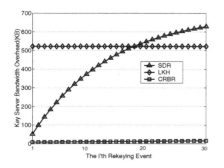
Fig. 3. Rekeying cost of LKH, SDR, and CRBR in different rekeying times.

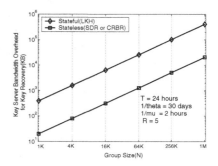
Fig. 4. The bandwidth overhead of key server for unicasting keys to nodes.

Scenario II: Unicast Cost. When the key server distributes its security update, none of the N_o offline nodes receive it. As we showed earlier, S of these nodes come back online during T. When LKH is employed, these S nodes would need to ask the key server for retransmission of the current group key to decrypt the current data because of the statefulness property of LKH, whereas in SDR and CRBR, these nodes can get retransmission from other nodes.

Next we show the overall retransmission cost in these schemes. In SDR or CRBR, only the current group key (no KEKs) is retransmitted to a requesting node. Thus the overall bandwidth overhead is S keys if we do not count other packet overhead. In LKH, a node needs to receive the current group key and some of its KEKs that have been updated. We assume that in LKH, a node that comes online needs to receive on average $h/2$ keys, where h is the height of the key tree maintained by the key server. Therefore, during T, the key server needs to retransmit $\frac{Sh}{2}$ keys.

Figure 4 plots the bandwidth overhead for unicast-based key updating in LKH and SDR/CRBR with the same network characteristics as in the previous comparison. We can observe that the key server bandwidth overhead is nontrivial and it increases linearly with group size. For example, for a group of size of $65,536$, in LKH the key server has to transmit 25.6 MB to help nodes update keys. In SDR or CRBR, the cost is 1.28 MB. When N reaches one million, the cost in LKH becomes greater than 400 MB.

Overall, the analysis of these two scenarios shows that CRBR outperforms LKH and SDR in terms of bandwidth for the applications under consideration. Moreover, our simulation (although not shown) indicates that in many cases we can greatly reduce the size of the CRL by compressing it using a compression program, e.g.,"zip", before performing digital signing.

5   A DoS-Resilient Key Distribution Scheme (k-RIP)

This section describes our DoS-Resilient key distribution scheme called k-RIP. The scheme can also be used for distribution of other small-size but critical information (e.g., new virus and worm signatures, CRLs) in overlay multicast group.

In overlay multicast, messages are normally injected into the network from the distribution server (i.e., the root node), and are then forwarded hop-by-hop to all the other nodes in the tree. If a malicious node in the tree intentionally discards the message it receives from its parent node, its downstream nodes will not receive the message. This attack is specially severe when the malicious node is very close to the root. We note that this attack is also effective to non-tree based delivery infrastructure. Schemes [19, 21, 22] based on more complex graphs are more resilient to the attack in general, but they are still subject to selective attacks in which an attacker selectively compromises several nodes close to the injection point.

Note that we cannot solely rely on detection and retransmission mechanisms to address this attack. If every node that detects message losses asks the key server for retransmission, the key server will become the performance bottleneck. Therefore, it is very important that the majority of the member nodes could receive messages even in the presence of DoS attacks.

5.1   Scheme Overview

To address the above attacks, we propose that in addition to propagating its message through the root node, the key server also randomly picks k nodes (not including the root) in the tree and sends its message to these k nodes. All these k nodes propagate the message towards their children (if any) as well as their parents if their children or parents have not received the message yet. Thus, if a small number of nodes do not forward the message, other nodes might still be able to get it from their children or parents with high probability.

In this scheme, we can simply use sequence numbers to suppress duplicated messages, thus every node only receives one copy of the message and forwards the message to another node at most once. Moreover, this scheme has the additional benefit of reducing the overall latency for all online nodes to receive the message. On the other hand, this scheme incurs the bandwidth overhead for the key server to transmit k additional copies of the message. However, for small-size messages (e.g., tens or hundreds of kilobytes) and a small k (e.g., ≤ 20), in practice this transmission overhead should not be a big concern for the key server.

5.2 Node Selection

The very first question is which k nodes to select? To answer this question, we need to consider two factors: latency and DoS-resilience. Ideally, we should select k nodes such that the overall latency is minimized and the number of nodes that can receive messages is maximized. In practice, it is hard to achieve the above goal because the key server might not have the precise knowledge of the tree topology due to the presence dynamics of the member nodes. The key server might know which nodes have joined the tree from a rendezvous point (RP) in many routing algorithms [2, 24] because a joining node contacts a RP for information assisting the node to find a position in the tree. However, for scalability the RP does not keep track of the position of a specific node in the tree or if a node is online or offline. Thus, for our scheme to work, a practical issue is to determine which nodes are online.

A heuristic selection algorithm. A simple solution works as follows. The key server randomly selects its member nodes to connect to. If a member node is unreachable, it picks another one. The key server repeats this process until it discovers k online nodes. One problem with this scheme is that the key server might not know the IP addresses of its member nodes because nodes might have dynamic IP addresses. This problem can be addressed by letting the RP record the IP addresses of the nodes that have recently contacted it. Because nodes normally do not change their IP addresses during a session, the key server can use these IP addresses directly[1].

Using the same group characteristics as that used in Section 4.4, we know that for a system that has the registered population of N and the average network size of $N_a = \frac{N}{R+1}$, the key server needs to try an average number of $\frac{kN}{N_a} = k(R+1)$ times to find k online nodes. This shows that the efficiency of this algorithm relies on the node presence dynamics. For a small R, this selection algorithm should work fine. When R is large, we may exploit the following heuristics to increase the hit ratio. The idea is that the key server could make a good guess of online members based on the joining times of the members. Again, we assume that presence durations in a multicast session approximately follow an exponential distribution [1]. Assume that the mean of presence durations is $1/\theta$, which can be calculated if every member node records its every presence period and reports its mean presence time to the RP when joining the tree.

The probability $p_i(t)$ that a member node i is still online t time after it joins is $p_i(t) = e^{-\theta \cdot t}$. $p_i(t)$ decreases with t, indicating that the nodes joining more recently are more likely to be online than those joining earlier. Thus, the RP simply tells the key server the ids of m distinct nodes that joined the tree most recently, such that $\sum_{i=1}^{m} p_i(t_i) \geq \varphi k$, where t_i ($1 \leq i \leq m$) is the time difference between the current time and the joining time of that node. Here $\varphi \geq 1$ is a parameter reflecting the

---

[1] Note that for nodes behind network address translators(NATs), if they can join the overlay network [10], they should also be reachable to the server.

probability that the key server finds k online nodes from m candidates, and it is variable and should be determined by the presence dynamics of an actual application.

We note that there is a potential attack against this selection algorithm if the message (e.g., the CRL in CRBR) is distributed periodically, because multiple malicious nodes may join the tree just before the distribution time point. Based on our selection algorithm, the RP will likely report their ids to the key server. Thus, these malicious nodes are selected as injection points, reducing the effectiveness of our scheme. To mitigate this attack, it is important that the key server randomly picks nodes from the m candidates for presence test, not preferring the nodes that joined more recently.

5.3 Evaluation of Effectiveness

This subsection reports the effectiveness of our k-RIP scheme in increasing DoS-resilience. Due to space limit, we refer the reader to our technical report [25] for our simulation results on the effectiveness of our scheme in reducing propagation latency. We first show the analytical model, followed by simulations.

Analytical model. Figure 5 depicts an example multicast tree that has degree of $d = 2$ and group size of N_a nodes (excluding the root node that is the distribution server). The solid nodes are good nodes and the empty one is a compromised node that drops messages going through it. Let h be the height (in hops) of the compromised node from the root and s be the number of nodes in the subtree rooted at the compromised node. Then we have $s = \frac{N_a}{d^h} - \frac{1-(\frac{1}{d})^{h-1}}{d-1}$.

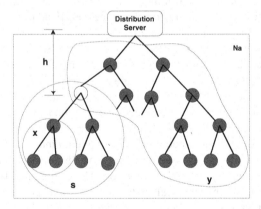

Fig. 5. An example tree of size N_a excluding the root. The empty node is a compromised node whose tree size is s.

Let z be the number of good nodes that can receive messages. Let base scheme be the one in which only a single copy of a message is injected via the root node. It is easy to see that in base scheme $z = N_a - s$. In our k-RIP scheme, besides the root node, k randomly picked nodes also inject the message into the tree simultaneously. If a good node in the subtree rooted at a child node of the compromised node is selected , all the nodes in this subtree will receive the message. If one good node is selected from each subtree rooted at each child node of the compromised nodes, all the good nodes in the network will receive the message. More generally, denote $p(i)$ as the probability that at least one node is selected from each of i ($0 \leq i \leq d$) subtrees rooted at i child nodes (but no nodes are selected from the other $(d - i)$ subtrees) of the compromised node. Further denote $x = (s - 1)/d$ and $y = N_a - s + 1$, as shown in Figure. 5. Basic probability and combinatorics arguments can be used to derive $p(i)$:

$$
p(i) = \begin{cases} \binom{y}{k}/\binom{N_a}{k} & (i = 0) \\ \\ \binom{y+ix}{k}/\binom{N_a}{k} - \sum\limits_{j=0}^{i-1} \binom{i}{j} p(j) & (0 < i \leq d) \end{cases}
$$

The expected value of z is:

$$
E[z] = \sum_{i=0}^{d} \binom{d}{i} p(i)(y - 1 + ix). \tag{2}
$$

This analytic result has been validated by simulations.

Simulation setting. We first generate a random graph of 10,000 nodes and then construct a tree out of the graph based on the joining algorithm that is also used in [12, 24]. Specifically, every joining node searches from the root downwards along the tree for the (possible) nearest node as its parent, thus geometrically adjacent nodes become neighbors in the tree. The link delay between any two nodes is randomly selected from a uniform distribution between 10 and 200 ms, and the outdegree of a node is a random number between 1 and 5. Our simulation programs were written using the Csim simulation library [9]. We use the method of independent replications for our simulations and all our results have 95% confidence intervals that are within 5% of the reported values.

Evaluation results. Figure 6 illustrates the effectiveness of our k-RIP scheme compared to the base scheme, based on eqn. 2. We observe that in the base scheme, a compromised node with the height $h = 1$ could prevent half of existing nodes from receiving the message, whereas our scheme allows a much larger fraction of nodes to receive the message. For example, when $k = 3$, about 80% nodes can receive the message. More nodes get the message when k increases. For example, when $k = 10$, about 97% nodes could receive it. In addition, the figure indicates that in the base scheme, to cause denial of service to more nodes, an attacker should manage to become as close to the root as possible. However, when our scheme is deployed, that is not necessarily the best strategy for the attacker. For example, when $k = 10$, becoming a node with $h = 2$ or $h = 3$ gives the attacker a little more advantage than becoming a node with $h = 1$.

Next we study the effectiveness of our heuristic selection algorithm that selects k nodes from mostly recently joined m nodes (denoted as k-RIP-h, dashed lines in Figure 7), compared with the base scheme in which we randomly select k nodes from N_a nodes (denoted as k-RIP, solid lines). We set the outdegree of a node $d = 3$ and the size of the candidate set $m = 50$. Figure 7 indicates that except when $h = 1$, the effectiveness of k-RIP is only slightly affected when choosing k ($k \leq 20$) nodes from 50 most recently joined nodes instead of choosing from all $N_a = 10,000$ nodes.

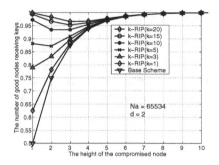
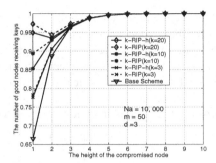

Fig. 6. The fraction of nodes that can receive messages as a function of the location of one single compromised node in the multicast tree and k.

Fig. 7. The effectiveness of our heuristic selection algorithm (through simulation, 95% C.I. is within 5% interval of a reported value.)

6   Conclusions and Future Work

We have presented a bandwidth efficient scheme that integrates network access control and group key management. Performance analysis and simulation study show that our scheme incurs much smaller communication overhead than two other well-known schemes. We also proposed a DoS-resilient information distribution scheme that delivers small-size but critical messages (e.g., keys) to a large fraction of nodes with high probability even if an attacker can selectively compromise nodes in the multicast data delivery hierarchy. The scheme has only considered to distribute one message and used a fixed k. In the future, we will consider selecting k dynamically based on the receiving status in the past.

Acknowledgements

We thank Wensheng Zhang, Lingyu Wang, Shiping Chen and the anonymous reviewers for their valuable comments and suggestions.

References

1. K. Almeroth and M. Ammar, Multicast Group Behavior in the Internet's Multicast Backbone (Mbone), IEEE Communications, June 1997.
2. S. Banerjee, B. Bhattacharjee, C. Kommareddy. Scalable Application Layer Multicast. In Proc. of ACM Sigcomm, 2002.
3. S. Banerjee, S. Lee, B. Bhattacharjee, A. Srinivasan. Resilient Multicast Using Overlays. In Proc. of ACM Sigmetrics 2003.
4. G. Badishi, I. Keidar, and A. Sasson. Exposing and Eliminating Vulnerabilities to Denial of Service Attacks in Secure Gossip-Based Multicast. In Proc. of Dependable Systems and Networks (DSN), 2004.
5. D. Balenson, D. McGrew, and A. Sherman. Key Management for Large Dynamic Groups: One-Way Function Trees and Amortized Initialization. IETF Internet draft (work in progress), August 2000.

6. CCITT Recommendation X.509: The Directory-Authentication Framework. 1988.
7. Y. Chu, S. Rao, S. Seshan, and H. Zhang. Enabling conferencing applications on the internet using an overlay multicast architecture. In Proc. of ACM SIGCOMM 2001.
8. Y. Chu, S. Rao, and H. Zhang. A case for endsystem multicast. In Proc. of ACM Sigmetrics'00, 2000.
9. http://www.mesquite.com/.
10. B. Ford, P. Srisuresh, and D. Kegel. Peer-to-Peer Communication Across Network Address translators. In Proc. of USENIX Annual Technical Conference, 2005.
11. H. He, T. Hardjono, and B. Cain. Simple Multicast Receiver Access Control. draft-irtf-gsec-smrac-00.txt, Nov. 2001.
12. J. Jannotti, D. Gifford, K. Johnson, M. Kaashoek, and J. O'Toole. Overcast: Reliable, Multicasting with an Overlay Network. In Proc. of 4th USENIX OSDI Symposium, 2000.
13. D. Liu, P. Ning, and K. Sun. Efficient Self-Healing Group Key Distribution with Revocation Capability. In Proc. of the 10th ACM CCS, 2003.
14. J. Li, P. Reiher, and G. Popek. Resilient Self-Organizing Overlay Networks for Security Update Delivery. IEEE Journal on Selected Areas in Communications, Vol.22., January 2004.
15. L. Mathy, N. Blundell, V. Roca, and A. Elsayed. Impact of Simple Cheating in Application-Level Multicast. In Proc. of IEEE Infocom 2004.
16. D. Naor, M. Naor, and J. Lotspiech. Revocation and Tracing Schemes for Stateless Receivers. In Advances in Cryptology - CRYPTO 2001. Springer-Verlag Inc. LNCS 2139, 2001, 41-62.
17. S. Setia, S. Koussih, S. Jajodia, and E. Harder. Kronos: A Scalable Group Re-Keying Approach for Secure Multicast. In Proc. of the IEEE Symposium on Security and Privacy, Oakland CA, May 2000.
18. S. Setia, S. Zhu and S. Jajodia. A Comparative Performance Analysis of Reliable Group Rekey Transport Protocols for Secure Multicast. In Performance Evaluation 49(1/4): 21-41 (2002), special issue Proceedings of Performance 2002, Rome, Italy, Sept 2002.
19. D. Song, D. Zuckerman, and J. Tygar. Expander Graphs for Digital Stream Authentication and Robust Overlay Networks. In Proc. of IEEE Symp. on Security & Privacy, 2002.
20. C. Wong, M. Gouda, S. Lam. Secure Group Communication Using Key Graphs. In Proc. of SIGCOMM 1998, Vancouver, British Columbia, 68-79.
21. R. Wright, P. Lincoln, and J. Millen. Efficient Fault-Tolerant Certificate Revocation. In Proc. of ACM CCS 2000.
22. H. Yang, H. Luo, Y. Yang, S. Lu, and L. Zhang HOURS: Achieving DoS Resilence in an Open Service Hierarchy. In Proc. of Dependable Systems and Networks (DSN), 2004.
23. Y. Yang, X. Li, X. Zhang and S. Lam. Reliable group rekeying: Design and Performance Analysis. In Proc. of ACM SIGCOMM 2001.
24. B. Zhang, S. Jamin, and L. Zhang. Host Multicast: a Framework for Delivering Multicast to End Users. In IEEE Infocom 2002.
25. S. Zhu, C. Yao, D. Liu, S. Setia, and S. Jajodia. Efficient Security Mechanisms for Overlay Multicast-based Content Distribution. Tech-report, CSE, PSU Feb., 2005. Http://www.cse.psu.edu/~szhu/overlay.pdf.

A Traitor Tracing Scheme Based on RSA
for Fast Decryption

John Patrick McGregor, Yiqun Lisa Yin, and Ruby B. Lee

Princeton Architecture Laboratory for Multimedia and Security (PALMS)
Department of Electrical Engineering
Princeton University
{mcgregor,yyin,rblee}@princeton.edu

Abstract. We describe a fully k-resilient traitor tracing scheme that utilizes RSA as a secret-key rather than public-key cryptosystem. Traitor tracing schemes deter piracy in broadcast encryption systems by enabling the identification of authorized users known as traitors that contribute to unauthorized pirate decoders. In the proposed scheme, upon the confiscation of a pirate decoder created by a collusion of k or fewer authorized users, contributing traitors can be identified with certainty. Also, the scheme prevents innocent users from being framed as traitors. The proposed scheme improves upon the decryption efficiency of past traitor tracing proposals. Each authorized user needs to store only a single decryption key, and decryption primarily consists of a single modular exponentiation operation. In addition, unlike previous traitor tracing schemes, the proposed scheme employs the widely deployed RSA algorithm.

1 Introduction

Broadcast encryption is beneficial in scenarios where a content provider wishes to securely distribute the same information to many users or subscribers. The broadcast content is protected with encryption, and only legitimate users should possess the information (e.g., decryption keys) necessary to access the content. These keys can be embedded in software or in tamper-resistant hardware devices such as smart cards.

Current tamper-resistant hardware is vulnerable to a variety of attacks [1], however. Furthermore, truly tamper-resistant software, which includes programs that resist unauthorized tampering or inspection of code and data, has yet to be developed. Thus, authorized users can extract decryption keys from a legitimate software or hardware decoder. These users can then circumvent the security of the system by divulging the compromised decryption keys to unauthorized users. Alternatively, the authorized users may employ the compromised keys to generate new decryption keys for distribution to unauthorized users. The authorized users who illegally extract and distribute decryption keys are *traitors*, and the unauthorized users who unfairly obtain the keys are *pirates*. The illegal decoder software or hardware devices created by the traitors are *pirate decoders*.

J. Ioannidis, A. Keromytis, and M.Yung (Eds.): ACNS 2005, LNCS 3531, pp. 56–74, 2005.

Traitor tracing schemes, which are also called *traceability schemes*, protect keys by enabling the identification of the source of pirated broadcast decryption keys. In systems that incorporate a traitor tracing scheme, it is possible to identify one or more contributing traitors upon confiscation of a pirate decoder using a *traitor tracing algorithm*. For a traitor tracing algorithm to be valuable, the scheme must be *frameproof*. The frameproof property ensures that a collusion of traitors cannot create a pirate decoder that would implicate an innocent user as being a traitor.

Past traitor tracing proposals have focused on providing an extensive suite of security services while reducing encryption and network communication requirements. However, decryption is often slow: existing traceability schemes may require dozens of modular exponentiations or thousands of symmetric-key decryptions per user per broadcast secret. In this work, we introduce a new secret-key traitor tracing system that improves upon the decryption performance of existing proposals by enabling decryption to be performed with essentially a single modular exponentiation operation.

The paper is organized as follows. In Section 1, we discuss past work in traitor tracing research and the contributions of this paper. In Section 2, we present the system model and discuss the RSA encryption algorithm. In Section 3, we present the implementation of the new traceability scheme. We analyze the security of the scheme in Section 4, and we present the traitor tracing algorithms in Section 5. In Section 6, we analyze the performance and implementation costs of the scheme, and we conclude in Section 7.

1.1   Past Work

Fiat and Naor introduced broadcast encryption in [14]. In their scheme, there exists a set of n authorized users, and a content provider can dynamically specify a privileged subset (of size $\leq n$) of authorized users that can decrypt certain encrypted messages. A message can be securely broadcast to such a privileged subset unless a group of $k+1$ or more authorized users not belonging to the privileged subset collude to construct a pirate decoder to recover the message. The communication overhead, i.e., the factor increase in message size, is $O(k^2 \log^2 k \log n)$. Also, each user must store $O(k \log k \log n)$ decryption keys. Many improvements to this scheme have been presented, but few enable the identification of traitors that collude to distribute pirate decryption keys to unauthorized users.

To combat such piracy of decryption keys, Chor, Fiat and Naor introduced traitor tracing schemes in [7, 8]. These schemes are *k-resilient*, which means if k or fewer traitors contribute to the construction of the pirate decoder, at least one of those traitors can be identified. In the deterministic symmetric-key one-level scheme of [7, 8], the computation and communication costs depend on the total number of users, n, and on the largest tolerable collusion size, k. Each user must store $O(k^2 \log n)$ decryption keys, and each user must perform $O(k^2 \log n)$ operations to decrypt the content upon receipt of the broadcast transmission. The one-level scheme also increases the communication cost of broadcasting secret content by a factor of $O(k^4 \log n)$. The deterministic symmetric-key two-level scheme of [7, 8] reduces the encryption complexity and communication overhead relative to the one-level scheme at the cost of increasing the decryption complexity and the number of decryption keys per user.

Pfitzmann introduced the concept of *asymmetric* traitor tracing in [26]. This feature allows a content provider to unambiguously convince a third party of a traitor's guilt. Previous proposals for traitor tracing were *symmetric*, which means the content provider shares all secret information with the set of authorized users. In a symmetric scheme, a dishonest content provider can frame an innocent authorized user as being a traitor by building an "unauthorized" decoder that contains a particular user's decryption key.

Public-key k-resilient traitor tracing schemes have also been introduced (e.g., [5, 19, 22, 36]). In such a scheme, publicly known encryption keys can be used to encrypt and subsequently transmit a secret to the entire set of authorized users. The authorized users then employ their respective private decryption keys to decode the transmission. The public-key scheme presented in [5] is symmetric, and the one described in [22] is asymmetric but requires a trusted third party. Asymmetric public-key traitor tracing schemes that do not require a trusted third party are described in [19, 36].

In some situations, a traitor may decrypt the broadcast information and then transmit the plaintext result to pirates rather than distribute a pirate decoder that contains valid decryption keys. Researchers have suggested combining digital fingerprinting and traitor tracing to prevent such piracy [15, 27, 29]. The systems discussed in [27] employ provably secure, robust digital watermark constructions presented in [6, 9]. More efficient and effective integrated fingerprinting and traceability schemes are described in [15, 29]. However, as illustrated by attacks on digital fingerprinting technologies, it can be difficult to design a practical fingerprinting scheme that a savvy attacker cannot thwart [10]. In this paper, we consider only those scenarios in which traitors do not command the resources necessary to distribute decrypted content efficiently; we assume that traitors can only distribute decryption keys.

Researchers have presented many other traceability schemes and traitor tracing algorithms that employ a rich variety of mathematical tools (e.g., [8, 13, 17, 20–22, 24, 25, 32, 34, 35]). For instance, Kurosawa and Desmedt describe a highly efficient k-resilient symmetric traceability scheme in [22]. Their scheme incurs a communication overhead of $O(k)$ and requires each user to store 1 decryption key and to perform $O(k)$ decryption operations per transmitted secret. Kiayias and Yung propose a public key traitor tracing scheme with "constant transmission overhead" [21]. However, in that scheme, the minimum size of the broadcast message may be impractical if protection against large collusions is desired. Researchers present systems that efficiently incorporate broadcast encryption and some degree of traceability in [13, 17, 24, 35]. For example, in [24], a highly efficient trace-and-revoke scheme is described that allows pirate decoders to be disabled upon confiscation of a pirate decoder without incurring significant re-keying costs. However, the scheme does not guarantee identification of the contributing traitors.

Table 1. Past work comparison (k is the maximum traitor collusion size, n is the total number of authorized users, and M is an RSA modulus).

Traitor Tracing Scheme	Communication Overhead	Decryption Complexity (Dominant Component) per User	Number of Decryption Keys per User
One-level [7, 8]	$O(k^4 \log n)$	$O(k^2 \log n)$ sym. decryptions	$O(k^2 \log n)$
Two-level [7, 8]	$O(k^3 \log^4 k \log(n/k))$	$O(k^2 \log^2 k \log n)$ sym. decryptions	$O(k^2 \log^2 k \log(n/k))$
Public-key [5, 19, 22, 36]	$O(k)$	$O(k)$ exponentiations	$O(1)$
Our Proposal	$O(\max(k \log n, k \log \log M / \log k))$	~ 1 exponentiation	1

Table 1 summarizes the performance and characteristics of certain traitor tracing schemes that can *identify* members of a traitor collusion of k or fewer traitors with certainty. We do not compare our results to trace-and-revoke schemes or probabilistic traceability schemes that do not guarantee traitor identification upon confiscation of a pirate decoder. In the table, n is the maximum number of authorized users, k is the maximum tolerable collusion size, and M is a typical value for an RSA modulus (e.g., $\sim 2^{1024}$). "Sym. decryptions" means symmetric-key decryption operations.

1.2   Our Contributions

We propose Traitor Tracing using RSA (TTR), a fully k-resilient traceability scheme based upon the RSA encryption algorithm. Although we employ RSA, TTR is not public-key: we apply RSA as a secret-key cryptosystem rather than as a public-key cryptosystem. This design choice enables many security features, including the prevention of common modulus attacks [11, 33]. Our system enables traceability against collusions of k or fewer traitors if the factoring problem is hard, and the encryption scheme is secure against known and chosen plaintext attacks if the RSA problem is hard. Furthermore, TTR prevents traitor collusions from framing innocent users.

We present both clear-box and black-box traitor tracing algorithms for TTR. The efficient clear-box algorithm can always identify at least one of the traitors in a collusion of size k or fewer. The efficient black-box algorithm can identify all of the contributing traitors in a collusion of size k or fewer, even when keys cannot be explicitly extracted from the pirate decoder, but only for a limited and special class of pirate decoders.

TTR improves decryption performance relative to past proposals at the cost of increasing the computation and transmission requirements of the content provider. As shown in Table 1, TTR requires only a single modular exponentiation operation and a relatively insignificant number of modular multiplication operations to perform decryption upon receipt of a broadcast secret[1]. Though modular exponentiations are computationally more expensive than symmetric key encryptions, TTR still exhibits the highest decryption performance for realistic numbers of users and traitors. Furthermore, TTR only requires each authorized user to store a single decryption key, which may be only 256 bytes in size in realistic scenarios. The communication overhead and encryption complexity of TTR are $O(\max(k \log n, k \log \log M / \log k))$.

2 Preliminaries

2.1 System Model

The broadcast encryption system model used in this paper involves several entities:

- **Content Provider.** The content provider prepares, encrypts, and transmits broadcast messages.
- **Universe of Users.** Broadcast messages are transmitted to the universe of all authorized and unauthorized users, U.
- **Authorized Users.** Only the members of the set of authorized users, T, are provided with the information needed to decode broadcast messages. The maximum number of authorized users is n, so $T = \{t_1, t_2, \ldots, t_n\}$, and $T \subseteq U$.

We present an open traceability scheme in which the methods employed to perform encryption and decryption are public, but the keys used to perform these operations are private. The content provider does not reveal the secret encryption keys to the users, and authorized users (who are not traitors) do not reveal their personal decryption keys to other users.

The following six components typically comprise an open traceability scheme:

- **Provider Initialization.** A content provider generates initial values required to produce the broadcast encryption keys and the user decryption keys.
- **User Initialization.** An authorized user t_i is added to the set of authorized users, T, by requesting that the content provider generate and securely distribute a user decryption key to t_i.
- **Encryption.** The content provider encrypts a message one or more times using one or more secret encryption keys.
- **Transmission.** The content provider transmits the encrypted message to all users.
- **Decryption.** Upon receipt of an encrypted message from the content provider, each authorized user decrypts the secret using his respective decryption key.
- **Traitor Tracing Algorithms.** Upon confiscation of a pirate decoder, the content provider invokes a tracing algorithm to identify contributing traitors.

---

[1] $(1 + O(\log n / \log M))$ exponentiations are required by a TTR decryption, which is ~ 1 exponentiation for realistic values of n and M (see Section 6.4).

2.2   RSA

Since TTR is based upon the RSA encryption algorithm, we will briefly describe the operation of standard RSA. In RSA, security is related to the computational difficulty of factoring large integers [28]. Let M be the product of two large prime integers, p and q, where p and q are roughly the same size. We call M the RSA modulus. Now, find two integers e and d such that $ed \equiv 1 \bmod \phi(M)$, where ϕ is Euler's totient function: $\phi(M) = (p-1)(q-1)$. The integers e and d are called the encryption exponent and the decryption exponent, respectively. The pair $\langle M, e \rangle$ is the encryption key, and the pair $\langle M, d \rangle$ is the decryption key. Given a plaintext block $a \in \mathbf{Z}_M^*$, a sender can encrypt a to produce a ciphertext c using the public key by computing $c = a^e \bmod M$. The receiver can decrypt c using the private key by computing $a = c^d \bmod M$. There are many minor implementation details required to fortify protocols using RSA against potential attacks. Boneh summarizes several attacks on RSA implementations in [3].

Consider a very simple traitor tracing scheme based on RSA: the content provider generates a common modulus M and a key pair $\langle e_i, d_i \rangle$ for each user t_i. The provider keeps the encryption exponent e_i secret (i.e., unknown to t_i) and passes the decryption key $\langle M, d_i \rangle$ to t_i. To broadcast information to authorized users, the provider simply encrypts messages individually for each user. However, this scheme is very inefficient, since the number of encryption keys and the communication overhead are the same as the number of users, n.

We can improve upon the performance of this simple scheme. Using the multiplicative properties of RSA, we can generate ciphertexts with a few encryption keys that can be decrypted using many decryption keys. The general method, which employs techniques also used in RSA-based threshold cryptosystems (initiated in [12]), operates as follows. Given a plaintext block a and a modulus M, we generate L ciphertexts $C = \{c_1, c_2, \ldots, c_L\}$ encrypted using L different non-zero positive encryption exponents $e_1, e_2, \ldots, e_L$:

$$c_j = a^{e_j} \bmod M \qquad (1)$$

Now, a user can multiply all L ciphertexts modulo M to obtain a "product ciphertext", c_{PROD}, that is equivalent to encrypting a one time using a single encryption exponent that is the sum of the L encryption exponents:

$$c_{PROD} = \prod_{i=1}^{L} c_i \bmod M = \left(\prod_{i=1}^{L} a^{e_i} \bmod M \right) \bmod M = a^{e_{SUM}} \bmod M, \qquad (2)$$

where $e_{SUM} = \sum_{i=1}^{L} e_i$. A user could subsequently decrypt the c_{PROD} using a decryption exponent $d_{SUM} \equiv e_{SUM}^{-1} \bmod \phi(M)$.

In general, upon obtaining the L ciphertext blocks, a user can multiply (modulo M) a subset of the ciphertexts in C to obtain a different product ciphertext. This new product ciphertext could be decrypted using a new decryption exponent. Since there exist $2^L - 1$ nonempty subsets of C, there exist $2^L - 1$ product ciphertexts that can be decrypted with $2^L - 1$ decryption keys. Hence, we can generate ciphertexts that can be deciphered using up to $2^L - 1$ decryption keys by performing only L encryptions with L encryption keys.

3   A Traceability Scheme Using RSA

TTR takes advantage of the multiplicative properties of RSA to generate and
support many decryption keys using relatively few encryption keys. TTR is parameterized by M, n, k, s, L, and α. M is the RSA modulus, and n is the
number of authorized users in T. The parameter k represents the maximum tolerable traitor collusion size, and s is the security parameter of the scheme. For
example, in a scenario with $k = 10$ and $s = 20$, any collusion of size at most 10
can produce a non-traceable key with probability at most 2^{-20}.

The parameters L and α are based on the values of M, n, k, and s. L
represents the number of encryption exponents in the scheme, and the value of
L is as follows:

$$L = O(\max(k \log n, k \log \log M / \log k)). \tag{3}$$

The parameter α equals the probability that an element in a user's decryption
vector (described below) equals 1, and $\alpha = 1/k$. The rationale for the values of
L and α will be presented in Section 4.4.

We now present the provider initialization, user initialization, encryption,
transmission, and decryption components of the new scheme. The traitor tracing
algorithms are presented in Section 5.

3.1   Provider Initialization

During provider initialization, the content provider creates the secret encryption
keys and the information required to generate future user decryption keys. First,
the content provider generates a RSA modulus $M = pq$, where p and q are both
prime. For performance reasons, we require that p and q be safe primes, i.e.,
the integers $(p-1)/2$ and $(q-1)/2$ are also prime. Second, the content provider
randomly generates a vector E of L unique encryption exponents for M. For each
$e_j \in E$, $e_j \sim M$. The content provider keeps all of the encryption exponents and
the values of p, q, and $\phi(M)$ secret.

We assume that the content provider's secrets are contained in a single device, but we note that the content provider is not required to be centralized. We
could improve security by using RSA threshold techniques (initiated in [12]) to
securely store the content provider's secrets and to securely perform key generation operations across multiple devices. Furthermore, the encryption exponents
and operations can be distributed across multiple content provider devices using
known RSA threshold techniques. Applying such techniques would require an
attacker to compromise most or all of the devices in order to successfully expose
E or $\phi(M)$.

3.2   User Initialization

When an authorized user t_i joins the system, the content provider generates and
securely distributes a user decryption key DK_i to t_i as follows:

1. Randomly generate an L-dimensional Boolean vector $v^{(i)}$. Each element in the vector is set to 1 with probability α, and each element in the vector is set to 0 with probability $1 - \alpha$. In addition, $v^{(i)}$ must not consist of all zeroes, and no two $v^{(i)}$'s are the same. Repeat until $v^{(i)}$ is found where $\sum_{j=1}^{L} v_j^{(i)} e_j$ is relatively prime to $\phi(M)$.
2. Using the extended Euclidean algorithm, calculate a decryption exponent d_i such that:

$$d_i = \left(\sum_{j=1}^{L} v_j^{(i)} e_j \right)^{-1} \mod \phi(M) \qquad (4)$$

If d_i is probabilistically prime, proceed to the next step; otherwise, return to Step 1 and restart the process.
3. Distribute $DK_i = \langle v^{(i)}, d_i, M \rangle$ to t_i via a secure channel.

3.3   Encryption, Transmission, and Decryption

To encrypt a plaintext message P using this scheme, the content provider performs L RSA encryptions on P using each of the encryption exponents in E. The resulting ciphertext C is:

$$C = \langle P^{e_1} \mod M, ..., P^{e_L} \mod M \rangle. \qquad (5)$$

To ensure semantic security, all plaintext messages P should be prepared using Optimal Asymmetric Encryption Padding (OAEP) [2, 4, 16, 31] or a similar method. OAEP is a provably secure mechanism for padding and encoding plaintext messages prior to RSA encryption.

The resulting ciphertext C is then broadcast to all users in U.

Upon receiving the ciphertext C, an authorized user t_i in T can decrypt the ciphertext using his decryption key $DK_i = \langle v^{(i)}, d_i, M \rangle$ as follows:

$$P = \left(\prod_{j=1}^{L} (c_j)^{v_j^{(i)}} \right)^{d_i} \mod M, \text{ where } c_j = P^{e_j} \mod M. \qquad (6)$$

It is easy to see that decryption works by the definition of the decryption keys.

4   Security Analysis

We now analyze the security properties of TTR. Proof sketches are provided for each of the theorems introduced in this section, and detailed proofs of the theorems are presented in the full version of this paper. Also, throughout this section, the terms "polynomial number", "polynomial size", and "polynomial time" imply that a number or running time is bounded by a function that is polynomial in a reasonable security parameter, such as s or the number of bits in the chosen modulus M.

4.1   Resilience Against Known Attacks on RSA

All authorized users possess unique decryption keys based upon the same RSA modulus M. However, the system is *not* vulnerable to the common modulus attacks described in [11, 33].

We classify common modulus attacks into two types. In the first type of common modulus attack, if an adversary has knowledge of two (or more) RSA encryption exponents used to encrypt the same message, the adversary can recover the message using the two (or more) ciphertexts without requiring knowledge of $\phi(M)$ or any decryption exponents [33]. The proposed scheme defends against this attack by treating RSA as a *secret-key cryptosystem* rather than as a *public-key cryptosystem*. The encryption keys employed by the content provider are not revealed to the authorized users, and therefore neither a collusion of users nor a passive adversary can implement this attack.

The second type of common modulus attack operates as follows. If an adversary has knowledge of an encryption key and the corresponding decryption key for a given RSA modulus M, the adversary can factor the modulus using a probabilistic algorithm or can calculate the decryption key corresponding to any encryption key [11]. Neither unauthorized nor authorized users can realize such attacks in the proposed scheme, however, for they do not possess knowledge of both the encryption and decryption keys for the modulus M.

4.2   Security of TTR Encryption

We begin the security analysis with two theorems concerning the security of TTR encryption. Theorem 1 shows that it is difficult for a *passive* unauthorized user to decrypt a given ciphertext in the proposed encryption scheme. For certain applications, however, it may also be desirable for the scheme to be semantically secure against an *active* adversary that can prepare specific content (i.e., plaintext) for the content provider to encrypt. Theorem 2 demonstrates semantic security for TTR against chosen plaintext attacks.

Theorem 1. *Given an RSA modulus M and a polynomial number of known plaintext-ciphertext pairs, a passive adversary cannot decrypt a new ciphertext with non-negligible probability in TTR, assuming the intractability of the RSA problem.*

Proof Sketch. Assume that there exists a polynomial-time algorithm A such that a passive adversary can use algorithm A to decrypt a new ciphertext with non-negligible probability given a polynomial number of plaintext-ciphertext pairs. We can show how to construct a polynomial time algorithm B that finds a solution to the RSA problem by using A as a subroutine.

At a high level, given the inputs of an RSA modulus M, a random encryption exponent e, and a ciphertext $C = P^e \bmod M$, B operates as follows. B first randomly defines (but does not explicitly calculate) a set E of L encryption exponents that are based on a function of the input e. Using these definitions, B

computes a polynomial number, R, of plaintext-ciphertext pairs that are consistent with E and M. With these results, B prepares a new $(R+1)$th ciphertext that is based on the input C. B applies this new ciphertext with the R plaintext-ciphertext pairs as inputs to A, and then A returns a valid plaintext P that is the solution to the instance of the RSA problem. $\square$

Theorem 2. *The TTR encryption scheme is semantically secure against chosen plaintext attacks, assuming the intractability of the RSA problem.*

Proof Sketch. Using similar ideas as presented in the proof of Theorem 1, we can show that the encryption scheme is semantically secure against chosen plaintext attacks (CPA) if RSA-OAEP is semantically secure against CPA. It is well known that RSA-OAEP is semantically secure against CPA assuming the intractability of the RSA problem [2, 4, 16, 31]. $\square$

4.3   Security Against Traitor Collusions

We now discuss the security of TTR against traitor collusions of authorized users in T. We show that a collusion of up to k traitors cannot produce an "untraceable" decryption key, i.e., a key that does not implicate at least one member of the collusion as being a traitor. Furthermore, we show that for sufficient values of L, a collusion of up to k traitors cannot produce any key that would implicate an innocent user as being a traitor.

We define a "traceable key" as follows. Recall that each authorized user is issued a distinct key with a distinct decryption exponent. We say that a pirate key is traceable to an authorized user t_i if the decryption exponent associated with t_i divides one of the integer components of the pirate key. More formally stated, given a user t_i with a key $\langle v^{(i)}, d_i, M \rangle$, a pirate decryption key of the form $\langle v^*, d^*, M \rangle$ is traceable to the user t_i if d_i divides v_j^* for any $1 \leq j \leq L$ or d_i divides d^*. Thus, an "untraceable key" produced by a traitor collusion is a new key in which neither the decryption exponent nor any of the vector elements are divisible by any of the decryption exponents of the traitors' original keys.

We consider the following two classes of keys that may be produced by a traitor collusion:

- The first class includes new valid decryption keys of the standard form defined by the scheme.
- The second class includes new decryption keys that are *not* of the form as defined by the scheme but can be used to successfully decrypt ciphertext and obtain correct plaintext.

We will demonstrate security for TTR against keys from both of these classes. In particular, the vector $v^{(i)}$ generated by the collusion is not required to be a Boolean vector, and the decryption exponents generated by the collusion are not required to be large prime numbers. Instead, each vector entry can be any integer, and each decryption exponent can be any integer. We remark that this

is a much stronger result than only showing that the collusion cannot produce
a decryption key of the standard form.

We need only to prove security against the strongest possible collusion, i.e.,
a collusion of k traitors with knowledge of k linearly independent decryption
keys. If the k or fewer decryption vectors of the traitor collusion's decryption
keys are not linearly independent, then there exists a feasible attack that may
allow the collusion to factor M and defeat the scheme. Thus, the vectors must be
constructed by the content provider such that any k vectors chosen at random
will be linearly independent. As we will explain in Section 4.4, our choice for the
value of L ensures that, with overwhelming probability, a collusion's decryption
vectors are always linearly independent.

We now present two theorems on the security of TTR against traitor collusions. Theorem 3 states that collusions cannot create untraceable keys, and
Theorem 4 states that collusions cannot frame innocent users as being traitors.

Theorem 3. *No collusion of k or fewer authorized users can create an untraceable decryption key with probability greater than 2^{-s} if $L \geq (k-1)(s + \log_2 k +
\log_2 n)/(e \log_2 e)$, assuming the difficulty of factoring.*

Proof Sketch. Assume that there exists a polynomial-time memoryless algorithm
A such that a collusion of k authorized users can employ algorithm A to create
a new, untraceable decryption key with non-negligible probability given their k
decryption keys. We show how to construct a polynomial time algorithm B that
factors a given modulus M by using A as a subroutine.

At a high level, on input $M(=pq)$, algorithm B operates as follows. B begins
by randomly generating k valid and unique decryption keys $DK_i = \langle v^{(i)}, d_i, M \rangle$
of the same form described in the scheme. These keys represent the keys of the
traitor collusion. B then applies the k keys as inputs to A to obtain a new
decryption key, DK_{NEW}. Next, the algorithm B generates an additional $(L-k)$
decryption keys of a special form. We can show that B can use the first k valid
keys, DK_{NEW}, and the additional $(L-k)$ decryption keys to obtain a multiple
of $\phi(M)$. If the multiple is non-zero, B can efficiently factor M [11]. If the
multiple is zero, we can show that with overwhelming probability given an L of
the required size, the key DK_{NEW} is traceable; at least one of the first k d_i's
must divide one of the vector elements or the decryption exponent of DK_{NEW}.
□

Theorem 4. *If the number of possible valid decryption keys exceeds 2^s, then the
probability is exponentially small in s that a collusion of k authorized users can
create a decryption key of size that is polynomial in s and that implicates an
innocent user as a traitor.*

Proof Sketch. Assume that a collusion of up to k authorized users can use
their respective decryption keys to create a new decryption key. In the proposed
scheme, the selection of the $(n-k)$ innocent users' decryption vectors and exponents can be performed entirely independently of the selection of the k traitor
keys. That is, the keys that represent the innocent authorized users may be any

$(n - k)$-subset chosen uniformly at random from the set of $(2^s / \log M - k)$ possible decryption keys that do not belong to the traitor collusion. Given these facts, we can show that the probability is exponentially small in s that the new decryption key will implicate one of the $(n - k)$ innocent authorized users. □

4.4   Choosing the Parameters

We now discuss the requirements for the values of the parameters α and L. As stated in Section 3, $\alpha = 1/k$. It may possible for this value to be increased or decreased; determining the optimal value of α is a subject for future work. We note that, as shown in the full version of this paper, some values of α will cause the scheme to be insecure. For example, setting α to $1/2$ prevents traceability in some scenarios.

The value of L depends on several factors. First, to satisfy several of the theorems stated above, we require the following lower bound for the value of L:

$$L \geq (k - 1)\,(s + \log_2 k + \log_2 n)\,/\,(e \log_2 e) \tag{7}$$

Second, we must ensure that there are enough possible distinct decryption keys to accommodate all of the users in the system. In addition, to satisfy the frameproofing theorem, we must ensure that the number of possible distinct decryption keys exceeds 2^s. Since the expected number of 1's in a vector of length L is $L\alpha$, the number of possible vectors is roughly $\binom{L}{L\alpha} = \binom{L}{L/k}$. However, only a subset of these vectors will correspond to a prime (and therefore valid) decryption exponent. Considering that the probability that a large exponent is prime is approximately $1/\log M$, we have $\binom{L}{L/k} \geq n \log M$, and $\binom{L}{L/k} \geq 2^s \log M$, where log is the natural logarithm. Using Stirling's approximation, a simple calculation shows that $L \geq (k(s + \log_2 n + \log_2 \log M))/ \log_2 ek$ is sufficient.

Third, we must ensure that any k vectors produced by the scheme are linearly independent. Otherwise, a traitor collusion of size k or fewer may be able to factor M. Hence, to maintain security, L should be large enough such that, with overwhelming probability, a set of k randomly generated Boolean vectors of length L are linearly independent. In [18], it is shown that the probability of linear independence is at least $1 - O((1 - \epsilon)^L)$ for some $\epsilon > 0$ if $k \leq L$. Thus, the lower bound for L cited above is sufficient, as that bound requires $L > s$, and therefore the probability of linear dependence will be exponentially small in the security parameter s.

Hence, we have the following expression for L:

$$L \geq \max\left(\frac{(k - 1)\,(s + \log_2 k + \log_2 n)}{e \log_2 e},\ \frac{ks + k \log_2 n + k \log_2 \log M}{\log_2 ek}\right) \tag{8}$$

If the security parameter s is treated as a constant, the size of L and the communication overhead of the scheme is $O(\max(k \log n, k \log \log M/ \log k))$. In most scenarios, $\log n > \log \log M$, so the communication overhead would be $O(k \log n)$.

Finally, we note that the system can be implemented *without* requiring decryption vectors to be prime. We choose to require all d_i's to be prime in order to simplify the proofs of security.

5   Traitor Tracing Algorithms

Upon confiscation of a pirate decoder device, the content provider invokes traitor tracing algorithms to identify the authorized users that contributed to the construction of the device. First, we explore the "clear-box" case, where it is possible to explicitly extract the representations of all the keys embedded in the pirate decoder. Using the clear-box tracing algorithm, we can always efficiently identify at least one of the traitors who contributed to a pirate decoder. Second, we present a limited "black-box" tracing algorithm. In this case, we cannot extract keys from the pirate decoder, but we can apply inputs to the decoder and observe the resulting outputs. Unlike the clear-box algorithm, the black-box algorithm enables the tracing of keys only in special cases.

5.1   A Clear-Box Tracing Algorithm

We assume that a pirate decoder contains easily recognizable representations of one or more valid decryption keys; these keys are employed by the decoder to perform all message decryptions. As shown in Section 4, a traitor collusion can generate new decryption keys only of a certain form. That is, assuming we choose appropriate values for L, α, and s, traitors cannot create untraceable keys (Theorem 3) or create traceable keys that implicate innocent users as traitors (Theorem 4). Hence, we can use the keys in a pirate decoder to identify contributing traitors.

The clear-box tracing algorithm simply compares components of the decryption keys within the pirate device to all existing user decryption keys. The algorithm proceeds as follows:

1. Let $\langle v^*, d^*, M \rangle$ be a pirate key extracted from a pirate decoder, where $v^* = \{v_1^*, ..., v_L^*\}$. For $1 \leq i \leq n$, repeat the following for each authorized user t_i (whose decryption exponent is d_i):
   (a) If d_i divides v_j^* for any $1 \leq j \leq L$ or d_i divides d^*, then user t_i is a traitor.

We now present a theorem stating that, without framing innocent users, this clear-box algorithm can identify at least one of the traitors that colluded to build the pirate decoder.

Theorem 5. *Given a pirate decryption key generated by a collusion of at most k traitors using their respective decryption keys, then with probability exceeding $1 - 2^{-s}$, the clear-box traitor tracing algorithm can identify at least one traitor in the collusion without implicating any innocent users.*

Proof Sketch. As shown by Theorem 3, no group of traitors of size fewer than $k+1$ can generate a new decryption key with non-negligible probability that does not implicate at least one of the colluding traitors using the clear-box traitor tracing algorithm. Furthermore, as shown by Theorem 4, no collusion of traitors of size fewer than $k + 1$ can generate a new decryption key with non-negligible probability that implicates an innocent user. □

Upon discovering the presence of one or more traitors using the proposed scheme, the content provider must re-issue decryption keys to the set of authorized users. We can address this issue by constructing a protocol that distributes new decryption keys to individual, legitimate users at fixed intervals, similar to that described in [30].

5.2   A Limited Black-Box Tracing Algorithm

For the black-box algorithm, we wish to achieve the same goals as desired for the clear-box tracing algorithm, i.e., the identification of at least one contributing traitor and no false implications of guilt. We achieve these goals for a limited class of pirate decoders: *limited-ability pirate decoders*. We define a limited-ability pirate decoder to be a device that contains k or fewer decryption keys that are identical to k or fewer keys issued by the content provider; any one and only one of these keys can be used to perform a single decryption for a given broadcast message. Restricting the pirate device model to limited-ability pirate decoders is reasonable in several practical situations. In a smart card-based decoder or a mass-produced ASIC decoder, storage space may be available only for a single decryption key from a single traitor. Also, it may not be feasible for a pirate decoder to perform multiple decryptions per broadcast message and maintain adequate throughput.

In the black-box algorithm, we identify traitors by applying random data as ciphertext input to the pirate decoder. The decryption of the random data using a decryption key (issued by the content provider) will yield a different and predictable plaintext result for each distinct decryption key. Thus, we can infer which keys are stored in a limited-ability pirate decoder without performing explicit inspection of the pirate device's contents. The decryption key for authorized user t_i is $DK_i = \langle v^{(i)}, d_i, M \rangle$, and the black-box algorithm operates as follows:

1. Randomly generate a set C of L $\lceil \log_2 M \rceil$-bit values, $C = \{c_1, c_2, ..., c_L\}$.
2. Repeat for all i such that $1 \leq i \leq n_{CUR}$, where n_{CUR} is the current number of authorized users:
   (a) Randomly select an integer z such that $v_z^{(i)} = 1$.
   (b) Construct $C' = \{c'_1, c'_2, ..., c'_L\}$ such that $c'_j = c_j$ for $j = z$, and $c'_j = 1$ for $j \neq z$.
   (c) Apply C' to the pirate decoder to obtain decrypted result P.
   (d) Compute $P_{TEST} = \left(\prod_{j=1}^{L} (c'_j)^{v_j^{(i)}} \right)^{d_i} \mod M$. If P_{TEST} equals P, user t_i is a traitor.

When ciphertext input is applied to a limited-ability pirate decoder, the device chooses one of its keys and employs that key to perform the decryption operation. As a result, the black-box tracing algorithm may identify only one of the many keys stored in the device. To find all traitors with high probability, one can simply repeat the black-box tracing algorithm a number of times that is a multiple of k, e.g., $10k$ times, assuming the decryption keys are chosen at random by the pirate decoder.

Without framing innocent users, the black-box algorithm can identify at least one of the traitors that colluded to build a limited-ability pirate decoder. The straightforward proof of this statement is given in the full version of the paper.

6 Performance Analysis

This section investigates the computation and storage costs of TTR.

6.1 Provider Initialization Costs

The computation and storage costs of the provider initialization procedure described in Section 3.1 are as follows. The one-time computation required to generate M and E includes $O(\log^2 M)$ ($\log M$)-bit probabilistic primality tests such as Miller-Rabin (a summary of which can be found in [23]) and $O(L + \log^2 M)$ ($\log M$)-bit random number generations. For convenience of user initialization and encryption of broadcast messages, it is prudent for the content provider to store E, M, and $\phi(M)$. Thus, the expected storage requirement for the content provider is at minimum $L\lceil \log_2 M \rceil + 2\lceil \log_2 M \rceil$ bits.

6.2 User Initialization Costs

The computation and storage costs of the 3-step user initialization procedure described in Section 3.2 are as follows. Since the probability of the summation in Step 1 being relatively prime to $\phi(M)$ is $1/2$, and since the probability that a possible decryption exponent is prime is approximately $1/\log M$, Step 1 will be executed fewer than $2\log M$ times on average, and Step 2 will be executed fewer than $\log M$ times on average. Hence, the total time required by Steps 1 and 2 to generate a prime decryption key is dominated by $O(\log M)$ ($\log M$)-bit probabilistic primality tests and $O(\log M)$ L-bit random number generations. Following key generation, the costs required to securely distribute the user decryption key in Step 3 highly depend on the method that is chosen to secure the channel.

A user decryption key, which consists of a Boolean vector v, a prime decryption exponent d, and a modulus M, requires at most $L + 2\lceil \log_2 M \rceil$ bits of storage. This equates to a decryption key size of approximately 256 bytes in realistic scenarios when using a 1024-bit modulus. The content provider also needs to store a copy of each issued decryption key to avoid issuing the same decryption key to two different users.

Table 2. Decryption computation cost for $2^{-s} = 2^{-80}$.

Number of	Number of exponentiations			
Users (n)	$k = 2$	$k = 10$	$k = 100$	$k = 1000$
2	1.006	-	-	-
10	1.006	1.012	-	-
100	1.007	1.013	1.015	-
1000	1.007	1.013	1.015	1.016
1 million	1.008	1.015	1.017	1.018
1 billion	1.010	1.016	1.019	1.019

6.3   Encryption and Transmission Costs

To encrypt a broadcast message in TTR as described in Section 3.3, the content provider must perform L multiple-precision modular exponentiations using L different encryption exponents. We note that we can reduce the bit length of the encryption exponents to improve the speed of the encryption operations without compromising security. Since one encrypted block is transferred for each encryption exponent, the communication overhead is $O(L)$. Though L may range in the hundreds, in many broadcast encryption systems, the transmission costs may apply only to a small portion (e.g., the header) of broadcast messages.

6.4   Decryption Costs

To decrypt a broadcast message in TTR as described in Section 3.3, an authorized user must perform αL multiple-precision modular multiplications and a single multiple-precision modular exponentiation. For reasonable values of M, n, and k, the $O(\alpha L) = O(\max(\log n, \log \log M / \log k))$ modular multiplications require much less computation than the single modular exponentiation.

Table 2 lists the computation required to perform decryption for various sizes of n and k when $2^{-s} = 2^{-80}$. The values in the table are normalized to a single random 1024-bit modular exponentiation. For example, a value of 1.015 indicates that the decryption operation requires 1.5% more computation than an average 1024-bit modular exponentiation. Some table cells do not have entries because the maximum collusion size k cannot exceed the number of users. If $k = 10$, $2^{-s} = 2^{-80}$, and n equals one million users, then L is 237. The number of modular multiplications required to obtain the product ciphertext is therefore $L\alpha - 1 = 237/10 - 1 \approx 23$. If the size of the RSA modulus is 1024 bits, the exponentiation requires 1535 modular multiplications on average [23]. Hence, in this case, generating product ciphertext requires only 1.48% of the computation involved in decryption. As shown in Table 2, the cost of generating the product ciphertext never exceeds 2% of the overall decryption computation.

In practice, a 1024-bit modular exponentiation can be 1000 times slower per decrypted bit than a 128-bit symmetric key decryption operation [23]. However, for realistic numbers of authorized users and traitors, the new scheme still exhibits the highest decryption performance among the past proposals listed in

Table 1. When k is 10 or greater, TTR outperforms the schemes of [8]. In a realistic implementation where n is one million and k is 10, the decryption speedup of TTR over the schemes of [8] exceeds 7.86x.

6.5   Tracing Algorithm Costs

The clear-box tracing algorithm runs in polynomial time. The algorithm requires at most $O(nL)$ integer division operations to identify a traitor. We note that the actual computational complexity of the algorithm is a function of n_{CUR}, which is the current number of authorized users, rather than a function of n, which is the maximum number of authorized users. This is an important distinction, as the values of n_{CUR} and n can differ by orders of magnitude in practice.

The limited black-box tracing algorithm runs in polynomial time. The values of P_{TEST} for each user can be precomputed (at user initialization time) and can be stored in a hash table. Using this precomputed hash table, the expected computation required by the black-box tracing algorithm for single-key decoders is 1 modular exponentiation and an insignificant number (i.e., $O(\alpha L)$) of modular multiplications. In the multiple-key case, we repeat the algorithm $O(k)$ times, so the computation would be $O(k)$ modular exponentiations and $O(k\alpha L)$ modular multiplications.

7   Conclusion

We presented TTR, a fully k-resilient traitor tracing scheme based on RSA that improves upon the decryption efficiency of past traitor tracing proposals. The scheme employs a single RSA modulus that is shared by multiple users, and we realize our security goals by applying RSA as a secret-key cryptosystem rather than a public-key cryptosystem. TTR is also frameproof against collusions of k or fewer traitors, and the scheme enables black-box traitor tracing in certain scenarios. In future work, we will investigate parameter optimizations and extensions to this scheme to enable higher performance and other security features. Furthermore, we will explore constructions for generalizing TTR and other traceability schemes based on similar cryptographic primitives.

Acknowledgements

The authors thank Scott Contini, Jeremy Horwitz, Joe Kilian, and Benny Pinkas for their suggestions and pointers regarding the security analysis. The authors also thank the anonymous reviewers for their helpful comments.

References

1. R. Anderson, *Security Engineering: A Guide to Building Dependable Distributed Systems*, John Wiley and Sons, Inc., New York, 2001.
2. M. Bellare and P. Rogaway, "Optimal Asymmetric Encryption," *Proc. of EURO-CRYPT '94*, Springer-Verlag LNCS, vol. 950, pp. 92–111, 1995.

3. D. Boneh, "Twenty Years of Attacks on the RSA Cryptosystem," *Notices of the American Mathematical Society*, vol. 46, no. 2, pp. 203–213, 1999.
4. D. Boneh, "Simplified OAEP for the RSA and Rabin Functions," *Proc. of CRYPTO '01*, Springer-Verlag LNCS, vol. 2139, pp. 275–291, 2001.
5. D. Boneh and M. Franklin, "An Efficient Public Key Traitor Tracing Scheme," *Proc. of CRYPTO '99*, Springer-Verlag LNCS, vol. 1666, pp. 338–353, 1999.
6. D. Boneh and J. Shaw, "Collusion-Secure Fingerprinting for Digital Data," *Proc. of CRYPTO '95*, Springer-Verlag LNCS, vol. 963, pp. 452–465, 1995.
7. B. Chor, A. Fiat, and M. Naor, "Tracing Traitors," *Proc. of CRYPTO '94*, Springer-Verlag LNCS, vol. 839, pp. 257–270, 1994.
8. B. Chor, A. Fiat, M. Naor, and B. Pinkas, "Tracing Traitors," *IEEE Transactions on Information Theory*, vol. 46, no. 3, pp. 893–910, May 2000.
9. I. J. Cox, J. Kilian, T. Leighton, and T. Sharmoon, "A Secure Robust Watermark for Multimedia," *Proceedings of the First Information Hiding Workshop – IHW '96*, Springer-Verlag LNCS, vol. 1174, pp. 185–206, 1996.
10. S. A. Craver, J. P. McGregor, M. Wu, B. Liu, A. Stubblefield, B. Swartzlander, D. S. Wallach, D. Dean, and E. W. Felten, "Reading Between the Lines: Lessons from the SDMI Challenge," Princeton Univ. CS Technical Report TR-657-02, 2002.
11. J. M. DeLaurentis, "A Further Weakness in the Common Modulus Protocol for the RSA Cryptoalgorithm," *Cryptologia*, vol. 8, no. 3, pp. 253–259, 1984.
12. Y. Desmedt and Y. Frankel, "Shared Generation of Authenticators and Signatures," *Proc. of CRYPTO '91*, Springer-Verlag LNCS, vol. 576, pp. 457–469, 1991.
13. Y. Dodis, N. Fazio, A. Kiayias, and M, Yung, "Fully Scalable Public-Key Traitor Tracing," *Proceedings of Principles of Distributed Computing (PODC-2003)*, July 2003.
14. A. Fiat and M. Naor, "Broadcast Encryption," *Proc. of CRYPTO '93*, Springer-Verlag LNCS, vol. 773, pp. 480–491, 1993.
15. A. Fiat and T. Tassa, "Dynamic Traitor Tracing," *Proc. of CRYPTO '99*, Springer-Verlag LNCS, vol. 1666, pp. 354–371, 1999.
16. E. Fujisaki, T. Okamoto, D. Pointcheval, and J. Stern, "RSA-OAEP Is Secure under the RSA Assumption," *Proc. of CRYPTO '01*, Springer-Verlag LNCS, vol. 2139, pp. 260–274, 2001.
17. E. Gafni, J. Staddon, and Y. L. Yin, "Efficient Methods for Integrating Traceability and Broadcast Encryption," *Proc. of CRYPTO '99*, Springer-Verlag LNCS, vol. 1666, pp. 372–387, 1999.
18. J. Kahn, J. Komlos, and E. Szemeredi, "On the Probability that a Random $+/-1$ Matrix Is Singular," *Journal of the AMS*, vol. 8, no. 1, pp. 223–240, Jan. 1995.
19. A. Kiayias and M. Yung, "Breaking and Repairing Asymmetric Public-Key Traitor Tracing," *Proceedings of the ACM Workshop on Digital Rights Management*, 2002.
20. A. Kiayias and M. Yung, "Self Protecting Pirates and Black-box Traitor Tracing," *Proc. of CRYPTO '01*, Springer-Verlag LNCS, vol. 2139, pp. 63–79, 2001.
21. A. Kiayias and M. Yung, "Traitor Tracing with a Constant Transmission Rate," *Proc. of EUROCRYPT '02*, Springer-Verlag LNCS, vol. 2332, pp. 450–465, 2002.
22. K. Kurosawa and Y. Desmedt, "Optimum Traitor Tracing and Asymmetric Schemes," *Proc. of EUROCRYPT '98*, Springer-Verlag LNCS, vol. 1403, pp. 145–157, 1998.
23. A. J. Menezes, P. C. van Oorschot, and S. A. Vanstone, *Handbook of Applied Cryptography*, CRC Press, LLC, Boca Raton, FL, 1997.
24. D. Naor, M. Naor, and J. Lotspiech, "Revocation and Tracing Schemes for Stateless Receivers," *Proc. of CRYPTO '01*, Springer-Verlag LNCS, vol. 2139, pp. 41–62, 2001.

25. M. Naor and B. Pinkas, "Threshold Traitor Tracing," *Proc. of CRYPTO '98*, Springer-Verlag LNCS, vol. 1462, pp. 502–517, 1998.
26. B. Pfitzmann, "Trials of Traced Traitors," *Proceedings of the First Information Hiding Workshop – IHW '96*, Springer-Verlag LNCS, vol. 1174, pp. 49–64, 1996.
27. B. Pfitzmann and M. Waidner, "Asymmetric Fingerprinting for Larger Collusions," *Proceedings of the ACM Conference on Computer and Communications Security*, pp. 145–157, 1997.
28. R. L. Rivest, A. Shamir, and L. M. Adleman, "A Method for Obtaining Digital Signatures and Public-key Cryptosystems," *Communications of the ACM*, vol. 21, no. 2, pp. 120–126, February 1978.
29. R. Safavi-Naini and Y. Yang, "Sequential Traitor Tracing," *Proc. of CRYPTO '00*, Springer-Verlag LNCS, vol. 1880, pp. 316–332, 2000.
30. S. Setia, S. Koussih, S. Jajodia, and E. Harder, "Kronos: A Scalable Group Re-keying Approach for Secure Multicast," *Proceedings of the 2000 IEEE Symposium on Security and Privacy*, pp. 215–228, 2000.
31. V. Shoup, "OAEP Reconsidered," *Proc. of CRYPTO '01*, Springer-Verlag LNCS, vol. 2139, pp. 239–259, 2001.
32. A. Silverberg, J. Staddon, and J. Walker, "Efficient Traitor Tracing Algorithms using List Decoding," *Proc. of ASIACRYPT '01*, Springer-Verlag LNCS, vol. 2248, pp. 175–192, 2001.
33. G. J. Simmons, "A Weak Privacy Protocol Using the RSA Cryptosystem," *Cryptologia*, vol. 7, no. 2, pp. 180–182, 1993.
34. D. Stinson and R. Wei, "Combinatorial Properties and Constructions of Traceability Schemes and Frameproof Codes," *SIAM Journal on Discrete Mathematics*, vol. 11, no. 1, 1998.
35. D. Stinson and R. Wei, "Key Preassigned Traceability Schemes for Broadcast Encryption," *Proceedings of Selected Areas in Cryptology – SAC '98*, Springer-Verlag LNCS, vol. 1556, pp. 144–156, 1999.
36. Y. Watanabe, G. Hanaoka and H. Imai, "Efficient Asymmetric Public-Key Traitor Tracing without Trusted Agents," *Progress in Cryptology – CT-RSA 2001*, Springer-Verlag LNCS, vol. 2020, pp. 392–407, 2001.

N-Party Encrypted Diffie-Hellman Key Exchange Using Different Passwords*

Jin Wook Byun and Dong Hoon Lee

Center for Information Security Technologies (CIST),
Korea University, Anam Dong, Sungbuk Gu, Seoul, Korea
{byunstar,donghlee}@korea.ac.kr

Abstract. We consider the problem of password-authenticated group *Diffie-Hellman* key exchange among N parties, N−1 clients and a single-server, using *different* passwords. Most password-authenticated key exchange schemes in the literature have focused on an authenticated key exchange using a *shared* password between a client and a server. With a rapid change in modern communication environment such as ad-hoc networks and ubiquitous computing, it is necessary to construct a secure end-to-end channel between clients, which is a quite different paradigm from the existing ones. To achieve this end-to-end security, only a few schemes of three-party setting have been presented where two clients exchange a key using their own passwords with the help of a server. However, up until now, no formally treated and round efficient protocols which enable group members to generate a common session key with clients' distinct passwords have been suggested.

In this paper we securely and efficiently extend three-party case to N-party case with a formal proof of security. Two provably secure N-party EKE protocols are suggested; N-party EKE-U in the unicast network and N-party EKE-M in the multicast network. The proposed N-party EKE-M is provable secure and provides forward secrecy. Especially, the scheme is of constant-round, hence scalable and practical.

Keywords: Password, Encrypted key exchange, N-party authentication, different password authentication, authenticated key exchange, dictionary attacks.

1 Introduction

To communicate securely over an insecure public network it is essential that secret keys are exchanged securely. An authenticated key exchange protocol allows two or more parties to agree on a common secret key over an insecure public network in a secure and authenticated manner. That is, no adversary can impersonate any participant during the protocol or learn any information about the value of the agreed secret. An authenticated key exchange protocol is essential for building secure communications between parties, and commonly used

---

* This research was supported by the MIC(Ministry of Information and Communication), Korea, under the ITRC(Information Technology Research Center) support program supervised by the IITA(Institute of Information Technology Assessment).

J. Ioannidis, A. Keromytis, and M.Yung (Eds.): ACNS 2005, LNCS 3531, pp. 75–90, 2005.

in cryptographic protocols such as IPsec, SSL, et al. In a distributed system, a password-authenticated key exchange (PAKE) scheme is practical, where key exchange is done using only a human-memorable password. Actually, the setting such that users are only capable of storing human-memorable passwords is arisen more often in practice because of its mobility and efficiency. However a password has a low-entropy because it is drawn from a relatively small dictionary. This makes PAKE schemes susceptible to a dictionary attack. Even tiny amounts of redundancy in the flows of the protocol could be used by an adversary to mount a dictionary attack.

1.1   Related Works

Over the years, there have been much research on password-authenticated key exchange protocols. Most password-authenticated key exchange schemes in the literature have focused on the *shared password-authentication* (SPWA, for short) model which provides password-authenticated key exchange using a shared password between a client and a server [4, 7, 11, 17, 27, 28, 34, 41]. In the SPWA model two parties, client and server, use a shared password to generate a common session key and perform key confirmation. Bellovin and Merrit first proposed Encrypted Key Exchange (EKE) scheme secure against dictionary attacks [7]. EKE scheme has been basis for many of the subsequent works in the SPWA model. Recently Bresson et al. proposed a password-authenticated group *Diffie-Hellman* key exchange protocol which allows group members to generate a session key with a shared password [11].

Few schemes have been presented to provide password-authenticated key exchange between two clients with their different passwords [2, 19, 32, 33, 35]. In this *different password-authentication* (DPWA, for short) model two clients generate a common session key with their distinct passwords by the help of a server. This DPWA model is particularly well-suited for applications that require secure end-to-end communication between light-weight mobile clients. Steiner et al. proposed 3-party EKE which provides a password-authenticated key exchange between two clients using a single-server [35]. However, Ding and Horster showed that 3-party EKE protocol had a weakness under an undetectable on-line guessing attack [23]. In [32] Lin et al., pointed out that 3-party EKE was susceptible to an off-line password guessing attack, and proposed LSH-3PEKE protocol in which the server holds publicly known keys to prevent both attacks above. However, LSH-3PEKE protocol requires a high burden on the clients such that clients have to obtain and verify the public key of the server. Lin et al. presented LSSH-3PEKE protocol which is resistant to both off-line and undetectable on-line password guessing attacks but does not require server public keys [33]. Byun et al. [19] proposed two secure C2C-PAKE schemes; one for a cross-realm setting where two clients are in two different realms and hence there exist two servers involved, the other for a single-server setting where two clients are in the same realm. They have proved that the schemes are secure against all attacks considered. Unfortunately, the scheme was found to be flawed. Chen firstly pointed out that in the scheme with a cross-realm setting one malicious server can mount a dictionary attack to obtain the password of client who belongs to the other realm [20]. This attack was recently mentioned in [30, 40] too. Very recently, Abdalla et al. [2] give formal treatments and provable security for this three-party setting. They also present a generic construction of a three-party protocol based on any two-party authenticated key exchange protocol.

1.2   Our Contribution

In this paper we extend three-party case in the DPWA to *N-party* case which allows group members holding different passwords to agree on a group session key with the help of a single-server. In the SPWA, as mentioned above, Bresson et al. combined password-based authentication with group *Diffie-Hellman* key exchange protocols and presented a password-authenticated group *Diffie-Hellman* key exchange protocols when group members share a same password [11]. However the setting such that all group members have a same password is not practical since a password is not a common secret but a secret depending on an individual. Generally, in a mobile computing environment and distributed environment such as an ad-hoc network, the setting in which group mobile users have different passwords is more suitable. Furthermore, the scheme in [11] requires $O(n)$ rounds and $O(n)$ modular exponentiation per party to establish a group key. So the scheme is inefficient when the number of group members is large.

In our paper we consider two network environments, unicast network and multicast network. In the unicast network, we assume that one client can send messages one by one to the next client in one direction. To establish a common key among the clients in the unicast network, the keying messages should be conveyed to the all clients, and hence it is inevitable that the round complexity required is linear in the number of group members. In the unicast network we propose an N-party EKE-U scheme which requires $O(n)$ round complexity to establish a group key. Many applications in the mobile ad-hoc network (MANET) are based upon unicast communication [9, 21, 31]. For example, mission-critical matters such as emergency rescue and military operations may occur in the setting which is absent from fixed infrastructure and advanced multicast routing network. So N-party EKE-U scheme may be well suited for making a secure session in the unicast routing MANET [3, 29].

In the multicast network, any client can send messages to multiple recipients only in one round—one round includes all the messages that can be sent in parallel during the protocol. Therefore more round-efficient group key exchange protocols can be designed under multicast network than under unicast network. We design a constant round N-party EKE-M scheme in the multicast network. N-party EKE-M protocol can be used to assure multicast message confidentiality or multicast data integrity in the various multicast scenarios. For example, the scheme can be used under ad-hoc network environment such as BSS (Basic Service Set), which is a component of the IEEE 802.11 architecture [26]. IEEE 802.11 supports multicast and broadcast messages. In a BSS infrastructure network (that is, network using an access point), multicasts are only sent from an access point to mobile devices, while mobile devices are not allowed to send broadcast messages directly. The access point first makes a group master key (GMK), then derives a group transient key (GTK) from the GMK. After each pairwise secure connection between access point and mobile devices is established, the access point sends the GTK to mobile devices by the secure pairwise connection. Finally the mobile users generate a group key by using the GTK.

The process of group key generation in N-party EKE-M protocol is very similar to the process of the above one. Clients and a server in our scheme generate intermediate keys, then they generate a common group key by using the intermediate keys. Hence, our protocol is well-suitable for the protection of multicast and broadcast messages in the IEEE 802.11.

Other examples are collaborative works, personal area networking (PAN), video conference and multiplayer game. For these scenario, the proposed scheme may be used for attractive security method that establishes a session key to protect a session.

The proposed N-party EKE-U protocol allows clients to generate a common session key using their own different passwords in the unicast networks. We prove the proposed scheme is secure under the *Diffie-Hellman*-like assumptions such as group computational *Diffie-Hellman* [11, 36], computational *Diffie-Hellman*, and multi-decisional *Diffie-Hellman* [12]. Above all, to construct a secure N-Party EKE-U protocol in the DPWA model, we must consider insider adversaries who may perform dictionary attacks on one specific password using all other $n-1$ passwords. Preventing insider attacks is not an easy work. To prevent this serious attack in our model, keying materials generated by each client are blinded by the server using a *Transformation Protocol* (**TF**, for short) between the client and the server. In **TF**, the server first decrypts keying materials encrypted by the client's password, blinds and encrypts the materials with the other client's password. Actually all clients with distinct passwords can generate a common session key by executing **TF**. We construct a secure N-Party EKE-U protocol containing **TF** in the DPWA model by modifying a password-authenticated group *Diffie-Hellman* key exchange protocol in [11] which provides a group *Diffie-Hellman* key exchange in the SPWA model.

The proposed N-party EKE-M protocol is also strong against insider dictionary attacks. We prove that the protocol is secure under the assumption of computational *Diffie-Hellman*. As mentioned above, N-party EKE-M protcol requires only a constant number of rounds to establish a session key. Accurately, one round is demanded by clients, and two rounds are demanded by a server. Furthermore only 2 modular exponentiations are required by each client. The proposed N-party EKE-M is the first constant round and provable secure scheme with forward secrecy in the group DPWA model.

1.3   Organization

The remainder of this paper is organized as follows. In Section 2 we newly define our model and security for our proofs. In Section 3 we present an N-party EKE-U protocol in the unicast network and prove its security formally in the random oracle and ideal cipher models. In Section 4, we present an N-party EKE-M protocol in the multicast network and prove its security.

2   Model and Definition

In this section we formalize the adversary capabilities and the security definitions in N-party EKE protocols. We modify the adversary model and the definition of security defined in [4, 11, 12], based on priori work of [6, 8]. The model of [11] are designed to enable n clients to generate a session key with a priori shared password. In the model of [12], each client possesses a distinct strong secret key, not a password, to generate a session key. For the DPWA model of N-party case, we need a security model to allow n clients to possess different passwords. We construct the model by combining two models in [11, 12] to be suitable for the DPWA model of N-party case. That is, by giving different passwords to N parties and modifying adversary abilities of the model in [12], we construct DPWA security model for N-party case. As compared with the previous results a significant change in our model is that clients have different weak secrets. Notation of participants, session ID (SID) and partner ID (PID) are slightly changed. We also give a security definition of a DPWA protocol for N-party case according to the changed setting. Other security notions and adversary abilities are similar to those in the previous models [4, 6, 11].

2.1   Communication Model

PARTICIPANTS. We have two types of protocol participants, clients and a server. Let $ID = Clients \cup Server$ be a non-empty set of protocol participants, and the set ID remains stable. We assume that $Server$ consists of a single-server S, and $Clients=\{C_1, ..., C_{n-1}\}$ consists of identities of $n-1$ clients. Each client $C_i \in Clients$ has a secret password pw_i, and server S keeps password verifiers in its database. A client $C_i \in Clients$ may execute a key exchange protocol multiple times with different partners, and we denote the t-th instance of the protocol executed by entity C_i (S) as oracle C_i^t (S^t, respectively).

ALGORITHM. An N-party EKE protocol requires the following two probabilistic polynomial time algorithms.

- **Password Generation Algorithm** $\mathcal{G}_{pw}$ is given an input of 1^k, where k is a security parameter, and then provides each client $C_i \in Clients$ with password pw_i.
- **Registration Algorithm** $\mathcal{R}$ is given an input of a fixed client $C_i \in Clients$, and then registers each password pw_i of C_i at S

To define the notion of security, we define capabilities of an adversary. We allow the adversary to potentially control all communication in the network via access to a set of oracles as defined below. We consider an *experiment* in which the adversary asks queries to oracles, and the oracles answer back to the adversary. Oracle queries model attacks which the adversary may use in the real system. We consider the following types of queries in this paper.

- A query $\mathsf{Send}(C_i^t, M)$ is used to send a message M to instance C_i^t. When C_i^t receives M, it responds according to the key-exchange protocol. The adversary may use this query to perform *active* attacks by modifying and inserting the messages of the key-exchange protocol. Hence, impersonation attacks and man-in-the-middle attacks are possible using this query.

- A query $\mathsf{Execute}(Clients)$ represents passive eavesdropping of the adversary on an execution of the protocol between honest clients in $Clients$. Namely, all clients in $Clients$ execute the protocol without any interference from the adversary, and the adversary is given the resulting transcript of the execution. (Although the output of an $\mathsf{Execute}$ query can be simulated by repeated Send oracle queries, this particular query is needed to define a forward secrecy[1].)

- A query $\mathsf{Reveal}(C_i^t)$ models the *known key* attacks (or Denning-Sacco Attacks [22]) in the real system. The adversary is given the session key of the specified instance C_i^t.

- A query $\mathsf{Corrupt}(C_i)$ models exposure of the long-term password of C_i. The adversary is assumed to be able to obtain long-term passwords of clients, but cannot control the behavior of these clients directly (of course, once the adversary has asked a query $\mathsf{Corrupt}(C_i)$, the adversary may impersonate C_i in subsequent Send queries).

- A query $\mathsf{Test}(C_i^t)$ is used to define the advantage of an adversary. If C_i^t is a fresh oracle (defined in Section 2.3), then the oracle C_i^t flips a coin b. If b is 1, then a session key is returned. Otherwise, a string randomly drawn from a session key distribution is returned. The adversary is allowed to make a single Test query, at any time during the experiment.

2.2 Security Definition and Assumption

SESSION IDS, PARTNERING, FRESHNESS. For unicast communication, there are well established definitions with respect to session IDS and partnering [11–13]. In the unicast network (for instance, in N-party EKE-U protocol), we directly use these notions defined in [12] without modification. For N-party EKE-M protocol, we define newly session IDS and partnering in the multicast communication as follows.

Definition 2.1 [Session IDS (SIDS)]. Suppose that S and $n - 1$ clients, $C_1,..,C_{n-1}$, participate in an N-party EKE-M protocol. First, SIDS for any C_i is defined as $\mathrm{SIDS}(C_i) = \{SID_{1,..,n-1} : C_1,..,C_{n-1} \in Clients\}$, where $SID_{1,..,n-1}$

---

[1] The definition of forward secrecy is introduced in the full version of paper, informally. Here we do not give a formal treatment on the forward secrecy for simplicity of security proofs. For a formal definition, refer to [4].

is the concatenation of all flows between oracles $C_1^{s_1},..,C_{n-1}^{s_{n-1}}$ and S^u. The values of s_i and u are instances of the protocol executed by C_i and S for $1 \leq i \leq n - 1$. Note that the multicast setting allows all the messages to be sent to all participating clients in parallel during the protocol, hence all participating clients can make SIDS. By using SIDS, we formally define **partnering** as follows.

Definition 2.2 [Partnering, PIDS]. The notion of **partnering** captures that the participating oracles, $C_1^{s_1},..,C_{n-1}^{s_{n-1}}$ and S^u have jointly run a protocol in the multicast network. After running the protocol, the oracles $C_1^{s_1},..,C_{n-1}^{s_{n-1}}$, S^u where $\{C_1,..,C_{n-1}\} \in Clients$, *are partnering if* the all oracles accept with same session key and same SIDS. The partner IDS, PIDS$(C_i^{s_i})$, is a set of clients' IDs which are partnered with oracles $C_i^{s_i}$ for $1 \leq i \leq n - 1$.

Definition 2.3 [Freshness]. An oracle C_i^t *is fresh if* neither C_i^t nor one of its partners have been asked for a Reveal query after oracle C_i^t and its partners have computed a session key sk.

SECURITY DEFINITION. Now we formally define an advantage of an adversary against N-party EKE (NEKE) protocols. Our model is designed for different password-authenticated key exchange between clients using a single-server. The goal of our protocols is for clients to share a common session key sk which is known to nobody but participants under passive or active adversaries. The output session key must be indistinguishable from a random key by the adversary. The property that a session key is indistinguishable is a well-known security condition in key exchange protocols. However we note that if an adversary initiates m ($\leq |\mathcal{D}|$, which is a size of dictionary) instances of a password-authenticated key exchange protocol, and guesses an appropriate password in each initiation, then it will succeed in guessing the password with probability $m/|\mathcal{D}|$. So the given password-authenticated protocol is considered secure if the active adversary can not do significantly better than this trial bound. We define this formally as follows.

Definition 2.4 [NEKE Security] Consider the following experiment. Firstly, a password is assigned to each client by running the password generation algorithm $\mathcal{G}_{pw}$, and the password is registered in the server S by running the registration algorithm $\mathcal{R}$. Then an adversary $\mathcal{A}$ is run. It will interact with finite oracles by asking queries defined above during the experiment. The adversary $\mathcal{A}$ can ask a Test query to a fresh oracle only once at any time. When $\mathcal{A}$ asks a Test query, then experiment flips a coin for bit b. If it lands $b = 1$, a real session key is returned to the adversary. Otherwise, a random key is returned to the adversary. After $\mathcal{A}$ is given a random or a real key, $\mathcal{A}$ may ask other queries continuously and perform an on-line password guessing attacks adaptively. Eventually $\mathcal{A}$ guesses b, outputs the guessed bit b' and terminates the experiment. Let $\mathbf{Succ}_{\mathcal{A}}^{neke}$ be the event that $b' = b$. The session key advantage of $\mathcal{A}$ in attacking protocol P is defined as

$$\mathbf{Adv}_P^{neke}(\mathcal{A}) = 2Pr[\mathbf{Succ}_{\mathcal{A}}^{neke}] - 1.$$

A given N-party EKE protocol P *is secure if* the following condition is satisfied:

- **Indistinguishability:** For all probabilistic polynomial time adversary $\mathcal{A}$, every finite dictionary $\mathcal{D}$, and for all $m \leq |\mathcal{D}|$,

$$\mathbf{Adv}_P^{neke}(\mathcal{A}) \leq \frac{m}{|\mathcal{D}|} + \varepsilon(k).$$

where $\varepsilon(k)$ is a negligible function and k is a security parameter.

COMPUTATIONAL ASSUMPTIONS. For our formal proofs, we require well-known intractable assumptions such as the computational *Diffie-Hellman* (CDH), group computational *Diffie-Hellman* (GCDH), and multi-decisional *Diffie-Hellman* (MDDH) assumptions. The MDDH assumptions were shown to be reasonable by relating it to the DDH assumption in [11]. Formal descriptions and notions of these assumptions are presented in the full version of the paper.

3   N-Party EKE-U Protocol

In this section we describe an N-party EKE-U protocol which enables $n - 1$ clients to generate a common session key, sk, by the help of a single-server S in the unicast network. Let $G = \langle g \rangle$ be cyclic group of prime order q. A common session key between clients is $sk = \mathcal{H}(Clients\|K)$ where $K = (g^{x_1 \cdots x_{n-1}})^{v_1 \cdots v_n}$ for random values $x_1, .., x_{n-1}, v_1, .., v_n$. $\mathcal{H}$ is an ideal hash function from $\{0, 1\}^*$ to $\{0, 1\}^l$. We assume that $\mathcal{E}$ is an ideal cipher which is a random one-to-one function such that $\mathcal{E}_K : M \rightarrow C$, where $|M| = |C|$. Several methods to instantiate an ideal cipher for practical use are described in [16].

3.1   Description of N-Party EKE-U

In N-party EKE-U protocol, as illustrated in Fig. 1, participants (clients $C_1, ..,$ C_{n-1} and sever S) are arranged on a line, and there are two stages: up-flow and down-flow. In the up-flow, each client raises the received intermediate values to the power of its own secret and forwards the resulting values to the next client (or sever S in the last step) on the line. Note that this process makes N-party EKE-U protocol contributory. In the down-flow, server S computes a keying material and distributes it to each client, encrypted with the receiver's password. In the up-flow, each client receives the values encrypted with the password of the client who sends them. To decrypt the values, each client needs to execute a **TF** protocol with server S. As illustrated in Fig. 2, S in **TF** protocol plays a role of interpreter by transforming the message encrypted with other's password into the one encrypted with the requesting client's password. Since a client does not know other clients' passwords, the intervention of server S is inevitable in the DPWA model.

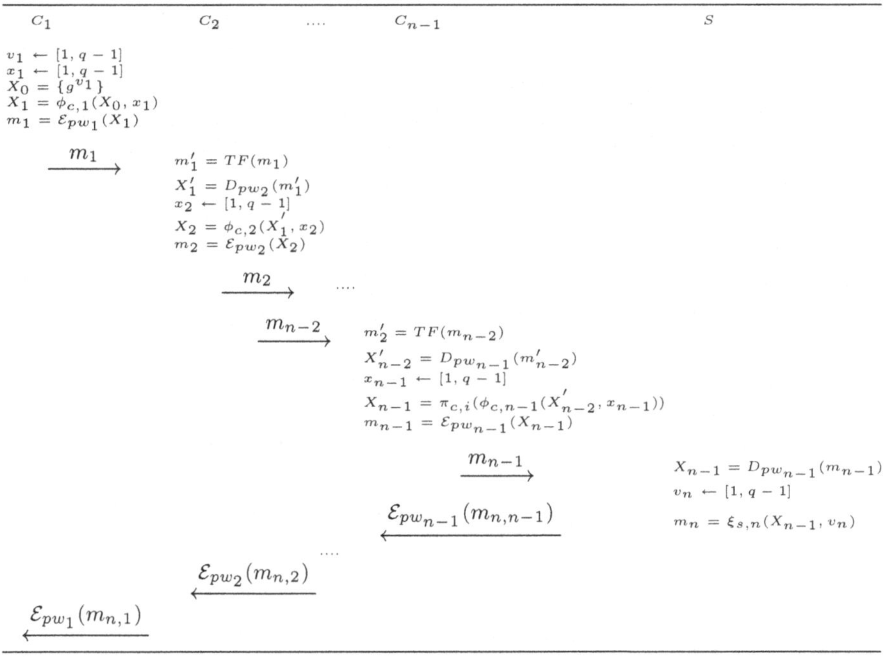

C_1	C_2	....	C_{n-1}	S

$v_1 \leftarrow [1, q-1]$
$x_1 \leftarrow [1, q-1]$
$X_0 = \{g^{v_1}\}$
$X_1 = \phi_{c,1}(X_0, x_1)$
$m_1 = \mathcal{E}_{pw_1}(X_1)$

$\xrightarrow{\quad m_1 \quad}$

$m_1' = TF(m_1)$
$X_1' = D_{pw_2}(m_1')$
$x_2 \leftarrow [1, q-1]$
$X_2 = \phi_{c,2}(X_1', x_2)$
$m_2 = \mathcal{E}_{pw_2}(X_2)$

$\xrightarrow{\quad m_2 \quad}$ ....

$\xrightarrow{\quad m_{n-2} \quad}$ $m_2' = TF(m_{n-2})$
$X_{n-2}' = D_{pw_{n-1}}(m_{n-2}')$
$x_{n-1} \leftarrow [1, q-1]$
$X_{n-1} = \pi_{c,i}(\phi_{c,n-1}(X_{n-2}', x_{n-1}))$
$m_{n-1} = \mathcal{E}_{pw_{n-1}}(X_{n-1})$

$\xrightarrow{\quad m_{n-1} \quad}$ $X_{n-1} = D_{pw_{n-1}}(m_{n-1})$
$v_n \leftarrow [1, q-1]$
$m_n = \xi_{s,n}(X_{n-1}, v_n)$

$\xleftarrow{\mathcal{E}_{pw_{n-1}}(m_{n,n-1})}$

.... $\xleftarrow{\mathcal{E}_{pw_2}(m_{n,2})}$

$\xleftarrow{\mathcal{E}_{pw_1}(m_{n,1})}$

Fig. 1. N-party EKE-U.

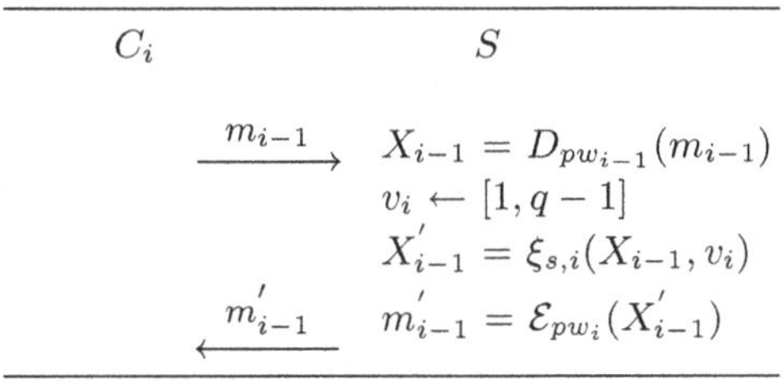

C_i	S

$\xrightarrow{\quad m_{i-1} \quad}$ $X_{i-1} = D_{pw_{i-1}}(m_{i-1})$
$v_i \leftarrow [1, q-1]$
$X_{i-1}' = \xi_{s,i}(X_{i-1}, v_i)$
$\xleftarrow{\quad m_{i-1}' \quad}$ $m_{i-1}' = \mathcal{E}_{pw_i}(X_{i-1}')$

Fig. 2. TF protocol.

In our protocol three types of functions are used. All clients or server contribute to generation of a common session key by using function $\phi_{c,i}$, $\pi_{c,i}$, and $\xi_{s,i}$ for positive integer i. The description of functions are as follows:

$$\phi_{c,i}(\{\alpha_1, .., \alpha_{i-1}, \alpha_i\}, x) = \{\alpha_1^x, .., \alpha_{i-1}^x, \alpha_i, \alpha_i^x\},$$
$$\pi_{c,i}(\{\alpha_1, .., \alpha_i\}) = \{\alpha_1, .., \alpha_{i-1}\},$$
$$\xi_{s,i}(\{\alpha_1, \alpha_2, .., \alpha_i\}, x) = \{\alpha_1^x, \alpha_2^x, .., \alpha_i^x\}.$$

We now describe the protocol in detail. In the up-flow, C_1 first chooses two numbers in $[1, q-1]$ randomly, calculates $X_1 = \phi_{c,1}(X_0, x_1) = \{g^{v_1}, g^{v_1 x_1}\}$, and sends m_1 to C_2, which is an encryption of X_1 with the password pw_1. Upon receiving m_1, C_2 executes a **TF** protocol with server S. In the **TF** protocol,

C_2 sends m_1 to S. Then S selects a random number v_2 and calculates $X_1' = \xi_{s,2}(X_1, v_2)$. The purpose of using v_2 is to prevent an insider dictionary attack. Since S knows all clients' passwords, it can construct $m_1' = \mathcal{E}_{pw_2}(X_1')$ and sends it back to C_2. This is the end of **TF** protocol. On receiving $m_1' = \mathcal{E}_{pw_2}(X_1')$, C_2 decrypts it to get X_1'. Next C_2 chooses its own random number x_2 and computes $X_2 = \phi_{c,2}(X_1, x_2)$. Finally C_2 sends a ciphertext $m_2 = \mathcal{E}_{pw_2}(X_2)$ to the next client C_3. The above process is repeated up to C_{n-2}. The last client C_{n-1} chooses a random number x_{n-1}, and calculates $X_{n-1} = \pi_{c,n-1}(\phi_{c,n-1}(X_{n-2}', x_{n-1}))$. The function $\pi_{c,n-1}$ only eliminates the last element of $\phi_{c,n-1}(X_{n-2}', x_{n-1})$. Finally the client C_{n-1} encrypts X_{n-1} with pw_{n-1}, and sends the ciphertext, m_{n-1} to the server S. By using the function $\pi_{c,n-1}$, the protocol does not allow the server to get the last element of $\phi_{c,n-1}(X_{n-2}', x_{n-1})$, hence the server is not able to compute a session key.

In the down-flow, S first decrypts m_{n-1} to get X_{n-1}, chooses a random number v_n, and computes $m_n = \xi_{s,n}(X_{n-1}, v_n)$. For $1 \le i \le n-1$, let $m_{n,i} = (g^{x_1 \cdots x_{i-1} x_{i+1} \cdots x_{n-1}})^{v_1 \cdots v_n}$ which is the i-th component of m_n. S encrypts each $m_{n,i}$ with password pw_i and sends the resulting ciphertexts to the clients. Each client C_i decrypts $\mathcal{E}_{pw_i}(m_{n,i})$ to obtain $m_{n,i}$. Next, C_i computes session key $sk = \mathcal{H}(Clients \| K)$ where $K = (m_{n,i})^{x_i} = (g^{x_1 \cdots x_{n-1}})^{v_1 \cdots v_n}$ and $Clients = \{C_1, ..., C_{n-1}\}$. In Fig. 3, we present an example of execution of the protocol with three clients and a sever S where $K = (g^{x_1 x_2 x_3})^{v_1 v_2 v_3 v_4}$ and $sk = \mathcal{H}(Clients \| K)$.

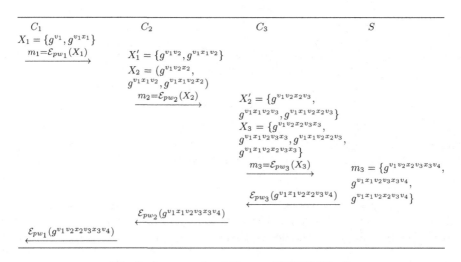

Fig. 3. An example of N-party EKE-U (N=4).

3.2   Mutual Authentication

If clients want to make sure that other clients really have computed the agreed key, then key confirmation for all clients can be incorporated into the key exchange protocol, so-called mutual authentication. That is, mutual authentication provides an assurance that all clients participated in the protocol have actually computed the agreed key. To add mutual authentication to our scheme, we use an additional *authenticator* structure described in [12]. The authenticator is computed as the hash of the session key sk and some other information such as client index. The client C_i makes an authenticator $Auth_i = \mathcal{H}(i||sk)$, where $sk = \mathcal{H}(Clients||K)$, and then sends $Auth_i$ to all clients. The client C_i verifies the received $n - 2$ authenticators $Auth_i$ $(i \neq j)$.

In [12], Bresson et al. design a generic transformation which transforms a group key exchange protocol into a protocol with mutual authentication by using the authenticator structure. They also proved that the transformation is secure in the random-oracle model. That is, authenticator transformation for mutual authentication preserves the indistinguishability security of the original session key. So, in the paper, we do not consider a security of mutual authentication.

3.3   Security of N-Party EKE-U

In this section we prove that the proposed N-party EKE-U protocol is secure under the group computational *Diffie-Hellman* and multi-decisional *Diffie-Hellman* assumptions in the ideal hash and ideal cipher paradigms. We show that N-party EKE-U satisfies that an advantage of an adversary $\mathcal{A}$ in attacking session key **Indistinguishability** security is bounded above by $\mathcal{O}(q_s/|\mathcal{D}|) + \varepsilon(k)$, for some negligible function $\varepsilon(\cdot)$. The first term is an advantage from on-line guessing attacks. As mentioned in Section 2, the on-line attacks can not be avoided and hence the success probability of the on-line attacks may be considered as a lower bound of an advantage of any adversary. By **Theorem 3.1** bellow, we show that the best thing any adversary can do is only on-line password-guessing attacks.

Theorem 3.1 *P is an N-party EKE-U protocol of Fig. 1, and passwords are chosen from a finite dictionary of size $|\mathcal{D}|$. Let $\mathcal{A}$ be a probabilistic polynomial time adversary which asks q_s send, q_h hash, and $q_{\mathcal{E}}$ encryption/decryption queries. Then*

$$\mathbf{Adv}_P^{neke}(\mathcal{A}) \leq \frac{q_{\mathcal{E}}^2}{(q-1)} + \frac{q_s}{|\mathcal{D}|} + 4n \cdot \mathbf{Adv}_{\mathcal{D}}^{mddh}(T_{\mathcal{D}}) + 2q_h \cdot \mathbf{Adv}_{\Delta}^{gcdh}(T_{\Delta}).$$

*where $T_{\mathcal{D}}$ and T_{Δ} is polynomial running time of **MDDH** adversary algorithm $\mathcal{A}_{\mathcal{D}}$ and **GCDH** adversary algorithm $\mathcal{A}_{\Delta}$ such that $T_{\Delta} \leq T + (q_s + q_{\mathcal{E}})(\tau_G + \tau_{\mathcal{E}})$ and $T_{\mathcal{D}} \leq T + (q_s + q_{\mathcal{E}})(\tau_G + \tau_{\mathcal{E}})$, respectively. τ_G and $\tau_{\mathcal{E}}$ are computational time for exponentiation and encryption. q is the prime order of G.*

Theorem 3.2 *An N-party EKE-U protocol P provides a forward secrecy under the group computational Diffie-Hellman assumption.*

The proofs of the theorems will appear in the full version of the paper.

4   N-Party EKE-M Protocol

In this section we design an N-Party EKE-M protocol in the multicast channel. We assume that a server S keeps clients' passwords $pw_1,..,pw_{n-1}$ and all entities know participating parties in a session in advance. Our N-party EKE-M protocol consists of two rounds. In the first round we run a well-known 2-party password-authenticated key exchange scheme to set up secure channels between all clients $\in Clients$ and a server. In the second round, the server distributes a common keying value on the secure channel. Finally all clients generate a group session key using the common keying value. In Fig. 4, we illustrate a general framework of our construction.

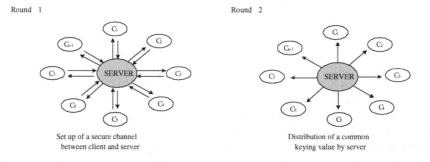

Round 1

Set up of a secure channel
between client and server

Round 2

Distribution of a common
keying value by server

Fig. 4. Framework of N-party EKE-M.

Concretely, to set up secure channels, we use a 2-party encrypted key exchange scheme BPR [4]. The scheme assumes the ideal cipher, hence our whole security results are naturally based on the ideal cipher model. If we adopt a 2-party password-authenticated key exchange scheme such as KOY [28] whose security is in the standard model, then our construction does not need the ideal cipher model in the proofs. However, as compared with BPR protocol, KOY protocol has disadvantages in computational and communicational aspects while it has advantage in the security assumption. For efficiency we adopt the BPR protocol to set up secure channels.

4.1   Description of N-Party EKE-M

Notations. Let G=$\langle g \rangle$ be cyclic group of prime order q. $sk_i(= \mathcal{H}_1(sid'||g^{x_i s_i}))$ is an ephemeral key generated between S and client C_i in the first round, where $sid' = \mathcal{E}_{pw_1}(g^{x_1})||\mathcal{E}_{pw_2}(g^{x_2})||...||\mathcal{E}_{pw_{n-1}}(g^{x_{n-1}})$. A common group key between clients is $sk = \mathcal{H}_2(SIDS||N)$, where $SIDS = sid'||sk_1 \oplus N||sk_2 \oplus N||...||sk_{n-1} \oplus N$ and N is a random value chosen from $[1, q-1]$.

Descriptions. In the first round, the single server S sends $\mathcal{E}_{pw_i}(g^{s_i})$ to $n-1$ clients concurrently. Simultaneously each client C_i, $1 \le i \le n-1$, also sends

$\mathcal{E}_{pw_i}(g^{x_i})$ to the single-server concurrently in the first round. After the first round finished S and C_i, $1 \le i \le n-1$, share an ephemeral *Diffie-Hellman* key, $sk_i = \mathcal{H}_1(sid'||g^{x_i s_i})$.

In the second round, S selects a random value N from $[1, q-1]$ and hides it by exclusive-or operation with the ephemeral key sk_i. S sends $N \oplus sk_i$ to C_i, $1 \le i \le n-1$, concurrently. After the second round finished all clients can get a random secret N using its sk_i, and generate a common session key, $sk = \mathcal{H}_2(SIDS||N)$. To add the mutual authentication (key confirmation) to N-party EKE-M protocol, we can use the additional *authenticator* structure described in [12], as mentioned in Section 3.

4.2 Security Theorem of N-Party EKE-M

We prove that an advantage of session key that an adversary $\tilde{\mathcal{A}}$ tries to get is negligible under the computational *Diffie-Hellman* assumption in both the ideal cipher and random oracle models. In the proof of **Theorem 4.1** we define sequences of experiments and get the advantage of the adversary in each experiment. At the end of proof we show the advantage of adversary in the real experiment is negligible. The security result is similar to the result of N-party EKE-U protocol except that the term about advantage of **GCDH** is replaced with the term about advantage of **CDH**. This result means that the best thing any adversary does in the multicast channel is also on-line guessing attacks. The security theorem is as follows.

Theorem 4.1 *P' is an N-party EKE-M protocol of Fig. 5, and passwords are chosen from a finite dictionary of size $|\mathcal{D}|$. Let $\tilde{\mathcal{A}}$ be a probabilistic polynomial time adversary which asks $\tilde{q}_s$ send, $\tilde{q}_h$ hash, and $\tilde{q}_\mathcal{E}$ encryption/decryption queries. Then*

$$\mathbf{Adv}_{P'}^{neke}(\tilde{\mathcal{A}}) \le \frac{\tilde{q}_\mathcal{E}^2}{(q-1)} + \frac{2\tilde{q}_s}{|\mathcal{D}|} + 2\tilde{q}_h \cdot \mathbf{Adv}_{\tilde{\mathcal{A}}}^{cdh}(T_{\tilde{\mathcal{A}}})$$

*where $T_{\tilde{\mathcal{A}}}$ is polynomial running time of **CDH** adversary algorithm $\mathcal{A}_{\tilde{\mathcal{A}}}$ such that $T_{\tilde{\mathcal{A}}} \le T + (\tilde{q}_s + \tilde{q}_\mathcal{E})(\tilde{\tau}_G + \tilde{\tau}_\mathcal{E})$. $\tilde{\tau}_G$ and $\tilde{\tau}_\mathcal{E}$ are computational time for exponentiation and encryption. q is the prime order of G.*

	S	C_1	C_2	...	C_{n-1}
Round 1	$s_i \leftarrow [1, q-1]$	$x_1 \leftarrow [1, q-1]$	$x_2 \leftarrow [1, q-1]$	...	$x_{n-1} \leftarrow [1, q-1]$
	$\mathcal{E}_{pw_i}(g^{s_i})$	$\mathcal{E}_{pw_1}(g^{x_1})$	$\mathcal{E}_{pw_2}(g^{x_2})$	...	$\mathcal{E}_{pw_{n-1}}(g^{x_{n-1}})$
	$N \leftarrow [1, q-1]$				
Round 2	$sk_1 \oplus N||...||sk_{n-1} \oplus N$				

Fig. 5. N-party EKE-M.

Theorem 4.2 *An N-party EKE-M protocol P' provides a forward secrecy under the computational Diffie-Hellman assumption.*

The proofs of the theorems will appear in the full version of the paper.

5 Conclusion and Further Research

In this paper we first presented two secure N-party EKE protocols in which clients are able to generate a common group session key only with their different passwords, and proved its security based on the group computational *Diffie-Hellman*, computational *Diffie-Hellman*, and multi-desional *Diffie-Hellman* assumptions. Further works may be to design N-Party EKE protocols in dynamic scenario and prove our schemes in the standard assumption.

Acknowledgement

We thank Dr. Ik Rae Jeong for helpful discussions about the security proofs and useful comments on an early version of this paper. We also thank anonymous referees for their valuable comments.

References

1. M. Abdalla, M. Bellare, and P. Rogaway, "The oracle diffie-hellman assumptions and an analysis of DHIES", *In proceedings of CT-RSA 2001*, LNCS Vol. 2020, pp. 143-158, Springer-Verlag, 2001.
2. M. Abdalla, P. Fouque, and D. Pointcheval, "Password-based authenticated key exchange in the three-party setting", *In proceedings of PKC'05*, LNCS Vol. 3386, pp. 65-84, Springer-Verlag, 2005.
3. R. Beraldi and R. Baldoni, "Unicast routing techniques for mobile ad hoc networks", ISBN:0-8493-1322-5, CRC Press, Inc. 2003.
4. M. Bellare, D. Pointcheval, and P. Rogaway, "Authenticated key exchange secure against dictionary attacks", *In proceedings of Eurocrypt'00*, LNCS Vol.1807, pp. 139-155, Springer-Verlag, 2000.
5. M. Bellare and P. Rogaway, "Random oracles are practical: a paradigm for designing efficient protocols", *In proceedings of the First ACM Conference on Computer and Communications Security, ACM*, 1995
6. M. Bellare and P. Rogaway, "Entity authentication and key distribution", *In proceedings of Crypto'93*, LNCS Vol. 773, pp. 232-249. Springer-Verlag, 1994.
7. S. Bellovin and M. Merrit, "Encrypted key exchange: password based protocols secure against dictionary attacks", *In proceedings of the Symposium on Security and Privacy*, pp.72-84, IEEE, 1992.
8. S. Blake-Wilson, D. Jhonson, and A. Menezes, "Key agreement protocols and their security analysis", *In proceedings of IMA international conference*, LNCS Vol. 1361, pp. 30-45, Springer-Verlag, 1997.
9. C. Basile, M-O. Killijian, and D. Powell, "A survey of dependability issues in mobile wireless networks", Technical Report, LAAS CNRS Toulouse, France, February, 2003. Availabe at http://www.crhc.uiuc.edu/~basilecl/papers/mobile.ps

10. C. Boyd and A. Mathuria, "Key establishment protocols for secure mobile communications : a selective survey", *In proceedings of ACISP 98'*, LNCS Vol. 1438, pp. 344-355, Springer-Verlag, 1998.
11. E. Bresson, O. Chevassut, and D. Pointcheval, "Group diffie-hellman key exchange secure against dictionary attacks", *In proceedings of Asiacrypt'02*, LNCS Vol. 2501, pp. 497-514, Springer-Verlag, 2002.
12. E. Bresson, O. Chevassut, D. Pointcheval, and J. J. Quisquater, "Provably authenticated group diffie-hellman key exchange", *In proceedings of 8th ACM Conference on Computer and Communications Security*, pp. 255-264, 2001.
13. E. Bresson, O. Chevassut, D. Pointcheval, and J. J. Quisquater, "Provably authenticated group diffie-hellman key exchange in the dynamic case", *In proceedings of Asiacrypt'01*, LNCS Vol. 2248, pp. 290-309, Springer-Verlag, 2001.
14. E. Bresson, O. Chevassut, and D. Pointcheval, "Dynamic group diffie-hellman key exchange under standard assumptions", *In proceedings of Eurocrypt'02*, LNCS Vol. 2332, pp. 321-336, 2002.
15. E. Bresson, O. Chevassut, and D. Pointcheval, "The group diffie-hellman problems", *In proceedings of SAC'02*, LNCS Vol. 2595, pp. 325-338, Springer-Verlag, 2002.
16. J. Black and P. Rogaway, "Ciphers with arbitrary finite domains", *In proceedings of CT-RSA conference*, LNCS Vol. 2271, pp. 114-130, Springer-Verlag, 2001.
17. V. Boyko, P. MacKenzie, and S. Patel, "Provably secure password-authenticated key exchange using diffie-hellman", *In proceedings of Eurocrypt'00*, LNCS Vol. 1807, pp. 156-171, Springer-Verlag, 2000.
18. M. Burmester and Y. Desmedt, "A secure and efficient conference key distribution system", *In proc. of Eurocrypt'94* LNCS VOL. 950, pp. 275-286, Springer-Verlag, 1994.
19. J. Byun, I. Jeong, D. Lee, and C. Park, "Password-authenticated key exchange between clients with different passwords", *In proceedings of ICICS'02*, LNCS Vol. 2513, pp. 134-146, Springer-Verlag, 2002.
20. L. Chen, "A Weakness of the Password-Authenticated Key Agreement between Clients with Different Passwords Scheme", ISO/IEC JTC 1/SC27 N3716.
21. C. Cordeiro and D. Agrawal, "Mobile ad hoc networking", *Tutorial/Short Course in 20 th Brazilian Symposium on Computer Networks*, pp. 125-186, May, 2002.
22. D. Denning and G. Sacco, "Timestamps in key distribution protocols", *In Communications of the ACM*, Vol. 24, No. 8, pp. 533-536, 1981.
23. Y. Ding and P. Horster, "Undetectable on-line password guessing attacks", *In ACM Operating Systems Review*, Vol. 29, No. 4, pp. 77-86, 1995.
24. O. Goldreich and Y. Lindell, "Session-key generation using human passwords only", *In proceedings of Crypto'01*, LNCS Vol. 2139, pp. 408-432, Springer-Verlag, 2001.
25. S. Halevi and H. Krawczyk, "Public-key cryptography and password protcols", *In proceedings ACM Conference on Computer and Communications Security*, ACM press, pp. 63-72, 1999.
26. IEEE P802.11i/D10.0, "Wireless medium access control (MAC) and physical layer (PHY) specifications : medium access control (MAC) security enhancements", April 2004.
27. D. Jablon, "Strong password-only authenticated key exchange", *In Computer Communication Review*, Vol.26, No.5, pp. 5-26, 1996.
28. J. Katz, R. Ostrovsky, and M. Yung, "Efficient password-authenticated key exchange using human-memorable passwords", *In proceedings of Eurocrypt'01*, LNCS Vol. 2045, pp. 475-494, Springer-Verlag, 2001.

29. A. Kashyap, H. Nishar, and P. Agarwal, "Survey on unicast routing in mobile ad hoc networks", 2001. This paper is available at http://www.cs.unibo.it/people/ faculty/bononi/Sim2003/Papers/surveyrouting..pdf
30. J. Kim, S. Kim, J. Kwak, and D. Won, "Cryptanalysis and Improvements of Password Authenticated Key Exchange Scheme between Clients with Different Passwords", In Proceedings of ICCSA 2004, LNCS Vol. 3044, pp. 895-902, Springer-Verlag, 2004.
31. P. Kuosmanen, "Classification of ad hoc routing protocols", 2003. Available at http://eia.udg.es/~lilianac/docs/classification-of-ad-hoc.pdf
32. C. Lin, H. Sun, and T. Hwang, "Three-party encrypted key exchange: attacks and a solution", In ACM Operating Systems Review, Vol. 34, No. 4, pp. 12-20, 2000.
33. C. Lin, H. Sun, M. Steiner, and Tzonelih Hwang, "Three-party Encrypted Key Exchange Without Server Public-Keys", In IEEE Communications Letters, Vol. 5, No. 12, pp. 497-499, IEEE Press, 2001.
34. S. Lucks, "Open key exchange: how to defeat dictionary attacks without encryting public keys", In proceedings of the security protocol workshop '97, pp. 79-90, 1997.
35. M. Steiner, G. Tsudik, and M. Waider, "Refinement and extension of encrypted key exchange", In ACM Operation Sys. Review, Vol. 29, No. 3, pp. 22-30, 1995.
36. M. Steiner, G. Tsudik, and M, Waidner, "Diffie-hellman key distribution extended to groups", In proceedings of ACM CCS'96, ACM Press, 1996.
37. V. Shoup, "OAEP reconsidered", In proceedings of Crypto01', LNCS Vol. 2139, pp. 239-259, 2001.
38. W. Tzeng, "A secure fault-tolerant conference-key agreement protocol", In IEEE Transaction on Computers, Vol. 51, No. 4, 2002.
39. V. Varadharajan and Y. Mu, "On the design of security protocols for mobile communications", In proceedings of ACISP'96, LNCS Vol. 1172, pp. 134-145, 1996.
40. S. Wang, J. Wang, and M. Xu, "Weakness of a Password-authenticated Key Exchange Protocol Between Clients with Different Passwords", In Proceedings of ACNS 2004, LNCS Vol. 3089, pp. 414-425, Springer-Verlag, 2004.
41. T. Wu, "Secure remote password protocol", In proceedings of the Internet Society Network and Distributed System Security Symposium, pp. 97-111, 1998.

Messin' with Texas Deriving Mother's Maiden Names Using Public Records

Virgil Griffith and Markus Jakobsson

School of Informatics, Indiana University Bloomington, Bloomington, IN 47408

Abstract. We have developed techniques to automatically infer mother's maiden names from public records. We demonstrate our techniques using publicly available records from the state of Texas, and reduce the entropy of a mother's maiden name from an average of close to 13 bits down to below 6.9 bits for more than a quarter of the people targeted, and down to a zero entropy (i.e., certainty of their mothers maiden name) for a large number of targeted individuals. This poses a significant risk not only to individuals whose mothers maiden name can easily be guessed, but highlights the vulnerability of the system as such, given the traditional reliance of authentication by mother maiden names for financial services. While our techniques and approach are novel, it is important to note that these techniques – once understood – do not require any insider information or particular skills to implement. This emphasizes the need to move away from mothers maiden names as an authenticator. Using the techniques described, during testing we were able to deduce the mother's maiden name for approximately 4,105,111 Texans.

1 Introduction

Within the security community the secrecy of your mother's maiden name (MMN) is known to not to be the strongest form of authentication. However, the MMN is frequently used by the commercial sector including banks, credit cards agencies, internet service providers, and many websites. This may be largely for convenience, but by and large the MMN is considered to be suitably secure against all but the most targeted attacks or those by close family friends. However, our study shows that by mining and cross-correlating public records information (which is required by US law to be public), an attacker can determine or "compute" MMNs with startling accuracy. Utilizing large numbers of identities for the purposes of laundering is an immense asset to both terrorist organizations and other more traditional organized crime.

The ubiquity of birth and marriage information constitutes the most direct threat of MNN compromise by means of public records. Marriage records are a reliable way of obtaining large numbers of maiden names, while birth records provide the identities of offspring. By using them in conjunction, all that remains for a successful compromise is linking a child to the appropriate parents, and then printing the bride's maiden name as listed within the marriage record. The cross-correlation of birth and marriage data is not only effective as a general

J. Ioannidis, A. Keromytis, and M.Yung (Eds.): ACNS 2005, LNCS 3531, pp. 91–103, 2005.

approach to MMN compromise, but also has numerous non-obvious special cases that make MMN derivation alarmingly easy. For example, if a groom has a very uncommon last name, then it becomes very easy to match him with any of his children simply by their uncommon last name. Secondly, if the birth record denotes that the child is suffixed "Jr.", "III", etc., an attacker can drastically narrow down the number of candidate parents. Third, if the child's last name is hyphenated, rarely will an attacker have any trouble matching the child with the appropriate marriage. While these special cases make up only a relatively small portion of the population, as we increase in scale, even the smallest tricks and statistical regularities will result in thousands of compromises. Moreover, for every victim that an attacker succeeds to infer the MMN, he narrows the number of choices for other potential victims (except for siblings). The ability to deduce secret information from supposedly innocuous information has been discussed previously [8]. However, we are not aware of any previous instances of deduction of personal authenticating information on this scale. Although no extensive survey has been done, the use of mother's maiden name as a security authenticator seems to be a practice unique to Canada and the United States. Other countries (particularly in Europe) use better security practices such as one-time use random numbers or insisting that they call customers back at their registered phone number.

The availability and exact information contained within birth and marriage records varies slightly from state to state. So, for purposes of illustration, we decided to focus on only one. Naturally, we wanted as large a sample size as possible to ensure that our methods scaled well to very large datasets, but also to assure that any conclusions pertaining to the sample would be worthy of attention in their own right. This left us with two prominent choices for in-depth analysis: California and Texas. The most recent US Census [4] indicates that Texas is substantially more representative of the entire country than California. Particularly, the ethnic composition of Texas is closer to that of the nation than California. This is of special relevance considering that marriage patterns as well as last names (and therefore maiden names) are strongly influenced by ethnicity. Texas is also more representative in the percentage of foreign-born residents, and the frequency of households moving to other states. Overall, this made Texas a natural choice for our studies. It should be clear that although we chose Texas because of its statistical proximity to the national averages, these same techniques can be used to derive MMNs in other states (especially large states with digitized records) with success rates likely on the same order as our findings. California has also made their records digitally available; we anticipate very similar results to those presented here.

Although these techniques are to the best of our knowledge completely novel, now that they've been discovered the replication and application of them can be done by anyone with Internet access. However, we do not believe that the publication of this information is immoral, and rather see it as a necessary alert of a problem bound to occur no matter what.

2   Availability of Texas Marriage, Birth, and Death Information

In smaller states, vital information is usually held by the individual counties in which the events took place, and in larger states there is an additional copy provided to a central state office. Texas is no exception to this pattern. Yet, regardless of where the physical records happen to be stored, all such records remain public property and are with few exceptions fully accessible to the public. The only relevance of where the records are stored is that of ease of access. State-wide agencies are more likely have the resources to put the information into searchable digital formats, whereas records from smaller local counties may only be available on microfilm (which they will gladly ship to you for a modest fee). However, as time progresses, public information stored at even the smallest county offices will invariably start being digitized.

The Texas Bureau of Vital Statistics website [16] lists all marriages state-wide from 1966–2002; records from before 1966 are available from the individual counties. Texas birth records are also available online but the *fields containing the names of the mother and father* are "aged" for 50 years (meaning they are withheld from the public until 50 years have passed). This means that for anyone born in Texas who is over 50, a parent-child linking has conveniently already been done. It may seem obvious if we think about it, but it's worth mentioning that the average American lives well beyond the age of 50, making this security measure insufficient. By means of this policy alone, every single person born in Texas that was born from 1923–1949 currently has their MMN completely compromised in plaintext. From these records alone we are able to fully compromise 1,114,680 males. Females are somewhat more difficult because if they have been married we would not know their current last name. However, our marriage records from 1966–2002 contain the age of both the groom and bride, by matching brides not only by name but also by year of birth, we were able to compromise 288,751 women (27%). In many cases older people make much better targets for fraud as they are likely to have more savings than younger adults.

Here it is worth noting that in October 2000, Texas officially took down the online access to their birth indexes (death indexes were similarly taken down as of June 2002 [3]) due to concerns of adopted children discovering the identities of their biological parents [2] (which is illegal). Additionally, they increased the aging requirement for both the partially redacted and full birth records to 75 years, and even then will only provide birth and death records in microfiche. However, before they were taken down partial copies of the state and county indexes had already been mirrored elsewhere where we were able to find and make use of them. We found two sizable mirrors of the birth and death information. One was from Brewster Kahle's famous *Wayback Machine* [1], and the other from the user-contributed grass-roots genealogy site Rootsweb.com [11] which had a even larger compilation of partial indexes from the state and county level. Oddly, despite these new state-level restrictions, county records apparently do not require aging and many county level birth and death records all the way up to the present remain freely available in microfilm or through their websites [13].

Of particular amusement, even though the death indexes available on Rootsweb and the Internet Archive were put up before they were supposedly taken down in June 2002, the full death indexes are still available (although not directly linked) over 2 1/2 years later from the Texas Dept. of Vital Statistic's own servers at *exactly the same URL they were at before* [19]! All of this is particularly relevant because even though Texas is now doing a better job protecting their public records (although largely for unrelated reasons), the public is just as vulnerable as they were before.

3   Heuristics for MMN Discovery Through Marriage Records

We have already described how a cursory glance over birth and marriage records reveals a more than ample supply of low-hanging fruit. However, if this is not enough to persuade the discontinuation of MMN-based authentication, the correlation of marriage data (perhaps the best source of MMNs) with other types of public information comprises an effective and more general approach to linking someone to his or her mother's maiden name. When given a list of random people whether it be produced by partially redacted birth records, phonebooks, or your favorite social networking service, there are at least seven general observations that an attacker could use to derive someone's MMN with high probability. Naturally, as each heuristic is applied, the chance of MMN compromise will be increased.

1. We do not have to link a child to a particular marriage record, only to a particular maiden name. There will often be cases in which there are repetitions in the list of possible maiden names. This holds particularly true for ethnic groups with characteristic last names. An attacker does not have to pick the correct parents, just the correct MMN! This observation alone makes guessing MMNs much simpler than one might think.
2. Children will generally have the same last name as their parents.
3. Couples will typically have a child within the first five years of being married.
4. Children are often born in the same county in which their parents were recently married.
5. Parts of the parents' first, last, and middle names are often repeated within a child's first or middle name. (Conveniently, this is especially true for the mother's maiden name and the child's middle name.)
6. Children are rarely born after their parents have been divorced. In addition to this rule, all Texas divorce records [18] list the number of children under 18 bequeathed within the now dissolved marriage. So, divorce records are helpful not only by eliminating the likelihood of children being born to a couple beyond a divorce date, but they also tell us how many children (if any) we should expect to find, as well as the general birth range to expect for them. In Texas, every divorce affects on average 0.79 children [17]. As nation-wide divorce rates average about half that of marriage rates, divorce data can significantly complement any analysis of marriage or birth records.

7. Children cannot be born after the mother's death nor more than a year after the father's death. Texas death indexes are aged 25 years before release (full state-wide indexes for 1964–1975 are available online [19]). Death records are useful in that they not only contain the full name (First/Last/Middle/Suffix) of the deceased, but also the full name of any spouse. This seemingly innocuous piece of information is useful for easily matching up deaths of husbands and wives to their marriages, thus narrowing the list of possible marriages that can still produce offspring by the time of a victim's birth.

For our preliminary statistics, we have taken into account observations 1, 2, 3, and 4. The heuristics listed above certainly are not the only viable attacks an attacker could use, but they serve as a good starting point for the automated derivation of MMNs.

4   Experimental Design

With easy access to public records and no easy way to put the cat back in the bag, we should now be asking ourselves, "How effective are the above described attacks/heuristics in leading to further MMN compromise?", and "What percent of the population is at risk?" To answer these questions, we will use data entropy to measure the risk of MMN discovery from our attacks. Comparing the entropy of different sets of potential MMNs is a suitable and illustrative measurement for accessing the vulnerability to these attacks. Data entropy measures the amount of unpredictability within a distribution of potential MMNs. Its primary benefit over simply listing the number of possible marriage records after filtering is that entropy takes into account repetitions within the set of possible MMNs. For example, after correlating records you could have a set of 40 possible marriages from which the child could have come from. However, 30 of these marriages may have the maiden name "Martinez", and 5 of the remaining 10 marriages the maiden name "Lopez." Clearly, in this case there is a far greater than a 2.5% chance (1/40) of correctly guessing the MMN. (In this example, the entropy would be 1.351 bits.)

To provide a baseline comparison for assessing the increased vulnerability due to accessing attacks using public records, we calculated the data entropy across all maiden names in our database (1966–2002). This measurement is equivalent to an example situation in which an attacker does not use any public records data, but despite this tries calling a local bank and saying the target's MMN is "Smith", just hoping to guess correctly. ("Smith" is the most common last name in America consisting of about 0.9% of the population). The resulting baseline entropy for this attack is 12.92 bits.

5   Analysis of MMN Discovery in Marriage Records

By our methods, we get the following graph (Fig. 1) gauging the risk of MMN compromise from an attacker who makes use of marriage data and makes the

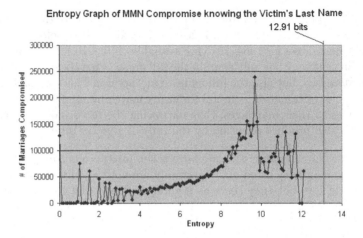

Fig. 1. Ability to determine MMNs from knowing the victim's last name.

assumption that the parents' marriage took place anytime from 1966 to 2002, but who knows nothing more than the victim's last name (i.e., has no knowledge of the victim's age, first or middle name, place of birth, etc.).

Unlike the entropy corresponding to a pure guess, public records allow the attacker to take advantage of the fact that we know the victim's last name (something the attacker would have to know anyway). Therefore, we will have different entropies, one for each last name. Naturally, deriving someone's MMNs based solely on the their last name will be more difficult for common last names than for uncommon last names given the larger pool of possible parents.

For example, if the attacker only knows the intended victim's last name is "Smith" (resulting entropy = 12.18 bits), this reduces the entropy only 0.74 bits from the original 12.91 bits. However, if it is a less common last name like "EVANGELISTA" (resulting entropy = 5.08 bits), or "AADNESEN" (resulting entropy = 0 bits), the attacker is immensely increasing the chances of correcting guessing the MMN. Note that for the absolute worst cases like "Smith" (12.18 bits) or "Garcia" (9.811 bits), these entropies will still be too high to compromise their bank accounts over the phone. However, these numbers quickly fall into the range of making brute-force an increasingly viable option for gaining assess to their web accounts. Moreover, knowledge of the victim beyond his or her last name(such as age, place of birth, etc.) can help the attacker eliminate large pools of candidate parents, and therefore improve the chances of determining the MMN. In summary, the use of public records to inform the most trivial search for vulnerable MMNs statistically increases the risk for everyone while enabling complete MMN compromise for children with the rarest of names. To allow effective comparison of different attacks, we will redraw Fig. 1 as a cumulative percentage of marriage records compromised.

A full zero-entropy compromise of approximately 2% of marriages may not initially seem so terrible, but the table above shows that even the smallest per-

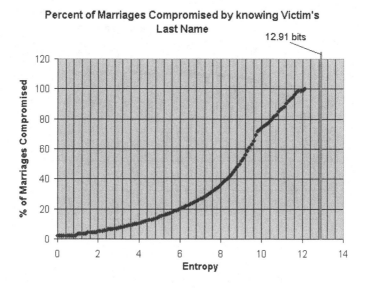

Fig. 2. Redrawing of Fig. 1 as cumulative percentage of marriages compromised.

Table 1. Using the unusual last names attack against our local birth records.

Entropy	# Children Compromised	% Birth Records Compromised	Chance to Guess MMN
= 0 bits	82,272	1.04	= 1/1
≤ 1 bit	148,367	1.88	≤ 1/2
≤ 2 bits	251,568	3.19	≤ 1/4
≤ 3 bits	397,457	5.04	≤ 1/8

centages will lead to massive compromise. The graph above is an accurate assessment of the risk of MMN compromise to an attacker armed with marriage records and Google phonebook [6].

5.1   MMN Compromise Looking Within Five Years and County of Victim's Birth

Although the first attack is the safest route to MMN compromise, in efforts to gain a greater yield there are times in which an attacker would be willing apply further assumptions, such as by creating a "window" of time in which it is reasonable to assume the victim's parents were married. This window of time could be as long or as short as the attacker desires. Naturally, longer windows increase the chances of including the parents' marriage record, while shorter windows yield higher percentages of compromised MMNs. In this example we assume the attacker knows not only the victim's last name, but his or her age (this information can be obtained from birth records or online social networks), and the county in which the victim was born (can be obtained from birth records). This

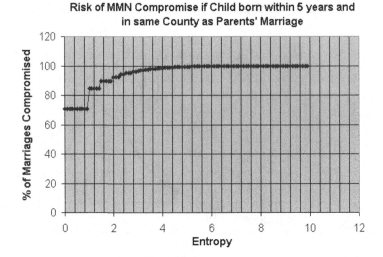

Fig. 3. 1970-2002: Risk of MMN compromise when parents' marriage county is known, and the marriage year known within five years.

attack uses a five year window up to and including the year the victim was born and deduces MMNs in accordance with the observation that couples frequently have a child within the first five years of being married. Naming statistics do vary from year to year, but for the reader's convenience we have averaged all years.

By narrowing our window in which to look for candidate marriages, the resulting entropies drop significantly. An attacker can increase or decrease the window size based upon the uncertainty of the marriage year. As the window increases, there are fewer zero-entropy compromises, but any compromises are more reliable as there is a better chance of the correct marriage record being included within the window.

5.2   MMN Compromise in Suffix'ed Children

Our final quantitative analysis is for an attack using public records in which the attacker has no knowledge of the victim's age but instead knows the victim's first

Table 2. Compromises from five year window + county attack against within local birth records.

Entropy	# Children Compromised	% Birth Records Compromised	Chance to Guess MMN
= 0 bits	2,355,828	29.8	= 1/1
≤ 1 bit	3,750,798	47.5	≤ 1/2
≤ 2 bits	3,750,798	47.5	≤ 1/4
≤ 3 bits	3,750,798	47.5	≤ 1/8

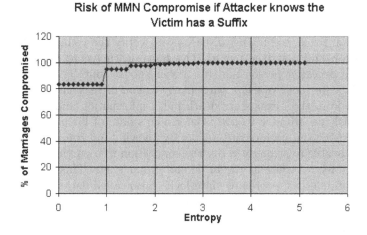

Fig. 4. Ability to determine MMN's for suffix'ed children.

name, last name, and suffix. Knowing that the victim has a suffix is immensely valuable as it tells the first name to look for within the parents' marriage record. Once again, naming statistics do vary from year to year, but for the reader's convenience we are printing only the average across all years.

Table 3. Compromises of suffix'ed children in our local birth records.

Entropy	# Children Compromised	% Birth Records Compromised	Chance to Guess MMN
= 0 bits	344,463	60.5	= 1/1
≤ 1 bit	345,211	60.6	≤ 1/2
≤ 2 bits	345,223	60.6	≤ 1/4
≤ 3 bits	345,223	60.6	≤ 1/8

6   Other Means for Deriving Mother's Maiden Names

Hereto we had focused on the use of birth and marriage records in compromising MMNs, and although birth and marriage information constitute the greatest threat to large scale MMN discovery, it is by no means the only viable route. The following is a sample of some of the more creative public records attacks that we have confirmed to work in our sample cases, yet remain largely unexplored.

6.1   Social Security Death Index

The Social Security Death Index (SSDI) [14] provides up-to-date information of people who have passed away. The SSDI was created as a security measure to prevent the mafia from selling the identities of deceased infants to illegal immigrants. As such, it is comprehensive, digitally available, and fully searchable. In the case of Texas, the SSDI can be used to verify the connection between a groom's death and marriage record. The state death record provides the full name of the deceased person and his or her spouse, but there is still always the possibility for name overlap, particularly as you increase in scale. By taking information from the Texas state death index information and plugging the it into the SSDI, we are able to learn the groom's date of birth, a fact that was unknowable from the state records alone. By knowing the groom's date of birth, an attacker is able to strongly verify the connection to a particular marriage as the marriage record contains the bride and groom's age. This is a reminder of the ability of different records to "interlock" (also called database aggregation) which allows for much stronger conclusions.

6.2   Voter Registration Records

In efforts to prevent voter fraud (a concern especially of late) voter registration records are by U.S. law [9] required to be public. But despite the good intentions, next to marriage and birth information, voter information constitutes the greatest threat to automated MMN discovery and can perhaps fill in the place of either a birth of marriage record. They contain the Full Name, "previous name" (the maiden name), date of birth, and county of residence [20]. Texas voting records for individual counties are sometimes available from the county websites, but for any significant coverage an attacker would have to purchase them from the state bureau. The database for voter registration records across the entire state costs approximately $1,100. As of 2000, 69% of voting-age Texans were registered to vote; this percentage has almost certainly increased since then due to efforts to "get-out-the-vote" during the 2004 elections.

6.3   Genealogy Websites

Not only a source for mirrored public records data, Rootsweb [12] is an all-purpose user-contributed genealogy website. Amazingly, more often than not, MMNs of currently living people can be read directly from the submitted family trees with no further analysis required for successful MMN compromise. In the off-chance that a security conscious genealogy researcher lists a mother under her husband's name, her first name, middle name, marriage date, date and place of birth are always given. With this much information already in hand, a marriage or birth record will allow for certain recovery of the maiden name. Online user-contributed family trees currently do not cover a large fraction of the population, but the submitted trees are still a complete map for MMN compromise and are available to anyone with Internet access. In our analysis we found Rootsweb.com to contain full family trees for 4,499 living Texans. Some genealogy resources such as the Church of Later-day Saints' FamilySearch.org avoids listing information about living people.

6.4   Newspaper Obituaries

Local newspapers frequently publish, both in print and online, obituaries of those who have recently died. Regardless of whether these obituaries happen to be analyzed by hand or via some clever natural language analysis, an obituary entry will generally give an attacker the deceased's name, date of birth, name of spouse, as well as the names of any children. The recently deceased is of no interest to an attacker, but the recent departure of a parent is a convenient opportunity for attacking any children. With the information contained in an obituary, the maiden name can be gotten easily from either the marriage or voting record. However, the children may have moved to other parts of the country, so simply looking them up in the local phonebook may not work. However, an attacker can look up the deceased's SSDI entry which lists a "zipcode of primary benefactor," which will almost invariably be the zipcode of one of the children. The combination of a name and zipcode is a surprisingly unique identifier and the location of the child can be easily queried using Google Phonebook [7].

6.5   Property Records

At our current scale property records are of relatively little value. But if we wanted to expand these techniques to a national scale, property records are a good option for tracking people who have moved to another state. Property records are required by law to be public and are usually freely available online [15]. In the absence of property records, mass aggregation of phonebooks from different years is also a viable option.

7   Conclusion

Just as cryptographic algorithms do with time require to be replaced, so do authentication mechanisms. Unlike the time when mother's maiden names first started being used as an authenticator, our analysis shows the MMN is increasingly vulnerable to the automated data-mining of public records. New data-mining attacks make it increasingly unacceptable to use documented facts as authenticators. Facts about the world are not true secrets. As a society, there are many ways to respond to this new threat. Texas' response to this threat was by legislating away easy and timely access to its public information. This approach has been largely ineffective, and has accomplished exceedingly little in diminishing the threat of MMN compromise to the public at large. If these actions have accomplished anything of significance, it is only the creation of a false sense of security. Access to public records of all types was created to strengthen government accountability and reduce the risk of government misconduct by allowing the public to watch over the government that it supports with its tax money. Some states find this governmental oversight so vital as to even write public records provisions directly into their state constitution [5]. We can only speculate as to the long term effects of policies which would routinely restrict access to otherwise valuable public information simply because it might also be valuable to those with less-than-noble intentions.

In today's society, the existence of a seperate mother's maiden name, much less a secret one, is slowly becoming obsolete. At one time, the mother's maiden name served as a convenient and reasonably secure piece of information. However, as sociological changes have made it increasingly socially permissible for a woman to keep her original name and have additionally brought about hyphenated names for children, new technologies have made for comprehensive and accurate record keeping as well as easy searching of these records. Using one of our methods (but expanding our search beyond the state of Texas), we established that the mother's maiden name of the current president of the United States is "Pierce," and the mother's maiden name of his two children is "Welch."

Acknowledgements

The primary author wishes to thank Henry Strickland for his suggestions on the entropy graph presentations.

References

1. Archive.org 21-Jun-2001: Bureau of Vital Statistics General and Summary Birth Indexes http://web.archive.org/web/20000621143352/http://www.tdh.state.tx.us/bvs/registra/birthidx/birthidx.htm
2. Archive.org 20-Nov-2001: Bureau of Vital Statistics, General and Summary Birth Indexes http://web.archive.org/web/20001120125700/http://www.tdh.state.tx.us/bvs/registra/birthidx/birthidx.htm
3. Archive.org Birth/Death Index mainpages for 19-Nov-2001 and 05-Jun-2002 Comparing http://web.archive.org/web/20011119121739/http://www.tdh.state.tx.us/bvs/registra/bdindx.htm to http://web.archive.org/web/20020605235939/http://www.tdh.state.tx.us/bvs/registra/bdindx.htm
4. Census 2000 Briefs www.census.gov/population/www/cen2000/briefs.html
5. Florida State Constitution, Section 24. http://www.flsenate.gov/Statutes/index.cfm?Mode=Constitution&Submenu=3&Tab=statutes#A01S24
6. Google Phonebook Search http://www.google.com/search?hl=en&q=phonebook%3A&btnG=Google+Search
7. Google Phonebook Search for "Smith" in zipcode 75201 (Dallas,TX) http://www.google.com/search?sa=X&oi=rwp&pb=r&q=Smith+75201
8. Sweeney, Latanya; Malin, Bradley: Journal of Biomedical Informatics. 2004; 37(3): 179-192 How (not) to protect genomic data privacy in a distributed network: using trail re-identification to evaluate and design anonymity protection systems.
9. National Voter Act of 1993 http://www.fvap.gov/laws/nvralaw.html
15. Texas State Property Records http://www.txcountydata.com
11. Rootsweb.com FTP server with complete copies of both the marriage and death indexes ftp://rootsweb.com/pub/usgenweb/tx/
12. RootsWeb.com Home Page http://www.rootsweb.com

13. SearchSystems.net listing of Texas Counties' online public record offerings http://searchsystems.net/list.php?nid=197   http://searchsystems.net/list.php?nid=344

14. Social Security Death Index http://ssdi.genealogy.rootsweb.com/

15. Texas State Property Records http://www.txcountydata.com

16. Texas Department of Health, Bureau of Vital Statistics, Marriage Indexes http://www.tdh.state.tx.us/bvs/registra/marridx/marridx.htm

17. Texas Department of Health, Divorce Trends in Texas, 1970 to 1999 www.tdh.state.tx.us/bvs/reports/divorce/divorce.htm

18. Texas Department of Health, Bureau of Vital Statistics, Divorce Indexes http://www.tdh.state.tx.us/bvs/registra/dividx/dividx.htm

19. Texas Department of Health, Bureau of Vital Statistics, General and Summary Death Indexes http://www.tdh.state.tx.us/bvs/registra/deathidx/deathidx.htm

20. TX Secretary of State Voter Information http://www.sos.state.tx.us/elections/voter/index.shtml

Mitigating Network Denial-of-Service Through Diversity-Based Traffic Management

Ashraf Matrawy, Paul C. van Oorschot, and Anil Somayaji

Carleton University, Ottawa, ON K1S 5B6, Canada
amatrawy@sce.carleton.ca, {paulv,soma}@scs.carleton.ca

Abstract. In this paper we explore the feasibility of mitigating network denial-of-service (NDoS) attacks (attacks that consume network
bandwidth) by dynamically regulating learned classes of network traffic.
Our classification technique clusters packets based on the similarity of
their contents – both headers and payloads – using a variation of n-grams
which we call (p, n)-grams. We then allocate shares of bandwidth to each
of these clusters using an adaptive traffic management technique. Our
design intent is that excessive bandwidth consumers (e.g. UDP worms,
flash crowds) are segregated so that they cannot consume bandwidth to
the exclusion of other network traffic. Because this strategy, under congestion conditions, increases the packet drop rate experienced by sets of
similar flows and thus reduces the relative drop rate of other, dissimilar
flows, we characterize this strategy as *diversity-based traffic management*.
We explain the approach at a high level and report on preliminary results
that indicate that network traffic can be quickly and concisely learned,
and that this classification can be used to regulate the bandwidth allocated to both constant packet and polymorphic flash UDP worms.

Keywords: network denial of service, flash worms, traffic shaping, network security, diversity

1 Introduction

In recent years the stability and usability of the Internet has been challenged
by numerous uses and abuses unforeseen by its original designers. Peer-to-peer
applications saturate links with searches and file transfers. Web servers and small
service providers are overwhelmed by flash crowds initiated by the rapid spread
of ideas and links on the "blogosphere" while email servers are flooded with vast
quantities of unsolicited commercial email. Most disturbingly, self-replicating
autonomous programs (worms and viruses) flood network connections through
scans and infection attempts, some spreading worldwide in seconds [1].

Many researchers have chosen to address each of these issues as isolated
problems; we believe, however, that progress can also be made by recognizing
what these problems have in common. In all of these situations, the actions of
a few applications can consume all available bandwidth and in so doing prevent
other hosts, applications, and users from communicating. While the denial-of-
service (DoS) problem in general has received much attention in recent years,

J. Ioannidis, A. Keromytis, and M.Yung (Eds.): ACNS 2005, LNCS 3531, pp. 104–121, 2005.

this type of bandwidth-consuming network DoS (NDoS) has received less study. NDoS is the one problem, however, to which no host or network is immune – no matter how well it is otherwise protected. Fundamentally, bandwidth forms a commons, in that it is a resource used by all but is completely controlled by nobody. Although it is possible to create mechanisms to allocate the bandwidth commons, such allocations will impose some limitations on communications – the primary purpose of the Internet. The question we pursue is that of how bandwidth may be allocated in a way that better reflects the differing needs of Internet users and applications. In doing so we try to prevent the actions of a few categories of excessive bandwidth consumers from disrupting the activities of other, more moderate consumers.

Rather than attempting to specifically identify undesirable sets of packets (whether they be malicious or simply less important by some measure), our approach is to allocate bandwidth on the basis of packet similarity. In some circumstances these commonalities may be shared destination ports or host IP addresses; in others, it may be recurring payload substrings. In our approach, packets sharing relatively high-frequency patterns (in header and/or payload) are identified as a set, and each of these sets is limited to a controlled fraction of network bandwidth. So long as such a set is "adequately represented" in the network flow, its bandwidth limit does not shrink – nor grow. Thus, while such sets are guaranteed representation in the outgoing packet stream, in the case of bandwidth starvation they must also share bandwidth with other identified packet sets. Because this strategy tends to increase the diversity of packets within a given network connection (under saturation conditions), we refer to it as *diversity-based network traffic management*.

To study the feasibility of this bandwidth management strategy, our research has focused on a simple pattern schema that we call (p, n)-grams. Like the better-known n-grams (cf. Section 2.2), (p, n)-grams are fixed-length strings of byte-length n; unlike n-grams, they are at a fixed offset p within a packet – thus allowing for very efficient pattern matching, even within payloads. More specifically, our work includes: (1) studying the patterns of (p, n)-grams present in captured network traffic; (2) creating and analyzing high-speed online algorithms for extracting sets of (p, n)-grams suitable for dividing packets into similarity sets; and (3) developing an architecture for dynamically allocating bandwidth between sets of similar packets.

Our Contributions. In this paper we propose that network denial-of-service attacks can be mitigated by adaptively clustering network packets and by allocating bandwidth on the basis of such clusters. To implement this strategy, we propose a new measure of packet similarity, namely (p, n)-grams, and a simple feedback algorithm for learning sets of (p, n)-grams that can be used to subdivide network traffic. We also propose an architecture for using this algorithm to regulate network traffic so as to minimize the impact of large aggregates of similar packets in congested conditions. We then present experimental data that indicates that the proposed algorithm can quickly and concisely learn the patterns of normal network traffic. With the injection of simulated worm traffic into live captured network data, we also show that the proposed mechanisms can limit the bandwidth allocated to both constant and random-payload UDP flash worms automatically and autonomously.

Outline. In what follows, Section 2 presents related work. Section 3 discusses the rationale for diversity-based network traffic management and our architecture for managing network traffic. Section 4 describes our approach to (p, n)-gram packet analysis. Section 5 presents the results of preliminary experiments. Concluding remarks in Section 6 include a discussion of ongoing challenges and plans for future work.

2   Related Work

Although it has been generally realized that network traffic must be managed to prevent communication disruptions, no central strategy has emerged that is effective at dealing with all aspects of the problem. Instead, researchers have developed many different mechanisms, each designed to address certain circumstances. To organize our review of past work, we divide these mechanisms into two classes: those that address the congestion control problem by managing overly aggressive bandwidth consumers, and those that identify and respond to malicious network traffic.

2.1   Congestion Control for Aggregates of Flows

Congestion control has been a basic design principle of the Internet from its earliest days. Indeed, the robustness of the Internet can be attributed in part to the end-to-end congestion control mechanisms built-in to TCP [2]. End-to-end congestion control, however, is based on the assumption that implementors of network protocols and applications are willing to cooperate to maximize network efficiency and fairness. While such assumptions were once well-founded, this is no longer the case.

Perhaps the first signs of trouble were in the form of UDP-based media applications. Early versions of these systems were not good network citizens, in that they would not throttle their communications in response to developing congestion. Therefore, they would gain an unfair share of bandwidth when competing with TCP streams that would honor such implicit congestion messages. The situation was even worse for multimedia multicast applications. These issues motivated a new area of research and development: unicast [3] and multicast [4] TCP-friendly protocols and applications. While the performance of these TCP-friendly mechanisms is satisfactory in some cases, the growing need for better congestion management has resulted in the development of mechanisms such as Explicit Congestion Notification [5] and Random Early Detection Gateways [6] where the network provides some congestion control support to end systems.

The main characteristic of the above architectures and mechanisms is that they are targeted at misbehaving *individual* flows. A flow is normally defined as a set of IP packets that are exchanged on fixed TCP or UDP ports between two IP addresses. As noted by Estan and Varghese [7], a large fraction of network bandwidth is sometimes consumed by a few large flows (e.g. by large file transfers, multimedia streams, etc.). In such situations, a sampling strategy can be used to find these "heavy hitters"; in the case of flash crowds and distributed network denial-of-service attacks, though, there are no such heavy hitters to identify. To address this limitation, network analysis systems such as AutoFocus [8] cluster flow state descriptors in order to discover sets of shared features in the high-dimensional space defined by IP addresses, protocols, and ports.

Rather than focus on network analysis, others have developed tools with which to manage network bandwidth. Systems such as Diffserv [9, 10] label and prioritize traffic according to pre-negotiated quality of service classes. Traffic shaping mechanisms [11, 12] can be used to limit the bandwidth allocated to specific quality-of-service classes, hosts, and/or ports. Existing traffic shaping systems are very good at managing traffic according to pre-established policies; however, static rules are not sufficient to manage the transient problems created by flash crowds, worms, or NDoS attacks.

Other researchers have recognized these limitations and have sought solutions. In particular, Mahajan et al. [13] (see also [14]) proposed that DDoS attacks be dealt with as an *aggregate congestion control* (ACC) problem. They combined a local mechanism (at the routers) to detect signatures of flow aggregates that are causing congestion, and a co-operative mechanism – called *pushback* – to notify other routers of these signatures so that they may take action against these aggregates to limit their impact. The local mechanism uses the destination address to detect high-bandwidth aggregates, which are represented using *congestion signatures*; these signatures are passed to other routers by the pushback mechanism when it is deemed necessary to communicate a deteriorating congestion status at a certain router. The intent is to stop the spread of high-bandwidth aggregates as close as possible to their source. As originally conceived, pushback would seem to require routers to store large amounts of information on flow state; work such as that by Yaar et al. [15], however, shows that this need not be the case if end points explicitly manage their bandwidth commitments.

While pushback has the potential to stop certain classes of NDoS, it also has some fundamental limitations. First, pushback requires that routers coordinate their responses to misbehaving flows. A large number of routers would need to adopt the pushback mechanism for it to be effective; such adoption may not be wise, however, since if the pushback communications channel is compromised, pushback itself could become a very effective tool for NDoS. A more fundamental issue, though, is that there may not be any identifiable set of flows (at least at the level of IP addresses and ports) that are responsible for observed congestion. Such a situation may arise if the congestion comes from a flash crowd or a rapidly propagating worm.

2.2 Network-Level Anomaly Detection

Another perspective for addressing the DoS problem arises from the observation that malicious network traffic typically has different structure and content from non-malicious traffic. If all non-malicious traffic can be profiled as "normal," then any observed abnormal traffic can be classified as malicious. While there are many methods for detecting security violations at the network level, anomaly detection is arguably the approach that is most capable of detecting attacks that exploit previously-unseen vulnerabilities. Because malware developers discover new vulnerabilities on almost a daily basis, and because attacks by worms and viruses are both fast and automated, there is a pressing need for methods that can both detect and respond automatically to such "zero-day" threats.

One of the earliest methods for detecting anomalous network traffic was Heberlein et al.'s Network Security Monitor (NSM) [16]. Their system used a centralized monitoring host to record the 5-tuples associated with normal network flows. After a training period, any new 5-tuples were classified as an anomaly. In 1999, Hofmeyr developed LISYS [17], an intrusion detection system similar to NSM except that its architecture permitted the set of normal network flows to be distributed across a set of hosts. While this model of intrusion detection is useful in a relatively static network environment, the rapid evolution of new services, protocols, and servers on today's Internet means that the presence of a novel 5-tuple connection is not sufficient to indicate malicious traffic.

More recently several approaches to automatically characterize and respond to rapidly propagating worms have been proposed. Among the most promising is Singh et al.'s *EarlyBird* system [18, 19], which relies on two basic observations associated with fast worm propagation: (1) most such worms produce a substantial volume of traffic containing identical payload substrings; and (2) these similar packets are relayed between an increasing number of distinct source and destination addresses. With these heuristics and a combination of several highly efficient, scalable algorithms such as Rabin fingerprints [20], EarlyBird is able to automatically identify packets with common substrings and worm-like propagation patterns. Once a worm has been identified, the observed payload substrings are then used to block subsequent worm packets. In online experiments over the course of several months, their system is reported to have detected many previously known worms along with new, previously unseen worms, all with zero false positives. However, in order to avoid false positives, they had to create a packet "white list" that included such patterns as the protocol identification strings of HTTP and SMTP and the repeated packets corresponding to some BitTorrent-based P2P file sharing.

While EarlyBird is (to our knowledge) the first to report a working online implementation, similar systems are in development. Kreibick and Crowcroft's [21] *Honeycomb* system also detects worms by extracting high-frequency substrings within packets; a novel aspect is to extract common substrings only in *honeypots* to increase the likelihood of finding malicious traffic. A similar system also based on packet content inspection, *Autograph* [22], uses a simple port-scan-based flow classifier to reduce the amount of traffic on which signature extraction is applied.

In another approach to network intrusion detection, Wang and Stolfo [23] propose a system which builds byte distributions (taking into consideration port number and packet length) of "normal traffic". Incoming packets are compared with these distributions to measure their similarity with normal traffic. Packet similarity is measured by computing the Mahalanobis distance [24] between distributions.

While these systems use packet classification methods ranging from simple heuristics to complex statistical models, what they have in common is that they classify network traffic into two groups: legitimate and illegitimate traffic. The difference between these two classes, however, is not always obvious even to a human observer. For example, "legitimate" flash crowds can be created maliciously, e.g. by posting a targeted web server's home page to a popular weblog. This ambiguity has been one of the prime motivators for our research.

3   Diversity-Based Traffic Management

While many of the known approaches to managing network traffic have appealing characteristics, we believe current approaches will fail to address the threats of tomorrow, especially as attackers adapt and attempt to subvert deployed anomaly detection systems – especially those targeted at flash worms [25] (see [26]). One way to avoid the trap of attacker innovation is to simply re-frame the problem by dividing it in two. Proceeding in this direction, we separate the problem of protecting vulnerable hosts from that of managing network bandwidth. For host protection, many mechanisms are at our disposal: virus scanners, automated code patches, buffer overflow defenses, code diversity, and even host-based (personal) firewalls and intrusion prevention systems. Some combination of these and future technologies should be adequate to provide a reasonable level of practical protection for any host that a user chooses to secure. To protect the network from less well-maintained systems, though, we need mechanisms that prevent any collection of hosts or services from consuming an excessive share of bandwidth.

General Approach. With this framework, security threats such as flash worms and distributed denial-of-service attacks simply become additional types of overly aggressive applications, ones that can potentially be managed in the same way as flash crowds, spam, and peer-to-peer file sharing systems. An initial thought might be not trying to determine "good" versus "bad," but rather "disruptive" versus "non-disruptive" traffic. However, this change in perspective does not necessarily make the problem easier. By our definition, *disruptive network traffic* is that which prevents the transmission of other packets due to congestion. Because disruptive traffic can only be recognized in relation to other traffic flows, it is defined by context, not content. Moreover, that context implies a value judgment that some are the "disruptors" while others are "being disrupted." As with the problem of identifying worm traffic, it can be dangerous for an automated system to make value judgments; it can be too easy for a computer to make a mistake.

Thus, what we really want is a technique for managing disruptive network traffic without ever having to explicitly identify what is disruptive. One general way to accomplish this goal is to classify packets (as explained below) into multiple sets and then apportion bandwidth between these sets. If attackers do not know the (current) basis upon which packet sets are defined, or if they cannot create packets belonging to arbitrary sets, then attackers cannot consume all available bandwidth; instead, they can only consume the bandwidth fraction that is assigned to the sets in which their packets fall.

Rather than using an explicit, static tag (as in Diffserv [9, 10]), we propose to classify packets using their "intrinsic" properties. We assume that attackers can create and inject arbitrary packets into network connections, and thus we cannot consistently use features such as source IP addresses to sort packets – otherwise an attacker could consume an arbitrary fraction of bandwidth by injecting packets with those same features. Instead, we dynamically choose classification patterns from those present in observed traffic. If we assume that an attacker cannot observe or accurately model most traffic at a given Internet routing nexus, then the hope is that such a bandwidth allocation scheme cannot be directly subverted by an attacker[1]. Our research, then, has been focused on methods for grouping packets on the basis of features present in actual network traffic, with the goal of using these groupings to manage bandwidth allocation.

Since we allocate bandwidth on the basis of packet features, our strategy is designed to give small sets of packets with unusual shared features a larger share of bandwidth than they would normally be allocated under link saturation. Because outgoing packets will have a higher frequency of such unusual patterns than they would otherwise (when congested), we characterize our method as increasing the diversity of packets. Thus, we avoid the problems of distinguishing between disruptive and non-disruptive traffic by favoring increased diversity of network flows.

Architecture. Recall that we are not differentiating between legitimate and illegitimate traffic; we cannot simply drop certain kinds of packets. Rather, we characterize packets (see above, and below) and then forward them based upon their class membership. To do this, we propose to use traffic shaping mechanisms to differentially queue and forward packets. Traffic shapers [11, 12] are typically used to allocate bandwidth between ISP customers or to limit commonly used applications that are heavy bandwidth users (e.g. multimedia streaming, peer-to-peer file sharing) – in other words, they are used to regulate traffic based upon port and IP address patterns. We propose to augment such traffic shaping mechanisms with more flexible and adaptive methods for classifying packets.

To be more specific, consider the traffic shaping architecture in Figure 1. In the context of a simple LAN connected to the Internet, our traffic shaping mechanism would be implemented on the LAN's local router (to manage outgoing packets) and on the Internet Service Provider's router (to manage packets inbound to the LAN). As packets arrive, they are placed by the classifier into one of a number of packet queues associated with an outbound interface. Packets from these queues are chosen for forwarding in a round-robin fashion. Periodically the classification rules are updated by a traffic analysis module that runs in parallel and works on periodically sampled packets. While this basic architecture implies that all packets are to be forwarded on a best-effort basis, we can also support multiple quality-of-service bands by replicating this system for

---

[1] As suggested by the wording, we have yet to prove this.

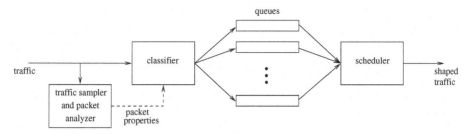

Fig. 1. Typical architecture for an adaptive traffic-shaping system.

each band; similarly, more complex topologies can be accommodated by placing a shaping module in front of any outbound interface within a given router.

Given a sufficiently efficient packet classification mechanism, this architecture can be implemented both at core routers and edge routers. In either case, it will help the router manage network bandwidth in the face of a surge in disruptive traffic. Currently this architecture is more appropriate for bandwidth-limited edge routers rather than the (apparently) over-provisioned core of the Internet. However, the introduction of new bandwidth-demanding applications may increase the utility of bandwidth management schemes such as ours in core routers.

Given this simple architecture, we next need a packet classification method that can group packets quickly (at router speeds) but in a way that cannot be easily predicted by an attacker. Although our classification may be approximate – it need not divide packets into any human-recognizable categories – our chances of limiting bandwidth allocation to disruptive traffic will be higher if packets within a given queue are somehow related (e.g. worm packets ideally should be classified within a set distinct from non-worm traffic, and to limit the worm bandwidth allocation to that allocated to one queue, or at worst a small number of queues). Thus, we have focused on developing an online method for finding common features between packets – features that can be used to assign packets to queues. The method we chose to develop is based on a simple scheme, which we call (p, n)-grams.

4   Packet Classification Using (p, n)-Grams

We now describe how we use a variation of n-grams to classify traffic, and explain our variation of traffic shaping using a set of queues managed adaptively, based on the continuous analysis of incoming traffic.

4.1   The Introduction of Position p into n-Grams

As described earlier, a (p, n)-gram is a byte string of length n located at an offset p in a packet within a data stream. Other systems (see Section 2.2) classify packets using the presence of substrings or the the relative distribution of 1-grams; in contrast, we combine substrings and offset positions in our representation for two reasons.

First, position matters in the context of an IP packet, especially within IP, TCP, UDP, and application-level protocol headers. For example, a four-byte IP address within a packet can have many different meanings depending upon its position within the packet: it can represent an IP source address, an IP destination address, a HTTP referrer host, or even a distant SMTP relay. Thus, by including position we have a method for capturing the important semantic features of IP packets.

Our second motivation for using an offset is speed for the online classification stage. To check for the presence of a (p, n)-gram in our system, one needs to perform a position computation (to find the offset p within the packet) and then a comparison of n bytes. (Note that such an offset/substring comparison is what a router does when identifying the destination address of an IP packet.) In contrast, typical position-independent n-gram techniques require a comparison with every byte within a packet. Techniques such as Rabin fingerprints [20] can significantly reduce the cost of multiple n-gram comparisons; nonetheless, (p, n)-gram comparisons are simple and efficient enough to scale to high speed links.

4.2   Adaptive Learning and Classification

While it is necessary to have a simple pattern schema (such as (p, n)-grams) with which to classify incoming packets, such a schema is not sufficient for our purposes. Because we have no pre-specified notion of how packets should be classified, we also need a learning algorithm that can discover appropriate classes autonomously. While this learning algorithm need not run at wire speeds, it must be fast enough that it can update the set of patterns frequently (e.g. every few minutes). While there are numerous classification and clustering algorithms in the literature, for performance reasons we have focused on a simple feedback learning strategy based on candidate (p, n)-grams extracted from samples of incoming packets. When the existing set of classification (p, n)-grams are not matching incoming traffic with sufficient fidelity, appropriate candidate (p, n)-grams are chosen as supplements and replacements.

More specifically, our system iteratively builds up a set of (p, n)-grams that allow network traffic to be partitioned into multiple "equivalence classes". The (p, n)-grams selected are initially those having the highest frequency in recent traffic; by merging sets of (p, n)-grams describing small aggregates and splitting ones describing large aggregates, though, this method attempts to converge on a description of "normal network traffic". When bandwidth becomes scarce, this iterative process is halted and the learned (p, n)-gram sets are used to (implicitly) decide which packets get dropped, i.e. the unserviced packets in long queues.

For example, assume we have a router with interfaces A and B, and we wish to shape traffic coming in from A and out to B. To do this shaping, we establish a fixed number q of queues Q associated with the outgoing interface B. When a packet is received on A that is destined for B, it is placed in one of the queues.

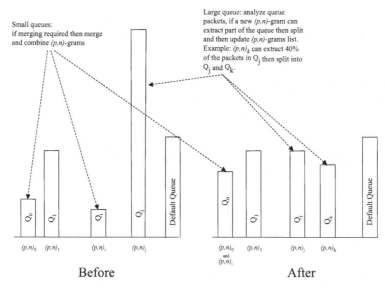

Fig. 2. The adaptive split/merge operation of queues.

Packets from the queues are selected in a round-robin[2]. fashion and are sent out interface B.

Associated with each queue $Q_i \in Q$ is a bounded set of (p, n)-grams. Note that the position p in a (p, n)-gram may specify anywhere in an IP packet, including in protocol headers and application-level payloads. To choose the queue in which to place a packet s, we first see whether any of the (p, n)-grams associated with Q_0 is present in s; if so, then s is placed in queue Q_0. Otherwise, test the next queue in the same fashion. Queue Q_{q-1} (called the *default queue*) is special, as it has no (p, n)-grams associated with it; if s is not placed into any of the other queues, it is placed in Q_{q-1}.

Initially, each queue is associated with a recently observed frequent (p, n)-gram. At fixed time intervals (e.g. every five minutes), the performance of the selected (p, n)-grams is examined and the system determines whether too many packets are falling into the default queue, and whether the distribution of packets between the queues is too imbalanced. If the currently selected (p, n)-grams are performing poorly according to this criteria, and if we have not dropped any packets over another fixed time interval (e.g. one hour), we then re-balance the queues (with respect to future traffic) by updating the sets of (p, n)-grams associated with each poorly-performing queue. Alternately, if we have dropped packets by exceeding the maximum length of any queue, then we *do not* re-balance the queues.

---

[2] Currently we use round-robin to allocate an equal share of bandwidth to every queue. Later we plan to study the effect of the service mechanism and the effect of the drop policy (currently we are using simple drop-tail).

The sets of queue-associated (p, n)-gram sets are updated in three ways. First, small queues are enlarged through merging: the (p, n)-gram sets associated two or more small queues are merged to form one new queue. Second, to reduce the number of (p, n)-grams in the system, when necessary the least frequently used (p, n)-grams are removed from the system. The third way (p, n)-gram sets are updated is through *splitting*: large queues are split through the creation of a new (p, n)-gram set that matches a subset of the large queue's traffic. To this end, we maintain a buffer of recent packets (e.g. the past 1000) that were placed within each queue. To split a queue, the (p, n)-grams contained within the queue's buffer are extracted and sorted by frequency. One or more of these (p, n)-grams are then selected such that they match a significant fraction, but not all, of the packets within the queue's buffer (e.g. (p, n)-grams that together match more than 20% but less than 50%). These new (p, n)-grams are then used to create a new queue. Splitting and merging are depicted in Figure 2.

As should be apparent, there are a number of parameters and implementation details that are not specified in the above description. Indeed, here we have defined an entire class of learning algorithms. Section 5 describes preliminary results obtained with one instance of this class. While the tested instance performs well in many respects, ongoing work is focused on studying other variants.

4.3 Malicious Encrypted and Polymorphic Traffic

The use of position in (p, n)-grams introduces the specific drawback that a small change in a string's position will prevent a match. This problem would be very significant if we were concerned about adversaries attempting to evade our packet classification system using encrypted or polymorphic traffic. However, so long as there are sufficient number of high-frequency (p, n)-grams present in other packets, we believe such behavior will actually hurt, not help an adversary, as now explained.

Packets with random contents (both header and payload) are highly unlikely to match any of the (p, n)-grams associated with queues; thus, streams with encrypted payloads and no repeated header patterns – e.g. a polymorphic flash worm – will be assigned to the default queue. At the same time, we expect that by construction normal traffic (future packets) will match many of the selected (p, n)-grams, and thus will be allocated most of the router's outgoing bandwidth.

An attacker wishing to consume a maximal amount of bandwidth may pursue a strategy of trying to construct packets that match at least one (p, n)-gram assigned to each queue – perhaps by adaptively constructing packets or by somehow causing the classification algorithm to replace (p, n)-grams matching normal traffic with ones matching malicious traffic. So long as selected (p, n)-grams are dependent on the specifics of local network traffic to which the attacker has no direct access, we believe it will be very difficult for an attacker to predict the constantly-changing set of (p, n)-grams corresponding to normal traffic. It may be possible for an attacker, however, to gradually train the system to increase his bandwidth allocation; we plan to study such adaptation (and appropriate algorithmic countermeasures) in future work.

5   Preliminary Experiments

To date we have focused on using offline experiments to evaluate the feasibility of (p, n)-grams for managing network traffic. In particular, we have focused on three central questions. First, are there a sufficient number of high-frequency (p, n)-grams (both in headers and in payloads) to enable the partitioning of network traffic? Second, does there exist a feedback learning algorithm that is able to learn a relatively small set of (p, n)-grams with which to partition network traffic? And finally, would this algorithm properly manage flash worm-like activity?

Table 1. Details of selected data sets analyzed.

Run#	Capture Date	Packets	% UDP	% TCP	% Other
1	Aug. 16, 2004	3437573	52%	16%	31%
2	Aug. 17, 2004	2156483	83%	16%	2%
3	Aug. 18, 2004	1283486	25%	71%	3%
4	Aug. 19, 2004	1006355	33%	63%	4%

To address these questions, we have studied the distribution of (p, n)-grams in packets captured on the link between the outside world and one of our small labs of seven Linux workstations, three Windows XP workstations, and four Linux servers. (Packets travelling from our network to the Internet were not analyzed, but only downstream ones.) For this paper, we report analysis of four days of captured traffic, the details of which are listed in Table 1; graphs presented, however, are based on the traffic of August 17, 2004. Data from other days shows a similar level of variability. Because this lab is essentially self-contained and is used for common tasks such as email (using an independent email server within the lab) and web surfing, traffic on our uplink, while not generally representative of Internet traffic, nevertheless has proven to be a rich data source that has helped us test and refine our ideas.

To understand the feasibility of using (p, n)-grams to classify network traffic, we first studied the distribution of (p, n)-grams. This distribution is best characterized as a "heavy-tail" distribution, with a few members having very high frequencies but most having relatively low frequencies (see Figure 3). We have found that high frequency (p, n)-grams typically match structural features of packets such as the IPv4 version number and padding fields. Such structural patterns are the exception, though – most (p, n)-grams present in a fixed data set will be located in the payload (assuming payloads are on average significantly longer than the IP headers), and most of these (p, n)-grams will match the payloads of a small number (perhaps no more than one) of these packets.

While such analysis told us something about the data, it could not directly tell us whether traffic could be effectively classified using (p, n)-grams. So, we then proceeded to implement a version of our feedback learning algorithm suitable for simulating queuing behavior using an offline data set. Our implementa-

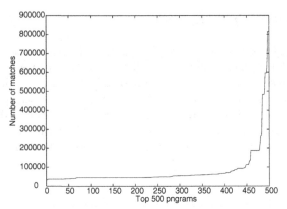

Fig. 3. Frequency graph of the 500 most frequent (p, n)-grams, with p allowed to vary over the entire packet length. Graph is based on the August 17, 2004 dataset with $n = 4$.

tion reads in packet capture files in `libpcap` format, one file at a time, classifies these packets into (p, n)-gram queues, and rebalances the queues before reading the next file. Since our captures are stored in 10-minute increments, this means that rebalancing happens at the same time intervals.

The classification program fixes $n = 4$ and starts with 50 queues, with the 1000 frequent (p, n)-grams (from an earlier day) initially assigned to these queues (most frequent (p, n)-gram to least, highest priority queue to lowest, assigned in a round-robin fashion one (p, n)-gram at a time). Traffic is then classified in 10-minute intervals, with (p, n)-gram frequency statistics being preserved for the most recent 3 hours of traffic. After processing a file, all queues are examined. If a queue received more than 2% of recently observed packets (i.e. within the past 3 hours), it is split. Similarly, queues are merged with the nearest lower priority queue if they each have received less than 0.25% of recently observed packets. The default queue is never merged with any other queue; however, it is split if the 2% threshold is exceeded. To prevent the accumulation of non-matching (p, n)-grams, ones that have not matched any packets for the last 3 hours are deleted.

When a queue is split, the program looks for a (p, n)-gram present in the last 10 minutes of packets placed in the queue (up to 1000 packets) that matches at least 20% of these packets but no more than 50%. (The search proceeds from the most frequent to the least frequent (p, n)-gram.) If no such (p, n)-gram is found, the queue is not split during the current time slice (but it may be split on the next time slice). When the new queue is created, we do not have a history of its behavior; thus, we allow it to exist for three hours (our history window) before allowing it to be merged or deleted.

Note that in this implementation there is not a fixed number of queues, and further there is not an upper bound on the total number of queues that may be created; however, in practice the merge/split bounds regulate the number of queues, as will be seen.

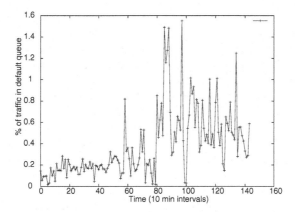

Fig. 4. Percentage of packets placed in the default queue. Despite the variation, note that the default queue is almost always below the target of 2% (the maximum value on the vertical axis). Graph is based on the August 17, 2004 dataset with $n = 4$.

We found that this feedback algorithm was able to successfully subdivide traffic on a regular basis. As indicated in Figure 4, the default queue size remained consistently small. Occasionally surges of traffic would appear within it; if they persisted or were large, then an attempt was made to split the default queue to bring it back down to a reasonable size. We were concerned that the system might accumulate an excessive number of low-traffic queues; even with the 3-hour minimum queue lifetime, however, the system used between 100 and 200 queues at any given time, with approximately 10 (p, n)-grams per queue on most time intervals. Thus, the feedback algorithm was able to consistently learn a relatively small set of (p, n)-grams with which to describe recent network traffic.

Note that the above results are for $n = 4$. By reducing the size n of matching substrings, we should be able to reduce the number of (p, n)-grams necessary to describe normal network traffic. We plan to study alternative learning algorthims that automatically adjusts the size of n so as to minimize the number of (p, n)-grams needed to divide network traffic into a fixed number of queues.

Simulated UDP Worm. To examine how the system might respond to a surge of malicious traffic, we simulated the activity of a constant payload UDP worm (such as SQL Slammer [27]) and a random payload (pseudo-polymorphic) UDP worm. For each case, we generated UDP packets using the `nemesis` packet generation tool using random source ports, source IP addresses, and destination IP addresses. The constant payload worm had a fixed (random string) payload of 714 bytes and a constant destination port of 1434. The random payload worm had a payload size between 357 and 1434 bytes and a random destination port.

As we expected (and hoped), both simulated worms initially saturate the default queue. On the first split operation, the constant-payload worm is placed in its own queue. On subsequent iterations (over the next 30–60 minutes), with no simulated packet dropping, every other non-default queue is merged into a second queue (pairwise merging happens on every time step). This merging happens because the large number of "worm" packets distort the overall packet statistics. By instead simulating dropped packets from overflowing queues, though, the program turns off rebalancing and keeps the (p, n)-gram assignments from before the attack, and the worm stays in the default queue.

The random payload worm behaves much the same; however, because it has no high-frequency (p, n)-grams, even without finite queues its packets remain in the default queue. Like the constant-payload worm, though, without finite queues the large number of worm packets bias the queue statistics and cause all remaining normal traffic to be placed into one queue after several iterations of the algorithm.

These results suggest that (p, n)-grams can be used to regulate network traffic, at least in the case of traffic destined for a small network. Further, this regulation appears to be effective at limiting the bandwidth that would be allocated to simple flash worms, even if they were polymorphic. While these results do not necessarily generalize to the behavior of larger, more complex networks, they are promising enough to warrant further experimentation and research.

6   Discussion and Concluding Remarks

We start this discussion by summarizing the methodology we are using in this approach. We have proposed to address the NDoS problem by adaptively learning sets of network traffic and then apportioning network bandwidth between these sets. We have also hypothesized that network traffic can be flexibly subdivided through the (p, n)-gram measure of packet similarity. Even though our framework and algorithm do not distiguish between malicious and non-malicious network traffic, nonetheless they appear to be able to mitigate the effects of some kinds of flash worms. We also hypothesize that the same mechanisms will be able to moderate the bandwidth consumption of other disruptive traffic such as flash crowds and high-volume spam.

Given the results of the previous section, we believe that there is much potential in our approach to managing network traffic. However, as itemized below, a number of important issues require further attention.

a) *The nature of (p, n)-gram learning:* For diversity-based traffic management to work against a hostile adversary, it is essential for normal traffic to be partitioned into groupings that are non-random yet cannot be easily predicted or overly affected by an attacker. If the partitioning is random, then malicious traffic will be placed into many different queues, thereby negating the advantage using separate queues; if the partitioning is too predictable, then an adversary may be able to increase his bandwidth allocation by constructing packets that will match many queues; if the partitioning can be too easily influenced, then the attacker can change it to suit his needs. The input dependence and non-linear feedback of our current algorithm seems to preclude simple analysis and would seem to require significant effort for an attacker to overly influence; nevertheless, we do not have enough data to ascertain how our algorithm will behave in practice. We are encouraged, though, that our offline experiments indicate that this algorithm tends to find fuzzy groupings that vary over time.

b) *The impact of packet re-ordering:* Since TCP and UDP flows are sometimes split across multiple queues, it is likely that packets within such flows will be re-ordered and differentially delayed. We have not specifically studied this issue, but we do not think that such perturbations will significantly impact end-to-end performance in non-congested situations. If it does turn out to be a concern, then such reordering can be eliminated by using the queue structure only to determine which packets should be dropped (with no congestion, packets would be relayed in the order received).

c) *Randomized payloads:* If a polymorphic worm has no repeated pattern of inter-packet (p, n)-grams, then our classifier will place most worm packets into the default queue. Since other encrypted traffic, such as the payloads in SSH and SSL, will also lack such structure, the worm may end up overwhelming such legitimate connections. One way to minimize this problem is to partition encrypted packets by header (p, n)-grams which match on IP addresses and ports. It remains to be determined whether special code will be needed to do such partitioning, or whether such patterns will be learned automatically.

d) *The composition and distribution of (p, n)-grams in more complex environments over longer time periods:* Are there a sufficient number of high-frequency (p, n)-grams such that the traffic of an enterprise or a university can be effectively partitioned? If we have sufficient (p, n)-grams, then is it also feasible for an attacker to predict which (p, n)-grams we will choose? It is possible that the greater sample sizes of larger networks will cause our method to always find similar sets of (p, n)-grams across different networks. If this turns out to be the case, then we may need new strategies for core Internet routers.

e) *Conflict with existing network policies:* One capability that we may need to provide is the ability for network administrators to intervene in the automatic learning and classification process to change the allocation of (p, n)-grams to queues. This would allow administrators to enforce certain policies in cases where the automatic learning and classification process contradicts established service provider's policies.

Despite the number and magnitude of questions that remain unanswered, we are optimistic that diversity-based traffic management holds the promise to address problems that other approaches cannot. As a community, we will have to develop strategies for managing overly aggressive bandwidth consumers within an environment where nobody has complete control over the hardware, network software, or applications; at the same time, though, we cannot make *a priori* decisions as to what traffic patterns and uses are permissible without jeopardizing the very flexibility that has fueled the net's growth. The Internet needs to be able to automatically and autonomously balance the myriad demands placed upon it by both malicious and non-malicious applications. We believe that our (p, n)-gram approach to diversity-based traffic management is a small step towards meeting this need.

Acknowledgments

We thank Evan Hughes and James Kelly, especially for their implementation and analysis work related to (p, n)-grams. We thank Miguel Vargas Martin and Tao Wan for their many contributions to this project, including work on earlier reports. We also thank Jean-Marc Robert and Emanuele Jones, for their guidance, many helpful discussions, and literature references.

We would like to acknowledge Alcatel and Canada's MITACS program for funding the initial stages of this project. We also wish to acknowledge Canada's National Sciences and Engineering Research Council (NSERC) for providing all three authors with NSERC Discovery Grants. The second author also wishes to acknowledge NSERC for funding his Canada Research Chair in Network and Software Security.

References

1. Staniford, S., Moore, D., Paxson, V., Weaver, N.: The Top Speed of Flash Worms. In: Proceedings of ACM Workshop on Rapid Malcode (WORM). (2004)
2. Floyd, S., K.Fall: Promoting the Use of End-to-End Congestion Control in the Internet. IEEE/ACM Transactions on Networking **7** (1999) 458–472
3. Widmer, J., Denda, R., Mauve, M.: A Survey of TCP-Friendly Congestion Control. IEEE Network (2001)
4. Matrawy, A., Lambadaris, I.: A Survey of Congestion Control Schemes for Multicast Video Applications. IEEE Communications Surveys and Tutorials **5** (2003) 22–31
5. Floyd, S.: TCP and Explicit Congestion Notification. ACM Computer Communications Review (1994) 10–23
6. Floyd, S., Jacobson, V.: Random Early Detection Gateways for Congestion Avoidance. IEEE/ACM Trans. on Networking (1993) 397–413
7. Estan, C., Varghese, G.: New Directions in Traffic Measurement and Accounting: Focusing on Elephants, Ignoring the Mice. ACM Trans. on Computer Systems **21** (2003) 270–313
8. Estan, C., Savage, S., Varghese, G.: Automatically Inferring Patterns of Resource Consumption in Network Traffic. In: Proceedings of ACM SIGCOMM'03, Germany (2003) 270–313
9. Clark, D., Fangand, W.: Explicit Allocation of Best Effort Packet Delivery Service. IEEE/ACM Trans. on Networking **6** (1988) 362–373
10. Blake, S., Black, D., Carlson, M., Davies, E., Wang, Z., Weiss, W.: An Architecture for Differentiated Services. RFC 2475 (1988)
11. Georgiadis, L., Guérin, R., Peris, V., Sivarajan, K.N.: Efficient Network QoS Provisioning Based on Per-Node Traffic Shaping. IEEE/ACM Transactions on Networking **4** (1996) 482–501

12. Elwalid, A., Mitra, D.: Traffic Shaping at a Network Node: Theory, Optimum Design, Admission Control. In: Proceedings of IEEE InfoCom'97. (1997)
13. Mahajan, R., Bellovin, S., Floyd, S., Ioannidis, J., Paxson, V., Shenker, S.: Controlling High Bandwidth Aggregates in the Network. Computer Communications Review (2002)
14. Ioannidis, J., Bellovin, S.: Implementing Pushback: Router-based Defense against DDoS Attacks. In: Proceedings of NDSS'02. (2001)
15. Yaar, A., Perrig, A., Song, D.X.: SIFF: A Stateless Internet Flow Filter to Mitigate DDoS Flooding Attacks. In: IEEE Symposium on Security and Privacy. (2004)
16. Heberlein, L., Dias, G., Levitt, K., Mukherjee, B., Wood, J., Wolber, D.: A Network Security Monitor. In: Proceedings of the IEEE Symposium on Security and Privacy. (1990)
17. Hofmeyr, S.: An Immunological Model of Distributed Detection and its Application to Computer Security. PhD thesis, University of New Mexico (1999)
18. Singh, S., Estan, C., Varghese, G., Savage, S.: The EarlyBird System for Real-time Detection of Unknown Worms. Technical report - cs2003-0761, UCSD (2003)
19. Singh, S., Estan, C., Varghese, G., Savage, S.: Automated Worm Fingerprinting. In: Proceedings of OSDI '04, San Francisco CA (2004)
20. Rabin, M.: Fingerprinting by Random Polynomials. Technical report 15-81, Harvard University (1981)
21. Kreibich, C., Crowcroft, J.: Honeycomb - Creating Intrusion Detection Signatures Using Honeypots. In: Proceedings of HOTNETS-II. (2003)
22. Kim, H., Karp, B.: Autograph: Toward Automated, Distributed Worm Signature Detection. In: Proceedings of the 13th Usenix Security Symposium. (2004)
23. Wang, K., Stolfo, S.J.: Anomalous Payload-based Network Intrusion Detection. In: Proceedings of RAID'04. (2004)
24. Mahalanobis, P.: On the generalized distance in statistics. Proc. Natl. Institute of Science of India 2 (1936)
25. Staniford, S., Paxson, V., Weaver, N.: How to Own the Internet in Your Spare Time. In: Proceedings of the 11th USENIX Security Symposium. (2002)
26. Matrawy, A., Somayaji, A., van Oorschot, P.: The Threat of Attacker Innovation to Flash Worm Defenses. Manuscript in Preparation (2005)
27. Moore, D., Paxson, V., Savage, S., Shannon, C., Staniford, S., Weaver, N.: The Spread of the Sapphire/Slammer Worm. Technical report, CAIDA et al. (2003) http://www.caida.org/analysis/security/sapphire/.

Searching for High-Value Rare Events
with Uncheatable Grid Computing

Wenliang Du[1] and Michael T. Goodrich[2]

[1] Department of Electrical Engineering and Computer Science, Syracuse University
wedu@ecs.syr.edu
[2] Department of Computer Science, University of California, Irvine
goodrich@acm.org

Abstract. High-value rare-event searching is arguably the most natural application of grid computing, where computational tasks are distributed to a large collection of clients (which comprise the computation *grid*) in such a way that clients are rewarded for performing tasks assigned to them. Although natural, rare-event searching presents significant challenges for a computation supervisor, who partitions and distributes the search space out to clients while contending with "lazy" clients, who don't do all their tasks, and "hoarding" clients, who don't report rare events back to the supervisor. We provide schemes, based on a technique we call *chaff injection*, for efficiently performing uncheatable grid computing in the context of searching for high-value rare events in the presence of coalitions of lazy and hoarding clients.

Keywords: Grid computing, cryptographic hash functions, obfuscation, security, cheating.

1 Introduction

Searching for high-value rare events is a natural use for grid computing environments, where computational tasks are farmed out to a collection of clients that comprise the computational *grid*. That is, such tasks naturally give rise to a large search space that can be explored in a parallel fashion to find a small handful of important inputs that deserve further attention. For example, rare-event searching forms the core of the most well-known grid computing applications, such as SETI@home, whose tasks involve processing large numbers of extraterrestrial signals for signs of intelligent life, and distributed.net, whose tasks involve performing search-space explorations that implement brute-force attacks on cryptographic algorithms.

Most grid computing environments provide an economic incentive for clients, which could involve something tangible, like digital cash, or something intangible, such as an identification of the fastest clients or the clients who have performed the most tasks. Searching for high-value rare events introduces additional economic complications in a grid computing environment, however. For example, such a system must contend with lazy clients, who can request payment for simply saying "I didn't find anything" and be assured that their answer is almost certainly correct. In addition, a system must contend with coalitions of hoarding participants, who may auction or ransom the rare events

J. Ioannidis, A. Keromytis, and M. Yung (Eds.): ACNS 2005, LNCS 3531, pp. 122–137, 2005.

they find rather than reporting them back to the supervisor of the grid environment[1]. Here *supervisor* refers to the server that assigns the tasks to the grid participants.

The risks posed by coalitions of cheaters in grid computing environments are real and immediate. SETI@home's director, Dr. David Anderson, is quoted [8] as stating that security has been a major problem, requiring roughly fifty percent of the project's resources. For example, he mentioned that the SETI@home software had been hacked to make it look like more work had been performed (to improve leader board rankings).

Although some well-known rare-event searching tasks, such as looking for extraterrestrial intelligence or breaking cryptographic functions, are arguably of philosophical or recreational interest, some natural grid-computing searching tasks may involve identifying rare events that have significant economic value. For example, a drug company may wish to use a computational grid to identify promising drugs for treating certain diseases (e.g., by performing molecule docking simulations for a large number of candidate drug configurations). Unfortunately, coalitions of greedy, hoarding clients in a computational grid performing such a search could pose a serious obstacle for the drug company. Knowing that a drug is effective against a certain disease via grid computing, the coalition could sell the result to another drug company. This of course assumes that the participants can interpret the results.

In some computations, although the supervisor can also disguise the input so that participants cannot make direct uses of the rare events, this does not fully protect the grid supervisor from coalitions of hoarding clients. For, even if a participant cannot directly use an identified rare-event result, the coalition may be able to derive economic benefit through other means, such as ransoming the result back to the supervisor or buying stock in the supervisor's company (in the case when a rare-event discovery could boost the stock value of the company).

We provide schemes for efficiently performing uncheatable grid computing for searching for high-value rare events. Our techniques, which we call *chaff injection* methods, involve introducing elements to task inputs or outputs that provide rare-event obfuscation. Output-chaff injection applies to contexts where rare-events are not immediately identifiable by clients (as in the distributed.net application of breaking cryptographic functions). It involves the use of one-way hash functions applied to computation outcomes in a way that defends against coalitions of hoarding clients. Input-chaff injection applies to contexts where rare-events are easily identified by clients (as in the SETI@home application of finding patterns of intelligence in extraterrestrial signals). It involves the injection of a number of obfuscated inputs that will test positive as rare events. We show that distributing such inputs efficiently in an unpredictable way provides defense against coalitions of hoarding clients at a cost that is lower than existing input duplication and distribution methods.

Organization. The rest of the paper is organized as follows. Section 2 discusses related work. Section 3 formulates the problem. Section 4 presents our general chaff injection approach for protecting rare events. Section 5 describes an input-chaff injection scheme, while Section 6 describes an output-chaff injection scheme. Finally we draw the conclusion and lay out our future work in Section 7.

---

[1] The participant who auctions or ransoms the rare events must be anonymous; otherwise the supervisor can get the correct results by redoing the tasks assigned to this identified participant.

2   Related Work

2.1   Uncheatable Grid Computing with Lazy Participants

Although it is an issue grid practitioners have had to contend with for some time [8], uncheatable grid computing was introduced by Golle and Sutbblebine [5]. In their paper, they advocate double-checking computational grid results by probabilistic redundant execution of the tasks (SETI@home employs a simple double-redundancy scheme [8]). A redundancy-based approach can reduce the incentive for isolated lazy cheaters when the number of potentially lazy cheaters is small, but it is less effective against large coalitions of lazy cheaters and potentially ineffective against hoarding cheaters. Indeed, we are not aware of any prior work that addresses the risks posed by hoarding cheaters.

Subsequent work on uncheatable grid computing has focused on stronger schemes to defeat lazy cheaters, that is, participants claiming credit for work left undone. Golle and Mironov propose a *ringer* scheme [4], which can protect against coalitions of lazy cheaters provided that the computational tasks all involve the Inversion of a One-Way Function (IOWF), f, for a given value y, as in the distributed.net attacks on cryptographic functions (but not the SETI@home application or other grid applications that don't involve IOWFs). In the ringer scheme, during the initialization stage for each participant, the supervisor randomly selects several inputs x_i that will be assigned to that participant and computes $f(x_i)$ for each one. Then, in addition to the value, y, that the supervisor wishes to invert, the supervisor also sends to that participant all the "ringers" the supervisor has computed for him. The participant must report the pre-images of all the ringers (as well as the pre-image of y if he was lucky enough to discover it). That is, the participant needs to compute f on x for all x in his input domain D and return the pre-image of y if found, and he also has to return all the ringer pre-images he finds. By remembering the ringers for each participant, the supervisor can easily verify whether each participant has found all his ringers or not. If he has, then the supervisor is assured with reasonable probability that the participant has indeed conducted all his computations. Golle and Mironov also discuss some ways to augment this basic ringer scheme – using bogus ringers to prevent participants from knowing the total number of ringers planted and magic sets to prevent direct images from being sent to the participants.

Szada, Lawson, and Owen [13] further extend the ringer scheme to deal with lazy cheaters for other classes of computations, including optimization and Monte Carlo simulations, by proposing effective ways to choose ringers for these computations. It is unknown whether the schemes proposed in [13] can be extended further to arbitrary computations.

Du *et al.* [3] propose a different approach to achieve uncheatable grid computing to defeat lazy participants. In their scheme, the supervisor randomly selects and verifies some samples from the task domain assigned to a participant. To prevent the participant from cheating on those samples, the participant must commit a digest of his/her entire computation results before being checked. Du *et al.* describe a commitment-based sampling scheme based on Merkle hash trees.

While the existing studies on uncheatable grid computing [3–5, 13] prevent participants from claiming credit for work they have not done, our study focuses on preventing participants from lying about the rare events they may have found, that is, defeating hoarding cheaters. The previous schemes do not seem useful against hoarding cheaters, particularly in the case of rare-event searching. Participants in a ringer scheme are not induced to report the desired inverse of the one-way function[2], and participants in the commitment-sampling scheme can simply lie about the commitment of a discovered rare event (which is unlikely to be chosen by the supervisor as a test).

As it turns out, our schemes provide some protection against lazy cheaters. In fact, even though previous works use scoring computations like SETI@home as motivating examples, our input chaff injection scheme is the first scheme for uncheatable grid computing that applies to applications that involve a scoring function that is computed in floating point and may have device-dependent rounding errors. These rounding errors don't significantly impact the correctness of requested computations but they prevent previous checking schemes, like ringers and commitment sampling, from validating otherwise acceptable computations. In the cases of other grid computing applications (with device-independent computations), protection against lazy cheaters can be strengthened by combining our schemes with one of the existing ringer or commitment-sampling techniques. Nevertheless, for the remainder of this paper, our primary emphasis will be on ways to defend against hoarding cheaters in grid computing applications.

2.2 Other Related Work

An alternative way to defeat cheating of many kinds is to use tamper-resistant software for all participants. Code obfuscators would be used in this context to convert programs to equivalent programs that are much harder to understand and reverse-engineer. Thus, it becomes hard for malicious attackers to modify the programs to accomplish what they want. However the tamper-resistant approach is only heuristically secure, and many tamper-resistant schemes cannot withstand attacks from coalitions of determined attackers [11].

The problem of uncheatable grid computing is close to another body of literature: the problem of malicious hosts in the study of mobile agents [15, 18]. Several practical solutions have been proposed for such problems, which include remote auditing [11, 14], code obfuscation with timing constraints [7], computing with encrypted functions [12], and replication and voting [17]. The major difference between the mobile-agent work and our grid-computing work is the threat model. The mobile-agent work assumes a malicious cheating model, i.e., a malicious host can do whatever it takes to cheat, including spending more CPU cycles than the honest behavior. Our study focuses on a different model, however, in which it is irrational for a participant to cheat with a cost more expensive than honest behavior.

Various cryptographic protocols, such as Private Information Retrieval (PIR) [2] and Probabilistically Checkable Proofs (PCP) [16] can also be used to achieve uncheatable grid computing. However, their expensive computation cost makes them inappropriate choice for grid computing in practice. We are interested in this paper on solutions that could be of efficient use in practice.

---

[2] Even if the hash value y would be randomly mixed with the ringer set for each participant, two cooperating cheaters could easily separate y from their respective ringers.

3   Problem Definition

In this section, we formally define the problem of rare-event searching with uncheatable grid computing, including definitions of the kinds of cheating we wish to defend against.

3.1   Model of Grid Computing

We consider a grid computing environment in which *untrusted participants* are taking part. The computation is organized by a *supervisor*. Formally, such computations are defined in our model by the following elements:

- **A task function $f : X \mapsto T$ defined on a finite domain X.** The goal of the computation is to evaluate f on all $x \in X$. For the purpose of distributing the computation, the supervisor partitions X into subsets. The evaluation of f on subset X_i is assigned to participant i.
- **A screening function S.** The screener is a function that takes as input a pair of the form $((x, f(x)); y)$ for $x \in X$, and returns a string $s = S((x, f(x)); y)$, where y represents the criterion. S is intended to screen for "valuable" outputs of f that are reported to the supervisor by means of the string s.

In the case of rare-event searching, we are interested in finding a small (possibly single-ton) previously-unknown subset R of X such that $f(x)$ is some desired value, for each $x \in R$. Minimally, the screening function S should catch all $x \in R$.

3.2   Models of Cheaters

A participant can choose to cheat for a variety of reasons. We categorize the cheating using the following three models. We assume each participant is given a domain $D \subset X$, and his task is to compute $f(x)$ for all $x \in D$. From now on, we use D as the domain of f for a given participant.

- *Lazy Cheater Model:* In this model, the participant follows the supervisor's compu-tations with one exception: for $x \in \check{D} \subset D$, the participant uses $\check{f}(x)$ as the result of $f(x)$. Function $\check{f}$ is usually much less expensive than function f; for instance, $\check{f}$ can be a random guess. In other words, the participant does not compute the re-quired function f on inputs $x \in \check{D}$. The goal of the cheating participant in this model is to reduce the amount of computations, such that it can maximize its gain by "performing" more tasks during the same period of time. If the participants are getting paid, the cheating participant might be guided by the lure of money. This type of cheating behavior is a cheating on the task function f.
- *Hoarding Cheater Model:* In this model, the participant conducts all the required computations. However, the participant will keep the computation results if the results are valuable. For example, if the computation is to search for a rare event, a "lucky" participant who has found a rare event might report a negative result because of the value of such a result. This type of cheating behavior is a cheating on the screening function S.

– *Malicious Cheater Model:* In this model, the behavior of the participant can be arbitrary. For example, a malicious participant might have calculated function f on all $x \in D$, but when it computes the screener function S, instead of returning $S((x, f(x)); y)$, it might return a random value. In other words, the participant intentionally returns wrong results to the supervisor, for the purpose of disrupting the computations. A malicious cheater may be a competitor, or a non-serious participant playing pranks.

Defending against the lazy cheaters is the main purpose of the schemes proposed in [3–5, 13]. In this paper, we focus primarily on defeating the second type of cheaters – hoarding cheaters. Namely, we want to prevent the participant who has found high-value rare events (members of R) from lying about the discovery. Moreover, we even want to prevent participants from determining which are the high-value rare inputs, that is, we would like to prevent participants from learning R with any certainty.

For the sake of simplicity, we assume that participants, including the hoarding participants, honestly conduct all the tasks assigned to them (i.e., they do not cheat on f). This honesty behavior can be guaranteed by the uncheatable grid computing schemes proposed previously [3–5, 13]. In other words, by combining our scheme with the schemes such as ringers, we can successfully defeat both lazy cheaters and hoarding cheaters.

3.3 Types of Rare Events

Recall that in the screener function S, there is an certificate y, which defines the criterion to justify whether a rare event is found or not. We categorize grid computing problems into the following two types, and we will describe solutions for each of them:

1. **Obvious Rare Events (ORE):** In some grid computing scenarios, the criterion y for identifying rare events is obvious. That is, given x and $f(x)$, a participant can easily determine if x is a desired rare-event input. For example, in the Hamiltonian-cycle problem, a rare event is a permutation of the vertices that forms a Hamiltonian cycle, and verifying this fact is straightforward based on the well-known definition of Hamiltonian cycles. Indeed, every member of the complexity class NP has an effective verification algorithm, by definition. Likewise, the SETI@home application has obvious rare events – input signals that have high correlations scores for patterns of intelligence.
2. **Camouflaged Rare Events (CRE):** In some grid computing scenarios, given x and $f(x)$ alone, it is not at all clear whether x is a rare event or not. For example, to find the inverse of a one-way hash value y, i.e., to find x that generates $y = h(x)$, where h is the one-way hash function and each participant is given the value of y. Since y provided to the participants might not be the actual valuable one, even if a participant finds the corresponding x, it will not be able to decide whether this is the valuable rare event.

To prevent participants from keeping the rare events, it is necessary to hide the criterion y, so that the participants cannot identify whether an input is a rare event or not.

Hiding y for the CRE problem is relatively easier than hiding y for the ORE problem, because y is given by the supervisor in CRE problems, while y is a public knowledge in ORE problems. In the remainder of this paper, for each type of rare events, we describe our solutions for performing uncheatable grid computing in the presence of hoarding cheaters.

4   Protecting Rare Events via Chaff Injection

In this section, we give a high-level description of *chaff injection* for protecting high-value rare events in grid computing. Like a true rare event (a member of R), a piece of chaff is also a rare event, but it is generated by the supervisor. Participants cannot distinguish chaff from an actual rare event. Only the supervisor knows which one is chaff and which one is an actual rare event he/she is searching for. We use the term *semi-rare* events to refer to sets that consist of the chaff and the actual rare events.

The main idea of chaff injection is the following:

1. The supervisor injects a number of chaff items into the computations
2. Participants report to the supervisor all the semi-rare events they find
3. The supervisor filters the results and discards the chaff.

If some participants decide not to return the chaff they have found, the supervisor can easily catch such cheaters. As long as the number of chaff items is sufficiently large, participants will have no incentive to hide semi-rare events, because the results might be useless chaff and their cheating can be caught. On the other hand, chaff should not be too dense, because receiving and processing those chaff consume bandwidth and CPU cycles of the supervisor. Since the supervisor has a high bandwidth connection and a large number of available CPU cycles, introducing millions of chaff items does not introduce much burden to the supervisor, but this amount is already large enough for participants to lose their cheating incentives.

4.1   Our Approaches to Chaff Injection

Two approaches can be used to introduce new chaff, which we respectively refer to as *input chaff* injection and *output chaff* injection.

One technique involves the replacement of the criterion y with a new criterion $\hat{y}$ so many non-rare events also become a semi-rare events, while maintaining the condition for defining actual rare events. Since the criterion y is used at the output, we call this chaff approach the *output chaff injection* scheme. Formally speaking, the screen function should satisfy the following predicate:

$$S((x, f(x)); y) = 1 \longrightarrow S((x, f(x)); \hat{y}) = 1.$$

The predicate states that if an event x is a rare event, then x should also be a semi-rare event. This way, we guarantee that the set of semi-rare events is a superset of rare events.

The output chaff injection scheme is suitable for CRE problems, because the criterion y is a secret information that is known only to the supervisor. In ORE problems, where y is public knowledge, replacing y with a new criterion $\hat{y}$ cannot hide y. There-fore, we use the output chaff scheme for CRE problems. There are two different ways to transform a criterion y in this case, however, one through *expansion* and the other one through *reduction*.

For ORE problems, where y cannot be disguised, to inject chaff, we turn to the input. In this case we replace the input domain X with $X \cup C$, where C is a set of chaff items that are guaranteed to test positive for the task function f. Depending on the particular application, we may assign a participant a set of inputs that include items from both X and C, or we may probabilistically choose to send a participant a set of inputs exclusively from X or C. The key property that we must maintain for input chaff is that it must be computationally expensive for a participant to determine if his input domain includes chaff or not. The efficiency challenge for an input-chaff injection scheme is to define the size of C to be large enough for rare events to become semi-rare while also keeping the size of C to be a small fraction of the size of X.

5   Obvious Rare Events with Input Chaff

In this section, we present *input chaff injection* schemes to protect high-value rare events in grid computing for ORE problems. Because the criterion y is already publicly known in this case; obfuscating y cannot prevent participants from knowing whether a rare event has occurred. We provide solutions to three types of computations, while solutions to generic computations are still an open problem.

5.1   Graph Isomorphism

As an illustration of how input-chaff injection can obfuscate rare events for hoarding cheaters, in this section we present an uncheatable grid computation for a problem often used to illustrate the concept of zero-knowledge proofs – the graph isomorphism problem. In the graph isomorphism problem, we are given two graphs $G = (V, E)$ and $H = (V, F)$, each having n vertices and m edges, and we are asked if there is a permutation map π, on V, so that $(a, b) \in E$ if and only if $(\pi(a), \pi(b)) \in F$. We view π as a permutation map because G and H have the same vertex sets; their lists of edges are different (but possibly isomorphic). The graph isomorphism problem is not known to be in P, nor is it known if the graph isomorphism problem is NP-complete. It is widely believed to be a difficult problem, however.

Suppose, then, that we are given two such graphs G and H (and that this appears to be a hard instance of the graph isomorphism problem). Suppose further that we are interested in performing a brute-force search for an isomorphism between G and H using a computational grid. Of course, the straightforward way of solving this problem is to give each participant the following tasks:

- Each participant is given, as input, G and H and a family Π of permutation maps on V. For each $\pi \in \Pi$, the participant should check if π maps each edge in G to an edge in H and that each edge in H has an edge mapped to it by π. If π is determined to define an isomorphism from G to H, this fact is to be reported back to the supervisor.

Thus, an exponential-sized search space is divided among the set of participants in a way that requires only polynomial space and bandwidth. The problem is that an isomorphism mapping from G to H is obvious; hence, it is easily hoarded.

To obfuscate this obvious rare event, we introduce some input chaff (and a further obfuscation of non-chaff inputs). Let $\mathcal{P} = \{\Pi_1, \Pi_2, \ldots, \Pi_k\}$ be the collection of permutation sets that are to be distributed to the participants, where we assume that the sets are represented in a way that allows composition with a permutation π to define a legitimate set of permutations in a way that does not reveal π. In addition, let $\{\pi_1, \pi_2, \ldots, \pi_{k+r}\}$ be a set of random permutations and let j be an index into this set (initially, $j = 1$). For a probability p set by the supervisor (e.g., $p = 1/100$ or $p = 1/1000$), the supervisor performs the following computation for each participant:

1. The supervisor generates a random bit with probability p. If this bit is 0, then the supervisor assigns the given participant, G and H, and the next set Π_i of permutation maps to as above, except that the supervisor disguises H and Π_i by applying π_j to both (this will not change the computation for the participant). The supervisor then increments i and j.
2. Otherwise, if the random bit is 1, then the supervisor randomly chooses a permutation π from Π_i and constructs a permutation G' of G using π. Then the supervisor sends the participant, G and G' and the family Π_i, after applying π_j to G' and Π_i. The supervisor then increments j (but not i).

Note that roughly p of the inputs are now guaranteed to test positive as isomorphisms between the two graphs given to the participants. Moreover, each participant is given the graph G and a graph that looks different for each participant but which will prove to be isomorphic to G with probability p.

Security. The security of the above chaff-injection scheme is derived from the inability of participants from determining whether they have been given chaff input or not. In this case, the argument is simple: for a participant to distinguish the chaff from a true input, they must be able to tell the difference between G' and H. But doing so would require them to solve essentially the same graph isomorphism problem the grid is collectively trying to solve. Note in addition that colluding cheaters may be able to determine that some of them were assigned the same permutation set Π_i, but, again, without solving the graph isomorphism problem itself, they will not be able to tell which of these tasks are chaff and which (if any) are a true input set. Each participant is given a different looking graph to test against G (even the ones assigned H); hence, colluding participants cannot determine which of them are given chaff and which are not (without solving the graph isomorphism problem itself, that is).

Analysis. The expected additional work involved in using this input chaff injection scheme is equal to p times the work needed by the original solution, which is not resistant to hoarding cheaters. That is, if we let e denote the additional work introduced by input chaff injection, then

$$E(e) = k \cdot p,$$

where k is the number of subproblems defined by the supervisor based on the size of her participant base (e.g., $k = 100,000$ or $k = 1,000,000$ are realistic values). Thus, if $p = 1/10$ or $p = 1/100$, this scheme introduces a small computational overhead of 10% or 1% to the process. For example, if $p = 1/100$ and $k = 1,000,000$, then $E(e) = 10,000$. But even with small values for p, rare events are significantly obfuscated. For, even if G and H are isomorphic, we have the following:

$$\Pr(\text{a participant finding an isomorphism that is not chaff}) = 1/e.$$

For example, if $e = 10,000$, then there is only a one in ten thousand chance that a discovered isomorphism is not chaff; hence, a 99.99% chance that a hoarding participant will be caught in this scheme (using these example parameters). Note that our chaff injection approach is therefore more efficient than task duplication approaches to uncheatable grid computing [5], which have a computational overhead of 46% to 243% for reasonable protection against lazy cheaters (while providing only modest protection against hoarding cheaters of rare events).

5.2 Data Filtering Problems

Having given a "warm-up" example of input-chaff injection, we turn in this section to a more practical set of grid computations – *data filtering* problems. In data filtering problems we are given a large set X of data instances and a Boolean filtering function f. The supervisor is interested in all the elements x of X such that $f(x) = 1$. Usually, the function f will involve some internal scoring function on each input x along with a threshold value such that if x scores above this value, then x is considered rare and interesting. This class of problems includes the SETI@home application, where X consists of extraterrestrial signals that are scored against what are considered to be patterns of intelligence. Likewise, this class of problems includes the drug screening example mentioned in the introduction.

By their very nature, it is not obvious which of the inputs in X will score positive for the filter f (for otherwise there would be no motivation for us to go to the trouble of using a grid computing environment to solve this problem). For example, a casual examination of the signals that have scored highest so far in the SETI@home scoring function does not yield any obvious patterns; to the naked eye they all appear as noise. Thus, for data filtering applications such as this, employing an input chaff injection scheme is easy.

To inject input chaff into the set of tasks, the supervisor needs only to have a set of instances Y such that determining if any member y_i is not in X is at least as difficult as computing $f(y_i)$. (The supervisor may not need to explicitly construct Y if she has a way of choosing elements from Y probabilistically.) Then the supervisor can randomly inject members of Y into the task sets $D \subset X$ for each participant (with some probability p) to provably obfuscate the rare events. For example, a true input x in the SETI@home application could be transformed into chaff simply by adding a pattern of intelligence to it.

Note that this chaff injection scheme has a finer granularity than our scheme for graph isomorphism, that is, in this case, each participant is likely to have some semi-rare chaff events to report, whereas in the graph isomorphism solution each participant was given an input that was entirely valid or entirely chaff. In any case, the security and analysis of this scheme for data filtering are similar to those given for the graph isomorphism solution given above.

5.3   Searching for Solutions to NP-Complete Problems

In this section, we present a chaff-injection solution for grid computations that involve searches for solutions to NP-complete problems. We begin with a template for building such schemes and we then give a solution for a well-known NP-complete problem – 3SAT. Since all NP problems can be reduced to 3SAT in polynomial time, this gives a chaff-injection scheme for any NP-complete problem. Of course, in practice, it may be more efficient for a supervisor setting up a grid search for solutions to a specific NP-complete problem to use our template and example as a guideline in setting up a specific scheme.

A Template for Chaff Injection for NP Solution Searching. By their nature, solutions to difficult instances of NP-complete problems are rare events, and, with the practical importance of many of these problems, such solutions may have economic value. Let us therefore provide a template for chaff injection for NP solution searching. Every language L in NP has a polynomial-time verification algorithm, A, that takes as input a problem instance x and a polynomial-sized certificate y, such that $x \in L$ if and only if A accepts x for some y (e.g., see [6]). Thus, we can set up a naive grid computation by dividing the set Y of all certificates into as many subsets as participants and asking each participant i to evaluate $A(x, y)$ for all y in his $Y_i \subset Y$. Of course, accepting inputs for A are obvious in this naive computation.

To set up a grid computation that defends against hoarding cheaters, we assume the existence of two functions, α and β, for L. The function α takes an input instance x and certificate set Y_i and produces a pair (x', Y_i') such that $A(x, y) = A(x', y')$, for each $y \in Y_i$ and $y' \in Y_i'$, but determining this fact is computationally difficult (e.g., at least as hard as the graph isomorphism problem). The function β takes a certificate set Y_i and returns a problem instance z for L such that $A(z, y) = 1$ from some $y \in Y_i$, but determining this fact is computationally hard (ideally, there should be only one accepting certificate in Y_i and locating it should be difficult). Moreover, it should be computationally difficult to determine whether or not z is isomorphic to x with respect to A. The template for a chaff-injection scheme, then, is for the supervisor to set a probability p (e.g., $p = 1/10$ or $p = 1/100$) and perform as follows for each participant:

1. The supervisor generates a random bit b with probability p. If $b = 0$, then she applies $\alpha(x, Y_i)$ to construct an isomorphic pair (x', Y_i') that is equivalent with respect to A to (x, Y_i). She then sends (x', Y_i') to the participant and increments i.
2. Otherwise, if $b = 1$, then the supervisor applies β on Y_i to generate at hard positive instance z of L on Y_i. She then applies α to the pair (z, Y_i) to yield an isomorphic pair (z', Y_i'), and she sends (z', Y_i') to the participant and does not increment i.

The participant in this scheme has no efficient way of determining if they got an input isomorphic to x or z; hence, each participant is induced to perform their computation. But roughly p of the inputs are now guaranteed to be rare events; hence, each rare event should be reported or a cheater will be discovered with high probability. The analysis and security of this scheme are therefore similar to that given for the graph isomorphism problem above.

A Specific Example for 3SAT. Since any NP-complete problem can be reduced to another NP-complete problem, we only need to describe our solution to one NP-complete problem. We choose the 3-CNF satisfiability problem, because it is traditionally the problem to which other problems in NP are reduced.

A *CNF formula* is a Boolean expression in a conjunctive normal form, i.e., each conjunct in the formula is a *clause*, which is itself the disjunction of literals. Each *literal* is either a *variable*, or the complement of a variable. A *3-CNF* formula consists of clauses each containing exactly 3 literals. A formula is *satisfiable* if there exists at least one assignment for those variables that will satisfy the formula. We use n and m to represent the number of variables and the number of clauses, respectively.

Finding whether a 3-CNF formula is satisfiable is NP-complete (e.g., see [6]). To apply our grid computing template, therefore, we need to show how to construct the functions α and β for this problem. Fortunately, building α for a formula x and certificate set Y_i is relatively simple in this case: we simply rename all the variable names in x (and change their respective names in Y_i in a corresponding way), and randomly permute the clauses in x. Determining if the output formula x' is equivalent to x is at least as hard as the graph isomorphism problem. For β, we can employ any of a number of schemes for constructing hard instances of 3SAT. For example, Achlioptas, Kautz, *et al.* [1, 9] have an interesting tunable scheme for generating hard instances of SAT, and Massacci and Marraro [10] show how to construct a satisfiable Boolean formula such that finding the satisfying assignment is as hard as breaking the DES encryption algorithm. Combining these techniques allows us to create difficult instances of 3SAT that would match the statistical properties of the input x, allowing us to create hard, satisfiable formulas that are difficult to distinguish as not being isomorphisms of x.

The statistical properties of two isomorphic 3-CNF formula are similar (e.g., the number of clauses are the same, and the number of occurrences for each variables are the same), while the statistical properties of chaff might be different from the original input and other chaff. Therefore, two colluding participants can compare their formulae to find out whether they are likely to have the chaff or the original input. There are two approaches to defeat the colluding attacks. First, we can make the statistical properties of the chaff match that of input x; second, the chaff can also be isomorphic to each other, so they also have similar statistical properties. Therefore, by comparing the statistical properties of their inputs, colluding participants are still unable to tell whether they have the original input x or chaff.

6   Camouflaged Rare Events with Output Chaff

In this section, we present our *output chaff injection* schemes to protect high-value rare events in grid computing when rare events are camouflaged.

6.1   An Chaff-Injection Scheme via Criterion Expansion

In the following, we give a generic solution for CRE problems, i.e. the criterion y is only known to the supervisor. We assume that the screen function is defined as the following:

$$S(f(x), y) = 1 \quad \text{iff} \quad f(x) == y.$$

For CRE problems, to obfuscate rare events, we introduce many other criteria. If an input x satisfies any of these criteria, it is considered as a semi-rare event. If the actual rare-event criterion is superficially indistinguishable from the introduced criteria, participants cannot tell whether a semi-rare event is the actual rare event or just chaff. The algorithms for CRE problems is described in the following:

1. The supervisor randomly selects m inputs $x_1, \ldots, x_m$ from the input domain X. Note that X is the global input domain, each participant only conducts tasks for a subset of X.
2. The supervisor generates m chaff by computing $c_i = hash(f(x_i))$, for $i = 1, \ldots, m$.
3. The supervisor sends the list $C = \{hash(y), c_1, \ldots, c_m\}$ to all the participants. C should be permuted to hide $hash(y)$.
4. For any input x assigned to each participant, the participant computes $hash(f(x))$ and compares the results with the list C. If a match occurs, the participant sends x back to the supervisor; otherwise x is discarded.
5. The supervisor can verify whether a returned x value is an actual rare event or chaff, by a simple lookup in C (say, by storing the elements of C in a hash table). The supervisor also checks whether the participant whose tasks include chaff has returned the chaff or not. This way, the cheater can be caught.

Security Analysis. When a participant finds a semi-rare event, because of the existence of chaff, the probability that this semi-rare event is an actual rare event is only $\frac{1}{m}$. Furthermore, because the participants all get the same list, i.e., the information about the rare events is the same, colluding does not bring any extra information to improve that probability. Incidentally, this scheme differs from the ringers scheme of Golle and Mironov [4] in two important ways. First, our output chaff injection scheme gives the same set of chaff to all participants, so collusion is useless in identifying chaff, unlike ringers. Second, unlike ringers, our output chaff cannot be distinguished from actual desired outputs (without performing the requested computation, that is).

In an actual grid computing application, of course, the rare event may or may not exist. Knowing whether a rare event exists or not might also be valuable, and needs to be protected. Our chaff scheme does prevent the participants from finding out this information. The only situation when the participants know that the rare event exists is when they have found the matches for all the elements in C. Because the chaff are selected uniformly randomly from the entire input domain, the chance that a group of cheating participants get all the chaff is p^m, where p is the portion of the cheating participants among all the participants. In practice, p is quite small. Therefore, p^m is negligible when m is large.

Computation Overhead. The extra computation cost added to this grid computing is that of computing a cryptographic hash function and the finding of matches among the list C (the lookup in C can be done using a non-cryptographic hash table). We have assumed that the cost of computing a hash function is negligible compared to the cost of computing the task function f. Moreover, finding the match can be quite efficient using the hash table data structure even if the list is long (i.e., the value of m is large). Therefore, the supervisor can afford to send a list containing tens of thousands chaff. As we have known, the longer the list is, the fewer incentives participants have.

6.2   Criterion Reduction for CRE Problems

Another way to increase the number of inputs that satisfy a criterion, and thereby introduce input chaff, is to reduce the amount of requirements that must be satisfied. For example, assume that the original criterion says that an input must satisfy five requirements to be considered as a rare event; we can reduce the number of requirements to three in the new criterion, thus increasing the number of satisfiable inputs.

1. The supervisor computes $h(y)$, and let $\hat{y}$ be the first k bits of the result, where k is a security parameter. The supervisor sends $\hat{y}$ to participants along with the task assignments.
2. For each assigned input x, a participant computes $f(x)$, and checks whether the first k bits of $h(f(x))$ equal $\hat{y}$. If true, the participant returns x and $h(f(x))$ to the supervisor; otherwise, discards x.
3. The supervisor verifies whether $h(f(x)) = h(y)$. If false, x is just chaff; else, x is a rare event.

Analysis. Just like the criterion-expansion scheme, we want to keep the number of semi-rare events sufficiently large, so participants will lose incentives to cheat. On the other hand, the number of semi-rare events must be kept within a range, otherwise, finding the actual rare events from the semi-rare events will consume too much time of the supervisor.

Because of the randomness of hash value, we can easily decide how many bits to disclose to the participants. Assume that the search space is 2^{64}, and hash values of outputs are uniformly distributed. Disclosing the first 44 bits of $h(y)$ will lead to a real-to-false ratio $1{:}2^{20}$. This is big enough for the participant to lose incentives, but small enough for the supervisor to find out the actual rare events (2^{20} means only 1 million of hash-function evaluations).

Compared to the criterion-expansion scheme, the criterion-reduction scheme introduces computation costs on the server side, although they are manageable. Another difference is that in criterion reduction, controlling the ratio between the rare and semi-rare events becomes difficult when the hash values of outputs are not uniformly distributed (this can happen, for example, when many outputs have the same values).

7   Conclusion and Future Work

This paper provides a first step towards disguising high-value rare events in the context of grid computing with hoarding cheaters. The techniques we employed involved the injection of input and/or output chaff, depending on whether the rare events were obvious or not. There are still many interesting open problems that could be studied in the future, including:

- Can we develop a generic scheme for all ORE problems?
- The difficulty with the ORE problems is the publically known indicator of rare events. Can we turn an obvious indicator to a non-obvious indicator, i.e., transform ORE problems into CRE problems? If this can be done, we could use solutions to CRE to solve ORE problems.

Acknowledgment

The authors acknowledge the supports from the United States National Science Foundation under grants ISS-0219560, IIS-0312366, CCR-0225642, CCR-0311720, CCR-0312760.

References

1. Dimitris Achlioptas, Carla P. Gomes, Henry A. Kautz, and Bart Selman. Generating satisfiable problem instances. In *AAAI/IAAI*, pages 256–261, 2000.
2. C. Cachin, S. Micali, and M. Stadler. Computationally private information retrieval with polylogarithmic communication. *Lecture Notes in Computer Science*, 1592:402–414, 1999.
3. W. Du, J. Jia, M. Mangal, and M. Murugesan. Uncheatable grid computing. In *The 24th International Conference on Distributed Computing Systems (ICDCS'04)*, pages 4–11, Tokyo, Japan, March 23–26 2004.
4. P. Golle and I. Mironov. Uncheatable distributed computations. *Lecture Notes in Computer Science*, 2020:425–440, 2001.
5. P. Golle and S. Stubblebine. Secure distributed computing in a commercial environment. In P. Syverson, editor, *Proceedings of Financial Crypto 2001*, volume 2339 of *Lecture Notes in Computer Science*, pages 289–304. Springer-Verlag, 2001.
6. M. T. Goodrich and R. Tamassia. *Algorithm Design: Foundations, Analysis, and Internet Examples*. John Wiley & Sons, New York, NY, 2002.
7. F. Hohl. Time limited blackbox security: Protecting mobile agents from malicious hosts. *Mobile Agents and Security, Lecture Notes in Computer Science,Springer-Verlag*, 1419:92–113, 1998.
8. L. Kahney. Cheaters bow to peer pressure. *Wired Magazine*, Feb. 15, 2001.
9. Henry A. Kautz, Yongshao Ruan, Dimitris Achlioptas, Carla P. Gomes, Bart Selman, and Mark E. Stickel. Balance and filtering in structured satisfiable problems. In *IJCAI*, pages 351–358, 2001.
10. F. Massacci and L. Marraro. Logical cryptanalysis as a SAT problem: The encoding of the Data Encryption Standard. *Journal of Automated Reasoning*, 24(1–2):165–203, 2000.
11. F. Monrose, P. Wykoff, and Aviel D. Rubin. Distributed execution with remote audit. In *Proceedings of ISOC Symposium on Network and Distributed System Security*, pages 103–113, February 1999.
12. T. Sander and C. F. Tschudin. Protecting mobile agents against malicious hosts, springer-verlag. *Lecture Notes in Computer Science*, 1419:44–60, 1998.
13. D. Szajda, B. Lawson, and J. Owen. Hardening functions for large scale distributed computations. *IEEE Symposium on Security and Privacy*, 2003.
14. G. Vigna. Protecting mobile agents through tracing. In *Proceedings of the 3rd Workshop on Mobile Object Systems*, June 1997.
15. G. Vigna, editor. *Mobile Agents and Security*, volume 1419 of *Lecture Notes in Computer Science*. Springer, 1998.

16. R. Ostrovsky W. Aiello, S. Bhatt and S. Rajagopalan. Fast verification of any remote procedure call: short witness-indistinguishable one-round proofs for np. In *Proceedings of the 27th International Colloquium on Automata, Languages and Programming*, pages 463–474, July 2000.

17. F. Schneider Y. Minsky, R. van Renesse and S. D. Stoller. Cryptographic support for fault-tolerant distributed computing. In *Proceedings of Seventh ACM SIGOPS European Workshop,System Support for Worldwide Applications*, pages 109–114, Connemara, Ireland, September 1996.

18. B. S. Yee. A sanctuary for mobile agents. In *Secure Internet Programming*, pages 261–273, 1999.

Digital Signatures Do Not Guarantee Exclusive Ownership

Thomas Pornin and Julien P. Stern

Cryptolog International, Paris, France
{thomas.pornin,julien.stern}@cryptolog.com

Abstract. Digital signature systems provide a way to transfer trust from the public key to the signed data; this is used extensively within PKIs. However, some applications need a transfer of trust in the other direction, from the signed data to the public key. Such a transfer is cryptographically robust only if the signature scheme has a property which we name *exclusive ownership*. In this article, we show that the usual signature algorithms (such as RSA[3] and DSS[4]) do *not* have that property. Moreover, we describe several constructs which may be used to transform a signature scheme into another signature scheme which provides exclusive ownership.

1 Introduction

Digital signature schemes based on public-key cryptography are now used in many communication protocols. Signatures are used to convey trust *from* a public key *to* the data which is signed: if the public key is known (by some other mean) to be associated with some entity who "owns" it (i.e., the entity has exclusive access to the corresponding private key), then a valid signature on some data "proves", in a way verifiable by third parties and non repudiable by the key owner, that the key owner had access to the data and deliberately agreed to that association between his public key and the data. This assumes, of course, that no other entity than the key owner has access to the private key, and that the signature and verification algorithms are uncrackable with today's technology. Various semantics can be attached to the signature; PKIs use it as a way to *certify* that the data is correct (the key owner formally guarantees the exactness of the data).

In this article, we are interested in the "reverse" problem, in which a signature on some data is known, and we want to know whether the existence of a public key which validates that signature implies that the corresponding private key was used to produce the signature in the first place. It so happens that usual signature algorithms such as RSA[3] and DSS[4] do *not* provide such guarantee; however, some applications, such as the certificate revocation process through CRLs in X.509[1], need that property. This problem has already been partially studied in [5].

We will first define, informally and then formally, what is the actual property that we are interested in; we call it *exclusive ownership* and we will define several

J. Ioannidis, A. Keromytis, and M.Yung (Eds.): ACNS 2005, LNCS 3531, pp. 138–150, 2005.

subdivisions. Then we will describe in detail how some widely used algorithms do not provide exclusive ownership. A further section will show how this can be fixed.

This work was partially supported by the French Ministry of Research RNRT X-CRYPT project.

1.1   Informal Definitions

We informally consider a signature scheme. An entity A owns a key pair which we note $(K_{\text{pub}}^A, K_{\text{priv}}^A)$ (the public key and the private key, respectively). We suppose that the signature scheme has the usual properties which make that we deem the scheme secure (i.e., it is computationaly infeasible, without knowledge of the private key, to compute existential forgeries[6]).

We now consider an external entity B which has no knowledge of the private key K_{priv}^A. B has access to a set of triplets (K_{pub}^A, m, s) where K_{pub}^A is A's public key, m is some binary message, and s is a valid signature of m relatively to K_{pub}^A. B will then try to produce a new triplet, which is accepted by the verification algorithm, and where some or all of the three triplet components are not part of the set of components issued by A. In other words, A has signed, using its (unique) private key, a set of distinct messages, and produced the corresponding signatures. B wants to produce a triplet comprising a public key, a message and a signature, such that the public key is distinct from A's public key, or the message is not one of those signed by A, or the signature is not one of those computed by A, or any combination of some of those properties. Moreover, we require the following properties:

– when the public key produced by B is not equal to A's public key, B knows the corresponding private key;
– when both the message m and the signature s are kept from the values issued by A, s must be a valid signature for m relatively to K_{pub}^A (in other words, if B keeps one of A's messages and one of A's signatures, the signature must apply to that message).

The figure 1 explicits the eight possible types of triplets that B may attempt to produce. In that figure, a triplet issued by B may contain:

– either A's public key K_{pub}^A, or a different public key K_{pub}^B for which B knows the corresponding private key K_{priv}^B;
– either one of the messages m signed by A, or a new message m';
– either one of the signatures s issued by A, or a new signature s'.

Transforms 1, 6 and 8 are trivial:

– for transform 1, B just selects one of the triplets issued by A;
– for transform 6, B creates its own key pair using the normal procedure, and then signs one of the messages issued by A;
– for transform 8, B creates its own key pair and signs an entirely different message.

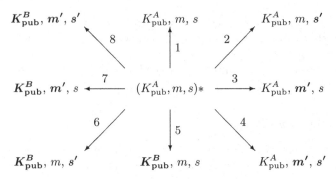

Fig. 1. Signature transforms.

Transforms 3 and 4 are computationaly infeasible for any good signature scheme: B must not be able to produce a new message and a signature which will be accepted by the verification algorithm relatively to A's public key. When either 3 or 4 is possible, it is called a *forgery attack*[6].

Transform 2 is subject to debate. For any given message m, that several distinct signatures are accepted relatively to the same public key is normal if the signature algorithm is randomized, which is a desirable property. If B can apply transform 2 without knowing the private key K^A_{priv}, the signature scheme is said to be *malleable*[7]. Whether malleability is acceptable for a signature scheme depends on the context. This paper does not deal any further with that question.

Transforms 5 and 7 are the purpose of this article. We define a new property which we call *exclusive ownership*. A signature scheme will be said to have conservative or destructive exclusive ownership if it is computationaly infeasible for B to apply, respectively, transform 5 or 7.

We will now define exclusive ownership formally.

1.2   Formal Definitions

Let us consider a signature scheme; it consists of the following three algorithms (as described in [6]):

- a *key generation algorithm* G which, on input 1^k (where k is the "security parameter"), outputs a pair (K_{pub}, K_{priv}) (a public key and a corresponding private key);
- a *signature algorithm* Σ which, using the private key K_{priv}, produces for a message m (in the space of messages $\mathcal{M}$) a signature $s = \Sigma(K_{priv}, m)$ (in the space of signatures $\mathcal{S}$);
- a *verification algorithm* V which takes as input a public key K_{pub}, a message m and a signature s, and returns **true** if the signature is "valid", **false** otherwise.

When K_{pub} and K_{priv} are such that, for every possible message m in $\mathcal{M}$, we have $V(K_{\mathrm{pub}}, m, \Sigma(K_{\mathrm{priv}}, m)) = \mathbf{true}$, then we say that K_{priv} *matches* K_{pub}. G must be such that it outputs only matching key pairs.

We now suppose that there exists an entity which has run the algorithm G and thus owns a key pair $(K_{\mathrm{pub}}, K_{\mathrm{priv}})$. That entity then proceeds with the signing of t messages $m_1, m_2,\ldots m_t$ using K_{priv}, thus producing $s_1, s_2,\ldots s_t$. Another entity, the "attacker", will try to produce a new key pair $(K'_{\mathrm{pub}}, K'_{\mathrm{priv}})$, a message m' and a signature s', such that:

- K'_{priv} matches K'_{pub};
- $V(K'_{\mathrm{pub}}, m', s') = \mathbf{true}$;
- s' is one of the $s_i (1 \leq i \leq t)$; we note it s_j.

Definition 1. *The signature scheme is said to provide* conservative exclusive ownership *(CEO) if it is computationaly infeasible for the attacker, given K_{pub} and t pairs (m_i, s_i) such that $V(K_{\mathrm{pub}}, m_i, s_i) = \mathbf{true}$ for $1 \leq i \leq t$, to produce values $K'_{\mathrm{pub}}, K'_{\mathrm{priv}}$ and m' such that $K'_{\mathrm{pub}} \neq K_{\mathrm{pub}}$, K'_{priv} matches K'_{pub}, $m' = m_j$ for some value j $(1 \leq j \leq t)$ and $V(K'_{\mathrm{pub}}, m_j, s_j) = \mathbf{true}$.*

Definition 2. *The signature scheme is said to provide* destructive exclusive ownership *(DEO) if it is computationaly infeasible for the attacker, given K_{pub} and t pairs (m_i, s_i) such that $V(K_{\mathrm{pub}}, m_i, s_i) = \mathbf{true}$ for $1 \leq i \leq t$, to produce values $K'_{\mathrm{pub}}, K'_{\mathrm{priv}}, m'$ and s' such that $K'_{\mathrm{pub}} \neq K_{\mathrm{pub}}$, K'_{priv} matches K'_{pub}, $s' = s_j$ for some value j $(1 \leq j \leq t)$, $m' \neq m_j$ and $V(K'_{\mathrm{pub}}, m', s_j) = \mathbf{true}$.*

Definition 3. *The signature scheme is said to provide* universal exclusive ownership *(UEO) if it is computationaly infeasible for the attacker, given K_{pub} and t pairs (m_i, s_i) such that $V(K_{\mathrm{pub}}, m_i, s_i) = \mathbf{true}$ for $1 \leq i \leq t$, to produce values $K'_{\mathrm{pub}}, K'_{\mathrm{priv}}, m'$ and s' such that $K'_{\mathrm{pub}} \neq K_{\mathrm{pub}}$, K'_{priv} matches K'_{pub}, $s' = s_j$ for some value j $(1 \leq j \leq t)$ and $V(K'_{\mathrm{pub}}, m', s_j) = \mathbf{true}$.*

Universal exclusive ownership naturally implies conservative and destructive exclusive ownership. However, there are no other implications. See section 3 for further details.

We call *second key construction* the process of defeating exclusive ownership, that is building a quartet $(K'_{\mathrm{pub}}, K'_{\mathrm{priv}}, m', s_j)$ which verifies the properties described above. Some distinctions can be made, depending on whether and when B chooses the messages that A signs (known messages, chosen messages and adaptive chosen messages second key construction).

1.3   Relevance to X.509 Revocation

X.509[1] is a standard for public-key infrastructures. Public keys owned by entities are *certified* by encapsulating them into certificates, which are digitally signed by certification authorities, whose public keys are themselves published within other certificates. A certificate establishes a binding between an identity and a public key. Certificate validation is the process of verifying those signatures, from an a priori trusted public key (often called a "root authority" or "trust anchor") downto an end-entity certificate. Validation uses signatures in the "proper" way: trust is transfered from knowledge of the public key to the signed data.

X.509 certificates can be revoked for a number of reasons, including private key compromise and normal rights management. Revocation is a way of externally "cancelling" a certificate, by declaring its signature invalid. The most common way to revoke a certificate is to publish a Certificate Revocation List (CRL) which contains the revocation status of the certificates issued by an authority. The paradigm here is that a given certificate has a unique issuer, and a unique revocation status. Applications use this unicity to implement caching strategies which prevent certificate validation from using too many computing resources.

The problem is that the validator considers a CRL as valid for a given certificate if it is signed relatively to the same public key than the certificate itself. If the signature algorithm lacks exclusive ownership, then a rogue authority could create a fake certificate issuer, with a constructed second key which validates the certificate. The rogue authority could then publish another CRL. From the point of view of the validator, the certificate has two issuers, and two relevant CRLs (both fulfill all validation procedures, including signature verification). The validation algorithm is then unsound, because it will return a result which depends upon which issuer is tried first by the validator. Moreover, for an application which uses a cache for certificate revocation status, the rogue authority can "contaminate" other certificate hierarchies, by declaring them as revoked, even though these certificates are not part of the authority subtree. This is in contradiction with the principle of a hierarchical PKI.

A detailed analysis of this weakness is presented in [2].

2   Usual Algorithms Lack Exclusive Ownership

The most widely used signature algorithms do not have the exclusive ownership property, neither conservative nor destructive. For some of them, we present here second key construction algorithms which work in the most adverse situations (only one signature is available on a known message, and the attacker arbitrarily chooses the message that will be validated by the signature relatively to the new public key).

2.1   RSA

Algorithm Description
RSA is a signature algorithm[1] whose principle was first described in [8]. The core operation is a modular exponentiation:

- the public key is (n, e) where n is a (big) composite number and e is an arbitrary value, usually small, which is relatively prime to $\phi(n)$;

---

[1] RSA is also an asymmetric encryption algorithm, but we consider here only the signature version.

- the private key is a number d;
- a value v (modulo n) is signed by computing $s = v^d \bmod n$;
- a signature s is verified by computing $w = s^e \bmod n$ and checking that $w = v$.

The private key d must be such that the verification algorithm works; it can be selected such that $ed = 1 \bmod \phi(n)$ (other private key values are possible, but this distinction is not important in this paper).

The core algorithm signs a value modulo n; several standards have been defined, which describe how an arbitrary binary message m is transformed into a value v in a way which makes RSA a secure signature scheme (this is called a *padding scheme* because it was historically done by concatenating the hashed message with some specific data). The most widely used standard is PKCS#1[3], which contains both a deterministic (old version, so-called "1.5") and a randomized (new version, named PSS) padding schemes. The resistance of these schemes to forgeries remains unchallenged; PSS even features strong security proofs.

Second Key Construction

Whatever the padding scheme used, as long as it does not use the value of n but only its size (which is the case for PKCS#1 padding schemes), RSA does not have the exclusive ownership property. We consider a public key (n, e) and a signature s on a message m; s is a positive integer strictly lower than n. We now consider another message m' which the padding scheme transforms into a value v' modulo n. We build a new public key (n', e') with the following process:

1. We select distinct random numbers q_i such that:
   - q_i is prime;
   - $p_i = 2q_i + 1$ is prime;
   - p_i is relatively prime to v' and s;
   - there exists some value d_i such that $v'^{d_i} = s \bmod p_i$ and d_i is relatively prime to $2q_i$ (this property is easily checked if q_i is small enough, e.g. by exhaustive search on d_i).
2. From the set of numbers p_i, we choose k of them (which we number from 1 to k), such that $n' = \Pi_{i=1}^{k} p_i$ has the appropriate size (n' must be greater than s but also small enough for v' to be a valid padding result with m' as message and n' as modulus).
3. We define the values e'_i to be such that $e'_i d'_i = 1 \bmod (p_i - 1)$.
4. By applying the Chinese remainder theorem[9], we compute values d' and e' which are such that $d' = d_i \bmod (p_i - 1)$ and $e' = e_i \bmod (p_i - 1)$ for all i from 1 to k.

This process yields n', d' and e' which are such that:

- (n', e') is a valid RSA public key and d' is a valid RSA private key matching that public key;
- $v'^{e'} \bmod n' = s$, which means that s is a valid signature of m' relatively to the public key (n', e').

This process is fast if the p_i are chosen such that the computation of each d_i value is fast. This is a discrete logarithm, which is easy if the p_i are small enough. The p_i values are chosen as $p_i = 2q_i + 1$ where q_i is prime, so that it is probable, for each such value p_i, that the value of d_i is relatively prime to $\phi(p_i) = p_i - 1 = 2q_i$. Besides, the primality of each q_i simplifies greatly the final reconstruction of d' and e' with the CRT.

A very naive implementation, in the Java programming language, on a simple and cheap PC, performs this second key construction in a few seconds for a 1024-bit original modulus n.

Remarks

• The message m' in the algorithm described above is chosen arbitrarily and may be equal to the message m. Thus, this algorithm demonstrates that RSA has neither CEO nor DEO.

• The algorithm described above produces an RSA modulus which is quite smooth: it is a product of small factors. The factors can be made bigger at the expense of a longer computation, to retrieve the values d_i. Detecting that the modulus is smooth depends on the size of the smallest of the p_i and implies a computational effort which is roughly of the same order than the one deployed by the attacker to compute each d_i. The attacker is therefore in a winning situation, since he usually has much more computing power than what any verifier is willing to spend before accepting a signature as valid.

• The produced public exponent e' is not controlled by the attacker, and as such is usually big. Most existing RSA public exponents are small (in order to speed up signature verification) and indeed some widely deployed implementations are not even able to handle public exponents bigger than 32 bits. Whether second key construction *with a small public exponent* is computationaly feasible is not currently known.

• Our intuition is that, with a fixed public exponent, RSA provides UEO. An intuitive argument runs thus: second key construction yields a key pair, from which a factorization of the modulus n' can be deduced. However, a pair (m', s) may accept only very few modulus values for which s will be a valid signature ($s^e \bmod n$ must be a valid padded value derived from m'). Hence, successful second key construction is a factorization algorithm on one of the modulus values n' for which $s^e \bmod n' = v'$. Easily factored integers of the size of a typical RSA modulus are scarce; hence, generic second key construction should not succeed in the general case.

Having a fixed public exponent means that the standard within which RSA is used specifies one unique public exponent which all public keys use. Although some values are popular (3, 17 and 65537), no clear consensus has yet been established on which value should always be used. Most protocols currently specify an RSA public key as a pair "modulus + public exponent", sometimes with restrictions on the public exponent size.

2.2 DSS

Algorithm Description
DSS is the American government Digital Signature Standard; it is described in
[4]. The base algorithm uses computations in a subgroup of invertible numbers
modulo p. The group parameters are:

- p, a 1024-bit prime number;
- q, a 160-bit prime number which divides $p - 1$;
- g, a multiplicative generator of a subgroup of order q (which means that
  $0 < g < p$, $g \neq 1$ and $g^q = 1 \mod p$).

A DSS private key is an arbitrary number x such that $0 < x < q$, and the
associated public key is $y = g^x \mod p$.

In order to sign a message m, a hash function (SHA-1 for basic DSS) is
applied to the message, yielding $H(m)$ (the size of $H(m)$ should be at least the
size of q). Then the signer chooses a random number k such that $0 < k < q$ and
computes the two following values:

$$r = (g^k \mod p) \mod q$$
$$s = k^{-1}(H(m) + xr) \mod q$$

The signature is the pair (r, s).

The signature verification algorithm is thus:

$$w = s^{-1} \mod q$$
$$u_1 = wH(m) \mod q$$
$$u_2 = wr \mod q$$
$$v = (g^{u_1} y^{u_2} \mod p) \mod q$$

The signature is accepted if and only if $v = r$.

Second Key Construction
We now consider that we have a valid triplet with a public key, a message and
a signature, with the notations described above. We choose a new message m'
and an arbitrary (e.g. random) number f such that $0 < f < q$. We now compute
the following values:

$$g' = (g^{u_1} y^{u_2})^f \mod p$$
$$x' = r^{-1}(sf^{-1} - H(m')) \mod q$$
$$y' = g'^{x'} \mod p$$

It can easily be seen that (r, s) then constitutes a valid signature for message
m' relatively to the public key y', with group parameters p, q and g'. x', the
private key corresponding to y', is known; thus, we have completed a successful
second key construction.

Remarks

- The message m' in the algorithm described above is chosen arbitrarily and may be equal to the message m. Thus, this algorithm demonstrates that DSS has neither CEO nor DEO.

- The "trick" used here is to use g^k (as advertised by the initial signer through the signature) as the basis for a new group generator. DSS security relies on the fact that discrete logarithm is hard: retrieving k from $g^k \bmod p$ is not computationaly feasible. By shifting the generator, we make that discrete logarithm easy. We still use the same group. Since q is prime, and thus relatively prime to both k and f, a random choice of f yields just any group element with equal probability. This makes the second key exactly as valid as the initial key: no test on the public key or group parameters may establish which of the two keys is the "correct" one.

- It is not possible to perform second key construction without altering the paramaters p, q and g. If such a second key was found, the signature and the private key could be used to retrieve the original k parameter used by the original signer; the whole process would then solve discrete logarithm (find k from $g^k \bmod p$), which is considered intractable.

- DSS defines (in [4]) a parameter generation algorithm, which uses internal pseudo-random number generators. Once the seed is determined, the parameter generation algorithm is deterministic; hence, with the seed, the parameter generation algorithm can be run again and the parameters checked. This validation algorithm defeats the second key construction described above, because it is not possible to find a seed which will match the new group generator g' (that such a seed exists at all is actually most improbable). However, the publication of the seed is optional in the usual public key formats, the validation is very expensive (thousands of times the cost of verifying the signature, up to dozens of seconds on a big modern PC), and the standard parameter generation is suboptimal (it does not include some basic optimisations which may speed up the process). The bottom line is that some parameter generation algorithms do not use the standard, verifiable algorithm, and almost none of the verifiers do actually validate the parameters.

- The second key construction algorithm can trivially be applied to variants of DSS based on elliptic curves, or other groups. It also works with other schemes based on discrete logarithm, such as Schnorr[10] and El-Gamal[11]. The basic principle remains the same: shift the generator, using the published (either directly, or indirectly as in DSS) value g^k as basis for the new generator.

3   Adding Exclusive Ownership

In the following sections, we will concatenate and apply hash functions on both messages and public keys; this assumes that a convenient unambiguous deterministic binary representation of messages and public key is defined. This is in any way true for almost all existing applications, for instance those which handle digital certificates.

3.1 Destructive Exclusive Ownership

Destructive exclusive ownership can be added to any signature scheme in the following way: from a scheme (G, Σ, V), define a new scheme (G', Σ', V') such that:

- $G' = G$;
- for any message m, $\Sigma'(K_{\mathrm{priv}}, m) = \Sigma(K_{\mathrm{priv}}, m) \| h(m)$ where $\|$ is the concatenation, and h is a cryptographically secure hash function;
- for any signature $s = s_1 \| t$ where t has the size of the output of h, s is accepted by V' if and only if s_1 is accepted by V and $t = h(m)$.

If the hash function h is collision-free (it is computationaly infeasible to exhibit a collision), that new scheme trivially provides DEO, because the signature is "branded" with the signed message, and hence cannot be used for any other message. Note that if the original scheme does not provide CEO, the new scheme does not provide it either.

3.2 Conservative and Universal Exclusive Ownership

Conservative exclusive ownership can be added to any signature scheme in the following way: from a scheme (G, Σ, V), define a new scheme (G', Σ', V') such that:

- $G' = G$;
- for any message m, $\Sigma'(K_{\mathrm{priv}}, m) = \Sigma(K_{\mathrm{priv}}, m) \| h(K_{\mathrm{pub}})$ where $\|$ is the concatenation, and h is a cryptographically secure hash function;
- for any signature $s = s_1 \| t$ where t has the size of the output of h, s is accepted by V' if and only if s_1 is accepted by V and $t = h(K_{\mathrm{pub}})$.

If the hash function h is collision-free, this scheme makes each signature exclusive to the public key which was used to generate it. Thus, the signature cannot be reused with any other public key. It so happens that this provides UEO, which is the union of CEO and DEO.

It is possible to create a contrived example which ensures CEO but *not* DEO: for instance, use DSS and define the signature to be the concatenation of a plain DSS signature on the message, and $h(m \oplus (p, q, g))$ where $\oplus$ is a bitwise exclusive or, and p, q and g are the public key parameters (some formatting and padding is needed in order to define this cleanly). Since second key construction on DSS requires changing the parameters (see section 2.2), m must also be modified in order to keep the total hash value unmodified; but such modification is easy since a simple bitwise exclusive or is used. Hence this scheme does not provide DEO. But it can be proven that if this modified DSS does not provide CEO, then the attacker can also produce existential forgeries on DSS.

This example shows that CEO does not imply UEO.

3.3 UEO Without Expanding Signatures

The method described in the previous section provides UEO but increases the signature size, which may be inappropriate for some applications. Unfortunately, we found no easy way to define a generic construction which provides UEO without increasing signature size. However, we do have a construction which works if the underlying signature scheme provides an additional property, which we explicit below.

Let us consider a secure signature scheme (G, Σ, V) which has the following property $\mathcal{P}$: for any given public key K_{pub} and signature value s that successfully pass the basic correctness tests that the verifier is willing to implement, and for random messages m taken in a defined space $\mathcal{H}$ (of cardinal $\#\mathcal{H}$), the probability over $\mathcal{H}$ that $V(K_{\mathrm{pub}}, m, s) = \mathbf{true}$ is negligeable (no more than 2^{-80} for instance). For the purpose of our construction, it is not needed that this property be true for any space $\mathcal{H}$, but only for the space of output values of a proper hash function h.

RSA has that property. The signature s and the public key (n, e) are sufficient to compute $s^e \bmod n$, which is the padded message, which is mostly the hashed message with additional features. For DSS, however, the situation is a bit more problematic: if the verifier does not perform some validation on the public key parameters, this property is not met (for a given signature, it is possible to devise a flawed public key such that the signature will be considered valid for many possible messages, for instance one message in three). The validation process must check that:

- q is prime;
- r and s (the two parts of the DSS signature) are strictly lower than q;
- g (the group generator) is greater than 1, lower than p, and has order q;
- y (the public key itself) is greater than 1, lower than p, and has order q.

Under those conditions, DSS has the required property $\mathcal{P}$. Performing these checks will slow down signature verification by a factor of about 2.5 in a typical implementation.

We will now build the new signature scheme (G', Σ', V') which provides UEO. We suppose that there exist:

- a secure hash function h which takes as input arbitrary bit strings;
- an unambiguous deterministic representation of the possible output values of h into messages m in $\mathcal{M}$.

Then we define:

- $G' = G$;
- $\Sigma'(K_{\mathrm{priv}}, m) = \Sigma(K_{\mathrm{priv}}, h(m||K_{\mathrm{pub}}))$ (where $||$ denotes concatenation);
- $V'(K_{\mathrm{pub}}, m, s) = V(K_{\mathrm{pub}}, h(m||K_{\mathrm{pub}}), s)$.

We place ourself in the (non-standard) model known as the Random Oracle Model, proposed in [12] after a suggestion by Fiat and Shamir[13]. If we consider h to be a random oracle, and if the original signature scheme has the property defined above, then this new signature scheme provides UEO. This is easily proven: the very nature of h as a random oracle means that second key construction has to work as a guess-work, where both m' and K'_{pub} are chosen prior to invoking the oracle, with a probability of success which is negligeable, thanks to the property of the initial signature scheme. And since K'_{pub} is distinct from K_{pub} (by definition of second key construction), none of those requests to the oracle may be performed by the initial user; thus, messages signed by the initial user are of no help to the attacker.

In most usual signature schemes, an appropriate hash function h' is already used, which means that the signature scheme operates on $h'(m)$ instead of m directly. We can thus merge that internal hash function h' with h. In that sense, we can give UEO to such a signature protocol by simply adding a copy of the public key (or a hash thereof) within the signed data. Note that, for any signature scheme which is deemed resistant to existential forgeries, signing $m||K_{pub}$ is *not* sufficient to guarantee UEO, unless resistance to existential forgeries is true for *all* possible keys, even the weak and potentially incorrect keys that the attacker may use. Hence the property $\mathcal{P}$ which we defined above.

4   Conclusion

We presented in this article the new notion of Exclusive Ownership, which usual signature algorithms do not provide. That notion is important to some real-world applications, such as the X.509 revocation system through CRLs. We showed how to defeat EO for some algorithms such as RSA and DSS; we also presented some generic ways to modify signature schemes in order to provide UEO, although these methods have shortcomings (either signature size increase, or restriction to algorithms which have a specific property, and the security proofs are in the random oracle model).

Our model describes the attack as recontructing a new key pair, which the attacker may later use to sign other messages. A slightly weaker attack model would be the following: the attacker builds a new public key K'_{pub}, which validates a previously issued signature $s' = s$ on some message m', and also a new signature s'' on another message m'', distinct from m'. In this model, the attacker needs not gain any knowledge of a private key K'_{priv} matching K'_{pub}. Our generic constructions for providing exclusive ownership also defeat this weaker attack model. It is yet an open question, whether RSA with a fixed or range-restricted public exponent provides exclusive ownership, either in our main attack model, or in this weaker model.

References

1. *Internet X.509 Public Key Infrastructure, Certificate and Certificate Revocation List (CRL) Profile*, R. Housley, W. Polk, W. Ford and D. Solo, RFC 3280, April 2002.
2. *On the Soundness of Certificate Validation in X.509 and PKIX*, T. Pornin and J. P. Stern, to appear in EuroPKI 2005.

3. *Public-Key Cryptography Standards (PKCS) #1: RSA Cryptography Specifications Version 2.1*, J. Jonsson and B. Kaliski, RFC 3447, February 2003.
4. *Digital Signature Standard*, National Institute of Standards and Technology (NIST), FIPS 186-2, 2000.
5. *Key-spoofing attacks on nested signature blocks*, R. Christianson and M. R. Low, Electronics Letters, vol. 31, no. 13, 1995, pp. 1043–1044.
6. *A Digital Signature Scheme Secure Against Adaptive Chosen-Message Attacks*, S. Goldwasser, S. Micali and R. Rivest, SIAM Journal on Computing, vol. 17, no. 2, 1988, pp. 281–308.
7. *Flaws in Applying Proof Methodologies to Signature Schemes*, J. Stern, D. Pointcheval, J. Lee and N. Smart, Lecture Notes in Computer Science, Proceedings of Crypto'02, 2002, pp. 93–110.
8. *A Method for Obtaining Digital Signatures and Public-Key Cryptosystems*, R. Rivest, A. Shamir and L. Adleman, Communications of the ACM, February 1978, pp. 120–126.
9. *Fast decipherment algorithm for RSA public-key cryptosystem*, J.-J. Quisquater and C. Couvreur, Electronics Letters, vol. 18, no. 21, October 1982, pp. 905–907.
10. *Efficient signature generation by smart cards*, G.P. Schnorr, Journal of Cryptology, vol. 4, 1991, pp. 161–174.
11. *A Public Key Cryptosystem and a Signature Scheme Based on Discrete Logarithms*, T. El-Gamal, Lecture Notes in Computer Science, Proceedings of Crypto'84, 1985, pp. 10–18.
12. *Random Oracles Are Practical: a Paradigm for Designing Efficient Protocols*, M. Bellare and P. Rogaway, Proceedings of the 1st CCS, ACM Press, 1993, pp. 62–73.
13. *How to Prove Yourself: Practical Solutions of Identification and Signature Problems*, A. Fiat and A. Shamir, Lecture Notes in Computer Science, Proceedings of Crypto'86, 1987, pp. 186–194.

Thompson's Group
and Public Key Cryptography

Vladimir Shpilrain[1,*] and Alexander Ushakov[2]

[1] Department of Mathematics, The City College of New York, New York, NY 10031
shpilrain@yahoo.com
[2] Department of Mathematics, CUNY Graduate Center, New York, NY 10016
aushakov@mail.ru

Abstract. Recently, several public key exchange protocols based on symbolic computation in non-commutative (semi)groups were proposed as a more efficient alternative to well established protocols based on numeric computation. Notably, the protocols due to Anshel-Anshel-Goldfeld and Ko-Lee et al. exploited the *conjugacy search problem* in groups, which is a ramification of the discrete logarithm problem. However, it is a prevalent opinion now that the conjugacy search problem alone is unlikely to provide sufficient level of security no matter what particular group is chosen as a platform.

In this paper we employ another problem (we call it the *decomposition problem*), which is more general than the conjugacy search problem, and we suggest to use R. Thompson's group as a platform. This group is well known in many areas of mathematics, including algebra, geometry, and analysis. It also has several properties that make it fit for cryptographic purposes. In particular, we show here that the word problem in Thompson's group is solvable in almost linear time.

1 Introduction

One of the possible generalizations of the *discrete logarithm problem* to arbitrary groups is the so-called *conjugacy search problem*: given two elements a, b of a group G and the information that $a^x = b$ for some $x \in G$, find at least one particular element x like that. Here a^x stands for $x^{-1}ax$. The (alleged) computational difficulty of this problem in some particular groups (namely, in braid groups) has been used in several group based cryptosystems, most notably in [1] and [6]. It seems however now that the conjugacy search problem alone is unlikely to provide sufficient level of security; see [7] and [8] for explanations.

In this paper we employ another problem, which generalizes the conjugacy search problem, but at the same time resembles the factorization problem which is at the heart of the RSA cryptosystem. This problem which some authors (see e.g. [3], [6]) call the *decomposition problem* is as follows:

Given an element w of a (semi)group G, a subset $A \subseteq G$ and an element $x \cdot w \cdot y$, find elements $x', y' \in A$ such that $x' \cdot w \cdot y' = x \cdot w \cdot y$.

* Research of the first author was partially supported by the NSF grant DMS-0405105.

J. Ioannidis, A. Keromytis, and M.Yung (Eds.): ACNS 2005, LNCS 3531, pp. 151–163, 2005.

The conjugacy search problem (more precisely, its subgroup-restricted version used in [6]) is a special case of the decomposition problem if one takes $x = y^{-1}$.

The usual factorization problem for integers used in the RSA cryptosystem is also a special case of the decomposition problem if one takes $w = 1$ and $G = \mathbf{Z}_p^*$, the multiplicative (semi)group of integers modulo p. It is therefore conceivable that with more complex (semi)groups used as platforms, the corresponding cryptosystem may be more secure. At the same time, in the group that we use in this paper (R. Thompson's group), computing (the normal form of) a product of elements is faster than in $\mathbf{Z}_p^*$.

A key exchange protocol based on the general decomposition problem is quite straightforward (see e.g. [6]): given two subsets $A, B \subseteq G$ such that $ab = ba$ for any $a \in A$, $b \in B$, and given a public element $w \in G$, Alice selects private $a_1, a_2 \in A$ and sends the element $a_1 w a_2$ to Bob. Similarly, Bob selects private $b_1, b_2 \in B$ and sends the element $b_1 w b_2$ to Alice. Then Alice computes $K_A = a_1 b_1 w b_2 a_2$, and Bob computes $K_B = b_1 a_1 w a_2 b_2$. Since $a_i b_i = b_i a_i$ in G, one has $K_A = K_B = K$ (as an element of G), which is now Alice's and Bob's common secret key.

In this paper, we suggest the following modification of this protocol which appears to be more secure (at least for our particular choice of the platform) against so-called "length based" attacks (see e.g. [4], [5]), according to our experiments (see our Section 3). Given two subsets $A, B \subseteq G$ such that $ab = ba$ for any $a \in A$, $b \in B$, and given a public element $w \in G$, Alice selects private $a_1 \in A$ and $b_1 \in B$ and sends the element $a_1 w b_1$ to Bob. Bob selects private $b_2 \in B$ and $a_2 \in A$ and sends the element $b_2 w a_2$ to Alice. Then Alice computes $K_A = a_1 b_2 w a_2 b_1$, and Bob computes $K_B = b_2 a_1 w b_1 a_2$. Since $a_i b_i = b_i a_i$ in G, one has $K_A = K_B = K$ (as an element of G), which is now Alice's and Bob's common secret key.

The group that we suggest to use as the platform for this protocol is Thompson's group F well known in many areas of mathematics, including algebra, geometry, and analysis. This group is infinite non-abelian. For us, it is important that Thompson's group has the following nice presentation in terms of generators and defining relations:

$$F = \langle x_0, x_1, x_2, \ldots \mid x_i^{-1} x_k x_i = x_{k+1} \ (k > i) \rangle. \tag{1}$$

This presentation is infinite. There are also finite presentations of this group; for example,

$$F = \langle x_0, x_1, x_2, x_3, x_4 \mid x_i^{-1} x_k x_i = x_{k+1} \ (k > i, \ k < 4) \rangle,$$

but it is the infinite presentation above that allows for a convenient normal form, so we are going to use that presentation in our paper.

For a survey on various properties of Thompson's group, we refer to [2]. Here we only give a description of the "classical" normal form for elements of F.

The classical normal form for an element of Thompson's group is a word of the form

$$x_{i_1} \ldots x_{i_s} x_{j_t}^{-1} \ldots x_{j_1}^{-1}, \tag{2}$$

such that the following two conditions are satisfied:

(NF1) $i_1 \leq \ldots \leq i_s$ and $j_1 \leq \ldots \leq j_t$

(NF2) if both x_i and x_i^{-1} occur, then either x_{i+1} or x_{i+1}^{-1} occurs, too.

We say that a word w is in *seminormal form* if it is of the form (2) and satisfies (NF1).

We show in Section 4 that the time complexity of reducing a word of length n to the normal form in Thompson's group is $O(|n| \log |n|)$, i.e., is almost linear in n.

Another advantage of cryptographic protocols based on symbolic computation over those based on computation with numbers is the possibility to generate a random word one symbol at a time. For example, in RSA, one uses random prime numbers which obviously cannot be generated one digit at a time but rather have to be precomputed, which limits the key space unless one wants to sacrifice the efficiency. We discuss key generation in more detail in our Section 3.

Acknowledgments. We are grateful to V. Guba for helpful comments and to R. Haralick for making a computer cluster in his lab available for our computer experiments.

2   The Protocol

Let F be Thompson's group given by its standard infinite presentation (1) and $s \in \mathbb{N}$ a positive integer. Define sets A_s and B_s as follows. The set A_s consists of elements whose normal form is of the type

$$x_{i_1} \ldots x_{i_m} x_{j_m}^{-1} \ldots x_{j_1}^{-1},$$

i.e. positive and negative parts are of the same length m, and

$$i_k - k < s \text{ and } j_k - k < s \text{ for every } k = 1, \ldots, s. \tag{3}$$

The set B_s consists of elements represented by words in generators $x_{s+1}, x_{s+2}, \ldots$. Obviously, B_s is a subgroup of F.

Proposition 1. *Let $a \in A_s$ and $b \in B_s$. Then $ab = ba$ in the group F.*

Proof. Let $a = x_{i_1} \ldots x_{i_m} x_{j_m}^{-1} \ldots x_{j_1}^{-1}$ and $b = x_{k_1}^{\varepsilon_1} \ldots x_{k_l}^{\varepsilon_l}$ where $k_q > s$ for every $q = 1, \ldots, l$. By induction on l and m it is easy to show that in the group F one has

$$ab = ba = x_{i_1} \ldots x_{i_m} \delta_m(b) x_{j_m}^{-1} \ldots x_{j_1}^{-1},$$

where δ_M is the operator that increases indices of all generators by M (see also our Section 4). This establishes the claim.

Proposition 2. *Let $s \geq 2$ be an integer. The set A_s is a subgroup of F generated by $x_0 x_1^{-1}, \ldots, x_0 x_s^{-1}$.*

Proof. The set A_s contains the identity and is clearly closed under taking inversions, i.e., $A_s = A_s^{-1}$. To show that A_s is closed under multiplication we take two arbitrary normal forms from A_s:

$$u = x_{i_1} \ldots x_{i_m} x_{j_m}^{-1} \ldots x_{j_1}^{-1}$$

and

$$v = x_{p_1} \ldots x_{p_l} x_{q_l}^{-1} \ldots x_{q_1}^{-1}$$

and show that the normal form of uv belongs to A_s. First, note that since the numbers of positive and negative letters in uv are equal, the lengths of the positive and negative parts in the normal form of uv will be equal, too (see the rewriting system in the beginning of our Section 4). Thus, it remains to show that the property (3) of indices in the normal form of uv is satisfied. Below we sketch the proof of this claim.

Consider the subword in the middle of the product uv marked below:

$$uv = x_{i_1} \ldots x_{i_m} \left(x_{j_m}^{-1} \ldots x_{j_1}^{-1} x_{p_1} \ldots x_{p_l} \right) x_{q_l}^{-1} \ldots x_{q_1}^{-1}$$

and find a seminormal form for it using relations of F (move positive letters to the left and negative letters to the right starting in the middle of the subword). We refer the reader to Algorithm 2 in Section 4 for more information on how this can be done. Denote the obtained word by w. The word w is the product of a positive and a negative word: $w = pn$. By induction on $l + m$ one can show that both p and n satisfy the condition (3).

Then we find normal forms for words p and n using relations of F (for p move letters with smaller indices to the left of letters with bigger indices, and for n move letters with smaller indices to the right of letters with bigger indices). By induction on the number of operations thus performed, one can show that the obtained words p' and n' satisfy the condition (3). Therefore, the word $w' = p'n'$ is a seminormal form of uv satisfying the condition (3).

Finally, we remove those pairs of generators in w' that contradict the property (NF2) (we refer the reader to our Algorithm 5 for more information). Again, by induction on the number of "bad pairs", one can show that the result will satisfy the condition (3). Therefore, uv belongs to A_s, i.e., A_s is closed under multiplication, and therefore, A_s is a subgroup.

Now we show that the set of words $\{x_0 x_1^{-1}, \ldots, x_0 x_s^{-1}\}$ generates the subgroup A_s. Elements $\{x_0 x_1^{-1}, \ldots, x_0 x_s^{-1}\}$ clearly belong to A_s. To show the inclusion $A_s \leq \langle x_0 x_1^{-1}, \ldots, x_0 x_s^{-1} \rangle$, we construct the Schreier graph of $\langle x_0 x_1^{-1}, \ldots, x_0 x_s^{-1} \rangle$ (depicted in Figure 1) and see that any word from A_s belongs to the subgroup on the right.

Now we give a formal description of the protocol based on the decomposition problem mentioned in the Introduction.

(0) Fix two positive integers s, M and a word $w = w(x_0, x_1, \ldots)$.
(1) Alice randomly selects private elements $a_1 \in A_s$ and $b_1 \in B_s$. Then she reduces the element $a_1 w b_1$ to the normal form and sends the result to Bob.

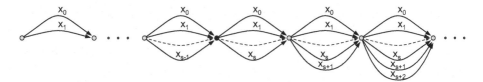

Fig. 1. The Schreier graph of the subgroup $H = \langle x_0 x_1^{-1}, \ldots, x_0 x_s^{-1} \rangle$. The black dot denotes the right coset corresponding to H.

(2) Bob randomly selects private elements $b_2 \in B_s$ and $a_2 \in A_s$. Then he reduces the element $b_2 w a_2$ to the normal form and sends the result to Alice.

(3) Alice computes $K_A = a_1 b_2 w a_2 b_1 = b_2 a_1 w b_1 a_2$, and Bob computes $K_B = b_2 a_1 w b_1 a_2$. Since $a_i b_i = b_i a_i$ in F, one has $K_A = K_B = K$ (as an element of F), which is now Alice's and Bob's common secret key.

3   Parameters and Key Generation

In practical key exchange we suggest to choose the following parameters.

(1) Select (randomly and uniformly) the parameter s from the interval $[3, 8]$ and the parameter M from the set $\{256, 258, \ldots, 318, 320\}$.

(2) Select the "base" word w as a product of generators

$$S_W = \{x_0, x_1, \ldots, x_{s+2}\}$$

and their inverses. This is done the following way. We start with the empty word v_0. When we have a current word v_i, we multiply it on the right by a generator from $S_B^{\pm 1}$ and compute the normal form of the product. The obtained word is denoted by v_{i+1}. We continue this process until the obtained word v_{i+1} has length M.

(3) Select a_1 and a_2 as products of words from

$$S_A = \{x_0 x_1^{-1}, \ldots, x_0 x_s^{-1}\}$$

and their inverses. This is done essentially the same way as above for w. We start with the empty word u_0. Let u_i be the currently constructed word of length less than M. We multiply u_i on the right by a randomly chosen word from $S_A^{\pm 1}$ and compute the normal form of the product. Denote the obtained normal form by u_{i+1}. Continue this process until the obtained word u_{i+1} has length M.

(4) Select b_1 and b_2 as products of generators from

$$S_B = \{x_{s+1}, x_{s+2}, \ldots, x_{2s}\}$$

and their inverses. To do that, start with the empty word v_0. Multiply a current word v_i on the right by a generator from $S_B^{\pm 1}$ and compute the normal form of the product. Denote the obtained word by v_{i+1}. Continue this process until the obtained word v_{i+1} has length M.

We would like to point out that the key space in the proposed scheme is exponential in M; it is easy to see that $|A_s(M)| \geq \sqrt{2}^M$.

The parameters above were chosen in such a way to prevent a length-based attack. Note that for Thompson's group, a length-based attack could be a threat since the normal form of any element represents a geodesic in the Cayley graph of F. Since ideas behind length-based attacks were never fully described, we present below a typical algorithm (adapted to our situation) implementing such an attack (Algorithm 1).

Define a directed labelled graph $\Gamma = (V(\Gamma), E(\Gamma))$ as follows:

– The set of vertices $V(\Gamma)$ corresponds to the set of all elements of the group F.
– The set of edges $E(\Gamma)$ contains edges $v_1 \xrightarrow{(w_1, w_2)} v_2$ such that $v_2 = w_1 v_1 w_2$ in the group F, with labels of two types:
  • $(w_1, 1)$, where $w_1 \in S_A^{\pm 1}$.
  • $(1, w_2)$, where $w_2 \in S_B^{\pm 1}$.

For an element $w \in F$ denote by Γ_w the connected component of Γ containing w. From the description of the protocol it follows that w and the element $w' = a_1 w b_1$ transmitted by Alice to Bob belong to $\Gamma_w = \Gamma_{w'}$, and breaking Alice's key is equivalent to finding a label of a path from w to w' in Γ_w.

To test our protocol, we performed a series of experiments. We randomly generated keys (as described above) and ran Algorithm 1 (see below) on them. Algorithm 1 keeps constructing Γ_w and $\Gamma_{w'}$ until a shared element is found. The sets S_w and $S_{w'}$ in the algorithm accumulate constructed parts of the graphs Γ_w and $\Gamma_{w'}$. The sets $M_w \subset S_w$ and $M_{w'} \subseteq S_{w'}$ are called the sets of marked vertices and are used to specify vertices that are worked out.

Algorithm 1 (Length-based attack)
INPUT. *The original public word w and the word w' transmitted by Alice.*
OUTPUT. *A pair of words $x_1 \in S_A$, $x_2 \in S_B$ such that $w' = x_1 w x_2$.*
INITIALIZATION. *Put $S_w = \{w\}$, $S_{w'} = \{w'\}$, $M_w = \emptyset$, $M_{w'} = \emptyset$.*
COMPUTATIONS.

A. *Find a shortest word $u \in S_w \setminus M_w$.*
B. *Multiply u by elements $S_A^{\pm 1}$ on the left and by elements $S_B^{\pm 1}$ on the right and add each result into S_w with the edges labelled accordingly.*
C. *Add u into M_w.*
D. *Perform the steps A–C with S_w and M_w replaced by $S_{w'}$ and $M_{w'}$, respectively.*
E. *If $S_w \cap S_{w'} = \emptyset$ then goto A.*
F. *If there is $\overline{w} \in S_w \cap S_{w'}$ then find a path in S_w from w to $\overline{w}$ and a path in $S_{w'}$ from $\overline{w}$ to w'. Concatenate them and output the label of the result.*

We performed a series of tests implementing this length-based attack; in each test we let the program to run overnight. None of the programs gave a result, i.e., the success rate of the length-based attack in our tests was 0.

4 The Word Problem in Thompson's Group

In this section, we show that the time complexity of reducing a word of length n to the normal form in Thompson's group F is $O(|n|\log|n|)$, i.e., is almost linear in n. Our algorithm is in two independent parts: first we reduce a given word to a seminormal form (Algorithm 4), and then further reduce it to the normal form by eliminating "bad pairs" (Algorithm 5). We also note that crucial for Algorithm 4 is Algorithm 3 which computes a seminormal form of a product of two seminormal forms. Our strategy for computing a seminormal form of a given $w \in F$ is therefore recursive ("divide and conquer"): we split the word w into two halves: $w = w_1 w_2$, then compute seminormal forms of w_1 and w_2, and then use Algorithm 3 to compute a seminormal form of w.

Recall that Thompson's group F has the following infinite presentation:

$$F = \langle x_0, x_1, x_2, \ldots \mid x_i^{-1} x_k x_i = x_{k+1} \ (k > i) \rangle.$$

The classical normal form for an element of Thompson's group (see [2] for more information) is described in the Introduction.

Let us denote by $\rho(w)$ the normal form for $w \in F$; it is unique for a given element of F. Recall that we say that a word w is in *seminormal form* if it is of the form (2) and satisfies (NF1) (see the Introduction). A seminormal form is not unique. As usual, for a word w in the alphabet X by $\overline{w}$ we denote the corresponding freely reduced word.

As mentioned above, the normal form for an element of Thompson's group can be computed in two steps:

1) Computation of a seminormal form.
2) Removing "bad pairs", i.e., pairs (x_i, x_i^{-1}) for which the property (NF2) fails.

The first part is achieved (Lemma 1) by using the following rewriting system (for all pairs (i, k) such that $i < k$):

$$
\begin{aligned}
x_k x_i &\rightarrow x_i x_{k+1} \\
x_k^{-1} x_i &\rightarrow x_i x_{k+1}^{-1} \\
x_i^{-1} x_k &\rightarrow x_{k+1} x_i^{-1} \\
x_i^{-1} x_k^{-1} &\rightarrow x_{k+1}^{-1} x_i^{-1}
\end{aligned}
$$

and, additionally, for all $i \in \mathbb{N}$

$$x_i^{-1} x_i \rightarrow 1$$

We denote this system of rules by $\mathcal{R}$. It is straightforward to check (using the confluence test, see [10, Proposition 3.1]) that $\mathcal{R}$ is confluent. The following lemma is obvious.

Lemma 1. $\mathcal{R}$ *terminates with a seminormal form. Moreover, a word is in a seminormal form if and only if it is $\mathcal{R}$-reduced.*

Let us now examine the action of $\mathcal{R}$ more closely. This action is similar to sorting a list of numbers, but with two differences: indices of generators may increase, and some generators may disappear.

By Lemma 1, for any word w in generators of F, the final result of rewrites by $\mathcal{R}$ is a seminormal form. Therefore, to compute a seminormal form we implement rewrites by $\mathcal{R}$. We do it in a special manner in Algorithm 3 in order to provide the best performance. For convenience we introduce a parametric function δ_ε, $\varepsilon \in \mathbb{Z}$, defined on the set of all words in the alphabet $\{x_0^{\pm 1}, x_1^{\pm 1}, \ldots\}$ by

$$x_i^{\pm 1} \overset{\delta_\varepsilon}{\mapsto} x_{i+\varepsilon}^{\pm 1}.$$

The function δ_ε may not be defined for some negative ε on a given word $w = w(x_{i_1}^{\pm 1}, x_{i_2}^{\pm 1}, \ldots)$, but when it is used, it is assumed that the function is defined.

4.1 Merging Seminormal Forms

Consider first the case where a word w is a product of w_1 and w_2 given in seminormal forms. Let $w_1 = p_1 n_1$ and $w_2 = p_2 n_2$, where p_i and n_i ($i = 1, 2$) are the positive and negative parts of w_i. Clearly, one can arrange the rewriting process for $p_1 n_1 p_2 n_2$ by $\mathcal{R}$ the following way:

1) Rewrite the subword $n_1 p_2$ of w to a seminormal form $p_2' n_1'$. Denote by $w' = p_1 p_2' n_1' n_2$ the obtained result.
2) Rewrite the positive subword $p_1 p_2'$ of w' to a seminormal form p. Denote by $w'' = p n_1' n_2$ the obtained result.
3) Rewrite the negative subword $n_1' n_2$ of w'' to a seminormal form n. Denote by $w''' = p n$ the obtained result.

The word $w''' = p n$ is clearly in a seminormal form and $w =_F w'''$. This process can be depicted as follows:

$$p_1 \underbrace{n_1 p_2} n_2$$
$$\Downarrow$$
$$p_1 p_2' \underbrace{n_1' n_2}$$
$$\Downarrow$$
$$p n$$

The next algorithm performs the first rewriting step from the scheme above, and the following Lemma 2 asserts that it correctly performs the first step in linear time.

Algorithm 2 (Seminormal form of a product of negative and positive seminormal forms)

SIGNATURE. $w = Merge_{-,+}(n, p, \varepsilon_1, \varepsilon_2)$.

INPUT. *Seminormal forms n and p (where $n = x_{j_t}^{-1} \ldots x_{j_1}^{-1}$ and $p = x_{i_1} \ldots x_{i_s}$), and numbers $\varepsilon_1, \varepsilon_2 \in \mathbb{Z}$.*

OUTPUT. *Seminormal form w such that $w =_F \delta_{\varepsilon_1}(n) \delta_{\varepsilon_2}(p)$.*

COMPUTATIONS.

A) If $s = 0$ or $t = 0$ then output a product np.
B) If $j_1 + \varepsilon_1 = i_1 + \varepsilon_2$ then
    1) Compute $w = Merge_{-,+}(x_{j_t}^{-1} \ldots x_{j_2}^{-1}, x_{i_2} \ldots x_{i_s}, \varepsilon_1, \varepsilon_2)$.
    2) Output w.
C) If $j_1 + \varepsilon_1 < i_1 + \varepsilon_2$ then
    1) Compute $w = Merge_{-,+}(x_{j_t}^{-1} \ldots x_{j_2}^{-1}, x_{i_1} \ldots x_{i_s}, \varepsilon_1, \varepsilon_2 + 1)$.
    2) Output $wx_{j_1+\varepsilon_1}^{-1}$.
D) If $j_1 + \varepsilon_1 > i_1 + \varepsilon_2$ then
    1) Compute $w = Merge_{-,+}(x_{j_t}^{-1} \ldots x_{j_1}^{-1}, x_{i_2} \ldots x_{i_s}, \varepsilon_1 + 1, \varepsilon_2)$.
    2) Output $x_{i_1+\varepsilon_2} w$.

Lemma 2. *For any seminormal forms n and p (where $n = x_{j_t}^{-1} \ldots x_{j_1}^{-1}$ and $p = x_{i_1} \ldots x_{i_s}$) and numbers $\varepsilon_1, \varepsilon_2 \in \mathbb{Z}$ the output $w = Merge_{-,+}(n, p,, \varepsilon_1, \varepsilon_2)$ of Algorithm 2 is a seminormal form for $\delta_{\varepsilon_1}(n)\delta_{\varepsilon_2}(p)$. Furthermore, the time complexity required to compute w is bounded by $C(|n| + |p|)$ for some constant C.*

Proof. Since in each iteration we perform the constant number of elementary steps and in each subsequent iteration the sum $|n| + |p|$ is decreased by one, the time complexity of Algorithm 2 is linear.

We prove correctness of Algorithm 2 by induction on $|n| + |p|$. Assume that $|n| + |p| = 0$. Then at step A) we get output $w = np$ which is an empty word. Clearly, such w is a seminormal form for np, so the base of induction is done.

Assume that $|n| + |p| = N + 1$ and for any shorter word the statement is true. Consider four cases. If $|n| = 0$ or $|p| = 0$ then one of the words is trivial and, obviously, the product np is a correct output for this case. If $j_1 + \varepsilon_1 = i_1 + \varepsilon_2$ then $x_{j_1+\varepsilon_1}^{-1} x_{i_1+\varepsilon_2}$ cancels out inside of the product $\delta_{\varepsilon_1}(n)\delta_{\varepsilon_2}(p)$, and by the inductive assumption we are done.

If $j_1 + \varepsilon_1 < i_1 + \varepsilon_2$ then $j_1 + \varepsilon_1$ is the smallest index in $\delta_{\varepsilon_1}(n)\delta_{\varepsilon_2}(p)$ and therefore, using $\mathcal{R}$, the word $\delta_{\varepsilon_1}(n)\delta_{\varepsilon_2}(p)$ can be rewritten the following way:

$$\delta_{\varepsilon_1}(n)\delta_{\varepsilon_2}(p) = x_{j_t+\varepsilon_1}^{-1} \ldots x_{j_2+\varepsilon_1}^{-1} x_{j_1+\varepsilon_1}^{-1} x_{i_1+\varepsilon_1} \ldots x_{i_s+\varepsilon_2} \xrightarrow{\mathcal{R}}$$
$$\xrightarrow{\mathcal{R}} x_{j_t+\varepsilon_1}^{-1} \ldots x_{j_2+\varepsilon_1}^{-1} x_{i_1+\varepsilon_1+1} \ldots x_{i_s+\varepsilon_2+1} x_{j_1+\varepsilon_1}^{-1}$$

Note that since $j_1 + \varepsilon_1$ is the smallest index in $\delta_{\varepsilon_1}(n)\delta_{\varepsilon_2}(p)$, the smallest index in $w = Merge_{-,+}(x_{j_t}^{-1} \ldots x_{j_2}^{-1}, x_{i_2} \ldots x_{i_s}, \varepsilon_1, \varepsilon_2)$ is not less than $j_1 + \varepsilon_1$. By the inductive assumption, w is a seminormal form for $\delta_{\varepsilon_1}(x_{j_t}^{-1} \ldots x_{j_2}^{-1})\delta_{\varepsilon_2}(x_{i_2} \ldots x_{i_s})$. Therefore, $wx_{j_1+\varepsilon_2+1}^{-1} =_F \delta_{\varepsilon_1}(n)\delta_{\varepsilon_2}(p)$ and it is a seminormal form.

The last case where $j_1 + \varepsilon_1 > i_1 + \varepsilon_2$ is treated similarly.

Using ideas from Algorithm 2 one can easily implement an algorithm merging positive words and an algorithm merging negative words, so that statements similar to Lemma 2 would hold. We will denote these two algorithms by $Merge_{-,-}(n_1, n_2, \varepsilon_1, \varepsilon_2)$ and $Merge_{+,+}(p_1, p_2, \varepsilon_1, \varepsilon_2)$, respectively. Thus, computation of a seminormal form of a product of two arbitrary seminormal forms has the following form.

Algorithm 3 (Seminormal form of a product of seminormal forms)

SIGNATURE. $w = Merge(w_1, w_2)$.

INPUT. *Seminormal forms w_1 and w_2.*

OUTPUT. *Seminormal form w such that $w =_F w_1 w_2$.*

COMPUTATIONS.

A) *Represent w_i as a product of a positive and negative word ($w_1 = p_1 n_1$ and $w_2 = p_2 n_2$).*

B) *Compute $w' = Merge_{-,+}(n_1, p_2, 0, 0)$ and represent it as a product of a positive and negative word $w' = p_2' n_1'$.*

C) *Compute $w'' = Merge_{+,+}(p_1, p_2', 0, 0)$.*

D) *Compute $w''' = Merge_{-,-}(n_1', n_2, 0, 0)$.*

E) *Output $w'' w'''$.*

Lemma 3. *For any pair of seminormal forms w_1 and w_2 the word $w = Merge(w_1, w_2)$ is a seminormal form of the product $w_1 w_2$. Moreover, the time-complexity of computing w is bounded by $C(|w_1| + |w_2|)$ for some constant C.*

Proof. Follows from Lemma 2.

4.2   Seminormal Form Computation

Algorithm 4 (Seminormal form)

SIGNATURE. $u = SemiNormalForm(w)$.

INPUT. *A word w in generators of F.*

OUTPUT. *A seminormal form u such that $u = w$ in F.*

COMPUTATIONS.

A) *If $|w| \leq 1$ then output w.*

B) *Represent w as a product $w_1 w_2$ such that $|w_1| - |w_2| \leq 1$.*

C) *Recursively compute*
   $u_1 = SemiNormalForm(w_1)$ *and*
   $u_2 = SemiNormalForm(w_2)$.

D) *Let $u = Merge(u_1, u_2)$.*

E) *Output u.*

Lemma 4. *Let w be a word in generators of F. The output of Algorithm 4 on w is a seminormal form for w. The number of operations required for Algorithm 4 to terminate is $O(C|w| \log |w|)$, where C is a constant independent of w.*

Proof. The first statement can be proved by induction on the length of w. The base of the induction is the case where $|w| = 1$. In this case w is already in a seminormal form, and the output is correct. The induction step was proved in Lemma 3.

To prove the second statement we denote by $T(n)$ the number of steps required for Algorithm 4 to terminate on an input of length n. Then clearly

$$T(n) = 2T(\frac{n}{2}) + C \cdot n,$$

where the last summand $C \cdot n$ is the complexity of merging two seminormal forms with the sum of lengths at most $|n|$. It is an easy exercise to show that in this case $T(n) = O(C \cdot n \log n)$.

4.3   Normal Form Computation

The next lemma suggests how a pair of generators contradicting the property (NF2) can be removed and how all such pairs can be found.

Lemma 5. *Let* $w = x_{i_1} \ldots x_{i_s} x_{j_t}^{-1} \ldots x_{j_1}^{-1}$ *be a seminormal form,* $(x_{i_a}, x_{j_b}^{-1})$ *be the pair of generators in* w *which contradicts (NF2), where* a *and* b *are maximal with this property. Let*

$$w' = x_{i_1} \ldots x_{i_{a-1}} \delta_{-1}(x_{i_{a+1}} \ldots x_{i_s} x_{j_t}^{-1} \ldots x_{j_{b+1}}^{-1}) x_{j_{b-1}}^{-1} \ldots x_{j_1}^{-1}.$$

Then w' *is in a seminormal form and* $w =_F w'$. *Moreover, if* $(x_{i_c}, x_{j_d}^{-1})$ *is the pair of generators in* w' *which contradicts (NF2) (where* a *and* b *are maximal with this property), then* $c < a$ *and* $d < b$.

Proof. It follows from the definition of (NF2) and seminormal forms that all indices in $x_{i_{a+1}} \ldots x_{i_s} x_{j_t}^{-1} \ldots x_{j_{b+1}}^{-1}$ are greater than $i_a + 1$ and, therefore, indices in $\delta_{-1}(x_{i_{a+1}} \ldots x_{i_s} x_{j_t}^{-1} \ldots x_{j_{b+1}}^{-1})$ are greater than i_a. Now it is clear that w' is a seminormal form. Then doing rewrites opposite to rewrites from $\mathcal{R}$ we can get the word w' from the word w. Thus, $w =_F w'$.

There are two possible cases: either $c > a$ and $d > b$ or $c < a$ and $d < b$. We need to show that the former case is, in fact, impossible. Assume, by way of contradiction, that $c > a$ and $d > b$. Now observe that if $(x_{i_a}, x_{j_b}^{-1})$ is a pair of generators in w contradicting (NF2), then $(x_{i_a+\varepsilon}, x_{j_b+\varepsilon}^{-1})$ contradicts (NF2) in $\delta_\varepsilon(w)$. Therefore, inequalities $c > a$ and $d > b$ contradict the choice of a and b.

By Lemma 5 we can start looking for bad pairs in a seminormal form starting from the middle of a word. The next algorithm implements this idea. The algorithm is in two parts. The first part finds all "bad" pairs starting from the middle of a given w, and the second part applies δ_ε to segments where it is required. A notable feature of Algorithm 5 is that it does not apply the operator δ_{-1} immediately (as in w' of Lemma 5) when a bad pair is found, but instead, it keeps the information about how indices must be changed later. This information is accumulated in two sequences (stacks), one for the positive subword of w, the other one for the negative subword of w. Also, in Algorithm 5, the size of stack S_1 (or S_2) equals the length of an auxiliary word w_1 (resp. w_2). Therefore, at step B), x_a (resp. x_b) is defined if and only if ε_1 (resp. ε_2) is defined.

Algorithm 5 (Erasing bad pairs from a seminormal form)
SIGNATURE. $w = EraseBadPairs(u)$.
INPUT. *A seminormal form* $u = x_{i_1} \ldots x_{i_s} x_{j_t}^{-1} \ldots x_{j_1}^{-1}$.
OUTPUT. *A word* w *which is the normal form of* u.
INITIALIZATION. *Let* $\delta = 0$, $\delta_1 = 0$, $\delta_2 = 0$, $w_1 = 1$, *and* $w_2 = 1$. *Let* $u_1 = x_{i_1} \ldots x_{i_s}$ *and* $u_2 = x_{j_t}^{-1} \ldots x_{j_1}^{-1}$ *be the positive and negative parts of* u. *Additionally, we set up two empty stacks* S_1 *and* S_2.

COMPUTATIONS.

A. Let the current $u_1 = x_{i_1} \ldots x_{i_s}$ and $u_2 = x_{j_t}^{-1} \ldots x_{j_1}^{-1}$.

B. Let x_a be the leftmost letter of w_1, x_b the rightmost letter of w_2, and ε_i $(i = 1, 2)$ the top element of S_i, i.e., the last element that was put there. If any of these values does not exist (because, say, S_i is empty), then the corresponding variable is not defined.

    1) If $s > 0$ and $(t = 0$ or $i_s > j_t)$, then:
       a) multiply w_1 on the left by x_{i_s} (i.e. $w_1 \leftarrow x_{i_s} w_1$);
       b) erase x_{i_s} from u_1;
       c) push 0 into S_1;
       d) goto 5).

    2) If $t > 0$ and $(s = 0$ or $j_t > i_s)$, then:
       a) multiply w_2 on the right by $x_{j_t}^{-1}$ (i.e. $w_2 \leftarrow w_2 x_{j_t}^{-1}$);
       b) erase $x_{j_t}^{-1}$ from u_2;
       c) push 0 into S_2;
       d) goto 5).

    3) If $i_s = j_t$ and (the numbers $a - \varepsilon_1$ and $b - \varepsilon_2$ (those that are defined) are not equal to i_s or $i_s + 1$), then:
       a) erase x_{i_s} from u_1;
       b) erase $x_{j_t}^{-1}$ from u_2;
       c) if S_1 is not empty, increase the top element of S_1;
       d) if S_2 is not empty, increase the top element of S_2;
       e) goto 5).

    4) If 1)-3) are not applicable (when $i_s = j_t$ and (one of the numbers $a - \varepsilon_1$, $b - \varepsilon_2$ is defined and is equal to either i_s or $i_s + 1$)), then:
       a) multiply w_1 on the left by x_{i_s} (i.e. $w_1 \leftarrow x_{i_s} w_1$);
       b) multiply w_2 on the right by $x_{j_t}^{-1}$ (i.e. $w_2 \leftarrow w_2 x_{j_t}^{-1}$);
       c) erase x_{i_s} from u_1;
       d) erase $x_{j_t}^{-1}$ from u_2;
       e) push 0 into S_1;
       f) push 0 into S_2;
       g) goto 5).

    5) If u_1 or u_2 is not empty then goto 1).

C. While w_1 is not empty:
    1) let x_{i_1} be the first letter of w_1 (i.e. $w_1 = x_{i_1} \cdot w_1'$);
    2) take (pop) c from the top of S_1 and add to δ_1 (i.e. $\delta_1 \leftarrow \delta_1 + c$);
    3) multiply u_1 on the right by $x_{i_1 - \delta_1}$ (i.e. $u_1 \leftarrow u_1 x_{i_1 - \delta_1}$);
    4) erase x_{i_1} from w_1.

D. While w_2 is not empty:
    1) let $x_{j_1}^{-1}$ be the last letter of w_2 (i.e. $w_2 = w_2' \cdot x_{j_1}^{-1}$);
    2) take (pop) c from the top of S_2 and add to δ_2 (i.e. $\delta_2 \leftarrow \delta_2 + c$);
    3) multiply u_2 on the left by $x_{j_1 - \delta_2}^{-1}$ (i.e. $u_2 \leftarrow x_{j_1 - \delta_2}^{-1} u_2$);
    4) erase $x_{j_1}^{-1}$ from w_2.

E. Return $u_1 u_2$.

Proposition 3. *The output of Algorithm 5 is the normal form w of a seminormal form u. The number of operations required for Algorithm 5 to terminate is bounded by $D \cdot |u|$, where D is a constant independent of u.*

Proof. The first statement follows from Lemma 5. The time estimate is obvious from the algorithm since the words u_1, u_2 are processed letter-by-letter, and no letter is processed more than once.

As a corollary, we get the main result of this section:

Theorem 1. *In Thompson's group F, the normal form of a given word w can be computed in time $O(|w| \log |w|)$.*

References

1. I. Anshel, M. Anshel, D. Goldfeld, *An algebraic method for public-key cryptography*, Math. Res. Lett. **6** (1999), 287–291.
2. J. W. Cannon, W. J. Floyd, and W. R. Parry, *Introductory notes on Richard Thompson's groups*, L'Enseignement Mathematique (2) **42** (1996), 215–256.
3. J. C. Cha, K. H. Ko, S. J. Lee, J. W. Han, J. H. Cheon, *An Efficient Implementation of Braid Groups*, ASIACRYPT 2001, Lecture Notes in Comput. Sci. **2248** (2001), 144–156.
4. D. Hofheinz and R. Steinwandt, *A practical attack on some braid group based cryptographic primitives*, in Public Key Cryptography, 6th International Workshop on Practice and Theory in Public Key Cryptography, PKC 2003 Proceedings, Y.G. Desmedt, ed., Lecture Notes in Computer Science **2567**, pp. 187–198, Springer, 2002.
5. J. Hughes and A. Tannenbaum, *Length-based attacks for certain group based encryption rewriting systems*, Workshop SECI02 Securitè de la Communication sur Intenet, September 2002, Tunis, Tunisia.
   http://www.storagetek.com/hughes/
6. K. H. Ko, S. J. Lee, J. H. Cheon, J. W. Han, J. Kang, C. Park, *New public-key cryptosystem using braid groups*, Advances in cryptology—CRYPTO 2000 (Santa Barbara, CA), 166–183, Lecture Notes in Comput. Sci. **1880**, Springer, Berlin, 2000.
7. V. Shpilrain, *Assessing security of some group based cryptosystems*, Contemp. Math., Amer. Math. Soc. **360** (2004), 167–177.
8. V. Shpilrain and A. Ushakov, *The conjugacy search problem in public key cryptography: unnecessary and insufficient*, Applicable Algebra in Engineering, Communication and Computing, to appear.
   http://eprint.iacr.org/2004/321/
9. V. Shpilrain and G. Zapata, *Combinatorial group theory and public key cryptography*, Applicable Algebra in Engineering, Communication and Computing, to appear.
10. C. Sims, *Computation with finitely presented groups*, Encyclopedia of Mathematics and its Applications, **48**. Cambridge University Press, Cambridge, 1994.

Rainbow, a New Multivariable Polynomial Signature Scheme

Jintai Ding[1] and Dieter Schmidt[2]

[1] Department of Mathematical Sciences
University of Cincinnati
Cincinnati, OH, 45221, USA
ding@math.uc.edu
[2] Department of Electrical & Computer Engineering and Computer Science
University of Cincinnati
Cincinnati, OH, 45221, USA
dieter.schmidt@uc.edu

Abstract. Balanced Oil and Vinegar signature schemes and the unbalanced Oil and Vinegar signature schemes are public key signature schemes based on multivariable polynomials. In this paper, we suggest a new signature scheme, which is a generalization of the Oil-Vinegar construction to improve the efficiency of the unbalanced Oil and Vinegar signature scheme. The basic idea can be described as a construction of multi-layer Oil-Vinegar construction and its generalization. We call our system a Rainbow signature scheme. We propose and implement a practical scheme, which works better than Sflash^{v2}, in particular, in terms of signature generating time.

Keywords: public-key, multivariable, quadratic polynomials, Oil and Vinegar

1 Introduction

The subject we deal with here are generalizations of the Oil-Vinegar construction of public key authentication systems. It is part of a general effort to build secure and efficient public key authentication systems for practical applications, in particular, low cost smart cards. The key point of our work is the idea of a multi-layer Oil-Vinegar system. The main achievement is the creation of a multi-layer Oil-Vinegar system, which we call Rainbow. We show, that the system should be more secure and more efficient than any comparable system. The importance of the work lies in the potential application of the Rainbow system as a strongly secure and very efficient public key authentication system.

Since the arrival of the RSA cryptosystem people have been trying to build new public key cryptosystems. This includes systems based on multivariable polynomials. In particular, cryptosystems based on quadratic polynomials have undergone an intensive development in the last 10 years. The theoretical basis for these constructions is the proven theorem that solving a set of multivariable polynomial equations over a finite field, in general, is an NP-hard problem, although it does not necessarily guarantee the security of a multivariable cryptosystem.

J. Ioannidis, A. Keromytis, and M.Yung (Eds.): ACNS 2005, LNCS 3531, pp. 164–175, 2005.

This direction of research attracted a lot of attention with the appearance of the construction by Matsumoto and Imai [MI88]. However, Patarin [Pat95] proved that this scheme is insecure under an algebraic attack using linearization equations. Since then Patarin and his collaborators have made a great effort to develop secure multivariable cryptosystems.

One particular direction, which Patarin and his collaborators have pursued, is inspired by the linearization equations themselves. This type of construction includes Little Dragon, Dragon, Oil and Vinegar, Unbalanced Oil and Vinegar [Pat96,KPG99]. The construction of the last two schemes uses the idea that certain quadratic equations can be easily solved if we are allowed to guess a few variables. Let k be a finite field. The key construction is a map F from k^{o+v} to k^o:

$$F(x_1, .., x_o, x_1', .., x_v') = (F_1(x_1, .., x_o, x_1', .., x_v'), \ldots, F_o(x_1, .., x_o, x_1', .., x_v')),$$

and each F_l is in the form:

$$F_l(x_1, \ldots, x_o, x_1', \ldots, x_v') = \sum a_{l,i,j} x_i x_j' + \sum b_{l,i,j} x_i' x_j' + \sum c_{l,i} x_i + \sum d_{l,j} x_j' + e_l$$

where x_i, $i = 1, \ldots, o$, are the Oil variables and x_j', $j = 1, \ldots, v$, are the Vinegar variables in the finite field k. (Note the similarity of the above formula with the linearization equations.) We call such a type of polynomial an 'Oil and Vinegar polynomial'. The reason that it is called Oil and Vinegar scheme is due to the fact that in the quadratic terms the Oil and Vinegar variables are not fully mixed (like oil and vinegar). This allows us to find one solution easily for any equation of the form

$$F(x_1, \ldots, x_o, x_1', \ldots, x_v') = (y_1, \ldots, y_o),$$

when $(y_1, \ldots, y_o)$ is given. To find one solution, one just needs to randomly choose values for the Vinegar variables and plug them into the equations above, which will produce a set of o linear equations with o variables. This should, with a probability close to 1, give us a solution. If it does not, one can try again by selecting different values for the Vinegar variables, until one succeeds in finding a solution.

This family of cryptosystems is designed specifically for signature schemes, where we need only to find one solution for a given set of equations and not a unique solution.

Once we have this map F, we "hide" it by composing it from the left and the right sides by two invertible affine linear maps L_1 and L_2, in the same way as it was done in the construction of [MI88]. Since L_1 is on k^o and L_2 on k^{o+v}, this generates a quadratic map

$$\bar{F} = L_1 \circ F \circ L_2$$

from k^{o+v} to k^o ($\circ$ means composition of two maps).

The balanced Oil and Vinegar scheme is characterized by $o = v$, but it was defeated by Kipnis and Shamir [KS99] using matrices related to the bilinear forms defined by quadratic polynomials.

For the unbalanced Oil and Vinegar scheme, $v > o$, it was shown in [KPG99] that a specific attack has a complexity of roughly $q^{v-o-1}o^4$, when $v \approx o$. This means, that if o is not too large (< 100) and a given fixed field of size q, then $v - o$ should be large enough, but also not too large, to ensure the security of the scheme.

However, one must notice that in this scheme the document to be signed is a vector in k^o and the signature is a vector in k^{o+v}. This means that the signature is at least twice the size of the document and with a large $v + o$ the system becomes less efficient.

We propose in this paper a new construction that uses the Oil and Vinegar construction multiple times such that in the end the signature will be only slightly longer than the document. This scheme is therefore much more efficient. It is called Rainbow.

In the next section, we present the general construction and a practical example. Then we give a general cryptanalysis. We compare our scheme with Sflash and the original unbalanced Oil and Vinegar schemes. Finally we discuss ways to optimize the scheme and to generalize it further.

2   Rainbow, a Signature Scheme

In this section, we present first the general construction of Rainbow and then give an example of its practical implementation.

2.1   General Construction of Rainbow

Let S be the set $\{1, 2, 3, \ldots, n\}$. Let $v_1, \ldots, v_u$ be u integers such that $0 < v_1 < v_2 < \cdots < v_u = n$, and define the sets of integers $S_l = \{1, 2, \ldots, v_l\}$ for $l = 1, \ldots, u$, so that we have

$$S_1 \subset S_2 \subset \cdots \subset S_u = S.$$

The number of elements in S_i is v_i.

Let

$$o_i = v_{i+1} - v_i, \text{ for } i = 1, \ldots, u - 1.$$

Let O_i be the set such that

$$O_i = S_{i+1} - S_i, \text{ for } i = 1, \ldots, u - 1.$$

Let P_l be the linear space of quadratic polynomials spanned by polynomials of the form

$$\sum_{i \in O_l, j \in S_l} \alpha_{i,j} x_i x_j + \sum_{i,j \in S_l} \beta_{i,j} x_i x_j + \sum_{i \in S_{l+1}} \gamma_i x_i + \eta$$

We can see that these are Oil and Vinegar type of polynomials such that x_i, $i \in O_l$ are the Oil variables and x_i, $i \in S_l$ are the Vinegar variables. We call x_i, $i \in O_l$ an l-th layer Oil variable and x_i, $i \in S_l$ an l-th layer Vinegar variable.

We call any polynomial in P_l an l-th layer Oil and Vinegar polynomial. Clearly we have $P_i \subset P_j$ for $i < j$.

In this way, each P_l, $l = 1, \ldots, u - 1$ is a set of Oil and Vinegar polynomials. Each polynomial in P_l has x_i, $i \in O_l$ as its Oil variables and x_i, $i \in S_l$ as its Vinegar variables. The Oil and Vinegar polynomials in P_i can be defined as polynomials such that $x_i \in O_i$ are the Oil variables and x_i, $i \in S_i$ are the Vinegar variables. This can be illustrated by the fact that

$$S_{i+1} = \{S_i, O_i\}.$$

Now, we will define the map F of the Rainbow signature scheme. It is a map F from k^n to k^{n-v_1} such that

$$F(x_1, \ldots, x_n) = (\tilde{F}_1(x_1, \ldots, x_n), \ldots, \tilde{F}_{u-1}(x_1, \ldots, x_n))$$

$$= (F_1(x_1, \ldots, x_n), \ldots, F_{n-v_1}(x_1, \ldots, x_n)),$$

each $\tilde{F}_i$ consists of o_i randomly chosen quadratic polynomials from P_i. By a randomly chosen polynomial, we mean that we choose its coefficients at random.

In this way, we can see that F actually has $u - 1$ layers of Oil and Vinegar constructions. The first layer consists of o_1 polynomials $F_1, \ldots, F_{o_1}$ such that x_j, $j \in O_1$ are the Oil variables and x_j, $j \in S_1$ are the Vinegar variables. The i-th layer consists of o_i polynomials, $F_{v_i+1}, \ldots, F_{v_{i+1}}$, such that x_j, $j \in O_i$ are the Oil variables and x_j, $j \in S_i$ are the Vinegar variables. From this, we can build a rainbow of our variables:

$$[x_1, \ldots, x_{v_1}]; \{x_{v_1+1}, \ldots, x_{v_2}\}$$

$$[x_1, \ldots, x_{v_1}, x_{v_1+1}, \ldots, x_{v_2}]; \{x_{v_2+1}, \ldots, x_{v_3}\}$$

$$[x_1, \ldots, x_{v_1}, x_{v_1+1}, \ldots, x_{v_2}, x_{v_2+1}, \ldots, x_{v_3}]; \{x_{v_3+1}, \ldots, x_{v_4}\}$$

$$\ldots ; \ldots$$

$$[x_1, \ldots, \ldots, \ldots, \ldots, \ldots, \ldots, \ldots, \ldots, \ldots, x_{v_{u-1}}]; \{x_{v_{u-1}+1}, \ldots, x_n\}$$

Each row above represents a layer of the Rainbow. For the l-th layer above, the ones in [ ] are Vinegar variables, the ones in { } are Oil variables and each layer's Vinegar variables consists of all the variables in the previous layer.

We call F a Rainbow polynomial map with $u - 1$ layers.

Let L_1 and L_2 be two randomly chosen invertible affine linear maps, L_1 is on k^{n-v_1} and L_2 on k^n.

Let

$$\bar{F}(x_1, \ldots, x_n) = L_1 \circ F \circ L_2(x_1, \ldots, x_n),$$

which consists of $n - v_1$ quadratic polynomials with n variables.

We will now use the above to construct a public key **Rainbow** signature scheme.

1. Public Key

For a Rainbow signature scheme, the public key consists of the $n - v_1$ polynomial components of $\bar{F}$ and the field structure of k.

2. Private Key

The private key consists of the maps L_1, L_2 and F.

3. Signing a Document

To sign a document, which is an element $Y' = (y'_1, \ldots, y'_{n-v_1})$ in k^{n-v_1}, one needs to find a solution of the equation

$$L_1 \circ F \circ L_2(x_1, \ldots, x_n) = \bar{F}(x_1, \ldots, x_n) = Y'.$$

We can apply the inverse of L_1 first, then we have

$$F \circ L_2(x_1, \ldots, x_n) = L_1^{-1}Y' = \bar{Y}'.$$

Next we need to invert F. In this case, we need to solve the equation

$$F(x_1, \ldots, x_n) = \bar{Y}' = (\bar{y}'_1, \ldots, \bar{y}'_{n-v_1}).$$

We first randomly choose the values of $x_1, \ldots, x_{v_1}$ and plug them into the first layer of o_1 equations given by

$$\tilde{F}_1 = (\bar{y}'_1, \ldots, \bar{y}'_{o_1}).$$

This produces a set of o_1 linear equations with o_1 variables, $x_{o_1+1}, \ldots, x_{v_2}$, which we solve to find the values of $x_{o_1+1}, \ldots, x_{v_2}$. Then we have all the values of x_i, $i \in S_2$.

Then we plug these values into the second layer of polynomials, which will again produce o_2 number of linear equations, which then gives us the values of all x_i, $i \in S_3$. We repeat the procedure until we find a solution.

If at any time, a set of linear equations does not have a solution, we will start from the beginning again by choosing another set of values for $x_1, \ldots, x_{v_1}$. We will continue until we find a solution. We know from [Pat96], that with a very high probability we can expect to succeed if the number of layers is not too large.

Then we apply the inverse of L_2, which gives us a signature of Y', which we will denote by $X' = (x'_1, \ldots, x'_n)$.

4 Verifying the Signature

To verify a signature, one only needs to check if indeed

$$\tilde{F}(X') = Y'.$$

In order to sign a large document, one can go through the same procedure for Flash as in [PCG01] by applying a hash function first, then sign the hash value of the document.

2.2   A Practical Implementation of Rainbow

For a practical implementation we have chosen k to be a finite field of size $q = 2^8$.

Let $n = 33$ and S be the set $\{1, 2, 3, \ldots, 33\}$.

Let $u = 5$ and $v_1 = 6$, $v_2 = 12$, $v_3 = 17$, $v_4 = 22$, $v_5 = 33$.

We have $o_1 = 6$, $o_2 = 5$, $o_3 = 5$, $o_4 = 11$.

In this case, both $\bar{F}$ and F are maps from k^{33} to k^{27}.

The public key consists of 27 quadratic polynomials with 33 variables. The total number of coefficients for the public key is $27 \times 34 \times 35/2 = 16,065$, or about 15 KB of storage.

The private key consists of 11 polynomials with 22 Vinegar variables and 11 Oil variables, 5 polynomials with 17 Vinegar and 5 Oil variables, 5 polynomials with 12 Vinegar and 5 Oil variables, and 6 polynomials with 6 Vinegar and 6 Oil variables plus the two affine linear transformations L_1 and L_2. The total size is about 10 KB.

This signature scheme signs a document of size $8 \times 27 = 216$ bits with a signature of $8 \times 33 = 264$ bits.

3   Cryptanalysis

We will present a short cryptanalysis of the Rainbow signature scheme by looking at the cryptanalysis of the example above. There are several ways to attack, which we will deal with one by one. For those methods where quadratic forms are used one has to remember that the theory of quadratic forms over finite fields is different when the characteristic is 2 compared to the case when the characteristic is odd [D09].

3.1   Method of Rank Reduction

In [CSV97] a method of rank reduction is used to break the birational permutation signature scheme of Shamir. The reason this attack could work is that the space spanned by the polynomial components of the cipher of Shamir's scheme consists of a flag of spaces:

$$V_1 \subset V_2 \subset \cdots \subset V_t,$$

where V_t is the space spanned by the polynomial components of the cipher, each V_i is a proper subset of V_{i+1} and the rank of the corresponding bilinear form corresponding to the elements in $V_{i+1} - V_i$ is strictly larger than the ones in V_i and the difference of the dimensions between V_i and V_{i+1} is exactly 1. Due to these properties, in particular the last one, it allows one to easily find this flag of spaces, namely all the V_i by first finding V_{n-1} then V_{n-2} and so on by rank reduction.

But this attack method can not work against our scheme anymore. The reason for this is that even though in our case, there also exists such a flag of spaces such that

1) the number of components is exactly the number of layers;
2) the dimension of each component of the flag corresponds exactly to the one of V_{i+1}, $i = 1, \ldots, u - 1$;

but

3) the difference in the dimensions of the last two big spaces is exactly O_{u-1}, which we have chosen specifically to be a rather large number 11 unlike in Shamir's case where it is 1.

The property 3) above is exactly the reason why the attack in [CSV97] can not work anymore. The rank reduction method can not be used here due to the fact that $o_{u-1} = 11$ and no longer 1. The "thick last layer of Oil" enables our scheme to resist the rank reduction attack in [CSV97].

3.2 Method of Attack for Oil-Vinegar Schemes

One can see that the action of L_1 is to mix all polynomial components of F. Therefore, each component of the cipher $\bar{F}$ now belongs to the top layer of Oil-Vinegar polynomials, namely they are all elements in P_4. These are Oil and Vinegar polynomials with 22 Vinegar variables and 11 Oil variables.

We can apply the method in [KPG99] for an unbalanced Oil and Vinegar signature scheme in order to try to attack the system, which will allow us to separate the top layer Oil and Vinegar variables. For this, what we need to do is to separate the top (or the final) layer of 11 Oil variables and 22 Vinegar variables. According to the cryptanalysis in [KPG99], the attack complexity of this first step is $q^{22-11-1} \times 11^4 > 2^{90}$.

3.3 Method of Minrank

There are two totally different ways of using the Minrank method. The first one is to search for the polynomial whose associated matrix has the lowest rank among all possible choices. This set of polynomials with 6 Vinegar and 6 Oil variables belongs to the first layer, that is P_1, and was denoted by $\tilde{F}_1$. To do this, we first associate to each polynomial a bilinear form, which has a matrix of size 33×33. We then can use linear combinations of the matrices associated with the components of $\bar{F}$ to derive a polynomial, whose associated matrix has rank 12.

Now, to attack the system, the problem becomes a search for a rank 12 matrix among a group of 27 matrices of size 33×33. From the Minrank method [Cou01] we know that the complexity to find such a matrix is $q^{12} \times 27^3$, which is much larger than 2^{100}.

Another possibility it to search for polynomials corresponding to the polynomials in the second last layer, namely the one that belong to P_3 and come from linear combinations of $\tilde{F}_i$, $i < 4$. In this case, the Minrank method definitely can not be used, because those are of rank 22 in general. One way surely is to randomly search for it. Because the dimension of P_3 is 16, this becomes a problem to search for an element in a subspace of dimension 16 in a total space of dimension 27. Therefore, such a random search needs at least q^{11} searches to find one, but we also need to determine if indeed the rank is lower than 22 for each search. In this case, the total complexity should be at least $q^{11} \times (22 \times 33^2/3) > 2^{100}$. This attack idea is actually related to the attack method in [CSV97], and the argument above explains why the method in [CSV97] can no longer work.

From the most recent e-print results in this direction [WBP], where they study a very general system called STS, we know that their method can also be applied to our case. In accordance with their estimate, the security of our system is at least $27 \times 33^3 \times (2^8)^{12} \times 5 > 2^{100}$

3.4 The Attack Using the Structure of Multi-layers

For the case of Matsumoto-Imai cryptosystem, Patarin [Pat95] realized that if the cipher is made of several independent parallel "branches", we can perform a separation of variables such that all polynomials in the cipher are derived as linear combinations of polynomials over each group of variables. This property actually can be used to attack the system. At first glance, one would think that our layers look like different "branches". Nevertheless, one should realize that our layers are in no way "independent", because each layer is build upon the previous one. In simple terms one can say that all layers stick together and there is no way we can do any kind of separation of variables. This is clear by looking at the polynomials in the last layer P_4. Therefore the attack using the property of the parallel independent branches in [Pat95] cannot work here. Similarly one can argue that the attack using syszygies cannot work here neither, due to the fact there are no branches and everything is actually "glued together".

3.5 General Methods

Other methods that could be used to attack our signature scheme are those, which solve polynomial equations directly, for example the XL method and its various generalizations, or those, which use Gröbner bases.

Surely, it is very difficult to solve a set of 27 equations with 33 variables, because there are too many solutions for this set of equations. In general, it is much better to solve an equation with only one variable.

Because of the nature of design of our system, one can guess the values for any set of $v_1 = 6$ variables and we have the probability $1/e < 1/2.71828 < 0.37$ to have a unique solution. Now the problem becomes a problem to solve a set of 27 quadratic equations with 33 variables. We should think of it as if it is a set of randomly chosen quadratic equations. According to what is commonly believed, to solve this set of equations, the complexity is at least $2^{3 \times 27} > 2^{81}$.

From this we conclude that the total complexity to attack our example is at least 2^{80}.

3.6 General Security Analysis

From the discussion above, we can see that in order to attack the system, one can approach it either from the top layer or form the bottom layer. The security of the bottom layer depends on how effectively the Minrank method can be used. The attack complexity in general is $q^{(v_2-1)}o_{u-1}^3$ if $v_1 > o_1$ or $q^{2v_1}o_{u-1}^3$ if $v_1 \leq o_1$. From this we know that we can not let $v_2 = o_1 + v_1$ be too small.

From the most recent e-print results [WBP], the security of our system is at least $(n - v_1) \times n^3 \times (q)^{o_1+v_1} \times u$, which surely requires $o_1 + v_1$ not to be small.

172 Jintai Ding and Dieter Schmidt

As for the case of attack from the top, the attack method for unbalanced Oil and Vinegar method tells us that $v_{u-1} - o_{u-1}$ can not be too small. Also to avoid random search attacks o_{u-1} should not be too small.

4 Comparison with Other Multivariable Signature Schemes

In this section, we will present the differences between our new system and two similar multivariable cryptosystems, the unbalanced Oil and Vinegar scheme and the Sflash scheme.

4.1 Comparison with Unbalanced Oil and Vinegar

First, our new system is a generalization of the original Oil and Vinegar construction and the original scheme can be interpreted as just a single layer Rainbow scheme, where $u = 2$.

Let us assume that we want to build an unbalanced Oil and Vinegar scheme, which has the same length for a document that can be signed as our practical example above.

In this case, we choose k again to be a finite field of size $q = 2^8$ and we know that the number of Oil variables should be 27. Because of the attack for unbalance Oil and Vinegar schemes [KPG99], we know that the number of Vinegar variables should be at least $27 + 11 = 38$ in order to have the same level of security.

In this case, the public key consists of 27 polynomials with $38 + 27 = 65$ variables. The size of public key is therefore $27 \times (67 \times 66/2)$ bytes, which is about 116 KB, about 10 times the size of our practical example. This implies that the public computation of verifying the signature will take at least 10 times as long.

The private key for the unbalanced Oil and Vinegar scheme consists of one affine linear transformation on k^{27} and another one on k^{65} and a set of 27 Oil and Vinegar polynomials with 27 Oil variables and 38 Vinegar variables. This means that the private key is about 40 KB. This implies that the private calculation to sign the document will take about four times longer compared to our example.

The length of the signature is $65 \times 8 = 520$ bits, which is also about twice the size of the signature of our example.

From this, we conclude that our scheme should be a much better choice in general in terms of both security and efficiency.

4.2 Sflash

NESSIE, New European Schemes for Signatures, Integrity, and Encryption, is a project within the Information Society Technologies Programme of the European Commission. It made its final selection of the crypto algorithm after a process of more than 2 years. (www.cosic.esat.kuleuven.ac.be/nessie)

Sflash^{v2}, a fast multivariate signature scheme was selected by the Nessie Consortium and was recommended for low-cost smart cards. However, due to security concerns, the designer of Sflash once recommended that Slash^{v2} should not be used, instead a new version Sflash^{v3} is recommended [PGC98]. It is a simple extension of Sflash^{v2} by increasing the length of the signature. Sflash^{v3} has the signature length of 469 bits and a public key of 112 KBytes. But more recently Sflash^{v2} was again deemed to be secure and we compared our implementation to that of Sflash^{v2}.

Sflash^{v2} has a signature of length $37 \times 7 = 259$ for a document of $26 \times 7 = 182$ bits. Our example has a signature of length $33 \times 8 = 264$ for a document of $27 \times 8 = 216$ bits. In terms of per bits efficiency the two are essentially the same.

For a comparison of the running times on a PC, we implemented Sflash^{v2} as described in [ACDG03]. The generation of the signature is about twice as fast for our example with Rainbow when compared to Sflash. The times for the verification of a signature is of course nearly identical.

From this, we conclude that our scheme should be a good choice in terms of both security and efficiency.

4.3   TTS

We can also compare our system with the new TTS schemes [YC03], but these schemes are broken as was shown in a presentation in IWAP'04 [DY04]. One should also see, that the Tractable Rational Map Signature, as presented in [WHLCY], is very similar to TTS and can be viewed as a very special examples of our scheme.

5   Optimization of Rainbow and Further Generalization

Because of all the possible choices of the design, one has to ask what is the best design. In the practical example above, we presented a very simple realization of Rainbow to make it easier to understand. In this section, we will look at the possibility in general to optimize the scheme for both key size and computational efficiency under the same security requirement.

Let us assume that we want to build a rainbow system to sign a document of size $m \times r$ bits in the space k^n, where k is a finite field of size $q = 2^r$. A question one has to ask is: What is the most efficient choice, if we are given a requirement of a security level of 2^θ?

For a document of length m the length of the signature is $v_u = (m + v_1)$. The security level is determined on the one side by $2^{3r(v_2-1)}$ due the possibility of the Minrank attack. We should choose $v_1 > o_1$ to make the system more efficient, and from this we know that $v_2 = o_1 + v_1$ should be at least $1 + \theta/3r$. But if we want to make the signature as short as possible, the private key as small as possible, and the private calculations as easy as possible, we can see that we should choose v_1 and o_1 such that the difference between o_1 and v_1 should be 0 or 1.

Now assume that we have fixed v_2, o_1, and v_1 already. Due to the security requirement, we know that we should make sure that $q^{v_u - v_{u-1} - 1}(o_{u-1})^4$ is larger than 2^θ.

Let us assume that we have chosen $v_u - v_{u-1}$. The next choice are the layers in-between. Clearly, we can see that the best choice is $v_{i+1} = v_i + 1$, as it has the shortest secret key, the fastest computation speed and it does not affect at all the security of the system. In this case each $\tilde{F}_i$ has only one polynomial.

We suggest to further improve the scheme with an even better choice. For this we set all coefficients of any quadratic term to zero, which mixes the one Oil variable with its Vinegar variables at its layer, and only the coefficient of the linear term of Oil variable is chosen to be a nonzero element. This will ensure that the corresponding linear equation in the signing process always has a solution. It also makes the process faster and does not at all affect the security. We call this type of polynomial, a linear Oil and Vinegar polynomial.

If one wants to make sure to have the maximum probability for success in finding a signature, even the lowest layer should have the same construction, namely $v_2 - v_1 = 1$ and the Oil- and Vinegar polynomial is chosen in the same way. In this case, the only possible place for the signing process will be the top layer. This type of construction, can be viewed also as a combination of the Oil and Vinegar method with the method first suggested in [Sha98].

As for the case of an attack from the top, the attack method for unbalanced Oil and Vinegar method tells us that $v_{u-1} - o_{u-1}$ can not be too small. Also to avoid random search attack o_{u-1} should not be too small.

For example, we can improve our practical example such that $u = 13$ and $v_1 = 6$, $v_2 = 12$, $v_3 = 13$, $v_4 = 14, \ldots, v_{12} = 22$, $v_{13} = 33$, $o_1 = 6$, $o_2 = 1, \ldots, o_{11} = 1$, $o_{12} = 11$. This now is a 12 layer Rainbow scheme.

Another possibility for optimization is to use sparse polynomials when we choose at random the coefficients of the Oil-Vinegar polynomials. Nevertheless, this is a very subtle and delicate task, as it opens up the possibility of new, often hidden and unexpected weakness. The use of sparse polynomial in the new TTS scheme caused it to be broken in [DY04]. Therefore we strongly suggest that such a method should not be used except if one can establish a way to prove that the security level has not been changed.

6 Conclusion

In this paper, we presented a generalization of the Oil and Vinegar signature scheme. It, in general, improves the efficiency of the system. We also suggested to further improve the system by using linear Oil and Vinegar polynomials. We believe that our construction produces excellent multivariable polynomial signature schemes for practical applications.

Acknowledgments

We would like to thank the referees for their helpful comments. The first author also would like to thank the Charles Phelps Taft Research Center for travel support, and Lei Hu, Louis Goubin and Tsuyoshi Takagi for their useful discussions.

References

[ACDG03] Mehdi-Laurent Akkar, Nicolas T. Courtois, Romain Duteuil, and Louis Goubin. A fast and secure implementation of Sflash. In *PKC 2003, LNCS*, volume 2567, pages 267–278. Springer, 2003.

[Cou01] Nicolas T. Courtois. The security of hidden field equations (HFE). In C. Naccache, editor, *Progress in cryptology, CT-RSA, LNCS*, volume 2020, pages 266–281. Springer, 2001.

[CSV97] D. Coppersmith, J. Stern, and S. Vaudenay. The security of the birational permutation signature schemes. *J. Cryptology*, 10(3):207–221, 1997.

[D09] Dickson, Leonard Eugene. Definite forms in a finite field. *Trans. Amer. Math. Soc.*, volume 10, pages 109–122, 1909.

[DY04] Jintai Ding and Z Yin. Cryptanalysis of TTS and Tame–like signature schemes. In *Third International Workshop on Applied Public Key Infrastructures*. Springer, 2004.

[KPG99] Aviad Kipnis, Jacques Patarin, and Louis Goubin. Unbalanced oil and vinegar signature schemes. In *Eurocrypt'99, LNCS*, volume 1592, pages 206–222. Springer, 1999.

[KS99] Aviad Kipnis and Adi Shamir. Cryptanalysis of the HFE public key cryptosystem by relinearization. In M. Wiener, editor, *Advances in cryptology – Crypto '99, LNCS*, volume 1666, pages 19–30. Springer, 1999.

[MI88] T. Matsumoto and H. Imai. Public quadratic polynomial-tuples for efficient signature verification and message encryption. In C. G. Guenther, editor, *Advances in cryptology – EUROCRYPT '88, LNCS*, volume 330, pages 419–453. Springer, 1988.

[Pat95] J. Patarin. Cryptanalysis of the Matsumoto and Imai public key scheme of Eurocrypt'88. In D. Coppersmith, editor, *Advances in Cryptology – Crypto '95, LNCS*, volume 963, pages 248–261, 1995.

[Pat96] J. Patarin. Hidden field equations (HFE) and isomorphism of polynomials (IP): Two new families of asymmetric algorithms. In U. Maurer, editor, *Eurocrypt'96, LNCS*, volume 1070, pages 33–48. Springer, 1996.

[PCG01] Jacques Patarin, Nicolas Courtois, and Louis Goubin. Flash, a fast multivariate signature algorithm. In *LNCS*, volume 2020, pages 298–307. Springer, 2001.

[PGC98] Jacques Patarin, Louis Goubin, and Nicolas Courtois. C^*_{-+} and HM: variations around two schemes of T. Matsumoto and H. Imai. In K. Ohta and D. Pei, editors, *ASIACRYPT'98, LNCS*, volume 1514, pages 35–50. Springer, 1998.

[Sha98] Adi Shamir. Efficient signature schemes based on birational permutations. In *LNCS, Advances in cryptology – CRYPTO '98 (Santa Barbara, CA, 1998)*, volume 1462, pages 257–266. Springer, 1998.

[WHLCY] Lih-Chung Wang, Yuh-Hua Hu, Feipei Lai, Chun-Yen Chou, Bo-Yin Yang Tractable Rational Map Signature In Serge Vaudenay, editors, *Public Key Cryptosystems, PKC-2005, LNCS*, volume 3386, pages 244-257 Springer, 2005.

[WBP] Christopher Wolf, An Braeken, and Bart Preneel. Efficient cryptanalysis of RSE(2)PKC and RSSE(2)PKC. http://eprint.iacr.org/2004/237.

[YC03] B. Yang and J. Chen. A more secure and efficacious TTS signature scheme. *ICISC'03*, 2003. http://eprint.iacr.org/2003/160

Badger – A Fast and Provably Secure MAC

Martin Boesgaard, Thomas Christensen, and Erik Zenner

CRYPTICO A/S
Fruebjergvej 3
2100 Copenhagen
Denmark
info@cryptico.com

Abstract. We present Badger, a new fast and provably secure MAC based on universal hashing. In the construction, a modified tree hash that is more efficient than standard tree hashing is used and its security is proven. Furthermore, in order to derive the core hash function of the tree, we use a novel technique for reducing Δ-universal function families to universal families. The resulting MAC is very efficient on standard platforms both for short and long messages. As an example, for a 64-bit tag, it achieves performances up to 2.2 and 1.3 clock cycles per byte on a Pentium III and Pentium 4 processor, respectively. The forgery probability is at most $2^{-52.2}$.

Keywords: MAC, universal hash, tree, pseudo-random generator

1 Introduction

A Message Authentication Code (MAC) provides a way to detect whether a message has been tampered with during transmission. The usual model for authentication includes three participants: a transmitter, a receiver and an opponent. The transmitter sends a message over an insecure channel, where the opponent can introduce new messages as well as alter existing ones. Insertion of a new message by the opponent is called impersonation, and modification of an existing message by the opponent is called substitution. In both cases the opponent's goal is to deceive the receiver into believing that the new message is authentic.

In many applications, it is of significant importance that the receiver can verify the integrity of a message. In some cases this is even more important than encryption [13]. Often encryption and authentication are both required. With the emergence of fast software-based encryption algorithms like Rijndael [9], SNOW [11], Rabbit [7] etc., the need for fast software-based message authentication codes is increasing. Some attempts have been made to construct integrated MAC and encryption algorithms, e.g. Helix [14]. However, such approaches make it hard to prove the security of the MAC part. In contrast, MACs that can be proven secure with respect to an underlying cryptographic primitive exist. Prominent examples are HMAC [17] and the universal hashing approach [8].

The construction presented here is based on the universal hashing paradigm introduced by Carter and Wegman [8, 27]. They proposed to hash a given message with a randomly chosen function from a strongly universal family of hash

J. Ioannidis, A. Keromytis, and M.Yung (Eds.): ACNS 2005, LNCS 3531, pp. 176–191, 2005.
© Springer-Verlag Berlin Heidelberg 2005

functions, whereafter the output is encrypted with a one-time-pad (OTP) in order to obtain the MAC tag. Since universal hash functions are only required to fulfill, in a cryptographical sense, a rather simple combinatorial property, they can usually be constructed to be very fast. Recent research has been successful in achieving high speed for long messages. Notable examples can be found in [4, 5, 12, 15, 23]. However, for short messages, these algorithms lose some of their efficiency due to initialization and finalization overhead; a problem that was addressed, e.g., by Poly1305 [2] and by new versions of UMAC [18].

It is the aim of this paper to construct a Wegman-Carter based MAC which is fast on both short and long messages. The performance on short messages is important, as e.g. the MAC function used in IPsec operates on 43-1500 bytes (see chapter 3 of [18]) and the MAC function used in TLS operates on 0-17 kilobytes. In addition, the setup procedure must be simple and fast, as the number of messages and amount of data processed per setup is small in many applications, e.g. TLS. Finally, the MAC should provide verifier-selectable assurance[1].

In order to achieve high performance we introduce new families of universal hash functions especially well suited for tree-like hashing. These are obtained using a novel technique for reducing Δ-universal hash families to universal hash families. This results in significant performance gains for small compressions. Furthermore, we develop an effective tree-like hashing procedure which basically consists of combining a tree hash with a linear hash. The construction is provably secure (relative to a cryptographic primitive) with simple proofs.

Organization: The paper is organized as follows. In section 2 we present the definitions of the different classes of universal hash families, we review composition theorems and sketch our construction. In section 3 we introduce a simple method to reduce Δ-universal hash families to universal hash families. A modification of the standard tree hashing scheme is presented in section 4. Section 5 discusses how to build a strongly universal hash family from this scheme. Section 6 contains the specification of Badger, and performance results are presented in section 7. We conclude in section 8.

2 Universal Hashing and Message Authentication

In 1981, Wegman and Carter [27] showed that randomly chosen elements from a strongly universal hash function family can be used to compress a given message and encrypt the output using a OTP[2]. We describe briefly in the following why this is possible, and how it will be used in our design.

---

[1] For a more detailed description of verifier-selectable assurance, see [18]. In short, this means that the receiver can choose to verify to lower assurance levels than for the full tag in order to increase performance.

[2] Of course, a cryptographic pseudo-random generator (PRG) can also be used to generate a pseudo-random pad, but then the security depends on the security of the PRG, as described in [20].

Universal hash function families: The following definitions of universal hash function families are well-known from the literature.

Definition 1. *[8, 24] An ϵ-almost universal (ϵ-AU) family H of hash functions maps from a set A to a set B, such that for any distinct elements $a, a' \in A$:*

$$\Pr_{h \in H} [h(a) = h(a')] \leq \epsilon \tag{1}$$

H is universal (U) if $\epsilon = 1/|B|$.

Definition 2. *[16, 26] Let $(B, +)$ be an Abelian group. A family H of hash functions that maps from a set A to the set B is said to be ϵ-almost Δ-universal (ϵ-AΔU) w.r.t. $(B, +)$, if for any distinct elements $a, a' \in A$ and for all $\delta \in B$:*

$$\Pr_{h \in H} [h(a) - h(a') = \delta] \leq \epsilon \tag{2}$$

H is Δ-universal (ΔU) if $\epsilon = 1/|B|$.

Definition 3. *[24, 27] An ϵ-almost strongly-universal (ϵ-ASU) family H of hash functions maps from a set A to a set B, such that for any distinct elements $a, a' \in A$ and all $b, b' \in B$:*

$$\Pr_{h \in H} [h(a) = b] = 1/|B| \qquad and \tag{3}$$

$$\Pr_{h \in H} [h(a) = b, h(a') = b'] \leq \epsilon/|B| \tag{4}$$

H is strongly universal (SU) if $\epsilon = 1/|B|$.

The Wegman-Carter MAC: From the definitions it follows that strongly universal hashing can be used for message authentication. If we denote the probability for an impersonation attack to succeed by P_i and the probability for a substitution attack to succeed by P_s, we have the following theorem:

Theorem 1. *[22, 25, 27] There exists an ϵ-ASU family of hash functions from A to B if and only if there exists an authentication code with $|A|$ messages, $|B|$ authenticators and $k = |H|$ keys, such that $P_i = 1/|B|$ and $P_s \leq \epsilon$.*

The particular Wegman-Carter MAC can be defined as follows:

Definition 4. *Given an ϵ-ASU family $\mathcal{H}$ of hash functions mapping from a set A to a set B, a nonce n, and an OTP $r(n)$, then the Wegman-Carter MAC is*

$$\mathrm{MAC}_{\mathrm{WC}}(M; h, r(n)) = h(M) \oplus r(n), \tag{5}$$

where h is a random hash function from $\mathcal{H}$ and M is the message.

A new nonce must be used for each application of the MAC to ensure the unconditional security of the construction.

Composition rules: Hash families can be combined in order to obtain new hash families. The below composition rules (see [25]) describe what happens to the resulting ϵ, domains, and ranges.

Composition 1 *If there exists an ϵ_1-AU family H_1 of hash functions from A to B and an ϵ_2-AU family H_2 of hash functions from B to C, then there exists an ϵ-AU family H of hash functions from A to C, where $H = H_1 \times H_2$, $|H| = |H_1| \cdot |H_2|$, and $\epsilon = \epsilon_1 + \epsilon_2 - \epsilon_1\epsilon_2$.*

Composition 2 *If there exists an ϵ_1-AU family H_1 of hash functions from A to B and an ϵ_2-ASU family H_2 of hash functions from B to C, then there exists an ϵ-ASU family H of hash functions from A to C, where $H = H_1 \times H_2$, $|H| = |H_1| \cdot |H_2|$, and $\epsilon = \epsilon_1 + \epsilon_2 - \epsilon_1\epsilon_2$.*

Our construction: In the following, we will use composition rule 2 to construct a Wegman-Carter MAC. First, we will use an ϵ_{H^*}-AU universal function family H^* to hash messages of all sizes onto a fixed size. Subsequently, we will use an ϵ_F-ASU function family F to guarantee for the strong universality of the overall construction. Thus, the strongly universal hash family used for our MAC can be described as $\mathcal{H} = H^* \times F$. Note that the following theorem follows immediately from composition rule 2:

Theorem 2. *The hash function family $\mathcal{H} = H^* \times F$ is $\epsilon_F + (1 - \epsilon_F)\epsilon_{H^*}$-ASU.*

We proceed by describing H^* in sections 3 and 4 and F in section 5.

3   Reducing AΔU Families to AU Families

Reducing function families: Note that for the classes of hash function families defined in definitions 1-3, the latter are contained in the former, i.e. an AΔU family is also an AU family a.s.o. On the other hand, a stronger family can be reduced to a weaker one. This is, of course, only relevant when a performance gain can be achieved. In the following, we will describe a method to reduce Δ-universal hash functions to universal hash functions. It turns out that these new universal hash families are particularly well-suited for tree structures.

Theorem 3. *Let H^Δ be an ϵ-AΔU hash family from a set A to a set B. Consider a message $(m, m_b) \in A \times B$. Then the family H consisting of the functions $h(m, m_b) = h^\Delta(m) + m_b$ is ϵ-AU.*

Proof. From the definitions above we have

$$\Pr_{h \in H}[h(m, m_b) - h(m', m'_b) = 0] = \Pr_{h^\Delta \in H^\Delta}[h^\Delta(m) + m_b - h^\Delta(m') - m'_b = 0]$$

$$= \Pr_{h^\Delta \in H^\Delta}[h^\Delta(m) - h^\Delta(m') = m'_b - m_b].$$

If $m \neq m'$, then this probability is at most ϵ, since H^Δ is an ϵ-AΔU family. If $m = m'$ but $m_b \neq m'_b$, then the probability is trivially 0.   □

Constructing the ENH family: A very fast universal hash family is the NH family used in UMAC [18]:

$$\text{NH}_K(M) = \sum_{i=1}^{l/2} (k_{2i-1} +_w m_{2i-1}) \cdot (k_{2i} +_w m_{2i}) \bmod 2^{2w}, \tag{6}$$

where '$+_w$' means 'addition modulo 2^w', and $m_i, k_i \in \{0, ..., 2^w - 1\}$. It is a 2^{-w}-$A\Delta U$ hash family. In [18], the $A\Delta U$ property is mentioned, but only the AU property is explicitly proven.

Lemma 1. *The following version of NH is 2^{-w}-$A\Delta U$:*

$$\text{NH}_K(M) = (k_1 +_w m_1) \cdot (k_2 +_w m_2) \bmod 2^{2w}. \tag{7}$$

Proof. This proof is just a slight modification of the one presented in [18]. We must show that

$$\Pr_{k_1, k_2} [(k_1 +_w m_1)(k_2 +_w m_2) - (k_1 +_w m_1')(k_2 +_w m_2') = \delta] \leq 2^{-w}.$$

where all arithmetic is carried out modulo 2^{2w}. Assume that $m_2 \neq m_2'$. Define $c = k_2 + m_2$ and $c' = k_2 + m_2'$. By assumption it follows that $c \neq c'$. So we have

$$\Pr_{k_1, k_2} [(k_1 +_w m_1)c - (k_1 +_w m_1')c' - \delta = 0] \leq 2^{-w}.$$

since from lemma 2.4.3 in [18], the equality will only be satisfied by one k_1.   □

Choosing $w = 32$ and applying theorem 3, we obtain the 2^{-32}-AU function family ENH, which will be the basic building block of our MAC:

$$\text{ENH}_{k_2, k_1}(m_4, m_3, m_2, m_1)$$
$$= (m_1 +_{32} k_1)(m_2 +_{32} k_2) +_{64} m_3 +_{64} 2^{32} m_4, \tag{8}$$

where all arguments are 32-bit and the output is 64-bit.

4   The Modified Tree Construction

The standard tree construction: The ENH function family maps 128-bit inputs to 64-bit outputs. An immediate use of such a function is in a tree-like structure that allows hashing of messages of arbitrary length. More generally, assume a block length b, a universal hash family H that maps from bc to b bits, and a message of length $|M| = b \cdot c^n$, for some suitable value n. Let $m||m'$ denote the concatenation of two strings m, m', and let $f \circ f'$ denote the successive execution of function f' and f. Then a hash tree can be defined by a succession of n parallel hashes, as follows [1, 8]:

Definition 5. *Let H be a universal hash family, taking bc bits to b bits. Given a message $M = m_1||...||m_{c^n}$ with length $|M| = bc^n$, we hash c blocks at a time with a function $h \in H$ and concatenate the results. The result is a string of length bc^{n-1}. We denote the hash family by H^{par} and a member by h^{par}.*

$$h^{par}(M) = h(m_1, ..., m_c)||...||h(m_{c^n-c+1}, ..., m_{c^n}) \qquad (9)$$

It is easy to see that if H has a collision bound of ϵ then so does the parallel hash, H^{par}. We define the standard tree construction as follows:

Definition 6. *Let M and H be as in definition 5. We define a new hash family by applying h_i^{par} n times, each time with a new random $h_i \in H$. We denote the resulting function family by H_n^{tree} and a member by h_n^{tree}:*

$$h_n^{tree}(M) = h_n^{par} \circ h_{n-1}^{par} \circ ... \circ h_1^{par}(M).$$

Theorem 4. *The function family H_n^{tree} is a $1-(1-\epsilon)^n$-universal family of hash functions for equal length messages.*

Proof. Let us define ϵ_i as the collision bound for H_i^{tree}, then we have for H_{i+1}^{tree}:

$$\Pr[h_{i+1}^{par}(h_i^{tree}(m)) - h_{i+1}^{par}(h_i^{tree}(m')) = 0] \leq \epsilon_i(1-\epsilon) + \epsilon.$$

Solving the recurrence we get:

$$\Pr[h_n^{par}(h_{n-1}^{tree}(m)) - h_n^{par}(h_{n-1}^{tree}(m')) = 0]$$

$$\leq (1-\epsilon)^{n-1}\epsilon + \epsilon \sum_{i=1}^{n-2}(1-\epsilon)^i + \epsilon$$

$$= 1 - (1-\epsilon)^n \qquad \qquad \square$$

The modified tree construction: Consider, as an example, the case $c = 2$, yielding a binary tree. Then the message length must be $b \cdot 2^n$, for some suitable n. If that is not the case, Wegman and Carter propose [27] to break the message into substrings of length $2b$ and if necessary pad the last substring with zeroes. The resulting string is hashed with the parallel hash. If necessary, the resulting string is again padded with zeroes. This is repeated until the resulting string has length b. This procedure is illustrated in fig. 1a.

Note that this algorithm is not always optimal, because for message lengths not equal to a power of two, extra applications of the universal hash function are required. Of course, this is only significant for short messages. We start constructing a modified tree hash by defining a modified parallel hash, as follows:

Definition 7. *Given a universal hash family, H, whose members h take bc bits to b bits, consider the message $M = m_1||..||m_q$ where $|M| = bq$. Let $r = q \bmod c$, then the modified parallel hash can be defined as:*

$$h^{mpar}(M) =$$
$$\begin{cases} h(m_1, .., m_c)||..||h(m_{q-c+1}, .., m_q) & \text{if } r = 0 \\ h(m_1, .., m_c)||..||h(m_{q-c-r+1}, .., m_{q-r})||m_{q-r+1}||..||m_q & \text{if } r \neq 0 \end{cases} \qquad (10)$$

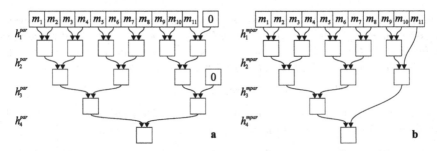

Fig. 1. Figure (a) illustrates the standard tree construction using the parallel hash and figure (b) illustrates the modified tree construction using the modified parallel hash.

Lemma 2. *The modified parallel hash is ϵ-AU on equal length messages.*

Proof. In the first case, where q is a multiple of c we simply have a parallel hash and the bound on the collision probability is ϵ. In the case where q is not a multiple of c, there are two possible situations. Either the difference in the messages M and M' is in the part, which is processed by h, or in the part which is not processed but simply concatenated to the result. In the first situation the bound on the collision probability is ϵ. In the second situation the collision probability is trivially zero. Thus, the collision probability is at most ϵ.   □

It is straightforward to define a modified tree hash, i.e. define it as in Definition 6 but use the modified parallel hash instead of the usual parallel hash.

Corollary 1. *Given a message with length $|M| = bq$, where $c^{n-1} < q \leq c^n$, the modified tree hash defines a $1 - (1 - \epsilon)^n$-AU family of hash functions on equal length messages.*

Proof. This follows from theorem 4, when the usual parallel hash is replaced by the modified parallel hash, since both are ϵ-AU, and the number of levels is the same in both cases[3].   □

The binary case: Again, consider $c = 2$. The message is divided into blocks of size b. If the message length is not a multiple of b, zeros are appended to the message such that the length becomes a multiple of b. If the length hereafter is a multiple of $2b$, the hash function is applied to each block and the results are concatenated. If the length is an odd multiple of b, the hash function is applied to each block except the last block. The results and the last block are concatenated. The procedure is repeated until the size of the result is b. The construction is illustrated in Fig. 1b.

---

[3] In a Wegman-Carter binary tree hash, a message consisting of an odd number of blocks is padded such that the number of blocks is even. This is done after each application of the parallel hash. The number of levels is equal to the number of levels for a message whose length is the nearest larger power of two. Now it is easy to convince oneself that the number of levels of the modified tree hash is exactly the same.

A different view: Note that the construction can be defined in an alternative way. Considering again the case $c = 2$, the message length can be described by $|M| \equiv b \sum_{i=0}^{n} a_i 2^i$ with $a_i \in \{0,1\}$. To each term $a_i = 1$ in the sum there corresponds a tree with i levels. We order these trees according to size with the largest tree first. More precisely, we use the tree hash for each group of data corresponding to a term in the sum, concatenate the result, and linearly hash it backwards, i.e. take the b-bit block as output from the last tree and hash it with the result of the second to last tree and so on, until only one b-bit string is left. In other words, the construction consists of a series of concatenated tree hashes followed by a linear hash [1]. For the example in Fig. 1b, the message length can be written as: $|M| = b(2^3 + 2^1 + 2^0)$. There is one tree with 3 levels, one with 1 level and one with 0 levels. The hash results if the outputs of those trees are linearly hashed starting with the result from the smallest tree.

The function family H^*: The above construction is only AU for equal length messages. To ensure universality for different length messages, we simply concatenate the length of the given message in a fixed z-bit format [1, 18]:

Definition 8. *Fix $z > 0$ and let the message M (before padding) have any length less than 2^z. Define $L_z = |M|$ to be the z-bit representation of the length and define the family H^* by its members h^*, as follows:*

$$h^*(M) = L_z || h(M). \tag{11}$$

We then have the following property:

Lemma 3. *The hash function family H^* is $1 - (1 - \epsilon)^n$-AU.*

Proof. In the case $|M| \neq |M'|$, the collision probability is trivially zero. In the case $|M| = |M'|$, the collision probability is defined according to corollary 1 by the number of levels necessary to compress the message.   □

Note that for Badger, we will use $H = \text{ENH}$. This immediately yields a binary tree with a block size of 64 bit. The input size of the function family H^* is defined to be between 0 and $2^{64} - 1$ bit. Consequently, the output size is 128 bit, 64 bit each for the hash and for the message length. Also note that the tree will contain between 1 and 58 levels, yielding a collision probability between $\epsilon_{H^*} \leq 2^{-32}$ for small and $\epsilon_{H^*} = 1 - (1 - 2^{-32})^{58} \leq 2^{-26.14}$ for large trees.

5   The Function Family F

Strenghtening a function family: What is left now according to theorem 1 is to construct a suitable SU family F, such that the overall function family $\mathcal{H} = H^* \times F$ is both efficient and secure. Note that without considering the details of H^*, the input size of F is $b + z$ bit, and its output size should be equivalent to the security of the overall scheme.

In section 3, we reduced a strong class of universal hash functions to a weaker one. In order to construct the strongly universal function familiy F, we will do the opposite: In accordance with lemma 1 from [12], we will transform the Δ-universal hash family, MMH*, proposed by Halevi and Krawczyk [15] based on [8], into a strongly universal hash family. This is accomplished by adding an additional key, k_{l+1}, in the following way:

$$\text{MMH}_K^{\text{su}}(M) = \sum_{i=1}^{l} m_i k_i + k_{l+1} \bmod p, \tag{12}$$

where p is a prime number, $M = m_1||...||m_n$, and $m_i, k_i \in \{0, ..., p-1\}$.

Key material: It is easily seen that for a given message M, the amount of key material, $N_{\mathcal{H}}(M)$, needed to choose a function from the family $\mathcal{H}$ is defined by

$$N_{\mathcal{H}}(M) = N_H \lceil \log_c(|M|/b) \rceil + N_F, \tag{13}$$

where N_H is the amount of key material needed for the H-function in the tree and N_F is the amount of key material needed for the F-function. Note that the amount of key material required is the same as for the usual tree MAC.

The choice for Badger: Remember from section 4 that H^* produces a 128-bit output, which is also the minimum input size for F. Also remember that the collision probability for the H^*-function ranges from 2^{-32} to $2^{-26.14}$, depending on the size of the tree. Since the overall security can not get better than that (according to theorem 2), an output size of 32 bit for the F-function is sufficient, since additional bits do not improve the security.

Consequently, we use a 32-bit version of the MMH^{su}-construction. We take p to be the largest 32-bit prime number, which is $p = 2^{32} - 5$. In order to process a 128-bit input, we have to choose $n = 5$ and obtain:

$$\text{F}_K(M) = \sum_{i=1}^{5} q_i k_i + k_6 \bmod \left(2^{32} - 5\right). \tag{14}$$

Note that the 128-bit output of H^* has to be divided into five input blocks q_i in some way. For Badger, it is padded with 7 leading zeroes and then split into 27-bit blocks[4].

6   The Badger Specification

For the algorithmic description of Badger, the following pseudocode calls to external functions are made:

---

[4] Note that the security claims for the SU function family also hold if not all messages from $\{0, ..., 2^{32}-6\}$ are actually used as inputs, as long as all keys from $\{0, ..., 2^{32}-6\}$ occur with equal probability.

$$L = |M|$$
if $L = 0$
$\quad M^1 = \ldots = M^u = 0$
$\quad$ Go to finalization
$r = L \bmod 64$
if $r \neq 0$:
$\quad M = 0^{64-r} || M$
for $i = 1$ to u:
$\quad M^i = M$
$\quad v' = \max\{1, \lceil \log_2 L \rceil - 6\}$
$\quad$ for $j = 1$ to v':
$\quad\quad$ divide M^i into 64-bit blocks, $M^i = m_t^i || \ldots || m_1^i$
$\quad\quad$ if t is even:
$\quad\quad\quad M^i = \mathrm{ENH}(k_j^i, m_t^i, m_{t-1}^i) || \ldots || \mathrm{ENH}(k_j^i, m_2^i, m_1^i)$
$\quad\quad$ else:
$\quad\quad\quad M^i = m_t^i || \mathrm{ENH}(k_j^i, m_{t-1}^i, m_{t-2}^i) || \ldots || \mathrm{ENH}(k_j^i, m_2^i, m_1^i)$

Fig. 2. Pseudo-code of the processing phase.

- PRG_KeySetup(K): Initializes PRG with the 128-bit key K.
- PRG_IVSetup(N): Initializes PRG with the 64-bit nonce N.
- PRG_Nextbit(n): Returns n bit of pseudorandom output.

As above, p denotes the prime number $2^{32} - 5$. The standard construction gives 32-bit tags; if larger tags are required, the algorithm is run u times in parallel. By v, we denote the maximum number of tree levels required when computing the function family H^*. The notation $a||b$ refers to a concatenation of strings.

Key generation: To generate the key material for the H^*- and F-functions, any secure PRG can be used, as long as the key length is at least 128 bit. For each tree, we require v 64-bit keys for the H^*-function and 6 keys from the interval $\{0, ..., 2^{32} - 6\}$ for the F-function. Note that (as opposed to the key material for the pseudo-random pad), this key material can be computed once and then be re-used for the computation of all future MACs under the same key.

Processing phase: In order to compute the function family H^*, we use the core function ENH as described in section 3. If $x \in \{0,1\}^{64}$, we denote the 32 least significant bits by $L(x)$ and the 32 most significant bits by $U(x)$. Then ENH $:\{0,1\}^{64} \times \{0,1\}^{128} \rightarrow \{0,1\}^{64}$ hashes a 128-bit string $m_2||m_1$ under a 64-bit key k to a 64-bit string, as follows:

$$\mathrm{ENH}(k, m_2, m_1) = (L(m_1) +_{32} L(k)) \cdot (U(m_1) +_{32} U(k)) +_{64} m_2 .$$

Using this function and denoting the level keys by k_j^i, the processing of a message can proceed as described in figure 2.

```
PRG_KeySetup(K)
PRG_IVSetup(N)
for i = 1 to u:
    Q^i = 0^7||L||M^i
    divide Q^i into 27-bit blocks , Q^i = q_5^i|| ... ||q_1^i
    S^i = (∑_{j=1}^{5} q_j^i K_j^i) + K_6^i mod p
S = S^u|| ... ||S^1
S = S ⊕ PRG_Nextbit(u · 32)
return S
```

Fig. 3. Pseudo-code of the finalization phase.

Finalization: The length of the message in bit (before padding) is represented as a 64-bit number and concatenated to the 64-bit result. The resulting 128-bit block is prefixed with 7 zeroes, divided into five 27-bit blocks and run through the F-function. The final tag is generated by xor-ing the output of the hash function with a pseudo-random pad, according to Definition 4. Denoting the finalization keys by K_j^i, this procedure is given in figure 3.

Note that no output of the PRG must ever be re-used; this can be achieved by running the PRG without resetting, or by using a new IV for every new message. In the second case, the initial state of the PRG has to be reconstructed and PRG_IVSetup(N) has to be run each time, making this approach more computationally expensive.

Forgery probability: The forgery probability is $\epsilon \leq \epsilon_F + (1 - \epsilon_F)\epsilon_{H^*}$, according to theorem 2. Remember that depending on the message length, the upper bound on ϵ_{H^*} can range from 2^{-32} to $2^{-26.14}$. Also note that $\epsilon_F = 1/(2^{32} - 5) \approx 2^{-32}$. Using these values, it can be seen that the overall forgery probability has an upper bound ranging from 2^{-31} for extremely short to $2^{-26.12}$ for extremely long messages.

Forgery probabilities of up to $2^{-26.12}$ are insufficient for most applications. However, a simple method to reduce the forgery probability is to hash the message u times with independent keys and concatenate the results. This results in a forgery probability of ϵ^u. To obtain 128-bit security, we need to hash the message 5 times, yielding bounds on the forgery probability of between 2^{-155} and $2^{-130.6}$ and a tag size of 160 bits. In particular, this leads to the verifier-selectable assurance as each 32-bit tag can be verified independently[5].

---

[5] At first glance, it seems that the Toeplitz construction (proposed by Krawczyk in [16]) is applicable here, i.e. that the u parallel MACs are calculated using $(k_1, \ldots, k_{58})$, $(k_2, \ldots, k_{59})$ etc. However, this only makes sense if the resulting forgery probability is at most ϵ^u, and experiments with smaller versions of the H^*-function indicate that this is not the case here. Thus, the Toeplitz construction is not used with Badger.

Table 1. Performance results with and without IV-setup. "Key setup" generates all keys for the ϵ-AU and SU hash functions, "Universal hash" processes the tree, and "Finalization" includes the F-function and generates the pseudo-random pad.

Function	Pentium III	Pentium 4
Key setup	4093 cycles	5854 cycles
Universal hash	2.2 cycles/byte	1.3 cycles/byte
Finalization without IV	175 cycles	220 cycles
Finalization with IV	433 cycles	800 cycles

7 Performance

On the testing environment: Performance of the Badger algorithm was measured on a 1.0 GHz Pentium III and on a 1.7 GHz Pentium 4 processor. The speed-optimized versions were programmed in assembly language inlined in C and compiled using the Intel C++ 7.1 compiler. All performance results in this section are based on generating a $2 \cdot 32$ bit tag. The pseudo-random material required for the algorithm was generated using the stream cipher Rabbit [6, 7], which is very fast in software. Note that since Badger is designed with speed being a main objective, it makes sense to use a fast stream cipher (instead of, e.g., using a block cipher like AES in a suitable stream cipher mode).

On IV-setup: Note that the pseudo-random pad can be generated either with or without an explicit IV-setup. If an explicit IV is used, the stream cipher has to be re-initialized for each message. Without an explicit IV, the key material for successive messages is produced by continuous extraction of bytes from the stream cipher, yielding a performance advantage. This corresponds to interpreting the message number as the IV. However, this technique is only applicable if messages are guaranteed to be received in the same order as generated, which is often not the case (e.g. in IPsec communication). Table 1 gives performance numbers both with and without explicit IV-setup.

On short messages: Since the amount of key material required for Badger depends on the length of the message, optimized versions can be used in applications where the message length is upper bounded. For example, in typical IPsec applications, the message length cannot exceed 1500 bytes and when authenticating TLS protected data, each message cannot exceed 17 kilobytes [10]. Furthermore, the evaluation of the F-function is simplified since part of the input is zero, see eq. (12). The properties of Badger when the message length is limited are shown in Table 2.

Note that the performance numbers for the key setup and finalization (which are dependent on the PRG in use) are partially based on estimates. The numbers for the universal hash function, however, are independent of the PRG and are fully based on measurements. A comparison to the fastest published MAC designs is given in appendix A.

Table 2. Badger properties for various restricted message lengths. "Memory req." denotes the amount of memory required to store the internal state including key material and the inner state of the Rabbit stream cipher. "Setup" denotes the key setup, and "Fin." denotes finalization with IV-setup.

Max. message size	Forgery bound	Memory req.	Pentium III		Pentium 4	
			Setup	Fin.	Setup	Fin.
2^{11} bytes (e.g. IPsec)	$2^{-57.7}$	400 bytes	1133 cycles	409 cycles	1774 cycles	776 cycles
2^{15} bytes (e.g. TLS)	$2^{-56.6}$	528 bytes	1370 cycles	421 cycles	2100 cycles	788 cycles
2^{32} bytes	$2^{-54.2}$	1072 bytes	2376 cycles	421 cycles	3488 cycles	788 cycles
$2^{61} - 1$ bytes	$2^{-52.2}$	2000 bytes	4093 cycles	433 cycles	5854 cycles	800 cycles

8   Conclusion

We presented a new fast and provably secure MAC called Badger, based on universal hashing. In the construction, a modified tree hash was introduced that basically combines a tree hash with a linear hash. The modified tree hash is more efficient than the standard tree hash, and its security has being proven. Furthermore, in order to derive the core hash function of the tree, we introduced a novel technique for reducing Δ-universal function families to universal families. The resulting MAC is very efficient on standard processors both for short and long messages. As an example, for a 64-bit tag, it achieves performances of up to 2.2 and 1.3 clock cycles per byte on a Pentium III and Pentium 4 processor, respectively. The key material necessary for the hash functions is only 976 bytes, and the forgery probability is at most $2^{-52.2}$.

References

1. M. Bellare and P. Rogaway. Collision-resistant hashing: Towards making UOWHFs practical. In B. Kaliski, editor, *Proc. Crypto '97*, volume 1294 of *LNCS*, pages 470–484. Springer, 1997.
2. D. Bernstein. The Poly1305-AES message-authentication code. In *Proc. Fast Software Encryption '05*.
3. D. Bernstein. Poly1305-AES speed tables. http://notabug.com/2002/cr.yp.to/mac/speed.html, 2005.
4. J. Bierbrauer, T. Johansson, G. Kabatianskii, and B. Smeets. On families of hash functions via geometric codes and concatenation. In D. Stinson, editor, *Proc. Crypto '93*, volume 773 of *LNCS*, pages 331–342. Springer, 1994.
5. J. Black, S. Halevi, H. Krawczyk, T. Krovetz, and P. Rogaway. UMAC: Fast and secure message authentication. In M. Wiener, editor, *Proc. Crypto '99*, volume 1666 of *LNCS*, pages 216–232. Springer, 1999.
6. M. Boesgaard, T. Pedersen, M. Vesterager, and E. Zenner. The Rabbit stream cipher - design and security analysis. In *Workshop Record of the State of the Arts of Stream Ciphers Workshop*, pages 7–29. ECRYPT Network of Excellence in Cryptography, October 2004.
7. M. Boesgaard, M. Vesterager, T. Pedersen, J. Christiansen, and O. Scavenius. Rabbit: A new high-performance stream cipher. In T. Johansson, editor, *Proc. Fast Software Encryption 2003*, volume 2887 of *LNCS*, pages 307–329. Springer, 2003.

8. J. Carter and M. Wegman. Universal classes of hash functions. *Journal of Computer and System Sciences*, 18:143–154, 1979.

9. J. Daemen and V. Rijmen. AES proposal: Rijndael.
http://csrc.nist.gov/encryption/aes/rijndael/Rijndael.pdf, 1999.

10. T. Dierks and C. Allen. The TLS protocol version 1.0, IETF RFC 2246.
http://www.ietf.org/rfc.html, 1999.

11. P. Ekdahl and T. Johansson. A new version of the stream cipher SNOW. In H. Heys and K. Nyberg, editors, *Proc. SAC 2002*, volume 2595 of *LNCS*, pages 47–61. Springer, 2002.

12. M. Etzel, S. Patel, and Z. Ramzan. Square Hash: Fast message authentication via optimized universal hash functions. In M. Wiener, editor, *Proc. Crypto '99*, volume 1666 of *LNCS*, pages 234–251. Springer, 1999.

13. N. Ferguson and B. Schneier. *Practical Cryptography*. Wiley, 2003.

14. N. Ferguson, D. Whiting, B. Schneier, J. Kelsey, S. Lucks, and T. Kohno. Helix: Fast encryption and authentication in a single cryptographic primitive. In T. Johansson, editor, *Proc. Fast Software Encryption 2003*, volume 2887 of *LNCS*, pages 330–346. Springer, 2003.

15. S. Halevi and H. Krawczyk. MMH: Software message authentication in the Gbit/second rates. In E. Biham, editor, *Proc. Fast Software Encryption '97*, volume 1267 of *LNCS*, pages 172–189. Springer, 1997.

16. H. Krawczyk. LFSR-based hashing and authentication. In Y. Desmedt, editor, *Proc. Crypto '94*, volume 839 of *LNCS*, pages 129–139, Berlin, 1994.

17. H. Krawczyk, M. Bellare, and R. Canetti. HMAC: Keyed-hashing for message authentication IETF RFC 2104. http://www.ietf.org/rfc.html, 1997.

18. T. Krovetz. *Software-Optimized Universal Hashing and Message Authentication*. PhD thesis, UC Davis, September 2000.

19. T. Krovetz. UMAC performance.
http://www.cs.ucdavis.edu/~rogaway/umac/2004/perf04.html, 2004.

20. S. Lucks and V. Rijmen. Evaluation of Badger. http://www.cryptico.com, 2005.

21. New European Schemes for Signatures, Integrity, and Encryption (NESSIE).
https://www.cosic.esat.kuleuven.ac.be/nessie/.

22. W. Nevelsteen and B. Preneel. Software performance of universal hash functions. In J. Stern, editor, *Proc. Eurocrypt '99*, volume 1592 of *LNCS*, pages 24–41. Springer, 1999.

23. P. Rogaway. Bucket hashing and its application to fast message authentication. In D. Coppersmith, editor, *Proc. Crypto '95*, volume 963 of *LNCS*, pages 29–42. Springer, 1995.

24. D. Stinson. Universal hashing and authentication codes. In J. Feigenbaum, editor, *Proc. Crypto '91*, volume 576 of *LNCS*, pages 74–85. Springer, 1992.

25. D. Stinson. Universal hashing and message authentication codes. *Designs, Codes, and Cryptography*, 4(4):369–380, 1994.

26. D. Stinson. On the connection between universal hashing, combinatorial designs and error-correcting codes. In *Proc. Congressus Numerantium 114*, pages 7–27, 1996.

27. M. Wegmann and J. Carter. New hash functions and their use in authentication and set equality. *Journal of Computer and System Sciences*, 22:265–279, 1981.

A   A Performance Comparison

Badger, UMAC and Poly1305: Figure 4 plots the processing performance of Badger against that of UMAC-64 [18][6] and Poly1305 [2][7]. In order to make a comparison possible, the performance figures have been normalized to 64-bit tags. Since Poly1305 provides only 128-bit tags, the cycle count for this MAC has been halved (which is slightly in favour of Poly1305, since it also halves the processing time of the final AES encryption, which is not possible in practice). Also note that we do not discuss the key setup times here since for UMAC-64 and Poly1305, no performance figures for the key setup are available.

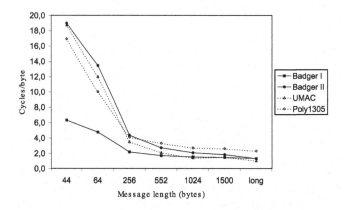

Fig. 4. Performance for Badger, UMAC-64 and Poly1305 on Pentium 4 processor. Badger I runs without IV setup, while Badger II uses IV setup.

A cautionary note on performance comparisons: The authors would like to point out that such a performance comparison has to be taken with at least one grain of salt. The comparison works with the figures provided by the authors of the respective MACs, and those figures can be influenced by, e.g.,

- the scope of the implementation (Does it include key setup, IV setup, and final encryption? Does is measure the time required for message and key loading, function calls, and so on? Does it take care of data alignment or starting addresses?),
- the amount of optimization done on the algorithm implementation,

---

[6] The figures for UMAC were obtained from the web page [19]. It is not clear from these figures whether or not they include the final AES encryption of the hash output or not.

[7] The figures for Poly1305 were obtained from the file `speed-173601.txt` available from [3]. We used the first entry of type `A4444KD` for each message size, ignoring the first two measurements. The resulting figures are the best ones available for Poly1305.

- the exact choice of the message lengths under consideration[8],
- the choice of the underlying cryptographic primitive (like Rabbit, AES etc.),
- the amount of optimization done on the implementation of this primitive,
- the amount of memory used to optimize, e.g. by using lookup tables, and
- the computer (processor, memory, cache, bus, etc.) the performance tests have been conducted on.

When using performance numbers provided by others, it is often not clear how at least some of the above parameters have been chosen. On the other hand, when implementing the competitor's algorithm oneself, it is quite likely that one would (even if inadvertently) optimize one's own brainchild better than the competitor's. Thus, we conclude that a fair performance comparison can only be based on the implementation by an independent entity - the figures provided here can only give an indication of the right order of magnitude.

Conclusion: Keeping these observations in mind, the following can be concluded from figure 4:

- Badger, UMAC, and Poly1305 are faster than widespread designs like HMAC-SHA-1 or CBC-MAC-AES by at least one order of magnitude (see, e.g., [21]). These MACs require roughly 25 cycles/byte for long messages and are thus left out of this consideration.
- If run without IV setup, Badger is clearly faster than its competitors on small messages.
- When run with IV setup, Badger, UMAC, and Poly1305 provide similar performance. Given the current numbers, it is not entirely clear which MAC would perform best under identical testing conditions. However, the authors of this work strive to provide such a comparison in an upcoming paper.

---

[8] Many algorithms have criticals lengths where the performance suddenly decreases dramatically by increasing the message length by just one bit. This is due to the fact that computers have limited register and cache sizes and that by exceeding those sizes, things suddenly get more complicated. By deliberately choosing the message lengths in one's own favour, the outcome of a performance comparison could be severely influenced.

IDS False Alarm Reduction Using Continuous and Discontinuous Patterns

Abdulrahman Alharby and Hideki Imai

Institute of industrial Science, The university of Tokyo
4-6-1, Komaba, Meguro-ku, Tokyo, 153-8505 Japan
alharby@imailab.iis.u-tokyo.ac.jp, imai@iis.u-tokyo.ac.jp

Abstract. Intrusion Detection Systems *(IDSs)* are widely deployed in computer networks to stand against a wide variety of attacks. IDSs deployment raises a serious problem, namely managing of a large number of triggered alerts. This problem becomes worse by the fact that some commercial IDSs may generate thousands of alerts per day. Identifying the real alarms from the huge volume of alarms is a frustrating task for security officers. Thus, reducing false alarms is a critical issue in IDSs efficiency and usability. In this paper, we mine historical alarms to learn how future alarms can be handled more efficiently. First, an approach is proposed for characterizing the "normal" stream of alarms. In addition, an algorithm for detecting anomalies by using continuous and discontinuous sequential patterns is developed, and used in preliminary experiments with real-world data to show that the presented model can handle IDSs alarms efficiently.

Keywords: Intrusion detection, alarm reduction, sequential patterns.

1 Introduction

Over the past decade, the number as well as the severity of computer attacks has significantly increased. CSO magazine conducted a survey on the 2004 cyber crimes, the survey shows a significant increase in reported electronic crimes. Compared to the previous year, more than 40% of intrusions and electronic crimes are reported. Also, 70% of the respondents reported at least one electronic crime or intrusion was committed against their organization [1]. According to collected statistics, electronic crimes have an incredible impact on economy. Reports say that electronic crimes have cost more that $600 million in 2003.

In response, security services strongly recommend to deploy and implement suitable protection technology. Besides the first defence protections (e.g. firewalls, authentication, and cryptography), IDSs are recommended for attacks detection and to alert security officers for further actions. IDS has become one of the corner stones in computer security because of its triggered alarms to intrusive activities can greatly reduce the possible harm and data leakage due to attacks.

Although IDSs have been deployed widely across data networks during the last decade, and their value as security components have been demonstrated.

J. Ioannidis, A. Keromytis, and M.Yung (Eds.): ACNS 2005, LNCS 3531, pp. 192–205, 2005.

Most of them suffer from high false alarms rate. In fact, during their normal operation they generate thousands of fake alarms per day.

In this paper, we report our filtration technique to reduce fake alarms rate. In the remaining of this introduction, we describe intrusion detection methods, fake alarms problem, and the basic requirements of filtration algorithm. Section 2 shows our proposed model. Section 3 shows the experiments. In section 4 we discuss the experiments results. Our method is contrasted with existing methods in section 5. Finally, in section 6 we conclude the paper.

1.1 Detection Methodologies

IDSs are considered as powerful security tools in computer systems environments. These systems collect activities within the protected network and analyze them in order to detect intrusions. System activities are usually collected from two main sources, network packet streams and host log files. Once the information is collected, the detection algorithm starts looking for any evidence for intrusions existence.

There are two general methodologies of detection: *misuse* and *anomaly* detection [2, 3]. *Misuse* detection systems such as STAT [4] look for a known malicious behavior or signature, once it is detected an alarm is raised for further actions. While this type is useful for detecting known attacks, it can't detect novel attacks, and its signatures database needs to be upgraded frequently. The main feature of this model is its low false alarm rate. *Anomaly* detection models (e.g. IDES [5]) compare reference model of normal behavior with the suspicious activities and flag deviations as anomalous and potentially intrusive. Unlike *misuse* detection, *anomaly* detection systems identify unknown intrusions. The two detection approaches can be combined to detect attacks more efficiently. The most apparent drawback of these systems is the high rate of false alarms.

1.2 IDS False Positive Alarms Problem

A false positive alarm in IDSs is an attack alarm that is raised incorrectly. Suppose an IDS detects someone attempting to run *Nmap* and it turns out that the traffic pattern that caused the alarm reveals someone was running a peer-to-peer application: that is a false positive [8]. But if that scan is against a nonexistent machine, this alarm is not a false positive, someone actually was attempting malicious activities.

An ideal detection system is the one that has 0% of miss-classified normal behavior with 100% attack detection. However, current detection systems suffer from high false alarms and low attack detection rate [6]. IDSs can be fine-tuned to reduce false alarm generation, but this may degrade the security level. Usually, with *anomaly-based IDSs* the abnormality is determined by measuring the distance between the suspicious activities and the norm, and based on a chosen threshold the observed behaviour is classified. Increasing this threshold leads directly to induce more false alarms, while many of them are actually not true. In case of *misuse-based IDSs* the detection depends on a set of rules or signatures to detect intrusive behaviour, the tighter the rule set, the higher the false alarms rate. On the other hand, the higher threshold in the case of anomaly detection and the tighter the rules set in the case of misuse detection, the stronger the security can be achieved. Reducing anomaly detection threshold and relaxing some misuse detection rules can reduce the number of generated false alarms, but such action is most risky, causing IDS to be unable to detect major attacks. Therefore, the tuning problem actually is a trade-off between reducing false alarms and maintaining system security.

1.3 An Overview and Basic Requirements

In this section, we propose an overview of our reduction method for IDSs false positive alarms that significantly reduces operators' workload. When the network is under attack, we believe that IDSs behave in a different way from the free-attack situation. This fact makes it clear that we can distinguish between the alarms sequences generated when the system is under attack from those sequences generated in a normal situation. In other words, the basic idea of our approach is simple: Frequent behaviour, over an extended period of time, is likely to be normal. A combination of specific alarm types occurring regularly in the same order, and within a certain time window, is most likely less suspicious than a sudden burst of alarms never seen before. We believe that any prospective technique for alarms reduction should satisfy the following requirements:

Scalability: Since IDSs can generate thousands of alarms per day, the reduction algorithm should be able to handle such huge amount of alarms.
Noisy data: Since IDSs trigger alarms subjected to be very noisy as detailed in [7, 8], the reduction model should be able to consider that property of IDSs alarms.
Alarm attributes: The model should support any type of attributes contained in the alarms, alarm attributes detailed by Julisch in [9].
Independency: Detection-Reduction processes should be independent, which allows the reduction algorithm to be applied to any type of IDSs.
Cost: To support automated reduction, the model should be efficient in terms of computation cost.

Below we will introduce our method to model normal alarms sequences and how to detect deviations from the norm.

2 An Approach

2.1 Methodology

Consider a finite set $U = \{X_1, X_2, ..., X_N\}$ of different sequences of a certain distinct alarm attribute. Each sequence X_i contains a different number of ordered alarms, the number of those alarms is called the length of the sequence. These sequences represent ordered alarms generated by IDS, furthermore, they are defined as "normal" if they are generated under conditions not associated with intrusion attacks. We believe that every single element in the sequence has a value and contains important information. In addition to considering all possible subsequences, our intention is to make sure that each single alarm within the sequence is included in the normal model. In general, we have to expand each sequence to its basic components which is called sequential patterns. Formally, for any alarms sequence $X_i = \{x_1, x_2, ..., x_m\}$ of m elements within a time window of size W, a number n of sequential patterns can be extracted. In other words, sequential patterns: $X_i^{sq} = \{S_1, S_2, ..., S_n\}$, each S_i contains a number of ordered alarms. For any sequence X_i, the sequential patterns can be extracted as $X_i^{sq} = f(X_i)$ where $f(\cdot)$ functions as a sequential patterns generator. Normal sequential patterns are extracted from normal alarm sequences via $f(\cdot)$, which form the basis of a normal profile of the triggered alarms. Furthermore, $U^{sq} = \{X_1^{sq}, X_2^{sq}, ..., X_N^{sq}\}$ describes the normal alarms profile that can be used to classify the next coming sequence with a satisfactory threshold.

Sequential patterns data mining are popular and have been extensively studied because of their numerous applications, many algorithms were proposed [10–13]. In our experiments, and because of its ability to mine both types of patterns (continuous and discontinuous), we adopted the algorithm proposed by Chen to extract the sequential patterns, a brief description about the algorithm given in appendix A.

In the next sections more details are given about sequential patterns types, sequential patterns generation, and how a single sequence of alarms can be classified as normal or intrusive.

2.2   Alarm Sequences Classification

The alarms sequential pattern S_i can be classified into two classes, continuous and discontinuous. Precisely, suppose a sequential pattern S_i extracted from the alarms sequence $X_i = \{x_1, x_2, ..., x_m\}$ and contains a number of alarms, that is, $S_i = \{s_1, s_2, ..., s_l\}$. The pattern S_i is considered as a continuous pattern if all contained elements appear in consecutive positions of the sequence X_i, such that, there is an integer r such that; $s_1 = x_r$, $s_2 = x_{r+1}$, ..., $s_d = x_{r+l-1}$. For example, the continuous pattern (s_3, s_4) occurs in sequence: $X_1 = (s_1, s_2, s_3, s_4, s_5, s_6)$. The second category is the discontinuous patterns, we say that s_i is a discontinuous pattern if the contained elements don't appear in consecutive positions of the sequence X_i, that is, if there are existing integers $r_1 < r_2 < ... < r_l$ such that $s_1 = x_{r_1}$, $s_2 = x_{r_2}$, ..., $s_l = x_{r_l}$. For example, the pattern (s_1, s_3) in sequence X_1 is a discontinuous pattern.

While continuous patterns reflect a clean alarm sequences, discontinuous patterns represent the sequences mixed with noisy data. Precisely, alarm streams can be mixed with undesirable data, thus, discontinuous patterns are very suitable to mine and then analyze noisy alarms. We believe that both of them - continuous and discontinuous - are generated by most of the IDSs. Any alarm sequences may consist of several continuous sub-sequences that are not adjacent. Ignoring such patterns leads to missing very meaningful patterns. For example, patterns:

(s_1, s_2) and (s_5, s_6) contained in sequence X_1, each one of them may have no meaning by itself, but if they are combined in one pattern like: $(s_1, s_2, *, s_5, s_6)$, they may represent a very useful meaningful pattern, where " $*$ " means a variable number of intermediate elements. In the next section, for a certain alarms sequence, we show how the two different types of sequential patterns can be extracted.

2.3   Extraction of Alarms Sequential Patterns

Let $X_i = \{x_1, x_2, ..., x_m\}$ denote all alarms in one sequence of length m, also, let the star " $*$ " denote a subsequence of any length of consecutive alarms $\{x_l, x_{l+1}, ...\}$, including zero length, which may be contained in X_i for $2 \leq l \leq m-1$. The sequence X_i can be expanded to a number of patterns called sequential patterns. In addition to the items themselves, sequential patterns are generated by extracting all possible forward combinations. Basically, forward combinations are sequences of items representing continuous and discontinuous patterns that may be contained in the sequence.

An alarm sequence of length m can be expanded to a number n of sequential patterns, including a number n_c as continuous, and n_d as discontinuous patterns. Two different methods are used to calculate n_d depending on the value of m whether it is an even or an odd value while using the same formula to calculate n_c. Table 1 shows the different formulas that were used to calculate the number of extracted sequential patterns from a certain sequence of length m.

Table 1. Different used formulas to calculate the number of sequential patterns $n = n_c + n_d$ that can be extracted from a sequence of length m.

Sequence length, m	Continuous (n_c)	Discontinuous (n_d)
Even	$0.5(m^2 + m)$	$1 + 2\sum_{i=1}^{0.5m-1}(m-1)i - i^2$
Odd	$0.5(m^2 + m)$	$1 + 2(m-2) + 0.25(m-1)^2 + 2\sum_{i=2}^{0.5(m-3)}(m-1)i - i^2$

Any extracted combination $S_i = \{s_1, s_2, ..., s_l\}$ from X_i can be considered as a sequential pattern if the following constraints are satisfied:

- $s_i \in X_i$
- $s_1, s_l \in X_i$
- If $s_i = $ " $*$ " then $s_{i+1}, s_{i-1} \in X_i$, for $1 < i < l$

By definition, the sequential pattern never starts or ends by " $*$ ". For example, if we have a sequence $X_i = ABCD$, we may have these continuous patterns AB, BCD, and ABC, or this discontinuous pattern $A * CD$. Because of the definition of the " $*$ ", the discontinuous one implicitly has two other patterns: ACD,

Table 2. Example of two sequences and their related Continuous & Discontinuous sequential patterns.

Sequence	Continuous	Discontinuous
ABC	A, B, C, AB, BC, ABC	A*C
ABCD	A,B,C,D,AB,BC,CD,ABC,BCD,ABCD	A*C,B*D,A*D,A*CD,AB*D

and *ABCD*. Table 2 shows an example of extracted continuous and discontinuous sequential patterns of two sequences. In the next section, we will show how deviation from the norm can be detected.

2.4   Alarms Deviation Detection

To classify a newly arrived sequence, corresponding sequential patterns are extracted in the same way described above. Then the similarity between sequential patterns of the new sequence and those of the normal sequences is calculated using the similarity algorithm. Each single extracted sequential pattern that is represented in the normal sequential patterns set is given a weight $w = 1/n$, where n is the total number of all extracted sequential patterns of that specific testing alarm sequence, and it can be obtained programmatically, or by using formulas given in table 1. The value of w falls in the range $0 \leq w \leq 1$. By calculating the total summation weights *sum* of all matches, strength of the deviation signal can be determined. If the total weights summation exceeds a certain threshold, the testing sequence is classified as normal. Otherwise, it is an anomalous sequence. An abstract of the pseudo code of the used similarity algorithm is given below:

```
1 Extract normal alarms sequential patterns;
2 for each new suspicious sequence X Do
3    extract all corresponding sequential patterns;
4    get n value; // number of extracted patterns
5    calculate sum; // all matched patterns
6        if sum/n ≥ threshold then
7            X is normal;
8        else then
9            X is abnormal;
```

3   Experiments

Experiments with DARPA 1999 data set have been conducted to evaluate the proposed approach. DARPA off-line data sets [14] were developed to evaluate any proposed techniques for intrusion detection. These data sets contain contents of every packet transmitted between hosts inside and outside a simulated military base. There were a collection of data including *tcpdump* and *BSM* audit data.

In our experiments we use the *tcpdump* data. There are three weeks of training data, week 1 and week 3 are free of attacks whereas week 2 is labelled with attacks.

3.1   The Detection System

In our experiments we examined the network traffic with a well-known IDS named *Snort* [15, 16]. *Snort* is a signature-based lightweight network intrusion detection system, it is available as an open source code on the internet. It can perform both protocol analysis, and content matching. *Snort* is capable of performing real-time traffic analysis and detect a variety of attacks. It looks for attacks signs by comparing the incoming packets with its own set of attacks signatures. Each detected attack is recorded in a database with relevant information called alarm attribute [9], such as: *alarm type, timestamp, source IP address, destination IP address*, and other information. In this work, we examine only the *alarm type*, the rest of the alarm attributes are planned to be our future work. *Snort* is capable of processing different types of protocols such as *TCP, UDP, ICMP, ARP, IPv6*, and others.

Our experiments were performed with *Snort 2.3.0RC2*. We processed the three weeks of DARPA 1999 training data set. The total generated alarms by *Snort* with its default setting were 97257 alarms with more than 6400 alarms per day on average. There were 76 different types of attacks. Experiments show that among the alarms, there are a limited number of alarms that have the most contribution. Table 3 shows the most frequent generated alarm types with the percentage of their occurrence. In the next section, we will show how we constructed our normal data set.

3.2   Normal Alarm Model

Since the first and third weeks of DARPA 1999 data set are free-attacks traffic, any triggered alarms of these two weeks are false positive alarms. After running *Snort*, we found 78972 alarms triggered within these two weeks which are considered as false alarms. For a certain time period, *Snort* generates hundreds of false alarms sequences. Obviously, a shorter time window would increase the total number of alarm sequences. Once alarm sequences are collected, the sequential patterns are extracted as described in the previous section.

Table 3. The most frequent triggered alarm types and their percentage of occurrence.

Alarm type	Occurrence
SNMP public access udp	72 %
ICMP PING NMAP	9.3 %
FTP CWD	7.2 %
TELNET access	2.3 %
SCAN FIN	1.3 %

The extracted sequential patterns of the first and third weeks false alarms represent the behaviour of the *Snort* as an IDS system in the free-attack environment, and we called them "normal" sequential patterns data. If a new sequential patterns data set is similar to this normal data set, it is considered as normal. Otherwise, abnormality appears and further investigations are needed. The experiment setup is shown in Figure 1. The next section shows the results of our experiments.

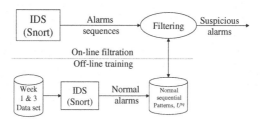

Fig. 1. Experiment setup shows the relation of the IDS and the proposed filtration process.

3.3   Experimental Results

This section assesses the proposed approach with respect to its ability to reduce the false alarms. To judge the effectiveness of applying continuous and discontinuous sequential patterns for alarms reduction, we ran two sets of experiments. In the first set, we fixed the parameter *threshold* to be 0.7, also, we fixed the sequence length m to be 15, and let the reduction algorithm run over all 15 days (i.e the three weeks). Figure 2 shows the alarms load reduction attained

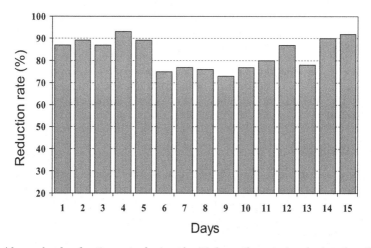

Fig. 2. Alarms load reduction rate during the 15 days, the rate is calculated at *threshold* 0.7 and sequence length $m = 15$.

in weeks 1, 2, and 3. Alarm reduction rate calculated as the ratio of triggered alarms with the filter to those triggered without the filter. Clearly, from the figure, approximately 80% of the alarms were discarded.

In the second set of the experiments, we ran the algorithm for the second week data set, and let m and the *threshold* vary. Figure 3 shows the alarms load reduction achieved for different sequence m length and *threshold*, the Results presented in the figure are encouraging. We found that the proposed approach is able to reduce the alarms up to 93% without filtering out any true alarms detected by the IDS. As the *threshold* goes up the reduction rates decrease because more sequential patterns are classified as abnormal and the alarm sequences corresponding to these sequential patterns haven't been filtered. For *threshold*=0.3 and during week 2, about 90% of false alarms are filtered when sequence length m is fixed at 20. The false alarms reduction rate drops to 62% when the *threshold* jumps to 0.85. Clearly, reducing the *threshold* leads to higher reduction rate, but to go further in decreasing the threshold leads to missing out some true alarms. The next section presents more discussion about the effects of the parameters m and *threshold* on the alarms load reduction rate.

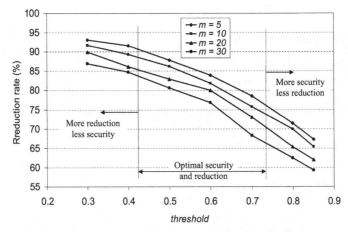

Fig. 3. False alarm reduction rate for different *threshold* and length m. The rate is calculated as the result of the division of the total number of triggered alarms during *week 2* with the filter and the total number of triggered alarms without the filter during the same period.

4   Discussions

For the proposed model to be efficient it must meet some basic operational requirements. In this section, we discuss some factors that we believe have apparent effects on the model efficiency, and form its main characteristics.

4.1   Critical Parameters

To achieve the most optimal parameters setting many preliminary experiments are performed. The three parameters values that have been tested are time window W, alarm sequence length m, and similarity *threshold*. During the experiments, we noticed that for a certain time window we have different lengths of alarm sequences. Since the sequence length has a direct effect on the number of extracted patterns, consequently, the performance of the filter, we fixed the sequence length value for each experiment regardless of the time window. Different m values have been tested, from 5 to 30. For each value of m, we worked out the alarms reduction rates with different *thresholds*. The larger the value of m, the more sequential patterns are extracted and the higher the similarity between the tested sequential patterns set and the normal ones.

The second tested parameter (i.e. the *threshold*) plays an important role when judging whether a sequence of alarms is abnormal. When classifying new sequential patterns data set (new sequence), the average of the total matching weights summation is taken as the similarity score of the sequential patterns set. If the score is larger than the *threshold*, the new sequence is classified as normal. Obviously, high *threshold* values would lead to higher similarity, consequently, to higher normality, and more security would be achieved, but the classifier will suffer from high false alarms rate. On the other hand, lower *threshold* leads to lower security with lower false alarms rate. Since alarms reduction techniques are recommended only if the security level is maintained, we don't prefer very low *threshold*. However, very low *threshold* leads to misclassifying true alarms and it is not desirable and not accepted. Figure 3 shows three regions of possible operation based on *threshold* value. The optimal operation limits can be decided based on the security policy, which is a trade-off between security and reduction rate.

4.2   Model Efficiency

In section 1.3 we have listed some requirements that alarms reduction model should satisfy. In this section, we discuss how well the proposed model meets these requirements:

`Scalability`: It is something to think about whether you have processed one alarm or one million alarms. Our approach shows good performance in terms of scalability. For instance, our implementation of the model can process more than one million alarms and *execute* the similarity algorithm in less than 3 minutes when it is run on 1.5 GHz Pentium 4 CPU with 256MB RAM. Moreover, our approach is scalable in another sense. Since network traffics are very dynamic and changeable, and subsequently normal alarm streams, new extracted normal patterns can be added to the normal pattern data set without any need to reconstruct the whole data set.

`Noisy data`: Typical IDSs can generate very noisy alarms, where undesirable data are mixed with real alarms. Our approach can handle these noisy data efficiently by exploiting discontinuous sequential patterns to represent noisy alarm sequences.

`Alarm attributes`: In general, commercial IDSs alarms contain many attributes such as time, numerical, categorical, and free-text. The most efficient model has to support any type of alarm attributes. Since sequential patterns extraction is never affected by the values of different attributes, the proposed approach is able to handle any attribute regardless of its type. In our current implementation we use *alarm type* (free-text) for alarms reduction.

Independency: Our proposed alarms reduction processes are totaly independent from the detection function. Therefore our model can be applied to most commercially-available IDSs without changing the existing security policy or system configuration. Since the normal model is constructed from alarms raised by IDSs under no attacks, and then used by the reduction algorithm in which incoming alarm streams are filtered, we believe that the entire reduction process can be seen as a plug-in to IDSs. Figure 1 shows the relationship of detection-reduction processes and how they are independent.

Cost: One of the critical issues in the reduction algorithm development is the cost. For extracting normal patterns of a number k of normal sequences of length m, we found that the suggested generator is an $O(km)$ cost. Since the normal model is built in off-line state this cost has no effect on the efficiency of the model. Similarity algorithm has a cost of an $O(n)$ where n is the total extracted patterns from the tested sequence.

Now, we will contrast the existing related alarms reduction methods with ours.

5   Related Works

There has been extensive considerable work in representing and reducing IDSs alarms. Here we only mention those efforts that contribute to the current proposal. In [17] Clifton and Gengo used episode data mining techniques to construct filtering rules. This work was extended by Julisch from IBM in [9], he introduced a clustering technique and used it in the design. In addition to discussing the main properties, Julisch observed that about 90% of false alarms are caused by a small number of root causes. Also related is the work by Manganaris, he applied association rules for false alarms reduction [18], he suggested an alarm filtration framework to handle IBM's network operation center based on extracted association rules. His approach classified incoming alarms based on frequent alarm set with minimum occurrence in bursts of alarms, non-frequent alarm sets flagged as suspicious. Our work, by contrast, uses different data mining techniques, it aspires to use continuous and discontinuous data mining for alarms filtering.

The other related work is done by Barbara *et al.* in [19] who enhanced anomalous patterns detection in computer networks by applying incremental data mining techniques. In [20] Lee *et al.* used data mining to construct the necessary features that help to detect the intrusions. In general, the last two works have overcome some limitations of existing detection systems by constructing more systematic models. By contrast, our approach is independent. It works with any IDSs and can handle any triggered alarms.

The works in [21, 22] focus on alarms grouping where each group contains the alarms of the same phenomenon. In that way, those works focus on the users features that have apparent effects on security issues raised by IDSs. In our work, we advocate exploratory data mining that needs no prior knowledge about the users where users privacy can be partially maintained. In general, we employ sequential patterns data mining to handle IDSs alarms in a more efficient way.

6 Conclusion

We have presented a new approach for dealing with IDS false alarms. Some systems use pattern matching for *misuse* detection while others use *anomaly* detection. Both approaches have their advantages and disadvantages. In this paper, we have attempted to combine these approaches, by performing anomaly detection on the voluminous results produced by a misuse detection system *"Snort"*. We have found our preliminary results with real-world data set encouraging: sequential patterns classification can be used to support investigation of a large number of alarms, the proposed approach employs historical alarms to build the norm and, more importantly, the viability of the proposed approach is demonstrated.

Our analysis of DARPA alarm traffic also produced interesting results. It showed that sequential patterns technique is suitable for false alarms reduction. Obviously, the basic value of using this technique is its ability to break the alarm sequence to its basic patterns. Moreover, the results have shown that alarm streams are very homogeneous, and contain very repetitive hidden useful patterns.

We have also investigated the suitability of using attribute *alarm type* for our purposes. It turned to work well in our framework. Our future work will focus on the validity of using other alarm attributes.

References

1. The 2004 E-Crime Watch survey, available at:
   http://www.csoonline.com/releases/ecrimewatch04.pdf
2. Kumar, S., Spafford E. H.: A Software Architecture to Support Misuse Intrusion Detection. In Proceedings of the 18th National Information Security Conference. (1995) 194-204
3. Forrest, S., Hofmeyr, S. A., Somayaji, A., Logstaff, T. A.: A Sense of Self for Unix process, Proceedings of 1996 IEEE Symposium on Computer Security and Privacy. (1996) 120-128
4. Ilgun, K., Kemmerer, R. A., Porras, P. A.: State Transition Analysis: A Rule-Based Intrusion Detection System. IEEE Transactions on Software Engineering, 21(3). (1995) 181-199
5. Javitz, H. S., Valdes, A.: The SRI IDES Statistical Anomaly Detector. In IEEE Symposium on Security and Privacy, Oakland, CA. SRI International. (May 1991)
6. Yihua, L., Vemuri, V. R.: Use of K-Nearest Neighbor classifier for intrusion detection. Computers & Security 21(5). (2002) 439-448
7. Bellovin, S. M.: Packets Found on an Internet. Computer Communications Review, 23(3). (1993) 26-31
8. Paxson, V., Bro,: A System for Detecting Network Intruders in Real-Time. Computer Networks, 31(23-24). (1999) 2435-2463

9. Julisch, K.: Mining Alarm Clusters to Improve Alarm Handling Effciency. In 17th Annual Computer Security Applications Conference (ACSAC). (December 2001) 12-21

10. Yen-Liang, C., Shih-Sheng, C., Ping-Yu H.: Mining hybrid sequential patterns and sequential rules. Information Systems V 27, 5. (2002) 345-362

11. Agrawal, R., Srikant, R.: Mining sequential patterns. Proceedings of the 7th International Conference on Data Engineering, Taipei, Taiwan, IEEE Computer Society. (1995) 3-14

12. Chen, M.S., Park, J.S., Yu, P.S.: Efficient data mining for path traversal patterns, IEEE Trans Knowledge Data Eng, 10(2). (1998) 209-221

13. Han, J., Pei, j., Yin, Y.: Mining frequent patterns without candidate. in proceedings of the 2000 ACM SIGMOD International Conference on Management of Data, Dallas, Texas, ACM Press, New York. (2000) 1-12

14. DARPA Dataset: http://www.ll.mit.edu/IST/ideval/

15. *Snort*: http://www.snort.org/

16. Roesch, M.: Snort – lightweight intrusion detection system for networks. In: Proceedings of USENIX LISA'99. (1999)

17. Clifton, C., Gengo, G.: Developing Custom Intrusion Detection Filters Using Data Mining. In Military Communications Int'l Symposium (MILCOM2000). (October 2000)

18. Manganaris, S., Christensen, M., Zerkle, D., Hermiz, K.: A Data Mining Analysis of RTID Alarms. Computer Networks, 34(4). (October 2000) 571-577

19. Barbara, D., Couto, J., Jajodia, S., Popyack, L., Wu, N.: ADAM: Detecting Intrusions by Data Mining. In IEEE Workshop on Information Assurance and Security. (2001)

20. Lee, W., Stolfo, S. J.: A Framework for Constructing Features and Models for Intrusion Detection Systems. ACM Transactions on Information and System Security, 3(4). (2000) 227-261

21. Valdes, A., Skinner, K.: Probabilistic Alert Correlation. In 4th Workshop on Recent Advances in Intrusion Detection (RAID), LNCS, Springer Verlag. (2001) 54-68

22. Staniford, S., Hoagland, J. A., McAlerney, J. M.: Practical Automated Detection of Stealthy Portscans. In ACM Computer and Communications Security IDS Workshop. (2000) 1-7

A   GFP1

Yen-Liang et al. in [10] formulated the definition of sequential patterns, and proposed an algorithm GFP1 to mine hybrid (continuous and discontinuous) patterns.

In this work, we adopted GFP1 to discover and extract all continuous and discontinuous sequential patterns. In the following a brief description of this algorithm will be given, the details can be found in Yen-Liang paper.

Algorithm GFP1

1 Generate $C_{1,0}$
2 Determine $L_{1,0}$ by scanning the database

3 For $(k = 2; L_{k-1,k-2} \neq 0; k + +)$ do
4    $C_{k,k-1} = GetJoin(L_{k-1,k-2})$
5   Determine $L_{k,k-1}$ by scanning the database
6   For $(j = 2; j = k; j + +)$ do
7       $C_{k,k-1} = GetNextCandidate(L_{k,k-j+1})$
8   Determine $L_{k,k-j}$ by scanning the database

In the above algorithm, some steps need to be further explained. Each $C_{i,j}$ contains all candidate and possible sequential patterns, and each $L_{i,j}$ contains all frequent sequential patterns that exceed some support value, where i is the number of elements and j is the number of stars within each pattern. In the first phase, we need to find $C_{1,0}$, i.e, all candidate patterns with only one known element and zero " $*$ ".

GFP1 algorithm includes two functions *GetJoin* and *GetNextCandidate*.

GetJoin function is used to generate the candidate patterns $C_{k,k-1}$ of length k from the frequent pattern set $L_{k-1,k-2}$. By joining the patterns in $L_{k-1,k-2}$, we can find a set of candidate patterns which contains all frequent patterns in $L_{k,k-1}$ with a *support* value exceeding a certain threshold, *Support* parameter value required for GFP1, it describes the minimum frequent number required for a single sequential pattern to be considered as a useful pattern and then mined.

Function *GetNextCandidate* is used to generate $C_{k,k-j}$ from the frequent pattern set $L_{k,k-j+1}$. The candidate $C_{k,k-j}$ can be found by removing the star from all the frequent patterns in $L_{k,k-j+1}$.

Indexing Information for Data Forensics

Michael T. Goodrich[1], Mikhail J. Atallah[2], and Roberto Tamassia[3]

[1] University of California, Irvine
goodrich@uci.edu
[2] Purdue University
mja@cs.purdue.edu
[3] Brown University
rt@cs.brown.edu

Abstract. We introduce novel techniques for organizing the indexing structures of how data is stored so that alterations from an original version can be detected and the changed values specifically identified. We give forensic constructions for several fundamental data structures, including arrays, linked lists, binary search trees, skip lists, and hash tables. Some of our constructions are based on a new reduced-randomness construction for nonadaptive combinatorial group testing.

Keywords: data forensics, data integrity, data marking, combinatorial group testing, information hiding, tamper detection, data structures

1 Introduction

Computer forensics [71] deals with methods for extracting digital evidence after a computer crime has been committed. Typically, such crimes involve modifying documents, databases, and other data structures to an attacker's advantage. Examples could include a student changing a grade in a registrar's database, a dishonest speculator altering online financial data for a certain company, an identity thief modifying personal information of a victim, or a computer intruder altering system logs to mask a virus infection. It would be ideal in such cases if an investigator could identify, after the fact, which pieces of information were changed and, in so doing, be able to implicate the attacker. In the rest of this section, we describe our motivation, model, and related work, and we summarize our contributions. But before doing so, we briefly give a simplified and intuitive overview of what this paper is about.

A cryptographic one-way hash is a commonly used way of detecting unauthorized or otherwise malicious modification of a file or other digital object (e.g., [5, 44, 62], to mention a few of many examples). This is done by storing a keyed cryptographic hash of the item and using it later as a reference for comparison. This paper is about going beyond the yes/no afforded by this common use of cryptographic hashes: given n items, we now seek to store as few hashes as possible so as to enable the pinpointing of *which* of these n items were modified (by comparing the computed hashes to the stored hash values). Of course a hash is now applied to (a concatenation of) a subset of the n items. But *which* subsets, and *how many* of them, are needed so as to pinpoint the modifications of up to d of the n items ? We show that remarkably few hashes suffice. Why it is so important to use few hashes will become apparent when we consider the

J. Ioannidis, A. Keromytis, and M. Yung (Eds.): ACNS 2005, LNCS 3531, pp. 206–221, 2005.

application we describe for the above-mentioned combinatorial result: the case when the n items are in the nodes of a data structure, and we seek to store the hashes within the topology of the data structure, i.e., *without using any additional space* (and, of course, without modifying any of the n items stored in the data structure). In other words, this forensic marking comes "for free" as far as the space of the data structure is concerned.

Motivation. As mentioned above, in this paper we initiate an investigation into methods for encoding information in the way data is indexed so as to identify if it has been altered, and if so, to determine exactly the pieces of information that have changed. Formally, we model this problem in terms of a data structure D that is stored on a semi-trusted machine, which under normal circumstances, would use D for some desired purpose. If there is an indication or suspicion that D has been altered in a malicious way, then we would like to enable a computer investigator, whom we call the *auditor*, to examine the current state of D to determine what, if anything, has changed. Of course, a trivial solution would be for the auditor to cache a copy of D in protected memory and do a simple comparison of this copy of D to the current version. This solution would achieve the desired goal of identifying exactly the parts of D that have changed, but it would also require a tremendous amount of storage for the auditor, who is potentially responsible for a large community of users and computers. Thus, we additionally restrict solutions to use no storage at the auditor (or equivalently in protected memories), other than possibly some small number of administrative values, such as a master key for "unlocking" information encoded in D. We refer to this problem as that of *indexing information for data forensics*, or *data forensics marking*, for short.

Model. We are further interested only in solutions where marking the indexing structure of data leaves the actual data values unchanged, since changing data values could alter the outcome of queries in unintended ways. Unlike well-known digital water-marking techniques [18], we want to encode authentication information only in the organizational structure of a data structure D, not in the values stored in it. We allow ourselves the possibility of modifying non-data fields in D, but we require that any such changes we carry out be stealthy, that is, not immediately detectable by the adversary. In information-hiding terminology, we view the information hidden in D to be steganographic rather than a watermark (which, strictly speaking, does not require stealthiness, whereas steganography requires that even the presence of hidden information be undetectable). Ideally, we want to encode information only in the topology of D's pointers and the ordering of D's memory blocks, yet we desire there to be sufficient information so as to specifically identify any portions of D that have been changed by an attacker. Note that this requirement for pinpointing of the changes goes beyond the notion of making the structure tamper-evident in the usual yes/no sense, something usually achieved using HMACs and digital signatures, but whose yes/no outcome has too coarse a granularity for our purposes.

Our model of the adversary is as follows. The adversary has access to the data structure D after it has been deployed on the semi-trusted machine and can modify the values of D, but not the topology of D's pointers and the ordering of D's memory blocks. This assumption is realistic in many practical applications for the following two reasons. First, regular users typically provide data to an application through the application's user interface but cannot modify the application's internal storage or the application's code to alter the memory arrangement of the data. Second, even if the user were able to alter the data organization, the user may not think about doing it because of the stealthiness of the marking.

The adversary is successful if he can modify some values of D without such changes being detected by the auditor. The adversary has knowledge of the algorithm the auditor will use to perform a forensic analysis of D. However, we do not allow the adversary to know the cryptographic master key maintained by the auditor, nor of any keys that are derived from such a master key. This is the usual (and preferred) "white box" security requirement. Although in practice one may gain additional "security through obscurity", it is wiser to assume the adversary knows all but the keys. We illustrate this model in Figure 1.

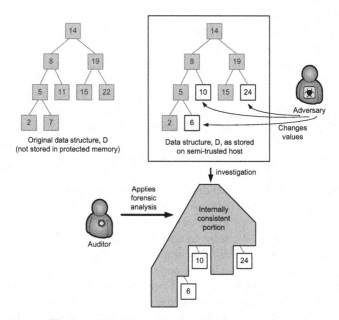

Fig. 1. An illustration of data forensics marking.

Prior Related Work. Computer forensics has been applied to software authorship detection [43, 63], the integrity of audit logs using external protected memories [59], tracing IP packets during denial-of-service attacks [29, 57], and e-mail author identification [20]. We are not familiar with any previous work on data forensics marking, however. Nevertheless, there has been considerable prior work in the theoretical computer science literature on a number of related areas, including digital watermarking, combinatorial group testing, program checking, property testing, and authenticated data structures. We review some of this prior work here.

Digital watermarking [18] deals with methods for hiding a mark (usually identifying information) in digital content in a manner that is resilient, i.e., hard to remove by an adversary without considerably damaging the object. There are many applications of watermarking, including inserting ownership information, inserting purchaser information, placing caption information, etc. Most watermarking work has been on multimedia content, where minor degradation of the quality of the media is acceptable in order to make the mark more resilient. There have been some notable exceptions, dealing with watermarking software, semi-structures (XML), and relational databases. Collberg and Thomborson [17, 19], Chang and Atallah [15], Horne, Matheson, Sheehan, and Tarjan [38] and Venkatesan, Vazirani, and Sinha [70], present schemes for watermarking software. Qu and Potkonjak [55] propose a watermarking scheme for graph colorings. Khanna and Zane [39] describe a scheme for encoding information in the weights of a graph representing a map so as to preserve shortest paths. Gross-Amblard [35] studies ways of changing values to encode identifying information in a database or XML document so as to preserve the answers to certain queries. Marking XML structures is also the topic of Sion et al. [60]. Database watermarking that slightly degrades the data was proposed by Agarwal et al. [1] and Sion et al. [61]. This watermarking work is related to data forensics marking in that it is directed at encoding information in digital content. It differs from data forensics marking, however, in that digital watermarking allows data values to change (in hopefully imperceptible ways) and is not interested in identifying the specific places where content has changed.

Several researchers have studied combinatorial group testing and its applications to cryptography and information encoding (e.g., see [16, 26]). This area is directed at performing group tests on subsets of a given set S to identify defective elements in S. The area has not to date been applied to data index integrity, but in this paper we show an interesting connection between data forensics marking and a new reduced-randomness construction of a nonadaptive combinatorial group testing scheme, which may be of independent interest. As evidence for this claim, we observe that Kurosawa, Johansson, and Stinson [45] explore other applications of reduced-randomness constructions in cryptography, and Stinson, van Trung, and Wei [65] explore applications of group testing to key distribution in cryptography.

Following early work on program checking (see, e.g., [7, 66, 67]), efficient schemes have been developed for checking the results of various data structures and algorithms (see, e.g., [4, 8–10, 23, 24, 27, 40, 48, 49]). These schemes typically utilize linear space with checking algorithms that run faster than the construction algorithms they are checking, and they are directed at detecting if an algorithm has performed correctly or not. We are not aware, however, of any prior work on program checking that, in addition to detecting an error state, also identifies all the places in a program or structure that have become invalid. Likewise, the related area of property testing is directed at determining if a combinatorial structure satisfies a certain property or is "far" from such a structure (e.g., see [56]), and it too does not identify all property violations.

Prior work in the area of authenticated data structures [3, 11, 13, 14, 21, 22, 28, 30–34, 41, 42, 47, 52, 54, 68, 69] has focused on disseminating information from a single, trusted source so that an alteration to the data structure could be detected, but not specifically identified. That is, they do not provide solutions to the data forensics marking problem. Related work on committed databases has recently been presented in [53].

Our Contributions. In this paper, we introduce the data forensics marking framework and give several results for this model that use no additional storage at the auditor other than a master key. The security of our methods are based on standard cryptographic assumptions. Namely, we assume the existence of the *message authentication code (MAC)* cryptographic primitive, which is a key-dependent one-way collision-resistant function (see, e.g., [50, 58, 64]). A message authentication code can be constructed from a standard cryptographic hash function.

We give forensic constructions for several fundamental data structures, including arrays, linked lists, binary search trees, skip lists, and hash tables. Some of our constructions are based on a new reduced-randomness construction for nonadaptive combinatorial group testing, which is of independent interest.

All of our data forensics marking constructions involve two phases of computation. In the first phase, we build a program P and authentication information A for S so that P can detect and identify up to some number, d, of changes to S in the indexing structure D using A. In the second phase, we encode P and A in the organizational and topological structure of D in a way that is probabilistically difficult for the adversary to reproduce, yet it also preserves the accuracy of P with high probability or it still allows P to restrict the changed values in S to a small set of candidates (which is often sufficient for forensics). The challenge, of course, is to design the encoding of P and A in D so that it can survive up to d alterations of the values in S, as stored in D, that the adversary might make.

Our contributions can be summarized as follows:

- We develop a new reduced-randomness construction for nonadaptive combinatorial group testing. In particular, we show how to construct a $t \times n$ d-disjunct binary matrix M encoding a nonadaptive combinatorial group test for n items that can detect up to d defective items, with t being $O(d^2 \log n)$. Our construction uses only $O(d^3 \log n \log d)$ random bits and is correct with high probability, whereas previous schemes use $\Theta(d^2 n \log n)$ random bits and are not high-probability constructions. Thus, we can encode matrix M using $O(\log n)$ bits when d is a constant, a polylogarithmic number of bits when d is polylogarithmic, or $o(n)$ bits when d is $o(n^{1/3}/\log^{2/3} n)$, which is of independent interest.
- We give efficient forensic constructions of several fundamental data structures, including binary search trees, skip lists, arrays, linked lists, and hash tables. The number of changes we can detect and identify for a data structure D storing a set S of n elements is $O(n^{1/3}/\log^{2/3} n)$ for balanced search trees and skip lists, $O(n^{1/4}/\log^{1/4} n)$ for arrays and linked lists, and $O(1)$ for hash tables.

In the next section, we describe our reduced-randomness construction of a nonadaptive combinatorial group test. In Section 3, we outline our two-phase constructions of indexing structures for data forensics marking schemes. We conclude in Section 4.

2   Blood Testing and Forensics

As mentioned above, some of our solutions utilize a reduced-randomness construction of a nonadaptive combinatorial group testing scheme. Combinatorial group testing [26] (or "CGT") schemes identify "bad" members of a set S of n elements using group tests. A *group test* consists of selecting a test sample $T \subset S$ and performing a single experiment to determine whether or not T contains a bad element. A testing scheme that makes all its tests in a single round, with all test sets determined in advance, is said to be *nonadaptive*. Most efficient schemes are designed assuming there is an upper bound, d, on the number of possible bad members of the input set S, where $1 \leq d < n$. Combinatorial group testing was originally formulated for testing blood supplies during World War II, with a group test comprising a tester extracting a few drops from each blood sample in a test set, pooling them together, and testing the mixed sample for the syphilis antigen [25].

Reduced-Randomness Nonadaptive Combinatorial Group Testing. For the case $d = 1$, it is straightforward to design a nonadaptive scheme using $O(\log n)$ tests. For the general case, $d > 1$, however, designing efficient general testing schemes is more challenging. Adaptive schemes generally make fewer total tests, in terms of d and n, than nonadaptive schemes. In particular, the best known general-purpose adaptive schemes use $O(d \log(n/d))$ tests, whereas the number of tests used by the best known general-purpose nonadaptive schemes is $O(d^2 \log n)$ [26]. Even so, adaptive schemes are not applicable in many contexts, including DNA sequence analysis and the context of this paper.

Our application of combinatorial group testing to data forensics marking is based on the use of nonadaptive CGT schemes. Unfortunately, the known deterministic nonadaptive CGT schemes are asymptotically suboptimal or not designed for most values of d and n, and the known randomized CGT schemes, for $d \geq 2$, utilize $\Theta(d^2 n \log n)$ random bits (e.g., see [26]). These drawbacks make existing nonadaptive combinatorial group testing schemes infeasible for data forensics marking, where we wish to limit the memory requirements of the auditor.

In this section, we present a simple, randomized nonadaptive combinatorial group testing scheme, for $d \geq 2$, where we reduce the needed random bits to be $O(d^3 \log n \log d)$. This reduced-randomness CGT scheme is based on applying the construction of Alon *et al.* [2] of almost k-wise independent random variables (see also [6, 51]) to the randomized CGT approach of Busschbach [12], and then showing that almost k-wise independent random variables can be used to achieve an efficient nonadaptive CGT with high probability (which is, in fact, a stronger result than the previous algorithm achieves using fully independent variables). The main idea of this approach is to construct a $t \times n$ binary matrix M, where each column corresponds to an element of S and each row corresponds to a test—so that $M[i, j] = 1$ if and only if element j is included in test i.

A $t \times n$ binary matrix M is d-disjunct [26] if, for any $d + 1$ columns with one of them designated, there always exists a row with a 1 in the designated column and 0's in the other d columns. Given a d-disjunct binary matrix M, we can immediately design a nonadaptive combinatorial group testing scheme—simply perform the test indicated by each row of M. With the results of these tests in hand, we can then remove each column of M that has a 1 in a row that returned a negative test result (recall that, in the testing framework, a negative is a good outcome). The remaining columns correspond to the "bad" elements. The correctness of this algorithm is derived directly from M being d-disjunct, for if we designate a "good" column together with a group of up to d bad

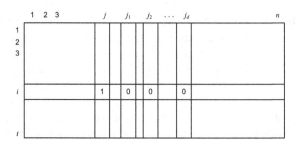

Fig. 2. An illustration of a $t \times n$ d-disjunct matrix.

columns, there must be a row (i.e., a test) that includes the good column and excludes the bad ones. See Figure 2.

Our algorithm for building a d-disjunct $t \times n$ matrix M is simply to set each $M[i, j] = 1$ with probability roughly $\frac{1}{d+1}$, by using "almost" k-wise independent random variables. The notion of being almost k-wise independent that we use is based on the following definition of Alon *et al.* [2]:

Definition 1. *A set of probability-$(1/2)$ random bits, $x_1, x_2, \ldots, x_n$, is (ϵ, k)-independent if, for any k-bit vector α and k positions $i_1 < i_2 < \cdots < i_k$, we have*

$$| \Pr[x_{i_1} x_{i_2} \cdots x_{i_k} = \alpha] - 2^{-k}| \le \epsilon.$$

Alon *et al.* [2] establish the following important fact:

Lemma 1. *Let $N = 2^r - 1$ and let k be an odd integer. Then, using*

$$2 \left(\left\lceil \log \frac{1}{\epsilon} + \log \left(1 + \frac{(k-1)r}{2} \right) \right\rceil \right)$$

probability-$(1/2)$ random bits, one can construct a set of N probability-$(1/2)$ bits that are (ϵ, k)-independent. That is, the number of needed random bits is roughly $2 \log \left(\frac{k \log N}{2\epsilon} \right)$.

Given Lemma 1, we would like to set t so that the $t \times n$ random matrix M we construct will be d-disjunct with high probability.

Theorem 1. *Given integers d and n such that $2 \le d < n$, one can construct a $t \times n$ binary matrix M that is d-disjunct with high probability, using $O(d^3 \log n \log d)$ random bits, where t is $\Theta(d^2 \log n)$.*

Proof. Let R be a set of tnl probability-$(1/2)$ random bits that are $(\epsilon, (d + 1)tl)$-independent, where $l = \lceil \log(d+1) \rceil$ and t and ϵ will be set in the analysis. Considering these bits l at a time, we can convert this set into a set R' of probability-p bits, where $p = 1/2^l$, so that $1/2(d+1) < p \le 1/(d+1)$. We use the bits in R' to define the matrix M so that $M[i, j] = 1$ if and only if the corresponding bit in R' is equal to 1. (Note:

Azar, Motwani, and Naor [6] have an alternate, more general, approach for constructing almost k-independent probability-p bits, but their construction is more complicated
than what is needed here.)

Consider now a particular column j and d other columns $j_1, j_2, \ldots, j_d$ in matrix M.
For any row i in M, had the random variables in R' been at least $(d+1)$-wise independent, then the probability that $M[i, j] = 1$ and $M[i, j_s] = 0$, for $s = 1, 2, \ldots, d$, would
be $p(1 - p)^d$. Thus, had the variables in R' been at least $(d+1)t$-wise independent,
then the probability that no such row exists (a *failure*) among these columns would be

$$\left[1 - p(1 - p)^d \right]^t .$$

Notice that this probability is actually determined by $(d+1)tl$ bits in R. Let $\mathcal{F}$ denote
the set of all vectors of values for these $k = (d+1)tl$ bits $x_{i_1} x_{i_2} \ldots x_{i_k}$ that result in
a failure event for column j and the d other columns, and note that $|\mathcal{F}| \leq 2^k$. Then, by
Lemma 1, for each vector α in $\mathcal{F}$, we have

$$\left| \Pr[x_{i_1} x_{i_2} \cdots x_{i_k} = \alpha] - 2^{-k} \right| \leq \epsilon.$$

That is, we obtain

$$2^{-k} - \epsilon \leq \Pr[x_{i_1} x_{i_2} \cdots x_{i_k} = \alpha] \leq 2^{-k} + \epsilon.$$

In other words, this probability is bounded from above by ϵ plus the value it would have
been had these bits been k-wise independent. Therefore, we have

$$\sum_{\alpha \in \mathcal{F}} \Pr[x_{i_1} x_{i_2} \cdots x_{i_k} = \alpha] \leq \left[1 - p(1 - p)^d \right]^t + 2^k \epsilon.$$

There are $(d+1) \binom{n}{d+1}$ ways of distinguishing a column j and d other columns in M.
Moreover, the probability that any column j and d others determine a failure is certainly
no more than the probability that all such groups determine a failure, which, irrespective
of any considerations about the independence of the underlying random variables, is no
more than

$$(d+1) \binom{n}{d+1} \left[1 - p(1 - p)^d \right]^t + (d+1) \binom{n}{d+1} 2^k \epsilon.$$

By the definition of p, this probability is at most

$$(d+1) \binom{n}{d+1} \left[1 - \frac{1}{2(d+1)} \left(1 - \frac{1}{d+1} \right)^d \right]^t + (d+1) \binom{n}{d+1} 2^k \epsilon.$$

Using the inequalities $(1 - 1/(d+1))^d > 1/3$ and $(d+1) \binom{n}{d+1} \leq n^{d+1}$, for $d \geq 2$,
and substituting in the value for k, we can further simplify this probability as being at
most

$$n^{d+1} \left(1 - \frac{1}{6(d+1)} \right)^t + n^{d+1} 2^{(d+1)tl} \epsilon.$$

For our claim to hold with high probability, we would like each of the above terms to be at most $1/n$. To bound the first term by $1/n$, we can use the inequality $-\ln(1-x) \geq x$, for $0 \leq x < 1$, and we can set

$$t = 6(d+1)(d+2)\lceil \ln n \rceil,$$

which is $\Theta(d^2 \log n)$. Given this value for t, to then bound the second term by $1/n$, we can set

$$\epsilon = n^{-(d+2)} 2^{-6(d+1)^2(d+2)\lceil \ln n \rceil \lceil \log d \rceil}.$$

According to Lemma 1, the number of random bits needed for this construction is

$$2\left(\left\lceil \log \frac{1}{\epsilon} + \log\left(1 + \frac{(k-1)\log N}{2}\right)\right\rceil\right).$$

That is, the number of random bits needed is $O(d^3 \log n \log d)$.

Having a reduced-randomness construction, as specified in Theorem 1, allows us to encode a $t \times n$ d-disjunct binary matrix M simply by storing the $O(d^3 \log n \log d)$ random bits used to generate M.

3   Specific Constructions for Data Forensics Marking

We use Theorem 1 in many of our data forensics marking solutions, which we briefly outline in this section. Throughout this discussion, we assume the reader is familiar with the fundamental data structures mentioned. In addition, throughout this section we assume that the auditor and data structure designer share a secret key K that is easily derived from the auditor's master key and the data structure designer's identity. We also assume the existence of a message authentication code (MAC) function $f_K(x)$ with key K. (see, e.g., [50, 58, 64]).

From Test Samples to Set Integrity Checking.   Given a nonadaptive combinatorial group test (CGT) for detecting up to d defectives in a set of n items, we can convert this into a test of the integrity of a collection S of n items stored in a data structure. For each test T specified by the CGT, compute its *authentication value* a_T defined by

$$a_T = f_K(x_1 \| x_2 \| \cdots \| x_m),$$

where f_K is a MAC function and $x_1, \cdots x_m$ are the items of S included in test T, in sorted order. We can then recompute a_T on an altered copy of S to determine if this value has changed. If so, then we know that an item in T has been modified. Thus, performing all these comparisons for all the tests in the CGT would give us a determination of which items in S have changed.

Lemma 2. *We can construct a forensic scheme for a set of n elements so as to detect and identify which of up to d of its elements have been changed, with high probability, using $O(d^3 \log^2 n)$ bits of authentication information.*

The problem, of course, is that the auditor does not have enough memory to store an encoding of a CGT. Nevertheless, Theorem 1 gives a way of avoiding storing anything at the auditor, for it implies that we can encode a nonadaptive CGT for detecting d defective elements among n using only $O(d^3 \log n \log d)$ bits. The number of tests determined by these bits is $O(d^2 \log n)$. For each test T defined by this CGT, we need to store the authentication value a_T, Note that a_T is determined by a message authentication code based on the key K, which is unknown to the adversary. Thus, the CGT and its associated authentication values can be represented using $O(d^3 \log^2 n)$ bits. Our solution, then, to avoid any storage at the auditor, is to encode these bits in the data structure itself.

Balanced Binary Search Trees. A balanced binary search tree holding n items has $O(\log n)$ depth. Its structure can also easily encode $O(n)$ bits in a simple recursive fashion. Given a set S of comparable items, we have $n/2$ items that we can pick for the root's value (from the middle half of elements from rank $n/4$ to $3n/4$). The exact choice allows us to encode $\log(n/2)$ bits at the root level, and we can then repeat this construction recursively at each child. Since we can encode in the tree a total of $O(n)$ bits we picking d that is $o(n^{1/3}/\log^{2/3} n)$.

By Lemma 2, we obtain the following result:

Theorem 2. *We can construct a forensic scheme for a balanced binary tree storing n elements so as to detect and identify which of up to $O(n^{1/3}/\log^{2/3} n)$ of its values have been changed, with high probability.*

Skip Lists. We can use, for skip lists, a scheme similar to the one developed for binary search trees. At each level of the skip list structure, about half of the (say) m elements of that level will survive to the next (higher) level. This allows us to encode at that level a number of bits equal to

$$\log \binom{m}{m/2} \geq \log(2^{m/2}) = m/2,$$

Hence, the overall encoding capacity in an n-element skip list is $O(n)$ bits. Thus, just as for the balanced binary tree case, by Lemma 2, we obtain the following result:

Theorem 3. *We can construct a forensic scheme for a skip list storing n elements so as to detect and identify which of up to $O(n^{1/3}/\log^{2/3} n)$ of its values have been changed, with high probability.*

Arrays and Linked Lists. Arrays and linked lists allow up to $O(n \log n)$ bits to be encoded in the permutation of the items stored in the list or array. But this information is stored implicitly, since the ordering itself could be altered should the adversary change values. Our solution in this case is to replicate the CGT and its expected values $d + 1$ times and spread these multiple encodings evenly across the bits encoded by the permutation. By a pigeon-hole argument, even if the adversary changes d values, there will still be a large enough contiguous run of unchanged values that encode the CGT and its expected values so as to allow us to determine which values might have changed.

In this case we need $O(d^4 \log^2 n)$ bits. Therefore, by Lemma 2, we have the following result:

Theorem 4. *We can construct a forensic scheme for an array or linked list storing n elements so as to detect and identify which of up to $O(n^{1/4}/\log^{1/4} n)$ of its values have been changed, with high probability.*

This construction can also be applied to relational databases that use a data-independent index number or unique ID to name records. In this case we can treat the index number in the same way we used positions in an array or linked list.

Hash Tables. A hash table for a set S of n elements consists of a bucket array B of size $O(n)$ and a hash function h which maps elements of S to cells of B under some collision-handling rule. Let us assume that h is based on a simple, standard linear function, so that $h(x) = \alpha x + \beta \bmod p$, for each x in S, where p is a prime on the order of n. There is not a lot of variability in such a hash table that we can exploit for forensic analysis, but there is nevertheless enough for the following:

Theorem 5. *A hash table has a forensic construction that can detect and identify a single value insertion or deletion and can isolate a changed value to a set of constant expected size.*

Proof. Our construction begins by choosing p to be a random prime on the order of n (for hash table efficiency, it is good that p is slightly larger than n) such that $p \bmod 4 = n \bmod 4$. Sort the elements of S and compute value α defined as follows:

$$\alpha = f_K(x_1 \,\|\, x_2 \,\|\, \cdots \,\|\, x_n \,\|\, p),$$

where $x_1, \cdots x_n$ are the items of S in sorted order. We then compute value β as follows:

$$\beta = x_1 \oplus x_2 \oplus \cdots \oplus f_0(p).$$

We then define the hash function h for the hash table as $h(x) = \alpha x + \beta \bmod p$.

Let us consider the forensic capabilities of this structure. If an item is deleted, then we can detect this case using α and we can recompute the deleted value from the XOR of β and the remaining values in the hash table. If a value is added, then we can detect this case using α and we can compute the complement of this value from the XOR of β and the existing values in the hash table. If a value is changed, then we can detect this case using α and β. For each element x in the hash table, we can use β to determine what its value should have been were x the item that changed, and then recompute α to verify that this is the case. The expected number of values that will be determined to have possibly changed will be $O(1)$ and the adversary cannot control this value, since he does not know K and is assumed to be unable to invert f.

Security. The security of our constructions is based on the fact that a successful adversary will have to invert or find collisions in the message authentication function f_K used or recover the secret key K shared by the data structure designer and auditor. A complete security proof will be given in the full version of the paper.

Extension. We can extend our results to a stronger adversarial model, where the adversary can also modify a constant fraction of the authentication information hidden in the data structure. For this purpose, we encode the authentication information using the cryptographic variation of the Guruswami-Sudan list decoder [36, 37] presented in [46]. Even with this stronger model, we obtain results analogous to those given in Theorems 2–4. Details will be given in the full version of the paper.

4 Conclusion

We have introduced the topic of information indexing for data forensics marking, given a new reduced-randomness construction for nonadaptive combinatorial group testing, and applied this and other techniques to design efficient and robust constructions of forensic schemes for several kinds of data indexing structures. We believe there is still a considerable amount of additional work that could be done in this area. In particular, it would be useful to have efficient forensic schemes for data that is changing over time. Such a solution would solve the problem of maintaining forensic data for audit logs and dynamic databases.

Acknowledgements

The work of the first author was supported in part by NSF Grants IIS-0325345, IIS-0219560, IIS-0312357, and IIS-0242421, ONR Contract N00014-02-1-0364, by sponsors of the Center for Education and Research in Information Assurance and Security, and by Purdue Discovery Park's e-Enterprise Center. The work of the second author was supported in part by NSF Grants CCR-0312760, CCR-0311720, CCR-0225642, and CCR-0098068. The work of the third author was supported in part by NSF Grants CCR-0311510, IIS-0324846 and CNS-0303577 and by a research gift from Sun Microsystems.

References

1. R. Agrawal and J. Kiernan. Watermarking relational databases. In *Proceedings of the 2002 ACM SIGMOD International Conference on Management of Data, Hong Kong*, pages 155–166. ACM Press, 2002.
2. N. Alon, O. Goldreich, J. Håstad, and R. Peralta. Simple construction of almost k-wise independent random variables. *Random Structures and Algorithms*, 3:289–304, 1992.
3. A. Anagnostopoulos, M. T. Goodrich, and R. Tamassia. Persistent authenticated dictionaries and their applications. In *Proc. Information Security Conference (ISC 2001)*, volume 2200 of *LNCS*, pages 379–393. Springer-Verlag, 2001.
4. S. Ar, M. Blum, B. Codenotti, and P. Gemmell. Checking approximate computations over the reals. In *Proc. ACM Symp. on the Theory of Computing*, pages 786–795, 1993.
5. W. Arbaugh, D. Farber, and J. Smith. A secure and reliable bootstrap architecture, 1997.
6. Y. Azar, R. Motwani, and J. Naor. Approximating probability distributions using small sample spaces. *Combinatorica*, 18(2):151–171, 1998.
7. M. Blum and S. Kannan. Designing programs that check their work. *J. ACM*, 42(1):269–291, Jan. 1995.

8. J. D. Bright and G. Sullivan. Checking mergeable priority queues. In *Digest of the 24th Symposium on Fault-Tolerant Computing*, pages 144–153. IEEE Computer Society Press, 1994.

9. J. D. Bright and G. Sullivan. On-line error monitoring for several data structures. In *Digest of the 25th Symposium on Fault-Tolerant Computing*, pages 392–401. IEEE Computer Society Press, 1995.

10. J. D. Bright, G. Sullivan, and G. M. Masson. Checking the integrity of trees. In *Digest of the 25th Symposium on Fault-Tolerant Computing*, pages 402–411. IEEE Computer Society Press, 1995.

11. A. Buldas, P. Laud, and H. Lipmaa. Eliminating counterevidence with applications to accountable certificate management. *Journal of Computer Security*, 10(3):273–296, 2002.

12. P. Busschbach. Constructive methods to solve the problems of: s-sujectivity conflict resoltuion, coding in defective memories. Unpublished manuscript, cited in [26], 1984.

13. J. Camenisch and A. Lysyanskaya. Dynamic accumulators and application to efficient revocation of anonymous credentials. In M. Yung, editor, *Advances in Cryptology — CRYPTO 2002*, volume 2442 of *Lecture Notes in Computer Science*, pages 61–76. Springer Verlag, 2002.

14. S. Cannella, M. Shin, C. Straub, R. Tamassia, and D. J. Polivy. Secure visualization of authentication information: A case study. In *Proc. IEEE Symp. on Visual Languages and Human-Centric Computing*, 2004.

15. H. Chang and M. Atallah. Protecting software code by guards. In T. Sander, editor, *Security and Privacy in Digital Rights Management*, volume 2320 of *Lecture Notes in Computer Science*, pages 160–175. Springer-Verlag, 2002.

16. C. J. Colbourn, J. H. Dinitz, and D. R. Stinson. Applications of combinatorial designs to communications, cryptography, and networking. In Walker, editor, *Surveys in Combinatorics*, volume 187 of *London Mathematical Society Lecture Note Series*, pages 37–100. Cambridge University Press, 1993.

17. C. Collberg and C. Thomborson. On the limits of software watermarking. Technical Report 164, Department of Computer Science, The University of Auckland, Private Bag 92019, Auckland, New Zealand, Aug. 1998.

18. C. Collberg and C. Thomborson. Software watermarking: Models and dynamic embeddings. In *ACM Symp. on Principles of Programming Languages (POPL)*, pages 311–324, 1999.

19. C. Collberg and C. Thomborson. Software watermarking: models and dynamic embeddings. In *ACM SIGPLAN–SIGACT POPL'99*, San Antonio, Texas, USA, Jan. 1999.

20. O. de Vel, A. Anderson, M. Corney, and G. Mohay. Mining e-mail content for author identification forensics. *SIGMOD Record*, 30(4):55–64, 2001.

21. P. Devanbu, M. Gertz, A. Kwong, C. Martel, G. Nuckolls, and S. G. Stubblebine. Flexible authentication of XML documents. In *Proc. ACM Conf. on Computer and Communications Security*, pages 136–145, 2001.

22. P. Devanbu, M. Gertz, C. Martel, and S. G. Stubblebine. Authentic data publication over the internet. *Journal of Computer Security*, 11(3):291 – 314, 2003.

23. O. Devillers, G. Liotta, F. P. Preparata, and R. Tamassia. Checking the convexity of polytopes and the planarity of subdivisions. *Comput. Geom. Theory Appl.*, 11:187–208, 1998.

24. G. Di Battista and G. Liotta. Upward planarity checking: "Faces are more than polygons". In S. H. Whitesides, editor, *Graph Drawing (Proc. GD '98)*, volume 1547 of *Lecture Notes Comput. Sci.*, pages 72–86. Springer-Verlag, 1998.

25. R. Dorfman. The detection of defective members of large populations. *Ann. Math. Statist.*, 14:436–440, 1943.

26. D.-Z. Du and F. K. Hwang. *Combinatorial Group Testing and Its Applications*. World Scientific, 2nd edition, 2000.

27. U. Finkler and K. Mehlhorn. Checking priority queues. In *Proc. 10th ACM-SIAM Symp. on Discrete Algorithms*, pages S901–S902, 1999.

28. I. Gassko, P. S. Gemmell, and P. MacKenzie. Efficient and fresh certification. In *Int. Workshop on Practice and Theory in Public Key Cryptography (PKC '2000)*, volume 1751 of *LNCS*, pages 342–353. Springer-Verlag, 2000.

29. M. T. Goodrich. Efficient packet marking for large-scale IP traceback. In *9th ACM Conf. on Computer and Communications Security (CCS)*, pages 117–126, 2002.

30. M. T. Goodrich, M. Shin, R. Tamassia, and W. H. Winsborough. Authenticated dictionaries for fresh attribute credentials. In *Proc. Trust Management Conference*, volume 2692 of *LNCS*, pages 332–347. Springer, 2003.

31. M. T. Goodrich and R. Tamassia. Efficient authenticated dictionaries with skip lists and commutative hashing. Technical report, Johns Hopkins Information Security Institute, 2000. Available from `http://www.cs.brown.edu/cgc/stms/papers/hashskip.pdf`.

32. M. T. Goodrich, R. Tamassia, and J. Hasic. An efficient dynamic and distributed cryptographic accumulator. In *Proc. of Information Security Conference (ISC)*, volume 2433 of *LNCS*, pages 372–388. Springer-Verlag, 2002.

33. M. T. Goodrich, R. Tamassia, and A. Schwerin. Implementation of an authenticated dictionary with skip lists and commutative hashing. In *Proc. 2001 DARPA Information Survivability Conference and Exposition*, volume 2, pages 68–82, 2001.

34. M. T. Goodrich, R. Tamassia, N. Triandopoulos, and R. Cohen. Authenticated data structures for graph and geometric searching. In *Proc. RSA Conference—Cryptographers' Track*, pages 295–313. Springer, LNCS 2612, 2003.

35. D. Gross-Amblard. Query-preserving watermarking of relational databases and XML documents. In *ACM Symp. on Principles of Database Systems (PODS)*, pages 191–201, 2003.

36. V. Guruswami. *List Decoding of Error-correcting Codes*. PhD thesis, Massachusetts Institute of Technology, Boston, MA, 2001.

37. V. Guruswami and M. Sudan. Improved decoding of Reed-Solomon and algebraic-geometric codes. In *IEEE Transactions on Information Theory*, pages 45:1757–1767, 1999.

38. B. Horne, L. Matheson, C. Sheehan, and R. Tarjan. Dynamic self-checking techniques for improved tamper resistance. In T. Sander, editor, *Security and Privacy in Digital Rights Management*, volume 2320 of *Lecture Notes in Computer Science*, pages 141–159. Springer-Verlag, 2002.

39. S. Khanna and F. Zane. Watermarking maps: Hiding information in structured data. In *ACM/SIAM Symp. on Discrete Algorithms*, pages 596–605, 2000.

40. V. King. A simpler minimum spanning tree verification algorithm. In *Workshop on Algorithms and Data Structures*, pages 440–448, 1995.

41. P. Kocher. A quick introduction to certificate revocation trees (CRTs), 1998. http://www.valicert.com/resources/whitepaper/bodyIntroRevocation.html.

42. P. C. Kocher. On certificate revocation and validation. In *Proc. Int. Conf. on Financial Cryptography*, volume 1465 of *LNCS*. Springer-Verlag, 1998.

43. I. Krsul and E. H. Spafford. Authorship analysis: Identifying the author of a program. *Computers and Society*, 16(3):248–259, 1997.

44. M. Kuhn. The trustno1 cryptoprocessor concept. Technical Report CERIAS-1997-04-30, Purdue University, 1997.

45. K. Kurosawa, T. Johansson, and D. R. Stinson. Almost k-wise independent sample spaces and their cryptologic applications. *Journal of Cryptology*, 14:231–253, 2001.

46. A. Lysyanskaya, R. Tamassia, and N. Triandopoulos. Multicast authentication in fully adversarial networks. In *Proceedings of IEEE Symposium on Security and Privacy*, pages 241–255, May 2004.

47. C. Martel, G. Nuckolls, P. Devanbu, M. Gertz, A. Kwong, and S. G. Stubblebine. A general model for authenticated data structures. *Algorithmica*, 39(1):21–41, 2004.
48. K. Mehlhorn and S. Näher. *LEDA: A Platform for Combinatorial and Geometric Computing.* Cambridge University Press, Cambridge, UK, 2000.
49. K. Mehlhorn, S. Näher, M. Seel, R. Seidel, T. Schilz, S. Schirra, and C. Uhrig. Checking geometric programs or verification of geometric structures. *Comput. Geom. Theory Appl.*, 12(1–2):85–103, 1999.
50. A. J. Menezes, P. C. van Oorschot, and S. A. Vanstone. *Handbook of Applied Cryptography.* CRC Press, 1997.
51. J. Naor and M. Naor. Small-bias probability spaces: Efficient constructions and applications. In *ACM Symposium on Theory of Computing*, pages 213–223, 1990.
52. M. Naor and K. Nissim. Certificate revocation and certificate update. In *Proc. 7th USENIX Security Symposium*, pages 217–228, Berkeley, 1998.
53. R. Ostrovsky, C. Rackoff, and A. Smith. Efficient consistency proofs for generalized queries on a committed database. In *Proc. 31th International Colloquium on Automata, Languages and Programming (ICALP)*, 2004.
54. D. J. Polivy and R. Tamassia. Authenticating distributed data using Web services and XML signatures. In *Proc. ACM Workshop on XML Security*, 2002.
55. G. Qu and M. Potkonjak. Analysis of watermarking techniques for graph coloring problem. In *IEEE/ACM Int. Conf. on Computer-Aided Design*, pages 190–193, 1998.
56. D. Ron. Property testing. In P. M. Pardalos, S. Rajasekaran, J. Reif, and J. D. P. Rolim, editors, *Handbook of Randomized Computing*, pages 597–649. Kluwer Academic Publishers, 2001.
57. S. Savage, D. Wetherall, A. R. Karlin, and T. Anderson. Practical network support for IP traceback. In *SIGCOMM*, pages 295–306, 2000.
58. B. Schneier. *Applied Cryptography: Protocols, Algorithms, and Source Code in C.* John Wiley and Sons, Inc., New York, NY, USA, second edition, 1996.
59. B. Schneier and J. Kelsey. Secure audit logs to support computer forensics. *ACM Trans. on Information and System Security*, 2(2):159–176, 1999.
60. R. Sion, M. J. Atallah, and S. K. Prabhakar. Resilient information hiding for abstract semi-structures. In *Proc. of the Workshop on Digital Watermarking (IWDW), Seoul, Korea*, LNCS. Springer-Verlag, 2003.
61. R. Sion, M. J. Atallah, and S. K. Prabhakar. Rights protection for relational data. In *Proc. 2003 ACM International Conference on Management of Data (SIGMOD), San Diego, California*, pages 98–109. ACM Press, 2003.
62. E. H. Spafford and G. Kim. The design and implementation of tripwire: A file system integrity checker. In *2d ACM Conf. on Computer and Communication Security (CCS)*, 1994.
63. E. H. Spafford and S. A. Weeber. Software forensics: Tracking code to its authors. *Computers and Society*, 12(6):585–595, 1993.
64. D. R. Stinson. *Cryptography: Theory and Practice, Second Edition.* CRC Press Series, 2002.
65. D. R. Stinson, T. van Trung, and R. Wei. Secure frameproof codes, key distribution patterns, group testing algorithms and related structures. *Journal of Statistical Planning and Inference*, 86:595–617, 2000.
66. G. F. Sullivan and G. M. Masson. Certification trails for data structures. In *Digest of the 21st Symposium on Fault-Tolerant Computing*, pages 240–247. IEEE Computer Society Press, 1991.
67. G. F. Sullivan, D. S. Wilson, and G. M. Masson. Certification of computational results. *IEEE Trans. Comput.*, 44(7):833–847, 1995.
68. R. Tamassia. Authenticated data structures. In *Proc. European Symp. on Algorithms*, volume 2832 of *Lecture Notes in Computer Science*, pages 2–5. Springer-Verlag, 2003.

69. R. Tamassia and N. Triandopoulos. Computational bounds on hierarchical data processing with applications to information security. In *Proc. Int. Colloquium on Automata, Languages and Programming (ICALP)*, LNCS. Springer-Verlag, 2005.

70. R. Venkatesan, V. Vazirani, and S. Sinha. A graph theoretic approach to software watermarking. In *4th Int. Workshop on Information Hiding*, volume 2137 of *LNCS*, pages 157–168. Springer-Verlag, 2001.

71. A. Yasinsac and Y. Manzano. Policies to enhance computer and network forensics. In *IEEE Workshop on Information Assurance and Security*, pages 289–295, 2001.

Model Generalization
and Its Implications on Intrusion Detection

Zhuowei Li[1,2], Amitabha Das[1], and Jianying Zhou[2]

[1] School of Computer Engineering, Nanyang Technological University
50 Nanyang Avenue, Singapore 639798
zhwei.li@pmail.ntu.edu.sg, asadas@ntu.edu.sg
[2] Institute for Infocomm Research, 21 Heng Mui Keng Terrace, Singapore 119613
jyzhou@i2r.a-star.edu.sg

Abstract. To make up for the incompleteness of the known behaviors of a computing resource, model generalization is utilized to infer more behaviors in the behavior model besides the known behaviors. In principle, model generalization can improve the detection rate but may also degrade the detection performance. Therefore, the relation between model generalization and detection performance is critical for intrusion detection. However, most of past research only evaluates the overall efficiency of an intrusion detection technique via detection rate and false alarm/positive rate, rather than the usefulness of model generalization for intrusion detection. In this paper, we try to do such evaluation, and then to find the implications of model generalization on intrusion detection. Within our proposed methodology, model generalization can be achieved in three levels. In this paper, we evaluate the first level model generalization. The experimental results show that the first level model generalization is useful mostly to enhance the detection performance of intrusion detection. However, its implications for intrusion detection are different with respect to different detection techniques. Our studies show that in general, though it is useful to generalize the normal behavior model so that more normal behaviors can be identified as such, the same is not advisable for the intrusive behavior model. Therefore, the intrusion signatures should be built compactly without first level generalization.

Keywords: Security, Machine Learning, Intrusion Detection, Generalization, Intrusion, Security Infrastructure.

1   Introduction

Intrusion detection has become a very important defense mechanism in the face of increasing vulnerabilities exposed in today's computer systems and the Internet (Debar et al.[3]), where authentication, cryptography, and access control mechanisms routinely prove inadequate in preventing new and increasingly numerous and disastrous attacks. In general, there exist two approaches for detecting intrusions (Denning[4]): signature-based intrusion detection (SID, a.k.a. misuse detection), where an intrusion is detected if its behavior matches existing intrusion signatures, and anomaly-based intrusion detection (AID), where

J. Ioannidis, A. Keromytis, and M.Yung (Eds.): ACNS 2005, LNCS 3531, pp. 222–237, 2005.

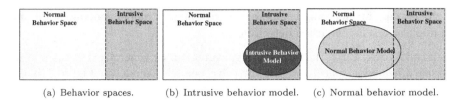

(a) Behavior spaces.   (b) Intrusive behavior model.   (c) Normal behavior model.

Fig. 1. Behavior Spaces and Models.

an intrusion is detected if the resource behavior deviates from known normal behaviors significantly. From another aspect, there are two behavior spaces in a computing resource for intrusion detection (Figure 1.a): *normal behavior space* and *intrusive behavior space*, and they are complementary to each other. Conceptually, SID is based on knowledge in intrusive behavior space, and AID is based on knowledge in normal behavior space(Chari et al.[2]). Perfect detection of intrusions can be achieved only if we have a complete model of any one of the two behavior spaces, because what is not bad is good and vice versa ideally.

Motivations: However, it is difficult to model such behavior spaces completely and correctly in reality. Figure 1 (b) and (c) illustrate real behavior models for signature-based (i.e., *intrusive behavior model*) and for anomaly-based intrusion detection (i.e., *normal behavior model*)(Chari and Cheng[2]). As the figure indicates, there exist model errors in the behavior models for SID techniques as well as AID ones. These model errors are called the *inaccuracy* in the behavior models. For example, a part of intrusive behavior model falls into normal behavior space. In addition, the intrusive behavior model cannot cover all intrusive behavior space, and the normal behavior model cannot cover all normal behavior space either. This is referred to as the *incompleteness* in the behavior models. In summary, there are two quality factors in every behavior models, namely *inaccuracy* and *incompleteness*. To build a practical intrusion detection system, it is critical to know the precise influence of these two quality factors on its performance.

On the other hand, the behavior models for intrusion detection are generally built from known knowledge of the protected resource. Thus, the quality of the behavior model is determined by the known knowledge as well as the '*model building*' technique. In reality, it is hard to guarantee the completeness of known knowledge under most scenarios (e.g., with 'concept drifting' problem, Li et al.[10]) as we do not know the future behaviors of a computing resource. To make up for the incompleteness, most existing '*model building*' techniques try to infer the unknown behaviors via *model generalization*(Debar et al.[3], Lee et al.[9], Chan et al.[13]). However, model generalization may lead to model inaccuracy (Figure 1), and model generalization cannot solve the incompleteness problem completely under most scenarios where it infers part but not all of unknown behaviors. Thus, the quality factors in the behavior models are completely determined by model generalization. In order to get the precise influence of the two quality factors, it is necessary to evaluate model generalization and its implications for intrusion detection.

Related Work: First, the intrusion signatures can be generalized to cover more intrusive behavior space, i.e., the intrusive behavior model in Figure 1 is extended. Anchor et al. [1] have done the only work on this to our knowledge. Using the evolution programming with a fitness function which depends on false positive rate and detection rate, they optimized the degree of generalization for intrusion signatures (represented by a *finite state transducer*). In general, the model generalization on intrusion signatures can solve the intrusion variations detection problem partially. Secondly, the normal behavior model of anomaly-based intrusion detection can be generalized as well, and it can be done in several ways. Based on a distance metric and a threshold (Denning[4], Eskin[5], Liao[12], Wang[16]), the instances in the existing audit trails are clustered unsupervisedly, and the new instances are labeled by the existing instances in their clusters. In statistical methods for intrusion detection (MADAM ID[9], LERAD[13], NIDES[7] etc.), the (statistical) resource usage profiles are mined from the existing audit trails. The novel instances are detected according to whether they fall into these profiles. In these two approaches, the existing audit trails are modeled inexactly to accommodate more resource behaviors in the profiles, and thus to achieve the model generalization.

Most of past research only credited the overall efficiency of an intrusion detection technique to such model generalization, and there is hardly any evaluation of the effect of the model generalization. This is partially due to the difficulty of pinpointing the contribution of model generalization to the overall efficiency. Fortunately, our methodology not only overcomes the problem, it also allows one to adjust the extent of model generalization.

Our Contributions: First, a new intrusion detection methodology with promising properties is introduced briefly. Then, an evaluation framework for model generalization is designed using our methodology, and an average detection cost function is defined to quantify the detection performance for intrusion detection. Finally, the experiments are done on a typical dataset to get the exact implications of model generalization for intrusion detection.

The remaining parts of this paper are organized as follows. Section 2 describes a formal intrusion detection methodology in brief. In section 3, model generalization is introduced and quantified, and its evaluation framework is designed. Experiments in section 4 reveals the implications of model generalization on intrusion detection. Lastly, we draw conclusions and lay out the future work on model generalization in section 5.

2   Retrospection: An Intrusion Detection Methodology

Any intrusion detection system builds the behavior models of the resources using a set of features, or a *feature vector* $FV = \{F_1, F_2, \ldots, F_n\}$, where F_i denotes one of its features. Every feature in the feature vector can be one of these types: A feature associated with an instant of time (e.g., *the fields in the current packet*), or with a time interval (e.g., *the number of SYN packets within 2 seconds*), or with the context of a current event (e.g., *the system-call events in stide [6], the state events in STAT [15]*). The context is defined over the timeline preceding the point in time when the event in question happens. In general, a feature F_i in the feature vector can be categorized into *nominal*, *discrete* or *continuous* one. A feature vector for intrusion detection can contain any number of nominal, discrete, and/or continuous features. In addition, a feature can also be as complex as a compound feature (see Section 2.3).

In this methodology [11], we assume that there is a training audit trail, which consists of normal and intrusion audit trails. We also assume that the training audit trails represent the known (or past) knowledge about the computing resource. Then, the instances of the feature vector are collected from the training audit trails as $\{I_{FV}^1, I_{FV}^2, I_{FV}^3, \ldots\}$. For each instance I_{FV}^i, there is a **status** that indicates the label of audit trails where it is collected. For example, if an instance I_{FV}^i is produced by an intrusion 'Nimda', its status is 'Nimda'.

2.1   Basic Concepts and Notations

For a specific feature F, several of its concepts are defined as follows.

- Its feature space $Dom(F)$ is the defining domain w.r.t. a computing resource.
- Any value in $Dom(F)$ is defined as a <u>feature value</u> v_F, and $v_F \in Dom(F)$. In general, there are many feature values in the feature space $Dom(F)$.
- A <u>feature range</u> R_F is an interval between any two feature values v_F^1 and v_F^2 in its feature space, which includes all feature values falling between v_F^1 and v_F^2. For a discrete or continuous feature, $R_F = [v_F^1, v_F^2]$. For a nominal feature, every feature value is independent. Thus, each nominal feature value is referred to as a feature range so that for a nominal feature F, $R_F = [v_F^i] = [v_F^i, v_F^i]$. If a feature value v_F^j is within the bounds of a feature range, we say that it falls within it, denoted as $v_F^j \in R_F$. The concept of *feature range* is used to treat uniformly every (nominal, discrete, or continuous) feature. For the range R_F, we further define $upper(R_F) = v_F^1$ and $lower(R_F) = v_F^2$.

Notations. We describe here the notations used in the subsequent expressions. Note that in order to avoid cluttering the expressions, we have dropped the subscript of F. If $F \in FV$,

- $v(I_{FV}^i, F)$ is the feature value of the feature F in the instance I_{FV}^i.
- $I(v_F, F)$ is the set of instances whose values of F are equal to v_F.

$$I(v_F, F) = \{I_{FV}^k | v_F = v(I_{FV}^k, F)\}$$

- $I(R_F, F)$ is the set of instances whose values of F fall in the feature range R_F.

$$I(R_F, F) = \{I_{FV}^k | v(I_{FV}^k, F) \in R_F\}$$

2.2   NSA Label

Definition 1 (NSA label of a feature value). *If a feature value v_F occurs only in the normal audit trails, it is normal. If it occurs only in the intrusive audit trails, for example, intrusion signatures, it is labeled as anomalous. Otherwise, i.e., if it occurs in both normal and intrusive audit trails, it is labeled as suspicious. For brevity, we will refer to the normal, suspicious, or anomalous label as the **NSA label** of the feature value v_F, denoted as $L(v_F) \in \{`N', `S', `A'\}$.*

It is worth noting that a feature value is either normal or anomalous in a specific instance, but its NSA label is collected from all related instances. We will further extend the concept of **NSA label** to feature ranges of a feature.

NSA Labels of Feature Ranges. From $Dom(F)$, we can collect a set of mutually exclusive feature ranges $\{R_F^1, R_F^2, \ldots\}$, such that **(1)** there is no common feature value v_F, which falls in R_F^j and R_F^k at the same time $(j \neq k)$, and **(2)** $I(R_F^i, F) \neq \emptyset$ $(i \geq 1)$. Then, the concept of NSA labels can be extended to these feature ranges as follows. For the feature range R_F,

$$L(R_F) = `N' \Leftrightarrow \forall i(v(I_{FV}^i, F) \in R_F \rightarrow L(v(I_{FV}^i, F)) = `N')$$
$$L(R_F) = `A' \Leftrightarrow \forall i(v(I_{FV}^i, F) \in R_F \rightarrow L(v(I_{FV}^i, F)) = `A')$$
$$L(R_F) = `S' \Leftrightarrow \exists i \exists j(v(I_{FV}^i, F) \in R_F \wedge L(v(I_{FV}^i, F)) = `A')$$
$$\wedge (v(I_{FV}^j, F) \in R_F \wedge L(v(I_{FV}^j, F)) = `N')$$

Feature Subspaces. Based on NSA labels, we can partition the feature space $Dom(F)$ into *three* feature subspaces: *normal, suspicious and anomalous*, denoted as $N(F)$, $S(F)$ and $A(F)$, respectively. Thus we have,

$$N(F) = \{R_F^j | j \geq 1, L(R_F^j) = `N'\}$$
$$S(F) = \{R_F^j | j \geq 1, L(R_F^j) = `S'\}$$
$$A(F) = \{R_F^j | j \geq 1, L(R_F^j) = `A'\}$$

We also define $\Omega(F) = N(F) \cup S(F) \cup A(F)$, so that it is a collection of all feature ranges found in the training audit trails.

2.3   Compound Feature

Definition 2 (compound feature). *A compound feature F_{12} is an ordered pair $\{F_1, F_2\}$, such that $\Omega(F_{12})$ is a subset of the cartesian product of $\Omega(F_1)$ and $\Omega(F_2)$. It also requires that each element in $\Omega(F_{12})$ represents at least one feature vector instance in the training audit trails. Mathematically,*

$$\Omega(F_{12}) = \{(R_{F_1}^a, R_{F_2}^b) | R_{F_1}^a \in \Omega(F_1), R_{F_2}^b \in \Omega(F_2), I((R_{F_1}^a, R_{F_2}^b), F_{12}) \neq \emptyset\}$$

Based on the definition of *cartesian product*, for any instance recognized by a compound feature range $(R_{F_1}^a, R_{F_2}^b)$, $I_{FV}^i \in I((R_{F_1}^a, R_{F_2}^b), F_{12})$, it will be recognized by feature ranges $R_{F_1}^a$ and $R_{F_2}^b$ as well (i.e., $I_{FV}^i \in I(R_{F_1}^a, F_1)$ and $I_{FV}^i \in I(R_{F_2}^b, F_2)$), and vice versa. Therefore, $I((R_{F_1}^a, R_{F_2}^b), F_{12}) = I(R_{F_1}^a, F_1) \wedge I(R_{F_2}^b, F_2)$. To avoid any ambiguity, we will refer to a single feature as an *atomic* feature. When a compound feature is formed from two component features, the ranges of the compound feature that are generated as a result of the process of composition are also mutually exclusive just like the feature ranges of the component features. This property is expressed in the following theorem, the proof of which is given in the appendix.

Theorem 1. *The feature ranges of a compound feature are mutually exclusive, i.e., for two different feature ranges, $(R_{F_1}^a, R_{F_2}^b)$ and $(R_{F_1}^c, R_{F_2}^d)$, there is no such instance I_{FV}^i so that $I_{FV}^i \in I((R_{F_1}^a, R_{F_2}^b), F_{12})$ and $I_{FV}^i \in I((R_{F_1}^c, R_{F_2}^d), F_{12})$.*

A compound feature space can be partitioned into three feature subspaces like an atomic feature, i.e., $\Omega(F_{12}) = N(F_{12}) \cup S(F_{12}) \cup A(F_{12})$.

Compounding More Features. In summary, the compound feature built from two atomic features shows the same properties as any of its component atomic features. Therefore, we can treat the compound feature as an atomic one to build higher order compound features. Using this recursive procedure, the feature vector FV for intrusion detection can be converted into an equivalent n-order compound feature $F_{1...n}$ with normal $N(F_{1...n})$, suspicious $S(F_{1...n})$ and anomalous $A(F_{1...n})$ subspaces.

2.4   Behavior Signatures

Definition 3 (behavior signature). *Assuming that there exists a feature vector $FV = \{F_1, F_2, \ldots, F_n\}$, and that the feature ranges of every feature are determined beforehand. A behavior signature Sig_{FV}^i is a feature range of the compound feature $F_{1...n}$ with its NSA label. In other words, the behavior signature is the combination of feature ranges of all the features in the feature vector.*

As indicated in the above definition, every behavior signature[1] represents a state of the resource at a specified time point. According to NSA labels of signatures, the behavior model can be split into three parts: normal, suspicious, and intrusion behavior models. In AID, only the normal behavior model is utilized, but SID identifies intrusions based on the intrusive behavior model. However, the best scenario is to do intrusion detection using the complete behavior models.

Detecting Instances via Signatures. Suppose that $FV = \{F_1, \ldots, F_n\}$, and the signatures are $Sig_{FV}^1, Sig_{FV}^2, \ldots, Sig_{FV}^m$, where $Sig_{FV}^i = (R_{F_1}^{i_1}, R_{F_2}^{i_2}, \ldots, R_{F_n}^{i_n})$, and the set of instances recognized by Sig_{FV}^i is $I(Sig_{FV}^i, F_{1...n})$. According to the definition of the compound feature $F_{1...n}$

$$I(Sig_{FV}^i, F_{1...n}) = I(R_{F_1}^{i_1}, F_1) \wedge I(R_{F_2}^{i_2}, F_2) \wedge \ldots \wedge I(R_{F_n}^{i_n}, F_n)$$

---

[1] For brevity, '*behavior signature*' will be simplified as '*signature*' in this paper.

For every instance of the computing resource, for example I_{FV}^j,

$$I_{FV}^j \in I(Sig_{FV}^i, F_{1...n})$$
$$\Leftrightarrow v(I_{FV}^j, F_1) \in R_{F_1}^{i_1}, v(I_{FV}^j, F_2) \in R_{F_2}^{i_2}, \ldots, v(I_{FV}^j, F_n) \in R_{F_n}^{i_n}$$

In order to detect I_{FV}^j, all of its feature values must fall in their corresponding feature ranges in the signature. Then, the relation between the NSA label of a signature and the instance is utilized in intrusion detection. In the behavior model, if the NSA label of the signature is 'N', the instance is detected as 'normal'. If the NSA label of the signature is 'S', the instance is detected as 'anomalous'. Otherwise, i.e., if its NSA label is 'A', the instance will be labeled by the respective intrusion(s). Significantly, if there is no signature in the behavior model that recognizes the instance, the instance will be detected as 'anomalous' because we lack knowledge about the '*new*' instance in the behavior model.

Note that the methodology thus introduced has a number of very desirable properties that make it attractive for intrusion detection, such as

(1)**Incremental:** it is possible to append a new feature in the feature vector, and it is also possible to append a new feature range to an existing feature dynamically;

(2)**Distributed:** as mentioned earlier, a feature can also be an output of a meta-intrusion detection system. Thus, different (atomic or compound) features can be deployed distributively and/or hierarchically;

(3)**Privacy protection:** The information in a feature has been replaced by the index of its corresponding feature range, and thus, the privacy in the instance has been protected;

(4)**Uniqueness:** signatures in the behavior models are mutually exclusive, thus there is no ambiguity in detecting an instance;

(5)**Quantified behavior models/spaces:** the behavior spaces/models can be quantified as the numbers of signatures in them. For this reason, we can define intrusion detection and analyze existing problems in a quantified manner;

(6)**Adjustable quality factors:** This methodology can describe the known knowledge precisely and extend the knowledge via a configurable degree of model generalization.

In the following section, we will use the *adjustable quality factors* to evaluate the usefulness of model generalization for intrusion detection.

3   Model Generalization

In general, *model generalization can improve the detection rate by identifying more novel behaviors (e.g., normal behaviors) but may also degrade the detection performance by mis-identifying novel behaviors due to generalization errors (Valdes et al.[14]).* Therefore, it is necessary to articulate the relation between model generalization and the detection performance. In our methodology, the task of model generalization is to make every signature in the behavior models identify more instances, and it can be achieved in three levels described below.

Note that, without model generalization, the known behaviors in the training audit trails can be represented in the behavior models precisely.

L1: [**Generalizing feature ranges**]. In the *feature range collection strategies*, the feature ranges can be generalized to cover more unknown parts of feature space other than the known feature values.

L2: [**Generalizing the behavior model**]. At the same time, using the *crossover* operations (or other generalization operations), especially on two signatures with the same NSA label, some signatures that are not in the training audit trails are augmented into the behavior model. Thus, the behavior model is generalized as well. To some degree, the effect of this generalization is to ignore several features in building signatures.

L3: [**Generalizing signatures during detection**]. With a *distance metric*, the model generalization introduces some signatures that are not in the training audit trails but within a distance threshold from existing signatures.

Figure 2 illustrates the three levels for model generalization using a simple but representative scenario, in which there are two features and 9 instances (*the points A to I in the figure*) initially. The light squares with label 'L1', which include initial instances, represent signatures due to the L1 generalization. The squares with 'L2' represent signatures introduced by L2 generalization. Lastly, the dark squares with label 'L3' represent signatures introduced by L3 generalization. Note that we have not illustrated all possible signatures from L2 and L3 model generalization in Figure 2.

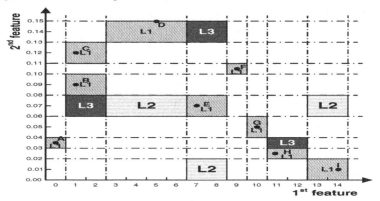

Fig. 2. Three levels for model generalization.

It is obvious that L1 generalization is the basis for L2 and L3 generalization. Thus, we will first discuss the model generalization introduced by collection strategies (*i.e., L1 model generalization*). In other words, we will evaluate the relation between model generalization introduced by collection strategies and the detection performance for intrusion detection.

For every feature, to achieve L1 generalization, we assume that the unknown parts in the feature space have the same NSA label as its nearest feature values.

Algorithm 1 Expanding the initial feature ranges for a discrete feature.

Require: (1) Initial feature ranges $R_{F_d}^i$ and $R_{F_d}^{i+1}$; (2) v_i and v_{i+1}; and (3) λ_d.

1: FUNCTION: **Expand**($R_{F_d}^i$, $R_{F_d}^{i+1}$, v_i, v_{i+1}, λ_d)
2:   $expand_i = 0$; $expand_{i+1} = 0$;
3:   $gap = v_{i+1} - v_i - 1$;
4:   **if** $gap = 0$ **then** return;
5:   **if** $gap \geq 2\lambda_d$ **then**
6:     $expand_i = \lambda_d$; $expand_{i+1} = \lambda_d$;
7:   **else**
8:     **if** $gap\%2 = 0$ **then**
9:       $expand_i = gap/2$; $expand_{i+1} = gap/2$;
10:     **else**
11:       $expand_i = (gap-1)/2$; $expand_{i+1} = (gap-1)/2$;
12:       Randomly select a value in {0,1}, and assign it to Rnd;
13:       $expand_i+ = Rnd$; $expand_{i+1}+ = 1 - Rnd$;
14:     **end if**
15:   **end if**
16:   Increasing the upper bound of $R_{F_d}^i$ by $expand_i$;
17:   Decreasing the lower bound of $R_{F_d}^{i+1}$ by $expand_{i+1}$;

Obviously, we indicate that there is a distance concept in L1 model generalization. However, because there is no distance concept for nominal features, L1 model generalization is not applicable to them actually. Therefore, we will only discuss the L1 model generalization on discrete/continuous features in this paper, and regard every feature value of a nominal feature as a feature range.

3.1   Model Generalization by Collection Strategies

Before applying the collection strategies, an initial feature range is formed for every feature value, and both its upper and lower bounds are equal to the feature value. With these initial feature ranges, the signatures can represent the behaviors in the training audit trails correctly and precisely. The model generalization is performed to cover more unknown feature space.

A Collection Strategy for Discrete Features. For a discrete feature F_d, other than feature values in all instances, there are some feature values that do not occur in the training audit trails. The collection strategy is to extend the initial feature ranges to embrace these non-occurring feature values. For example, $\Omega(F_d) = [0, 20]$, and the feature values in the training audit trails are {0,2,3,11,13,18,19,20}. Thus, the non-occurring feature values are {[1,1],[4,10], [12,12],[14,17]}, and the task of the collection strategy is to infer NSA labels for all of them. To achieve it, the unknown feature values will be labeled by its nearest known feature values, where the concept of 'nearest' is represented by a generalization parameter λ_d.

Given the generalization parameter λ_d, the collection strategy is designed as follows. Suppose that existing feature values are $v_1, v_2, \ldots, v_m$ in an incremental order. The initial feature ranges $R_{F_d}^i$ and $R_{F_d}^{i+1}$ will be expanded by the unknown feature values between v_i and v_{i+1} ($1 \leq i \leq m-1$). Algorithms 1 and 3 show the pseudo codes for the collection strategy of discrete features.

Algorithm 2 Expanding the initial feature ranges for a continuous feature.

Require: (1) Initial feature ranges $R_{F_c}^i$ and $R_{F_c}^{i+1}$; (2) v_i and v_{i+1}; and (3) λ_c.
1: FUNCTION: **Expand**($R_{F_c}^i$, $R_{F_c}^{i+1}$, v_i, v_{i+1}, λ_c)
2: $expand = 0$;
3: **if** $\lambda_c > 0.5$ **then** $L = 0.5$;
4: $gap = v_{i+1} - v_i$;
5: $expand = gap \times \lambda_c$;
6: Increasing the upper bound of $R_{F_c}^i$ by $expand$;
7: Decreasing the lower bound of $R_{F_c}^{i+1}$ by $expand$;

Algorithm 3 The Splitting Strategy for a Discrete or Continuous Feature F.

Require: (1) Initial feature ranges R_F^1, R_F^2, and R_F^l; (2) $v_1, \ldots, v_l$; and (3) λ.
{If the feature F is discrete, λ represents λ_d, otherwise, λ_c.}
1: **for** $i = 1$ to $l - 1$ **do**
2:    **Expand**(R_F^i, R_F^{i+1}, v_i, v_{i+1}, λ);
3: **end for**
4: i=1;
5: **while** $i = l$ **do**
6:    **if** No additional feature subspace between R_F^i and R_F^{i+1}, and $L(R_F^i) = L(R_F^{i+1})$ **then**
7:       Merging R_F^{i+1} into R_F^i;
8:       Deleting R_F^{i+1}; {The index of every following feature range is decreased by 1}
9:       $l = l - 1$;
10:    **else**
11:       $i = i + 1$;
12:    **end if**
13: **end while**

A Collection Strategy for Continuous Features. Similarly, for a continuous feature F_c, there are feature values in the training audit trails, $v_1, v_2, \ldots, v_l$, in an incremental order, and the initial feature ranges are $R_{F_c}^1, R_{F_c}^2, \ldots, R_{F_c}^l$, where, for every feature range $R_{F_c}^i$, $lower(R_{F_c}^i) = upper(R_{F_c}^i) = v_i$. However, unlike the collection strategy for discrete features, there always exist non-occurring feature space between any two consecutive initial feature ranges, and the objective of its collection strategy is to split these non-occurring feature space. For example, $\Omega(F_c) = [0, 1.0]$, and the feature values in the training audit trails are $\{0, 0.02, 0.03, 0.12, 0.23, 0.40, 1.0\}$. Thus, the non-occurring feature space are $\{[0,0.02], [0.02,0.03], [0.03,0.12], [0.12,0.23], [0.23,0.40], [0.40,1.0]\}$, and the task of its collection strategy is to label them with NSA label(s). Similar to discrete features, there is another generalization parameter λ_c to infer the NSA labels of unknown feature parts in the feature space of the continuous feature F_c.

Given the generalization parameter λ_c, the collection strategy is done as follows. For every feature value v_i $(1 \leq i \leq l - 1)$ in the existing audit trails, the initial feature space $R_{F_c}^i$ and $R_{F_c}^{i+1}$ will be expanded by non-occurring feature ranges between v_i and v_{i+1}. Algorithms 2 and 3 show the pseudo codes for the collection strategy of continuous features.

Ultimately, for every pair of parameters $\langle \lambda_d, \lambda_c \rangle$, the feature ranges for all features in the feature vector will become determined. Then, the signatures are collected from all instances in the training audit trails. In the detection phase, the instances in the test audit trails are utilized to measure the performance of the behavior model with parameter pair $\langle \lambda_d, \lambda_c \rangle$. In the following section, an average cost function for every instance of the detection performance is designed.

3.2   Measuring the Detection Performance

The two main objectives of intrusion detection are (1) to detect the intrusions correctly (as anomalies), and (2) to identify the behaviors correctly (i.e., normal behaviors or its original intrusions). Considering these two objectives, we calculate the average detection cost (Lee et al.[8]) of an instance in the test audit trails as in Table 1. If the behavior is identified correctly, the cost is 0. Otherwise, we can give some penalty for the detection result. In our cost scheme, we assume that the detection of an intrusion as an anomaly is useful but it is less useful than intrusion identification. Lastly, the average cost of every instance in the test audit trails is utilized to quantify the detection performance of the behavior model.

Suppose that there are T instances in the test audit trails. Based on the detection results, several statistics are further defined as follows.

Table 1. Detection Results and Costs.

INDEX	NOTATIONS	ORIGINAL CLASS	DETECTION RESULTS	COST
1	$\#_{(N,N)}(\lambda_d, \lambda_c)$	normal	normal	0
2	$\#_{(N,A)}(\lambda_d, \lambda_c)$	normal	anomaly	3
3	$\#_{(I,I)}(\lambda_d, \lambda_c)$	intrusion	original intrusion	0
4	$\#_{(I,A)}(\lambda_d, \lambda_c)$	intrusion	anomaly	1
5	$\#_{(I,N)}(\lambda_d, \lambda_c)$	intrusion	normal	3

With respect to generalization parameters $\langle \lambda_d, \lambda_c \rangle$, the average cost of every instance in the test audit trails is defined as:

$$cost(\lambda_d, \lambda_c) = (\#_{(N,A)}(\lambda_d, \lambda_c) \times 3 + \#_{(I,N)}(\lambda_d, \lambda_c) \times 3 + \#_{(I,A)}(\lambda_d, \lambda_c) \times 1) \times \frac{1}{T} \quad (1)$$

In our framework, the average cost at $\lambda_d = \lambda_c = 0$ is the detection performance baseline as there are no model errors. In practice, the usefulness of model generalization with $\langle \lambda_d, \lambda_c \rangle$ is reflected in $cost(\lambda_d, \lambda_c)$. If $cost(\lambda_d, \lambda_c) > cost(0,0)$, the efficiency for intrusion detection has been degraded by such model generalization. Otherwise, the model generalization is useful for intrusion detection.

4   Experiments

We have chosen a typical dataset for network intrusion detection from KDD CUP 1999 contest. This is because the dataset meets the requirements of our formal framework: *labeled audit trails and a intrusion-specific feature vector.* The specifications of the dataset are listed as follows: *training-4898431 records, test-311029 records.* Table 2 lists all the features used in our experiments. For a

Table 2. Features in the Connection Records.

Types (41)	Features
nominal (9)	protocol type, service, flag, land, logged_in, root shell, su_attempted, is_hot_login, is_guest_login
discrete (15)	duration, src_bytes, dst_bytes, wrong_fragments, urgent, hot, num_failed_logins, num_compromised, num_root, num_file_creations, num_shells, num_access_files, num_outbound_cmds, count, srv_count
continuous (17)	serror_rate, srv_serror_rate, rerror_rate, srv_rerror_rate, same_srv_rate, diff_srv_rate, srv_diff_host_rate, dst_host_count, dst_host_srv_count, dst_host_same_srv_rate, dst_host_diff_srv_rate, dst_host_same_src_port_rate, dst_host_srv_diff_host_rate, dst_host_serror_rate, dst_host_srv_serror_rate, dst_host_rerror_rate, dst_host_srv_rerror_rate

detailed description of the datasets, especially for the intrusions in the datasets, please refer to '*http://www-cse.ucsd.edu/users/elkan/clresults.html*'.

4.1 Evaluating L1 Model Generalization

In our experimental evaluations, the model parameters $\langle \lambda_d, \lambda_c \rangle$ is adjusted to simulate different degrees of model generalization. Within our following experimental layout, the model generalization parameters are assigned from several specific values: $\lambda_d \in [0, 19]$, and $\lambda_c \in \{0, 0.1, 0.2, 0.3, 0.4, 0.5\}$.

Experimental Results. To increase the significance of model generalization in the behavior model, only part of the training audit trails(i.e., the first 500000 instances, around 10%) is utilized in our experiments. In our experimental results, the detection performance baseline with $\lambda_d = \lambda_c = 0$ is $cost(0,0) = 0.805$. Thus, for a specific parameter pair $\langle \lambda_d, \lambda_c \rangle$, the usefulness of model generalization for intrusion detection is determined by the relation between $cost(\lambda_d, \lambda_c)$ and cost(0,0)(=0.805).

Figure 3(a) illustrates the influence of L1 model generalization on detection performance. It is obvious that the average cost of every instance is decreased with the increase of λ_d. However, it is slightly strange that, for every value of λ_d, $cost(\lambda_d, 0) = cost(\lambda_d, 0.1) = cost(\lambda_d, 0.2) = cost(\lambda_d, 0.3) = cost(\lambda_d, 0.4)$, but $cost(\lambda_d, 0.5)$ is dropped. Further study about the training audit trails and our proposed collection strategy for continuous features shows that the phenomenon is caused by the following reasons. First, the precision of continuous features in the training audit trails is 0.01, thus, there are no non-occurring feature spaces between v_i and v_{i-1} if $v_i - v_{i-1} = 0.01$. Secondly, almost all feature values of continuous features within the precision occur in the training audit trails. Therefore, the influence of model generalization on continuous features is very small. Thirdly, in our designed evaluation methodology, the neighboring feature ranges with same NSA labels will be combined into a novel feature range only when $\lambda_c = 0.5$ (Algorithm 3). Thus, the combination of neighboring feature ranges with same NSA labels is the only reason for the average cost dropping when $\lambda_c = 0.5$. In view of the above, we will only consider the model generalization with $\lambda_c = 0$ and $\lambda_c = 0.5$ in the following discussion.

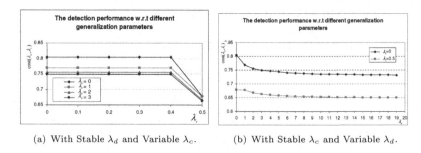

(a) With Stable λ_d and Variable λ_c.   (b) With Stable λ_c and Variable λ_d.

Fig. 3. Evaluation of L1 Model Generalization.

Overall Evaluation for L1 Model Generalization Figure 3(b) illustrates the overall influence of model generalization on intrusion detection. When $\lambda_c = 0$ (*corresponding to the upper curve*), there is no generalization for continuous features, i.e., there is only generalization for discrete features. It is obvious that the model generalization for discrete features is useful to enhance the efficiency of intrusion detection, indicated by the lower cost after more generous model generalization. The difference between the two curves implies the usefulness of model generalization for continuous features (when $\lambda_c = 0.5$). In other words, the combination of the neighboring feature ranges with the same NSA labels is useful for intrusion detection. Therefore, it can be concluded that model generalization can enhance the detection performance for intrusion detection. We provide the statistics of the detection results in the appendix.

Next, the influence of model generalization on normal behavior model and intrusive behavior model will be analyzed by our experimental results respectively. To achieve it, the average cost for normal instances is calculated by assuming that $\#_{(I,I)}(\lambda_d, \lambda_c) = \#_{(I,A)}(\lambda_d, \lambda_c) = \#_{(I,N)}(\lambda_d, \lambda_c) = 0$. Similarly, $\#_{(N,N)}(\lambda_d, \lambda_c) = \#_{(N,A)}(\lambda_d, \lambda_c) = 0$ for calculating the average cost for intrusive instances. Figure 4 gives the detection performance for normal and intrusive instances in the test audit trails.

L1 Model Generalization of the Normal Behavior Model. In Figure 4(a), it is obvious that the average cost for every normal instance is dropping with the increase of model generalization parameters (i.e., λ_d and λ_c). Thus, it is useful to generalize the behavior model, and then to enhance the detection performance for the normal behaviors. At the same time, a normal behavior is identified if it matches a signature in the normal behavior model. Thus, the enhanced detection performance is achieved by the generalization of the normal behavior model. In other words, it is profitable and necessary to generalize the normal behavior model, and then to identify more normal behaviors.

L1 Model Generalization of the Intrusive Behavior Model. The difference between Figure 4(b) and Figure 4(a) is so significant that we can reach a

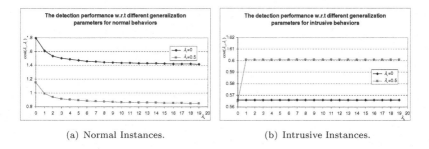

(a) Normal Instances.   (b) Intrusive Instances.

Fig. 4. Detection Performance for Normal and Intrusive Instances.

contrary conclusion to the one for normal behavior model. That is, the model generalization in intrusive behavior model is not advisable for intrusion detection. Even worse, it will aggravate the detection performance. In the experimental results, $\#_{(I,N)}(0,0) = 0$ but $\#_{(I,N)}(i,0.5) \geq 4814$ $(1 \leq i \leq 19)$, indicate that the generalization of the normal behavior model will accommodate more intrusive signatures. Thus, the average cost of every instance when $\lambda_c = 0.5$ is increased considerably in Figure 4(b) at $\lambda_d = 1$.

In summary, the generalization of the normal behavior model is necessary to cover more normal signatures, but it is limited by the intrusion signatures in the generalized normal behavior model due to the generalization errors. On the other hand, the intrusion signatures should be built compactly as model generalization applied to the intrusive behavior model cannot enhance (or even can aggravate) the detection performance.

5   Conclusions and Future Work

In this paper, we designed a formal framework to evaluate the usefulness of model generalization and its implications on intrusion detection. As the first step, we only evaluated the L1 model generalization for intrusion detection for the time being. The preliminary results are identified as follows (which are consistent with the observations in [14]). With respect to L1 model generalization, the normal behavior model can be generalized more generously to accommodate more unknown normal behaviors to enhance its detection efficiency, but the intrusive behavior model should be generalized a little stingily to describe the attacks more correctly as the generalized intrusive behavior model cannot identify more intrusions. In general, the formal framework can be applied to the datasets in other fields to articulate the usefulness of model generalization as well.

Due to the time and space limits, our experiments only gave the preliminary results for the evaluation about L1 model generalization on intrusion detection. The future work is to evaluate L2 & L3 model generalization. Actually, the abstraction attack scenario in STAT family sensors (Kemmerer and Vigna[15]) is achieved by L2 & L3 model generalization. Considering that STAT is successful in detecting new intrusions, it can be envisioned that L2 & L3 model generalization may give different pictures compared with L1 model generalization.

References

1. K.P. Anchor, J.B. Zydallis, G.H. Gunsch, and G.B. Lamont. Extending the computer defense immune system: Network intrusion detection with a multiobjective evolutionary programming approach. In *ICARIS 2002: 1st International Conference on Artificial Immune Systems Conference Proceedings*, 2002.
2. S.N. Chari and P. Cheng. BlueBox: A Policy-Driven, Host-based Intrusion Detection System. *ACM Transaction on Infomation and System Security*, 6(2):173–200, May 2003.
3. H. Debar, M. Dacier, and A. Wespi. A revised taxonomy for intrusion detection systems. *Annales des Telecommunications*, 55(7–8):361–378, 2000.
4. D.E. Denning. An intrusion detection model. *IEEE Transaction on Software Engineering*, SE-13(2):222–232, Feburary 1987.
5. E. Eskin, A. Arnold, M. Prerau, L. Portnoy, and S. Stolfo. A geometric framework for unsupervised anomaly detection: Detecting intrusions in unlabeled data. *In D. Barbara and S. Jajodia (editors), Applications of Data Mining in Computer Security, Kluwer*, 2002.
6. S.A. Hofmeyr, S. Forrest, and A. Somayaji. Intrusion detection using sequences of system calls. *Journal of Computer Security*, 6(3):151–180, 1998.
7. H. Javits and A. Valdes. The NIDES statistical component: Description and justification. SRI Anual Report A010, SRI International, Computer Science Laboratory, March 1993.
8. W. Lee, M. Miller, and S. Stolfo. Toward cost-sensitive modeling for intrusion detection. Technical Report No. CUCS-002-00, Computer Science,Columbia University, 2000.
9. W. Lee and S.J. Stolfo. A framework for contructing features and models for intrusion detection systems. *ACM Transactions on Information and System Security*, 3(4):227–261, Nov. 2000.
10. Zhuowei Li and Amitabha Das. Analyzing and Improving the Performance of a Class of Anomaly-based Intrusion Detectors. In *CoRR cs.CR/0410068*, 2004.
11. Zhuowei Li, Amitabha Das, and Jianying Zhou. Unifying Signature-based and Anomaly-based Intrusion Detection. In *Proceedings of the Ninth Pacific-Asia Conference on Knowledge Discovery and Data Mining (PAKDD-05)*, Hanoi, Vietnam, May. 2005. Lecture Notes in Artificial Intelligence.
12. Y. Liao and V.R. Vemuri. Using text categorization techniques for intrusion detection. In *Usenix: Security 2002*, Aug. 2002.
13. M.V. Mahoney and P.K. Chan. Learning Nonstationary Models of Normal Network Traffic for Detecting Novel Attacks. In *SIGKDD 2002*, July 23-26 2002.
14. Alfonso Valdes and Keith Skinner. Adaptive, model-based monitoring for cyber attack detection. In *Recent Advances in Intrusion Detection (RAID 2000)*, number 1907 in Lecture Notes in Computer Science, pages 80–92, Toulouse, France, October 2000. Springer-Verlag.
15. G. Vigna and R.A. Kemmerer. NetSTAT: A Network-based Intrusion Detection System. *Journal of Computer Security*, 7(1):37–71, 1999.
16. K. Wang and S.J. Stolfo. Anomalyous payload-based network intrusion detection. In *Proceedings of RAID*, 2004.

A   Proof of Theorem 1

Proof. We prove this by contradiction. If there exists an instance I_{FV}^i so that $I_{FV}^i \in I((R_{F_1}^a, R_{F_2}^b), F_{12})$ and $I_{FV}^i \in I((R_{F_1}^c, R_{F_2}^d), F_{12})$.

$$I_{FV}^i \in I((R_{F_1}^a, R_{F_2}^b), F_{12})$$
$$\Leftrightarrow I_{FV}^i \in I(R_{F_1}^a, F_1) \wedge I(R_{F_2}^b, F_2)$$
$$\Leftrightarrow v(I_{FV}^i, F_1) \in R_{F_1}^a, v(I_{FV}^i, F_2) \in R_{F_2}^b \tag{2}$$

Similarly,

$$I_{FV}^i \in I((R_{F_1}^c, R_{F_2}^d), F_{12})$$
$$\Leftrightarrow v(I_{FV}^i, F_1) \in R_{F_1}^c, v(I_{FV}^i, F_2) \in R_{F_2}^d \tag{3}$$

Recall that there is no common feature value v_F, which falls into R_F^j and R_F^k simultaneously $(j \neq k)$. From (1) and (2), we can get $R_{F_1}^a = R_{F_1}^c$ and $R_{F_2}^b = R_{F_2}^d$. Thus, $(R_{F_1}^a, R_{F_2}^b) = (R_{F_1}^c, R_{F_2}^d)$. This contradicts the assumption that the two feature ranges are different.

B   Detection Results

Table 3. The Statistics of Detection Results.

$\lambda_c \rightarrow$	$\lambda_c = 0$					$\lambda_c = 0.5$				
$\lambda_d \downarrow$	$\#_{(N,N)}$	$\#_{(N,A)}$	$\#_{(I,I)}$	$\#_{(I,A)}$	$\#_{(I,N)}$	$\#_{(N,N)}$	$\#_{(N,A)}$	$\#_{(I,I)}$	$\#_{(I,A)}$	$\#_{(I,N)}$
0	24367	36226	108712	141724	0	37369	23224	109555	140599	282
1	28097	32496	108712	141724	0	40550	20043	109555	136067	4814
2	29557	31036	108712	141723	1	41610	18983	109555	136067	4814
3	30213	30380	108712	141723	1	42067	18526	109555	136065	4816
4	30527	30066	108712	141723	1	42357	18236	109555	136065	4816
5	30787	29806	108712	141723	1	42550	18043	109555	136065	4816
6	31080	29513	108712	141723	1	42709	17884	109555	136064	4817
7	31193	29400	108712	141723	1	42838	17755	109555	136064	4817
8	31427	29166	108712	141723	1	42944	17649	109555	136063	4818
9	31487	29106	108712	141723	1	43004	17589	109555	136063	4818
10	31601	28992	108712	141723	1	43085	17508	109555	136063	4818
11	31647	28946	108712	141723	1	43134	17459	109555	136062	4819
12	31676	28917	108712	141723	1	43184	17409	109555	136062	4819
13	31718	28875	108712	141723	1	43228	17365	109555	136062	4819
14	31755	28838	108712	141723	1	43267	17326	109555	136062	4819
15	31829	28764	108712	141723	1	43313	17280	109555	136062	4819
16	31879	28714	108712	141723	1	43346	17247	109555	136062	4819
17	31889	28704	108712	141723	1	43369	17224	109555	136062	4819
18	31920	28673	108712	141723	1	43400	17193	109555	136062	4819
19	31986	28607	108712	141723	1	43439	17154	109555	136062	4819

Intrusion-Resilient Secure Channels
(Extended Abstract)

Gene Itkis*, Robert McNerney Jr.**, and Scott Russell***

Boston University Computer Science Dept.
111 Cummington St.
Boston, MA 02215, USA
{itkis,robmcn,srussell}@bu.edu

Abstract. We propose a new secure communication primitive called an *Intrusion-Resilient Channel (IRC)* that limits the damage resulting from key exposures and facilitates recovery. We define security against passive but mobile and highly adaptive adversaries capable of exposing even expired secrets. We describe an intuitive channel construction using (as a black box) existing public key cryptosystems. The simplicity of the construction belies the technical challenges in its security proof.

Additionally, we outline a general strategy for proving enhanced security for two-party protocols when an IRC is employed to secure all communication. Specifically, given a protocol proven secure against adversaries with restricted access to protocol messages, we show how the use of an IRC allows some of these adversary restrictions to be lifted. Once again, proving the efficacy of our intuitive approach turns out to be non-trivial. We demonstrate the strategy by showing that the intrusion-resilient signature scheme of [IR02] can be made secure against adversaries that expose even expired secrets.

1 Introduction

1.1 Motivation and Contributions

BACKGROUND. One of the most basic problems in cryptography is that of secure communication between two parties, call them Alice and Bob. Typically, Alice and Bob ensure confidentiality and integrity of their conversation by using a primitive called a *secure channel* that encrypts and authenticates their messages using coordinated secret key(s). As long as only Alice and Bob know these secret keys, the channel guarantees their messages remain secure. Once another party learns these keys, confidentiality of all messages sent using these keys is lost.

Due to its importance, the secure channel problem has been widely researched, leading to numerous results, many of which have been implemented in

---

* Supported in part by National Science Foundation grant No. CCR-0311485.
** Supported by U.S. Dept. of Education GAANN award #P200A040102
*** Supported in part by first author's NSF grant and by a National Physical Science Consortium Fellowship with stipend support from the National Security Agency.

J. Ioannidis, A. Keromytis, and M.Yung (Eds.): ACNS 2005, LNCS 3531, pp. 238–253, 2005.

practice. Widely deployed cryptographic secure channels include SSH, TLS/SSL, IPSEC, various VPNs, etc. See [MVV97] for a survey of the rich history of this problem. Secure channels also form an important building block in protocols for performing more complex tasks ranging from on-line auctions to secure multi-party computation. Much of the relevant work to date has focused on initializing the channel, leading to the study of (authenticated) key exchange: from the earliest ideas of Diffie and Hellman [DH76] to the more refined and formalized extensions of [BR93,BCK98,Sho99,CK01], to name just a few.

In contrast, our main goal is to limit the loss of confidentiality due to exposures of Alice and/or Bob's secret keys and to facilitate channel recovery. For signatures and encryption these goals are achieved in *intrusion-resilient* schemes [IR02,DFK$^+$03] by combining key evolution ideas from forward-secure schemes [And97,BM99] and secret-sharing from proactive schemes [OY91,HJJ$^+$97]. Key evolution changes the secret key over time in such a way that prior keys cannot be computed from the current key, thus limiting the loss of confidentiality to messages sent with current and future keys. Secret-sharing distributes shares of the secret among multiple parties who proactively refresh the sharing by exchanging refresh messages. Consequently, to learn the secret an adversary must expose shares of multiple parties at the same time.

CHANNEL DEFINITION AND CONSTRUCTION. In Section 2 we formulate a new secure two-party communication primitive called an *Intrusion-Resilient Channel (IRC)* that uses familiar key-evolution and proactive techniques to limit propagation of exposures both forward and backward in time and facilitates restoration of confidential communication. In Section 3 we describe $g\mathcal{IRC}$, our intrusion-resilient channel construction based on any semantically secure public key encryption scheme with sufficiently large domain[1]. $g\mathcal{IRC}$ uses public key encryption in a straightforward way to secure the two-way channel traffic. Either party may proactively refresh the channel by generating new key pairs and sending the appropriate public and private keys to the other party. Despite the simplicity of the construction, its proof of security requires a surprising amount of work, since refresh messages include new private keys for the recipient.

CHANNEL APPLICATIONS. In Section 4 we explore the message hiding capabilities of general two-party protocols augmented with an intrusion-resilient channel. Specifically, in Section 4.3 we outline a general strategy for proving the increased security of channel-augmented protocols. To demonstrate the strategy, we prove the intrusion-resilient signature scheme of [IR02] secure against adversaries with greater temporal adaptivity than was previously proven. We believe the strategy is applicable to other two-party protocols as well, such as intrusion-resilient encryption [DFK$^+$03] and proactive two-party signatures [NKDM03].

Our proofs utilize a modified definition of a protocol simulator developed in Section 4.1 in which success, i.e. indistinguishability, is measured with respect to specified *subsets* of the views generated by the simulator. This type of simulator may be of independent interest and applicable in other contexts.

---

[1] The public key encryption scheme must also be key-indistinguishable as defined in [BBDP01] for $g\mathcal{IRC}$ to be used as a secure sub-protocol (see Section 4).

1.2   Adversary Models and Assumptions

PROTOCOL ADVERSARIES.   General protocol adversaries may be *static* or *mobile*. Parties corrupted by static adversaries remain corrupted until the protocol terminates. Mobile adversaries, introduced in [OY91], capture the idea that corrupted parties may be able to detect intrusions and execute a recovery mechanism, effectively removing the adversary and restoring the party to an uncorrupted state. When considering mobile adversaries, it is useful to talk about *secret exposures* rather than full corruption in order to specify to a finer degree the knowledge the adversary learns as the result of various actions.

Adaptive adversaries determine their next action based on the results of all previous exposures and other queries, whereas *non-adaptive* adversaries must specify their entire activity schedule at the time of protocol initialization.

Active adversaries may modify messages sent by uncorrupted parties and exert complete control over corrupted parties, for example by arbitrarily modifying their internal state and messages and causing them to deviate from the protocol. In contrast, *passive* adversaries are only allowed to observe the internal state of corrupted parties, and may read protocol messages without modifying them.

OUR MODEL AND ASSUMPTIONS.   Adversaries in this work are assumed to be adaptive and mobile (even able to access "expired" information) but passive. Parties are not assumed to possess long term secrets which cannot be exposed, but all parties are assumed to have access to independent sources of *private randomness*, that is, they can privately generate truly random bits (even *after* exposure). To simplify the proofs communication is assumed to be *synchronous*, that is, all messages are delivered instantaneously and reliably. In practice only an ordered, reliable datagram delivery mechanism similar to TCP is needed.

Although results exist for *active*, adaptive and mobile adversaries (see Section 1.3), restricting to passive adversaries allows us to provide the desired resiliency and recovery capability via a simple, generic construction. In particular, we avoid altogether the need for authentication which is difficult to maintain against active adversaries. Despite its simplicity, significant technical challenges are encountered in proving the message-privacy properties of our construction.

1.3   Comparison with Previous Work

ADAPTIVE MOBILE ADVERSARIES.   In [CHH00] Canetti et al. show how to restore authenticity to a party in the presence of active, adaptive and mobile adversaries. This is accomplished by using a "proactive distributed signature scheme" which they realize in a setting without authenticated communication. Other proactive threshold[2] schemes include [FMY99], built on the non-adaptive scheme of [FGMY97], and [HJJ+97], based on [HJKY95] (see below). All such threshold schemes require an honest majority of communicating parties, and thus are not applicable to the case of two-party protocols.

---

[2] A *threshold* scheme remains secure provided the number of *simultaneously* compromised parties never exceeds the given threshold.

[CK02] recasts the classical notion of secure channels into the powerful universally composable (UC) model [Can01] by defining key exchange and secure channel functionalities in the presence of *active*, adaptive and mobile adversaries. They realize relaxed versions of these functionalities by using a modification to the UC model called "non-information" oracles. These oracles help bridge the differences between indistinguishability and simulation-based security. However, their exposure model assumes that the active adversary does not learn the long-term authentication secret of a party, allowing them to avoid the complexities of impersonation attacks considered in [CHH00].

In contrast, to avoid authentication altogether we assume an adversary that is passive but who learns the *entire* state of a party upon exposure. This allows us to focus on damage containment and recovery, the hallmarks of existing intrusion-resilient schemes, at the expense of the secure composability of the UC model. Indeed, the security proofs of the intrusion-resilient signature and encryption schemes of [IR02,DFK+03], two potential applications for our IRC, are not in the UC model. An interesting line of future research would be to combine the intrusion-resilient and UC models together.

NON-ADAPTIVE MOBILE ADVERSARIES. Secret sharing in the presence of non-adaptive mobile adversaries is handled in [HJKY95]. To aid recovery, all parties broadcast channel refresh messages according to a proactive "private key renewal protocol". In contrast, in this paper a refresh consists of a single party sending a single message. This was done to provide consistency with the existing intrusion-resilient signature and public key encryptions schemes of [IR02] and [DFK+03]. The proof techniques in this paper should suffice to prove the key renewal protocol of [HJKY95] intrusion-resilient (and "spliceable"; see Section 2.3) against *adaptive* adversaries. We emphasize that this key renewal protocol was not articulated as a stand-alone primitive.

2   Definitions

2.1   Functional Definition: Two-Party Key-Evolving Channel

Let $u \in \{0,1\}$ and $\bar{u} = 1 - u$ denote the identities of the two communicating parties, and let $\tau > 0$ be a natural number denoting a time period. The channel is fully bi-directional, so that in all that follows u and $\bar{u}$ may be interchanged. Let $SK_\tau^{[u]}$ denote the secret key for party u in period τ. Similarly, $R_\tau^{[u]}$ denotes the key refresh message *received* by party u for period τ which is generated and sent by party $\bar{u}$. Party u combines refresh information in $R_\tau^{[u]}$ with its current key $SK_\tau^{[u]}$ to obtain its new key $SK_{\tau+1}^{[u]}$ for the next period $(\tau + 1)$ and then deletes the expired $SK_\tau^{[u]}$, thereby completing the *refresh protocol*. The current period τ thus gives the number of refreshes executed since channel initiation. It is assumed that τ is explicitly part of both $SK_\tau^{[u]}$ and $R_\tau^{[u]}$. For convenience let the array U contain the identity of the refresh message receiver for each period, that is $U[\tau] \in \{0,1\}$ denotes the receiver for period τ. Note that the channel communicates two types of messages[3]: data and refresh.

Definition 1. *A* two-party key-evolving channel $\mathcal{KEC} = (InitKeys, EncM, DecM, GenR, ProcR;$ $\underline{SendMesg},$ $\underline{RefKeys})$ *is a quintuple of algorithms and pair of protocols as described in Figure 2.1.*

$\mathcal{KEC}.InitKeys(1^k) \to \langle SK_0^{[0]}, SK_0^{[1]} \rangle$: channel initialization algorithm
   In: Security parameter k (in unary)
   Out: Key pair $\langle SK_0^{[0]}, SK_0^{[1]} \rangle$ to be used by the channel endpoints
$\mathcal{KEC}.EncM_{SK_\tau^{[u]}}(m) \to c$: message encryption algorithm
   In: Message m to be sent from party u to party $\bar{u}$, current period secret key $SK_\tau^{[u]}$ of the sending party
   Out: Ciphertext c
$\mathcal{KEC}.DecM_{SK_\tau^{[\bar{u}]}}(c) \to m'$: message decryption algorithm
   In: Ciphertext c (received by party $\bar{u}$ from party u), current period secret key $SK_\tau^{[\bar{u}]}$ of the receiving party
   Out: Message m', where $\forall m\ DecM_{SK_\tau^{[\bar{u}]}}(EncM_{SK_\tau^{[u]}}(m)) = m$
$\mathcal{KEC}.GenR(SK_\tau^{[u]}) \to \langle SK_{\tau+1}^{[u]}, R_\tau^{[\bar{u}]} \rangle$: key refresh generation algorithm
   In: Current period secret key $SK_\tau^{[u]}$
   Out: Refreshed secret key $SK_{\tau+1}^{[u]}$ and key refresh message $R_\tau^{[\bar{u}]}$ for party $\bar{u}$.
   Party u sends $R_\tau^{[\bar{u}]}$ to $\bar{u}$, securely deletes $SK_\tau^{[u]}$ and $R_\tau^{[\bar{u}]}$, and sets $\tau = \tau + 1$.
$\mathcal{KEC}.ProcR_{SK_\tau^{[\bar{u}]}}(R_\tau^{[\bar{u}]}) \to SK_{\tau+1}^{[\bar{u}]}$: key refresh processing algorithm
   In: Secret key $SK_\tau^{[\bar{u}]}$, key refresh $R_\tau^{[\bar{u}]}$ (received by party $\bar{u}$ from party u)
   Out: Refreshed secret key $SK_{\tau+1}^{[\bar{u}]}$. Party $\bar{u}$ securely deletes $SK_\tau^{[\bar{u}]}$ and $R_\tau^{[\bar{u}]}$, and sets $\tau = \tau + 1$.
$\mathcal{KEC}.SendMesg$: Protocol for party u to securely send message m to party $\bar{u}$.
   1. Party u calls $EncM_{SK_\tau^{[u]}}(m)$ and sends output c to $\bar{u}$.
   2. The other party $\bar{u}$ on receipt of data message c from u, calls $DecM_{SK_\tau^{[\bar{u}]}}(c)$ to retrieve the sent plaintext data message m.
$\mathcal{KEC}.RefKeys$: Protocol for refreshing the secret keys of both parties.
   1. Party u initiates refresh by calling $GenR(SK_\tau^{[u]})$ which outputs $(SK_{\tau+1}^{[u]}, R_\tau^{[\bar{u}]})$.
   2. Party u sends refresh message $R_\tau^{[\bar{u}]}$ to $\bar{u}$ ($GenR$ securely deletes $SK_\tau^{[u]}$ and $R_\tau^{[\bar{u}]}$, and increments τ by 1).
   3. The other party $\bar{u}$ on receipt of $R_\tau^{[\bar{u}]}$ completes the refresh cycle by calling $ProcR_{SK_\tau^{[\bar{u}]}}(R_\tau^{[\bar{u}]})$ which returns $SK_{\tau+1}^{[\bar{u}]}$ ($ProcR$ securely deletes $SK_\tau^{[\bar{u}]}$ and $R_\tau^{[\bar{u}]}$, and increments τ by 1).

Fig. 1. Two-party Key-evolving Channel $\mathcal{KEC}$ Algorithms and Protocols (underlined).

---

[3] In practice, a mechanism for distinguishing the two types is needed, e.g. a distinguished 1-bit flag in the (unencrypted) message header. We omit this detail henceforth.

2.2   Security Definition: Channel Intrusion-Resilience

A $\mathcal{KEC}$ adversary $\mathcal{A}$ is modeled as a probabilistic polynomial-time (PPT) Turing machine that conducts an adaptive chosen-ciphertext (CCA2) attack[4] against $\mathcal{KEC}$ with the aid of the oracle set O_t according to the security experiment $\mathbf{Exp}_{\mathcal{KEC},\mathcal{A}}^{channel-ind-b}$; see Figure 2 for details. Let Q denote the sequence of all oracle queries made by $\mathcal{A}$ during a run of experiment $\mathbf{Exp}_{\mathcal{KEC},\mathcal{A}}^{channel-ind-b}(k)$. In addition to being exposed *directly* by querying $Okey$, keys may be exposed *indirectly* due to the combined results of specific $Okey$ and $Oref$ queries. This leads to a notion of key exposure analogous to that in [IR02].

Definition 2 (Q-Exposure). *For a sequence of adversary oracle queries Q and time period τ, we say that the key $SK_\tau^{[u]}$ is Q-exposed[5]:*

[directly] *if $(u, \tau) \in Q$; or*
[via evolution] *if $SK_{\tau-1}^{[u]}$ is Q-exposed **and** $U[\tau - 1] = u$ **and** $\tau - 1 \in Q$*
(Given $SK_{\tau-1}^{[u]}$ and $R_{\tau-1}^{[u]}$, $\mathcal{A}$ can compute $SK_\tau^{[u]}$ via $ProcR_{SK_{\tau-1}^{[u]}}(R_{\tau-1}^{[u]})$).

CHANNEL COMPROMISE AND RECOVERY.   Whereas key exposure models the "internal" side of a security breach, compromise refers to its "external" aspect. We say that party u is (Q, τ)-compromised if $SK_\tau^{[u]}$ is Q-exposed. When party u is (Q, τ)-compromised, the adversary can read all messages directed toward u by simply decrypting them using $SK_\tau^{[u]}$. If both sides of the channel are (Q, τ)-compromised for the same period τ then the channel is totally compromised for period τ, i.e. neither refresh nor data messages can be securely exchanged.

An important feature of intrusion-resilient channels, due the passive adversary assumption, is their ability to recover from even a total compromise. Party u recovers from a compromise as soon as it sends a refresh message, even if this message is observed and read. Party $\bar{u}$, if also compromised, can likewise recover by initiating its own refresh after receiving party u's. Thus, channel recovery is achieved whenever both parties send refreshes without any intervening direct exposures. Moreover, if the adversary ever fails to intercept a refresh, then both the refresh sender and receiver simultaneously recover from compromise.

SECURITY EXPERIMENT.   As in the standard security definitions for public key cryptosystems (see for example [BDPR98]), the adversary $\mathcal{A}$ is divided into probing and distinguishing subcomponents: $\mathcal{A}_{probe}$ and $\mathcal{A}_{dist}$. Note that $\mathcal{A}_{probe}$ maintains state during the experiment, and passes its final state to $\mathcal{A}_{dist}$. $\mathcal{A}$ specifies the timing and direction of each channel refresh. $\mathcal{A}$ can obtain encryptions and decryptions on adaptively chosen messages for the party (direction), and time period of its choice via the oracle set O_t. Eventually, $\mathcal{A}$ requests a

---

[4] Appropriately restricting the set O_t yields definitions of intrusion-resilient security against ciphertext-only and adaptive chosen-message attacks. Additional definitions can be created by specifying the appropriate oracles for these notions.

[5] Alternate models allowing additional exposure types may have more efficient constructions with weaker security and are not explored in this paper.

challenge ciphertext for a message pair, party (direction), and time period of its choice, and attempts to distinguish. It is required that $\mathcal{A}$ not query $Odec$ on the challenge ciphertext or Q-expose the corresponding decryption secret.

Definition 3 (Intrusion-Resilience).
Let $\mathcal{KEC} = (InitKeys, EncM, DecM, GenR, ProcR; \underline{SendMesg}, \underline{RefKeys})$ *be a two-party key evolving channel scheme with security parameter* k, *and let* $\mathcal{A} = (\mathcal{A}_{probe}, \mathcal{A}_{dist})$ *be an adversary. The (CCA) advantage of* $\mathcal{A}$ *against the channel* $\mathcal{KEC}$ *is defined as:*

$$\mathbf{Adv}_{\mathcal{KEC},\mathcal{A}}^{channel-ind}(k) \stackrel{def}{=} \Pr[\mathbf{Exp}_{\mathcal{KEC},\mathcal{A}}^{channel-ind-1}(k)=1] - \Pr[\mathbf{Exp}_{\mathcal{KEC},\mathcal{A}}^{channel-ind-0}(k)=1].$$

$\mathcal{KEC}$ *is (CCA)* intrusion-resilient *if* $\mathbf{Adv}_{\mathcal{KEC},\mathcal{A}}^{channel-ind}(\cdot)$ *is negl. for all PPT* $\mathcal{A}$.

2.3   Channel Spliceability

As we will see when we explore the message-hiding capabilities of two-party protocols augmented with an intrusion-resilient channel in Section 4, our results rely on an additional hiding property of our channel. Namely, data messages sent over the channel should hide the specific key instance used to encrypt them. In the context of public key cryptosystems this property is called *key indistinguishability* and was introduced by Bellare, et al. in [BBDP01]. For our channels we formulate an appropriate version of this property called *spliceability*, which we define in detail in [IMR05].

3   A Generic Intrusion-Resilient Channel Construction

This section describes $g\mathcal{IRC}$, our intrusion-resilient channel, which can be constructed using any semantically secure, public key cryptosystem[6] $\mathcal{S} = (\mathcal{G}, \mathcal{E}, \mathcal{D})$. $g\mathcal{IRC}$ consists of two bi-directional sub-channels, one to secure data messages and the other to secure refresh messages. Each party holds a pair of public keys for sending and a pair of secret keys for receiving on each sub-channel. Either party may proactively refresh the channel by generating a complete set of new keys for both sides of the channel. The generating party retains its own new sub-channel keys. It sends the complimentary keys to the other party in a refresh message encrypted under the appropriate (expiring) refresh sub-channel key. A detailed description of $g\mathcal{IRC}$ appears in Figure 3.

Despite the simplicity of $g\mathcal{IRC}$, its security proof (see proof sketch below) is complicated by the fact that refresh messages include the recipient's new secret keys.

Theorem 1 ($g\mathcal{IRC}$ is Intrusion-Resilient). *If* $\mathcal{S}$ *is a CCA semantically-secure public-key encryption scheme,* $g\mathcal{IRC}$ *is an intrusion-resilient channel.*

---

[6] See, for example, [BDPR98] for the definition of a public key cryptosystem. Any $\mathcal{E}$ with domain sufficiently large enough to accommodate the messages described in Figure 3 can be used. If $\mathcal{E}$ is also key-indistinguishable then the resulting $g\mathcal{IRC}$ is spliceable.

Oracle Set[a] O_t

$Okey_t(u,\tau)$: key exposure oracle

    on input party identifier u and period $\tau \leq t$ returns $SK_\tau^{[u]}$.

$Oenc_t(u,\tau,m)$: message encryption oracle

    on input party identifier u, period $\tau \leq t$, and message m returns $EncM_{SK_\tau^{[u]}}(m)$.

$Odec_t(\bar{u},\tau,c)$: message decryption oracle

    on input party identifier $\bar{u}$, period $\tau \leq t$, and ciphertext c returns $DecM_{SK_\tau^{[\bar{u}]}}(c)$.

$Oref_t(\tau)$: key refresh message oracle

    on input period $\tau \leq t$ returns $R_\tau^{[U[\tau]]}$.

Experiment $\mathbf{Exp}_{\mathcal{KEC},\mathcal{A}}^{channel-ind-b}(k)$

INIT:

    $t \leftarrow 0;\ q \leftarrow \mathrm{ref}(0,1);\ c \leftarrow \perp;$

    $\langle SK_t^{[0]}, SK_t^{[1]} \rangle \leftarrow InitKeys(1^k);$

PROBE:

    while q in $(\mathrm{ref}(w,\bar{w}),\text{"test"})$ do

        $q \leftarrow \mathcal{A}_{probe}^{O_t}(1^k)$

        CASE q

          $\mathrm{ref}(w,\bar{w})$: % *send refresh from party w to party $\bar{w}$*

            $\langle SK_{t+1}^{[w]}, R_t^{[\bar{w}]} \rangle \leftarrow GenR(SK_t^{[w]})$ % *party w generates new key and refresh*

            $SK_{t+1}^{[\bar{w}]} \leftarrow ProcR_{SK_t^{[\bar{w}]}}(R_t^{[\bar{w}]})$ % *party $\bar{w}$ receives refresh and updates its key*

            $U[t] \leftarrow \bar{w}$ % *party $\bar{w}$ is recorded as the receiver for period t*

            $t \leftarrow t+1$ % *time period incremented*

          "test": % *output challenge*

            if $c \neq \perp$ then break % *only one challenge allowed[b]*

            $(u,\bar{u},\tau,m_0,m_1) \leftarrow \mathcal{A}_{probe}^{O_t}(1^k)$ % *request period τ challenge, $(u,\bar{u})$ direction[c]*

            $c \leftarrow Oenc(m_b,u,\tau)$ % *encrypt challenge with $SK_\tau^{[u]}$; decryptable with $SK_\tau^{[\bar{u}]}$*

            $\mathcal{A}_{probe}^{O_t}(1^k,c)$ % *$\mathcal{A}_{probe}$ receives challenge c*

DIST:

    $s \leftarrow \mathcal{A}_{probe}^{O_t}(1^k)$ % *$\mathcal{A}_{probe}$ outputs final state s*

    $\hat{b} \leftarrow \mathcal{A}_{dist}^{O_t}(1^k,s)$ % *$\mathcal{A}_{dist}$ outputs distinguishing guess $\hat{b}$ for challenge bit b*

    if $SK_\tau^{[\bar{u}]}$ not Q-exposed % *decryption key not exposed (receiver not compromised)*

      and $(\mathcal{A}_{probe}, \mathcal{A}_{dist})$ did not query $Odec$ with $(\bar{u},\tau,c)$ % *challenge not decrypted*

      then return $\hat{b}$

    else return $\perp$

---

[a] O_t denotes the set of oracles to which $\mathcal{A}$ has access during period t. All oracles take as input τ, the period in which the adversary is interested. Queries about the future $(\tau > t)$ are prohibited, and result in the oracle returning $\perp$. Without loss of generality, we assume this never happens.

[b] Limiting $\mathcal{A}$ to a single challenge is not an essential restriction. Given an adversary $\mathcal{A}'$ which is allowed $poly(k)$ challenges, one can easily construct an $\mathcal{A}$ with advantage one over $poly(k)$ the advantage of $\mathcal{A}'$.

[c] We require that u, w, and $\hat{b}$ all be from $\{0,1\}$. If $\tau > t$, then $Oenc_t$ returns $\perp$. The adversarially chosen messages m_0 and m_1 must of course be in the domain of $EncM_{SK_\tau^{[u]}}(\cdot)$ and be of equal length, i.e. $|m_0| = |m_1|$.

Fig. 2. Intrusion-Resilience Security Experiment.

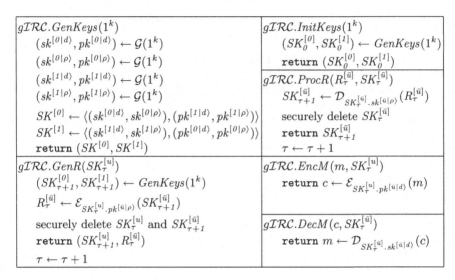

Fig. 3. Generic Intrusion-Resilient Channel $g\mathcal{IRC}$ Algorithms.

More precisely, given any $g\mathcal{IRC}$-adversary $\mathcal{A}$, one can construct a triple of $\mathcal{S}$-adversaries $\langle E_1, E_2, E_3 \rangle$ such that for each value of the security parameter k there exists some $i \in \{1, 2, 3\}$ such that, $\mathbf{Adv}_{\mathcal{S}, E_i}^{ind-cca}(k) \geq \mathbf{Adv}_{g\mathcal{IRC}, \mathcal{A}}^{channel-ind}(k) / (4q_{refr}^2 \cdot (3q_{refr} - 2))$, where q_{refr} is an upper bound on the number of refreshes requested by the adversary in experiment $\mathbf{Exp}_{g\mathcal{IRC}, \mathcal{A}}^{channel-ind-b}(k)$ (see Figure 2 in Section 2.2). The running times of the E_i are essentially the same as for $\mathcal{A}$.

Proof (Sketch). (Complete proof available in [IMR05]). There are two cases to consider: the ciphertext challenge and refresh message beginning the challenge period specified by the adversary have either the *same* or *opposite* direction. If the direction is the same, a straightforward reduction to the semantic security of $\mathcal{S}$ is used. In the opposite case, a two step reduction is used. First the channel security is reduced to the security of a chain of $\mathcal{S}$ instances where the secret key of the next instance is encrypted under the public key of the current instance and given to the adversary. The security of this $\mathcal{S}$ chain is then reduced to the semantic security of a single $\mathcal{S}$ instance.

Theorem 2 ($g\mathcal{IRC}$ is Spliceable). *If $\mathcal{S}$ is a CCA semantically-secure public-key encryption scheme and $\mathcal{S}$ is CCA key-indistinguishable (IK-CCA) in the sense of [BBDP01], then $g\mathcal{IRC}$ is spliceable.*

Proof. Proof available in [IMR05].

4   More Secure Two-Party Protocols via Intrusion Resilient Channels

In this section we explore the message-hiding capabilities of general two-party protocols augmented with an intrusion-resilient channel. Suppose a two-party protocol $\mathcal{P}$ is secure against all adversaries who can only access a protocol message by exposing the receiver during the same period in which it was sent. Any messages for which this is not the case are called "forbidden" and are never seen by the adversary. One would expect $\mathcal{P}'$, an IRC-augmented version of $\mathcal{P}$, to be secure against adversaries who can view *any* protocol message, even forbidden ones.

However, this seems difficult to prove in the *adaptive* adversary setting considered here, since the set of messages which are forbidden depends dynamically on the adversary's query sequence. Indeed, a straightforward security reduction is frustrated by the fact that a simulator does not know ahead of time which messages will ultimately be forbidden. Consequently, at the time of a message query the simulator does not know whether or not it should substitute "garbage" in place of the true protocol message.

To help avoid this dilemma, commonly known as the "selective-decryption problem", in Section 4.1 we add an extra restriction to our definition of forbidden messages (Definition 4, condition 2), require the order of adversary exposures to be "refresh-receiver-biased" (Definition 6), and introduce a new type of protocol simulator (Definition 8). The success of these simulators is measured in terms of indistinguishability on a subset of their output (Definition 7).

These restrictions suffice to prove a result about simulators but not adversaries (Theorem 3 in Section 4.2). However, in Section 4.3 we outline a general proof strategy for applying Theorem 3 to prove that if the two-party protocol $\mathcal{P}$ is secure against refresh-receiver-biased adversaries who cannot expose any forbidden messages, then the channel-augmented version $\mathcal{P}'$ is secure against any refresh-receiver-biased adversary who *can* expose forbidden messages. To demonstrate the strategy, we prove the intrusion-resilient signature scheme of [IR02] secure against adversaries with greater temporal adaptivity than in the proof of [IR02].

4.1   Protocol Security Model

In what follows, all protocol parties are modeled as interactive Turing machines (ITMs) [Gol01]. Recall that ITMs have a random tape, a work tape, local input and output tapes, and a pair of communication tapes for incoming and outgoing protocol messages. Let $\mathcal{P}$ be any two-party protocol with security parameter[7] κ, initial input $\gamma_{\mathcal{P}}$, and randomness $r_{\mathcal{P}}$. Let $\mathcal{A}$ be an adversary for $\mathcal{P}$ with input $\gamma_{\mathcal{A}}$ and randomness $r_{\mathcal{A}}$. $\mathcal{A}$ also gets security parameter κ (in unary) as an input.

Correspondingly, let $\mathcal{A}'$ denote an adversary for $\mathcal{P}'$, a protocol identical to $\mathcal{P}$ but augmented so that all inter-party communication is protected using $\mathcal{IRC}$, a spliceable, intrusion-resilient channel. $\mathcal{P}'$ is constructed from $\mathcal{P}$ as follows. At the beginning of protocol $\mathcal{P}'$, in addition to the usual protocol secrets the parties also receive their respective initial keys for $\mathcal{IRC}$. Next, whenever in $\mathcal{P}$ party u sends message m, $\mathcal{P}'$ instead sends an encryption of m under party u's current

---

[7] If more than one, let κ denote a vector of security parameters.

channel key[8]. The sender u then executes a channel refresh and sends $\bar{u}$ the resulting channel refresh message[9].

PROTOCOL ADVERSARY INTERFACE. In attacking $\mathcal{P}$, the adversary $\mathcal{A}$ interacts with the protocol $\mathcal{P}$ via its user interface, which includes the ability to execute cryptographic routines and specify protocol control commands to effect the evolving state of the protocol. In addition, $\mathcal{A}$ has "attack" capabilities, such as the ability to expose secret keys and protocol messages or exert greater influence over the evolution $\mathcal{P}$. In the following O_t denotes the set of oracles[10] which mediate these interactions between $\mathcal{A}$ and $\mathcal{P}$. Similarly, O_t' denotes the oracle set for $\mathcal{A}'$ attacking $\mathcal{P}'$.

ADVERSARY QUERY CLASSES. Let Q denote the sequence of all oracle queries and control commands made by $\mathcal{A}$ while interacting with a particular execution of $\mathcal{P}$, and let $\mathcal{Q}$ denote a set of adversary query sequences, i.e. a set of Qs. Let Q' and $\mathcal{Q}'$ be similarly defined for adversary $\mathcal{A}'$ and protocol $\mathcal{P}'$.

Definition 4. *A message m sent in period τ using a key-evolving channel $\mathcal{KEC}$ is Q-forbidden if: 1) the receiver of m is not Q-exposed for period τ, and 2) the sender of m sent the previous (period $\tau - 1$) refresh.*

Let $Q_{FM} \subset Q$ denote the set of all Q-forbidden messages. Generalizing, let $\mathcal{Q} \setminus \mathcal{Q}_{FM}$ denote the set of query sequences derived from $\mathcal{Q}$ by removing from each $Q \in \mathcal{Q}$ its corresponding Q_{FM}.

Definition 5. *An interactive Turing machine I is $\mathcal{Q}$-restricted if its sequence of outgoing messages Q is always in $\mathcal{Q}$.*

Definition 6. *An adversary exposure sequence Q is* **refresh-receiver-biased** *if for all periods τ in which both ends of the channel are Q-exposed, the $\tau - 1$ refresh receiver is Q-exposed before the sender. A class $\mathcal{Q}$ of exposure query sequences is refresh-receiver-biased if $\forall Q \in \mathcal{Q}$, Q is refresh-receiver-biased. An adversary $\mathcal{A}$ is refresh-receiver-biased if $\mathcal{A}$ is $\mathcal{Q}$-restricted and $\mathcal{Q}$ is refresh-receiver-biased.*

INDISTINGUISHABILITY WITH RESPECT TO SUBSETS OF DISTRIBUTIONS. The following notion of indistinguishability is needed for the modified definition of protocol simulators used in Theorem 3. Let X and Y denote distributions over

---

[8] The granularity of channel time periods may differ from that of the protocol. Also, if necessary, m can be fragmented into multiple sub-messages prior to encryption.

[9] Other compositions are possible. For example, after every message sent, both parties could execute refreshes one right after the other, etc.

[10] While queries pertaining to past and current time periods are permissible, queries about the future and non-existent messages are prohibited (return value $\perp$). WLOG, we assume this never happens. In cases where $\mathcal{A}$ is given protocol control capability beyond that available to an honest $\mathcal{P}$ user, the particulars of this interface are handled by the security experiment in which $\mathcal{A}$ is participating. Note when the adversary is interacting with a simulator for $\mathcal{P}$, all oracle queries are handled by the simulator.

length n sequences of bit-strings. For a sequence of bit-strings x, $x[i]$ denotes the ith bit-string. Let $J \subseteq \{1, \ldots, n\}$ be an index subset. $\mathcal{D}^x$ denotes oracle access to x by $\mathcal{D}$ on a per bit-string basis.

```
Experiment Exp_{X/Y,D}^{J-ind-b}(κ)
  if b = 0 then x ← X
  if b = 1 then x ← Y
  b̂ ← D^x
  if D queried for bit-string x[j] for j ∉ J
      then output ⊥    % D may only view bit-stings indexed by J
  else output b̂
```

Definition 7 (J-indistinguishable distributions). *Let J, X, and Y be as in the above experiment, and $\mathcal{D}$ be a distinguishing adversary. The J-distinguishing advantage of $\mathcal{D}$ against distributions X and Y is defined as:*

$$\mathbf{Adv}_{X/Y,\mathcal{D}}^{J-ind}(\kappa) \stackrel{def}{=} \Pr[\mathbf{Exp}_{X/Y,\mathcal{D}}^{J-ind-0}(\kappa) = 1] - \Pr[\mathbf{Exp}_{X/Y,\mathcal{D}}^{J-ind-1}(\kappa) = 1].$$

The two distributions X and Y are J-indistinguishable, denoted $X \approx_J Y$, if $\mathbf{Adv}_{X/Y,\mathcal{D}}^{J-ind}(\cdot)$ is negligible for all PPT $\mathcal{D}$. More generally, the two distributions X and Y are $\mathcal{J}$-indistinguishable, denoted $X \approx_{\mathcal{J}} Y$, if $\forall J \in \mathcal{J}$, $\mathbf{Adv}_{X/Y,\mathcal{D}}^{J-ind}(\cdot)$ is negligible for all PPT $\mathcal{D}$.

MODIFIED SIMULATORS. Let $\mathsf{VIEW}_{\mathcal{A}}^{\mathcal{P},\mathcal{A}^{O_t}}(\gamma_{\mathcal{P}}, r_{\mathcal{P}} | \gamma_{\mathcal{A}}, r_{\mathcal{A}})$ denote adversary $\mathcal{A}$'s view of its interaction with an instance of protocol $\mathcal{P}$ via the oracle set O_t. Recall that $\gamma_{\mathcal{A}}$ and $r_{\mathcal{A}}$ (resp. $\gamma_{\mathcal{P}}$ and $r_{\mathcal{P}}$) denote the input and randomness for $\mathcal{A}$ (resp. $\mathcal{P}$), and the security parameter κ is an implicit input to all parties. This view consists of the sequence of all queries made by $\mathcal{A}$ along with the corresponding responses received. Similarly, let $\mathsf{VIEW}_{\mathcal{A}'}^{\mathcal{P}',\mathcal{A}'^{O_t'}}(\gamma_{\mathcal{P}'}, r_{\mathcal{P}'} | \gamma_{\mathcal{A}'}, r_{\mathcal{A}'})$ denote the view of $\mathcal{A}'$ interacting via the oracle set O_t' with an instance of $\mathcal{P}'$. In the definition below $J_{Q'} \subseteq Q'$ denotes a unique (non-empty) subset of query sequence Q' used to qualify the indistinguishability of the views. $\mathcal{J}$ denotes the collection of all such $J_{Q'}$ for all $Q' \in \mathcal{Q}'$.

Definition 8. *An ITM Sim is a $\mathcal{Q}'$-answering, $\mathcal{Q}$-restricted, ε-good $\mathcal{J}$-simulator for protocol $\mathcal{P}$ with security parameter κ if*

1. *Sim is $\mathcal{Q}$-restricted,*
2. *Sim interactively generates query sequence $Q \in \mathcal{Q}$ to ask $\mathcal{P}$ in response to interactive query sequence Q'*
3. *$\exists$ an efficiently computable predicate $Sim.OK : \mathcal{Q}' \times \mathcal{Q} \to \{0, 1\}$*
4. *$\forall Q' \in \mathcal{Q}'$, $\Pr[Sim.OK(Q', Q) = 1] \geq \varepsilon(\kappa)$ taken over the random choices of Sim*
5. *$\forall$ ITM $\mathcal{A}$ asking $Q' \in \mathcal{Q}'$, if Q satisfies $Sim.OK(Q', Q) = 1$, then*
   $$\mathsf{VIEW}_{\mathcal{A}}^{\mathcal{P},\mathcal{A}^{O_t}}(\gamma_{\mathcal{P}}, r_{\mathcal{P}} | \gamma_{\mathcal{A}}, r_{\mathcal{A}}) \approx_{J_{Q'}} \mathsf{VIEW}_{\mathcal{A}}^{Sim,\mathcal{A}^{O_t}}(\gamma_{Sim}, r_{Sim} | \gamma_{\mathcal{A}}, r_{\mathcal{A}}).$$

Intuitively, *Sim* simulates answers to any query sequence $Q' \in \mathcal{Q}'$ by asking a transformed query sequence $Q \in \mathcal{Q}$ of $\mathcal{P}$. *Sim* succeeds with probability at least ε in producing a view which is indistinguishable when judged with respect to the *smaller* query set $J_{Q'} \subseteq Q'$.

4.2   Intrusion-Resilient and Spliceable Channels Hide Forbidden Messages

In what follows, let Sim' denote the ITM obtained by augmenting Sim with $\mathcal{IRC}$ in the same way that $\mathcal{P}'$ is obtained from $\mathcal{P}$. That is, Sim' augments the view produced by Sim to include $\mathcal{IRC}$ encrypted messages and keys. Sim' passes query sequence Q' to Sim which in turn interactively generates query sequence Q to answer the Q' queries. Note that $Sim'.OK \stackrel{def}{=} Sim.OK$[11].

Theorem 3. *Let $\mathcal{P}'$ be instantiated with an intrusion-resilient and spliceable channel. If $\mathcal{Q}'$ is refresh-receiver-biased and Sim is a $\mathcal{Q}'$-answering, Q-restricted, ε-good $\mathcal{Q}' \setminus \mathcal{Q}'_{FM}$-simulator for $\mathcal{P}$, then Sim' is a $\mathcal{Q}'$-answering, Q-restricted, ε-good $\mathcal{Q}'$-simulator for $\mathcal{P}'$.*

Theorem 3 says that composing an intrusion-resilient and spliceable channel with a simulator Sim which answers query sequences $Q' \in \mathcal{Q}'$ but may only be indistinguishable when forbidden messages are excluded, i.e. for $Q' \setminus \mathcal{Q}'_{FM}$, yields a simulator Sim' answering the same set of query sequences $\mathcal{Q}'$ and which is indistinguishable even on forbidden messages. For forbidden message queries Sim need only generate responses of the correct length. Note that Sim may have to deal with arbitrary simultaneous compromise of both ends of the channel, and thus a total compromise of $\mathcal{P}'$.

Proof. Proof available in [IMR05].

4.3   Improved Two-Party Protocol Security

A SPECIFIC EXAMPLE. Let SiBIR2 denote the channel-augmented version of SiBIR1, the Signer-Base Intrusion-Resilient signature scheme of [IR02], in which all message traffic is secured via some spliceable, intrusion-resilient channel $\mathcal{IRC}$, as was described for general two-party protocols in the beginning of Section 4.1. Recall in SiBIR1 the long-term signing secrets are shared between Base and Signer modules (the two parties), whereas the complete signing secret for the current time period is always held by the Signer.

For SiBIR2, let $\mathcal{Q}'$ be any refresh-receiver-biased class of query sequences Q which have at least one time period for which the Signer keys are not Q-exposed[12]. Provided these two conditions are satisfied, a sequence $Q' \in \mathcal{Q}'$ may contain both Base and Signer key exposures and message exposures in any order.

---

[11] For all pairs (Q',Q), it should be the case that $Sim'.OK(Q',Q) = 1$ whenever $Sim.OK(Q',Q) = 1$, since if Sim does not need to abort with unencrypted simulated messages, Sim' with encrypted simulated messages should not have to either. The reverse implication may not always hold, but by assuming it we only underestimate the success (non-abort) probability of Sim'.

[12] This is reasonable since no successful forger can expose the Signer keys for the forgery period.

Theorem 4. SiBIR2 *is secure against all Q'-restricted adversaries $\mathcal{A}'$, in particular any time-adaptive adversary restricted to refresh-receiver-biased query sequences.*

Proof (Sketch). (Proof available in [IMR05].)

1. Select a suitably restricted SiBIR1 adversary query class Q.
2. Prove SiBIR1 secure against all Q-restricted adversaries.
3. Exhibit a Q'-answering, Q-restricted, ε-good $Q' \setminus Q'_{FM}$ simulator for SiBIR1.
4. Apply Theorem 3 to get a simulator which reduces any SiBIR2 adversary to a SiBIR1 adversary.
5. The advantage lost in the reduction is just an $\varepsilon = 1/T$ factor, where T is the number of time periods.

GENERAL STRATEGY. We believe the strategy outlined in the proof sketch of Theorem 4 can also be used to prove enhanced security for other channel-augmented two-party cryptographic protocols, including intrusion-resilient encryption [DFK+03] and proactive two-party signatures [NKDM03]. To do so, first decide on a query class Q'. Then follow the steps outlined above, replacing SiBIR1 and SiBIR2 with $\mathcal{P}$ and $\mathcal{P}'$ respectively. Note that the challenge lies in selecting appropriate adversary query classes Q and Q' such that Steps 2 and 3 can be simultaneously accomplished.

References

[And97]   Ross Anderson. Invited lecture. In *Fourth ACM Conference on Computer and Communication Security* [CCS97]. (see also [And02]).

[And02]   Ross Anderson. Two remarks on public key cryptology. Technical Report UCAM-CL-TR-549, University of Cambridge, Computer Laboratory, December 2002. http://www.cl.cam.ac.uk/TechReports/UCAM-CL-TR-549.pdf.

[BBDP01] Mihir Bellare, Alexandra Boldyreva, Anand Desai, and David Pointcheval. Key-privacy in public-key encryption. In Colin Boyd, editor, *Advances in cryptology — ASIACRYPT 2001: 7th International Conference on the Theory and Application of Cryptology and Information Security, Gold Coast, Australia, December 9–13, 2001: proceedings*, volume 2248 of *Lecture Notes in Computer Science*, pages 566–??, New York, NY, USA, 2001. Springer-Verlag Inc.

[BCK98]   Mihir Bellare, Ran Canetti, and Hugo Krawczyk. A modular approach to the design and analysis of authentication and key exchange protocols (extended abstract). In ACM, editor, *Proceedings of the Thirtieth Annual ACM Symposium on Theory of Computing*, Dallas, Texas, 23–26 May 1998.

[BDPR98] Mihir Bellare, Anand Desai, David Pointcheval, and Phillip Rogaway. Relations among notions of security for public-key encryption schemes. In Hugo Krawczyk, editor, *Advances in Cryptology—CRYPTO '98*, volume 1462 of *Lecture Notes in Computer Science*, pages 26–45. Springer-Verlag, 23–27 August 1998.

[BH93]   Donald Beaver and Stuart Haber. Cryptographic protocols provably secure against dynamic adversaries. In Rainer A. Rueppel, editor, *Advances in Cryptology – EUROCRYPT ' 92*, volume 658 of *Lecture Notes in Computer Science*, pages 307–323. International Association for Cryptologic Research, Springer-Verlag, Berlin Germany, 1993.

[BHNS99]   Boaz Barak, Amir Herzberg, Dalit Naor, and Eldad Shai. The proactive security toolkit and applications. In Gene Tsudik, editor, *Proceedings of the 5th ACM Conference on Computer and Communications Security*, pages 18–27, Singapore, November 1999. ACM Press.

[BM99]   Mihir Bellare and Sara Miner. A forward-secure digital signature scheme. In Michael Wiener, editor, *Advances in Cryptology—CRYPTO '99*, volume 1666 of *Lecture Notes in Computer Science*, pages 431–448. Springer-Verlag, 15–19 August 1999. Revised version is available from `http://www.cs.ucsd.edu/~mihir/`.

[BR93]   Mihir Bellare and Phillip Rogaway. Entity authentication and key distribution. In Douglas R. Stinson, editor, *Advances in Cryptology—CRYPTO '93*, volume 773 of *Lecture Notes in Computer Science*, pages 232–249. Springer-Verlag, 22–26 August 1993.

[Can01]   Ran Canetti. Universally composable security: A new paradigm for cryptographic protocols. In *42nd Annual Symposium on Foundations of Computer Science*, pages 136–145, New York, October 2001. IEEE.

[CCS97]   *Fourth ACM Conference on Computer and Communication Security*. ACM, April 1–4 1997.

[CHH00]   Ran Canetti, Shai Halevi, and Amir Herzberg. Maintaining authenticated communication in the presence of break-ins. *Journal of Cryptology*, 13(1):61–105, January 2000.

[CK01]   Ran Canetti and Hugo Krawczyk. Analysis of key-exchange protocols and their use for building secure channels. In Birgit Pfitzmann, editor, *Advances in Cryptology—EUROCRYPT 2001*, volume 2045 of *Lecture Notes in Computer Science*, pages 451–472. Springer-Verlag, 6–10 May 2001.

[CK02]   Ran Canetti and Hugo Krawczyk. Universally composable notions of key exchange and secure channels. In Lars Knudsen, editor, *Advances in Cryptology—EUROCRYPT 2002*, Lecture Notes in Computer Science, pages 337–351. Springer-Verlag, 28 April–2 May 2002.

[Des97]   Y. Desmedt. Some recent research aspects of threshold cryptography. In *Proc. 1st International Information Security Workshop*, pages 158–173, 1997.

[DFK+03]   Y. Dodis, M. Franklin, J. Katz, A. Miyaji, and M. Yung. Intrusion-resilient public-key encryption. In *Progress in Cryptology — CT-RSA 2003*, volume 2612 of *Lecture Notes in Computer Science*, pages 19–32. Springer-Verlag, 2003.

[DH76]   Whitfield Diffie and Martin E. Hellman. New directions in cryptography. *IEEE Transactions on Information Theory*, IT-22(6):644–654, 1976.

[FGMY97]   Y. Frankel, P. Gemmell, P. D. MacKenzie, and M. Yung. Proactive RSA. In *Proc. 17th International Advances in Cryptology Conference – CRYPTO '97*, pages 440–454, 1997.

[FMY99]   Yair Frankel, Philip D. MacKenzie, and Moti Yung. Adaptively-secure optimal-resilience proactive rsa. In Kwok-Yan Lam, Eiji Okamoto, and Chaoping Xing, editors, *Advances in Cryptology—ASIACRYPT '99*, volume 1716 of *Lecture Notes in Computer Science*, pages 180–194, Singapore, 14–18 November 1999. Springer-Verlag.

[Gol01]   Oded Goldreich. *Foundations of Cryptography: Basic Tools*. Cambridge University Press, 2001.

[HJJ+97]   Amir Herzberg, Markus Jakobsson, Stanisław Jarecki, Hugo Krawczyk, and Moti Yung. Proactive public key and signature systems. In *Fourth ACM Conference on Computer and Communication Security* [CCS97], pages 100–110.

[HJKY95]   Amir Herzberg, Stanislaw Jarecki, Hugo Krawczyk, and Moti Yung. Proactive secret sharing or: How to cope with perpetual leakage. In Don Coppersmith, editor, *Advances in Cryptology—CRYPTO '95*, volume 963 of *Lecture Notes in Computer Science*, pages 339–352. Springer-Verlag, 27–31 August 1995.

[IMR05]   Gene Itkis, Robert McNerney, and Scott Russell. Intrusion-resilient secure channels. Cryptology ePrint Archive, Report 2005/247, 2005. http://eprint.iacr.org/.

[IR02]   Gene Itkis and Leonid Reyzin. SiBIR: Intrusion-resilient signatures, or towards obsoletion of certificate revocation. In Yung [Yun02]. Available from http://eprint.iacr.org/2002/054/.

[JL00]   Stanisław Jarecki and Anna Lysyanskaya. Adaptively secure threshold cryptography: Introducing concurrency, removing erasures. In Bart Preneel, editor, *Advances in Cryptology—EUROCRYPT 2000*, volume 1807 of *Lecture Notes in Computer Science*, pages 221–242. Springer-Verlag, 14–18 May 2000.

[MVV97]   A. J. (Alfred J.) Menezes, Paul C. Van Oorschot, and Scott A. Vanstone. *Handbook of applied cryptography*. The CRC Press series on discrete mathematics and its applications. CRC Press, 2000 N.W. Corporate Blvd., Boca Raton, FL 33431-9868, USA, 1997.

[NKDM03]   A. Nicolosi, M. Krohn, Y. Dodis, and D. Mazières. Proactive two-party signatures for user authentication. In *Proceedings of the Symposium on Network and Distributed Systems Security (NDSS '03)*, 2003.

[OY91]   Rafail Ostrovsky and Moti Yung. How to withstand mobile virus attacks. In *10-th Annual ACM Symp. on Principles of Distributed Computing*, pages 51–59, 1991.

[Sho99]   Victor Shoup. On formal models for secure key exchange. Research Report RZ 3120 (#93166), IBM Research, April 1999. A revised version 4, dated November 15, 1999, is available from http://www.shoup.net/papers/.

[Yun02]   Moti Yung, editor. *Advances in Cryptology—CRYPTO 2002*, Lecture Notes in Computer Science. Springer-Verlag, 18–22 August 2002.

Optimal Asymmetric Encryption and Signature Paddings

Benoît Chevallier-Mames[1,2], Duong Hieu Phan[2], and David Pointcheval[2]

[1] Gemplus, France
benoit.chevallier-mames@gemplus.com
[2] ENS, Paris, France
{david.pointcheval,duong.hieu.phan}@ens.fr

Abstract. Strong security notions often introduce strong constraints on the construction of cryptographic schemes: semantic security implies probabilistic encryption, while the resistance to existential forgeries requires redundancy in signature schemes. Some paddings have thus been designed in order to provide these minimal requirements to each of them, in order to achieve secure primitives.

A few years ago, Coron et al. suggested the design of a common construction, a *universal padding*, which one could apply for both encryption and signature. As a consequence, such a padding has to introduce both randomness and redundancy, which does not lead to an optimal encryption nor an optimal signature.

In this paper, we refine this notion of universal padding, in which a part can be either a random string in order to introduce randomness or a zero-constant string in order to introduce some redundancy. This helps us to build, with a unique padding, optimal encryption and optimal signature: first, in the random-permutation model, and then in the random-oracle model. In both cases, we study the concrete sizes of the parameters, for a specific security level: The former achieves an optimal bandwidth.

1 Introduction

When one deals with public-key encryption, chosen-ciphertext security [22] is by now the basic required security notion. Similarly, for signatures, resistance to existential forgeries against adaptive chosen-message attacks [10] is also the minimal requirement. But strong security is not enough, it has to be achieved in an efficient way, according to various criteria: time, bandwidth, but also size of the code.

The first two above criteria are the most usual goals, and improvements are continuously proposed. When dealing with public-key cryptography, one can indeed note that fast paddings have been proposed for encryption [3, 19] and signature [4]. About the bandwidth, Phan and Pointcheval recently addressed this problem for encryption [20, 21], and proposed an optimal padding, w.r.t. this criteria, by avoiding redundancy. Most signatures with message-recovery [18, 16, 4] improve the bandwidth, but these solutions are not optimal, since redundancy

J. Ioannidis, A. Keromytis, and M.Yung (Eds.): ACNS 2005, LNCS 3531, pp. 254–268, 2005.

and randomization are always added. The notable exception is the recent idea of Katz and Wang, that achieves tight security by using FDH, but also PSS-R, constructions [4] with only one additional bit, that is not random but dependent on the message [13].

The last criteria has been more recently considered, by Coron, Joye, Naccache and Paillier [6], with the so-called notion of *universal paddings*: the code size is reduced by using a common padding for both encryption and signature. For such a goal, they used a variant of PSS, called PSS-ES. Other solutions have thereafter been proposed, including those of Komano and Ohta [14]. But in all these constructions, the resulting encryption contains redundancy, and the signature is probabilistic.

1.1   Contribution

In this paper, we address this problem of efficiency, trying to optimize the three above criteria at the same time: for a time-efficient construction, we consider simple paddings; for a good bandwidth, we extend the work of [20, 21], by avoiding not only redundancy in encryption, but also randomization in signatures; additionally, we use the idea of the Katz-Wang construction [13] in order to achieve tight security in signature. Finally, about the size of the code, we optimize the common parts in the two paddings (for signature and encryption), by giving a relaxed version of *universal padding*. Furthermore, we analyze the security of these paddings, to be used for both encryption and signature, but in the extreme case where the same primitive (trapdoor one-way permutation which might optionally be assumed claw-free) is used for encryption and signature, at the same time, as already suggested in [12]: the same public/private key pair is used for encryption and signature.

More precisely, we study two paddings with the above *universal* property. The first one is based on the Full-Domain Permutation construction, studied in [11] for signature and in [20], for encryption, which can be proved optimal with the three above criteria in the random-permutation model. Hence the name of *Optimal Permutation-based Padding* (OPbP). Then, we also review the OAEP 3-rounds construction [20, 21] (OAEP3r), in the random-oracle model [2].

1.2   Redundancy and Randomness

A basic requirement for encryption, to achieve semantic security, is a probabilistic mechanism which is necessary to make distributions of ciphertexts indistinguishable. But until recently, chosen-ciphertext security was thought to furthermore imply redundancy in the ciphertext (for a kind of proof of knowledge/awareness of the plaintext [3, 1, 7].) However, this was not mandatory [20, 21], at least in the random-oracle model and in the ideal-cipher model. Existence of such schemes in the standard model is still an open problem.

Similarly, for signature, to prevent forgeries, some redundancy in the message-signature pair (or unique string in case of message-recovery feature) is required, which should be hard to satisfy without the signing key. But most of the signature schemes are probabilistic [23, 17, 4, 8], while it is not necessary (e.g. the FDH-signature, but with *loose* security). Recently, Katz and Wang proved that it was possible to achieve *tight* security with a deterministic construction very close to FDH-signature or PSS-R, by adding a single bit that is not random but dependent on the message [13]. More precisely, this additional bit should be not predictable by anyone else than the signer, and so Katz and Wang proposed that it results from a PRF computation.

1.3 Universal Paddings

The goal of universal padding is to design a padding which can not only be applied for signature and for encryption independently, but for both at the same time, with the same user's keys: the public key is used for both encryption and verification, while the private key is used for both decryption and signature.

In the security model, the adversaries (against either semantic security or existential unforgeability) are given access to both the signing and decryption oracles, which is not the security scenario considered when one deals with encryption and signature, independently. The decryption oracle may indeed help to forge signatures, and vice-versa.

2   Security Model

2.1   Signature Schemes

Digital signature schemes are the electronic version of handwritten signatures for digital documents: a user's signature on a message m is a string which depends on m, on public and secret data specific to the user and – possibly – on randomly chosen data, in such a way that anyone can check the validity of the signature by using public data only. In this section, we briefly review the main security notions [10].

Definitions. A signature scheme $S = (\mathcal{K}, \mathcal{S}, \mathcal{V})$ is defined by the three following algorithms:

- The *key generation algorithm* $\mathcal{K}$. On input 1^k, which is a formal notation for a machine with running time polynomial in k (1^k is indeed k in basis 1), the algorithm $\mathcal{K}$ produces a pair $(\mathsf{pk}, \mathsf{sk})$ of matching public and private keys. Algorithm $\mathcal{K}$ is probabilistic. The input k is called the security parameter. The sizes of the keys, or of any problem involved in the cryptographic scheme, will depend on it, in order to achieve an appropriate security level (the expected minimal time complexity of any attack).
- The *signing algorithm* $\mathcal{S}$. Given a message m and a pair of matching public and private keys $(\mathsf{pk}, \mathsf{sk})$ $\mathcal{S}$ produces a signature σ. The signing algorithm might be probabilistic.

- The *verification algorithm* $\mathcal{V}$. Given a signature σ, a message m, or just a part (possibly empty), and a public key pk, $\mathcal{V}$ possibly extracts the full message m and tests whether σ is a valid signature of m with respect to pk. In general, the verification algorithm need not be probabilistic.

Forgeries and Attacks. The simpler goal for an adversary is to build a new acceptable message-signature pair. This is called *existential forgery*. The corresponding security level is called *existential unforgeability* (EUF). On the other hand, the strongest scenario one usually considers is the so-called *adaptive chosen-message attack* (CMA), where the attacker can ask the signer to sign any message of its choice, in an adaptive way: it can adapt its queries according to previous answers. When signature generation is not deterministic, there may be several signatures corresponding to a given message. And then the notion of existential forgery may be ambiguous [24]: the original definition [10] says the adversary wins if it manages to forge a signature for a new message. Non-malleability [24] says the adversary wins if it manages to forge a new signature.

Thereafter, the security notion one wants to achieve is (at least) the resistance to existential forgeries under adaptive chosen-message attacks (EUF/CMA): one wants that the success probability of any adversary $\mathcal{A}$ with a reasonable time is small, where

$$\mathsf{Succ}_\mathsf{S}^{\mathsf{euf}/\mathsf{cma}}(\mathcal{A}) = \Pr\left[(\mathsf{pk}, \mathsf{sk}) \leftarrow \mathcal{K}(1^k), (m, \sigma) \leftarrow \mathcal{A}^{\mathcal{S}_\mathsf{sk}}(\mathsf{pk}) : \mathcal{V}(\mathsf{pk}, m, \sigma) = 1\right].$$

2.2 Public-Key Encryption

The aim of a public-key encryption scheme is to allow anybody who knows the public key of Alice to send her a message that she will be the only one able to recover, granted her private key.

Definitions. A public-key encryption scheme $\mathsf{S} = (\mathcal{K}, \mathcal{E}, \mathcal{D})$ is defined by the three following algorithms:

- The *key generation algorithm* $\mathcal{K}$. On input 1^k where k is the security parameter, the algorithm $\mathcal{K}$ produces a pair (pk, sk) of matching public and private keys. Algorithm $\mathcal{K}$ is probabilistic.
- The *encryption algorithm* $\mathcal{E}$. Given a message m and a public key pk, $\mathcal{E}$ produces a ciphertext c of m. This algorithm may be probabilistic. In the latter case, we write $\mathcal{E}_\mathsf{pk}(m; r)$ where r is the random input to $\mathcal{E}$.
- The *decryption algorithm* $\mathcal{D}$. Given a ciphertext c and the private key sk, $\mathcal{D}_\mathsf{sk}(c)$ gives back the plaintext m. This algorithm is necessarily deterministic.

Security Notions. The most widely admitted goal of an adversary is the distinction of ciphertexts (IND). One thus wants to make it unable to distinguish between two messages, chosen by the adversary, which one has been encrypted, with a probability significantly better than one half. On the other hand, an attacker can play many kinds of attacks. The strongest scenario consists in giving a full access to the decryption oracle, which on any ciphertext answers the corresponding plaintext. There is of course the natural restriction not to ask the challenge ciphertext to that oracle. This scenario which allows adaptively chosen ciphertexts as queries to the decryption oracle is named the *chosen-ciphertext attack* (CCA). Therefore, for any adversary $\mathcal{A}$, seen as a 2-stage attacker $(\mathcal{A}_1, \mathcal{A}_2)$, its advantage $\mathsf{Adv}_S^{\mathsf{ind/cca}}(\mathcal{A})$ should be negligible, where

$$\mathsf{Adv}_S^{\mathsf{ind/cca}}(\mathcal{A}) = 2 \times \Pr_{b,r} \left[\begin{array}{l} (\mathsf{pk}, \mathsf{sk}) \leftarrow \mathcal{K}(1^k), (m_0, m_1, s) \leftarrow \mathcal{A}_1^{\mathcal{D}_{\mathsf{sk}}}(\mathsf{pk}), \\ c = \mathcal{E}_{\mathsf{pk}}(m_b; r) : \mathcal{A}_2^{\mathcal{D}_{\mathsf{sk}}}(m_0, m_1, s, c) = b \end{array} \right] - 1,$$

2.3 Signature and Encryption

As already noticed, our motivation is to design a unified padding which one could use for both encryption and signature at the same time, and furthermore with the same asymmetric primitive. The goals of an adversary are thus the same as above: build an existential forgery (EUF) against the signature scheme, or distinguish ciphertexts (IND) against the encryption scheme. However, the means are the combination of the above attacks: it has access to both the signing oracle and the decryption oracle in a fully adaptive way, hence the CMA + CCA notation.

2.4 Claw-Free Permutations

In [13], Katz and Wang has shown that, by using trapdoor permutations induced by claw-free permutations, one can obtain a variant of FDH (just adding one more bit) with tight reduction. We can also use this technique for our construction. The existence of claw-free permutations seems be reasonable. In fact, any random self-reducible permutation can be seen as a trapdoor permutations induced by claw-free permutations [9] and almost all known examples of trapdoor permutations are self-reducible.

Definition 1 (Claw-Free Permutations). *A family of claw-free permutations is a tuple of algorithms* $\{\mathsf{Gen}; f_i; g_i | i \in I\}$ *for an index set I such that:*

- *Gen outputs a random index i and a trapdoor td.*
- *f_i, g_i are both permutations over the same domain D_i.*
- *there is an efficient sampling algorithm which, on index i, outputs a random $x \in D_i$.*
- *f_i^{-1} (the inverse of f_i) and g_i^{-1} (the inverse of g_i) are both efficiently computable given the trapdoor td.*

A claw is a pair (x_0, x_1) such that $f(x_0) = g(x_1)$. Probabilistic algorithm $\mathcal{A}$ is said to (t, ϵ)-break a family of claw-free permutations if $\mathcal{A}$ runs in time at most t and outputs a claw with probability greater than ϵ:

$$\Pr \left[(i, \mathsf{td}) \leftarrow \mathsf{Gen}(1^k), (x_0, x_1) \leftarrow \mathcal{A}(i) : f_i(x_0) = g_i(x_1) \right] \geq \epsilon$$

A family of claw-free permutations is (t, ϵ)-secure if no algorithm can (t, ϵ)-break it.

3   Optimal Permutation-Based Padding

3.1   Our Optimal Proposal

In the following, we propose a universal padding, based on the construction from [20], in the random-permutation model. It is optimal both for signing and encrypting, *i.e.*, that uses only 82 bits of randomness for encrypting and only 82 bits of redundancy for signing. After the description, we show it is indeed secure, in the random-permutation model. In the next section, we provide another construction, based on the OAEP-3 rounds construction from the same paper [20], which is secure in the random-oracle model, but just near optimal (161 bits of overhead instead of 82).

The encryption and signature schemes use a permutation $\mathcal{P}$, that we assume to behave like a truly random permutation. Let k be a security parameter. Let $\varphi_{\mathsf{pk}} : \{0,1\}^n \rightarrow \{0,1\}^n$ be a trapdoor one-way permutation (whose inverse is called ψ_{sk}). Messages to sign or to encrypt with our padding function will be of size $\ell = n - k - 1$. The symbol "$\|$" denotes the bit-string concatenation and identifies $\{0,1\}^k \times \{0,1\}^\ell \times \{0,1\}$ to $\{0,1\}^n$. Finally, in the following, $\mathsf{PRF}_\varrho()$ designs a PRF that uses a secret key ϱ.

The Padding. The padding is quite simple, since it takes as input a single bit γ, the message m and an additional data r, and $\mathsf{OPbP}(\gamma, m, r) = \mathcal{P}(\gamma\|m\|r) = t\|u$. Thereafter, the reverse operation is natural: $\mathsf{OPbP}^{-1}(t, u) = \mathcal{P}^{-1}(t\|u) = \gamma\|m\|r$.

Encryption Algorithm. The space of the plaintexts is $\mathcal{M} = \{0,1\}^\ell$, the encryption algorithm uses a random coin from the set $r \in \mathcal{R} = \{0,1\}^k$, a random bit γ, and outputs a ciphertext c into $\{0,1\}^n$: on a plaintext $m \in \mathcal{M}$, one computes $t\|u = \mathsf{OPbP}(\gamma, m, r)$ and $c = \varphi_{\mathsf{pk}}(t\|u)$.

Decryption Algorithm. On a ciphertext c, one first computes $t\|u = \psi_{\mathsf{sk}}(c)$, where $t \in \{0,1\}^k$ and $u \in \{0,1\}^{\ell+1}$, and then $\gamma\|m\|r = \mathsf{OPbP}^{-1}(t, u)$. The answer is m.

Signature Algorithm. The space of the messages is $\mathcal{M} = \{0,1\}^\ell$, the signature algorithm outputs a signature σ into $\{0,1\}^n$: on a message $m \in \mathcal{M}$, one computes $\gamma = \mathsf{PRF}_\varrho(m)$, and then $t\|u = \mathsf{OPbP}(\gamma, m, 0^k)$ and $\sigma = \psi_{\mathsf{sk}}(t\|u)$.

Verification Algorithm. On a signature σ, one first computes $t\|u = \varphi_{\mathsf{pk}}(\sigma)$, where $t \in \{0,1\}^k$ and $u \in \{0,1\}^{\ell+1}$, and then $\gamma\|m\|r = \mathsf{OPbP}^{-1}(t, u)$. If $r = 0^k$, the verification outputs "Correct" and recovers m, otherwise outputs "Incorrect".

3.2   Security Analysis

A variant of this padding has already been proved to lead to an IND/CCA secure encryption scheme [20], and to a EUF/CMA signature scheme [11], in the random-permutation model. However, there was not the additional bit of Katz and Wang, that just makes more randomness in the encryption. Here, we extend these results to IND/CMA + CCA and EUF/CMA + CCA:

Theorem 2. *Let $\mathcal{A}$ and $\mathcal{B}$ be both chosen-ciphertext (to the decryption oracle) and chosen-message (to the signing oracle) adversaries, against the encryption scheme (IND) and the signature scheme (EUF) respectively. Let us assume that $\mathcal{A}$ can break the semantic security with an advantage ε_E, or $\mathcal{B}$ can produce an existential forgery with success probability ε_S (within a time bound t, after q_p, q_s, q_d queries to the permutation oracles, signing oracle and decryption oracle respectively.) Then the permutation φ_{pk} can be inverted with probability ε' within time t' where either:*

$$\varepsilon' \geq \varepsilon_E - \frac{(q_p + q_d + q_s + 1)^2}{2^{k+\ell+1}} - \frac{(q_d + 1)^2}{2^\ell} - \frac{2q_p + q_d + q_s + 2}{2^k}, \ or$$

$$\varepsilon' \geq \frac{1}{q_p + q_s + 1} \cdot \left(\varepsilon_S - \frac{(q_p + q_d + q_s + 1)^2}{2^{k+\ell+1}} - \frac{(q_d + 1)^2}{2^\ell} - \frac{2q_p + q_d + q_s + 2}{2^k} \right).$$

Particularly, if the function φ_{pk} is induced by a (t', ε')-secure claw-free permutation, the latter can be rewritten by:

$$\varepsilon' \geq \frac{1}{2} \left(\varepsilon_S - \frac{(q_p + q_d + q_s + 1)^2}{2^{k+\ell+1}} - \frac{(q_d + 1)^2}{2^\ell} - \frac{2q_p + q_d + q_s + 2}{2^k} \right)$$

where $t' \leq t + (q_p + q_d + q_s + 1)T_f$, and T_f is the time for an evaluation of φ_{pk}.

Proof. We provide now the proof of this theorem, with incremental games, to reduce the inversion of the permutation φ_{pk} on a random instance y (*i.e.*, find x such that $y = \varphi_{\mathsf{pk}}(x)$) to an attack against either the encryption or the signature. We show that either $\mathcal{A}$ or $\mathcal{B}$ can help us to invert φ_{pk}.

Some parts of this proof are similar to [20]. We anyway provide the proof without the similar parts. The full proof can be found in the full version [5].

GAME $\mathbf{G}_0$:   This is the attack game, in the random-permutation model. Several oracles are thus available to the adversary: two random permutation oracles ($\mathcal{P}$ and $\mathcal{P}^{-1}$), the signing oracle $\mathcal{S}_{\mathsf{sk}}$, and the decryption oracle $\mathcal{D}_{\mathsf{sk}}$.

To break the encryption, the adversary $\mathcal{A} = (A_1, A_2)$ runs its attack in two steps. First, A_1 is given the public key pk, and outputs a pair of messages (m_0, m_1). Next a challenge ciphertext is produced by the challenger, which flips a coin b and computes a ciphertext $c^\star$ of $m^\star = m_b$. This ciphertext comes from a random $r^\star \xleftarrow{R} \{0,1\}^k$, a bit $\gamma^\star$ and $c^\star = \mathcal{E}(\gamma^\star, m_b, r^\star) = \varphi_{\mathsf{pk}}(\mathcal{P}(\gamma^\star, m_b, r^\star))$. In the second step, on input $c^\star$, A_2 outputs a bit b'. We denote by Dist_0 the event $b' = b$ and use the same notation Dist_n in any game $\mathbf{G}_n$.

To break the signature, the adversary $\mathcal{B}$ outputs its forgery, one checks whether it is actually valid or not. We denote by Forge_0 the event this forged signature is valid and use the same notation Forge_n in any game $\mathbf{G}_n$.

Note that the adversary is given access to the signing oracle $\mathcal{S}_{\mathsf{sk}}$ and the decryption oracle $\mathcal{D}_{\mathsf{sk}}$ at any time during the attack. Note also that if the adversary asks q_d queries to the decryption oracle, q_s queries to the signing oracle and q_p queries to the permutation oracles, at most $q_d + q_s + q_p + 1$ queries are asked to the permutation oracles during this game, since each decryption query or signing query may make such a new query, and the last verification step or the challenger step does too. By definition,

$$\varepsilon_E = \mathsf{Adv}_{\mathsf{OPbP}}^{\mathsf{ind/cma+cca}}(\mathcal{A}) = \Pr[\mathsf{Dist}_0] - 1/2$$
$$\varepsilon_S = \mathsf{Succ}_{\mathsf{OPbP}}^{\mathsf{euf/cma+cca}}(\mathcal{B}) = \Pr[\mathsf{Forge}_0].$$

GAME $\mathbf{G_1}$: We skip the easy steps, similar to [20] for the encryption part, and to [4] for the signature. Details can be found in the full version [5], which leads to the simulation presented in Figures 1 and 2, which is statistically indistinguishable from the initial one since the distance is bounded by:

$$\Delta_G \leq \frac{(q_p + q_d + q_s + 1)^2}{2^{k+\ell+1}} + \frac{(q_d + 1)^2}{2^\ell} + \frac{2q_p + q_d + q_s + 2}{2^k}.$$

In the following, depending on the goal of the adversary, namely against encryption or against signature, we complete the reduction to the inversion of the function ψ_{sk} on the given instance y.

Encryption Attack

GAME $\mathbf{G_{1.1}}$: We suppress the element $(\gamma^\star, m^\star, r^\star, \bot, \bot, c^\star)$ from P-List during the generation of the challenge.
▶**Rule** ChalAdd$^{(1.1)}$
| Do nothing.

The two games $\mathbf{G_{1.1}}$ and $\mathbf{G_1}$ are perfectly indistinguishable unless $(\gamma^\star, m^\star, r^\star)$ is asked for $\mathcal{P}$ (which event is included in event $\mathsf{BadP}_{1.1}$, already excluded) or $p^\star = \psi_{\mathsf{sk}}(c^\star)$ is asked to $\mathcal{P}^{-1}$. We define the latter event $\mathsf{AskInvP}_{1.1}$. We have: $\Delta_{1.1} \leq \Pr[\mathsf{AskInvP}_{1.1}]$. Since $(\gamma^\star, m^\star, r^\star, \bot, \bot, c^\star)$ does not appear in P-List, the

Challenger	For two messages (m_0, m_1), flip coins $\gamma^\star$ and b, set $m^\star = m_b$, and randomly choose $r^\star$.
	
	 ▶**Rule** Chal$^{(1)}$
	    | $p^\star = \mathcal{P}(\gamma^\star, m^\star, r^\star)$; $c^\star = \varphi_{\mathsf{pk}}(p^\star)$.
	
	 ▶**Rule** ChalAdd$^{(1)}$
	    | Add $(\gamma^\star, m^\star, r^\star, \bot, \bot, c^\star)$ in P-List.
	
	 Answer $c^\star$

$\mathcal{V}$-Oracle	The game ends with the verification of the output (σ) from the adversary. One first computes $t\|u = \varphi_{\mathsf{pk}}(\sigma)$, then asks for $(\gamma, m, r) = \mathcal{P}^{-1}(t\|u)$. Then he checks whether $r = 0^k$, in which case the signature is a valid signature of m.

Fig. 1. Simulation in the Game $\mathbf{G_1}$.

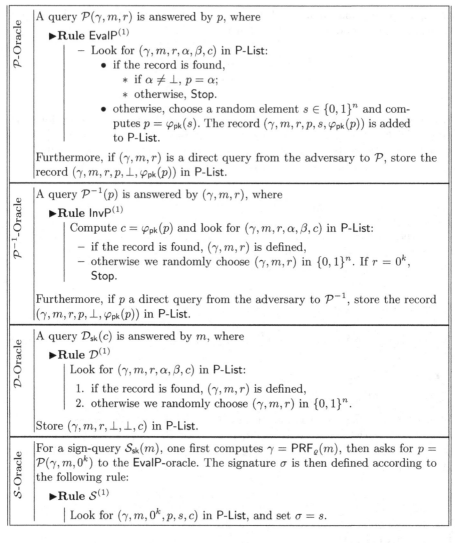

Fig. 2. Simulation in the Game $\mathbf{G}_1$.

adversary receives answers which are perfectly independent of the latter, and therefore, it has no advantage for guessing b: $\Pr[\mathsf{Dist}_{1.1}] = \frac{1}{2}$.

GAME $\mathbf{G}_{1.2}$:   Instead of choosing $c^\star = \varphi_{\mathsf{pk}}(p^\star)$, we choose $c^\star = y$, uniformly at random.

▶**Rule Chal**$^{(1.2)}$

$\quad | \ c^\star = y.$

So, one implicitly defines $p^\star = \psi_{\mathsf{sk}}(y)$. Since the tuple $(\gamma^\star, m^\star, r^\star, \bot, \bot, c^\star)$ is not used anywhere in the simulation, the two games $\mathbf{G}_{1.2}$ and $\mathbf{G}_{1.1}$ are perfectly indistinguishable: $\Delta_{1.2} = 0$.

Finally, it is clear that when the event $\mathsf{AskInvP}_{1.2}$ happens, one can easily compute ψ_{sk} on y: with a look up into P-List (which contains at most $q_p+q_d+q_s+1$ elements), one can extract p such that $y = \varphi_{\mathsf{pk}}(p)$. Therefore, $\Pr[\mathsf{AskInvP}_{1.2}] \leq \mathsf{Succ}_{\varphi}^{\mathsf{ow}}(t')$, where T_{φ} is the time for evaluating φ_{pk}, and $t' \leq t + (q_p + q_d + q_s + 1) \times T_{\varphi}$ is the running time of the simulation in the current game. This completes the first part of the proof.

Signature Attack (The General Case)

GAME $\mathbf{G}_{1.1}$:   In the following, we number calls to the permutation oracle, but only those which are of the form $(\gamma, \star, 0^k)$, which are those that are used for signature. We define a variable ν which is initialized to 0.

▶**Rule** EvalP$^{(1.1)}$

> Look for $(\gamma, m, r, \alpha, \beta, c)$ in P-List:
> - if the record is found,
>   - if $\alpha \neq \perp$, $p = \alpha$;
>   - otherwise, Stop.
> - otherwise,
>   - if $r = 0^k$, increment ν
>   - choose a random element $s \in \{0,1\}^n$ and computes $p = \varphi_{\mathsf{pk}}(s)$. The record $(\gamma, m, r, p, s, \varphi_{\mathsf{pk}}(p))$ is added to P-List.

Clearly, this leaves the game indistinguishable from the game $\mathbf{G}_1$: $\Delta_{1.1} = 0$.

GAME $\mathbf{G}_{1.2}$:   Since the verification process is included in the attack game, the output message is necessarily asked to the permutation oracle EvalP. Let us guess the index ν_0 of this (first) query. If the guess failed, we abort the game. Therefore, only a correct guess (event GoodGuess) may lead to a success.

$$\Pr[\mathsf{Forge}_{1.2}] \geq \Pr[\mathsf{Forge}_{1.1}]/(q_p + q_s + 1).$$

GAME $\mathbf{G}_{1.3}$:   We now incorporate the challenge y to the simulation of the permutation oracle. By this, we could extract the pre-image x. Our idea is to return y as the value of the guessed ν-th query:

▶**Rule** EvalP$^{(1.3)}$

> Look for $(\gamma, m, r, \alpha, \beta, c)$ in P-List:
> - if the record is found,
>   - if $\alpha \neq \perp$, $p = \alpha$;
>   - otherwise, Stop.
> - otherwise,
>   - if $r = 0^k$, increment ν
>   - if $\nu \neq \nu_0$ or if $r \neq 0^k$, choose a random element $s \in \{0,1\}^n$ and computes $p = \varphi_{\mathsf{pk}}(s)$.
>   - if $\nu = \nu_0$ and $r = 0^k$, sets $p = y$.
>   - The record $(\gamma, m, r, y, s, \varphi_{\mathsf{pk}}(p))$ is added to P-List.

Because of the random choice for the challenge y, this rule leaves the game indistinguishable from the previous one: $\Delta_{1.3} = 0$. It follows that the forgery leads to the pre-image of y: $\Pr[\mathsf{Forge}_{1.3}] = \mathsf{Succ}_{\varphi}^{\mathsf{ow}}(t + (q_p + q_d + q_s + 1)T_{\varphi})$. This concludes the second part of the proof.

Signature Attack (With (t', ε')-Secure Claw-Free Permutations). We assume that $(\varphi_{\mathsf{pk}}, \lambda_{\mathsf{pk}})$ are from a (t', ε')-secure claw-free permutations family.

GAME $\mathbf{G}_{1.1}$:   We now exploit the bit γ to the simulation of the permutation oracle, as it was proposed firstly by Katz and Wang [13]. The idea is to use φ_{pk} in the OPbP output, for one and only one value of bit γ, and otherwise use λ_{pk}. As this value of γ is not predictable by the attacker, its forgery will, with a probability $\frac{1}{2}$, produce a claw.

▶**Rule** EvalP$^{(1.1)}$

Look for $(\gamma, m, r, \alpha, \beta, c)$ in P-List:
- if the record is found,
    - if $\alpha \neq \perp$, $p = \alpha$;
    - otherwise, Stop.
- otherwise,
    - if $r \neq 0^k$ or $\gamma = \mathsf{PRF}_\varrho(m)$, choose a random element $s \in \{0,1\}^n$ and compute $p = \varphi_{\mathsf{pk}}(s)$.
    - if $r = 0^k$ or $\gamma \neq \mathsf{PRF}_\varrho(m)$, choose a random element $s \in \{0,1\}^n$ and compute $p = \lambda_{\mathsf{pk}}(s)$.
    - The record $(m, r, p, s, \varphi_{\mathsf{pk}}(p))$ is added to P-List.

Because of the random choice of s and so $\lambda_{\mathsf{pk}}(s)$, this rule leaves the game indistinguishable from the previous one: $\Delta_{1.1} = 0$.

Using arguments as in [13], one can easily see that the forgery leads to a claw with probability $\frac{1}{2}$. In fact, let us assume that the adversary can forge a signature $(\tilde{m}, \tilde{\sigma})$, where $(\tilde{m}, 0^k)$ has been asked to the permutation oracle $\mathcal{P}$ either in a permutation query or in the verification step. Since the bit $b_{\tilde{m}} = \mathsf{PRF}_\varrho(\tilde{m})$ is an unknown random bit in the view of the adversary, with probability of $\frac{1}{2}$, there exists an element $(\tilde{m}, \tilde{r}, \tilde{p} = \lambda_{\mathsf{pk}}(\tilde{s}), \tilde{s}, \varphi_{\mathsf{pk}}(\tilde{p}))$ in the P-List. In that case, the simulator can output a claw $\varphi_{\mathsf{pk}}(\tilde{\sigma}) = \lambda_{\mathsf{pk}}(\tilde{s})$.   □

3.3 Proposed Sizes for the Parameters

We say that a scheme achieves a security level of 2^κ, if the ratio between the running time t of the adversary, and its success probability ε, is at least 2^κ: this is an approximation of the expected time of success. Or similarly, we want $t/\varepsilon \leq 2^{-\kappa}$, with a usual security bound set with $\kappa = 80$.

First, we can simplify the above security result. Indeed, for practical purpose, where ℓ is the bit-size of the message, and k is the bit-size of the random/redundancy, the former is expected to be much larger than the latter: the quantity $Q/2^\ell$, or even $Q^2/2^\ell$, can be ignored in front of $Q/2^k$ (since Q, the global number of queries is bounded by 2^{80}). Therefore, the above reduction cost provides that

$$\frac{\varepsilon_E}{t} \leq \frac{\varepsilon'}{t} + \frac{2}{2^k} \qquad \text{and}$$

$$\frac{\varepsilon_S}{t} \leq \frac{Q\varepsilon'}{t} + \frac{2}{2^k} \qquad \text{in the general case}$$

$$\leq \frac{2\varepsilon'}{t} + \frac{2}{2^k} \qquad \text{if the function } \varphi_{\mathsf{pk}} \text{ is induced by a claw-free permutation}$$

In the latter case (the most interesting case, where one uses RSA) we can assume the message length sufficiently large (and thus the RSA modulus) so that ε'/t is lower than 2^{-82}. Due to the Lenstra-Verheul's estimation [15], for the case of RSA, we can use a 1024-bit modulus.

In the general case, we have to consider that the security parameter (and thus message length ℓ) large enough such that the ration between ε'/t is lower than 2^{-161}. But then the overhead $k = 82$ is enough too.

As a conclusion, for the general case, we can choose $k = 82$ if the security level of the function φ is about 2^{161}. For the particular case of RSA, we can use a 1024-bit modulus. We remark then that, with only 82 bits of redundancy, we obtain the same level of security than RSA-PSS [3], which, compared to our scheme, uses a lowest bandwidth. For the encryption security, we find again the result from [20]: 82 bits of randomness are enough to achieve semantic security, even under chosen-ciphertext and chosen-message attacks.

4   The OAEP-3 Rounds Construction

4.1   Description

In order to work in the more usual random-oracle model [2], we now consider the OAEP-3 rounds construction proposed in [20, 21]. As above, the security of this padding has already been studied for encryption, but without giving access to the signing oracle to the adversary. We thus extend the security model to deal with the two oracles access.

The encryption and signature schemes use three hash functions: $\mathcal{F}, \mathcal{G}, \mathcal{H}$ (assumed to behave like random oracles in the security analysis) where the security parameters satisfy $n = k + \ell + 1$:

$$\mathcal{F} : \{0,1\}^k \rightarrow \{0,1\}^{\ell+1} \qquad \mathcal{G} : \{0,1\}^{\ell+1} \rightarrow \{0,1\}^k \qquad \mathcal{H} : \{0,1\}^k \rightarrow \{0,1\}^{\ell+1}.$$

The encryption and signature schemes use any permutation family $(\varphi_{\mathsf{pk}})_{\mathsf{pk}}$ on the space $\{0,1\}^n$, whose inverses are respectively denoted ψ_{sk}, where sk is the private key associated to the public key pk. The symbol "$\|$" denotes the bit-string concatenation and identifies $\{0,1\}^k \times \{0,1\}^\ell \times \{0,1\}$ to $\{0,1\}^n$.

Padding OAEP3r and Unpadding OAEP3r^{-1}

$$\mathsf{OAEP3r}(\gamma, m, r) : s = (\gamma \| m) \oplus \mathcal{F}(r) \quad t = r \oplus \mathcal{G}(s) \quad u = s \oplus \mathcal{H}(t)$$

$$\mathsf{OAEP3r}(\gamma, m, r) = t \| u$$

$$\mathsf{OAEP3r}^{-1}(t, u) : \quad s = u \oplus \mathcal{H}(t) \qquad r = t \oplus \mathcal{G}(s) \quad \gamma \| m = s \oplus \mathcal{F}(r)$$

$$\mathsf{OAEP3r}^{-1}(t, u) = \gamma \| m \| r$$

Encryption Algorithm. The space of the plaintexts is $\mathcal{M} = \{0,1\}^\ell$, the encryption algorithm uses a random coin from the set $r \in \mathcal{R} = \{0,1\}^k$, a random bit γ and outputs a ciphertext c into $\{0,1\}^n$: on a plaintext $m \in \mathcal{M}$, one computes $t \| u = \mathsf{OAEP3r}(\gamma, m, r)$ and $c = \varphi_{\mathsf{pk}}(t \| u)$.

Decryption Algorithm. On a ciphertext c, one first computes $t\|u = \psi_{\mathsf{sk}}(c)$, where $t \in \{0,1\}^k$ and $u \in \{0,1\}^{\ell+1}$, and then $\gamma\|m\|r = \mathsf{OAEP3r}^{-1}(t, u)$. The answer is m.

Signature Algorithm. The space of the plaintexts is $\mathcal{M} = \{0,1\}^\ell$, the signature algorithm outputs a signature σ into $\{0,1\}^n$: on a plaintext $m \in \mathcal{M}$, one computes $\gamma = \mathsf{PRF}_\varrho(m)$, then computes $t\|u = \mathsf{OAEP3r}(\gamma, m, 0^k)$ and $\sigma = \psi_{\mathsf{sk}}(t\|u)$.

Verification Algorithm. On a signature σ, one first computes $t\|u = \varphi_{\mathsf{pk}}(\sigma)$, where $t \in \{0,1\}^k$ and $u \in \{0,1\}^{\ell+1}$, and then $\gamma\|m\|r = \mathsf{OAEP3r}^{-1}(t, u)$. If $r = 0^k$, the verification outputs "Correct" then recovers m, otherwise outputs "Incorrect"

4.2   Security Result

We extend the security result from [21] by the following theorem:

Theorem 3. *Let $\mathcal{A}$ and $\mathcal{B}$ be both chosen-ciphertext (to the decryption oracle) and chosen-message (to the signing oracle) adversaries, against the encryption scheme (IND) and the signature scheme (EUF) respectively. Let us assume that $\mathcal{A}$ can break the semantic security with the advantage ε_E, or $\mathcal{B}$ can produce an existential forgery with success probability ε_S (within a time bound t, after q_f, q_g, q_h, q_s, q_d queries to the oracles $\mathcal{F}$, $\mathcal{G}$, $\mathcal{H}$, signing oracle and decryption oracle respectively.) Then the permutation φ_{pk} can be inverted with probability ε' within time t' where either:*

$$\varepsilon' \geq \varepsilon_E - \left(q_d^2 \times \left(\frac{1}{2^{\ell+1}} + \frac{6}{2^k} \right) + \frac{4q_dq_g + q_g}{2^{\ell+1}} + \frac{5q_dq_f + q_gq_h + q_f + q_d}{2^k} \right) \quad or$$

$$\varepsilon' \geq \frac{1}{q_g + q_s + 1} \times$$
$$\left(\varepsilon_S - \left(q_d^2 \times \left(\frac{1}{2^{\ell+1}} + \frac{6}{2^k} \right) + \frac{4q_dq_g + q_g}{2^{\ell+1}} + \frac{5q_dq_f + q_gq_h + q_f + q_d}{2^k} \right) \right)$$

Particularly, if the function φ_{pk} is induced by a (t', ε')-secure claw-free permutation, the latter can be rewritten by:

$$\varepsilon' \geq \frac{1}{2} \times \left(\varepsilon_S - \left(q_d^2 \times \left(\frac{1}{2^{\ell+1}} + \frac{6}{2^k} \right) + \frac{4q_dq_g + q_g}{2^{\ell+1}} + \frac{5q_dq_f + q_gq_h + q_f + q_d}{2^k} \right) \right)$$

with $t' \leq t + (q_f + q_g + q_h + q_d)T_{lu} + q_d^2 T_{lu} + (q_d + 1)q_gq_h(T_\varphi + T_{lu})$, where T_φ is the time complexity for evaluating any function φ_{pk}, and T_{lu} is the time complexity for a look up in a list.

Proof. The full proof can be found in the full version [5]. The simulation of the oracles as well as the simulation of the decryption are similar to the ones in [21]. The simulation of the signature (after all the oracles are well simulated) is quite the same as in the random-permutation model case.   □

4.3   Proposed Sizes for the Parameters

Using similar arguments as in the previous construction, one can simplify the constraints on the security parameters:

- For encryption, one has:

$$\frac{\varepsilon_E}{t} \leq \frac{\varepsilon'}{t} + \frac{Q}{2^k}.$$

  Then, $k = 161$ is enough if the security parameters are large enough (*i.e.*, as soon as $\varepsilon'/t < 2^{-81}$).
- For signature, in the general case:

$$\frac{\varepsilon_S}{t} \leq \frac{Q\varepsilon'}{t} + \frac{Q}{2^k}.$$

  In the general case, $k = 161$ is also valid, as soon as $\varepsilon'/t < 2^{-161}$.
- For signature, in case the function φ_{pk} is induced by a claw-free permutation:

$$\frac{\varepsilon_S}{t} \leq \frac{2\varepsilon'}{t} + \frac{Q}{2^k}.$$

We have a similar expression as in the above encryption case (the term ε'/t is replaced by $2\varepsilon'/t$, which allows shorter security parameters. Anyway, $k = 161$ is required, as soon as $\varepsilon'/t < 2^{-82}$.

To sum up, for the interesting case of the RSA, one can choose $k = 161$, with a security parameter chosen so that the security level of the function φ is about 2^{82}, that is 1024-bit modulus.

Acknowledgement. The work described in this paper has been supported in part by the European Commission through the IST Programme under Contract IST-2002-507932 ECRYPT.

References

1. M. Bellare, A. Desai, D. Pointcheval, and P. Rogaway. Relations among Notions of Security for Public-Key Encryption Schemes. In *Crypto '98*, LNCS 1462, pages 26–45. Springer-Verlag, Berlin, 1998.
2. M. Bellare and P. Rogaway. Random Oracles Are Practical: a Paradigm for Designing Efficient Protocols. In *Proc. of the 1st CCS*, pages 62–73. ACM Press, New York, 1993.
3. M. Bellare and P. Rogaway. Optimal Asymmetric Encryption – How to Encrypt with RSA. In *Eurocrypt '94*, LNCS 950, pages 92–111. Springer-Verlag, Berlin, 1995.
4. M. Bellare and P. Rogaway. The Exact Security of Digital Signatures – How to Sign with RSA and Rabin. In *Eurocrypt '96*, LNCS 1070, pages 399–416. Springer-Verlag, Berlin, 1996.
5. B. Chevallier-Mames and D.H Phan and D. Pointcheval Optimal Asymmetric Encryption and Signature Paddings. In *Proc. of the ACNS*, LNCS 3531. Springer-Verlag, Berlin, 2005. Full version available from `http://www.di.ens.fr/users/pointche/`.

6. J.-S. Coron, M. Joye, D. Naccache, and P. Paillier. Universal Padding Schemes For RSA. In M. Yung, editor, *Advances in Cryptology – CRYPTO '02*, volume 2442 of *Lecture Notes in Computer Science*, pages 226–241. Springer-Verlag, Berlin, 2002.
7. R. Cramer and V. Shoup. A Practical Public Key Cryptosystem Provably Secure against Adaptive Chosen Ciphertext Attack. In *Crypto '98*, LNCS 1462, pages 13–25. Springer-Verlag, Berlin, 1998.
8. R. Cramer and V. Shoup. Signature Scheme based on the Strong RSA Assumption. In *Proc. of the 6th CCS*, pages 46–51. ACM Press, New York, 1999.
9. Y. Dodis and L. Reyzin. On the power of claw-free permutation. In *Security in Communication Networks*, 2002.
10. S. Goldwasser, S. Micali, and R. Rivest. A Digital Signature Scheme Secure Against Adaptive Chosen-Message Attacks. *SIAM Journal of Computing*, 17(2):281–308, April 1988.
11. L. Granboulan. Short Signatures in the Random Oracle Model. In *Asiacrypt '02*, LNCS 2501, pages 364–378. Springer-Verlag, Berlin, 2002.
12. S. Haber and B. Pinkas. Combining Public Key Cryptosystems. In *Proc. of the 8th ACM CSS*, pages 215–224. ACM Press, New York, 2001.
13. J. Katz and N. Wang. Efficiency improvements for signature schemes with tight security reductions. In *Proc. of the 10th CCS*, pages 155–164. ACM Press, Washington, 2003.
14. Y. Komano and K. Ohta. Efficient Universal Padding Schemes for Multiplicative Trapdoor One-Way Permutation. In D. Boneh, editor, *Advances in Cryptology – CRYPTO '03*, volume 2729 of *Lecture Notes in Computer Science*, pages 366–382. Springer-Verlag, Berlin, 2003.
15. A. Lenstra and E. Verheul. Selecting Cryptographic Key Sizes. In *PKC '00*, LNCS 1751, pages 446–465. Springer-Verlag, Berlin, 2000.
16. D. Naccache and J. Stern. Signing on a Postcard. In *Financial Cryptography '00*, LNCS 1962. Springer-Verlag, Berlin, 2001.
17. NIST. Digital Signature Standard (DSS). Federal Information Processing Standards PUBlication 186, November 1994.
18. K. Nyberg and R. A. Rueppel. Message Recovery for Signature Schemes Based on the Discrete Logarithm Problem. In *Eurocrypt '94*, LNCS 950, pages 182–193. Springer-Verlag, Berlin, 1995.
19. T. Okamoto and D. Pointcheval. The Gap-Problems: a New Class of Problems for the Security of Cryptographic Schemes. In *PKC '01*, LNCS 1992. Springer-Verlag, Berlin, 2001.
20. D. H. Phan and D. Pointcheval. Chosen-Ciphertext Security without Redundancy. In *Asiacrypt '03*, LNCS 2894, pages 1–18. Springer-Verlag, Berlin, 2003.
21. D. H. Phan and D. Pointcheval. OAEP 3-Round: A Generic and Secure Asymmetric Encryption Padding. In *Asiacrypt '04*, LNCS 3329, pages 63–77 Springer-Verlag, Berlin, 2004.
22. C. Rackoff and D. R. Simon. Non-Interactive Zero-Knowledge Proof of Knowledge and Chosen Ciphertext Attack. In *Crypto '91*, LNCS 576, pages 433–444. Springer-Verlag, Berlin, 1992.
23. C. P. Schnorr. Efficient Signature Generation by Smart Cards. *Journal of Cryptology*, 4(3):161–174, 1991.
24. J. Stern, D. Pointcheval, J. Malone-Lee, and N. Smart. Flaws in Applying Proof Methodologies to Signature Schemes. In *Crypto '02*, LNCS 2442, pages 93–110. Springer-Verlag, Berlin, 2002.

Efficient and Leakage-Resilient Authenticated Key Transport Protocol Based on RSA

SeongHan Shin, Kazukuni Kobara, and Hideki Imai

Institute of Industrial Science, The University of Tokyo,
4-6-1 Komaba, Meguro-ku, Tokyo 153-8505, Japan
shinsh@imailab.iis.u-tokyo.ac.jp, {kobara,imai}@iis.u-tokyo.ac.jp
http://imailab-www.iis.u-tokyo.ac.jp/imailab.html

Abstract. Let us consider the following situation: (1) a client, who communicates with a variety of servers, remembers only one password and has *insecure* devices with very-restricted computing power and built-in memory capacity; (2) the counterpart servers have enormous computing power, but they are not perfectly secure; (3) neither PKI (Public Key Infrastructures) nor TRM (Tamper-Resistant Modules) is available.
Our main goal of this paper is to provide its security against the leakage of stored secrets as well as to attain high efficiency on client's side. For those, we propose an efficient and leakage-resilient RSA-based Authenticated Key Establishment (RSA-AKE) protocol suitable for the above situation whose authenticity is based on password *and* an additional stored secret. The RSA-AKE protocol is provably secure in the random oracle model where an adversary is given the stored secret of client and the RSA private key of server. In terms of computation costs, the client is required to compute only one modular exponentiation with an exponent e ($e \geq 3$) in the protocol execution. We also show that the RSA-AKE protocol has several security properties and efficiency over the previous ones of their kinds.

1   Introduction

Since the discovery of public-key cryptography by Diffie and Hellman [7], one of the most important research topics is to design a practical and provably secure protocol for realizing secure channels. In the 2-party setting (e.g., a client and a server), this can be achieved by an authenticated key establishment (AKE) protocol at the end of which the two parties share a common session key to be used for subsequent cryptographic algorithms. Typically, for mutual authentication it requires some information that can be a (high-entropy) secret key (e.g., [4, 19]) to be shared between the parties or a private key corresponding to a public key (e.g., [8, 19, 20]) owned by the parties.

In practice, the high-entropy keys may be substituted by human-memorable passwords chosen from a relatively small dictionary size. Owing to the usability of passwords, password-based AKE protocols have been extensively investigated where a client remembers a short password and the corresponding server holds

J. Ioannidis, A. Keromytis, and M.Yung (Eds.): ACNS 2005, LNCS 3531, pp. 269–284, 2005.

the password or its verification data. However, there are existing two major attacks on passwords: on-line and off-line dictionary attacks. The on-line dictionary attack is a series of exhaustive search for a secret performed on-line, so that an adversary can sieve out possible secret candidates one by one communicating with the target party. In contrast, the off-line dictionary attack is performed off-line massively in parallel by simply guessing a secret and verifying the guessed secret with recorded transcripts of a protocol. While on-line attacks are applicable to all of the password-based protocols equally, they can be prevented by letting a server take appropriate intervals between invalid trials. But, we cannot avoid off-line attacks by such policies, mainly because the attacks can be performed off-line and independently of the server, resulting in many password-based protocols insecure [21].

At first sight, it seems paradoxical to design a secure AKE protocol with passwords. For that, Bellovin and Merritt opened the door by showing that a combination of symmetric and asymmetric (public-key) cryptographic techniques can provide insufficient information for an adversary to verify a guessed password and thus defeats off-line dictionary attacks [1]. By asymmetric cryptographic techniques, we can roughly divide AKE protocols into two categories: authenticated key agreement (e.g., incorporating the Diffie-Hellman protocol) and authenticated key transport (e.g., using RSA) ones. When it comes to the lower-power computing devices (especially, on client's side), RSA-based AKE protocols would be preferable to the Diffie-Hellman based ones since with an encryption exponent e to be a small prime (e.g., $e = 3$) the computation costs will be drastically decreased. In the next section, we revisit the previous AKE protocols (using password and RSA) from a point of view of how much the leakage of stored secrets affect on its security of each protocol.

1.1 Previous Works

Bellovin and Merritt first proposed Encrypted Key Exchange (EKE) protocols (including the RSA-based EKE) in [1] that was very influential and became the basis for what we call Password-Authenticated Key Exchange (PAKE) protocols[1]. In PAKE protocols, a client is required to remember his/her password *only* (without any device) whereas the counterpart server has its verification data that should be stored securely. In other words, if the stored secret (or, password verification data) of the server is leaked out, the password eventually can be retrieved through off-line dictionary attacks, simply by verifying password candidates one by one using the verification data. When implementing with the RSA function, RSA-based PAKE protocols have to verify whether a server's RSA public key (e, N) is correct or not (i.e., $\gcd(e, \varphi(N)) = 1$) due to the lack of PKI (Public Key Infrastructures). This yields extra computation costs or communication overheads.

Contrary to the PAKE protocols, Lomas et al., introduced an AKE protocol, resistant to off-line dictionary attacks, where a client remembers his/her

---

[1] A complete list of such protocols can be found in Jablon's research link [17].

password and holds a server's public key in advance whereas the corresponding server has password verification data and its private key both of which should be stored securely [15]. This type of AKE protocols were further studied by Gong [9] and formalized by Halevi and Krawczyk [11]. However, the leakage of one of the stored secrets (the verification data or the private key) may cause a serious problem enough to break its security of the AKE protocol. For example, the leakage of the verification data makes possible for an adversary to retrieve the password through off-line dictionary attacks and thus to impersonate the client. With the leaked private key, an adversary can impersonate the server so that she can get the password through off-line dictionary attacks as well.

Other AKE protocols based on PKI can be found in SSL/TLS (Secure Socket Layer/Transport Layer Security) [10, 13] and SSH (Secure SHell) [12] where a client remembers his/her password and holds a server's public key whereas the corresponding server has password verification data and its private key both of which should be stored securely. The difference from the above AKE protocols is that the parties first establish a secure channel with the server's public key and then the client sends the password for authentication through the secure channel. Note that the client must verify the server's certificate via CRL (Certificate Revocation Lists) or OCSP (Online Certificate Status Protocol), before running the actual protocol, which entails additional computation and communication costs. As for the leakage of the stored secrets, the same discussion of the above paragraph can be done.

1.2   Motivation

The previous password-based AKE protocols have been designed to be secure against an active adversary who controls the communications and usually based on the assumption that the stored secrets would not leak out. However, the leakage of stored secrets is a more practical risk rather than breaking a well-studied cryptographic hard problem. TRM (Tamper-Resistant Modules) of course may be one of the ways to reduce the probability of leakage, but they cannot prevent the damage caused by the leakage as well as it is still hard to make a perfect TRM with low cost. In the password-based AKE protocols, the leakage of stored secrets may occur more serious catastrophe in the following multiple server scenario: a client who would have access to a lot of different servers registered the same password to them for authentication. In this scenario either an adversary or a dishonest server administrator who finds out the password with the leaked stored secrets from one server can impersonate the client to the other remaining servers! The other motivation comes from the fact that all of the previous RSA-based AKE protocols couldn't achieve perfect forward secrecy, if an RSA key pair is fixed, without incorporating the Diffie-Hellman protocol.

1.3   Overview of Our Contributions

Let us consider the following situation for unbalanced wireless networks where a client holds some *insecure* devices (e.g., mobile phones or PDAs) with very-restricted computing power and built-in memory capacity, on the other hand, the counterpart server has enormous computing power but is *not perfectly secure* against various attacks (e.g., virus or hackers). In addition, neither PKI nor TRM is available. In this paper, we propose an efficient and leakage-resilient RSA-based AKE (RSA-AKE) protocol, suitable for the above situation, whose authenticity is based on the client's password *and* an additional stored secret both of which makes possible to extend to the multiple sever scenario with only one password. That is, the respective leakage of stored secret(s) from a client and servers doesn't reveal any information on the password. That implies the client need not change his/her password even if stored secrets are leaked out from either the client or servers.

We also prove its security of the RSA-AKE protocol in the random oracle model under the notion of LR-AKE security where an adversary is given the stored secret of client and the RSA private key of server. Though our protocol is a password-based AKE one, we can avoid even on-line dictionary attacks as long as the leakage of stored secret from client does not happen.

In the RSA-AKE protocol, the client is required to compute only one modular exponentiation with an exponent e ($e \geq 3$) and the remaining computation costs if the pre-computation is allowed are one modular multiplication and some negligible operations. This is because we provide perfect forward secrecy, when the RSA key pair is fixed, by taking a way to update each stored secret of client and server every session. Doing so, the RSA-AKE protocol becomes efficient mainly in aspects of both computation and communication costs.

Organization. This paper is organized as follows. In section 2, we introduce the security model and security definitions. In Section 3, we propose an efficient and leakage-resilient RSA-based AKE (RSA-AKE) protocol, followed by its security proof and discussion in Section 4. Section 5 is devoted to comparison with the previous RSA-based AKE protocols in aspects of security properties and efficiency.

2   Security Model and Definitions

In this section we introduce the security model (based on [6] but extended considering "Leak" queries) and security definitions for the notion of LR-AKE security.

We denote by $\mathcal{C}$ and $\mathcal{S}$ two parties that participate in a protocol P. Each of them may have several *instances* called oracles involved in distinct, possibly concurrent, executions of P where we denote $\mathcal{C}$ (resp., $\mathcal{S}$) instances by $\mathcal{C}^I$ (resp., $\mathcal{S}^J$), or by U in case of any instance. Let us show the capability of adversary $\mathcal{A}$ each query captures:

- Execute($\mathcal{C}^I, \mathcal{S}^J$): This query models passive attacks, where the adversary gets access to honest executions of P between $\mathcal{C}^I$ and $\mathcal{S}^J$ by eavesdropping.
- Send(U, m): This query models active attacks by having $\mathcal{A}$ send a message to instance U. The adversary $\mathcal{A}$ gets back the response U generates in processing the message m according to the protocol P.

- Reveal(U): This query handles the misuse of a session key by any instance U. The query is only available to $\mathcal{A}$ if the instance actually "holds" a session key and the latter is released to $\mathcal{A}$.
- Leak(U): This query handles the leakage of "stored" secrets by any instance U. The query is available to $\mathcal{A}$ since stored secrets might be leaked out due to a bug of the system or physical limitations.
- Test(U): This oracle is used to see whether the adversary can obtain some information on the challenge session key, by giving a hint on the latter. The Test-query can be asked at most once by the adversary $\mathcal{A}$ and is only available to $\mathcal{A}$ if the instance U is "fresh" in that the session key is not *obviously* known to the adversary. This query is answered as follows: one flips a (private) coin $b \in \{0, 1\}$ and forwards the corresponding session key SK (Reveal(U) would output) if $b = 1$, or a random value except the session key if $b = 0$.

The goal of the adversary is to break the privacy of the session key (a.k.a., semantic security) in the context of executing P. We denote LR-AKE advantage, by $\mathsf{Adv}_P^{\mathsf{lr-ake}}(\mathcal{A}) = 2\Pr[b = b'] - 1$, as the probability that $\mathcal{A}$ can correctly guess the value of b. The protocol P is said to be LR-AKE secure if $\mathcal{A}$'s advantage is negligible for any adversary $\mathcal{A}$ with polynomial running time t. We formally define the LR-AKE security; this will be necessary for stating meaningful results about our protocol (compared to the other protocols) in Section 5.

Definition 1 (LR-AKE Security) *A protocol P is said to be LR-AKE secure if, when adversary $\mathcal{A}$ asks q_s queries to Send oracle and passwords are chosen from a dictionary of size D, the adversary's advantage $\mathsf{Adv}_P^{\mathsf{lr-ake}}(\mathcal{A}) = 2\Pr[b = b'] - 1$ in attacking the protocol P is bounded by*

$$O(q_s/D) + \epsilon(k), \tag{1}$$

for some negligible function $\epsilon(\cdot)$ [2] in the security parameter k. The first term represents the fact that the adversary can do no better than guess a password during each query to Send oracle.

The LR-AKE security notion captures the intuitive fact that the protocol P is secure against on-line and off-line dictionary attacks *even if* the leakage of stored secrets from the involving parties happens.

3   An RSA-Based AKE (RSA-AKE) Protocol

Before presenting an RSA-based AKE (for short, RSA-AKE) protocol, we will start by giving some preliminary notations to be used. Let k and l denote the security parameters, where k can be thought of as the general security parameter

---

[2] Denote with $\mathbb{N}$ the set of natural numbers and with $\mathbb{R}^+$ the set of positive real numbers. We say that a function $\epsilon : \mathbb{N} \to \mathbb{R}^+$ is *negligible* (in k) if and only if for every polynomial $P(k)$ there exists an $n_0 \in \mathbb{N}$ such that for all $n > n_0$, $\epsilon(k) \leq 1/P(k)$.

for hash functions (say, 160 bits) and l ($l > k$) can be thought of as the security parameter for RSA (say, 1024 bits). We define the RSA function by $\mathsf{RSA}_{N,f}(w) \equiv w^f \bmod N$ for all $w \in \mathbb{Z}_N^\star$. Let D be a dictionary size (cardinality) of passwords (say, 36 bits for alphanumerical passwords with 6 characters). Let $\{0,1\}^\star$ denote the set of finite binary strings and $\{0,1\}^k$ the set of binary strings of length k. If A is a set, then $a \xleftarrow{R} A$ indicates the process of selecting a at random and uniformly over A. Let "$\|$" denote the concatenation of bit strings in $\{0,1\}^\star$.

Let us define secure one-way hash functions (e.g., SHA-1). While $\mathcal{G} : \{0,1\}^\star \rightarrow \mathbb{Z}_N^\star \backslash \{1\}$ denotes a full-domain hash (FDH) function, the other hash functions are denoted $\mathcal{H}_j : \{0,1\}^\star \rightarrow \{0,1\}^k$ for $j = 1, 2, 3$ and 4. Here $\mathcal{G}$ and $\mathcal{H}_j$ are distinct random functions one another. Let $\mathcal{C}$ and $\mathcal{S}$ be the identities of client and server, respectively, with representing each ID $\in \{0,1\}^\star$ as well.

3.1   The RSA-AKE Protocol

We consider the following scenario where a client is communicating with many disparate i servers[3]. We especially focus on unbalanced wireless networks where the client has *insecure* devices (e.g., mobile phones or PDAs) with very-restricted computing power but some memory capacity itself, on the other hand, each server has its database and enormous computing power enough to generate a pair of (public and private) keys of RSA and to perform the RSA decryption function, when e is a small prime number. The choice of RSA key pair $((e, N), (d, N))$ is in general left to the implementations. However, in order to speed-up computation of $\mathsf{RSA}_{N,e}$, e should be chosen to be a small prime with a small number of 1's in its binary representation (e.g., $e = 3$ or $2^{16} + 1$). In addition, neither PKI nor TRM is available at all. Here we propose an efficient and leakage-resilient RSA-based AKE (RSA-AKE) protocol suitable for the above-mentioned situation. The whole protocol is illustrated in Fig. 1.

[**Initialization**]. During the initialization phase, client $\mathcal{C}$ registers a verification data, computed by a secret and his password, to one of different servers $\mathcal{S}_i$ ($i \geq 1$). At first, server $\mathcal{S}_i$ sends its RSA public key (e, N), which is generated from $\mathsf{RSAKeyGen}(1^l)$, to the client. The latter picks a secret value α_{i1} randomly chosen in $\mathbb{Z}_N^\star$ and registers securely a verification data p_{i1} to server $\mathcal{S}_i$:

$$p_{i1} \equiv \alpha_{i1} + \alpha_0 \bmod N \tag{2}$$

and sets the term $\alpha_0 = pw$ where pw is the client's password[4]. Since both α_{i1} and p_{i1} are in the set of the same length, each of α_{i1} and p_{i1} is a share of $(2, 2)$-threshold secret sharing scheme for α_0 [18].

Then client $\mathcal{C}$ remembers his password pw *and* additionally stores the secret value α_{i1} and the RSA public key (e, N) on insecure devices (e.g., mobile devices

---

[3] For simplicity, we assign the servers consecutive integer $i \geq 1$ where $\mathcal{S}_i$ can be regarded as i-th server.

[4] The password pw is drawn from password space $\mathbb{D}_{\mathsf{Password}}$ according to a certain probability distribution.

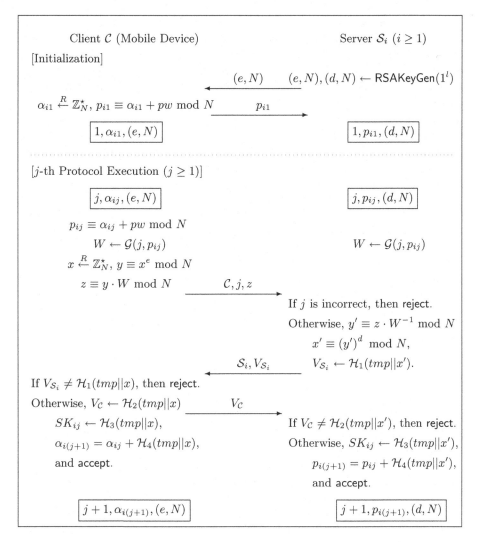

Fig. 1. The initialization and j-th protocol execution of RSA-based AKE (RSA-AKE) protocol where $tmp = \mathcal{C}||\mathcal{S}_i||j||z||p_{ij}$ and the enclosed values in rectangle represent stored secrets of client and server, respectively. The first flow of the protocol execution comprises a key exchange (concretely, key transport), followed by authenticators that are just the hashed values easily computable by both parties. Both of them check the received authenticator prior to accepting the session key.

or smart cards) which may happen to leak the secret α_{i1} and the key (e, N) eventually. The server $\mathcal{S}_i$ also stores the verification data p_{i1} and its RSA private key (d, N) on its databases both of which may be leaked out. Finally, they set a counter j as 1.

[**The j-th Protocol Execution**]. When client C wants to share an authenticated session key securely with server S_i, they run the j-th ($j \geq 1$) execution
of the RSA-AKE protocol as follows. At the start of the j-th protocol execution,
client C and server S_i hold $(j, \alpha_{ij}, (e, N))$ and $(j, p_{ij}, (d, N))$, respectively, where
$p_{ij} \equiv \alpha_{ij} + pw \bmod N$. The client C should recover the verification data p_{ij} by
adding the secret value α_{ij} stored on devices with the password pw kept in his
mind. Then the client chooses a random value x (as a keying material) from
$\mathbb{Z}_N^\star$ and sends (C, j, z) to server S_i, after calculating z using a mask generation
function as the product of an encryption of x under the RSA public key (e, N)
with a full-domain hash of (j, p_{ij}). If the received counter j is correct, the server
divides this encrypted value by a hash of the counter and its verification data
p_{ij}, and then decrypts the resultant value under its RSA private key (d, N) so as
to obtain the keying material x that is used to compute its authenticator V_{S_i} and
a session key SK. Upon receiving (S_i, V_{S_i}) from the server, client C computes
his authenticator V_C and a session key SK_{ij}, as long as the authenticator V_{S_i} is
valid, and sends V_C to server S_i. Of course, if V_{S_i} is not the case, client C wipes
off all the temporal data including the keying material and then terminates the
protocol. If the authenticator V_C is valid, server S_i actually computes a session
key SK_{ij} that will be used for their subsequent cryptographic algorithms.

At the end of the j-th protocol execution, client C refreshes the secret value
α_{ij} to a new one $\alpha_{i(j+1)}$ for $(j+1)$-th session:

$$\alpha_{i(j+1)} = \alpha_{ij} + \mathcal{H}_4(C||S_i||j||z||p_{ij}||x).$$

In the same way, server S_i also refreshes the verification data p_{ij} to a new
one: $p_{i(j+1)} = p_{ij} + \mathcal{H}_4(C||S_i||j||z||p_{ij}||x')$. Finally, client C stores $(j+1, \alpha_{i(j+1)}, (e, N))$ on his devices and server S_i stores $(j+1, p_{i(j+1)}, (d, N))$ on its databases
for the next session.

Only if client C inputs the right password pw and the corresponding secret
value α_{ij} to server S_i *and* server S_i uses the right verification data p_{ij} and its
RSA private key (d, N), they can generate the correct authenticators, share the
same session key and refresh each stored secret to a new one all of which are
derived from the keying material x. Without any leaked secret the probability
of guessing the other's keying material is $1/2^l$.

4   Security Proof for the RSA-AKE Protocol

In this section we show the RSA-AKE protocol of Fig. 1. is provably secure in the
random oracle model[5], under the assumption that inverting an RSA problem is

---

[5] To analyze the security of certain cryptographic constructions Bellare and Rogaway
introduced an idealized security model called the random oracle model [3]. Random
oracles are used to model cryptographic hash functions such as SHA-1 which produce
a random value for each new query. Note that security in the random oracle model is
only heuristic: it does not imply security in the real world. Nevertheless, the random
oracle model is a useful tool for validating natural cryptographic constructions.

hard. Informally speaking, an adversary cannot determine the correct password through off-line dictionary attacks, even if she knows the client's secret and the server's RSA private key, since generating the valid client's authenticator after computing z *or* generating the valid server's authenticator falls into on-line dictionary attacks (which can be easily prevented and detected).

4.1 Security Proof

In order to simplify the security proof, we only consider the first two flows of the j-th protocol execution (unilateral authentication of $\mathcal{S}$ to $\mathcal{C}$) [6]. This is due to the well-known fact that the basic approach in folklore for adding authentication to an AKE protocol is to use the distributed Diffie-Hellman key or the keying material to construct a simple "authenticator" for the other party [2, 6]. Therefore, the security proof with unilateral authentication can be extended to one with mutual authentication by simply adding the authenticator of $\mathcal{C}$ (the third flow) as in Fig. 1. However, this entails a more complicated proof.

Here we assert that the two-flows RSA-AKE protocol distributes semantically-secure session keys and provides unilateral authentication for the server $\mathcal{S}$ under the one-wayness of RSA. Since the security of the RSA-AKE protocol only depends on the password, the LR-AKE security can be proven with some adjustments and changes of the proof for the RSA-based PAKE protocol [6][7].

Theorem 1 (LR-AKE/UA Security) *Let P be the two-flows RSA-AKE protocol, where passwords are chosen from a dictionary of size D. For any adversary $\mathcal{A}$ within a polynomial time t, with less than q_s active interactions with the parties (Send-queries), q_p passive eavesdroppings (Execute-queries) and q_l leakages (Leak-queries), and asking q_g and q_h hash queries to $\mathcal{G}$ and any $\mathcal{H}_i$ respectively, $\mathsf{Adv}_P^{\mathsf{lr-ake}}(\mathcal{A}) \leq 4\varepsilon$ and $\mathsf{Adv}_P^{\mathsf{S-auth}}(\mathcal{A}) \leq \varepsilon$, with ε upper-bounded by*

$$(q_{\mathcal{C}} + 3q_{\mathcal{S}})/D + 6q_l \cdot \mathsf{Succ}_{RSA}^{\mathsf{ow}}\left(q_h^2, t + 2q_h^2\tau_{rsa}\right) + \frac{q_{\mathcal{C}}}{2^{k_1}} + \frac{2q_{\mathcal{C}} + (q_g + q_h)^2}{2^{l+1}} , \quad (3)$$

where $q_{\mathcal{C}}$ and $q_{\mathcal{S}}$ denote the number of $\mathcal{C}$ and $\mathcal{S}$ instances involved during the attack (each upper-bounded by $q_p + q_s$), k_1 is the output length of $\mathcal{H}_1$, l is the security parameter, and τ_{rsa} is the computational time needed for $RSA_{N,d}$.

Due to the lack of space, we omit the security model, formal definitions and the proof but those will appear in the full version. Here we justify the main terms in the security result. Some ways for the adversary $\mathcal{A}$ to break the protocol are: (1) guess a password and makes an on-line trial with respect to $\mathcal{C}^I$ and $\mathcal{S}^J$ involved during the attack. The RSA-AKE protocol is secure against on-line dictionary attacks since the advantage of $\mathcal{A}$ essentially grows with the ratio of

---

[6] For the sake of brevity, we omit the index i in the proof.

[7] The security reduction to the one-wayness of RSA is based on [5] where a challenge RSA problem is included in the answer of many hash queries so that the adversary is useful to the simulator with greater probability.

interactions to the number of passwords. Hence the term $(q_C + 3q_S)/D$; (2) use the authenticator V_S to check the correct password. But this requires the ability to compute $\mathsf{RSA}_{N,d}(z \times W^{-1})$. Hence the term $6q_l \cdot \mathsf{Succ}^{\mathsf{ow}}_{RSA}(\cdot, \cdot)$; (3) send a correct authenticator V_S, but being lucky. Hence the term $q_C/2^{k_1}$. Additional negligible terms come from very unlikely collisions. All the remaining kinds of attacks need some information about the password.

In the proof, the simulator has to "guess" which hash query to $\mathcal{G}$ will be used by the adversary to produce the correct bit b, resulting in a factor of q_l (the number of Leak-queries) in the success probability to invert the RSA encryption function.

4.2   Discussion

The only restriction on an adversary is that she cannot replace an RSA public key (e, N), stored on a client's devices, with a different one (e', N'). If it is possible, the adversary can store a fake RSA public key (e', N') such that $(e, N) \neq (e', N')$ and $\gcd(e', \varphi(N')) \neq 1$. As a result, the RSA encryption function $\mathsf{RSA}_{N',e'}(x) \equiv x^{e'} \bmod N'$ is no longer a permutation on $\mathbb{Z}^\star_{N'}$ which maps an element $x \in \mathbb{Z}^\star_{N'}$ to the set of e'-residues (a proper subset of $\mathbb{Z}^\star_{N'}$). Since the adversary knows the factorization of N', it is easy to check whether an element $x \in \mathbb{Z}^\star_{N'}$ is e'-residues or not. This is generally called e-residue attack that is one of the off-line dictionary attacks.

However, one has to notice the intrinsic distinction of adversary's behavior in the RSA-AKE and PAKE protocols. In the latter, an adversary is a kind of network adversary who can impersonate the involving parties and control all of the communications for e-residue attacks. On the other hand, an adversary, who is willing to perform e-residue attacks in the RSA-AKE protocol, should first steal a client's device, change an RSA public key and return back to the client. Then the adversary impersonates the corresponding server so as to narrow down the password candidates. (We call this "replacement attack" for convenience.)

One of the possible ways to thwart e-residue attacks in the RSA-AKE protocol is as follows. If the client has noticed the leakage of stored secrets $(\alpha_j, (e, N))$ or couldn't run the protocol within a fixed number of trials, he runs one of the RSA-based PAKE protocols (e.g., [6, 22]) by using p_j instead of the password pw. After establishing a secure channel, the client refreshes the secret α_j to α_{j+1} and stores the correct RSA public key. In this case, the adversary cannot mount e-residue attacks successively since its security now depends on the refreshed secret α_{j+1} as well as the latter is completely independent from α_j. In order to continue the e-residue attacks, the adversary should steal the device to get α_{j+1}, change the RSA public key, return back to the client, and then impersonate the server again.

More simple way against e-residue attacks is to exploit insecure devices in the practical point of view. Suppose that a client has a mobile phone on which a server's RSA public key (e, N) is stored, on the other hand, he also holds a memory card separately for the mobile phone where the fingerprint of (e, N) is kept. Of course, TRM is not needed at all. Whenever the client runs the RSA-AKE protocol with the server, he should at first do the integrity check for (e, N), as Halevi and Krawczyk's protocol [11] does[8], by inserting the memory card to the phone and confirming the correctness of (e, N).

5   Comparison

In this section we compare the RSA-AKE protocol of Section 3.1 with the previous AKE protocols using password and RSA. In order to be fair, we instantiate with the RSA function if a public key encryption is not specified in the relevant previous works. For simplifying its discussion, we omit additional computation and communication costs of SSL/TLS and SSH in order to verify the counterpart's certificate.

5.1   As for Security Properties

The RSA-AKE protocol may seem to be similar to Halevi and Krawczyk's protocol [11] since a client holds a server's RSA public key and remembers his password after the initialization phases of both protocols. However, in their protocol if an adversary changes the RSA public key (e, N), stored on the client's devices, with a one (e', N') generated by RSAKeyGen(1^l) of the adversary, she can discover the password through off-line dictionary attacks with only one interaction with the client.

As for several security properties, we show the comparative results in Table 1 and 2. For an easier comparison, the following three cases are considered.

- CASE1: This is the case that an adversary gets the stored secret associated with the password from client $\mathcal{C}$.
- CASE2: This is the case that an adversary gets the verification data associated with the password from server $\mathcal{S}$.
- CASE3: This is the case that an adversary gets the RSA private key from server $\mathcal{S}$.

In the RSA-AKE protocol, CASE1, CASE2 and CASE3 correspond to the leakage of $\alpha_{i(j+1)}$, $p_{i(j+1)}$ and (d, N), respectively. We can see in Table 1 that the RSA-AKE protocol guarantees semantic security of session keys even if CASE1 and CASE3 happen at the same time. In terms of semantic security against CASE2, the key-establishment part of SSL/TLS and SSH in the public-key based user authentication mode is the only survivor simply because the password is not used for client's authentication but for protecting the client's private key.

In terms of security of password against CASE1 and CASE2 (in Table 2), we claim the following theorem:

---
[8] For the integrity check in their protocol, a client receives a public key from a server and then compares the key with one stored on devices. Unfortunately, their protocol is insecure against the "replacement attack" described above (refer to Section 5).

Table 1. Comparison of RSA-based AKE protocols in a situation where no perfect TRM is available.

Protocols		Client's possessions			Semantic security of session key against			
		PW^{*1}	SS^{*2}	PI^{*3}	CASE1	CASE2	CASE3	CASE1∨ CASE3
P	RSA-IPAKE [6]							
A	PEKEP [22]	$\checkmark$						
K	CEKEP [22]				secure	insecure	secure	secure
E	SNAPI [16]							
	SNAPI-X [16]	$\checkmark$		$\checkmark^{*4}$				
MAKE^{*5} [11]		$\checkmark$		$\checkmark^{*7}$	secure	insecure	insecure	insecure
MA-DHKE^{*6} [11]		$\checkmark$		$\checkmark^{*4,*7}$	secure	insecure	insecure	insecure
SSL/TLS, SSH^{*8}		$\checkmark$		$\checkmark$	secure	insecure	insecure	insecure
SSL/TLS, SSH^{*9}		$\checkmark$	$\checkmark$	$\checkmark$	insecure^{*10}	secure	insecure	insecure
RSA-AKE		$\checkmark$	$\checkmark$	$\checkmark$	secure	insecure	secure	secure^{*11}

*1: Human-memorable secret (i.e., password)
*2: Stored secret: a secret value, a signing (decryption) key or a symmetric key
*3: Public information: a CA's verification key, an encryption key or its fingerprint
*4: Public parameters for the Diffie-Hellman protocol: let $\mathbb{G}$ be a finite, cyclic group of prime order q and g be a generator of $\mathbb{G}$
*5: Mutual Authentication and Key Exchange of Section 3.4
*6: Mutual Authentication and Diffie-Hellman Key Exchange of Section 3.4
*7: Cached server's RSA public key (e.g., $\mathcal{H}(e, N)$)
*8: Key-establishment part of SSL/TLS and SSH in the password-based user authentication mode
*9: Key-establishment part of SSL/TLS and SSH in the public-key based user authentication mode with a password-protected private key
*10: $E_{pw}(d)$ where d is an RSA private key and E is a symmetric encryption with pw as its key
*11: Theorem 1

Theorem 2 (Security of Password) *The password in the* RSA-AKE *protocol remains information-theoretically secure against off-line dictionary attacks even after either* CASE1 *or* CASE2 *happens.*

Proof. The proof is straightforward. First, we think of an adversary who obtains the stored secret $\alpha_{i(j+1)}$ of client $\mathcal{C}$ and is trying to deduce the password pw. Since $\alpha_{i(j+1)}$ is completely independent from pw, $\alpha_{i(j+1)}$ doesn't reveal any information about the password.

$$H(pw) = H\left(pw|\alpha_{i(j+1)}\right) \tag{4}$$

where $H(X)$ denotes the (Shannon) entropy of X and $H(X|Y)$ denotes the conditional entropy of X conditioned on Y. Second, we think of the security of password against an adversary who obtains the stored secret $p_{i(j+1)}$ of server

Table 2. Comparison of RSA-based AKE protocols in a situation where no perfect TRM is available (con't).

Protocols		Security[*1] of password CASE1	CASE2	Extension[*2]	Perfect forward secrecy (CASE1 ∨ CASE2 ∨ CASE3)
P	RSA-IPAKE [6]	○	X ($\triangle$[*3])	impossible	PFS can be achieved only if server $\mathcal{S}$ changes its RSA key pair every time.
A	PEKEP [22]				
K	CEKEP [22]				
E	SNAPI [16]				
	SNAPI-X [16]	○	$\triangle$[*4]		
MAKE [11]		○	$\triangle$[*3]	impossible	not achieved
MA-DHKE [11]		○	$\triangle$[*3]	impossible	achieved[*5]
SSL/TLS, SSH		○	X ($\triangle$[*3])	impossible	achieved[*5]
SSL/TLS, SSH		$\triangle$	○	possible	achieved[*5]
RSA-AKE		○[*6]	○[*6]	possible[*7]	achieved

*1: Security level against an adversary who either obtains client's devices (CASE1) or intrudes severs (CASE2) in order to retrieve the client's password in each case: ○ guarantees the security of password against both on-line and off-line dictionary attacks; $\triangle$ guarantees the security of password against on-line, but not off-line attacks; and X guarantees the security of password against neither on-line nor off-line attacks.

*2: Extension to the multiple server scenario with only one password

*3: A client registers password verification data computed with a particular one-way function of the password, $f(pw)$, to the server instead of pw. Doing this somewhat slows down off-line dictionary attacks of an adversary who obtained the server's database.

*4: $g^{\mathcal{H}_5(\mathcal{C}||\mathcal{S}||pw)}$ where $\mathcal{H}_4$ is a secure one-way hash function

*5: Due to the Diffie-Hellman protocol

*6: Information-theoretically secure

*7: The number of stored secrets α_{ij} grows linearly to the number of servers.

S_i and is trying to deduce the password pw. However, the adversary cannot get any information about the password, simply because $p_{i(j+1)}$ is one share of $(2,2)$-threshold (perfect) secret sharing scheme. As a result, the password is information-theoretically secure as a secret value of $(2,2)$-threshold secret sharing scheme. □

Contrary to the **RSA-AKE** protocol, the other AKE protocols don't have the security of password since their stored secrets in either the client or the server(s) contain enough information to succeed in retrieving the relatively short password with off-line dictionary attacks.

One of the important security properties is perfect forward secrecy. According to [20], we informally say that a protocol P achieves perfect forward secrecy if the disclosure of "long-term" secrets of the involving parties does not compromise the semantic security of session keys from previous sessions (even though that compromises the authenticity and thus the security of new sessions). In the RSA-AKE protocol, perfect forward secrecy can be interpreted as follows: if an adversary is given with $\alpha_{i(j+1)}, p_{i(j+1)}$ and (d, N), such that $p_{i(j+1)} = \alpha_{i(j+1)} + pw$, in the $(i + 1)$-th session, the adversary is trying to deduce the previous session key SK_{ij} for the i-th session[9]. In order to compute x

$$
x = \mathsf{RSA}_{N,d}(z/W) = \mathsf{RSA}_{N,d}(z)/\mathsf{RSA}_{N,d}\left(\mathcal{G}(j, \underline{p_{ij}})\right)
$$
$$
= \mathsf{RSA}_{N,d}(z)/\mathsf{RSA}_{N,d}\left(\mathcal{G}(j, \alpha_{ij} + pw)\right)
$$
$$
= \mathsf{RSA}_{N,d}(z)/\mathsf{RSA}_{N,d}\left(\mathcal{G}(j, p_{i(j+1)} - \mathcal{H}_4(\cdot|| \cdot || \cdot || \cdot ||\underline{p_{ij}}||\underline{x})))\right), \qquad (5)
$$

the adversary should know α_{ij} or p_{ij} both of which are completely independent from $\alpha_{i(j+1)}$ and $p_{i(j+1)}$ without x. Remember that α_{ij} and p_{ij} are uniformly distributed in $(\mathbb{Z}_N^\star)^2$. That is, the RSA-AKE protocol achieves perfect forward secrecy[10] even if server $\mathcal{S}_i$ would use the same RSA key pair for many sessions.

5.2   As for Efficiency

Since password-based AKE protocols have been motivated by the very practical implementations and widely used even in wireless networks, we analyze computation costs of client and communication overheads in the RSA-AKE protocol while comparing with those of each protocol execution, providing perfect forward secrecy, in Table 3. We denote by l (resp., k) the security parameter for the RSA function and the Diffie-Hellman protocol (resp., for the hash functions and random numbers). The number of modular exponentiations is a major factor to evaluate efficiency of a cryptographic protocol because that is the most power-consuming operation. So we count the number of modular exponentiations as computation costs of client $\mathcal{C}$. The figures in the parentheses are the remaining costs after pre-computation. For brevity, we denote by RSA-Exp. (resp., DH-Exp.) the number of RSA modular exponentiations with an exponent e (resp., the number of Diffie-Hellman modular exponentiations with an exponent of 160-bits long). In terms of communications overheads, the length of identities is excluded and $| \cdot |$ indicates its bit-length.

With respect to computation costs in the RSA-AKE protocol, client $\mathcal{C}$ is required to compute one modular exponentiation with an exponent e ($e \geq 3$) and one modular multiplication. In particular, the remaining costs after pre-computation is only one modular multiplication and additional operations for modular additions and hash functions. On the other hand, MAKE protocol doesn't allow pre-computation and doesn't provide perfect forward secrecy. With respect to communication overheads in the RSA-AKE protocol, it requires a bandwidth of $(l + 2k)$ bits approximately.

---

[9] The adversary is in the game to distinguish the i-th session key given by Test oracle.

[10] For an RSA-based AKE protocol without incorporating the Diffie-Hellman protocol, it seems impossible to prove perfect forward security in a sense of [2, 14] since this kind of protocol is actually a key transport one.

Table 3. Comparison of RSA-based AKE protocols as for efficiency.

Protocols		Computation costs of client $\mathcal{C}$		Communication
		DH-Exp.	RSA-Exp. with e	overheads
P	RSA-IPAKE [6]		$m + 1$ when $e \geq 3$, (m) *1	$(m+2)l + 3k$
	PEKEP [22]		$n + 1$ when $e \geq 3$, (n) *2	$2l + 4k + |e|$
A	CEKEP [22]		$2n$ when $e \geq 3$, $(2n-1)$ *3 or 2, (2) *4	$3l + 6k + |e| + |n|$
K	SNAPI [16]		Primality test of large e and 1 *5, (Primality test of e)	$2l + 4k + |e|$
E	SNAPI-X [16]	2, (2)	Primality test of large e and 1 *5, (Primality test of e)	$3l + 4k + |e|$
MAKE [11]			1 when $e \geq 3$, (1)	$2l + 3k + |e|$
MA-DHKE [11]		2, (1)	1 when $e \geq 3$, (1)	$4l + 3k + |e|$
SSL/TLS, SSH		2, (1)	1 when $e \geq 3$, (1)	$3l + |E|$
SSL/TLS, SSH		2, (1)	1 when $e \geq 3$ and 1 RSA-Exp. with d, (1 RSA-Exp. with d) *6	$3l$
RSA-AKE			1 when $e \geq 3$, (0)	$l + 2k$

*1: m is the system parameter
*2: $n = \lfloor \log_e N \rfloor$
*3: $n = \lceil \log_e \omega^{-1} \rceil$ where $0 < \omega \leq 2^{-80}$
*4: 2 modular exponentiations each having an exponent of $\lceil \log_e \omega^{-1} \rceil$ bits where $0 < \omega \leq 2^{-80}$
*5: 1 modular exponentiation with an exponent e having the following explicit requirements on e and N (in order to enforce the relative primality of e and $\varphi(N)$). One is to set e to be a prime, in the range of $2^l + 1 \leq e < 2^{l+1}$, greater than N. The other is to set e to be a prime such that $e \geq \sqrt{N}$ and $(N \bmod e) \nmid N$.
*6: 1 modular exponentiation with an exponent d

Acknowledgements

The authors appreciate anonymous reviewers for their helpful comments.

References

1. S. M. Bellovin and M. Merritt. Encrypted Key Exchange: Password-based Protocols Secure against Dictioinary Attacks. In *Proc. of IEEE Symposium on Security and Privacy*, pages 72-84. IEEE Computer Society, 1992.
2. M. Bellare, D. Pointcheval, and P. Rogaway. Authenticated Key Exchange Secure against Dictionary Attacks. In *Proc. of EUROCRYPT 2000*, LNCS 1807, pages 139-155. Springer-Verlag, 2000.
3. M. Bellare and P. Rogaway. Random Oracles are Practical: A Paradigm for Designing Efficient Protocols. In *Proc. of ACM CCS '93*, pages 62-73, 1993.
4. M. Bellare and P. Rogaway. Entity Authentication and Key Distribution. In *Proc. of CRYPTO '93*, LNCS 773, pages 232-249. Springer-Verlag, 1993.
5. M. Bellare and P. Rogaway. The Exact Security of Digital Signatures: How to Sign with RSA and Rabin. In *Proc. of Eurocrypt '96*, LNCS 1070, pages 399-416. Springer-Verlag, 1996.

6. D. Catalano, D. Pointcheval, and T. Pornin. IPAKE: Isomorphisms for Password-based Authenticated Key Exchange. In *Proc. of CRYPTO 2004*, LNCS 3152, pages 477-493. Springer-Verlag, 2004. The full version is available at `http://www.di.ens.fr/~pointche/slides.php?reference=CaPoPo04`.
7. W. Diffie and M. Hellman. New Directions in Cryptography. In *IEEE Transactions on Information Theory*, Vol. IT-22(6), pages 644-654, 1976.
8. W. Diffie, P. van Oorschot, and M. Wiener. Authentication and Authenticated Key Exchange. In *Proc. of Designs, Codes, and Cryptography*, pages 107-125, 1992.
9. L. Gong. Optimal Authentication Protocols Resistant to Password Guessing Attacks. In *Proc. of IEEE Computer Security Foundation Workshop*, pages 24-29, 1995.
10. A. Frier, P. Karlton, and P. Kocher. The SSL 3.0 Protocol. Netscape Communication Corp., 1996. available at `http://wp.netscape.com/eng/ssl3/`.
11. S. Halevi and H. Krawczyk. Public-Key Cryptography and Password Protocols. February 1999.
12. IETF (Internet Engineering Task Force). Secure Shell (secsh) Charter. `http://www.ietf.org/html.charters/secsh-charter.html`
13. IETF (Internet Engineering Task Force). Transport Layer Security (tls) Charter. `http://www.ietf.org/ html.charters/tls-charter.html`
14. J. Katz, R. Ostrovsky, and M. Yung. Forward Secrecy in Password-Only Key Exchange Protocols. In *Proc. of SCN 2002*, LNCS 2576, pages 29-44. Springer-Verlag, 2002.
15. M. Lamos, L. Gong, J. Saltzer, and R. Needham. Reducing Risks from Poorly Chosen Keys. In *Proc. of the 12th ACM Symposium on Operating System Principles*, ACM Operating Systems Review, pages 14-18, 1989.
16. P. MacKenzie, S. Patel, and R. Swaminathan. Password-Authenticated Key Exchange Based on RSA. In *Proc. of ASIACRYPT 2000*, LNCS 1976, pages 599-613. Springer-Verlag, 2000. The full version is available at `http://cm.bell-labs.com/who/philmac/bib.html`.
17. Phoenix Technologies Inc., Research Papers on Strong Password Authentication. available at `http://www.integritysciences.com/links.html`.
18. A. Shamir. How to Share a Secret. In *Proc. of Communications of the ACM*, Vol. 22(11), pages 612-613, 1979.
19. V. Shoup. On Formal Models for Secure Key Exchange. IBM Research Report RZ 3121, 1999.
20. S. B. Wilson, D. Johnson, and A. Menezes. Key Agreement Protocols and their Security Analysis. In *Proc. of IMA International Conference on Cryptography and Coding*, December 1997.
21. T. Wu. A Real-world Analysis of Kerberos Password Security. In *Proc. of Network and Distributed System Security Symposium*, February 1999.
22. M. Zhang. New Approaches to Password Authenticated Key Exchange based on RSA. In *Proc. of ASIACRYPT 2004*, LNCS 3329, pages 230-244. Springer-Verlag, 2004. Cryptology ePrint Archive, Report 2004/033, available at `http://eprint.iacr.org/2004/033`.

Identity Based Encryption Without Redundancy

Benoît Libert* and Jean-Jacques Quisquater

UCL Crypto Group
Place du Levant, 3, B-1348 Louvain-La-Neuve, Belgium
{libert,jjq}@dice.ucl.ac.be

Abstract. This paper presents a first example of secure identity based encryption scheme (IBE) without redundancy in the sense of Phan and Pointcheval. This modification of the Boneh-Franklin IBE is an hybrid construction that is proved to be secure (using proof techniques borrowed from those for KEM-DEM constructions) in the random oracle model under a slightly stronger assumption than the original IBE and turns out to be more efficient at decryption than the latter. A second contribution of this work is to show how to shorten ciphertexts in a recently proposed multiple-recipient IBE scheme. Our modification of the latter scheme spares about 1180 bits from a bandwidth point of view as, somewhat surprisingly, redundancies are not needed although all elements of the ciphertext space are not reachable by the encryption mapping. This shows that in public key encryption schemes, redundancies may be useless even when the encryption mapping is not a surjection.

Keywords: ID-based encryption, provable security, redundancies.

1 Introduction

Identity based cryptosystems were introduced by Shamir in 1984 [35] in order to simplify key management and avoid the use of digital certificates by letting a public key be publicly derivable from a human-memorizable information on its owner (e-mail address, IP address combined to a user name,...) while the associated private keys must be computed by a trusted Private Key Generator (PKG) thanks to a master secret. This paradigm avoids key management problems arising in traditional public key infrastructures: as long as a public key "is" its owner's identity, nothing must be certified except the PKG's public key and a single public key per domain is thus needed.

Finding a practical identity based encryption scheme (IBE) remained an long-standing open challenge until two independent works of Boneh-Franklin [10] and Cocks [14] which appeared in 2001. Among those solutions, Boneh and Franklin's one happens to be the most practical one.

In provable security purposes, motivated by the design of public key encryption schemes that provably reach the widely admitted required level of security against adaptive chosen-ciphertext attacks [34] in the random oracle model [6],

---

* This author is supported by the DGTRE's First Europe Program.

J. Ioannidis, A. Keromytis, and M.Yung (Eds.): ACNS 2005, LNCS 3531, pp. 285–300, 2005.
© Springer-Verlag Berlin Heidelberg 2005

Bellare and Rogaway introduced the notion of plaintext-awareness [7] that captures the general idea to render a decryption oracle useless by making impossible the creation of valid ciphertexts by the adversary. As mentioned in [21], several works [2, 13, 20, 31, 33], gave (knowingly or not) evidence that chosen-ciphertext security is achievable without plaintext-awareness in the random oracle model. Among them, salient results of Phan and Pointcheval [31, 33] showed designs of strongly secure [34] public key encryption schemes for which all ciphertexts are valid and have a corresponding plaintext. Those results were very recently extended by a work [13] exhibiting a 'redundancy-optimal' generic construction of IND-CCA secure public key encryption.

Meanwhile, Kurosawa and Matsuo [28] showed how to turn the DHIES [1] hybrid construction into a redundancy-free encryption scheme in the standard model (but under the non-standard oracle Diffie-Hellman assumption that actually looks as strong as the random oracle model) by removing the message authentication code (MAC) and replacing the IND-CPA symmetric encryption scheme with an IND-CCA one. Their approach is actually a KEM-DEM [17, 18, 36] construction that can also be proved secure in the random oracle model under a more standard assumption in the same way as the oracle Diffie-Hellman assumption was shown [1] to imply the Gap Diffie-Hellman assumption [30] in the random oracle model.

The contribution of the present paper is two-fold. We first extend the technique of Kurosawa and Matsuo to the identity based setting in the random oracle model and show a hybrid variant of the Boneh-Franklin IBE [10] that reaches the IND-ID-CCA2 security level (under a slightly stronger assumption) without introducing redundancies in ciphertexts that are thus shorter than in the FullIdent scheme of [10]. As a side effect, the decryption operation is more efficient in the resulting scheme than its counterpart in the fully secure original IBE [10]. We mention that an independent work [8] of ours recently considered identity based and certificateless [3] extensions of KEMs. When combined to a suitable symmetric encryption scheme, the first identity based KEM proposed in [8] provides a hybrid IBE that is quite similar to ours. However, as explained in section 3, our variant enjoys a better security reduction in the random oracle model.

The second contribution of the paper is a method to shorten ciphertexts produced by a recently proposed [5] multiple-receiver IBE by the size of an RSA modulus. The modified scheme has the particulary that, although the encryption function is not surjective, no validity checking must be performed at decryption and the decryption algorithm never returns any error message.

2   Preliminaries

2.1   Admissible Bilinear Maps

Let k be a security parameter and q be a $k-$bit prime number. Let us consider groups $\mathbb{G}_1$ and $\mathbb{G}_2$ of the same prime order q. For our purposes, we need a bilinear map $e : \mathbb{G}_1 \times \mathbb{G}_1 \to \mathbb{G}_2$ satisfying the following properties:

1. Bilinearity: $\forall\, P, Q \in \mathbb{G}_1$, $\forall\, a, b \in \mathbb{Z}_q^*$, we have $e(aP, bQ) = e(P, Q)^{ab}$.
2. Non-degeneracy: $\forall\, P \in \mathbb{G}_1$, $e(P, Q) = 1$ for all $Q \in \mathbb{G}_1$ iff $P = \mathcal{O}$.
3. Computability: $\forall\, P, Q \in \mathbb{G}_1$, $e(P, Q)$ can be efficiently computed.

As shown in [10], such non-degenerate admissible maps over cyclic groups can be obtained from the Weil or the Tate pairing over algebraic curves.

2.2 Underlying Hard Problems

This section recalls definitions of underlying hard problems on which the security of our scheme is shown to rely.

Definition 1. *Given groups $\mathbb{G}_1$ and $\mathbb{G}_2$ of prime order q, a bilinear map e : $\mathbb{G}_1 \times \mathbb{G}_1 \to \mathbb{G}_2$ and a generator P of $\mathbb{G}_1$,*

- *The **Bilinear Diffie-Hellman Problem** (BDH) in $(\mathbb{G}_1, \mathbb{G}_2)$ is, given elements $\langle P, aP, bP, cP \rangle$ for unknown $a, b, c \in \mathbb{Z}_q$, to compute $e(P, P)^{abc} \in \mathbb{G}_2$.*
- *The **Decision Bilinear Diffie-Hellman Problem** (DBDH) is to distinguish the distributions $D_1 := \{(P, aP, bP, cP, e(P, P)^{abc}) | a, b, c \xleftarrow{R} \mathbb{Z}_q^*\}$ and $D_2 := \{(P, aP, bP, cP, h) | a, b, c \xleftarrow{R} \mathbb{Z}_q^*,\ h \xleftarrow{R} \mathbb{G}_2\}$. Tuples from D_1 are denoted as "BDH tuples" in the sequel in contrast to those from D_2 which will be called "random tuples" .*
- *The **Gap Bilinear Diffie-Hellman Problem** (Gap-BDH) in $(\mathbb{G}_1, \mathbb{G}_2)$ consists of, given $\langle P, aP, bP, cP \rangle$, to compute $e(P, P)^{abc}$ with the help of a DBDH oracle.*

The security of the schemes presented in this paper relies on the Gap-BDH assumption which is the intractability of the latter problem.

2.3 Definition of IBE

We recall here the formalism introduced in [10] for identity based encryption. Such a primitive consists of the following algorithms.

Setup: is a probabilistic algorithm run by a private key generator (PKG) that takes as input a security parameter to output a public/private key pair (P_{pub}, mk) for the PKG (P_{pub} is its public key and mk is its master key that is kept secret).

Keygen: is a key generation algorithm run by the PKG on input of a master key mk and a user's identity ID to return the user's private key d_{ID}.

Encrypt: this probabilistic algorithm takes as input a plaintext M, a recipient's identity ID and the PKG's public key P_{pub} to output a ciphertext C.

Decrypt: is a deterministic decryption algorithm that takes as input a ciphertext C and the private decryption key d_{ID} to return a plaintext M or a distinguished symbol $\perp$ if C is not a valid ciphertext.

In sections 3 and 4, we shall use the above definition with the restriction that the decryption algorithm never outputs a rejection message.

2.4 Security Notions

Definition 2. *An identity based encryption scheme (IBE) is said to be **adaptively chosen-ciphertext secure (IND-ID-CCA2)** if no probabilistic polynomial time (PPT) adversary has a non-negligible advantage in the following game.*

1. *The challenger runs the Setup algorithm on input of a security parameter k and sends the domain-wide parameters to the cca-adversary $\mathcal{A}$.*
2. *In a find stage, $\mathcal{A}$ starts probing the following oracles:*
   - *Key extraction oracle: given an identity ID, it returns the extracted private key associated to it.*
   - *Decryption oracle: given an identity $ID \in \{0,1\}^*$ and a ciphertext C, it generates the private key d_{ID} associated to ID and returns a plaintext $M \in \mathcal{M}$ or (optionally, in schemes where ciphertexts may be invalid) a distinguished symbol $\perp$ indicating an ill-formed ciphertext.*

   $\mathcal{A}$ can present her queries adaptively in the sense that each query may depend on the answer to previous ones.
3. *$\mathcal{A}$ produces two equal-length plaintexts $M_0, M_1 \in \mathcal{M}$ and a target identity ID^* for which she has not corrupted the private key in stage 2.*
4. *The challenger computes $C = \mathsf{Encrypt}(M_b, ID^*)$, for a random hidden bit $b \xleftarrow{R} \{0,1\}$, which is sent to $\mathcal{A}$.*
5. *In the guess stage, $\mathcal{A}$ asks new queries as in the find stage but is restricted not to issue a key extraction request on the target identity ID^* and cannot submit C to the decryption/verification oracle for the identity ID^*.*
6. *$\mathcal{A}$ eventually outputs a bit b' and wins if $b' = b$.*

$\mathcal{A}$'s advantage is defined as $Adv(\mathcal{A}) := |2 \times Pr[b' = b] - 1|$.

As the modification of DHIES presented in [28], our hybrid modification of the Boneh-Franklin IBE [10] makes use of a symmetric cipher (i.e. a deterministic length-preserving symmetric encryption scheme) that is chosen-ciphertext secure in the find-then-guess sense instead of one that only withstands passive attacks as required by the Fujisaki-Okamoto transform [23].

Recall that a symmetric encryption scheme is a triple of algorithms $SE = (K, E, D)$. The key generation algorithm K generates a key $k \xleftarrow{R} \{0,1\}^\lambda$ for a security parameter λ. The encryption algorithm E takes a key k and a plaintext m to produce a ciphertext $c = E(k, m)$ while the decryption algorithm takes a key k and a ciphertext c to return $m/reject = D(k, c)$. In the definition of chosen-ciphertext security for symmetric encryption schemes, the adversary can query a decryption oracle $D(k, .)$ as well as an encryption oracle $E(k, .)$. We recall below a security notion for ciphers that is considered in [32] and [28].

Definition 3. *A symmetric cipher (E, D) is secure in the IND-CCA sense if no PPT adversary $\mathcal{A}$ has a non negligible advantage in the following game:*

1. *The challenger chooses a key $k \xleftarrow{R} \{0,1\}^\lambda$.*
2. *$\mathcal{A}$ queries the encryption oracle $E(k, .)$ and the decryption oracle $D(k, .)$.*
2. *$\mathcal{A}$ outputs (m_0, m_1) that were not submitted to $E(k, .)$ (which is deterministic) or obtained from $D(k, .)$ and gets $c^* = E(k, m_b)$ for $b \xleftarrow{R} \{0,1\}$.*

3. $\mathcal{A}$ *issues new queries[1] as in step 2 but is disallowed to ask for the decryption of c^* and the encryptions of m_0 and m_1.*
4. $\mathcal{A}$ *eventually outputs a guess b' for b.*

As usual, her advantage is $Adv^{sym}(\mathcal{A}) := |2 \times Pr[b' = b] - 1|$.

The modes of operations CMC [25] and EME [26] are both length preserving and they were shown to be secure in the sense of IND-CCA if the underlying block cipher is a strong pseudo-random permutation.

3   A Modification of the Boneh-Franklin IBE

This section presents a secure modification of the Boneh-Franklin IBE that is (almost) as efficient as its basic version (that is only secure against chosen-plaintext attacks and was called BasicIdent in [10]) while the original fully secure version of IBE (that was called FullIdent) has computational and bandwidth overheads induced by the application of the Fujisaki-Okamoto transform [23]. The new scheme, that we call Hybrid-IBE, produces shorter ciphertexts than the original FullIdent while it is slightly more efficient for the receiver who does not have to compute a scalar multiplication in $\mathbb{G}_1$ upon decryption.

We have to mention that other transformations such as REACT [29] or GEM [16] could be applied to BasicIdent or to some of its variants to turn them into fully secure identity based encryption schemes without requiring the receiver to

---

Setup: given security parameters k and λ so that λ is polynomial in k, this algorithm chooses a k-bit prime number q, groups $\mathbb{G}_1, \mathbb{G}_2$ of order q, a generator $P \in \mathbb{G}_1$, a bilinear map $e : \mathbb{G}_1 \times \mathbb{G}_1 \to \mathbb{G}_2$, hash functions $H_1 : \{0,1\}^* \to \mathbb{G}_1$, $H_2 : \mathbb{G}_1{}^2 \times \mathbb{G}_2 \to \{0,1\}^\lambda$, as well as a chosen-ciphertext secure cipher (E, D) of keylength λ. It finally picks a master key $\mathsf{mk} := s \xleftarrow{R} \mathbb{Z}_q^*$ and the corresponding public key $P_{pub} := sP \in \mathbb{G}_1$. The system-wide public key is

$$\mathsf{params} := \{q, \mathbb{G}_1, \mathbb{G}_2, P, P_{pub}, e, H_1, H_2, G, n, E, D, \lambda, l\}$$

where n denotes a bound on the size of plaintexts.
Keygen: given a user's identity $\mathsf{ID} \in \{0,1\}^*$, the PKG computes $Q_{\mathsf{ID}} = H_1(\mathsf{ID}) \in \mathbb{G}_1$ and returns a private key $d_{\mathsf{ID}} = sQ_{\mathsf{ID}} \in \mathbb{G}_1$.
Encrypt: to encrypt a message M using P_{pub} and an identity $\mathsf{ID} \in \{0,1\}^*$, compute $Q_{\mathsf{ID}} = H_1(\mathsf{ID}) \in \mathbb{G}_1$, pick a random $r \xleftarrow{R} \mathbb{Z}_q^*$ and output the ciphertext

$$C = \langle rP, E_{SK}(M) \rangle$$

where $SK = H_2(Q_{\mathsf{ID}}, rP, e(P_{pub}, Q_{\mathsf{ID}})^r) \in \{0,1\}^\lambda$
Decrypt: upon receiving a ciphertext $C = \langle A, B \rangle \in \mathbb{G}_1 \times \{0,1\}^n$, the recipient returns $M = D_{SK}(B)$ where $SK = H_2(Q_{\mathsf{ID}}, A, e(A, d_{\mathsf{ID}})) \in \{0,1\}^\lambda$.

Fig. 1. Hybrid-IBE

---

[1] Phan and Pointcheval showed in [32] that post-challenge queries are not of a significant additional help to adversaries.

perform a re-encryption in validity checking concerns. Unfortunately, these transformations should be applied to a OW-PCA[2] variant of BasicIdent for which a part of the ciphertext is obtained by multiplying the message with a $\mathbb{G}_2$ element. As those elements have a representation of at least 1024 bits for recommended parameters (see [10] or [11] for details), ciphertexts would be significantly longer than in our scheme. On the other hand, redundancy-free IBE schemes may also be obtained with the OAEP 3-round generic construction [33] but the security could only be proved in a relaxation of the security model of definition 2 and ciphertexts would also be longer than those of Hybrid-IBE. The security of the latter is claimed by the theorem below.

Theorem 1. *Let us assume that an IND-ID-CCA2 adversary $\mathcal{A}$ has an advantage ϵ against Hybrid-IBE when running in a time τ, asking q_{h_i} queries to oracles h_i $(i = 1, 2)$, q_D decryption queries and q_{KE} key extraction queries. Then, for any $0 \leq \nu \leq \epsilon$, there either exists*

- *a PPT algorithm $\mathcal{B}$ to solve the Gap-BDH problem with an advantage*

$$\epsilon' \geq \frac{1}{e(q_{KE} + 1)} \left(\epsilon - \frac{q_D}{2^k} - \nu \right)$$

  within time $\tau' \leq \tau + (q_{h_1} + q_{KE})\tau_{mult} + q_D\tau_{sym} + q_{h_2}\Phi$
- *an attacker that breaks the IND-CCA security of the symmetric encryption scheme (E, D) with advantage ν within a time τ'*

where e is the base of the natural logarithm, τ_{mult} is the cost of a multiplication in $\mathbb{G}_1$ while τ_{sym} and Φ respectively denote the complexity of a symmetric decryption and the one of a call to the decision oracle.

Proof. Let $(aP, bP, cP, \mathcal{O}_{DBDH})$ be an instance of the Gap-BDH problem where $\mathcal{O}_{DBDH}(.)$ is a decision[3] oracle that, on input (P, aP, bP, cP, ω), answers 1 if $\omega = e(P, P)^{abc}$ and 0 otherwise. We describe an algorithm $\mathcal{B}$ using $\mathcal{A}$ and the latter oracle to compute $e(P, P)^{abc}$.

Algorithm $\mathcal{B}$ initializes $\mathcal{A}$ with the system-wide public key $P_{pub} = aP$ and simulates the adversary's view as explained below. Wlog, we assume that H_1 queries on identities are distinct (otherwise, a list may be used to store inputs and responses) and that any key extraction, decryption or H_2 query involving an identity is preceded by a H_1 query on the same identity.

- H_1 queries: for such a query on an identity ID, $\mathcal{B}$ flips a bit $coin \in \{0, 1\}$ taking the value 0 with probability ξ and the value 1 with probability $1 - \xi$. If $coin = 0$, $\mathcal{B}$ returns $uP \in \mathbb{G}_1$ for some $u \xleftarrow{R} \mathbb{Z}_q^*$ and it answers $u(bP) \in \mathbb{G}_1$ if $coin = 1$. In both cases, a triple $(\text{ID}, u, coin)$ is stored in a list L_1.

---

[2] More precisely, this notion would be an identity based flavored extension of the One-Wayness against Plaintext-Checking Attacks characterizing schemes that remain computationally one-way even in the presence of an oracle deciding whether a given ciphertext encrypts a given message. See [29] for a more formal definition.

[3] In fact, it is a restricted decision oracle as some of its inputs (namely P and $aP \in \mathbb{G}_1$) do not change between all queries. The actual assumption is thus slightly weaker than the Gap-BDH one for which additional degrees of freedom are enabled in queries to the DBDH oracle.

- Private key queries: when the private key associated to an identity $\mathsf{ID} \in \{0,1\}^*$ is requested, $\mathcal{B}$ recovers the entry $(\mathsf{ID}, u, coin)$ from L_1. If $coin = 1$, $\mathcal{B}$ aborts since it is unable to coherently answer the query. Otherwise, it returns uP_{pub} as a private key.
- Queries to $H_2(.)$: according to a proof technique already used in [17, 18, 36] for KEMs, these queries are processed using three lists $L_{2,a}$, $L_{2,b}$ and $L_{2,c}$ which are initially empty:
  - $L_{2,a}$ contains triples $(Q_{\mathsf{ID}_i}, A_i, \omega_i)$ to which a hash value was previously assigned and the corresponding digest $h_{2,i} \in \{0,1\}^\lambda$.
  - $L_{2,b}$ contains triples $(Q_{\mathsf{ID}_i}, A_i, \omega_i)$ such that $(Q_{\mathsf{ID}_i}, A_i, \omega_i, h_{2,i})$ exists in $L_{2,a}$ for $h_{2,i} \in_R \{0,1\}^\lambda$ and $\mathcal{O}_{DBDH}(P, Q_{\mathsf{ID}_i}, A_i, P_{pub}, \omega_i) = 1$.
  - $L_{2,c}$ will contain triples $(Q_{\mathsf{ID}_i}, A_i, h_{2,i})$ for which $\mathcal{B}$ has implicitly assigned a value $h_{2,i} \xleftarrow{R} \{0,1\}^\lambda$ to $H_2(Q_{\mathsf{ID}_i}, A_i, \omega_i)$ although the value ω_i such that $\mathcal{O}_{DBDH}(P, Q_{\mathsf{ID}_i}, A_i, P_{pub}, \omega_i) = 1$ is unknown.

  More precisely, when $\mathcal{A}$ submits a triple $(Q_{\mathsf{ID}}, A, \omega)$ to $H_2(.)$,
  - $\mathcal{B}$ first checks if $L_{2,a}$ contains a tuple $(Q_{\mathsf{ID}}, A, \omega, h_2)$ for some $h_2 \in \{0,1\}^\lambda$ (meaning the a hash value was previously assigned to the same input). If it does, h_2 is returned to $\mathcal{A}$.
  - Otherwise, $\mathcal{B}$ submits $(P, Q_{\mathsf{ID}}, A, P_{pub}, \omega)$ to the $\mathcal{O}_{DBDH}(.)$ oracle which decides whether it is a valid BDH tuple.
    * If it is, then:
      · If $A = cP$ and $coin = 1$ (i.e. $H_1(\mathsf{ID})$ was defined to be $u(bP)$), $\mathcal{B}$ halts and outputs $\omega^{1/u}$ which is the searched solution. We denote by AskH_2 the event that such a hash query is made .
      · Otherwise, $\mathcal{B}$ continues and adds $(Q_{\mathsf{ID}}, A, \omega)$ in $L_{2,b}$.
      · If $L_{2,c}$ contains an entry $(Q_{\mathsf{ID}}, A, h_2)$ for some $h_2 \in \{0,1\}^\lambda$, the tuple $(Q_{\mathsf{ID}}, A, \omega, h_2)$ is stored in $L_{2,a}$ and h_2 is returned to $\mathcal{A}$. Otherwise, $\mathcal{B}$ continues.
    * It selects a string $h_2 \xleftarrow{R} \{0,1\}^\lambda$, inserts the tuple $(Q_{\mathsf{ID}}, A, \omega, h_2)$ into $L_{2,a}$ and answers h_2 to $\mathcal{A}$.
- Decryption queries: upon receiving a ciphertext $C = \langle A, B \rangle \in \mathbb{G}_1 \times \{0,1\}^n$ and an identity ID, the simulator $\mathcal{B}$ does the following:
  - it checks if $(Q_{\mathsf{ID}}, A, \omega)$ exists in $L_{2,b}$ for some $\omega \in \mathbb{G}_2$. If it does, $\mathcal{B}$ retrieves the tuple $(Q_{\mathsf{ID}}, A, \omega, h_2)$ that must be in $L_{2,a}$ and returns the symmetric decryption $D_{h_2}(B)$ of B using $h_2 \in \{0,1\}^\lambda$ as a symmetric key. Otherwise, it continues.
  - It tests whether $L_{2,c}$ contains a triple $(Q_{\mathsf{ID}}, A, h_2)$ for some string $h_2 \in \{0,1\}^\lambda$. In this case, the latter is used to compute a symmetric decryption $D_{h_2}(B)$ that is returned as a result. Otherwise, a random $h_2 \xleftarrow{R} \{0,1\}^\lambda$ is chosen and $(Q_{\mathsf{ID}}, A, h_2)$ is inserted into $L_{2,c}$ ($\mathcal{B}$ thereby implicitly assigns the hash value h_2 to the oracle H_2 on the unique input $(Q_{\mathsf{ID}}, A, \omega)$ for which $\mathcal{O}_{DBDH}(P, Q_{\mathsf{ID}}, A, P_{pub}, \omega) = 1$ although the relevant $\omega \in \mathbb{G}_2$ is still unknown) while $D_{h_2}(B)$ is returned to $\mathcal{A}$.

After the find stage, $\mathcal{A}$ comes with messages $M_0, M_1 \in \{0,1\}^n$ and a target identity ID^*. Let $(\mathsf{ID}^*, u^*, coin^*)$ be the corresponding entry in L_1. If $coin^* = 0$,

$\mathcal{B}$ aborts and reports "failure" because, in such a situation, $\mathcal{A}$ is of no help in $\mathcal{B}$'s endeavour. Otherwise, it sets $A^* = cP \in \mathbb{G}_1$, checks whether $L_{2,c}$ contains an entry $(Q_{\mathsf{ID}^*}, A^*, h_2^*)$ for $Q_{\mathsf{ID}^*} = h_1(\mathsf{ID}^*)$ and some $h_2^* \in \{0,1\}^\lambda$ (if not, $\mathcal{B}$ inserts it for a string $h_2 \xleftarrow{R} \{0,1\}^\lambda$ of its choice) to compute a symmetric encryption $B^* = E_{h_2^*}(M_d)$, for $d \xleftarrow{R} \{0,1\}$, and return the challenge $C^* = \langle A^*, B^* \rangle$. In the unlikely event (its probability is less than $q_D/2^k$) that C^* was previously submitted to the decryption oracle for the identity ID^*, $\mathcal{B}$ aborts.

At the second stage, $\mathcal{B}$ processes all queries as above and $\mathcal{A}$ eventually produces a bit d'. In a real game, we have $\Pr[d' = d] = (\epsilon + 1)/2$ and, provided the simulation is perfect, the latter equality still holds as $\mathcal{A}$'s view is indistinguishable from a real environment. It can be showed that the simulation is imperfect with a probability smaller than $e^{-1}(q_{KE} + 1)^{-1}(1 - q_D/2^k)$. Indeed, let us define the following events:

E_1: $\mathcal{B}$ does not abort as a result of a private key extraction query.
E_2: $\mathcal{B}$ does not abort during the challenge phase because $\mathcal{A}$ chooses a target identity ID^* for which $coin^* = 0$.
E_3: $\mathcal{B}$ does not fail because the constructed challenge C^* was previously queried to the decryption oracle for the identity ID^*.

Those events are independent. We observed that $\Pr[E_3] \geq 1 - q_D/2^k$. We also have $\Pr[E_1] = (1 - 1/(q_{KE} + 1))^{q_{KE}} \geq 1/e$ (as shown in the proof technique of [15]) and $\Pr[E_2] = 1/(q_{KE} + 1)$. It comes that if $\mathsf{Fail} = \neg E_1 \vee \neg E_2 \vee \neg E_3$, we have $\Pr[\neg\mathsf{Fail}] = e^{-1}(q_{KE} + 1)^{-1}(1 - q_D/2^k)$.

On the other hand, if AskH_2 does not occur and thus if $\mathcal{A}$ never makes the relevant $h_2(Q_{\mathsf{ID}^*}, A^*, \omega^*)$ query during the game, the only way for her to produce a correct guess for d is to succeed in a chosen-ciphertext attack against the symmetric cipher (E, D): indeed, in the latter case, each decryption query on a ciphertext $C' = (A^*, B)$, with $B \neq B^*$, for the target identity ID^* corresponds to a symmetric decryption request for a completely random key SK^*. It follows that, if (E, D) is a chosen-ciphertext secure symmetric encryption scheme, the event AskH_2 is very likely to happen and $\mathcal{B}$ is able to extract the Gap-BDH solution.

More formally, for any event E, if we denote by $\mathrm{pr}[E]$ the conditional probability $\Pr[E|\neg\mathsf{Fail}]$, we have

$$\mathrm{pr}[d' = d] = \mathrm{pr}[d' = d|\mathsf{AskH}_2]\mathrm{pr}[\mathsf{AskH}_2] + \mathrm{pr}[d' = d|\neg\mathsf{AskH}_2]\mathrm{pr}[\neg\mathsf{AskH}_2]$$
$$\leq \mathrm{pr}[\mathsf{AskH}_2] + \mathrm{pr}[d' = d|\neg\mathsf{AskH}_2](1 - \mathrm{pr}[\mathsf{AskH}_2])$$

and, since $\mathrm{pr}[d' = d] = (\epsilon + 1)/2$ and $\mathrm{pr}[d' = d|\neg\mathsf{AskH}_2] \leq (\nu + 1)/2$, it comes that

$$\frac{\epsilon + 1}{2} \leq \frac{\nu + 1}{2} + \frac{1 - \nu}{2}\mathrm{pr}[\mathsf{AskH}_2] \leq \frac{\nu + 1}{2} + \frac{1}{2}\mathrm{pr}[\mathsf{AskH}_2]$$

and hence $\mathrm{pr}[\mathsf{AskH}_2] \geq \epsilon - \nu$. When going back to non-conditional probabilities, we find the announced lower bound

$$\Pr[\mathsf{AskH}_2 \wedge \neg\mathsf{Fail}] \geq \frac{1}{e(q_{KE} + 1)}(1 - q_D 2^{-k})(\epsilon - \nu) > \frac{1}{e(q_{KE} + 1)}\left(\epsilon - \frac{q_D}{2^k} - \nu\right)$$

on $\mathcal{B}$'s probability of success.   □

The reason for which the symmetric encryption key is computed using a hash function taking U and Q_{ID} among its input is that it provides us with a more efficient reduction: the security of the scheme can still be proved if the symmetric key is derived from the sole bilinear Diffie-Hellman key but the reduction then involves $q_D q_{H_2}$ calls to the decision oracle. A similar observation was made by Cramer and Shoup [17] in their security proof of the Hashed El Gamal KEM.

The reduction given in theorem 1 is more efficient than the one obtained from the BDH assumption through the Fujisaki-Okamoto tranform [23] in the original IBE. Although our proof relies on a stronger assumption, we believe that this is a fact of interest because a tight reduction from a given assumption should always be preferred to a loose reduction from a potentially weaker assumption as argued in [27]. On the other hand, the Gap-BDH assumption does not appear as a much stronger assumption than the (already non-standard) BDH assumption.

Interestingly, if we compare our security reduction for Hybrid-IBE with the one of Galindo [24] for another variant of the Boneh-Franklin IBE obtained through the first Fujisaki-Okamoto transform [22], we find that ours is as efficient as Galindo's one (which relies on the DBDH assumption) but our Hybrid construction happens to be more efficient (as no re-encryption is needed for the receiver) and produces shorter ciphertexts thanks to the absence of redundancy.

As for Galindo's variant [24], an essentially optimal reduction can be obtained for Hybrid-IBE by applying a trick suggested in [27] at the cost of an additional pairing computation at encryption. We also mention that a similar technique can be applied to a variant of a certificateless encryption scheme [3] proposed in [4].

4   Shortening Ciphertexts in the Multiple-Receiver Case

A recent result [5] of Baek, Safavi-Naini and Susilo showed how to efficiently encrypt a message intended to N distinct recipients from their identities without having to compute more than one pairing. The security of their scheme in the selective-ID model considered in [12] and [9] (that is, the attacker has to announce the set of identities it intends to attack at the beginning of the game even before seeing the master-key of the scheme) was shown to rely on the Gap-BDH assumption and was obtained through the REACT transformation.

It is not hard to see that the construction we used in the previous section can also help to shorten the ciphertexts produced by the single-recipient version of the latter scheme since, in the same way as the use of an IND-CCA cipher instead of an IND-CPA one allows removing the message authentication code (MAC) from the DHIES construction [1] as shown in [28], it also allows removing the checksum from REACT (so that the resulting construction produces as short ciphertexts as the GEM conversion).

Interestingly, the same trick applies to the multiple-receiver case considered in [5] if we accept a loss of efficiency in the security reduction. The latter then involves a number of calls to the decision oracle that depends on the square of the number of adversarial queries. We thus believe the resulting hybrid multiple-recipient scheme (called Hybrid-IBE2 and depicted on figure 2) to be of interest because of its ciphertexts which are about 1184 bits shorter than in [5] as no checksum is needed and there is no need to encode a part of ciphertext as a $\mathbb{G}_2$ element.

4.1   The Selective-ID Security Model for Multiple-Receiver Schemes

The formal definition [5] of a multiple-receiver IBE scheme is identical to the definition of section 2.3 with two essential syntactic differences. First, the encryption algorithm takes as inputs a message M, system-wide parameters params and several identities $(\mathsf{ID}_1, \ldots, \mathsf{ID}_t)$ to produce an encryption C of M under $(\mathsf{ID}_1, \ldots, \mathsf{ID}_t)$. Secondly, the decryption algorithm is given a ciphertext C together with a receiver number $i \in \{1, \ldots, t\}$ and the associated private key d_{ID_i} and returns either a plaintext or a rejection message $\perp$. In the scheme described in this section, a ciphertext is never rejected.

Similarly to the authors of [5], we establish the security of our multiple-receiver construction in the selective-ID model recalled in the next definition. The reason for this is that, as in [5], a security reduction in the strongest model (where target identities are adaptively chosen) involves a loss of concrete security which is exponential in the number of receivers.

Definition 4 ([5]). *A multiple-receiver IBE scheme is said to be selective-ID secure against chosen-ciphertext attacks (or IND-sMID-CCA secure) if no PPT adversary has a non-negligible advantage in the game below.*

1. *The attacker $\mathcal{A}$ outputs a set of target identities $(\mathsf{ID}_1^*, \ldots, \mathsf{ID}_t^*)$.*
2. *The challenger $\mathcal{CH}$ runs the setup algorithm, transmits the public parameters params to $\mathcal{A}$ and keeps the master key mk to itself.*
3. *$\mathcal{A}$ issues a number of key extraction queries (as in definition 2) for identities $\mathsf{ID} \neq \mathsf{ID}_1^*, \ldots, \mathsf{ID}_t^*$ and decryption queries, each of which is denoted by (C, ID_i) for some $i \in \{1, \ldots, t\}$.*
4. *$\mathcal{A}$ produces messages (M_0, M_1) and obtains a challenge ciphertext $C^* = \mathsf{Encrypt}(M_b, \mathsf{params}, \mathsf{ID}_1^*, \ldots, \mathsf{ID}_t^*)$, for a random bit $b \xleftarrow{R} \{0,1\}$, from $\mathcal{CH}$.*
5. *$\mathcal{A}$ issues new queries with the same restriction as in step 3. Additionally, she is disallowed to ask for the decryption of C^* for any one of the target identities $(\mathsf{ID}_1^*, \ldots, \mathsf{ID}_t^*)$.*
6. *$\mathcal{A}$ outputs a bit $b' \in \{0,1\}$ and wins if $b' = b$. Her advantage is again $Adv(\mathcal{A}) = |2 \times Pr[b' = b] - 1|$.*

4.2   The Scheme

A strange feature of Hybrid-IBE2 is that, unlike Hybrid-IBE, it is not a public key encryption scheme without redundancy in the strict sense of [31] and [33]. Indeed, in the simplest single-recipient scenario, elements $\langle U, V, W \rangle$ of the ciphertext space for which $\log_P(U) \neq \log_{Q_{\mathsf{ID}}+Q}(V)$ can never be reached by a correct application of the encryption function and thus do not correspond to

> **Setup:** given security parameters k and λ, this algorithm selects a k-bit prime q, groups $\mathbb{G}_1, \mathbb{G}_2$ of order q, a generator $P \in \mathbb{G}_1$, a bilinear map $e : \mathbb{G}_1 \times \mathbb{G}_1 \to \mathbb{G}_2$, hash functions $H_1 : \{0,1\}^* \to \mathbb{G}_1$, $H_2 : \{0,1\}^* \to \{0,1\}^\lambda$ and an IND-CCA cipher (E, D) of keylength λ. It also picks $Q \xleftarrow{R} \mathbb{G}_1$, a master key $\mathsf{mk} := s \xleftarrow{R} \mathbb{Z}_q^*$ and the public key is $(P_{pub} := sP, Q)$. The public parameters are
>
> $$\mathsf{params} := \{q, \mathbb{G}_1, \mathbb{G}_2, P, Q, P_{pub}, e, H_1, H_2, n, E, D, \lambda\}$$
>
> where n denotes a bound on the size of plaintexts.
> **Keygen** is the same as in Hybrid-IBE.
> **Encrypt:** to encrypt a message M under the system-wide public key P_{pub} for identities $\mathsf{ID}_1, \ldots, \mathsf{ID}_t \in \{0,1\}^*$, compute $Q_{\mathsf{ID}_i} = H_1(\mathsf{ID}_i) \in \mathbb{G}_1$ for $i = 1, \ldots, t$, pick a random $r \xleftarrow{R} \mathbb{Z}_q^*$ and output the ciphertext
>
> $$C = \langle U, V_1, \ldots, V_t, W, \mathcal{L} \rangle = \langle rP, rQ_{\mathsf{ID}_1} + rQ, \ldots, rQ_{\mathsf{ID}_t} + rQ, E_{SK}(M), \mathcal{L} \rangle$$
>
> where $SK = H_2(U, V_1, \ldots, V_t, \mathcal{L}, \omega) \in \{0,1\}^\lambda$ with $\omega = e(P_{pub}, Q)^r$ and $\mathcal{L}$ is a label indicating how each part of ciphertext is associated to each receiver.
> **Decrypt:** given $C = \langle U, V_1, \ldots, V_t, W, \mathcal{L} \rangle \in \mathbb{G}_1^{t+1} \times \{0,1\}^n$ and his private key $d_{\mathsf{ID}_i} = sQ_{\mathsf{ID}_i}$, receiver $i \in \{1, \ldots, t\}$ computes $\omega = e(P_{pub}, V_i)/e(U, d_{\mathsf{ID}_i})$ and returns $M = D_{SK}(W)$ where $SK = H_2(U, V_1, \ldots, V_t, \mathcal{L}, \omega) \in \{0,1\}^\lambda$.

Fig. 2. Hybrid-IBE2

any plaintext. Nevertheless, the decryption oracle never returns an error message indicating a badly formed ciphertext and the receiver does not have to perform a validity checking (that could be made here by solving a DDH problem in $\mathbb{G}_1$) when decrypting a ciphertext. In any case, for an input $\langle U, V, W \rangle$, the decryption algorithm returns a symmetric decryption of W using a hash value of $e(P_{pub}, V)/e(U, d_{\mathsf{ID}})$ and other ciphertext components (it is essential to include them among the inputs of H_2 to prevent the scheme from being malleable) as a symmetric key so that inconsistent ciphertexts are decrypted into random messages but consistently encrypted messages are always correctly decrypted.

From a security point of view, theorem 2 shows that ill-formed ciphertexts do not have to be detected and that their existence does not induce security concerns: in the security proof, the simulator is always able to provide an attacker with a perfectly consistent emulation of the decryption oracle thanks to the power of the decision oracle. This result shows that the existence of incorrectly formed ciphertexts does not necessarily require the recipient to perform a validity checking for chosen-ciphertext security purposes.

Theorem 2. *Let $\mathcal{A}$ be an adversary having an advantage ϵ against the IND-sMID-CCA2 security of Hybrid-IBE2 when running in a time τ, making q_{H_i} queries to random oracles H_i $(i = 1, 2)$, q_D decryption queries and q_{KE} private key extraction queries. Then, for any $0 \leq \nu \leq \epsilon$, there either exists*

— a PPT algorithm $\mathcal{B}$ to solve the Gap-BDH problem with an advantage

$$\epsilon' \geq \epsilon - \nu - \frac{q_D}{2^k}$$

within time $\tau' \leq \tau + (q_{H_1} + q_{KE})\tau_{mult} + (2q_D + 1)q_{H_2}\Phi + q_D(\tau_{sym} + \tau_p)$

- an attacker that breaks the IND-CCA security of the symmetric encryption scheme (E, D) with an advantage ν within a time τ'

where τ_{mult} is the time to perform a multiplication in $\mathbb{G}_1$, τ_{sym} denotes the cost of a symmetric decryption, τ_p the cost of a pairing evaluation and Φ the complexity of a call to the decision oracle.

Proof. Given an instance $(aP, bP, cP, \mathcal{O}_{DBDH})$ of the Gap-BDH problem, $\mathcal{B}$ launches the adversary $\mathcal{A}$ who first announces the set of identities $(\mathsf{ID}_1^*, \dots, \mathsf{ID}_t^*)$ that she intends to attack. She then obtains the domain-public key $(P_{pub} = aP, Q = bP)$ from $\mathcal{B}$ that simulates her view as follows.

- queries $H_1(\mathsf{ID}_i)$: $\mathcal{B}$ draws $l_i \xleftarrow{R} \mathbb{Z}_q^*$. If $\mathsf{ID}_i = \mathsf{ID}_j^*$ for some $j \in \{1, \dots, t\}$, $\mathcal{B}$ returns $l_i P - Q$. Otherwise, it responds with $l_i P$ (so that the associated private key $d_{\mathsf{ID}_i} = l_i(aP)$ is always computable).

$H_2(.)$ queries and decryption queries are handled using two lists L_2 and L_2' which are initially empty.

- For decryption queries on a ciphertext $C = \langle U, V_1, \dots, V_t, W, \mathcal{L} \rangle$ for an identity ID_i and a receiver number $i \in \{1, \dots, t\}$, the simulator's strategy is to always return a symmetric decryption of W under a symmetric key that appears (or will subsequently appear) to $\mathcal{A}$ as a hash value of the tuple

$$(U, V_1, \dots, V_t, \mathcal{L}, e(P_{pub}, V_i)/e(U, d_{\mathsf{ID}_i}))$$

according to the specification of the decryption algorithm under recipient i's private key d_{ID_i}. To do so, $\mathcal{B}$ first retrieves $Q_{\mathsf{ID}_i} = H_1(\mathsf{ID}_i) \in \mathbb{G}_1$ and then searches list L_2 for entries of the form $(U, V_1, \dots, V_t, \mathcal{L}, \omega_j, \kappa_j)$ for pairs $(\omega_j, \kappa_j) \in \mathbb{G}_2 \times \{0,1\}^\lambda$ indexed by $j \in \{1, \dots, q_{h_2}\}$.
  - For each one of such entries, $\mathcal{B}$ checks whether

$$\mathcal{O}_{DBDH}(P, Q_{\mathsf{ID}}, U, P_{pub}, e(P_{pub}, V_i)/\omega_j) = 1$$

(meaning that $\omega_j = e(P_{pub}, V_i)/e(U, d_{\mathsf{ID}_i})$). If the unique $\omega \in \mathbb{G}_2$ satisfying the latter relation is found, $\mathcal{B}$ uses the corresponding κ to compute $M = D_\kappa(W)$ and return the result to $\mathcal{A}$.
  - If no entry of L_2 satisfies the above condition, $\mathcal{B}$ draws $\kappa \xleftarrow{R} \{0,1\}^\lambda$, stores the information $(U, V_1, \dots, V_t, \mathcal{L}, ?, \kappa, e(P_{pub}, V_i), Q_{\mathsf{ID}_i})$, where $?$ denotes an unknown $\mathbb{G}_2$ element, into L_2' and returns $M = D_\kappa(W)$ as a plaintext.
- $H_2(.)$ queries: for such a query on an input $(U, V_1, \dots, V_t, \mathcal{L}, \omega)$, $\mathcal{B}$ halts and outputs ω as a result if $\mathcal{O}_{DBDH}(P, aP, bP, cP, \omega) = 1$. Otherwise, it first checks whether H_2 was previously defined for that input. If so, the previously defined value is returned. Otherwise, $\mathcal{B}$ checks if the auxiliary list L_2' contains an entry of the form $(U, V_1, \dots, V_t, \mathcal{L}, ?, \kappa, \gamma, Q_{\mathsf{ID}_i})$ for some pair $(\kappa, \gamma) \in \{0,1\}^\lambda \times \mathbb{G}_2$ and some $Q_{\mathsf{ID}_i} \in \mathbb{G}_1$.

- If it does, $\mathcal{B}$ checks if $\mathcal{O}_{DBDH}(P, Q_{\mathsf{ID}_i}, U, P_{pub}, \gamma/\omega) = 1$ for each one of such triples $(\kappa, \gamma, Q_{\mathsf{ID}_i})$. If the decision oracle positively answers for one of them, the corresponding κ is returned as a hash value.
- Otherwise, $\mathcal{B}$ returns a randomly sampled string $\kappa \xleftarrow{R} \{0,1\}^\lambda$

In both case, $\mathcal{B}$ stores the information $(U, V_1, \ldots, V_t, \mathcal{L}, \omega, \kappa)$ in L_2.

In the challenge step, $\mathcal{A}$ produces messages $M_0, M_1 \in \{0,1\}^n$. The simulator $\mathcal{B}$ computes $U^* = cP, V_1^* = l_1^*(cP), \ldots, V_t^* = l_t^*(cP)$ and the corresponding label $\mathcal{L}^*$ where $l_1^*, \ldots, l_t^* \in \mathbb{Z}_q^*$ are finite field elements for which $H_1(\mathsf{ID}_j^*) = l_j^* P - Q$ for $j \in \{1, \ldots, t\}$. It then chooses a random $\kappa^* \xleftarrow{R} \{0,1\}^\lambda$ and computes $W^* = E_{\kappa^*}(M_d)$ for $d \xleftarrow{R} \{0,1\}$. The challenge ciphertext is set to $C^* = \langle U^*, V_1^*, \ldots, V_t^*, W^*, \mathcal{L}^* \rangle$. In the unlikely event (its probability is less than $q_D/2^k$) that C^* was queried to the decryption oracle at the find stage, $\mathcal{B}$ aborts.

All queries of the guess stage are processed as in the find stage and $\mathcal{A}$ eventually produces a bit d'. From a similar analysis to the one of theorem 1, we find that the relevant query $H_2(U^*, V_1^*, \ldots, V_t^*, \mathcal{L}^*, \omega^*)$, where $\omega^* = e(P, P)^{abc}$ is very likely to be made by $\mathcal{A}$ during the simulation. The Gap-BDH solution can thus be detected when handling $H_2(.)$ queries. $\qquad\square$

5   Another Way to Avoid the Re-encryption in IBE

This section presents an alternative method to achieve the chosen-ciphertext security in the original IBE system [10] without requiring a re-encryption for validity checking upon decryption and without having to encode of piece of ciphertext as a long $\mathbb{G}_2$ element. This method introduces a minimal amount of redundancies in ciphertexts (only 160 additional bits are needed w.r.t to BasicIdent) and is actually an extension of a construction originally designed by Bellare and Rogaway [6] for trapdoor permutations. Recall that this construction produces ciphertexts of the form $E(m, r) = \langle f(r), m \oplus G(r), H(m, r) \rangle$, where r denotes a random coin, f is a trapdoor permutation and G, H are random oracles. Actually, this construction (that was previously generalized into a generic conversion in [29]) can be instantiated with more general number theoretic primitives. For example, it can be applied to the El Gamal [19] cryptosystem and to the Boneh-Franklin identity based encryption scheme. The resulting scheme is called XBR-IBE (as a shorthand for eXtended Bellare-Rogaway like IBE) and depicted on figure 3.

As for the schemes described in the previous sections, the security relies on the Gap-BDH assumption. The security proof is omitted here because of space limitation but will be given in the full version of this paper.

Theorem 3. *If an IND-ID-CCA2 adversary $\mathcal{A}$ has advantage ϵ against XBR-IBE in a time τ when asking q_{h_i} queries to oracles h_i ($i = 1, 2, 3$), q_D decryption queries and q_{KE} private key queries, then a PPT algorithm $\mathcal{B}$ can solve the Gap-BDH problem with an advantage $\epsilon' \geq (e(q_{KE}+1))^{-1}(\epsilon - \frac{q_D}{2^{k-1}})$ within time $\tau' \leq \tau + (q_{h_1} + q_{KE})\tau_{mult} + 2(q_{h_2} + q_{h_3})\Phi$ where τ_{mult} is the cost of a scalar*

---

298 Benoît Libert and Jean-Jacques Quisquater

Setup: is the same as in Hybrid-IBE except that no cipher is needed and hash functions are $H_1 : \{0,1\}^* \to \mathbb{G}_1$, $H_2 : \{0,1\}^* \to \{0,1\}^{k_1}$ and $H_3 : \mathbb{G}_2 \to \{0,1\}^n$ where n still denotes the size of plaintexts and k_1 is a security parameter which is polynomial in $k = \log(|\mathbb{G}_1|)$.

Keygen is the same as in Hybrid-IBE and Hybrid-IBE2.

Encrypt: to encrypt a message M using an identity $\mathsf{ID} \in \{0,1\}^*$, compute $Q_{\mathsf{ID}} = H_1(\mathsf{ID}) \in \mathbb{G}_1$, pick a random $r \xleftarrow{R} \mathbb{Z}_q^*$ and output the ciphertext

$$C = \langle rP, m \oplus H_3(g_{\mathsf{ID}}^r), H_2(m\|rP\|\mathsf{ID}\|g_{\mathsf{ID}}^r)\rangle$$

where $g_{\mathsf{ID}} = e(P_{pub}, Q_{\mathsf{ID}}) \in \mathbb{G}_2$.

Decrypt: given $C = \langle U, V, W\rangle$, compute $\omega = e(U, d_{\mathsf{ID}})$ and $m = V \oplus H_3(\omega) \in \{0,1\}^n$. Output $m \in \{0,1\}^n$ if $W = H_2(m\|U\|\mathsf{ID}\|\omega)$ and $\perp$ otherwise.

Fig. 3. XBR-IBE

multiplication in $\mathbb{G}_1$, Φ denotes the cost of a call to the DBDH oralce and e is the base of the natural logarithm.

Interestingly, a similar method also applies to Baek et al.'s multiple-receiver scheme [5] and yields shorter ciphertexts (about 1024 bits are spared) which have the form $\langle rP, V_1, \ldots, V_t, m \oplus H_3(\omega), H_2(m, rP, V_1, \ldots, V_t, \mathcal{L}, \omega), \mathcal{L}\rangle$ where $V_i = rH_1(\mathsf{ID}_i) + rQ$ for $i = 1, \ldots, t$, $\omega = e(P_{pub}, Q)^r$ and the label $\mathcal{L}$ contains receivers'identities $\mathsf{ID}_1, \ldots, \mathsf{ID}_t$. The security of this second multiple-receiver scheme still relies the Gap-BDH assumption.

6 Conclusion

We presented two methods to avoid the re-encryption in chosen-ciphertext secure IBE systems. Among those methods, the hybrid construction yields more compact ciphertexts thanks to the absence of redundancies. We also explained how to shorten ciphertexts produced by a multiple-receiver IBE scheme. We finally gave an example of secure public key encryption scheme for which no validity checking is needed at decryption although the encryption mapping is not surjective.

Acknowledgements

Thanks to Damien Vergnaud for his helpful comments and to the anonymous referees for their useful feedback.

References

1. M. Abdalla, M. Bellare, P. Rogaway, *The Oracle Diffie-Hellman Assumptions and an Analysis of DHIES*, in Topics in Cryptology – CT-RSA'01, LNCS 2020, pp. 143–158, Springer, 2001.

2. M. Abe, *Combining Encryption and Proof of Knowledge in the Random Oracle Model*, Topics in Cryptology – CT-RSA'02, LNCS 2271, Springer, pp. 277–289, 2002.
3. S.-S. Al-Riyami , K.G. Paterson, *Certificateless Public Key Cryptography*, in Advances in Cryptology – Asiacrypt'03, LNCS 2894, pp. 452–473, 2003.
4. S.S. Al-Riyami , K.G. Paterson, *CBE from CL-PKE: A Generic Construction and Efficient Schemes* , in proc. of PKC'05, LNCS 3386, pp. 398–415, Springer, 2005.
5. J. Baek, R. Safavi-Naini, W. Susilo, *Efficient Mutli-Receiver Identity-Based Encryption and Its Application to Broadcast Encryption,* in proc. of PKC'05, LNCS 3386, pp. 380–397, Springer, 2005.
6. M. Bellare, P. Rogaway, *Random oracles are practical: A paradigm for designing efficient protocols*, in proc. of the 1st ACM Conference on Computer and Communications Security, pp. 62-73, 1993.
7. M. Bellare, P. Rogaway, *Optimal asymmetric encryption – How to encrypt with RSA*, in Advances in Cryptology – Eurocrypt 94, LNCS 950, Springer, pp. 92–111, 1995.
8. K. Bentahar, P. Farshim, J. Malone-Lee, N.P. Smart, *Generic Constructions of Identity-Based and Certificateless KEMs*, Cryptology ePrint Archive Report, available from http://eprint.iacr.org/2005/058.
9. D. Boneh, X. Boyen, *Efficient Selective-ID Secure Identity Based Encryption Without Random Oracles*, in Advances in Cryptology – Eurocrypt'04, LNCS 3027, Springer,pp. 223–238, 2004.
10. D. Boneh, M. Franklin, *Identity Based Encryption From the Weil Pairing*, in Advances in Cryptology – Crypto'01, LNCS 2139, pp. 213–229, Springer, 2001.
11. D. Boneh, B. Lynn, H. Shacham, *Short signatures from the Weil pairing*, in Advances in Cryptology – Asiacrypt'01, LNCS 2248, pp. 514–532. Springer, 2001.
12. R. Canetti, S. Halevi, J. Katz, *A Forward Secure Public Key Encryption Scheme*, in Advances in Cryptology – Eurocrypt'03, LNCS 2656, pp. 254–271, Springer, 2003.
13. Y. Chui, K. Kobara, H. Imai, *A Generic Conversion with Optimal Redundancy*, in Topics in Cryptology – CT-RSA'05, LNCS 3376, Springer, pp. 104–117, 2005.
14. C. Cocks, *An Identity Based Encryption Scheme Based on Quadratic Residues*, 8th IMA International Conference, LNCS 2260, Springer, pp. 360-363, 2001.
15. J.-S. Coron. *On the Exact Security of Full Domain Hash*, in Advances in Cryptology – Crypto'00, LNCS 1880, pp. 229–235, 2000.
16. J.-S. Coron, H. Handschuh, M. Joye, P. Paillier, D. Pointcheval, C. Tymen, *GEM: a Generic Chosen-Ciphertext Secure Encryption Method*, in Topics in Cryptology – CT-RSA'02, LNCS 2271, pp. 263–276, Springer, 2002.
17. R. Cramer, V. Shoup, *Design and analysis of practical public-key encryption schemes secure against adaptive chosen ciphertext attack*, in SIAM Journal of Computing 33:167-226, 2003.
18. A. Dent, *A Designer's Guide to KEMs*, in Cryptography and Coding, 9th IMA International Conference, pp. 133–151, Springer, 2003.
19. T. El Gamal, *A Public Key Cryptosystem and a Signature Scheme Based on Discrete Logarithms* , Advances in Cryptology – Crypto'84, LNCS 0196, pp. 10–18, Springer, 1984.
20. P.A. Fouque, D. Pointcheval, *Threshold Cryptosystems Secure against Chosen-Ciphertext Attacks*, Advances in Cryptology – Asiacrypt'01, LNCS 2248, Springer, pp. 351–368, 2001.
21. E. Fujisaki, *Plaintext Simulatability*, Cryptology ePrint Archive Report, available from http://eprint.iacr.org/2004/218.

22. E. Fujisaki, T. Okamoto, *How to Enhance the Security of Public-Key Encryption at Minimum Cost*, in proc. of PKC'99, LNCS 1560, pp. 53–68. Springer, 1999.
23. E. Fujisaki and T. Okamoto, *Secure integration of asymmetric and symmetric encryption schemes*, in Advances in Cryptology – Crypto'99, LNCS 1666, pp. 537–554. Springer, 1999.
24. D. Galindo, *The Exact Security of Pairing Based Encryption and Signature Schemes*, talk at INRIA Workshop on Provable Security, 2004.
25. S. Halevi, P. Rogaway, *A tweakable enciphering mode*, in Advances in Cryptology – Crypto'03, LNCS 2729, pp. 482–499, Springer, 2003.
26. S. Halevi, P. Rogaway, *A parallelizable enciphering mode*, in Topics in Cryptology – CT-RSA'04, LNCS 2964, pp. 292–304, Springer, 2004
27. J. Katz, N. Wang, *Efficiency improvements for signature schemes with tight security reductions*, in 10th ACM Conference on Computer and Communications Security, pp. 155–164, 2003.
28. K. Kurosawa, T. Matsuo, *How to Remove MAC from DHIES*, in proc. of ACISP 2004, LNCS 3108, pp. 236–247, Springer, 2004.
29. T. Okamoto, D. Pointcheval, *REACT: Rapid Enhanced-Security Asymmetric Cryptosystem Transform*, in Topics in Cryptology – CT-RSA'01, LNCS 2020, pp. 159–174, Springer, 2001.
30. T. Okamoto, D. Pointcheval, *The Gap-Problems: A New Class of Problems for the Security of Cryptographic Schemes*, in proc. of PKC'01, LNCS 1992, pp. 104–118, Springer, 2001.
31. D.H. Phan, D. Pointcheval, *Chosen-Ciphertext Security without Redundancy*, in Advances in Cryptology – Asiacrypt'03, LNCS 2894, pp. 1–18, Springer, 2003.
32. D.H. Phan, D. Pointcheval, *About the Security of Ciphers (Semantic Security and Pseudo-Random Permutations)*, Selected Areas in Cryptography (SAC'04), pp. 185–200, LNCS 3357, Springer, 2005.
33. D.H. Phan, D. Pointcheval, *OAEP 3-Round: A Generic and Secure Asymmetric Encryption Padding*, in Advances in Cryptology – Asiacrypt'04, LNCS 3329, pp. 63–78, Springer, 2004.
34. C. Rackoff, D. Simon, *Non-interactive zero-knowledge proof of knowledge and chosen ciphertext attack*, in Advances in Cryptology – Crypto'91, LNCS 576, Springer, pp. 433–444, 1991.
35. A. Shamir, *Identity Based Cryptosystems and Signature Schemes*, in Advances in Cryptology – Crypto' 84, LNCS 196, pp. 47-53, Springer, 1984.
36. V. Shoup, *A proposal for the ISO standard for public-key encryption (version 2.1)*, manuscript available from http://shoup.net/, 2001.

OACerts: Oblivious Attribute Certificates

Jiangtao Li and Ninghui Li

CERIAS and Department of Computer Science, Purdue University
250 N. University Street, West Lafayette, IN 47907
{jtli,ninghui}@cs.purdue.edu

Abstract. We propose Oblivious Attribute Certificates (OACerts), an attribute certificate scheme in which a certificate holder can select which attributes to use and how to use them. In particular, a user can use attribute values stored in an OACert obliviously, i.e., the user obtains a service if and only if the attribute values satisfy the policy of the service provider, yet the service provider learns nothing about these attribute values. This way, the service provider's access control policy is enforced in an oblivious fashion.

To enable the oblivious access control using OACerts, we propose a new cryptographic primitive called Oblivious Commitment-Based Envelope (OCBE). In an OCBE scheme, Bob has an attribute value committed to Alice and Alice runs a protocol with Bob to send an envelope (encrypted message) to Bob such that: (1) Bob can open the envelope if and only if his committed attribute value satisfies a predicate chosen by Alice, (2) Alice learns nothing about Bob's attribute value. We develop provably secure and efficient OCBE protocols for the Pedersen commitment scheme and predicates such as $=, \geq, \leq, >, <, \neq$ as well as logical combinations of them.

1 Introduction

In Trust Management and certificate-based access control systems [3, 11, 19, 34, 35], access control decisions are based on attributes of requesters, which are established by digitally signed certificates. Each certificate associates a public key with the key holder's identity and/or attributes such as employer, group membership, credit card information, birth-date, citizenship, and so on. Because these certificates are digitally signed, they can serve to introduce strangers to one another without online contact with the attribute authorities. Privacy becomes an important concern in the use of Internet and web services. When the attribute information in a certificate is sensitive, the certificate holder may want to disclose only the information that is absolutely necessary to obtain services. Consider the following example.

Example 1. A senior citizen Bob requests from a service provider Alice a document that can be accessed freely by senior citizens. Bob wants to use his digital driver license to prove that he is entitled to free access. Bob's driver license certificate has fields for an identification number, expiration date, name, address, birth-date, and so on; and Bob would like to reveal as little information as possible.

In the above example, it might seem that Bob needs to reveal at least the fact that he is a senior citizen, i.e., his birth-date is before a certain date. However, even this

J. Ioannidis, A. Keromytis, and M.Yung (Eds.): ACNS 2005, LNCS 3531, pp. 301–317, 2005.

seemingly minimal amount of information disclosure can be avoided. Suppose that the document is encrypted under a key and the encrypted document is freely available to everyone. Further suppose a protocol exists such that after the protocol is executed between Alice and Bob, Bob obtains the key if and only if the birth-date in his driver license is before a certain date and Alice learns nothing about Bob's birth-date. Under these conditions, Alice can perform access control based on Bob's attribute values while being oblivious about Bob's attribute information.

We call this *oblivious access control*, because Alice's access control policies for her resources are enforced without Alice learning any information about Bob's certified attribute values, not even whether Bob satisfies her policy or not. To enable such oblivious access control, we propose Oblivious Attribute Certificates (OACerts), a scheme for using certificates to document sensitive attributes. The basic idea of OACerts is quite simple. Instead of storing attribute values directly in the certificates, a certificate authority (CA) stores the cryptographic commitments [12, 16, 23, 39] of these values in the certificates. Using OACerts, a user can select *which* attributes to use as well as *how* to use them. An attribute value in an OACert can be used in several ways: (1) by opening a commitment and revealing the attribute value, (2) by using zero-knowledge proof protocols [5, 13, 18, 37] to prove that the attribute value satisfies a condition without revealing other information, and (3) by running a protocol so that the user obtains a message only when the attribute value satisfies a condition, without revealing any information about the attribute value. The idea of storing cryptographic commitments of attribute values in certificates was used in anonymous credentials [7–10, 36]; however, we are not aware of prior work on the oblivious usage of such attribute values.

In Example 1, suppose that the driver-license certificate that Bob has is an OACert. With attribute values committed rather than stored in the clear in her certificates, Bob can send his certificate to Alice without revealing his birth-date or any other attribute information. Using zero-knowledge proof protocols [5, 13, 18, 37], Bob can prove to Alice that his committed birth-date is before a certain date without revealing any other information. However, our goal is that Alice should learn nothing about Bob's birth-date, not even whether Bob is a senior citizen or not. To enable oblivious access control, we need to solve the following two-party Secure Function Evaluation (SFE) problem:

Problem 1. Let commit be a commitment algorithm, let Params be public parameters for commit, and Pred be a public predicate. Let a be a private number (Bob's attribute value), $c = \mathsf{commit}_{\mathsf{Params}}(a, r)$ be a commitment of a under the parameters Params with a random number r, and M be a private message (Alice wants Bob to see M if and only if a satisfies Pred). Alice and Bob jointly compute a family F of functions, parameterized by commit and Pred. Both parties have commit, Pred, Params, and c. Alice has private input M. Bob has private input a and r. The function F is defined as follows.

$$F[\mathsf{commit}, \mathsf{Pred}]_{Alice}(\mathsf{Params}, c, M, a, r) = 0$$
$$F[\mathsf{commit}, \mathsf{Pred}]_{Bob}(\mathsf{Params}, c, M, a, r)$$
$$= \begin{cases} M & \text{if } c = \mathsf{commit}_{\mathsf{Params}}(a, r) \land \mathsf{Pred}(a) = \text{true}; \\ 0 & \text{otherwise.} \end{cases}$$

where $F[\text{commit}, \text{Pred}]_{Alice}$ represents Alice's output, $F[\text{commit}, \text{Pred}]_{Bob}$ represents Bob's output. In other words, our goal is that Alice learns nothing and Bob learns M only when his committed attribute value satisfies the predicate Pred.

The preceding problem can be solved using general solutions to two-party SFE [25, 26, 44]; however, the general solutions are inefficient, as commitment verification is done within the SFE. We propose an Oblivious Commitment Based Envelope (OCBE) scheme that solves Problem 1 efficiently. Formal definition of OCBE will be given in Section 4. Informally, an OCBE scheme enables a sender Alice to send an envelope (encrypted message) to a receiver Bob, such that Bob can open the envelope if and only if his committed value satisfies the predicate. An OCBE scheme is *oblivious* if at the end of the protocol the sender cannot learn any information about the receiver's committed value. An OCBE scheme is *secure against the receiver* if a receiver whose committed value does not satisfy the predicate cannot open the envelope.

We develop efficient OCBE protocols for the Pedersen commitment scheme [39] and six kinds of comparison predicates: $=, \neq, <, >, \leq, \geq$, as well as conjunctions and disjunctions of multiple predicates. These predicates seem to be the most useful ones for testing attribute values in access control policies. We present a protocol (called EQ-OCBE) for equality predicates and a protocol (called GE-OCBE) for greater-than-or-equal-to predicates and prove that these protocols are provably secure in the Random Oracle Model [2]. These protocols use cryptography hash functions to efficiently derive symmetric encryption keys from a shared secret, and random oracles are used to model such usage of hash functions. We also show that it is easy to construct OCBE protocols for other comparison predicates using variants of EQ-OCBE, GE-OCBE. The contributions of this paper are as follows.

- We introduce the notions of OACerts and OCBE, which together enable oblivious access control. OACerts and OCBE may be of interests in other applications as well.
- We present efficient and provably secure OCBE protocols for the Pedersen commitment scheme [39] and several kinds of comparison predicates.

The rest of this paper is organized as follows. Section 2 discusses the related work. Section 3 presents the architecture and application of OACerts. Section 4 gives a formal definition of OCBE. Section 5 reviews the Pedersen commitment scheme. Section 6 presents several efficient and provably secure OCBE protocols. Section 7 describes our implementation and performance measurements. Section 8 concludes our paper.

2   Related Work

Recent works on using cryptographic protocols for certificate-based access control include Hidden Credentials [6, 22, 28], Secret Handshakes [1], and Oblivious Signature Based Envelope [32]. Using any of these schemes, the service provider Alice could send an encrypted message to a client Bob such that Bob can decrypt if and only if he has certificates whose contents are the same as those identified by Alice's policy; at the same time, Alice does not know whether Bob has those certificates or not. (In

Secret handshakes [1], Alice computes a key such that Bob can compute if and only if Bob has the required certificate.) These schemes can implement oblivious access control when Alice's policies have very specific forms. In Example 1, if Alice's policy is that Bob's birth-date is April 1st, 1974, then oblivious access control can be achieved using these existing schemes, as Alice could identify the contents of the certificates that would enable Bob to satisfy her policy. However, for the policy in Example 1 (birth-date in a certain range) where many possible attribute values would satisfy a policy, these schemes do not work well.

Our work is also closely related to anonymous credentials [7–10, 36]. Indeed, the ideas of storing commitments of attribute values in certificates and using zero-knowledge proofs to prove properties of these values appeared in the literature on anonymous credentials, e.g. [7]. These schemes differ from OACerts in that they provide orthogonal privacy protections. None of the existing anonymous credential schemes enables oblivious access control as the verifier learns whether the prover satisfies her policy or not. On the other hand, anonymous credentials enable Bob to use a credential anonymously, i.e., Alice and other service providers cannot link together transactions in which Bob's credential is used. For such protection to make sense, anonymous communication channels are required. The OACerts scheme does not provide anonymity protection and therefore does not require anonymous communication channels. Furthermore, anonymous credential schemes tend to involve protocols dramatically different from existing public-key infrastructure standards, whereas the OACerts scheme is compatible with existing standards, such as X.509 [29].

Crescenzo et al. [15] introduced a variant of oblivious transfer called Conditional Oblivious Transfer (Conditional OT), in which Alice and Bob each has a private input and shares with each other a public predicate that is evaluated over the private inputs. In the Conditional OT of a bit b from Alice to Bob, Bob receives the bit only when the predicate holds; furthermore, Alice learns nothing about Bob's private input or the output of the predicate. Crescenzo et al. [15] developed an efficient protocol for a special case of Conditional OT where the predicate is greater-than-or-equal-to. OCBE can be viewed as another special case of the Conditional OT problem, in which Alice has no private inputs, the commitment c of Bob's private input a is made public, and the public predicate for this Conditional OT is a conjunction of two conditions: (1) Bob's private input a must be the value he committed in c, and (2) Bob's private input a must also satisfy a predicate (e.g., greater-than-or-equal-to some value). The additional requirement of (1) makes OCBE quite different from Conditional OT for greater-than-or-equal-to predicate; therefore, the solution in [15] cannot apply to OCBE.

Crépeau [14] introduced the notion of Committed Oblivious Transfer (COT). In COT, Alice commits two bits: a_0 and a_1, and Bob commits a bit b. All three committed values are public knowledge. The goal of COT is enable Bob to learn a_b without learning anything else, while Alice learns nothing. Garay et al. [24] gave an efficient construction of COT in the universal composability framework. OCBE differs from COT in that Bob's input in OCBE is an integer whereas Bob's input in COT is a single bit. Furthermore, because the predicate in OCBE could be arbitrary, results in COT cannot apply directly to our OCBE protocol.

Our work is related to zero-knowledge proof protocols [5, 13, 18, 37] that prove a committed value satisfies some property. Our GE-OCBE protocol has similarities with the range proof protocol in [18, 37], which proves that a committed value lies within a range. Also, the details of our GE-OCBE protocol are reminiscent of the techniques used in the oblivious transfer protocols [38, 41] and the comparison method for millionaires [21].

3   Architecture and Applications of OACerts and OCBE

In this section, we present the architecture of OACerts and OCBE and outline their applications.

Architecture. There are three kinds of parties in the OACerts scheme: certificate authorities (CA's), certificate holders, and service providers. A CA issues OACerts for certificate holders. Each CA and each certificate holder has a unique public-private key pair. A service provider, when providing services to a certificate holder, performs access control based on the attributes of the certificate holder, as certified in OACerts.

An OACert is a digitally signed assertion about the certificate holder by a CA. Each OACert contains one or more attributes. We use $attr_1, \ldots, attr_m$ to denote the m attribute names in an OACert, and $v_1, \ldots, v_m$ to denote the corresponding m attribute values. Let $c_i = \mathsf{commit}_{\mathsf{Params}}(v_i, r_i)$ be the commitment of attribute value v_i for $1 \leq i \leq m$ with r_i being the secret random number. The attribute part of the certificate consists of a list of m entries, each entry is a tuple $\langle attr_i, c_i \rangle$. When the commitment scheme used is secure, the certificate itself does not leak any information about the sensitive attributes. Thus, an OACert's content can be made public. A certificate holder can show his OACerts to others without worrying about the secrecy of his attributes.

OACerts can be implemented on existing public-key infrastructure standards, such as X.509 Public Key Infrastructure Certificate [4, 29] and X.509 Attribute Certificate [20]. The commitments can be stored in X.509v3 extension fields, in which case a certificate includes also the following fields: serial number, validity period, issuer name, user name, certificate holder's public key, and so on. The distribution and revocation of OACerts can be handled using existing infrastructure and techniques. See Section 7 for our implementation and performance measurements of OAcerts.

There are four basic protocols in the OACerts scheme:

- **CA-Setup:** A CA picks a signature scheme Sig with a public-private key pair $(K_{\mathrm{CA}}, K_{\mathrm{CA}}^{-1})$, and a commitment scheme commit with public parameters Params. The public parameters of the CA are $\{\mathsf{Sig}, K_{\mathrm{CA}}, \mathsf{commit}, \mathsf{Params}\}$.
- **Issue Certificate:** A CA uses this protocol to issue an OACert to a user. A user Bob generates a public-private key pair (K_B, K_B^{-1}) and sends to the CA a certificate request that includes his public key K_B and attributes information $(attr_1, v_1), \ldots, (attr_m, v_m)$, and is signed by K_B^{-1}. After the CA verifies the correctness of $v_1, \ldots, v_m$ (most likely using off-line methods), it issues an OACert for Bob. In this process, the CA computes $c_i = \mathsf{commit}_{\mathsf{Params}}(v_i, r_i)$ and sends the certificate along with the secrets $r_1, \ldots, r_m$ to Bob. Bob stores the certificate and stores the values $(v_1, r_1), \ldots, (v_m, r_m)$ together with his private key K_B^{-1}. The role of the CA here is similar to the role of a CA in the traditional Public Key Infrastructure.

- **Alice-Bob Initialization:** Bob, a certificate holder, establishes a secure communication channel with Alice, a service provider, and at the same time proves to Alice the ownership of an OACert. In this protocol, Alice checks the signature and the validity period of the certificate, then verifies that the certificate has not been revoked (using, e.g., standard techniques in [29]). Alice also verifies that Bob possesses the private key corresponding to K_B in the OACert. All these can be done using standard protocols such as TLS/SSL [40]. Bob then requests the decryption key for an encrypted document, and Alice sends Bob her policy.
- **Alice-Bob Interaction:** Alice and Bob runs an interactive protocol so that in the end Bob obtains the decryption key if and only if his committed attribute satisfies Alice's policy.

Applications of OACerts. In addition to enabling oblivious access control, OACerts and OCBE can also be used to break policy cycles (see [32] for definition) in automated trust negotiation [42, 43, 45]. Consider the following scenario where Alice and Bob want to exchange their salary certificates. Alice's policy says that she can show her salary certificate only to those whose salary is great than $100k. Similarly, Bob will reveal his certificate only to other who earns more than $80k a year. Using current trust negotiation techniques, neither Alice nor Bob is willing to present her/his certificate first. The technique developed in [32] does not work well here neither, because the salary requirement in the policies is a range, not a specific value. Such problems can be solved using OACerts and OCBE.

4   Definition of Oblivious Commitment-Based Envelope (OCBE)

We now give a formal definition of OCBE. While the definition follows the usage scenario described in Section 3 in general, it abstracts away some of the details in the scenario that have been solved using OACerts and focuses on the parts that still need to solved by the OCBE protocol.

Definition 1 (OCBE). An Oblivious Commitment-Based Envelope (OCBE) scheme is parameterized by a commitment scheme commit. It involves a sender S, a receiver R, and a trusted CA, and has the following phases:

CA-Setup CA takes a security parameter t and outputs the following: the public parameters Params for commit, a set $\mathcal{V}$ of possible values, and a set $\mathcal{P}$ of predicates. Each predicate in $\mathcal{P}$ maps an element in $\mathcal{V}$ to either true or false. The domain of commit[Params] contains $\mathcal{V}$ as a subset.

CA-Commit R chooses a value $a \in \mathcal{V}$ (R's attribute value) and sends to CA. CA picks a random number r and computes the commitment $c = \text{commit}_{\text{Params}}(a, r)$. CA gives c and r to R, and c to S.

Recall that in the actual usage scenario, CA does not directly communicate with R. Instead, CA stores the commitment c in R's OACert certificate. The certificate is then sent by R to S, enabling S to have c as if it is sent from CA. Here we abstract these steps away to have CA sending c to S. We stress that CA does *not* participate in the interactions between S and R.

Initialization S chooses a message $M \in \{0,1\}^*$. S and R agree[1] on a predicate Pred $\in \mathcal{P}$.

Now S has Pred, c, and M. R has Pred, c, a, and r.

Interaction S and R run an interactive protocol, during which an envelope containing an encryption of M is delivered from S to R.

Open After the interaction phase, if Pred(a) is true, R outputs the message M; otherwise, R does nothing.

Observe that the receiver R's attributed value a is committed by a trusted CA. This is natural (and necessary) in our intended usage scenarios for OCBE.

4.1 Basic Cryptographic Assumptions

We say that a function f is *negligible* in the security parameter t if, for every polynomial p, $f(t)$ is smaller than $1/|p(t)|$ for large enough t; otherwise, it is *non-negligible*. The security of our OCBE protocols is based on two standard assumptions in cryptography and the random oracle model.

– *Discrete Logarithm (DL) Assumption.* Given a finite cyclic group G, a generator $g \in G$, and a group element y, there exists no polynomial-time algorithm that can compute $\log_g y$ with non-negligible probability.
– *Computational Diffie-Hellman (CDH) Assumption.* Given a finite cyclic group G, a generator $g \in G$, and group elements g^a, g^b, there exists no polynomial-time algorithm that can compute g^{ab} with non-negligible probability.
– *Random Oracle Model.* The random oracle model is an idealized security model introduced by Bellare and Rogaway [2]. Roughly speaking, a random oracle is a function $H: X \rightarrow Y$ chosen uniformly at random from the set of all functions $\{h : X \rightarrow Y\}$. Random oracles are used to model cryptographic hash functions such as SHA-1.

4.2 Security Definitions

Let an *adversary* be a probabilistic interactive Turing Machine [27]. An OCBE scheme must satisfy the following three properties. It must be sound, oblivious, and semantically secure against the receiver.

Sound. An OCBE scheme is *sound* if in the case that Pred(a) is true, the receiver can output the message M with overwhelming probability, i.e., the probability that the receiver cannot output M is negligible.

Oblivious. An OCBE scheme is *oblivious* if the sender learns nothing about a, i.e., no adversary $\mathcal{A}$ has a non-negligible advantage against the challenger in the game described in Figure 1 where the challenger emulates CA and the receiver, and the adversary emulates the sender. In other words, an OCBE scheme is *oblivious* if for every probabilistic interactive Turing Machine $\mathcal{A}$, $|\Pr[\mathcal{A}$ wins the game in Figure 1$] - \frac{1}{2}| \leq f(t)$, where f is a negligible function in t.

[1] The main effect of having both the sender and the receiver to affect the predicate is that in the security definitions both an adversarial sender and an adversarial receiver can choose the predicate they want to attack on.

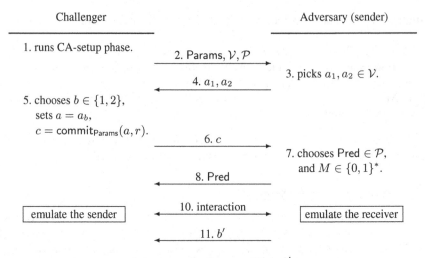

Adversary wins the game if $b = b'$.

Fig. 1. The attacker game for OCBE's oblivious property. We allow the adversary to pick a predicate Pred and two attribute values a_1, a_2 of her choice; yet the adversary still should not be able to distinguish a receiver with attribute a_1 from one with attribute a_2.

Secure against the receiver. An OCBE scheme is *secure against the receiver* if the receiver learns nothing about M when $\text{Pred}(a)$ is false, i.e., no adversary $\mathcal{A}$ has a non-negligible advantage against the challenger in the game described in Figure 2 where the challenger emulates CA and the sender, and the adversary emulates the receiver.

We now argue that OCBE is an adequate solution to the two-party SFE problem in Problem 1, by showing intuitively that the security properties defined for OCBE suffice to prove that the scheme protects the privacy of the participants in the malicious model [25]. Observe that our definitions allow arbitrary adversaries, rather than just those following the protocol (semi-honest adversaries). The oblivious property guarantees that the sender's view of any protocol run can be simulated using just the sender's input, because one can simulate a protocol run between the sender and receiver, and no polynomially bounded sender can figure out the receiver's input. Soundness and security against the receiver guarantee that the receiver's view can be simulated using just the receiver's input and output. If the receiver's committed value a satisfies Pred, then the message M is in the output, one can therefore simulates the sender S. If the receiver's committed value a does not satisfy Pred, one can simulate the sender with a arbitrary message M' and no polynomially bounded receiver can tell the difference.

The security properties defined for OCBE guarantee also the correctness [25] of the OCBE protocol against malicious receivers. Our security definitions do not cover the correctness of the protocol against malicious senders, i.e., if the receiver's value does not satisfy the predicate, a malicious sender may trick the receiver to output the message M which violates the correctness of the protocol[2]. However, this malicious

---

[2] In such case, the views of the sender and receiver cannot be simulated in the ideal model.

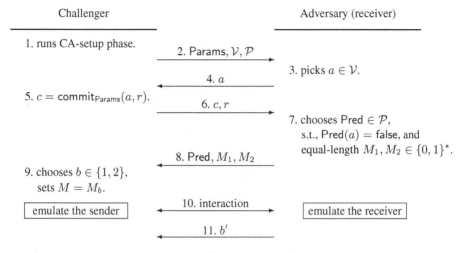

Challenger		Adversary (receiver)

1. runs CA-setup phase.

2. Params, $\mathcal{V}, \mathcal{P}$ →

3. picks $a \in \mathcal{V}$.

← 4. a

5. $c = \mathsf{commit}_{\mathsf{Params}}(a, r)$.

6. c, r →

7. chooses $\mathsf{Pred} \in \mathcal{P}$,
s.t., $\mathsf{Pred}(a) = \mathsf{false}$, and
equal-length $M_1, M_2 \in \{0,1\}^*$.

← 8. Pred, M_1, M_2

9. chooses $b \in \{1, 2\}$,
   sets $M = M_b$.

| emulate the sender |

← 10. interaction →

| emulate the receiver |

← 11. b'

Adversary wins the game if $b = b'$.

Fig. 2. The attacker game for OCBE's security property against the receiver. Even if we give the adversary the power to pick two equal-length messages M_1 and M_2 of her choice, she still cannot distinguish an envelope containing M_1 from one containing M_2. This formalizes the intuitive notion that the envelope leaks no information about its content.

behavior does not make sense in the applications. If a malicious sender does not want to send the message M, she can choose not to participate in the protocol; on the other hand, if a malicious sender wants the receiver to see M without satisfying her policy; she can choose to send M directly rather than participating in the protocol.

We assume that the interaction phase of the OCBE scheme is executed on top of a previously established private communication channel between the sender and the receiver. Recall that the certificate holder establishes an SSL channel with the service provider using OACerts described in Section 3.

5   The Pedersen Commitment Scheme

We now review the Pedersen commitment scheme [39], which will be used in the OCBE protocols.

Definition 2 (The Pedersen Commitment Scheme).

Setup A trusted third party T chooses two large prime numbers p and q such that q divides $p - 1$. It is typical to have p be 1024 bits and q be 160 bits. Let g be a generator of G_q, the unique order-q subgroup of $\mathbb{Z}_p^*$. We use $x \leftarrow \mathbb{Z}_q$ to denote that x is uniformly randomly chosen from $\mathbb{Z}_q$. T picks $x \leftarrow \mathbb{Z}_q$ and computes $h = (g^x \bmod p)$. T keeps the value x secret and makes the values p, q, g, h public.

Commit The domain of the committed values is $\mathbb{Z}_q$. For a party A to commit an value $a \in \mathbb{Z}_q$, A chooses $r \leftarrow \mathbb{Z}_q$ and computes the commitment $c = (g^a h^r \bmod p)$.

Open To open a commitment c, A reveals a and r, and a verifier verifies whether $c = (g^a h^r \bmod p)$.

The above setting is slightly different from the standard setting of commitment schemes, in which the verifier runs the setup program and does a zero-knowledge proof to convince A that the parameters are constructed properly. We use a trusted third party to generate the parameters, because this is done by a trusted CA in the OACerts scheme.

The Pedersen commitment scheme is *unconditionally hiding*: Even with unlimited computational power it is impossible for an adversary to learn any information about the value a from c, because the commitments of any two numbers in $\mathbb{Z}_q$ have exactly the same distribution. This commitment scheme is *computationally binding*: Under the DL assumption, it is computationally infeasible for an adversarial committer to open a value a' other than a in the open phase of the commitment scheme. Suppose an adversary finds a' (other than a) and r' such that $g^{a'}h^{r'} \equiv g^a h^r \pmod{p}$, then she can compute $\frac{a'-a}{r-r'} \bmod q$, which is $\log_g(h)$, the discrete logarithm of h with respect to the base g.

6   OCBE Protocols

In this section, we present two OCBE protocols using the Pedersen commitment scheme, one for equality predicates, the other for greater-than-or-equal-to predicates. We then sketch how to construct OCBE protocols for other comparison predicates. All arithmetic in this section is assumed to be mod p unless otherwise specified.

6.1   EQ-OCBE: An OCBE Protocol for Equality Predicates

Our EQ-OCBE protocol runs a Diffie-Hellman style key-agreement protocol [17] with the twist that the receiver can compute the shared secret if and only if the receiver's committed value a is equal to a_0.

Protocol 1 (EQ-OCBE) Let $\mathcal{E}$ be a semantically secure symmetric encryption scheme with keyspace $\{0,1\}^s$. Let $H : G_q \rightarrow \{0,1\}^s$ be a cryptographic hash function that extracts a key for $\mathcal{E}$ from an element in the group G_q, the order-q subgroup of $\mathbb{Z}_p^*$. EQ-OCBE involves a sender S, a receiver R, and a trust CA.

CA-Setup CA takes a security parameter t and runs the setup algorithm of the Pedersen commitment scheme to create Params $= \langle p, q, g, h \rangle$. CA also outputs $\mathcal{V} = \mathbb{Z}_q$ and $\mathcal{P} = \{\mathsf{EQ}_{a_0} \mid a_0 \in \mathcal{V}\}$, where $\mathsf{EQ}_{a_0} : \mathcal{V} \rightarrow \{\mathsf{true, false}\}$ is a predicate such that $\mathsf{EQ}_{a_0}(a)$ is true if $a = a_0$ and false if $a \neq a_0$.

CA-Commit R chooses an integer $a \in \mathcal{V}$ and sends to CA. CA picks $r \leftarrow \mathbb{Z}_q$ and computes the commitment $c = g^a h^r$. CA gives c and r to R, and c to S.

Initialization S chooses a message $M \in \{0,1\}^*$. S and R agree on a predicate $\mathsf{EQ}_{a_0} \in \mathcal{P}$. Now S has EQ_{a_0}, c, and M. R has EQ_{a_0}, c, a, and r.

Interaction S picks $y \leftarrow \mathbb{Z}_q^*$, computes $\sigma = (cg^{-a_0})^y$, and then sends to R the pair $\langle \eta = h^y, C = \mathcal{E}_{H(\sigma)}[M] \rangle$.

Open R receives $\langle \eta, C \rangle$ from the interaction phase. If $\mathsf{EQ}_{a_0}(a)$ is true, R computes $\sigma' = \eta^r$, and decrypts C using $H(\sigma')$.

To see that EQ-OCBE is sound, observe that when $\mathsf{EQ}_{a_0}(a)$ is true,

$$\sigma = (cg^{-a_0})^y = (g^a h^r g^{-a_0})^y = (g^{a-a_0} h^r)^y = (h^r)^y = (h^y)^r = \eta^r = \sigma'.$$

Therefore the sender and receiver share the same symmetric key.

Also observe that the interaction phase of the EQ-OCBE protocol is one-round; it involves only one message from the sender to the receiver. In the interaction and open phases, the sender does two exponentiations and the receiver does one exponentiation.

The key idea of EQ-OCBE is that if the receiver's committed value a is equal to a_0, the sender can compute $cg^{-a_0} = g^{a-a_0}h^r = h^r$. The sender now holds h^r such that the receiver knows the value r. This achieves half of the Diffie-Hellman key-agreement protocol [17], with h as the base. The sender then does the other half by sending h^y to the receiver. Thus both the sender and receiver can compute $\sigma = (cg^{-a_0})^y = h^{ry}$. If the receiver's committed value a is not equal to a_0, then it is presumably hard for him to compute $\sigma = (cg^{-a_0})^y$ from h^y and cg^{-a_0}. The receiver cannot effectively compute $\log_h(cg^{-a_0})$, because if the receiver is able to find a number $r' = \log_h(cg^{-a_0})$, he can break the binding property of the commitment scheme, i.e., he finds a (a_0, r') pair such that $g^{a_0}h^{r'} = g^a h^r$.

Theorem 1. *EQ-OCBE is oblivious.*

Theorem 2. *Under the CDH assumption on G_q, the order-q subgroup of $\mathbb{Z}_p^*$, and when H is modeled as a random oracle, EQ-OCBE is secure against the receiver.*

Due to space limitation, all the proofs are given in the full version of this paper [31].

6.2   GE-OCBE: An OCBE Protocol for Greater-Than-or-Equal-to Predicates

In this section, we present an OCBE protocol (GE-OCBE) for the Pedersen commitment scheme with greater-than-or-equal-to predicates. The basic idea of the GE-OCBE protocol is as follows. Let ℓ be an integer such that $2^\ell < q/2$. Let a and a_0 be two numbers in $[0..2^\ell - 1]$, and let $d = ((a - a_0) \mod q)$. Let $c = g^a h^r$ be a commitment of a where r is known to the receiver, then $cg^{-a_0} = g^{a-a_0}h^r = g^d h^r$ is a commitment of d that the receiver knows how to open. Notice that if $a \geq a_0$ then $d \in [0..2^\ell - 1]$, otherwise $d \notin [0..2^\ell - 1]$.

If $a \geq a_0$, the receiver generates ℓ new commitments $c_0, \ldots, c_{\ell-1}$, one for each of the ℓ bits of d. The sender picks a random encryption key k and split it into ℓ secrets $k_0, \ldots, k_{\ell-1}$. Then the sender and receiver run a "bit-OCBE" protocol for each commitment, i.e., if c_i is a bit-commitment, the receiver obtains k_i, otherwise he gets nothing, while the sender learns nothing about the value committed under c_i.

Protocol 2 (GE-OCBE) Let $\mathcal{E}$ be a semantically secure symmetric encryption scheme with keyspace $\{0,1\}^s$. Let $H : G_q \rightarrow \{0,1\}^s$ and $H' : \{0,1\}^{s\ell} \rightarrow \{0,1\}^s$ be two cryptographic hash functions. Our GE-OCBE protocol involves a sender S, a receiver R, and a trust CA.

CA-Setup CA takes two parameters, a security parameter t and a parameter ℓ (which specifies the desired range of the attribute values). CA runs the setup algorithm of the Pedersen commitment scheme to create $\text{Params} = \langle p, q, g, h \rangle$ such that $2^\ell < q/2$. CA also outputs $\mathcal{V} = [0..2^\ell - 1]$ and $\mathcal{P} = \{\text{GE}_{a_0} \mid a_0 \in \mathcal{V}\}$, where $\text{GE}_{a_0}: \mathcal{V} \rightarrow \{\text{true}, \text{false}\}$ is a predicate such that $\text{GE}_{a_0}(a)$ is true if $a \geq a_0$ and false otherwise.

CA-Commit R chooses an integer $a \in \mathcal{V}$ and sends to CA. CA picks $r \leftarrow \mathbb{Z}_q$ and computes the commitment $c = g^a h^r$. CA gives c and r to R, and c to S.

Initialization S chooses a message $M \in \{0,1\}^*$. S and R agree on a predicate $\mathsf{GE}_{a_0} \in \mathcal{P}$. Now S has GE_{a_0}, c, and M. R has GE_{a_0}, c, a, and r.

Interaction Let $d = ((a - a_0) \bmod q)$, $\mathsf{GE}_{a_0}(a) = \text{true}$ if and only if $d \in [0..2^\ell - 1]$. Note that $cg^{-a_0} = g^d h^r$ is a commitment of d that R can open.

1. R picks $r_1, \ldots, r_{\ell-1} \leftarrow \mathbb{Z}_q$ and sets $r_0 = r - \sum_{i=1}^{\ell-1} 2^i r_i \bmod q$. When $\mathsf{GE}_{a_0}(a) = \text{true}$, let $d_{\ell-1} \ldots d_1 d_0$ be the binary representation of d, i.e., $d = d_0 2^0 + d_1 2^1 + \cdots + d_{\ell-1} 2^{\ell-1}$. When $\mathsf{GE}_{a_0}(a) = \text{false}$, R randomly picks $d_1, d_2, \ldots, d_{\ell-1} \leftarrow \{0,1\}$, and sets $d_0 = d - \sum_{i=1}^{\ell-1} 2^i d_i \bmod q$. R computes, for $0 \le i \le \ell - 1$, the commitment $c_i = \mathsf{commit}(d_i, r_i) = g^{d_i} h^{r_i}$. R sends $c_0, \ldots, c_{\ell-1}$ to S.

2. S verifies that $cg^{-a_0} = \prod_{i=0}^{\ell-1}(c_i)^{2^i}$. S randomly chooses ℓ symmetric keys $k_0, \ldots, k_{\ell-1} \in \{0,1\}^t$ and sets $k = H'(k_0 \| \cdots \| k_{\ell-1})$. S picks $y \leftarrow \mathbb{Z}_q^*$, computes $\eta = h^y$ and $C = \mathcal{E}_k[M]$. For each $0 \le i \le \ell - 1$, S computes $\sigma_i^0 = (c_i)^y$, $\sigma_i^1 = (c_i g^{-1})^y$, $C_i^0 = H(\sigma_i^0) \oplus k_i$, and $C_i^1 = H(\sigma_i^0) \oplus k_i$. S sends to R the tuple $\langle \eta, C_0^0, C_0^1, \ldots, C_{\ell-1}^0, C_{\ell-1}^1, C \rangle$.

Open R receives $\langle \eta, C_0^0, C_0^1, \ldots, C_{\ell-1}^0, C_{\ell-1}^1, C \rangle$ from the interaction phase. If $\mathsf{GE}_{a_0}(a)$ is true, $d = \sum_{i=0}^{\ell-1} 2^i d_i$ where $d_i \in \{0,1\}$. For each $0 \le i \le \ell - 1$, R computes $\sigma_i' = \eta^{r_i}$, and obtains $k_i' = H(\sigma_i') \oplus C_i^{d_i}$. R then computes $k' = H'(k_0' \| \cdots \| k_{\ell-1}')$, and decrypts C using k'.

To see that the GE-OCBE protocol is sound, observe that when $\mathsf{GE}_{a_0}(a)$ is true, $d_0, \ldots, d_{\ell-1}$ are either 0 or 1. If the receiver follows the protocol, the sender will succeed in verifying $\prod_{i=0}^{\ell-1}(c_i)^{2^i} = \prod_{i=0}^{\ell-1}(g^{d_i} h^{r_i})^{2^i} = g^d h^r = cg^{-a_0}$. For each $0 \le i \le \ell - 1$, if $d_i = 0$, $\sigma_i^0 = (c_i)^y = (g^{d_i} h^{r_i})^y = (h^y)^{r_i} = \eta^{r_i} = \sigma_i'$, the receiver can compute $k_i = C_i^0 \oplus H(\sigma_i')$; if $d_i = 1$, $\sigma_i^1 = (c_i g^{-1})^y = (g^{d_i-1} h^{r_i})^y = (h^y)^{r_i} = \eta^{r_i} = \sigma_i'$, the receiver can compute $k_i = C_i^1 \oplus H(\sigma_i')$. As $k = H'(k_0 \| \cdots \| k_{\ell-1})$, the receiver can successfully obtain k. Thus the sender and receiver share the same symmetric key k if $\mathsf{GE}_{a_0}(a)$ is true.

The interaction phase of the GE-OCBE protocol is two rounds. The receiver does about 2ℓ exponentiations. The sender does about ℓ exponentiations (observe that σ_i^1 can be computed as $\sigma_i^0 g^{-y}$, where g^{-y} needs to be computed only once).

We briefly sketch the idea why the receiver cannot obtain M if $\mathsf{GE}_{a_0}(a)$ is false. If the receiver follows the protocol, then $d_1, \ldots, d_{\ell-1} \in \{0,1\}$ and $d_0 \notin \{0,1\}$. The receiver can successfully compute $k_1, \ldots, k_{\ell-1}$, but fails to compute k_0 because he can compute neither $\sigma_0^0 = (c_0)^y = (g^{d_0} h^r)^y$ nor $\sigma_0^0 = (c_0 g^{-1})^y = (g^{d_0-1} h^r)^y$. Even if the receiver does not follow the protocol, it is impossible for him to find $d_0, \ldots, d_{\ell-1} \in \{0,1\}$ and $r_0, \ldots, r_{\ell-1}$ such that $cg^{-a_0} = \prod_{i=0}^{\ell-1}(c_i)^{2^i}$ and $c_i = g^{d_i} h^{r_i}$. Suppose the receiver finds such $d_0, \ldots, d_{\ell-1} \in \{0,1\}$ and $r_0, \ldots, r_{\ell-1}$; let $d' = \sum_{i=0}^{\ell-1} d_i 2^i \in [0..2^\ell - 1]$ and $r' = \sum_{i=0}^{\ell-1} r_i 2^i \pmod q$, then

$$g^{a-a_0} h^r = cg^{-a_0} = \prod_{i=0}^{\ell-1}(c_i)^{2^i} = \prod_{i=0}^{\ell-1}(g^{d_i} h^{r_i})^{2^i}$$

$$= g^{\sum_{i=0}^{\ell-1} d_i 2^i} h^{\sum_{i=0}^{\ell-1} r_i 2^i} = g^{d'} h^{r'}.$$

As $a - a_0 \notin [0..2^\ell - 1]$ and $d' \in [0..2^\ell - 1]$, $d' \neq a - a_0$, the receiver is able to find $a - a_0, r, d'$, and r' such that $g^{a-a_0} h^r = g^{d'} h^{r'}$, which breaks the binding property of the Pedersen commitment scheme.

Theorem 3. *GE-OCBE is oblivious.*

Theorem 4. *Under the CDH assumption on G_q, the order-q subgroup of $\mathbb{Z}_p^*$, and when H and H' are modeled as random oracles, GE-OCBE is secure against the receiver.*

6.3   OCBE Protocols for Other Predicates

In this section, we first present two logical combination OCBE protocols, one for $\wedge$ (AND-OCBE), the other for $\vee$ (OR-OCBE). Then we describe OCBE protocols for comparison predicates: $>$ (GT-OCBE), $\leq$ (LE-OCBE), $<$ (LT-OCBE), $\neq$ (NE-OCBE). Finally, we present an OCBE protocol for range predicates (RANGE-OCBE). Due to space limitation, we only sketch the ideas. Note that similar techniques have been used before in [7, 33]. In what follows, we use $OCBE(\mathsf{Pred}, a, M)$ to denote an OCBE protocol with predicate Pred and committed value a, the receiver outputs M if $\mathsf{Pred}(a)$ is true.

1. **AND-OCBE**: Suppose there exists OCBE protocols for Pred_1 and Pred_2, the goal is to build an OCBE protocol for the new predicate $\mathsf{Pred} = \mathsf{Pred}_1 \wedge \mathsf{Pred}_2$. An $OCBE(\mathsf{Pred}_1 \wedge \mathsf{Pred}_2, a, M)$ can be constructed as follows: In the interaction phase, the sender picks two random keys k_1 and k_2 and sets $k = k_1 \oplus k_2$. The sender then runs the interaction phases of $OCBE(\mathsf{Pred}_1, a, k_1)$ and $OCBE(\mathsf{Pred}_2, a, k_2)$ with the receiver. Finally, the sender sends $\mathcal{E}_k[M]$ to the receiver. The receiver can recover M in the open phase only if both $\mathsf{Pred}_1(a)$ and $\mathsf{Pred}_2(a)$ are true.

2. **OR-OCBE**: An $OCBE(\mathsf{Pred}_1 \vee \mathsf{Pred}_2, M)$ can be constructed as follows: In the interaction phase, the sender picks a random key k. The sender then runs the interaction phases of $OCBE(\mathsf{Pred}_1, a, k)$ and $OCBE(\mathsf{Pred}_2, a, k)$ with the receiver. Finally, the sender sends $\mathcal{E}_k[M]$ to the receiver. The receiver can recover M in the open phase if either $\mathsf{Pred}_1(a)$ or $\mathsf{Pred}_2(a)$ is true.

3. **GT-OCBE**: For integer space, $a > a_0$ is equivalent to $a \geq a_0 + 1$. An $OCBE(>_{a_0}, a, M)$ protocol is equivalent to an $OCBE(\geq_{a_0+1}, a, M)$ protocol.

4. **LE-OCBE**: Observe that $a \leq a_0$ if and only if $d = ((a_0 - a) \bmod q) \in [0..2^\ell - 1]$. Let $c = g^a h^r$ be a commitment of a, then $g^{a_0} c^{-1} = g^{(a_0-a) \bmod q} h^{-r \bmod q}$ is a commitment of d such that the receiver knows how to open. The LE-OCBE protocol uses the same method as in GE-OCBE.

5. **LT-OCBE**: For integer space, $a < a_0$ is equivalent to $a \leq a_0 - 1$. An $OCBE(<_{a_0}, a, M)$ protocol is equivalent to an $OCBE(\leq_{a_0-1}, a, M)$ protocol.

6. **NE-OCBE**: $a \neq a_0$ is equivalent to $(a > a_0) \vee (a < a_0)$. Therefore, an $OCBE(\neq_{a_0}, a, M)$ can be built as $OCBE(>_{a_0} \vee <_{a_0}, a, M)$.

7. **RANGE-OCBE**: $a_0 \leq a \leq a_1$ is equivalent to $(a \geq a_0) \wedge (a \leq a_1)$. Therefore, a RANGE-OCBE can be built as $OCBE(\geq_{a_0} \wedge \leq_{a_1}, a, M)$.

7   Implementation and Performance

We have implemented a toolkit that generates X.509 certificates [29] that are also OACerts using Java v1.4.2 SDK and JCSI PKI Server Library [30]. In our implementation, both the parameters of the Pedersen commitment scheme and commitments of certificate holder's attributes are encoded in the X.509v3 extension fields. We assign each attribute in the certificate a unique object identifier (OID). We convert each attribute value into an octet string and place it together its corresponding OID in the extension fields as a non-critical extension. The CA can publish a list of attribute names and their corresponding OID, so that the service providers know which commitment corresponds to which attribute. Our OACerts can be recognized by OpenSSL.

We also implemented the OCBE protocols and some zero-knowledge proof protocols [12, 13, 16, 37] using Java 2 Platform v1.4.2 SDK. We use the Pedersen commitment scheme with security parameters $p = 1024$ bits and $q = 160$ bits. The size of a commitment is 128 bytes. In the implementation of the OCBE protocols, we use MD5 as the cryptographic hash function, AES as the symmetric key encryption scheme. In our setting, M is typically a 16-byte symmetric key.

We ran our implementation on a 2.53GMz Intel Pentium 4 machine with 384MB RAM running RedHat Linux 9.0. We simulate the certificate holder and the service provider on the same machine. The performance of two zero-knowledge proof protocols and two OCBE protocols is summarized in Table 1.

Table 1. Running time and size of communication on a 2.53GMz Intel Pentium 4 running RedHat Linux. Security parameters are $\ell = 32$, $p = 1024$ bits, and $q = 160$ bits.

	execution time	communication size
Zero-knowledge proof that $a = a_0$	28 ms	168 bytes
Zero-knowledge proof that $a \geq a_0$	2.2 s	15 KB
EQ-OCBE	75 ms	144 bytes
GE-OCBE	0.9 s	5.1 KB

8   Conclusion

In this paper, we proposed OACerts, an attribute certificate scheme that enables oblivious access control. We introduced the notion of OCBE, and developed provably secure and efficient OCBE protocols for the Pedersen commitment scheme and predicates such as $=, \geq, \leq, >, <, \neq$ as well as logical combinations of them. Future work includes developing efficient OCBE protocols for predicates other than comparison predicates.

Acknowledgement

This work is supported by NSF ITR grant CCR-0325951 and by sponsors of CERIAS. We would like to thank Dan Boneh for helpful discussions. We thank the anonymous reviewers for their helpful comments. We thank also Ziad Bizri, Ji-Won Byun, Klorida Miraj, and Mahesh V. Tipunitara for reading drafts of the paper and making suggestions that have improved the paper's presentation.

References

1. Dirk Balfanz, Glenn Durfee, Narendar Shankar, Diana Smetters, Jessica Staddon, and Hao-Chi Wong. Secret handshakes from pairing-based key agreements. In *Proceedings of the IEEE Symposium and Security and Privacy*, pages 180–196, May 2003.
2. Mihir Bellare and Phillip Rogaway. Random oracles are practical: A paradigm for designing efficient protocols. In *Proceedings of the 1st ACM Conference on Computer and Communications Security*, pages 62–73. ACM Press, 1993.
3. Matt Blaze, Joan Feigenbaum, and Jack Lacy. Decentralized trust management. In *Proceedings of the 1996 IEEE Symposium on Security and Privacy*, pages 164–173. IEEE Computer Society Press, May 1996.
4. Sharon Boeyen, Tim Howes, and Patrick Richard. Internet X.509 Public Key Infrastructure LDAPc2 Schema. IETF RFC 2587, June 1999.
5. Fabrice Boudot. Efficient proofs that a committed number lies in an interval. In *Advances in Cryptology: EUROCRYPT '00*, volume 1807 of *Lecture Notes in Computer Science*, pages 431–444. Springer, May 2000.
6. Robert Bradshaw, Jason Holt, and Kent Seamons. Concealing complex policies with hidden credentials. In *Proceedings of 11th ACM Conference on Computer and Communications Security*, October 2004.
7. Stefan A. Brands. *Rethinking Public Key Infrastructures and Digital Certificates: Building in Privacy*. MIT Press, August 2000.
8. Jan Camenisch and Els Van Herreweghen. Design and implementation of the idemix anonymous credential system. In *Proceedings of the 9th ACM Conference on Computer and Communications Security, CCS '02*, pages 21–30. ACM, nov 2002.
9. Jan Camenisch and Anna Lysyanskaya. An efficient system for non-transferable anonymous credentials with optional anonymity revocation. In *Advances in Cryptology: EUROCRYPT '01*, volume 2045 of *Lecture Notes in Computer Science*, pages 93–118. Springer, 2001.
10. David Chaum. Security without identification: Transaction systems to make big brother obsolete. *Communications of the ACM*, 28(10):1030–1044, 1985.
11. Dwaine Clarke, Jean-Emile Elien, Carl Ellison, Matt Fredette, Alexander Morcos, and Ronald L. Rivest. Certificate chain discovery in SPKI/SDSI. *Journal of Computer Security*, 9(4):285–322, 2001.
12. Ronald Cramer and Ivan Damgård. Zero-knowledge proof for finite field arithmetic, or: Can zero-knowledge be for free? In *Advances in Cryptology: CRYPTO '98*, volume 1462 of *Lecture Notes in Computer Science*, pages 424–441. Springer, 1998.
13. Ronald Cramer, Matthew K. Franklin, Berry Schoenmakers, and Moti Yung. Multi-authority secret-ballot elections with linear work. In *Advances in Cryptology: EUROCRYPT '96*, volume 1070 of *Lecture Notes in Computer Science*, pages 72–83. Springer, 1996.
14. Claude Crépeau. Verifiable disclosure of secrets and applications (abstract). In *Advances in Cryptology: EUROCRYPT '89*, volume 434 of *Lecture Notes in Computer Science*, pages 150–154. Springer, 1990.
15. Giovanni Di Crescenzo, Rafail Ostrovsky, and S. Rajagopalan. Conditional oblivious transfer and timed-release encryption. In *Advances in Cryptology: EUROCRYPT '99*, volume 1592 of *Lecture Notes in Computer Science*, pages 74–89, March 1999.
16. Ivan Damgård and Eiichiro Fujisaki. An integer commitment scheme based on groups with hidden order. In *Advances in Cryptology: ASIACRYPT '02*, volume 2501 of *Lecture Notes in Computer Science*, pages 125–142. Springer, December 2002.
17. Whitfield Diffie and Martin E. Hellman. New directions in cryptography. *IEEE Transactions on Information Theory*, 22:644–654, 1976.

18. Glenn Durfee and Matt Franklin. Distribution chain security. In *Proceedings of the 7th ACM Conference on Computer and Communications Security*, pages 63–70. ACM Press, 2000.
19. Carl Ellison, Bill Frantz, Butler Lampson, Ron Rivest, Brian Thomas, and Tatu Ylonen. SPKI certificate theory. IETF RFC 2693, September 1999.
20. Stephen Farrell and Russell Housley. An internet attribute certificate profile for authorization. IETF RFC 3281, April 2002.
21. Marc Fischlin. A cost-effective pay-per-multiplication comparison method for millionaires. In *CT-RSA 2001: Proceedings of the 2001 Conference on Topics in Cryptology*, volume 2020 of *Lecture Notes in Computer Science*, pages 457–472. Springer, 2001.
22. Keith B. Frikken, Mikhail J. Atallah, and Jiangtao Li. Hidden access control policies with hidden credentials. In *Proceedings of the 3rd ACM Workshop on Privacy in the Electronic Society*, October 2004.
23. Eiichiro Fujisaki and Tatsuaki Okamoto. Statistical zero knowledge protocols to prove modular polynomial relations. In *Advances in Cryptology: CRYPTO '97*, volume 1294 of *Lecture Notes in Computer Science*, pages 16–30. Springer, 1997.
24. Juan Garay, Philip MacKenzie, and Ke Yang. Efficient and universally composable committed oblivious transfer and applications. In *Theory of Cryptography, TCC 2004*, volume 2951 of *Lecture Notes in Computer Science*, pages 297–316. Springer, 2004.
25. Oded Goldreich. Secure multi-party computation, October 2002.
26. Oded Goldreich, Silvio Micali, and Avi Wigderson. How to play any mental game. In *Proceedings of the nineteenth annual ACM conference on Theory of computing*, pages 218–229, May 1987.
27. Shafi Goldwasser, Silvio Micali, and Charles Rackoff. The knowledge complexity of interactive proof systems. *SIAM Journal on Computing*, 18:186–208, feb 1989.
28. Jason E. Holt, Robert W. Bradshaw, Kent E. Seamons, and Hilarie Orman. Hidden credentials. In *Proceedings of the 2nd ACM Workshop on Privacy in the Electronic Society*, October 2003.
29. Russell Housley, Warwick Ford, Tim Polk, and David Solo. Internet X.509 Public Key Infrastructure Certificate and CRL Profile. IETF RFC 2459, January 1999.
30. JCSI. Java cryptographic secure implementation. Wedgetail Communications, 2004.
31. Jiangtao Li and Ninghui Li. OACerts: Oblivious attribute certificates. Technical Report CERIAS-TR-2005-26, Center for Education and Research in Information Assurance and Security, Purdue University, April 2005.
32. Ninghui Li, Wenliang Du, and Dan Boneh. Oblivious signature-based envelope. In *Proceedings of the 22nd ACM Symposium on Principles of Distributed Computing (PODC 2003)*. ACM Press, July 2003.
33. Ninghui Li, Wenliang Du, and Dan Boneh. Oblivious signature-based envelope. *Distributed Computing*, 2005. to appear.
34. Ninghui Li, John C. Mitchell, and William H. Winsborough. Design of a role-based trust management framework. In *Proceedings of the 2002 IEEE Symposium on Security and Privacy*, pages 114–130. IEEE Computer Society Press, May 2002.
35. Ninghui Li, William H. Winsborough, and John C. Mitchell. Distributed credential chain discovery in trust management. *Journal of Computer Security*, 11(1):35–86, February 2003.
36. Anna Lysyanskaya, Ronald L. Rivest, Amit Sahai, and Stefan Wolf. Pseudonym systems. In *Selected Areas in Cryptography, 6th Annual International Workshop, SAC '99*, volume 1758 of *Lecture Notes in Computer Science*, pages 184–199. Springer, 1999.
37. Wenbo Mao. Guaranteed correct sharing of integer factorization with off-line shareholders. In *Public Key Cryptography: PKC'98*, volume 1431 of *Lecture Notes in Computer Science*, pages 60–71. Springer, February 1998.
38. Moni Naor and Benny Pinkas. Efficient oblivious transfer protocols. In *Proceedings of SODA 2001 (SIAM Symposium on Discrete Algorithms)*, pages 448–457, January 2001.

39. Torben P. Pedersen. Non-interactive and information-theoretic secure verifiable secret sharing. In *Advances in Cryptology: CRYPTO '91*, volume 576 of *Lecture Notes in Computer Science*, pages 129–140. Springer, 1991.
40. Eric Rescorla. *SSL, TLS: Designing, and Building Secure Systems*. Addison-Wesley, 2001.
41. Wen-Guey Tzeng. Efficient 1-out-n oblivious transfer schemes. In *PKC '02: Proceedings of the 5th International Workshop on Practice and Theory in Public Key Cryptosystems*, number 2274 in Lecture Notes in Computer Science, pages 159–171. Springer, 2002.
42. William H. Winsborough and Ninghui Li. Safety in automated trust negotiation. In *Proceedings of the IEEE Symposium on Security and Privacy*, pages 147–160, May 2004.
43. William H. Winsborough, Kent E. Seamons, and Vicki E. Jones. Automated trust negotiation. In *DARPA Information Survivability Conference and Exposition*, volume I, pages 88–102. IEEE Press, January 2000.
44. Andrew C. Yao. How to generate and exchange secrets. In *Proceedings of the 27th IEEE Symposium on Foundations of Computer Science*, pages 162–167. IEEE Computer Society Press, 1986.
45. Ting Yu, Marianne Winslett, and Kent E. Seamons. Supporting structured credentials and sensitive policies through interoperable strategies for automated trust negotiation. *ACM Transactions on Information and System Security (TISSEC)*, 6(1):1–42, February 2003.

Dynamic k-Times Anonymous Authentication

Lan Nguyen and Rei Safavi-Naini

School of Information Technology and Computer Science
University of Wollongong, Wollongong 2522, Australia
{ldn01,rei}@uow.edu.au

Abstract. *k-times anonymous authentication* (k-TAA) schemes allow members of a group to be anonymously authenticated by application providers for a bounded number of times. k-TAA has application in e-voting, e-cash, electronic coupons and anonymous trial browsing of content. In this paper, we extend k-TAA model to *dynamic* k-TAA in which application providers can independently grant or revoke users from their own groups and so have the required control on their clients. We give a formal model for dynamic k-TAA, propose a dynamic k-times anonymous authentication scheme from bilinear pairing, and prove its security. We also construct an ordinary k-TAA from the dynamic scheme and show communication efficiency of the schemes compared to the previously proposed schemes.

1 Introduction

In many scenarios, it is required that authenticated users can anonymously access applications while application providers can decide the number of times users can access their applications. Teranisi et al. [15] proposed k-times anonymous authentication as a solution to this problem. In a k-TAA system, participants are a group manager (GM), a number of application providers (AP) and a group of users. The GM registers users into the group and each AP independently announces the number of times a user can access his application. A registered user can then be anonymously authenticated by APs within their allowed numbers of times and without the need to contact the GM. Dishonest users can be traced by anyone while no one, even the GM or APs, can identify honest users or link two authentication executions performed by the same user. Finally no one, even the GM, is able to successfully impersonate an honest user to an AP.

Applications of k-TAA to e-voting, e-cash, electronic coupons and trial browsing of content have been shown in [15]. A particularly interesting application is trial browsing of content, where each provider allows members of a designated group to anonymously and freely browse content (e.g. movies or music on trial) while he also wants to limit the number of times that users can access the service on trial. Users who try to go over the prescribed quota will be identified and removed. It is shown that none of the known related primitives such as identity escrow/group signature [1, 2, 12, 13], blind signature [7], multiple-show cash [5] and electronic coupon [11], can provide all required properties listed above.

J. Ioannidis, A. Keromytis, and M.Yung (Eds.): ACNS 2005, LNCS 3531, pp. 318–333, 2005.

However, k-TAA schemes are inflexible in the sense that the GM decides on the group membership and APs do not have any control over giving users access permission to their services. APs are passive and their role is limited to announcing the number of times a user can access their applications. This requires a lot of trust to be put on the GM and all group members to share all applications offered by all APs. In practice, APs want to select their user groups and grant or revoke access to users independently. For example, in the case of trial browsing, the AP may prefer to give access to users with good profile, or he may require some small fee to be included in his group. Another case is when the AP needs to put also an expiry date on the trial access. We introduce *dynamic* k-times anonymous authentication to provide these properties. In dynamic k-TAA, APs have more control over granting and revoking access to their services, and less trust and computation from the GM is required. Dynamic k-TAA allows APs to restrict access to their services based on not only the number of times but also other factors such as expiry date and so can be used in much wider range of realistic scenarios.

Our Contribution

We extend the formal model of k-TAA in [15] to a formal model of *dynamic* k-TAA schemes and construct a dynamic k-TAA scheme from bilinear pairings. We also construct a new k-TAA scheme, and prove security of both schemes under the Strong Diffie-Hellman (SDH) and the Decisional Bilinear Diffie-Hellman (DBDH) assumptions. Dynamic k-TAAs have two new procedures, i.e. granting access and revoking access, that allow APs to grant and revoke users' access, respectively. Security requirements of dynamic systems are similar to the original k-TAAs but are more complex to accommodate the dynamic property.

We propose a new assumption, (l, m, n)-DBDH, and prove that it is implied by the DBDH assumption. And we show that our schemes have lower communication costs than the TFS04 scheme. For example, for k-times authentication with a comparable level of security (1024 bit composite modulus for TFS04) the communication costs of our two schemes are $60k + 244$ bytes and $60k + 364$ bytes, respectively, while the cost of the TFS04 scheme is $60k + 1657$ bytes. The interactive protocols in our schemes achieve perfect zero-knowledge without any computational assumption whereas those in the TFS04 scheme only provide statistical zero-knowledge under the Strong RSA assumption. (We note that in all cases honest verifier model is used.) Adapting a revocation method proposed in [6] to our system, the revocation costs become independent of the group size and the number of revoked users.

The organization of the paper is as follows. We give the background in section 2 and present the model of dynamic k-TAA schemes in section 3. Section 4 gives descriptions of our dynamic and ordinary k-TAA schemes with their security proofs, and provides efficiency analysis of the schemes and comparison of communication costs with the TFS04 scheme.

2   Preliminaries

Notation. A function $f : \mathbb{N} \to \mathbb{R}^+$ is called *negligible*, if for every positive number α, there exists a positive integer κ_0 such that for every integer $\kappa > \kappa_0$, it holds that $f(\kappa) < \kappa^{-\alpha}$. Let PT denote polynomial-time, PPT denote probabilistic PT and DPT denote deterministic PT. For a PT algorithm $\mathcal{A}(\cdot)$, "$x \leftarrow A(\cdot)$" denotes an output from the algorithm. For a set $\mathbf{X}$, "$x \leftarrow \mathbf{X}$" denotes an element uniformly chosen from $\mathbf{X}$, and $\#\mathbf{X}$ denotes the number of elements in $\mathbf{X}$. Let "$Pr[Procedures|Predicate]$" denote the probability that $Predicate$ is true after executing the $Procedures$, $\mathcal{H}_{\mathbf{X}}$ denote a hash function from the set of all finite binary strings $\{0,1\}^*$ onto the set $\mathbf{X}$, and $PK\{x : R(x)\}$ denote a proof of knowledge of x that satisfies the relation $R(x)$.

2.1   Bilinear Groups

Let $\mathbb{G}_1, \mathbb{G}_2$ be additive cyclic groups generated by P_1 and P_2, respectively, whose orders are a prime p, and $\mathbb{G}_T$ be a cyclic multiplicative group with the same order p. Suppose there is an isomorphism $\psi : \mathbb{G}_2 \to \mathbb{G}_1$ such that $\psi(P_2) = P_1$. Let $e : \mathbb{G}_1 \times \mathbb{G}_2 \to \mathbb{G}_T$ be a bilinear pairing with the following properties:

1. **Bilinearity:** $e(aP, bQ) = e(P, Q)^{ab}$ for all $P \in \mathbb{G}_1, Q \in \mathbb{G}_2, a, b \in \mathbb{Z}_p$
2. **Non-degeneracy:** $e(P_1, P_2) \neq 1$
3. **Computability:** There is an efficient algorithm to compute $e(P, Q)$ for all $P \in \mathbb{G}_1, Q \in \mathbb{G}_2$

For simplicity, hereafter, we set $\mathbb{G}_1 = \mathbb{G}_2$ and $P_1 = P_2$ but the proposed schemes can be easily modified for the general case when $\mathbb{G}_1 \neq \mathbb{G}_2$.

We define a Bilinear Pairing Instance Generator as a PPT algorithm $\mathcal{G}$ that takes as input a security parameter 1^κ and returns a uniformly random tuple $\mathbf{t} = (p, \mathbb{G}_1, \mathbb{G}_T, e, P)$ of bilinear pairing parameters, including a prime number p of size κ, a cyclic additive group $\mathbb{G}_1$ of order p, a multiplicative group $\mathbb{G}_T$ of order p, a bilinear map $e : \mathbb{G}_1 \times \mathbb{G}_1 \to \mathbb{G}_T$ and a generator P of $\mathbb{G}_1$.

2.2   Complexity Assumptions

q-Strong Diffie-Hellman (q-SDH) Assumption. *For every PPT algorithm $\mathcal{A}$, the following function $Adv_{\mathcal{A}}^{q\text{-}SDH}(\kappa)$ is negligible.*

$$Adv_{\mathcal{A}}^{q\text{-}SDH}(\kappa) = Pr[(\mathcal{A}(\mathbf{t}, P, sP, \ldots, s^q P) = (c, \frac{1}{s+c}P)) \wedge (c \in \mathbb{Z}_p)]$$

where $\mathbf{t} = (p, \mathbb{G}_1, \mathbb{G}_T, e, P) \leftarrow \mathcal{G}(1^\kappa)$ and $s \leftarrow \mathbb{Z}_p^*$.

The q-SDH assumption is proposed by Boneh and Boyen [3] and is originated from an earlier (and weaker) assumption introduced by Mitsunari et. al. [10]. The assumption informally means that there is no PPT algorithm that can compute a pair $(c, \frac{1}{s+c}P)$, where $c \in \mathbb{Z}_p$, from a tuple $(P, sP, \ldots, s^q P)$, where $s \leftarrow \mathbb{Z}_p^*$.

Decisional Bilinear Diffie-Hellman (DBDH) Assumption. *For every PPT algorithm $\mathcal{A}$, the following function $Adv_{\mathcal{A}}^{DBDH}(\kappa)$ is negligible.*

$$Adv_{\mathcal{A}}^{DBDH}(\kappa) = |Pr[\mathcal{A}(\mathbf{t}, aP, bP, cP, e(P,P)^{abc}) = 1]$$
$$- Pr[\mathcal{A}(\mathbf{t}, aP, bP, cP, \Gamma) = 1]|$$

where $\mathbf{t} = (p, \mathbb{G}_1, \mathbb{G}_T, e, P) \leftarrow \mathcal{G}(1^{\kappa})$, $\Gamma \leftarrow \mathbb{G}_T^*$ and $a, b, c \leftarrow \mathbb{Z}_p^*$.

Informally, the DBDH assumption states that there is no PPT algorithm that can distinguish between a tuple $(aP, bP, cP, e(P,P)^{abc})$ and a tuple (aP, bP, cP, Γ), where $\Gamma \leftarrow \mathbb{G}_T^*$ and $a, b, c \leftarrow \mathbb{Z}_p^*$.

3   A Model for Dynamic k-TAA schemes

We propose a formal model for dynamic k-TAA and underline the differences between this model and the TFS04 model for ordinary k-TAA in [15].

3.1   Entities and Procedures

Entities in the model are the GM, APs and users; the procedures are setup, joining, bound announcement, granting access, revoking access, authentication and public tracing. In the setup procedure (SETUP), the GM obtains a group public key/group secret key pair, and each AP $\mathcal{V}$ obtains a pair of public and secret keys $(apk_{\mathcal{V}}, ask_{\mathcal{V}})$. AP $\mathcal{V}$ also has an *access group* $AG_{\mathcal{V}}$ which is the set user identities who can access his application, and also some other *public information* $PI_{\mathcal{V}}$. $AG_{\mathcal{V}}$ is initially empty.

The joining procedure $(\mathcal{U}_{JOIN-GM}, \mathcal{U}_{JOIN-U})$ allows a user i to join the group by obtaining a member public key/member secret key pair (mpk_i, msk_i) and the GM adds the user's identification and public key to an *identification list* LIST. In the bound announcement procedure (BD-ANN), an AP announces the number of times a group member can access his application by publishing his identity ID, and the upper bound k. An AP $\mathcal{V}$ uses the granting access procedure (GRAN-AP) to give selected group members permission to access the his application. He includes the new member in his access group $AG_{\mathcal{V}}$ and updates his public information $PI_{\mathcal{V}}$. Similarly, in the revoking access procedure (REVO-AP), AP $\mathcal{V}$ can stop a group member from accessing his application by excluding the member from his access group and updating his public information. The authentication procedure $(\mathcal{U}_{AUTH-AP}, \mathcal{U}_{AUTH-U})$, between a user i and AP $\mathcal{V}$ succeeds if and only if user i has been granted access and his access has not been revoked, and the number of accesses has not reached the allowed number. AP $\mathcal{V}$ records the transcripts of authentication executions in the authentication log LOG. Tracing procedure TRACE can be executed by anyone using the public information and the authentication log. Possible outputs of the procedure are user i's identity, GM, or NO-ONE which mean "user i tries to access more than the prescribed limit", "the GM published information is not correct", and "the public tracing procedure cannot find any malicious entity", respectively.

The main difference between dynamic k-TAA and the TFS04 model with regard to procedures is that an AP has a pair of public and secret keys and maintains his own access group using two new procedures, granting access and revoking access; and authentication procedure succeeds only if the user has been granted access, the access has not been revoked, and he has not accessed the application over the allowed number of times.

3.2   Oracles

The adversary· has access to a number of oracles and can query them according to the description below, to learn about the system and increase his success chance in the attacks.

List oracle model. We will use a *list* oracle $\mathcal{O}_{LIST}$ first defined in [15]. The oracle is used to ensure correct correspondence between the identity of a group member and his public key. In *list oracle model* there is a $\mathcal{O}_{LIST}$ oracle which manages the LIST that contains identities and the corresponding public key list. The response of the oracle to a query to view a group member's public key is the member's public key. The oracle allows an entity to choose and write a user's pair of identity and public key to the LIST only if the entity is the user or a colluder with the user. The oracle allows an entity to delete data from LIST only if the entity is the GM or a colluder with the GM.

Other oracles. Other oracles in our model are the *join GM* oracle $\mathcal{O}_{JOIN-GM}$, the *join user* oracle $\mathcal{O}_{JOIN-U}$, the *authentication AP* oracle $\mathcal{O}_{AUTH-AP}$, the *authentication user* oracle $\mathcal{O}_{AUTH-U}$, the *query* oracle $\mathcal{O}_{QUERY}$, the *granting user* oracle $\mathcal{O}_{GRAN-AP}$, the *revoking user* oracle $\mathcal{O}_{REVO-AP}$ and the *corrupting AP* oracle $\mathcal{O}_{CORR-AP}$. The $\mathcal{O}_{JOIN-GM}$ oracle, given a user specified by the adversary, performs joining procedure as executed by the honest GM on the user. The $\mathcal{O}_{JOIN-U}$ oracle, given an honest user specified by the adversary, performs joining procedure between the GM and the user. The $\mathcal{O}_{AUTH-AP}$ oracle, given an honest AP and a user from the adversary, makes the AP to perform an authentication procedure with the user. The $\mathcal{O}_{AUTH-U}$ oracle, given an honest user and an AP, makes the user to perform an authentication procedure with the AP. Oracles $\mathcal{O}_{LIST}$, $\mathcal{O}_{JOIN-U}$, $\mathcal{O}_{JOIN-GM}$ and $\mathcal{O}_{AUTH-AP}$ are the same as in TFS04 model and their formal definition can be found in [15].

The $\mathcal{O}_{QUERY}$ oracle gives the adversary the challenged authentication transcript in the D-Anonymity definition and more details can be found in this definition. The $\mathcal{O}_{QUERY}$ oracle first checks if input identities i_1 and i_2 are current members of the input AP with identity ID; if not, it outputs CHEAT. It then proceeds, as defined in [15], by randomly choosing one of the two identities and executing the authentication procedure between the chosen identity and the input AP. The $\mathcal{O}_{AUTH-U}$ oracle performs as defined in [15], but it takes one more input (ID, k) to indicate the AP. The formal definitions of $\mathcal{O}_{QUERY}$ and $\mathcal{O}_{AUTH-U}$ are presented in the full version [14].

We introduce three new oracles, $\mathcal{O}_{GRAN-AP}$, $\mathcal{O}_{REVO-AP}$ and $\mathcal{O}_{CORR-AP}$. The $\mathcal{O}_{GRAN-AP}$ oracle takes as input an honest AP and a user and executes the granting access procedure GRAN-AP by the AP to grant access to the user. The $\mathcal{O}_{REVO-AP}$ oracle takes as input an honest AP and a member of the AP's access group and executes the revoking access procedure REVO-AP by the AP to revoke access from the user. The $\mathcal{O}_{CORR-AP}$ oracle corrupts an AP specified by the adversary and maintains the set $S_{CORR-AP}$ of corrupted APs. The formal definitions and explanation of these oracles are presented in the full version [14].

3.3   Security Requirements

Security requirements of dynamic k-TAA are D-Correctness, D-Anonymity, D-Detectability, D-Exculpability for users and D-Exculpability for the GM. These are similar to requirements Correctness, Anonymity, Detectability, Exculpability for users and Exculpability for the GM defined in the TFS04 model.

In the following we give an informal definition of these requirements. D-Correctness requires that an honest member who is in the access group of an honest AP and has not performed the authentication procedure for more than the allowed number of times, be successfully authenticated by the AP. D-Anonymity means that it is computationally hard for the adversary to distinguish between authentication executions of two honest group members i_1 and i_2 who are in the access group of an AP, and have not performed authentication with the AP for more than the limited number of times, even if the GM, all APs, and all users except i_1 and i_2 are corrupted. D-Detectability means that if a subgroup of corrupted members have performed the authentication procedure with the same honest AP for more than the allowed number of times, then the public tracing procedure using the AP's authentication log outputs NO-ONE with negligible probability. D-Exculpability for users means that the tracing procedure does not output the identity of an honest user even if other users, the GM and all APs are corrupted. D-Exculpability for the GM means that the tracing procedure does not output the honest GM even if all users and all APs are corrupted. The difference between D-Detectability and Detectability is more significant and so the formal definition of D-Detectability is given below. The formal definitions of other requirements can be found in the full version [14].

D-Detectability. The adversary $\mathcal{A}$ is allowed to corrupt all members and the experiment has two stages. In the first stage, the adversary can query the three new oracles ($\mathcal{O}_{GRAN-AP}$, $\mathcal{O}_{REVO-AP}$ and $\mathcal{O}_{CORR-AP}$), $\mathcal{O}_{LIST}$, $\mathcal{O}_{JOIN-GM}$ and $\mathcal{O}_{AUTH-AP}$. After that, all authentication logs of all APs are emptied. Then the adversary continues the experiments, but without access to the revoking oracle $\mathcal{O}_{REVO-AP}$. The adversary wins if he can be successfully authenticated by an honest AP with identity ID and access bound k for more than $k \times \#AG_{ID}$, where $\#AG_{ID}$ is the number of members in the AP's access group. The set $S_{AUTH-AP}$ contains all APs' information used by the $\mathcal{O}_{AUTH-AP}$, and LOG_{ID} is the authentication log produced by $\mathcal{O}_{AUTH-AP}$ using information of the AP (ID, k). The formula of the experiment is as follows.

Experiment $\mathsf{Exp}_{\mathcal{A},\mathcal{H}}^{d-decis}(\kappa)$

$((gpk, gsk), \{(apk, ask)\}) \leftarrow SETUP(1^{\kappa})$.

$St \leftarrow \mathcal{A}^{ORACLES}(1^{\kappa})$ where $ORACLES = \{\mathcal{O}_{LIST}(\{GM\}^{c}, \cdot),$

$\quad \mathcal{O}_{JOIN-GM}(gpk, gsk, \cdot), \mathcal{O}_{AUTH-AP}(gpk, \cdot, \cdot), \mathcal{O}_{GRAN-AP}(gpk, \cdot, \cdot),$

$\quad \mathcal{O}_{REVO-AP}(gpk, \cdot, \cdot), \mathcal{O}_{CORR-AP}(\cdot)\}$.

Empty all LOGs.

$\mathcal{A}^{ORACLES\backslash\{\mathcal{O}_{REVO-AP}(gpk,\cdot,\cdot)\}}(St)$.

If $(\exists (ID, k) \in S_{AUTH-AP} \backslash S_{CORR-AP}$ s.t. $\#LOG_{ID} > k \times \#AG_{ID})$

$\quad$ Return $TRACE^{\mathcal{O}_{LIST}(\emptyset, \cdot)}(gpk, apk_{ID}, LOG_{ID})$.

Return $\bot$.

A dynamic k-TAA scheme provides D-Detectability if the following function $Adv_{\mathcal{A}}^{d-decis}(\kappa)$ is negligible.

$$Adv_{\mathcal{A}}^{d-decis}(\kappa) = \Pr[\mathsf{Exp}_{\mathcal{A},\mathcal{H}}^{d-decis}(\kappa) = \text{NO-ONE}]$$

Similar to arguments for group signatures [2], these requirements for dynamic k-TAA also imply *unforgeability, coalition resistance* and *traceability* that can be informally defined as follows. Unforgeability means that any adversary, who is not in the access group of an AP, can not be authenticated by the AP without colluding with some group members, or both of the GM and the AP. Coalition resistance means that a colluding subset of group members can not produce a new member public key/secret key pair which has not been generated in the joining procedure. Traceability means that if a user has accessed an AP for more than the bound number of times, then that user can be traced from the public information and the AP's authentication log.

4   A Dynamic k-TAA Scheme

4.1   Overview

Our proposed scheme is constructed in cyclic groups with bilinear mapping. For simplicity, we present the scheme when the groups $\mathbb{G}_1$ and $\mathbb{G}_2$ are the same but the scheme can be easily modified for the general case when $\mathbb{G}_1 \neq \mathbb{G}_2$. Note that the users do not need to perform any pairing operation in the authentication procedure.

Suppose a bilinear pairing tuple $(p, \mathbb{G}_1, \mathbb{G}_T, e, P)$ is given, the GM's group secret key is $\gamma \leftarrow \mathbb{Z}_p^*$ and group public key is $(P, P_{pub} = \gamma P, P_0 \leftarrow \mathbb{G}_1, H \leftarrow \mathbb{G}_1, \Delta = e(P, P))$. In the joining procedure, a user obtains a membership public key/secret key pair $((a, S), x)$ from the GM such that $S = \frac{1}{\gamma+a}(xP + P_0)$, where P and P_0 are in the GM's public key, γ is the GM's secret key and x is randomly generated by both the user and the GM but is only known to the user. The user can be anonymously authenticated as a group member by proving the knowledge of (a, S, x) such that $e(S, aP + P_{pub}) = e(xP + P_0, P)$.

An AP publishes k *tag bases* to be used for up to k times user access to the AP's service. A tag base is a pair $(\Theta_i, \check{\Theta}_i)$ of $\mathbb{G}_T$'s elements. In an authentication execution, a group member interacts with the AP and constructs a tag $(\Gamma, \check{\Gamma}) =$

$(\Theta_i^x, (\Delta^l \check{\Theta}_i)^x)$ to be sent to the AP, where $\Delta = e(P, P)$, and the AP has randomly selected l. The group member also proves the knowledge of (i, x) satisfying the above equation. If the member uses the same tag base to compute another tag $(\Gamma', \check{\Gamma}') = (\Theta_i^x, (\Delta^{l'} \check{\Theta}_i)^x)$, anyone can find these from the AP's authentication log (since $\Gamma = \Gamma'$) and use it to compute $(\check{\Gamma}/\check{\Gamma}')^{1/(l-l')} = \Delta^x$, which is published in the joining procedure. However, if the member does not use the same tag base twice, based on the DBDH assumption his anonymity is protected. Similar to [6], we will use dynamic accumulators to provide the dynamic property. However we will use a new accumulator scheme based on the SDH assumption. Each AP has a public key/secret key pair $((Q, Q_{pub}), s)$, where $Q_{pub} = sQ$. To grant access to a member with a public key (a, S), the AP accumulates the value a of the public key into an *accumulated value* $V \leftarrow (s + a)V$, and the member obtains the old accumulated value as the witness W. The member shows that the AP has granted access to him by proving the knowledge of (a, W) such that $e(W, aQ + Q_{pub}) = e(V, Q)$. To revoke access from a member, the AP computes a new *accumulated value* $V \leftarrow 1/(s + a)V$.

4.2   Description

Setup

<u>For GM</u>: On input a security parameter 1^κ, the Bilinear Pairing Instance Generator generates a tuple $(p, \mathbb{G}_1, \mathbb{G}_T, e, P)$ as in Section 2.2. GM selects $P_0, H \leftarrow \mathbb{G}_1$, $\gamma \leftarrow \mathbb{Z}_p^*$, and sets $P_{pub} = \gamma P$ and $\Delta = e(P, P)$. The group public and secret keys are $gpk = (P, P_{pub}, P_0, H, \Delta)$ and $gsk = \gamma$, respectively. The identification list LIST of group members is initially empty.

<u>For APs</u>: AP $\mathcal{V}$ selects $Q \leftarrow \mathbb{G}_1$, $s \leftarrow \mathbb{Z}_p^*$, $\Lambda, \Upsilon \leftarrow \mathbb{G}_T$, and sets $Q_{pub} = sQ$. The public and secret keys for the AP are $apk = (Q, Q_{pub}, \Lambda, \Upsilon)$ and $ask = s$, respectively. AP maintains an authentication log LOG, an *accumulated value*, which is published and updated after granting or revoking a member, and a public archive ARC (as the other public information PI in the formal model), which is a list of 3-tuples. The first component of the tuple is an element in the public key of a member, who was granted or revoked from accessing the AP. The second component is a single bit indicating whether the member was granted (1) or revoked (0). The third component is the accumulated value after granting or revoking the member. Initially, the accumulated value is set to $V_0 \leftarrow \mathbb{G}_1$ and LOG and ARC are empty.

Joining

A user U_i can join the group as follows.

1. User U_i selects $x', r \leftarrow \mathbb{Z}_p^*$, and sends a commitment $C' = x'P + rH$ of x' to the GM.
2. The GM sends $y, y' \leftarrow \mathbb{Z}_p^*$ to U_i.
3. User U_i computes $x = y + x'y'$ and $(C, \beta) = (xP, \Delta^x)$, then adds new data (i, β) to the identification list LIST. Next, U_i sends (C, β) to the GM with a standard proof $Proof_1 = PK\{(x, r') : C = xP \wedge yP + y'C' - C = r'H\}$ to show that C is correctly computed from C', y, y' and U_i knows x satisfying $C = xP$.

4. The GM verifies that (i, β) is an element of the LIST, $\beta = e(C, P)$ and the proof is valid. Then, the GM generates $a \leftarrow \mathbb{Z}_p^*$ different from all corresponding previously generated values, computes $S = \frac{1}{\gamma+a}(C+P_0)$, and sends (S, a) to user U_i.
5. User U_i confirms that equation $e(S, aP + P_{pub}) = e(C + P_0, P)$ is satisfied. The new member U_i's secret key is $msk = x$, and his public key is $mpk = (a, S, C, \beta)$.

Bound announcement
An AP publishes his identity ID and a number k as the bound. Let $(\Theta_j, \check{\Theta}_j) = \mathcal{H}_{\mathbb{G}_T \times \mathbb{G}_T}(ID, k, j)$ for $j = 1, ..., k$. We call $(\Theta_j, \check{\Theta}_j)$ the jth tag base of the AP.

Granting access
An AP grants access to a user U_i with public key $mpk = (a, \cdot, \cdot, \cdot)$, as follows. Suppose there are j tuples in the AP's ARC and the AP's current accumulated value is V_j. The AP computes a new accumulated value $V_{j+1} = (s + a)V_j$, adds $(a, 1, V_{j+1})$ to his ARC. The user U_i can form his access key $mak = (j + 1, W)$, where $W = V_j$. The user keeps a counter ι, which is initially set to 0.

Revoking access
An AP revokes access from a user U_i with public key $mpk = (a, \cdot, \cdot, \cdot)$, as follows. Suppose there are j tuples in the AP's ARC and the AP's current accumulated value is V_j. The AP computes a new accumulated value $V_{j+1} = 1/(s+a)V_j$, and adds $(a, 0, V_{j+1})$ to ARC.

Authentication
An AP (ID, k), whose public key and current accumulated value are $apk = (Q, Q_{pub}, \Lambda, \Upsilon)$ and V respectively, authenticates a member M with public and secret keys $mpk = (a, S, C, \beta)$ and $msk = x$, respectively, as follows.

1. Member M increases counter ι. If value $\iota > k$, then M sends $\perp$ to the AP and stops. Otherwise, M runs the algorithm Update (see Section 4.3 for this algorithm) to update his access key $mak = (j, W)$.
2. The AP sends a random integer $l \leftarrow \mathbb{Z}_p^*$ to M.
3. Member M computes tag $(\Gamma, \check{\Gamma}) = (\Theta_\iota^x, (\Delta^l \check{\Theta}_\iota)^x)$ using the ιth tag base $(\Theta_\iota, \check{\Theta}_\iota)$, and sends $(\Gamma, \check{\Gamma})$ to the AP with $Proof_2 = PK\{(\iota, a, S, x, W) : \Gamma = \Theta_\iota^x \wedge \check{\Gamma} = (\Delta^l \check{\Theta}_\iota)^x \wedge e(S, aP + P_{pub}) = e(xP + P_0, P) \wedge e(W, aQ + Q_{pub}) = e(V, Q)\}$.
4. If the proof is valid and if Γ is different from all corresponding tags in the AP's LOG, the AP adds tuple $(\Gamma, \check{\Gamma}, l)$ and the proof to the LOG, and outputs accept. If the proof is valid and Γ is already written in the LOG, the AP adds tuple $(\Gamma, \check{\Gamma}, l)$ and the proof to the LOG, outputs (detect,LOG) and stops. If the proof is invalid, the AP outputs reject and stops.

Public tracing
The identity of a malicious user can be traced from an AP's LOG as follows.

1. Look for two entries $(\Gamma, \check{\Gamma}, l, Proof)$ and $(\Gamma', \check{\Gamma}', l', Proof')$ in the LOG, such that $\Gamma = \Gamma'$ and $l \neq l'$, and that $Proof$ and $Proof'$ are valid. If no such entry can be found, output NO-ONE.

2. Compute $\beta = (\check{\Gamma}/\check{\Gamma}')^{1/(l-l')} = ((\Delta^l \check{\Gamma})^x/(\Delta^{l'} \check{\Gamma}')^x)^{1/(l-l')} = \Delta^x$, and look for a pair (i, β) from the LOG. Output member identity i, or if no such (i, β) can be found conclude that the GM has deleted some data from the LOG, and output GM.

4.3 Details

Proof$_2$

The member M computes the proof as follows:

1. Select $v \leftarrow \mathbb{Z}_p^*$, and compute the perfect commitment $\Omega = \Lambda^x \Upsilon^v$ of x.
2. Publish Ω and proofs of knowledge of the following:
   - $Proof_{2a} = PK\{(\iota, x, v) : \Gamma = \Theta_\iota^x \wedge \check{\Gamma} = (\Delta^l \check{\Theta}_\iota)^x \wedge \Omega = \Lambda^x \Upsilon^v\}$.
   - $Proof_{2b} = PK\{(a, S, x, W, v) : e(S, aP + P_{pub}) = e(xP + P_0, P) \wedge e(W, aQ + Q_{pub}) = e(V, Q) \wedge \Omega = \Lambda^x \Upsilon^v\}$.

The $Proof_{2a}$ can be constructed the same as proof 1 in [15] using the standard techniques. We describe $Proof_{2b}$ as follows.

1. Generate $r_1, ..., r_5, k_0, ..., k_7 \leftarrow \mathbb{Z}_p^*$ and compute $U_1 = r_1(aP + P_{pub})$; $U_2 = r_2 r_4 U_1 + r_3 H$; $U_3 = r_2 r_4 S$; $X = r_1 r_2 r_4(xP + P_0)$; $R_1 = r_4(aQ + Q_{pub})$; $R_2 = r_1 r_2 R_1 + r_5 H$; $R_3 = r_4^{-1} W$; $T_1 = k_1 P + k_2 P_{pub} + k_0 H$; $T_2 = k_3 P + k_2 P_0$; $T_4 = k_5 U_1 + k_0 H$; $T_3 = k_1 Q + k_2 Q_{pub} + k_4 H$; $T_5 = k_6 R_1 + k_4 H$; $\Pi = \Lambda^{k_3} \Upsilon^{k_7} \Omega^{-k_2}$
2. Compute $c = \mathcal{H}_{\mathbb{Z}_p}(P||P_{pub}||P_0||H||\Delta||Q||Q_{pub}||\Lambda||\Upsilon||\Omega||ID||k||l||V||X||U_1||U_2||U_3||R_1||R_2||R_3||T_1||...||T_5||\Pi)$
3. Compute in $\mathbb{Z}_p$: $s_0 = k_0 + cr_3$; $s_1 = k_1 + cr_1 r_2 r_4 a$; $s_2 = k_2 + cr_1 r_2 r_4$; $s_3 = k_3 + cr_1 r_2 r_4 x$; $s_4 = k_4 + cr_5$; $s_5 = k_5 + cr_2 r_4$; $s_6 = k_6 + cr_1 r_2$; $s_7 = k_7 + cr_1 r_2 r_4 v$
4. Output $(X, U_1, U_2, U_3, R_1, R_2, R_3, c, s_0, ..., s_7)$

Verification of $Proof_{2b}$. Checking the following equations (which can be done concurrently): $e(U_3, U_1) \stackrel{?}{=} e(X, P)$; $e(R_3, R_1) \stackrel{?}{=} e(V, Q)$; and $c \stackrel{?}{=} \mathcal{H}_{\mathbb{Z}_p}(P||P_{pub}||P_0||H||\Delta||Q||Q_{pub}||\Lambda||\Upsilon||\Omega||ID||k||l||V||X||U_1||U_2||U_3||R_1||R_2||R_3||s_1 P + s_2 P_{pub} + s_0 H - cU_2||s_3 P + s_2 P_0 - cX||s_1 Q + s_2 Q_{pub} + s_4 H - cR_2||s_5 U_1 + s_0 H - cU_2||s_6 R_1 + s_4 H - cR_2||\Lambda^{s_3} \Upsilon^{s_7} \Omega^{-s_2})$

Update

Suppose the AP's ARC currently has n tuples, the member M with the public key $(a, \cdot, \cdot, \cdot)$ and the access key (j, W_j) computes a new access key as follows.

```
for (k = j + 1; k + +; k ≤ n) do
    retrieve from ARC the kth tuple (u, b, Vk);
    if b = 1, then Wk = Vk−1 + (u − a)Wk−1
    else Wk = (1/(u − a))(Wk−1 − Vk) end if;
end for;
return (n, Wn);
```

Public Inspection

Any party can run this algorithm to assure the correctness of an AP's public archive ARC. With such an algorithm, we can assume that ARC is always updated correctly. Any party, after a change on ARC, can retrieve the new tuple (u, b, V_k). If $(b = 1)$ then he checks if $e(V_{k-1}, aQ + Q_{pub}) \stackrel{?}{=} e(V_k, Q)$; otherwise, he checks if $e(V_k, aQ + Q_{pub}) \stackrel{?}{=} e(V_{k-1}, Q)$;

4.4 Correctness and Security

Correctness and security of our scheme is stated in Theorem 1, whose proof can be found in the full version [14].

Theorem 1. *In the random oracle model and the list oracle model, our dynamic k-TAA scheme provides (i) Correctness; (ii) D-Anonymity under the Decisional Bilinear Diffie-Hellman assumption; (iii) D-Detectability under the q-Strong Diffie-Hellman assumption, where q is the upper bound of the group size; (iv) D-Exculpability for users under the Discrete Logarithm assumption on $\mathbb{G}_1$; (v) D-Exculpability for the GM under the q-Strong Diffie-Hellman assumption, where q is the upper bound of the group size.*

Theorem 1's proof is based on the following lemmas, definition and theorem. Lemma 1's proof can be found in the full version [14].

Lemma 1. *The interactive protocol corresponding to the $Proof_2$ by the Fiat-Shamir heuristic [8] is an honest verifier perfect zero-knowledge proof.*

Lemma 2. *Suppose a PPT adversary can corrupt all APs and all users and can query the oracle $\mathcal{O}_{JOIN-GM}$. Let $S = \{((a_i, S_i, \cdot, \cdot), x_i)\}_{i=1}^q$ be the set of public key/secret key pairs of all member which are obtained by the adversary using $\mathcal{O}_{JOIN-GM}$. If the adversary can output a new valid member public key/secret key pair $((a^*, S^*, \cdot, \cdot), x^*) \notin S$, then the q-SDH assumption does not hold.*

Proof. Suppose there is a PPT adversary $\mathcal{A}$ such that from set $S = \{((a_i, S_i, \cdot, \cdot), x_i)\}_{i=1}^q$ of public key/secret key pairs of all members, obtained by $\mathcal{O}_{JOIN-GM}$, $\mathcal{A}$ can generate the public key/secret key pair $((a^*, S^*, \cdot, \cdot), x^*) \notin S$ of a new valid member. We show a construction of a PPT adversary $\mathcal{B}$ that can break the q-SDH assumption. Suppose a tuple $challenge = (Q, zQ, \ldots, z^q Q)$ is given, where $z \leftarrow \mathbb{Z}_p^*$, we show that $\mathcal{B}$ can compute $(c, 1/(z+c)Q)$, where $c \in \mathbb{Z}_p$ with non-negligible probability. We consider two cases.

Case 1: This is a trivial case, where $\mathcal{A}$ outputs $S^* \in \{S_1, ..., S_q\}$ with non-negligible probability. In this case, $\mathcal{B}$ chooses $\gamma \leftarrow \mathbb{Z}_p^*$ and $H \leftarrow \mathbb{G}_1$, gives $\mathcal{A}$ the group public key $(P = Q, P_{pub} = \gamma P, P_0 = zQ, H, \Delta = e(P, P))$, simulates a GM and a set of possible users, and simulates a set of possible APs with their public/secret key pairs. Then $\mathcal{B}$ can simulate the oracle $\mathcal{O}_{JOIN-GM}$ that $\mathcal{A}$ needs to access. Suppose a set of keys $S = \{((a_i, S_i, \cdot, \cdot), x_i)\}_{i=1}^q$ is generated and $\mathcal{A}$ outputs a new $((a^*, S^*, \cdot, \cdot), x^*)$ with non-negligible probability such that $S^* \in \{S_1, ..., S_q\}$. Suppose $S^* = S_j$, where $j \in \{1, ..., q\}$, then $\frac{1}{a^*+\gamma}(x^* P + P_0) =$

$\frac{1}{a_j+\gamma}(x_jP+P_0)$, so $(a_j - a^*)P_0 = (a^*x_j - a_jx^* + x_j\gamma - x^*\gamma)P$. Therefore, z is computable by $\mathcal{B}$ from this, and so is $(c, 1/(z+c)Q)$, for any $c \in \mathbb{Z}_p$.

Case 2: This is when the first case does not hold. That means $\mathcal{A}$ outputs $S^* \notin \{S_1, ..., S_q\}$ with non-negligible probability. Then $\mathcal{B}$ plays the following game:

1. Generate $\alpha, a_i, x_i \leftarrow \mathbb{Z}_p^*$, $i = 1, ..., q$, where a_is are different from one another, and choose $m \leftarrow \{1, ..., q\}$.
2. Suppose $\gamma = z - a_m$ ($\mathcal{B}$ does not know γ). Then $\mathcal{B}$ can compute the following P, P_{pub}, P_0 from the tuple *challenge*.

$$P = \prod_{i=1,i\neq m}^{q} (z + a_i - a_m)Q$$

$$P_{pub} = \gamma P = (z - a_m) \prod_{i=1,i\neq m}^{q} (z + a_i - a_m)Q$$

$$P_0 = \alpha \prod_{i=1}^{q}(z + a_i - a_m)Q - x_m \prod_{i=1,i\neq m}^{q} (z + a_i - a_m)Q$$

3. Generate $H \leftarrow \mathbb{G}_1$ and give $\mathcal{A}$ the group public key $(P, P_{pub}, P_0, H, \Delta = e(P, P))$. Simulate a GM, a set of possible users and a set of possible APs with their public/secret key pairs.
4. $\mathcal{B}$ can simulate the oracle $\mathcal{O}_{JOIN-GM}$ that $\mathcal{A}$ needs to access as follows. Suppose $\mathcal{A}$ wants an execution of the joining procedure between the GM (controlled by $\mathcal{B}$) and a user (controlled by $\mathcal{A}$). As being able to extract information from $\mathcal{A}$, after receiving the commitment C' from $\mathcal{A}$, $\mathcal{B}$ can find x', r and generate y, y', a in the joining procedure so that the prepared a_i, x_i above are computed in the protocol to be the corresponding parts of the user i's keys. $\mathcal{B}$ can compute S_i as follows:
   - If $i = m$, then

   $$S_m = \frac{1}{a_m + \gamma}(x_mP + P_0) = \alpha \prod_{i=1,i\neq m}^{q} (z + a_i - a_m)Q$$

   This is computable from the tuple *challenge*.
   - If $i \neq m$, then

   $$S_i = \frac{1}{a_i + \gamma}(x_iP + P_0) =$$

   $$(x_i - x_m) \prod_{j=1,j\neq m,i}^{q} (z + a_j - a_m)Q + \alpha \prod_{j=1,j\neq i}^{q} (z + a_j - a_m)Q$$

   This is computable from the tuple *challenge*.
5. Get the output $((a^*, S^*, \cdot, \cdot), x^*)$ from $\mathcal{A}$, where

$$S^* = \frac{1}{a^* + \gamma}(x^*P + P_0) = \frac{1}{z + a^* - a_m}(\alpha z + x^* - x_m) \prod_{i=1,i\neq m}^{q} (z + a_i - a_m)Q$$

We can see that the case $\alpha z + x^* - x_m = \alpha(z + a^* - a_m)$ happens with negligible probability, as it results in $S^* = S_m$. So the case $\alpha z + x^* - x_m \neq \alpha(z + a^* - a_m)$ happens with non-negligible probability ϵ_1. Suppose in this case, the probability that $a^* \in \{a_1, ..., a_q\}$ is ϵ_2. Then the probability that $a^* \notin \{a_1, ..., a_q\} \backslash \{a_m\}$ is $\epsilon_1 - \frac{q-1}{q}\epsilon_2$ (as $m \leftarrow \{1, ..., q\}$), which is also non-negligible if q is bound by a polynomial of l. If $\alpha z + x^* - x_m \neq \alpha(z + a^* - a_m)$ and $a^* \notin \{a_1, ..., a_q\} \backslash \{a_m\}$, then $\frac{1}{z + a^* - a_m} Q$ is computable from the tuple $challenge$ and S^* and so $\mathcal{B}$ can compute $(c, \frac{1}{z+c}Q)$, where $c = a^* - a_m$.

4.5 Relationship Between DBDH and (l, m, n)-DBDH Assumptions

We now present the (l, m, n)-Decisional Bilinear Diffie-Hellman assumption and show that it is weaker than the DBDH assumption in Theorem 2.

(l, m, n)-Decisional Bilinear Diffie-Hellman Assumption. *For every PPT algorithm $\mathcal{A}$, the following function $Adv_{\mathcal{A}}^{(l,m,n)\text{-}DBDH}(\kappa)$ is negligible.*

$$Adv_{\mathcal{A}}^{(l,m,n)\text{-}DBDH}(\kappa) = |Pr[\mathcal{A}(\mathbf{t}, \{x_u P\}_{u=0}^{l}, \{e(P,P)^{x_u y_v z_w}\}_{(u,v,w)=(0,1,1)}^{(l,m,n)}) = 1]$$
$$- Pr[\mathcal{A}(\mathbf{t}, \{P_u\}_{u=0}^{l}, \{\Gamma_{uvw}\}_{(u,v,w)=(0,1,1)}^{(l,m,n)}) = 1]|$$

where $\mathbf{t} = (p, \mathbb{G}_1, \mathbb{G}_T, e, P) \leftarrow \mathcal{G}(1^\kappa)$ *and* $x_u, y_v, z_w \leftarrow \mathbb{Z}_p^*$, $P_u \leftarrow \mathbb{G}_1$, $\Gamma_{u,v,w} \leftarrow \mathbb{G}_T$, *for* $(u, v, w) = (0, 1, 1)...(l, m, n)$.

Theorem 2. *If the DBDH assumption holds then the (l, m, n)-DBDH assumption also holds.*

Proof. We first prove that if the DBDH assumption holds, then the $(1, 1, 1)$-DBDH assumption holds. We show that if a PPT algorithm $\mathcal{A}$ has non-negligible $Adv_{\mathcal{A}}^{(1,1,1)\text{-}DBDH}(\kappa)$ (i.e. the $(1, 1, 1)$-DBDH assumption does not hold), then we can build an algorithm $\mathcal{B}$ that has non-negligible $Adv_{\mathcal{B}}^{DBDH}(\kappa)$ (i.e. the DBDH assumption does not hold). Suppose $a, b, c \in \mathbb{Z}_p^*$ and $\Gamma \in \mathbb{G}_T^*$, we observe that if a and b are uniformly distributed in $\mathbb{Z}_p^*$, then $x = ab$ is also uniformly distributed in $\mathbb{Z}_p^*$ and if Γ is uniformly distributed in $\mathbb{G}_T^*$, then s is also uniformly distributed in $\mathbb{Z}_p^*$, where $\Gamma = e(P,P)^s$. So to distinguish between $(aP, bP, cP, e(P,P)^{abc})$ and (aP, bP, cP, Γ), the algorithm $\mathcal{B}$ can choose an uniformly random $d \in \mathbb{Z}_p^*$ and simply return the output by $\mathcal{A}$ when it takes as input $(\mathbf{t}, \{dP, dcP\}, \{e(aP, bP)^d, e(P,P)^{abcd}\})$ or $(\mathbf{t}, \{dP, dcP\}, \{e(aP, bP)^d, \Gamma^d\})$.

We now prove that if the (l, m, n)-DBDH assumption and the $(1, 1, 1)$-DBDH assumption hold, then the $(l+1, m, n)$-DBDH assumption holds. We show that if a PPT algorithm $\mathcal{A}$ has non-negligible $Adv_{\mathcal{A}}^{(l+1,m,n)\text{-}DBDH}(\kappa)$ (i.e. the $(l+1, m, n)$-DBDH assumption does not hold), then we can build a PPT algorithm $\mathcal{B}$ that has non-negligible $Adv_{\mathcal{B}}^{(l,m,n)\text{-}DBDH}(\kappa)$ (i.e. the (l, m, n)-DBDH assumption does not hold) or has non-negligible $Adv_{\mathcal{B}}^{(1,1,1)\text{-DBDH}}(\kappa)$ (i.e. the $(1,1,1)$-DBDH assumption does not hold). We define the following sets

$$\mathbf{S}_1 = \{(\{x_u P\}_{u=0}^{l+1}, \{e(P,P)^{x_u y_v z_w}\}_{(u,v,w)=(0,1,1)}^{(l+1,m,n)}) \mid x_u, y_v, z_w \leftarrow \mathbb{Z}_p^*\}$$

$$\mathbf{S}_2 = \{(\{P_u\}_{u=0}^{l+1}, \{\Gamma_{uvw}\}_{(u,v,w)=(0,1,1)}^{(l+1,m,n)}) \mid P_u \leftarrow \mathbb{G}_1; \Gamma_{u,v,w} \leftarrow \mathbb{G}_T; r \leftarrow \mathbb{Z}_p^*;$$
$$P_{l+1} = rP_l; \Gamma_{(l+1)vw} = \Gamma_{lvw}^r\}$$

$$\mathbf{S}_3 = \{(\{P_u\}_{u=0}^{l+1}, \{\Gamma_{uvw}\}_{(u,v,w)=(0,1,1)}^{(l+1,m,n)}) \mid P_u \leftarrow \mathbb{G}_1; \Gamma_{u,v,w} \leftarrow \mathbb{G}_T\}$$

A non-negligible $Adv_{\mathcal{A}}^{(l+1,m,n)\text{-DBDH}}(\kappa)$ means that $\mathcal{A}$ can distinguish between a random element of $\mathbf{S}_1$ and a random element of $\mathbf{S}_3$. It means $\mathcal{A}$ can distinguish either between a random element of $\mathbf{S}_1$ and a random element of $\mathbf{S}_2$ or between a random element of $\mathbf{S}_2$ and a random element of $\mathbf{S}_3$. We consider these 2 cases:

- We show that if $\mathcal{A}$ can distinguish between a random element of $\mathbf{S}_1$ and a random element of $\mathbf{S}_2$, then we can build an algorithm $\mathcal{B}$ that has non-negligible $Adv_{\mathcal{B}}^{(l,m,n)\text{-DBDH}}(\kappa)$. Suppose $\mathcal{B}$ is given an input $(\mathbf{t}, \{P'_u\}_{u=0}^{l}, \{\Gamma'_{uvw}\}_{(u,v,w)=(0,1,1)}^{(l,m,n)})$, $\mathcal{B}$ chooses an uniformly random x and computes $P'_{l+1} = xP'_l$ and $\Gamma'_{(l+1)vw} = \Gamma'^x_{lvw}$, for $v = 1, ..., m$ and $w = 1, ..., n$. $\mathcal{B}$ then return the output from $\mathcal{A}$ when it takes as input $(\mathbf{t}, \{P'_u\}_{u=0}^{l+1}, \{\Gamma'_{uvw}\}_{(u,v,w)=(0,1,1)}^{(l+1,m,n)})$.
- We show that if $\mathcal{A}$ can distinguish between a random element of $\mathbf{S}_2$ and a random element of $\mathbf{S}_3$, then we can build an algorithm $\mathcal{B}$ that has non-negligible $Adv_{\mathcal{B}}^{(1,1,1)\text{-DBDH}}(\kappa)$. Suppose $\mathcal{B}$ is given an input$(\mathbf{t}, \{P'_u, P'_{u+1}\}, \{\Gamma'_{lmn}, \Gamma'_{(l+1)mn}\})$. $\mathcal{B}$ chooses $P'_u \leftarrow \mathbb{G}_1, \Gamma'_{u,v,w} \leftarrow \mathbb{G}_T$, for $(u,v,w) = (0,1,1)$ $\cdots (l-1,m,n)$. $\mathcal{B}$ then return the output from $\mathcal{A}$ when it takes as input $(\mathbf{t}, \{P'_u\}_{u=0}^{l+1}, \{\Gamma'_{uvw}\}_{(u,v,w)=(0,1,1)}^{(l+1,m,n)})$.

Therefore, if the PPT algorithm $\mathcal{A}$ has non-negligible $Adv_{\mathcal{A}}^{(l+1,m,n)\text{-DBDH}}(\kappa)$, then the algorithm $\mathcal{B}$ has either non-negligible $Adv_{\mathcal{B}}^{(l,m,n)\text{-DBDH}}(\kappa)$ or non-negligible $Adv_{\mathcal{B}}^{(1,1,1)\text{-DBDH}}(\kappa)$.

It can be similarly proved that if the (l,m,n)-DBDH assumption and the $(1,1,1)$-DBDH assumption hold, then the $(l,m+1,n)$-DBDH assumption and the $(l,m,n+1)$-DBDH assumption hold. Therefore, by induction, Theorem 2 has been proved.

4.6   A New k-TAA Scheme

A dynamic k-TAA scheme can be converted into an ordinary k-TAA as follows. The setup procedure remains the same, except that the APs do not obtain any key, do not maintain any access group and other public information. The joining, the bound announcement and the public tracing procedures remain the same. The granting access and revoking access procedures are removed. In the authentication procedure for dynamic k-TAA, a user needs to prove to an AP three conditions: (i) he has been registered as a group member; (ii) he is in the access group of the AP; and (iii) he has not accessed the AP more than the allowable number of times. For ordinary k-TAA, the user do not have to prove condition (ii) and just needs to prove two conditions (i) and (iii).

Using the above approach we can construct a k-TAA scheme from the proposed dynamic scheme. The k-TAA scheme has the following differences with the dynamc one. In the setup procedure, the for APs part is removed and only the part for GM is performed. The joining, the bound announcement and the public tracing procedures remain the same. There is no granting access or revoking access. In the authentication procedure, a different $Proof_{2b}$ is used and there is no Update or Public Inspection algorithm. Security of the ordinary scheme is stated in Theorem 3. The authentication procedure and Theorem 3's proof are provided in the full version [14].

Theorem 3. *In the random oracle model and the list oracle model, our k-TAA scheme provides (i) Correctness; (ii) Anonymity under the Decisional Bilinear Diffie-Hellman assumption; (iii) Detectability under the q-Strong Diffie-Hellman assumption, where q is the upper bound of the group size; (iv) Exculpability for users under the Discrete Logarithm assumption on $\mathbb{G}_1$; (v) Exculpability for the GM under the q-Strong Diffie-Hellman assumption, where q is the upper bound of the group size.*

4.7   Efficiency

Our schemes have the same desirable features of the TFS04 scheme. The size of a group member's keys does not depend on the group size and the GM can add new members to the group without modifying the public key or secret key of group members. After being registered into the group, a user does not need to contact the GM. Each AP can independently determine his bound. In the dynamic scheme, each AP can independently decide which members are allowed to access his services. Without considering the Update algorithm the computational cost of authentication depends only on the bound of the AP.

Our schemes have higher communication efficiency compared to the TFS04 scheme. For instance, assume the scheme is implemented by an elliptic curve or hyperelliptic curve over a finite field. p is a 160-bit prime, $\mathbb{G}_1$ is a subgroup of an elliptic curve group or a Jacobian of a hyperelliptic curve over a finite field of order p. $\mathbb{G}_T$ is a subgroup of a finite field of size approximately 2^{1024}. Techniques in [9] can be used to compress elements of $\mathbb{G}_T$ by a factor of three. A possible choice for the parameters can be from Boneh *et al.* [4]: $\mathbb{G}_1$ is derived from the curve $E/GF(3^\ell)$ defined by $y^2 = x^3 - x + 1$. In addition, we assume that system parameters in the TFS04 scheme are $\nu = 1024$, $\varepsilon = \mu = \kappa = 160$. We summarize the comparison of communication costs, which are measured by the number of bytes sent, for authentication procedures in the following table.

	Bytes sent by AP	Bytes sent by User	Dynamic
The TFS04 scheme	40	60 k+ 1617	No
Our ordinary scheme	20	60 k+ 244	No
Our dynamic scheme	20	60 k+ 364	Yes

References

1. G. Ateniese, J. Camenisch, M. Joye, and G. Tsudik. A practical and provably secure coalition-resistant group signature scheme. CRYPTO 2000, Springer-Verlag, LNCS 1880, pp. 255-270.
2. M. Bellare, H. Shi, and C. Zhang. Foundations of Group Signatures: The Case of Dynamic Groups. Cryptology ePrint Archive: Report 2004/077.
3. D. Boneh, and X. Boyen. Short Signatures Without Random Oracles. EURO-CRYPT 2004, Springer-Verlag, LNCS 3027, pp. 56-73.
4. D. Boneh, B. Lynn, and H. Shacham. Short signatures from the Weil pairing. ASIACRYPT 2001, Springer-Verlag, LNCS 2248, pp. 514-532.
5. S. Brands. An Efficient Off-line Electronic Cash System Based On The Representation Problem. Technical Report CS-R9323, Centrum voor Wiskunde en Informatica.
6. J. Camenisch, and A. Lysyanskaya. Dynamic Accumulators and Application to Efficient Revocation of Anonymous Credentials. CRYPTO 2002, Springer-Verlag, LNCS 2442, pp. 61-76.
7. D. Chaum. Blind signature system. CRYPTO 1983, Plenum Press, pp. 153-153.
8. A. Fiat and A. Shamir. How to prove yourself: practical solutions to identification and signature problems. CRYPTO 1986, Springer-Verlag, LNCS 263, pp. 186-194.
9. R. Granger, D. Page, and M. Stam. A Comparison of CEILIDH and XTR. Algorithmic Number Theory, 6th International Symposium, ANTS-VI, pages 235-249. Springer, June 2004.
10. S. Mitsunari, R. Sakai, and M. Kasahara. A new traitor tracing. IEICE Trans. Vol. E85-A, No.2, pp.481-484, 2002. [29]
11. T. Nakanishi, N. Haruna, and Y. Sugiyama. Unlinkable Electronic Coupon Protocol with Anonymity Control. ISW 1999, Springer-Verlag, LNCS 1729, pp. 37-46.
12. L. Nguyen. *Accumulators from Bilinear Pairings and Applications.* RSA Conference 2005, Cryptographers' Track (CT-RSA), Springer-Verlag, LNCS 3376, pp. 275-292, 2005.
13. L. Nguyen and R. Safavi-Naini. *Efficient and Provably Secure Trapdoor-free Group Signature Schemes from Bilinear Pairings.* ASIACRYPT 2004, Springer-Verlag, LNCS 3329, pp. 372-386, 2004.
14. L. Nguyen and R. Safavi-Naini. *Dynamic k-Times Anonymous Authentication.* Full version.
15. I. Teranisi, J. Furukawa, and K. Sako. k-Times Anonymous Authentication. ASIACRYPT 2004, Springer-Verlag, LNCS 3329, pp. 308-322, 2004.

Efficient Anonymous Roaming
and Its Security Analysis

Guomin Yang, Duncan S. Wong*, and Xiaotie Deng

Department of Computer Science
City University of Hong Kong
Hong Kong, China
{csyanggm,duncan,deng}@cs.cityu.edu.hk

Abstract. The Canetti-Krawczyk (CK) model uses resuable modular components to construct indistinguishability-based key exchange protocols. The reusability of modular protocol components makes it easier to construct and prove new protocols when compared with other provably secure approaches. In this paper, we build an efficient anonymous and authenticated key exchange protocol for roaming by using the modular approach under the CK-model. Our protocol requires only four message flows and uses only standard cryptographic primitives. We also propose a one-pass counter based MT-authenticator and show its security under the assumption that there exists a MAC which is secure against chosen message attack.

Keywords: Authenticated Key Exchange, Anonymous Roaming

1 Introduction

Secure key-exchange (KE) protocols provide the basis to build secure communications using symmetric cryptography. But numerous claimed secure protocols have later been found insecure. In 1993, Bellare and Rogaway [3] proposed the first security model for provably secure KE protocols under the symmetric setting. In 1998, Bellare, Canetti and Krawczyk [2] proposed a different model which treats authentication and key exchange separately. The major advantage of this approach is that the proved building blocks can be reused to construct new provably secure protocols. Later, Canetti and Krawczyk [5] extended this work and changed the definition of secure key exchange from simulation-based to indistinguishability-based.

A traditional key exchange protocol involves two parties connected by wired networks, or three parties in the trusted third party setting. With the rapid development of mobile technology, wireless networks become widely available. People can travel around with their mobile devices without being limited by the geographical area of their home networks. This capability is called *roaming*. A

---

* The work was supported by a grant from the Research Grants Council of the Hong Kong Special Administrative Region, China (Project No. 9040904 (RGC Ref. No. CityU 1161/04E)).

J. Ioannidis, A. Keromytis, and M.Yung (Eds.): ACNS 2005, LNCS 3531, pp. 334–349, 2005.

typical roaming scenario involves three parties: *a roaming user, a foreign server,* and *a home server.* The roaming user subscribed to a home server is now in a foreign network and wants to get services from the foreign server. In order to ensure confidentiality of the communications, an authenticated key exchange protocol is carried out among the three parties, e.g. the 2G and 3G cellular network key exchange protocols.

Another important issue regarding the roaming scenario is user privacy. It concerns about hiding the roaming user's identity and movements from eavesdroppers and even the foreign servers, namely *user anonymity* and *user untraceability.* In cellular networks, the latest generation, 3GPP[1], is urging roaming services to be provided with some assurance on the privacy of mobile users. There are many other roaming networks that want user privacy. One is the inter-bank ATM networks or the credit card payment systems [1]. Ideally, a user should not have to reveal anything to the serving network (i.e. the foreign server) other than the confirmation of his good standing with respect to his ATM card or credit card issued by his home server. However, current systems are having users given out their personal information inevitably. Some other scenarios which require anonymous roaming include hopping across meshed WLANs (Wireless Local Area Networks) administered by different individuals, joining and leaving various wireless ad hoc networks operated by different foreign operators, etc.

There have been a number of work on anonymous and authenticated key exchange for roaming [6, 9]. In [9], there is a session key established in each protocol execution between a user and a foreign server. However, the key is also known to the user's home server. This is undesirable because when a roaming user is visiting a foreign server, services are actually provided by the foreign server to the user but not the home server. The home server is called in only as a guarantor for giving a promise that the user is indeed a legitimate subscriber of the home server. For example, in the WLAN Roaming, when a user accesses the Internet through a foreign server, the user may not want his home server to know which network sites he is visiting. In [6], a protocol was designed for protecting a roaming user's identity from all entities other than his home server and the serving foreign server. However, according to results from [11], a malicious server which is not communicating with the roaming user can launch an active attack to reveal the user's identity. In addition, it is recently found that both [9] and [6] cannot provide *Subscription Validation* as described below as both of them are vulnerable to the Deposit-Case Attack [12].

In this paper, we consider a key exchange protocol involving three parties: a user and two servers, namely a home server and a foreign server. In each protocol execution, the following five properties will be attained.

1. **(Server Authentication)** The user is sure about the identity of the foreign server.
2. **(Subscription Validation)** The foreign server is sure about the identity of the home server of the user.

---

[1] http://www.3gpp.org

3. (**Key Establishment**) The user and the foreign server establish a random session key which is known only to them and is derived from contributions of both of them. In particular, the home server should not obtain the key.
4. (**User Anonymity**) Besides the user himself and his home server, no one including the foreign server can tell the identity of the user.
5. (**User Untraceability**) Besides the user himself and his home server, no one including the foreign server is able to identify any previous protocol runs which have the same user involved.

Since this notion is very useful in the roaming scenario for users to travel from their home servers to foreign servers anonymously while at the same time establishing secure session keys with the foreign servers, we call such a scheme as an **Anonymous and Authenticated Key Exchange for Roaming Networks (AAKE-R)**. To our best knowledge, there is no protocol proposed previously which satisfies all the five properties above.

We adopt the modular approach of Canetti and Krawczyk [5] to construct an AAKE-R protocol from reusable building blocks. The protocol is not only provably secure but also network friendly. There are only four message flows and only standard cryptographic primitives are used. Hence efficient implementation of the protocol is possible by choosing appropriate primitives to use. Besides constructing an authenticated key exchange protocol for anonymous roaming, we also build one for conventional roaming (i.e. not anonymous). In fact, we start with some reusable building blocks based on the modular approach of Canetti and Krawczyk and build one for conventional roaming. Then, we extend it to a version which supports user anonymity and user untraceability. As a side-product of our construction, we propose a one-pass counter based MT-authenticator which is used as one of the building blocks in our protocols. Like other MT-authenticators, this new authenticator can be reused to build new protocols in the future.

Organization. In Sec. 2, we briefly introduce the Canetti-Krawczyk model and describe a new MT-authenticator. An authenticated key exchange protocol for roaming is then built in Sec. 3 and the anonymous version of the protocol is derived in Sec. 4. We conclude the paper in Sec. 5.

2   The CK Model and Some Reusable Building Blocks

In the Canetti-Krawczyk (CK) model [5], there is a system of n parties denoted by $P_1,...,P_n$, which may carry out multiple concurrent executions of a message-driven protocol over an adversary controlled network.

There are two models with respect to the adversary.

1. **Authenticated-links adversarial model (*AM*).** An *AM* adversary can corrupt any parties and sessions particular parties. However, the adversary is not allowed to inject or modify messages (except that the sender is corrupted or if the message belongs to an exposed session). The adversary is restricted to deliver messages faithfully, and the message is only to be delivered once

(i.e. all the messages the adversary received are in a set M of undelivered messages with format (m, P_i, P_j) where P_i and P_j are the sender and the receiver, m is some message, and once m is delivered, it is removed from M). However, the adversary can choose not to deliver it.

2. **Unauthenticated-links adversarial model** (UM). A UM adversary is essentially the same as an AM adversary but without those restrictions above on delivering messages.

For the rest of the paper, we denote an AM adversary by $\mathcal{A}$, and a UM adversary by $\mathcal{U}$. Let $AUTH_{\pi, \mathcal{A}}$ be the global output (i.e. the output of the adversary and all the parties in the system) of running π in AM and $UNAUTH_{\pi, \mathcal{U}}$ be that in UM.

Definition 1. *Let π and π' be n-party message-driven protocols in AM and UM, respectively. We say that π' **emulates** π in UM if for any UM-adversary $\mathcal{U}$ there exists an AM-adversary $\mathcal{A}$ such that $AUTH_{\pi, \mathcal{A}}$ and $UNAUTH_{\pi', \mathcal{U}}$ are computationally indistinguishable.*

Since the authentication in AM is explicitly ensured, if π' emulates π in UM, the authentication in UM is also ensured.

Definition 2 (Authenticator). *An authenticator $\mathcal{C}$ is an algorithm that for any protocol π in AM, the protocol $\mathcal{C}(\pi)$ emulates π in UM.*

The way to construct an authenticator is given in [2], where a layered approach is used. An authenticator $\mathcal{C}_\lambda$ can be constructed from an **MT-authenticator** λ which emulates the basic message transmission protocol. The basic idea is that whenever a party P_i wants to send or receive a message, we emulate it using λ. Readers can refer to [2] for details.

According to [5, Theorem 6], it states that if π is a SK-secure key-exchange protocol in AM and λ is a MT-authenticator, $\pi' = \mathcal{C}_\lambda(\pi)$ is a SK-secure key-exchange protocol in UM.

In the subsection below, we review some MT-authenticators and also introduce a new one which will be used to construct our protocols.

2.1   MT-Authenticators

MT-authenticators can be built from various cryptographic primitives. In case public key cryptosystems are used, it is assumed that each party has its private key and also knows the authentic public key of other parties. We also assume that each message m sent by a sender is different. This can be realized by adding a message-ID.

A Signature Based MT-Authenticator [2]

$$P_i \to P_j : m$$
$$P_i \gets P_j : m, N_j$$
$$P_i \to P_j : m, SIG_{P_i}(m, N_j, P_j)$$

The figure above illustrates a signature based MT-authenticator for party P_i to send a message m to party P_j in an authenticated way. Let k be a security parameter, $N_j \in_R \{0,1\}^k$ be a random challenge and SIG_{P_i} be the signature generation function of P_i. The signature scheme is assumed to be secure against chosen message attack [7].

An Encryption Based MT-Authenticator [2]

$$P_i \rightarrow P_j : m$$
$$P_i \leftarrow P_j : m, ENC_{P_i}(N_j)$$
$$P_i \rightarrow P_j : m, MAC_{N_j}(m, P_j)$$

This figure shows an encryption based MT-authenticator. As above, $N_j \in_R \{0,1\}^k$ is a random challenge. ENC_{P_i} denotes the public key encryption function of P_i and MAC_{N_j} denotes a MAC (Message Authentication) scheme under the key N_j. It is assumed that the encryption scheme is semantically secure against chosen ciphertext attack (CCA) [8] and the MAC scheme is secure against chosen message attack.

In this MT-authenticator, after P_i obtains N_j by decrypting the ciphertext from the message sent by P_j, P_i uses N_j as an authentication key to generate the MAC value in the third message. To thwart some interleaving attack which make use of information obtained from session-state reveal queries, we require that N_j is not part of the state information of the involving session of P_i. Instead, N_j should be handled in some secure part of P_i and destroyed once it is no longer needed, that is, after generating the MAC value in the third message.

A One-Pass Counter Based MT-Authenticator

We construct a new one-pass counter based MT-authenticator and propose to use it in authenticated key exchange protocols for simplifying the authentication procedures and improving the efficiency of the underlying mobile applications. The first attempt of constructing a counter based MT-authenticator is found in [2]. However, it has been pointed out in [5] that the security proof of the authenticator in [2] cannot be true due to several shortcomings in the definition of secure KE protocols. We now build a new one and show its security. The idea follows that proposed in [2], but we use a different composition.

Let π be a key exchange protocol in UM. Suppose a party P_i shares a session key κ with another party P_j by running one copy of π. Each of P_i and P_j initiates a counter starting with 0. Our one-pass counter based MT-authenticator λ_{COUNT} proceeds as follows.

- Whenever P_i wants to send a message m to P_j, P_i increases its local counter $COUNT_{P_i}$ by one, sends $m, COUNT_{P_i}, MAC_\kappa(m, COUNT_{P_i}, P_j)$ to P_j, and adds a message "P_i sent m to P_j" to P_i's local output.
- Upon receiving $m, COUNT_{P_i}, MAC_\kappa(m, COUNT_{P_i}, P_j)$, P_j verifies that the MAC is correct and $COUNT_{P_i} > COUNT_{P_j}$ where $COUNT_{P_j}$ is the local counter of P_j. If all of the verifications succeed, P_j outputs "P_j received m from P_i" and sets $COUNT_{P_j} = COUNT_{P_i}$.

Note that the receiver ID is included in the MAC in our scheme, which is not included in [2]. Here we argue that in case the receiver ID is not included and the same key is used for communications in both directions with two counters (one for send and one for receive) at each side, reflection attack will work.

Theorem 1 (One-Pass Counter Based MT-Authenticator). *If π is a SK-Secure key exchange protocol in UM, and MAC is secure against chosen message attack, the MT protocol λ_{COUNT} described above is an MT-authenticator.*

The proof is given in Appendix A.

Remark. Note that a delayed previous message will be rejected by the receiver after a later sent message is accepted in UM, while the delayed message will still be accepted in AM, but it will not affect $\mathcal{A}$ on emulating $\mathcal{U}$.

2.2 SK-Secure Key Exchange Protocols in AM

The Diffie-Hellman key-exchange protocol is SK-secure under the Decisional Diffie-Hellman (DDH) assumption [4]. Let G be a subgroup of prime order q of a multiplicative group $\mathbb{Z}_p^*$. Let g be a generator of G. Below is the review of the protocol which is proven SK-secure in AM [5]. P_i and P_j are two parties and s is the session ID.

Diffie-Hellman (DH) Key Exchange in AM

1. On input (P_i, P_j, s), P_i chooses $x \in_R \mathbb{Z}_q$ and sends $(P_i, s, \alpha = g^x)$ to P_j.
2. Upon receipt of (P_i, s, α), P_j chooses $y \in_R \mathbb{Z}_q$ and sends $(P_j, s, \beta = g^y)$ to P_i, then computes $\kappa = \alpha^y$, erases y, and outputs the session key κ under session ID s.
3. Upon receipt of (P_j, s, β), P_i computes $\kappa' = \beta^x$, erases x, and outputs the session key κ' under session ID s.

Theorem 2 (Theorem 8 of [5]). *Under the Decisional Diffie-Hellman (DDH) assumption, Diffie-Hellman (DH) Key Exchange above is SK-secure in AM.*

3 Authenticated Key Exchange for Roaming (AKE-R)

In the following, we design a key exchange protocol in the roaming scenario which satisfies the first three properties listed in Sec. 1: Server Authentication, Subscription Validation, and Key Establishment. Thanks for the modular approach, we will see that the separation of key exchange and authentication using the modular approach makes the design work and security analysis easier.

Let k be a system-wide security parameter. Let $\mathsf{C}(k) = \{C_1, \cdots, C_{Q_1(k)}\}$ be the set of roaming users (clients) in the system and $\mathsf{S}(k) = \{S_1, \cdots, S_{Q_2(k)}\}$ be the set of servers in the system, where Q_1 and Q_2 are some polynomials and $C_i, S_j \in \{0,1\}^k$ are the corresponding identities of the parties, for $1 \leq i \leq Q_1(k)$ and $1 \leq j \leq Q_2(k)$.

Subscription. The term 'subscribe' is commonly used to describe some special relationship between a user and a server without clear definition. Based on the widely-used concept of subscription in mobile communications, we give the following definition for subscription.

Definition 3 (Subscribe). *Given a security parameter k, 'subscribe' is a computable function Subscribe from $C(k)$ into $S(k)$. We say that C_A is 'subscribed' to S_H if $Subscribe(C_A) = S_H$ where $C_A \in C(k)$ and $S_H \in S(k)$.*

We assume that each user has subscribed to one and only one server, and the subscription is persistent. Hence scenarios related to changing subscriptions of users are excluded.

Based on the terminologies of mobile communications, S_H is said to be the home server of C_A and S_V is said to be a foreign server of C_A if $S_V \neq S_H$. We also assume that the inverse $Subscribe^{-1}$ is computable. Hence for any $S_H \in S(k)$, $Subscribe^{-1}(S_H)$ is the set of all $C_A \in C(k)$ such that $Subscribe(C_A) = S_H$.

3.1   The Security Definition of AKE-R

An AKE-R (Authenticated Key Exchange for Roaming) protocol is a message-driven protocol. In the CK-model, each session is modelled by running a sub-process within a party with input $(P_i, P_j, P_\ell, s, role)$. We extend the CK-model so that the parties are categorized as roaming users and servers. For a user C_A, the input of his session will be in the form $(C_A, S_V, S_H, s, \text{initiator})$ where the *role* must be initiator. For a server, the *role* can either be responder or credential. We say that three sessions of a user and two servers, C_A, S_V and S_H, respectively, are *3-party matching*, if in an execution of the AKE-R protocol, user C_A has a session with input $(C_A, S_V, S_H, s, \text{initiator})$, server S_V has a session with input $(S_V, C_A, S_H, s', \text{responder})$, server S_H has a session with input $(S_H, C_A, S_V, s'', \text{credential})$, and $s = s' = s''$ and $Subscribe(C_A) = S_H$.

Definition 4 (SK-Secure AKE-R Protocol). *An AKE-R protocol π runs among C_A, S_V, and S_H is called **SK-secure** if the following properties hold.*

1. *If uncorrupted C_A, S_V and S_H complete 3-party matching sessions, then upon the completion of the protocol, C_A and S_V output the same key.*
2. *The probability that anyone except C_A and S_V guesses correctly the bit b' (i.e., $b' = b$) is no more than $1/2$ plus a negligible fraction in the security parameter.*

Having an AKE-R protocol SK-secure is not enough in practice. In particular, the definition does not capture Subscription Validation. For example, suppose we extend the two-party Diffie-Hellman key exchange protocol which is proven SK-secure in *AM* (reviewed in Sec. 2.2) to a three-party version in such a way that C_A and S_V conduct the key exchange. After completed, S_V sends the session ID to S_H. Then S_H accepts and the protocol is completed. This three-party version can be shown to be SK-secure with respect to Def. 4 but obviously not satisfying the requirement of Subscription Validation.

For Subscription Validation, S_V has to make sure that a credential issued by a server has been received claiming that C_A is subscribed to the server and is connecting to S_V. In addition, C_A has to make sure that S_V has received a credential issued by S_H.

Definition 5 (Secure AKE-R Protocol). *An AKE-R protocol π run among C_A, S_V, and S_H is secure if the following properties hold.*

1. *π is SK-secure.*
2. *Upon the completion of the 3-party matching sessions,*
   (a) the matching session of S_H has sent the message below to S_V;
      `"C`$_A$` is subscribed to S`$_H$` and is talking to S`$_V$`"`
   (b) the matching session of S_V has received the message below from S_H;
      `"C`$_A$` is subscribed to S`$_H$` and is talking to S`$_V$`"`
   (c) the matching session of S_V has sent the message below to C_A;
      `"S`$_H$` claimed that C`$_A$` is its subscriber and is talking to S`$_V$`"`
   (d) the matching session of C_A has received the message below from S_V.
      `"S`$_H$` claimed that C`$_A$` is its subscriber and is talking to S`$_V$`"`

Remark: Based on Def. 5 above, if a server S_H outputs the message no matter the actual home server of C_A is S_H or not, then it relies on C_A to check (item (d) above) if S_H is cheating. This helps detect the Deposit-Case Attack [12].

In the following, we state an important theorem which allows us to reuse all the proven MT-authenticators given in Sec. 2 for constructing secure AKE-R protocols.

Theorem 3. *Let C_λ be an authenticator (Def. 2) constructed from an MT-authenticator λ exemplified in Sec. 2. If π is a secure AKE-R protocol in AM, then $\pi' = C_\lambda(\pi)$ is a secure AKE-R protocol in UM.*

Proof is given in Appendix B.

We now start describing our AKE-R protocol. Our protocol consists of two steps. In the first step, a user carries out a *Pre-authentication* protocol with his home server when he is in the network operated by his home server. In this step, a 'long-term' *user authentication key* will be established. This key will be used in the second step for authenticating the user.

In the second step, the user is roaming and communicating with a foreign server. The roaming key exchange protocol will be carried out by the user, the foreign server and the home server. The purpose of the protocol is to let the roaming user and the foreign server establish a fresh session key so that a secure channel can be built.

3.2   Pre-authentication

The purpose of pre-authentication is to have C_A and S_H establish a *user authentication key*, $authK_A$. One way to achieve the task is to run a SK-secure key exchange protocol. Alternatively, like in the cellular networks, the key has already been embedded in the SIM card. No matter in which of these two cases, we assume that $authK_A$ is randomly chosen and only shared by C_A and S_H.

After running the pre-authentication protocol, C_A stores $authK_A$ and a *counter* initialized to 0 in some secure and non-volatile memory location. S_H creates an entry for C_A in its own database and sets the attribute of $authK_A$ as the primary key of the database. In the entry for C_A, other attributes such as the identity of C_A and a counter value are included. The counter is also initialized to 0, and will be increased in each run of the AKE-R Main protocol below.

3.3   The AKE-R Main Protocol

We first describe our AKE-R Main Protocol in AM. Then we *compile* it to a secure AKE-R protocol in UM using those authenticators described in Sec. 2.1.

A Secure AKE-R Protocol in AM

We extend the two-party DH key exchange protocol which is SK-secure in AM (Sec. 2.2) to a three-party variant. Since the network is controlled by the adversary, here we use a virtual link between A and H although they are not physically linked in our target applications. In the following, we describe the AKE-R protocol in AM in an informal way. We think that the presentation below can give readers a better picture of the protocol. But it can always be converted to the form according to CK-model.

Extended DH Protocol in AM: (Fig. 1)

1. A roaming user C_A initiates the protocol execution by choosing $x \in_R \mathbb{Z}_q$ and sends $(C_A, S_V, s, \alpha = g^x)$ to S_H.
2. Upon receipt of (C_A, S_V, s, α), S_H checks if C_A is its subscriber, if not, it rejects and halts. Otherwise, S_H sends (S_H, C_A, s, α) to S_V.
3. Upon receipt of (S_H, C_A, s, α), S_V checks if S_H is a legitimate server in its server list, if not, it rejects and halts. Otherwise, S_V chooses $y \in_R \mathbb{Z}_q$, sends $(S_V, S_H, s, \beta = g^y)$ to C_A, then computes $\kappa = \alpha^y$, erases y, and outputs the session key κ under session ID s.
4. Upon receipt of (S_V, S_H, s, β), C_A checks if S_H is indeed its home server. If not, it rejects and halts. Otherwise, it computes $\kappa' = \beta^x$, erases x, and outputs the session key κ' under session ID s.

Corollary 1. *Under the DDH assumption, the Extended DH protocol is SK-secure in AM if S_H is uncorrupted and honest.*

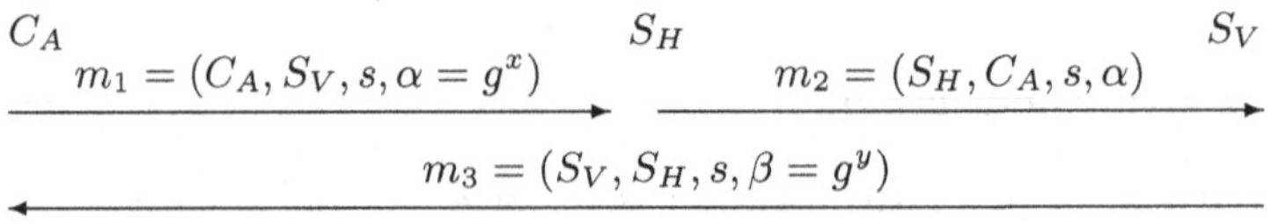

Fig. 1. Extended DH protocol in AM.

Proof. For the first condition in Def. 4, it is easy to see that if the protocol completes, and S_H is uncorrupted and behaves honestly, C_A and S_V share the same key. It is also straight forward that the second condition of Def. 4 is satisfied by following Theorem 2.   □

Corollary 2. *Under the DDH assumption, the Extended DH protocol is secure in AM.*

Proof. Trivial.   □

A Secure AKE-R Protocol in UM

An AKE-R protocol in UM can be derived by applying MT-authenticators to the Extended DH protocol in AM. We apply the one-pass counter based MT-authenticator to m_1, the signature based MT-authenticator to m_2, and the encryption based MT-authenticator to m_3. The resulting protocol is in Fig. 2.

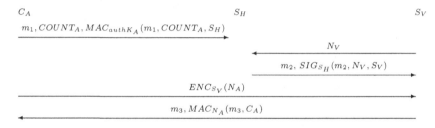

Fig. 2. Extended DH protocol in UM.

After deriving the AKE-R protocol in UM, an optimization [10] of message flows can be applied. And the final AKE-R protocol in UM is illustrated in Fig. 3.

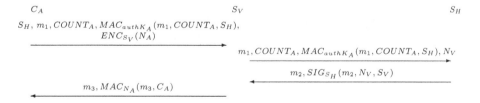

Fig. 3. Optimized Extended DH protocol in UM.

Remark: Note that the identity of the home server S_H is added in the first message from C_A to S_V (Fig. 3). This is required as the one-pass counter based MT-authenticator to m_1 from C_A is not sent directly to S_H. Instead, it is now relayed by S_V to S_H. This is because in our target applications, we assume that C_A is roaming in a foreign network and does not have a direct link with S_H. Therefore, C_A has to tell S_V the identity of his home server, which is S_H.

4   Anonymous and Authenticated Key Exchange for Roaming (AAKE-R)

We now start specifying the security definition of the *anonymous* version of an AKE-R protocol. This version of AKE-R protocol will satisfy all the five properties listed in Sec. 1. In particular, the protocol should provide User Anonymity and User Untraceability. We call such a protocol an Anonymous and Authenticated Key Exchange for Roaming (AAKE-R) protocol.

The adversarial model is based on the adversarial model UM defined in CK-model [5, Sec. 3.2]. The adversary controls the communications of the system and is free to choose any scheduling of activations and action requests of the AAKE-R protocol. The adversary can also adaptively corrupts parties in the system using corrupt a party query, session-state reveal query, and session-key reveal query. By following the notations of [5], we denote the adversary by $\mathcal{U}$.

4.1   The Security Definition of User Anonymity and Untraceability

Game A: "The game is carried out by a simulator $\mathcal{S}$ which runs an adversary $\mathcal{U}$. It is based on the adversarial model UM.

1. $\mathcal{S}$ sets up a system with users in $C(k)$ and servers in $S(k)$.
2. $\mathcal{S}$ then runs $\mathcal{U}$ and answers $\mathcal{U}$'s queries.
3. $\mathcal{U}$ can execute the AAKE-R protocol on any parties in the system by activating these parties and making queries.
4. Among all the parties in the system, $\mathcal{U}$ picks two users $C_i, C_j \in C(k)$ and two servers $S_V, S_H \in S(k)$ such that $Subscribe(C_i) = Subscribe(C_j) = S_H$.
5. $\mathcal{U}$ sends a test query by providing C_i, C_j, S_V and S_H.
6. The simulator $\mathcal{S}$ tosses a coin b, $b \xleftarrow{R} \{0,1\}$. If $b = 0$, the simulator emulates one AAKE-R protocol run among C_i, S_V and S_H. Otherwise, a protocol run among C_j, S_V and S_H are emulated. The simulator then returns to $\mathcal{U}$, all messages generated in the emulated protocol execution.
7. After receiving the response of the test query, $\mathcal{U}$ can still launch all the allowable attacks through queries and also activate parties for protocol executions as before.
8. At the end of $\mathcal{U}$'s run, it outputs a bit b' (as its guess for b)."

$\mathcal{U}$ wins the game if (1) S_H is uncorrupted. Note that C_i, C_j and S_V can be corrupted (so they are not in the restriction). (2) $\mathcal{U}$ guesses correctly the bit b (i.e. outputs $b' = b$.). Define $\mathbf{Adv}_{\pi,\mathcal{U}}(k)$ to be the probability that $\mathcal{U}$ wins the game.

Definition 6 (User Anonymity and Untraceability). *For sufficiently large security parameter k, $\mathbf{Adv}_{\pi,\mathcal{U}}(k)$ is negligible.*

The formulation of Def. 6 is very powerful and can be shown to ensure both user anonymity and user untraceability required by a good AAKE-R protocol.

4.2   A Secure AAKE-R Protocol

To provide user anonymity, the identity of the user should not be sent in clear. In addition, it should not be known to the foreign server according to the anonymity definition above. To do so, we first change the identity of C_a in m_1 and m_2 in Fig. 3 to a *temporary ID* or an *alias* which is a fixed-length binary string chosen randomly from $\{0, 1\}^k$. Then, put $authK_A$ into m_1 so that S_H is able to use $authK_A$ as the search key to get C_A's information from S_H's subscriber database. Also, encrypt the one-pass counter based MT-authenticator using S_H's public key encryption function E_{S_H}. Finally, since S_V does not know the real identity of C_A, the identity of the receiver in the MAC of the encryption based MT-authenticator (i.e. the last message in Fig. 3) has to be changed to *alias* which essentially identifies the initiator of the protocol execution.

In addition, for anonymity, all the counters used in the system should have the same length. We define a counter $COUNT \in \{0, 1\}^{Q_3(k)}$ for some polynomial Q_3 and assume that the value of $COUNT$ would not reach $2^{Q_3(k)} - 1$ in the lifetime of the system.

The complete AAKE-R main protocol is illustrated in Fig. 4.

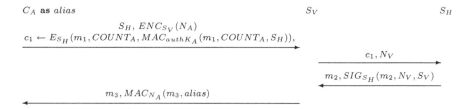

Fig. 4. The AAKE-R Main Protocol.

Theorem 4. *If E_{S_H} is CCA-secure, $\boldsymbol{Adv}_{\pi,\mathcal{U}}(k)$ is negligible.*

Proof is given in Appendix C.

5   Conclusions

Based on the modular approach of the CK-model, we build an anonymous and authenticated key exchange protocol for roaming which is provably secure and efficient. Our scheme requires only four message flows and is the first provably secure key exchange protocol for anonymous roaming. As a side-product from our modular construction, we propose a one-pass counter based MT-authenticator and show its security under the assumption that there exists a secure MAC against chosen message attack. Like other proven secure MT-authenticators, this new authenticator will also be reused to construct new protocols in the future.

References

1. G. Ateniese, A. Herzberg, H. Krawczyk, and G. Tsudik. On traveling incognito. In *Proc. of the IEEE Workshop on Mobile Systems and Applications*, Dec 1994.

2. M. Bellare, R. Canetti, and H. Krawczyk. A modular approach to the design and analysis of authentication and key exchange protocols. In *Proc. 30th ACM Symp. on Theory of Computing*, pages 419–428. ACM, May 1998.
3. Mihir Bellare and Phillip Rogaway. Entity authentication and key distribution. In *Proc. CRYPTO 93*, pages 232–249. Springer-Verlag, 1994. LNCS 773.
4. D. Boneh. The decision Diffie-Hellman problem. In *Proc. of the Third Algorithmic Number Theory Symposium*, pages 48–63. Springer-Verlag, 1998. LNCS 1423.
5. R. Canetti and H. Krawczyk. Analysis of key-exchange protocols and their use for building secure channels. In *Proc. EUROCRYPT 2001*, pages 453–474. Springer-Verlag, 2001. LNCS 2045. http://eprint.iacr.org/2001/040/.
6. J. Go and K. Kim. Wireless authentication protocol preserving user anonymity. In *Proc. of the 2001 Symposium on Cryptography and Information Security (SCIS 2001)*, pages 159–164, January 2001.
7. S. Goldwasser, S. Micali, and R. Rivest. A digital signature scheme secure against adaptive chosen-message attack. *SIAM J. Computing*, 17(2):281–308, April 1988.
8. C. Rackoff and D. R. Simon. Non-interactive zero-knowledge proof of knowledge and chosen ciphertext attack. In *Proc. CRYPTO 91*, pages 433–444. Springer, 1992. LNCS 576.
9. D. Samfat, R. Molva, and N. Asokan. Untraceability in mobile networks. In *Proc. of MobiCom '95*, pages 26–36, 1995.
10. Y. Tin, C. Boyd, and J. Gonzalez-Nieto. Provably secure key exchange: An engineering approach. In *Australasian Information Security Workshop (AISW2003)*, 2003.
11. D. Wong. Security analysis of two anonymous authentication protocols for distributed wireless networks. In *Proc. of the 3rd IEEE Intl. Conf. on Pervasive Computing and Communications Workshops (PerCom 2005 Workshops)*, pages 284–288. IEEE Computer Society, March 2005.
12. G. Yang, D. Wong, and X. Deng. Deposit-case attack against secure roaming. In *Information Security and Privacy, 10th Australasian Conference, ACISP 2005*. Springer, 2005. LNCS.

A Proof of Theorem 1

We start with the following lemma.

Lemma 1. *For sufficiently large security parameter k, if κ is replaced by an unknown random key from $\{0,1\}^k$ and MAC is secure against chosen message attack, λ_{COUNT} is an MT-authenticator.*

Proof. Here we assume that for the two communicating parties, one of them always has the role of initiator and the other always has the role of responder. But the proof also applies to the case when the communication is in bidirectional and both directions are using the same shared key but with two different counters (one for send and one for receive) at each side.

Let $\mathcal{U}$ be a UM adversary interacts with λ_{COUNT}. We define an AM adversary $\mathcal{A}$ which simulates $\mathcal{U}$ as follows.

$\mathcal{A}$ runs $\mathcal{U}$ on a simulated interaction with a set of parties running λ_{COUNT}. First, $\mathcal{A}$ chooses and distributes keys for the imitated parties, note that in this case, the shared secret keys are chosen and distributed. Then $\mathcal{A}$ proceeds its simulation as follows.

1. When $\mathcal{U}$ activates an imitated party $\tilde{P}_i$ for sending a message m to imitated party $\tilde{P}_j$, $\mathcal{A}$ activates P_i in AM for sending m to P_j.
2. When some imitated party $\tilde{P}_j$ outputs "$\tilde{P}_j$ received m from $\tilde{P}_i$", $\mathcal{A}$ activates party P_j in AM with incoming message m from P_i.
3. When $\mathcal{U}$ corrupts a party, $\mathcal{A}$ corrupts the same party in AM and hands the corresponding information (from the simulated run) to $\mathcal{U}$.
4. $\mathcal{A}$ outputs whatever $\mathcal{U}$ outputs.

Let $\mathbf{E}$ denote the event that imitated party $\tilde{P}_j$ outputs "$\tilde{P}_j$ received m from $\tilde{P}_i$" where $\tilde{P}_i$ is uncorrupted and the message (m, P_i, P_j) is not currently in the set M of undelivered messages. In other words, either P_i is not activated for sending m to P_j, or P_j has already had the same output before. Since neither $\tilde{P}_i$ nor $\tilde{P}_j$ is corrupted, $\mathbf{E}$ is also the event that either $\tilde{P}_i$ is not activated for sending m to $\tilde{P}_j$, or $\tilde{P}_j$ has already had the same output before.

If $\mathbf{E}$ never occurs, then $AUTH_{MT,\mathcal{A}}$ and $UNAUTH_{\lambda,\mathcal{U}}$ are equally distributed. It remains to show that $\mathbf{E}$ occurs only with negligible probability.

We prove it by contradiction. Assume $\mathbf{E}$ occurs with non-negligible probability, then we construct a forger $\mathcal{F}$ that breaks the MAC with non-negligible probability.

The forger $\mathcal{F}$ has a MAC oracle O_{MAC} that uses an unknown random key, $\mathcal{F}$ can request O_{MAC} on any message or any verification pair (m, σ). The task of $\mathcal{F}$ is to produce a valid (m, σ) pair but m has not been queried to the oracle before.

$\mathcal{F}$ starts by running $\mathcal{U}$ on a set of parties running λ_{COUNT}. $\mathcal{F}$ chooses and distribute shared keys between parties with one exception, $\mathcal{F}$ randomly chooses one pair of users $\tilde{P}_i$ and $\tilde{P}_j$, and whenever one party is required to produce or verify an MAC for some value, $\mathcal{F}$ queries the oracle and hands the result to that party. If $\mathcal{U}$ chooses to corrupt either $\tilde{P}_i$ or $\tilde{P}_j$, $\mathcal{F}$ fails and aborts.

Note that running λ_{COUNT} in this case is equivalent to a regular run. Assume $\mathbf{E}$ occurs with probability $v(k)$, the probability it occurs between $\tilde{P}_i$ and $\tilde{P}_j$ is then $\frac{2v(k)}{n(n-1)}$ since $\tilde{P}_i$ and $\tilde{P}_j$ are randomly chosen. Also note that when $\mathbf{E}$ occurs between $\tilde{P}_i$ and $\tilde{P}_j$, neither $\tilde{P}_i$ nor $\tilde{P}_j$ is corrupted.

In the case $\tilde{P}_i$ is not activated for sending m to $\tilde{P}_j$, $\mathcal{F}$ outputs the MAC value $\mathcal{U}$ delivered to $\tilde{P}_j$ in the last message as its forgery. On the other hand, if $\tilde{P}_j$ has already had the same output before, then $\tilde{P}_j$ has received m from $\tilde{P}_i$ with a counter, say $COUNT_{\tilde{P}_i}^{old}$ before. Now when $\tilde{P}_j$ accepts m the second time, then $\tilde{P}_j$ must have accepted another incoming message from $\tilde{P}_i$ with the same m but with a more updated counter value, say $COUNT_{\tilde{P}_i}^{new}$ such that $COUNT_{\tilde{P}_i}^{new} > COUNT_{\tilde{P}_i}^{old}$. However, $\tilde{P}_i$ ($\mathcal{F}$) has never queried with $(m, COUNT_{\tilde{P}_i}^{new}, \tilde{P}_j)$ because each message from $\tilde{P}_i$ to $\tilde{P}_j$ is assumed to be different. Hence $\mathcal{F}$ outputs the MAC value that $\mathcal{U}$ has delivered to $\tilde{P}_j$ in the last message as its forgery as well. Thus $\mathcal{F}$ successfully produces a forgery with probability $\frac{2v(k)}{n(n-1)}$. □

Since the SK-security of the key-exchange protocol guarantees that the session key is indistinguishable from a random key, Theorem 1 follows directly from Lemma 1 above.   □

B   Proof of Theorem 3

Proof. We prove it by showing that the following requirements are satisfied.

1. If π is SK-Secure, then π' is also SK-Secure:
   The proof follows that of Theorem 6 in [5] directly. Since that proof only requires π' emulates π, which is done due to the definition of $\mathcal{C}_\lambda$, and also it does not depend on the parties involved in the protocol. Therefore, if π is SK-Secure, $\pi' = \mathcal{C}_\lambda(\pi)$ "inherits" this property from π.
2. If π satisfies requirement 2 of Def. 5 in AM, π' satisfies the requirement in UM as well:
   Suppose π' does not satisfy this requirement. Then there exists an adversary $\mathcal{U}$ in UM such that the global output of running π' with $\mathcal{U}$ does not follow the requirement, but there has no adversary in AM can do this since π satisfies the requirement. Thus the global outputs are distinguishable, in contradiction to $\mathcal{C}_\lambda$ being an authenticator.   □

C   Proof of Theorem 4

Proof. We prove it by contradiction. Namely, if the protocol is not anonymous, that is, if $\mathcal{U}$ wins the game with non-negligible advantage, $\upsilon(k)$, over random guess (which is half chance), we construct a distinguisher $\mathcal{D}$ to break E_{S_H}.

We start by describing a game for the distinguisher $\mathcal{D}$. First, $\mathcal{D}$ adaptively queries a decryption oracle with any ciphertext. Then $\mathcal{D}$ chooses two messages msg_1 and msg_2 and asks the game simulator for a ciphertext. The simulator randomly picks $b \xleftarrow{R} \{0,1\}$ and gives $\mathcal{D}$ the ciphertext c such that $c = E_{S_H}(msg_b)$. After receiving c, $\mathcal{D}$ adaptively queries the decryption oracle with any ciphertext except c. $\mathcal{D}$ is to output a value $b' \in \{0,1\}$ as its guess for b.

Now we construct $\mathcal{D}$ which simulates Game A. First, $\mathcal{D}$ sets up the system appropriately by creating a set $\mathsf{C}(k)$ of users and another set $\mathsf{S}(k)$ of servers. It then initializes all the users in $\mathsf{C}(k)$ with randomly chosen authentication keys from $\{0,1\}^k$ and randomly chosen counter values from $\{0,1\}^{Q_3(k)}$, and initializes all the servers in $\mathsf{S}(k)$ with randomly chosen public key pairs for encryption and another set of public key pairs for signature. Afterwards, $\mathcal{D}$ randomly picks a server, S_H, and replace its encryption public key corresponding to E_{S_H}. Let $COUNT_{min}$ be the smallest counter value initialized for the users in $\mathsf{C}(k)$.

$\mathcal{D}$ runs $\mathcal{U}$ and answers all its queries and emulates all the responses of party activation due to protocol execution. If $\mathcal{U}$ picks S_H as the home server, two users C_i, C_j such that $Subscribe(C_i) = Subscribe(C_j) = S_H$, and some server S_V as the foreign server during the test query, $\mathcal{D}$ answers the query by providing the transcript of a protocol run constructed as follows.

First, $\mathcal{D}$ randomly chooses a in $\mathbb{Z}_q$, $alias$ in $\{0,1\}^k$, a session ID $s \in_R \{0,1\}^k$, and constructs two messages msg_1 and msg_2 as follows.

$$msg_1 = alias \parallel S_V \parallel s \parallel authK_{C_i} \parallel COUNT_{min} - t \parallel g^x$$
$$msg_2 = alias \parallel S_V \parallel s \parallel authK_{C_j} \parallel COUNT_{min} - t \parallel g^x$$

where $t \in_R \{0,1\}^{Q_3(k)}$ such that $COUNT_{min} - t \geq 0$. Note that the counter value is always encoded into a $Q_3(k)$-bit binary string. $\mathcal{D}$ queries the CCA-security simulator with msg_1 and msg_2. Suppose the CCA-security simulator returns a ciphertext c. Then, $\mathcal{D}$ constructs

$$message_1 = \langle\, S_H, ENC_{S_V}(N_A), c \,\rangle$$
$$message_2 = \langle\, c, N_V \,\rangle$$
$$message_3 = \langle\, S_H, alias, s, g^x, SIG_{S_H}(S_H, alias, s, g^x, N_V, S_V) \,\rangle$$
$$message_4 = \langle\, S_V, S_H, s, g^y, MAC_{N_A}(S_V, S_H, s, g^y, alias) \,\rangle.$$

where $N_A, N_V \in_R \{0,1\}^k$, ENC_{S_V} is S_V's public key encryption function, and Sig_{S_H} is the signature generation function of S_H.

The transcript returned by $\mathcal{D}$ to $\mathcal{U}$, as the response for $\mathcal{U}$'s **test** query, is $(message_1, message_2, message_3, message_4)$. $\mathcal{D}$ continues the game by answering all the queries made by $\mathcal{U}$ and emulating all the responses of party activation due to protocol execution. When $\mathcal{U}$ outputs a bit value b' as its guess, $\mathcal{D}$ outputs b' and halts.

If $\mathcal{U}$ does not pick S_H as the home server in his **test** query, $\mathcal{D}$ just randomly picks a value $b' \xleftarrow{R} \{0,1\}$, outputs it and halts.

Analysis: Let $\mathbf{E}$ be the event that $\mathcal{U}$ picks S_H as the home server in its **test** query. Since $\mathcal{D}$ chooses S_H from $\mathsf{S}(k)$ in the game uniformly, $\Pr[\mathbf{E}] = \frac{1}{Q_2(k)}$. Hence we have

$$\Pr[\mathcal{D} \text{ guesses } b \text{ correctly}] = (\frac{1}{2} + \upsilon(k))\Pr[\mathbf{E}] + \frac{1}{2}(1 - \Pr[\mathbf{E}])$$
$$= \frac{1}{2} + \frac{\upsilon(k)}{Q_2(k)}$$

which is non-negligible. $\square$

Quantifying Security
in Hybrid Cellular Networks

Markus Jakobsson[1] and Liu Yang[2]

[1] School of Informatics, Indiana University,
Bloomington, IN 47406, USA
markus@indiana.edu
[2] Software Engineering College, Sichuan University,
Chengdu, 610065, P.R. China
yangliutww@gmail.com

Abstract. We propose a micro-payment scheme for symmetric multi-hop cellular networks that encourages intermediaries to transmit packets and recipients to provide auditing information. Our scheme is an extension of [6], where the authors addressed the simpler asymmetric case. We then analyze the possible rational abuses to our protocol, and construct a detailed statistical model to detect attacks. We show that for typical applications, the statistical detection model we develop will detect cheating very rapidly. For example, in a VoIP application, one particular attack will be detected within a dozen of seconds.

1 Introduction

Multi-hop cellular networks [1, 13] is a new and promising paradigm for wireless communication. Several benefits [5, 7–9] can be expected from the use of this approach. For one thing, the energy consumption of the mobile device can be reduced, as the distance the signal has to cover is smaller. For another, the interference between nodes is reduced, which means more bandwidth. And then, the number of fixed antennas can be reduced, because packets travel between the user and base station by one or more hops. Finally, the coverage of the network can be increased. To make the communication between users go smoothly in such a scheme, users need to collaborate with each other by transmitting packets for others.

One approach to encourage *intermediaries* to collaborate in packet forwarding is to pay them. A micro-payment scheme based on [10] was proposed by Jakobsson, Hubaux, and Buttyán [6] to encourage collaboration in multi-hop cellular networks. The networks they considered consist of cellular nodes, base stations (connected to the backbone), and accounting and auditing centers. If an originator wants to send some packets to a recipient, each packet first needs to travel by one or more hops to the base station which the *originator* belongs to, then the packet is forwarded to the *recipient's* base station, after which this base station transmits the packet to the recipient by one hop. Such a structure is called an asymmetric cellular network.

J. Ioannidis, A. Keromytis, and M.Yung (Eds.): ACNS 2005, LNCS 3531, pp. 350–363, 2005.

Jakobsson, Hubaux, and Buttyán [6] suggested using a micro-payment scheme influenced by the work of Micali and Rivest [10] to allow payments for intermediaries who help forwarding packets. Therein, an intermediary is paid by checking whether packets it handles corresponds to winning tickets. Thus, instead of being paid per packet, intermediaries are given a "lottery ticket" for each packet. This allows for global aggregation of payment information, since intermediaries only record the winning tickets, and only forward the same to the accounting/auditing center. This approach is more efficient than being paid per packet because of the reduced cost of processing total payments. As records are being aggregated, though, detection of abuse becomes more challenging. In [6] , the notion of attack *footprints* was proposed; a footprint is a statistical aberration of audit information that can be associated with a given form of abuse. More in detail, they are ways to infer the likely occurrence of specific attacks by comparing a user's frequency as claimant, sending neighbor, and receiving neighbor, for some attacks also taking into consideration the frequency with which a potential offender is reported as sender vs. recipient by other nodes. While these footprints appear likely to be theoretically sound, it is not evident that they are practically meaningful. In other words, it is not clear that one could determine the presence of an attack (with reasonably small error margins) within a reasonable amount of time. Another potential drawback of [6] is the use of an asymmetric communication model. Namely, the scheme proposed therein uses an unusual multi-hop up / single-hop down communication model, which introduces routing complexities.

1.1   Our Contributions

Our first contribution is to extend the micro-payment scheme in [6] from the asymmetric case to the symmetric case, i.e. to a setting in which both the uplink and downlink are one or more hops. Here, *uplink* refers to the routing of a packet from an *originator* to the nearest base station; and *downlink* from the recipient's base station to the *recipient*. The symmetric case is fraught with two difficulties. First, the nodes on the downlink need to know where to send the packet (in the uplink it is always to the closest base station). Second, while the base station knows about all packets on the uplink (since it receives them), it does not automatically know what packets were successfully received by the recipient on the downlink. This is not a problem of the same magnitude if the downlink is one-hop, since then there is no risk a packet will be dropped on the route. If the base station knows nothing about the downlink transmission, cheating is undetectable. In our design, we not only encourage *intermediaries* to transmit packets, but also encourage recipient to report receipt of packets by checking winning tickets, and thereby address these problems. This constitutes an extension of the techniques proposed in [6].

The second contribution is to construct an efficient auditing model. We propose the following view of the packet flow: If two intermediaries transmit the same number of packets within a certain time interval, they are expected to get the same number of winning tickets on average. This is because each packet corresponds to a winning ticket with the same probability. (Note that one intermediary will win with a probability independent of whether other intermediaries win on the same packet.) Whether a ticket is winning or not depends on secret information associated with an intermediary, as well as on the contents of the packet. Because a winning intermediary also reports his *sending neighbor* – the neighbor who sent him the packet with the winning ticket, and the *receiving neighbor* – the neighbor he sent the packet to, we can expect that the frequency of an intermediary as winning claimant equal his frequencies as sending and receiving neighbor (in which case others will report the event.) After extending the analysis of [6] to the symmetric setting, and analyzing the characteristics of different attacks, we construct statistical models to detect them, and obtain the confidence intervals of some parameters related with winning frequency. Some attacks can be detected by hypothesis testing. Our construction allows for the detection or prevention of the following attacks: packet dropping, originator and recipient collusion, selective acceptance, packet tampering, intermediary credits a friend, ticket sniffing, greedy ticket collection, and packet replay. The simulation results show our method is practical, effective, and efficient.

Our third contribution is that we allow the recipient to verify authenticity of all packets without having to share a key with the sender, and without the use of costly public key operations. This is achieved by making each node share a key with its home base station (which has to be done anyway, for charging purposes.) The uplink message is authenticated by the originator's base station; and the downlink base station computes a MAC with a key shared with the recipient – thus, the recipient can verify the packet he received. Apart from being a beneficial feature to users, the authentication is also indirectly useful as part of the auditing mechanism.

1.2   Related Work

Probabilistic micropayments based on the use of electronic lottery tickets were first suggested by Rivest [11]. To illustrate the idea, a lottery ticket for a $1.00 prize with a 1/100 winning rate has the expected value of one cent. A payer can pay somebody one cent by giving him such a lottery ticket. Since the bank only needs to process winning tickets, this significantly reduces its effort, and the amount of storage and communication needed for both the winner and the bank. In [11], payers will be billed when the lottery tickets they issue win. This creates a psychological disincentive to use the scheme; an alternative version without this drawback was later proposed by Micali and Rivest [10].

Instead of using one payment token *per payee* (as is done in traditional micropayment schemes [10, 11]), Jakobsson, Hubaux, and Buttyán [6] used one token *per packet*, letting each relaying node verify whether this token corresponds to a winning ticket for him. In their scheme, payers (i.e., originators of packets) are charged per packet, and not per winning ticket, while users performing packet forwarding are paid per winning ticket. While there is only one payee per payer in traditional payment schemes, *each* node on a route in [6] may win for a ticket associated with one specific packet, which means one packet may result in more than (or less than) one winning ticket. The originator pays a cost that – on average – covers the cost of routing as well as other network maintenance. The cost an originator needs to pay for sending out a packet is a fixed value which does not depend on the number of winning tickets associated with this packet. Such an approach is a generalization of the averaging techniques proposed in [10].

Jakobsson, Hubaux, and Buttyán's work [6] is a packet based scheme, while Ben Salem, Buttyán, Hubaux, and Jakobsson considered a session based scheme in multi-hop cellular networks [12]. The latter differs from [6] in several aspects. The session based scheme needs exchanging some packets to authenticate users and set up a session, which results in a certain amount of overhead. If the nodes in a cell are highly mobile, the chance a session to be broken is high. Thus this scheme is suitable only in relatively stable networks. The packet based scheme has much less overhead for short sessions and can be used in networks with poor connection or large topology changes.

In [2], Avoine analyses potential weaknesses in the scheme by [6]. Some of these weaknesses relate to a modified version of [6], namely one in which transcripts are not encrypted before being transmitted. The protocol we propose herein inherits the general properties of [6], and exhibits the same vulnerabilities as well. However, these are easily overcome by the use of encryption of transcripts (as specified in [6]), along with an appropriate choice of the function used to determine what tickets win.

Like in [6], our approach is a packet based scheme, which is different from [12]. While [12] charges the recipient, we instead *pay* the recipient to encourage it to report receipt of packet, which is essential to detect cheating. (This payment simply becomes part of the charge to the packer originator.)

1.3   Outline

We begin by describing our work in general and covering some related work in the first part, and then detail our trust and communication models in section 2. In section 3, we describe the protocols for routing, trasmission, and reward recording. Abuse detection and simulation results are described in section 4. Details of our simulation are described in the Appendix.

2   Model

2.1   Trust Model

User model. Like in [6], we assume the existence of three types of participants: users, base stations, and one or more accounting and auditing centers. In addition, there may be multiple networks, each one of them considered the home network for some users.

Functional model. As in [6], users can be categorized to belong to one or more of the following classes: originators; recipients; and intermediaries.

Trust model. In our context, a node and a user refers to the same entity. We consider the user as a software module running on a multi-purpose computer, with an appropriate communicating module. Users, which can be modeled as polynomial time Turning Machines, may cheat in an arbitrary but rational manner: Users only abuse the protocol when they can benefit from doing so. Users trust base stations of their home network not to disclose their secret information; no such trust has to be placed on base stations outside their home network. All base stations are trusted to correctly transmit packets, and to forward billing and auditing information to the accounting center of the user's home network. Because the users are assumed to be selfish, and because they may depart from the protocol if they can benefit from it, we have that the base station cannot trust users to be honest in terms of routing, packet transmission, and reward claiming. Users do not trust each other, either. The accounting center, finally, is trusted by all to correctly perform billing and auditing.

Rewarding model. Our protocol encourages the intermediaries to transmit packets, and also encourages both intermediaries and the recipient to provide auditing information to the auditing center. This is achieved using micro-payments. Similar to the proposal by Micali and Rivest, our remuneration technique works by a probabilistic selection of payment tokens. A winning user records the ticket as well as his sending neighbor (where packet comes from) and receiving neighbor (where packet is sent to). Like in [6], all these three users are rewarded. The recorded claims are sent to the base station; the latter forwards all claims to accounting center periodically.

Abuse. Intermediaries may cheat if this could increase their profit or lower their effort. Thus, we need to consider detecting all possible rational attacks when designing our protocol. In particular, we prevent or detect the following abuses.

- *Packet dropping.* An intermediary agrees to forward packets, but does not retransmit them – whether he claims credit for winning tickets or not.
- *Originator and recipient collusion.* An originator helps a recipient gain a profit by sending packets with winning tickets. For example, an originator constructs a packet and checks if it contains a winning ticket for the recipient (by knowing the secret key of the recipient). If this is the case then he sends out the packet to the recipient; If no, then he makes a minor modification and checks again, until the packet contains a winning ticket to the recipient.
- *Selective acceptance.* An intermediary agrees to receive and forward packets with winning tickets, but not packets without winning tickets. (This attack can be combined with collusion between the originator and the intermediary, and has the same footprint on a per-originator basis; due to lack of space, we do not consider this special case in our description.)
- *Packet tampering.* An intermediary changes the payload of a packet before re-transmitting it.
- *Intermediary credits a friend.* An intermediary with a winning ticket claims to have received the packet from (or have sent to) a user different from the one he actually received it from (resp. sent it to).
- *Ticket sniffing.* A user claims credit for packets he intercepted, but neither agreed to re-transmit nor actually re-transmitted.

- *Greedy ticket collection.* This is a collection of cheating strategies which users try to claim credits in excess of what the protocol specifies – by collecting and sharing tickets with colluders.
- *Packet replay.* A user checks a packet and finds that it contains a winning ticket. Then he makes a copy of the packet and replays it one or more times to increase his profit.

We do not consider the communication attack mentioned in [2], since the attacker benefits nothing from performing it.

2.2   Communication Model

We consider a symmetric multi-hop hybrid network. In other words, as a packet travels from the originator to the receiver, it is transmitted in one or more hops to the closest base station. Then the packet is sent over the backbone to the base station where the recipient resides. The base station of the recipient transmits the packet to the recipient in one or more hops.

The routing of uplink transmission can be performed by either of the two approaches. In one of these, the base station infers topology changes from observed communications and signals, then maintains and propagates routing tables. Route discovery information of each cell is maintained and stored by each local base station, and the updates of routing information are sent to all local nodes periodically. In another approach, routing tables are maintained by the users themselves. Here, it is worth noting that uplink routing is relatively easy because there is only one destination, the base station. However, downlink routing is more complex. Therefore, we assume that the downlink routing is performed by the base station of the corresponding cell. We therefore use a source routing protocol (e.g., Dynamic Source Routing [3]) for the downlink, and a packet sent out by an originator will carry full routing information. In other words, the routing tables of users do not have to take downlink routing into consideration – this also translates into a privacy benefit as general user location data does not have to be propagated to peers.

3   Protocol

Setup. When a user registers to access the home network, he is assigned a pair (id_u, K_u), where id_u is its identity and K_u is a symmetric key.

Packet origination. First of all, the originator u_o of a packet p selects a route path r_p; then he calculates $\mu = MAC_{K_{u_o}}(p)$; finally, he assembles a tuple (p, u_o, u_r, r_p, μ) and transmits it to the next node indicated by the r_p. Here, u_r is the final recipient, and r_p is the route to the closest base station.

Transmission. For both uplink and downlink, each intermediary transmits the packet tuple according to r_p (resp. the downlink route, r'_p).

Network processing. When a packet $P = (p, u_o, u_r, r_p, \mu)$ is received by a base station in the originator's home network, the base station looks up the secret key K_{u_o} of the originator and verifies whether $\mu = MAC_{K_{u_o}}(p)$, dropping the packet if it does not hold.

If the verification of MAC succeeds, the base station (resp. home network register) transmits the packet portion p to the base station associated with the desired recipient, u_r.

The recipient's base station first selects a downlink route r'_p from its routing table or routing cache, then he looks up the recipient's secret key K_{u_r} and calculates $\mu_r = MAC_{K_{u_r}}(p)$. He then assembles a tuple (p, u_r, r'_p, μ_r) and transmits the tuple to the first downlink hop according to the routing path r'_p.

Packet receiving. When a recipient receives a tuple (p, u_r, r'_p, μ_r), he verifies its authenticity by calculating $MAC_{K_{u_r}}(p)$ and verifying whether this equals μ_r. If this holds, then he accepts the packet; otherwise he drops it. The recipient also checks if this was a winning ticket by performing the reward recording protocol.

Reward recording. After an intermediary u has forwarded a tuple $P = (p, u_o, u_r, r_p, \mu)$ (resp. $P = (p, u_r, r'_p, \mu_r)$), he verifies whether $f(\mu, K_u) = 1$ (resp. $f(\mu_r, K_u) = 1$) for some function f (we do not discuss the choice of f in this paper). If this holds, it means that the considered ticket is winning; he then records (u_1, u_2, μ) (resp. (u_1, u_2, μ_r)), where u_1 is the identity of the user (or base station) he received the the packet from, and u_2 is the identity of the user (or base station) he forwarded it to. To a recipient who gets a winning ticket, he just records (u_1, μ), where u_1 is the node who sent him this packet. We use M to denote the list of recorded reward tuples. u_1 is called the *sending neighbor*, and u_2 is referred to as the *receiving neighbor*.

Reward claim. A user periodically transmits claims (u, M, μ') to the base station, where $\mu' = MAC_{K_u}(hash(M))$. When a base station receives a claim, it verifies the correctness of μ' with the key K_u of user u. If the MAC is correct, then it records the claim and computes an acknowledgement $ack = MAC_{K_u}(\mu')$ that is sent to u; otherwise it ignores the claim. When u receives the ack, he verifies the ack and erases M if (but only if) it is correct. Within a time Δ, each base station forwards all recorded claims to an accounting center, and then erases the list.

4   Abuse Detection and Simulation

4.1   Flow Equations and Confidence Intervals

Not all users will collect the same expected number of winning tickets due to several factors, such as the users' location, energy, and power state (on or off). However, if we consider the packet flow (which can be approximated using the rate of winning tickets), we see that the flow-in should be equal to the flow-out, where flow-in denotes the number of packets sent to this node, and flow-out denotes that sent out by this node. Significant divergence in terms of the reported flows is indicative of network problems or attacks. The flows can be approximated using the claims for winning tickets. We use hypothesis testing to detect cheating.

Our attacks detecting approach is based on the following equalities (We suppose the probability of a node to get a winning ticket is s):

To a given cell within a certain period, the number of packets sent out by an originator (resp. base station in downlink) times the winning rate s is expected to be equal to the number of winning tickets reported by the recipient. In particular, to the downlink transmission:

$$N_{B_r} \cdot s = \tilde{w}_r \tag{1}$$

where $\tilde{w}_r$ is the expected value of winning frequency w_r of the recipient. The form of the equation is the same for the uplink transmission. (In the following statements, we focus on downlink transmission, noting that the uplink can be analyzed in the same way.)

Since each intermediary along a path has an equal probability to obtain a winning ticket, the winning frequency of each intermediary is expected to be equal to its frequency being reported as receiving neighbor, and also be equal to that being reported as sending neighbor.

$$\tilde{w}_i = \tilde{r}_i = \tilde{s}_i \tag{2}$$

Here, r_i is the frequency of u_i being reported as receiving neighbor; and s_i is the frequency of u_i being reported as sending neighbor. If someone reports a winning frequency either too high or too low, this indicates cheating may exist during the transmission. We will show that most attacks violate at least one of the above equalities.

Confidence intervals. Equation (1) and (2) hold probabilistically speaking, but may fail to do so in the short run. Thus, there might exist a difference between any two of w_i, r_i, and s_i for user u_i. To all users in a given cell, we denote $x_i = s_i - w_i$, $y_i = w_i - r_i$, $z_i = r_i - s_i$, and assume that x, y, and z are three random variables which satisfy the same normal distribution $N(0, \sigma)$, where σ is the standard deviation, and 0 is the expected value of x, y, and z.

To evaluate if all nodes in a given cell work well or not, we give out confidence intervals of variables x, y, and z which can be used for hypothesis testing to detect attacks. The process is as follows:

1. Make hypothesis $H_0 : e = 0$, equation (2) holds; and $H_1 : e \neq 0$, equation (2) was voilated; where e is the expected value of x, y, or z.
2. Construct statistics $t_x = \frac{\bar{x}-e}{S_x/\sqrt{n}}$, $t_y = \frac{\bar{y}-e}{S_y/\sqrt{n}}$, and $t_z = \frac{\bar{z}-e}{S_z/\sqrt{n}}$ satisfying a $t - distribution$ with freedom of $n - 1$, where n is the number of samples, and $S_x^2 = \frac{1}{n-1}\sum(x_i - \bar{x})^2$, $S_y^2 = \frac{1}{n-1}\sum(y_i - \bar{y})^2$, $S_z^2 = \frac{1}{n-1}\sum(z_i - \bar{z})^2$ are the square deviations of samples.
3. Choose a value of level of significance α and calculate the confidence interval of e:

$$CI_x = (-\frac{S_x}{\sqrt{n}}t_0, \frac{S_x}{\sqrt{n}}t_0); CI_y = (-\frac{S_y}{\sqrt{n}}t_0, \frac{S_y}{\sqrt{n}}t_0); CI_z = (-\frac{S_z}{\sqrt{n}}t_0, \frac{S_z}{\sqrt{n}}t_0) \tag{3}$$

4. Calculate sample means $\bar{x} = \frac{1}{n}\sum x_i$, $\bar{y} = \frac{1}{n}\sum y_i$, and $\bar{z} = \frac{1}{n}\sum z_i$. If $\bar{x} \in CI_x$, $\bar{y} \in CI_y$, and $\bar{z} \in CI_z$, we accept H_0; otherwise we reject H_0, which means abuses might have occurred during the transmission.

In the following statements, we show that all practical attacks we are aware of will violate at least one of the above equations or confidence intervals.

4.2 Analysis

Packet dropping. If an intermediary u_i consistently performs packet dropping, then the intended recipients will receive less packets than expected, and thus, will report fewer winning tickets; u_i will have a higher *claimant* frequency than being reported as *sending neighbor*. This can be expressed as the following model:

$$N_{B_r} \cdot s > w_r \tag{4}$$

$$w_i > s_i \tag{5}$$

$$\tilde{r}_i = \tilde{w}_i \tag{6}$$

equation (1) and (2) are violated. Inequalities (4) to (6) are equivalent to:

$$\frac{N_{Br} \cdot s}{w_r} \geq \delta_0; \ \bar{y} \in CI_y; \ \bar{x} < -\frac{S_x}{\sqrt{n}}t_0 \tag{7}$$

where $\delta_0 > 1$ is a threshold chosen by the auditing center. If $\frac{N_{Br} \cdot s}{w_r}$ exceeds this threshold, the difference between $N_{Br} \cdot s$ and w_r can not be ignored. The higher value we choose for δ_0, the more certain we are to declare a cheating. The above (7) shows: the recipient's winning frequency is unusually much lower than expected; $\bar{y}$ is still in its confidence interval; and $\bar{x}$ is smaller than the lower bound of its confidence interval.

A VoIP Example. Assume the nodes are running a VoIP application using G.711 Codec($Rate = 64kbit/s$) with a frame size (including the headers) of 200 bytes [4]. Then, an originator is able to send out 40 packets per second. If at least 40 packets need to be sent to detect the dropping, then the minimum time to detect this attack is 1 second. The minimum time t can be calculated by $t = \frac{minN_{sent}}{r}$, where $minN_{sent}$ denotes the minimum number of packets needed to be sent to detect the attack, and r is the packet rate of a node.

We use the above VoIP example to demonstrate the relationship among α, s, and $minN_{sent}$ (Figure 1). The second vertical axis in the figure indicates the time needed to detect this attack. We take standard deviation $\sigma = 5$, and $n = 16$ in the simulation. The details of the calculation are described in Appendix. Figure 1 shows:

- To a given point $D = (s, \alpha, N)$ in the 3-D space, if $\frac{N.s}{w_r} \geq \delta_0$, then one or more intermediaries are suspected of packet dropping; otherwise no dropping attack is believed to have occurred.
- Given a winning rate s, the minimum number of packets $minN_{sent}$ needed to be sent increases as the level of significance α decreases. This indicates that to detect packet dropping with higher accuracy (corresponding to higher $1 - \alpha$), more packets need to be sent.

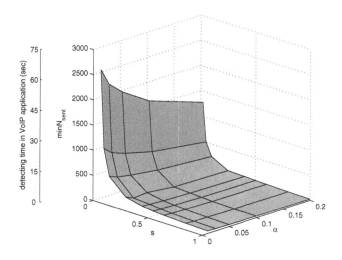

Fig. 1. Simulation of detecting packet dropping.

- Given a value of α, $minN_{sent}$ increases greatly as s decreases (proportional to $\frac{1}{s}$). This indicates that the smaller the winning rate is, the more packets need to be sent to detect a packet dropping attack.

Remark 1. Selective or probablistic packet dropping also results in a smaller number of winning tickets reported by the recipient, which corresponds to a case described in the above model.

Originator and recipient collusion. If an originator benefits a recipient by sending the latter winning tickets, then the recipient will have an unusually high winning rate. Equation (1) will be violated, but equation (2) still holds:

$$N_{B_r} \cdot s < w_r \tag{8}$$

$$\tilde{w}_i = \tilde{r}_i = \tilde{s}_i \tag{9}$$

Formulae (8) and (9) can be verified by the following conditions:

$$\frac{w_r}{N_{Br} \cdot s} \geq \delta_0 \tag{10}$$

$$\bar{x} \in CI_x, \bar{y} \in CI_y, \bar{z} \in CI_z \tag{11}$$

where $\delta_0 > 1$ is a threshold chosen by the auditing center. From (10) we also get $\delta_0 \cdot s \leq 1$ (because $w_r \leq N_{B_r}$).

Inequality (10) can be rewritten as $N_{Br} \leq \frac{w_r}{s \cdot \delta_0}$. We use an example to illustrate it: suppose $s = 0.05$, $\delta_0 = 1.3$, and $w_r = 20$, then we get $\frac{w_r}{s \cdot \delta_0} = 308$, which means if a recipient reports 20 or more (much higher than 308×0.05) winning tickets within 308 packets, then the originator and the recipient are suspected of colluding. The relationship among w_r, s, and N_{B_r} is shown in Figure 2 with

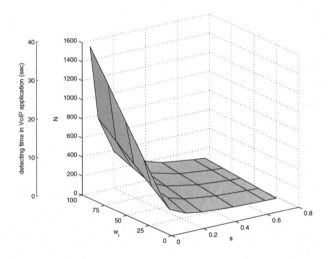

Fig. 2. Simulation when originator and recipient are colluding.

the same VoIP example. The second vertical axis indicates the time needed to detect such an attack. Figure 2 shows:

- To a given point $D = (w_r, s, N)$ in the 3-D coordinate system, if D is located in the upper side of the surface, no colluding attack is believed to have occurred; otherwise the originator and the recipient are suspected as colluding.
- The number of packets needed to be transmitted to detect this attack is proportional to w_r and $\frac{1}{s}$.

Remark 2. We note even if the cheaters only collude some of the time, the recipient will still report a higher number of winning tickets than a expected value ($N_{Br} \cdot s$). Thus this is a detectable case by our above model.

Other attacks. Selective acceptance does not work when the routing is under the control of the base station. Packet tampering is easy to be detected because: (1) both the base station of originator and recipient will verify the MAC of a packet; and (2) the base stations know the routing path. Intermediaries can not easily credit selected friends because they can not choose the routing path. This also affects the greedy ticket collection attack. Collusion between sender and intermediaries can be handled in the same way as collusion between sender and receiver. Ticket sniffing will be easily detected because the attacker will report a fake routing path different to that selected by the base station during a particular transmission. Packet replay will be traced because the attacker will have a too high winning frequency and the base station knows the routing path. Sequence numbers can also be used to avoid this attack.

5 Conclusion

We have extended the asymmetric micro-payment based routing scheme of [6] to the symmetric case, where both the uplink and downlink transmission are one or more hops. Our architecture not only encourages the intermediaries to transmit packets, but also encourages the recipient to report receipt of packet by checking for winning tickets. To discourage and detect dishonest users, we have proposed statistical models based on the perspective of packet flow. The conditions of different attacks in our models are easy to be verified by the auditing center. Our simulation results indicate that abuses will be detected within a short time (ranges from dozens of seconds to a couple of minutes) for common applications. Thus, our model is realistic and meaningful. Due to the space limit, we have not discussed abuse detection when routing is not controlled by the base station. This remains an open problem how to properly address, in particular given the increased complexity of this setting.

References

1. Aggélou G. N., Tafazolli R.: On the Relaying Capacity of Next-Generation GSM Cellular Networks. IEEE Personal Communications, February (2001)
2. Avoine G.: Fraud within Asymmetric Multi-Hop Cellular Networks. accepted by Financial Cryptography (2004)
3. Broch J., Johnson D. B., Maltz D. A.: The Dynamic Source Routing Protocol for Mobile Ad-Hoc Networks. Internet Draft, draft-ietf-manet-dsr-03.txt (1999)
4. Goode B.: Voice Over Internet Protocol (VoIP). Proceedings of the IEEE, Vol. 90. (2002) 1495-1517
5. Hsieh H.-Y., Sivakumar R.: Towards a Hybrid Network Model for Wireless Packet Data Networks. Proceedings of ISCC. IEEE (2002)
6. Jakobsson M., Hubaux J. P. , Buttyan L. : A Micro-payment Scheme Encouraging Collaboration in Multi-hop Cellular Networks. Proceeding of Financial Cryptography (2003)
7. Kubisch M., Mengesha S., Hollos D., Karl H., Wolisz A.: Applying Ad-hoc Relaying to Improve Capacity, Energy Efficiency, and Immission in Infrastructure-based WLANs. Proceedings of Kommunikation in Verteilten Systemen. Leipzig, Germany, KiVS (2003)
8. Lin Y.-D., Hsu Y.-C.: Multihop Cellular: A New Architecture for Wireless Communications. Proceedings of INFOCOM (2000)
9. Mantel O. C., Scully N., Mawira A.: Radio Aspects of Hybrid Wireless Ad Hoc Networks. Proceedings of VTC. IEEE (2001)
10. Micali S., Rivest R.: Micropayments Revisited. CT-RSA (2002) 149–163
11. Rivest R.: Electronic Lottery Tickets as Micropayments. Financial Cryptography (1997) 307–314
12. Salem N. B., Buttyan L., Hubaux J.P., Jakobsson M.: A Charging and Rewarding Scheme for Packet Forwarding in Multi-hop Cellular Networks. Annapolis, MD, USA, MobiHoc(2003)
13. Zadeh A. N., Jabbari B., Pickholtz R., and Vojcic B.: Self-Organizing Packet Radio Ad Hoc Networks with Overlay (SOPRANO). IEEE Communications Magazine (2002)

Appendix: Simulation in Details

Packet Dropping

Since standard deviation of samples S_x, S_y, and S_z are unknown before the experiment, we use a normal distribution as an approximation of t−distribution to simulate the attack. Thus the confidence interval CI_x can be expressed by $CI_x = (-\frac{\sigma}{\sqrt{n}}t_0, \frac{\sigma}{\sqrt{n}}t_0)$, where $\Phi(t_0) = 1 - \frac{\alpha}{2}$, and Φ is the distribution function of $N(0, \sigma)$. For example, if we take the level of significance $\alpha = 0.05, \sigma = 5$, and $n = 16$, we can calculate $CI_x = (-2.45, 2.45)$. To make packet dropping be detected, it is required that $\bar{x} < -2.45$, which means $\sum x_i < -2.45 \times 16 = -39.2$. This indicates at least 40 winning packets need to be dropped. The number of packets need to be dropped can be calculated by $N_{drop} \cdot s \leq -40$, where s is winning rate. If the nodes are running a VoIP application using G.711 Codec($Rate = 64kbit/s$) with a frame size (including the headers) of 200 bytes [4], then an originator can send out 40 packets per second. If at least 40 packets need to be sent to detect the dropping, then the minimum time to detect this attack is 1 second. The minimum time t can be calculated by:

$$t = \frac{minN_{sent}}{r} \tag{12}$$

where r is the packets rate of a node. Numerical results when $\alpha = 0.2, 0.1, 0.05$, 0.025, and 0.01 are listed in the following tables.

Table 1. Numerical results when $\alpha = 0.2$.

s	1	0.8	0.6	0.5	0.4	0.25	0.1	0.05	0.02	0.01
$minN_{drop}$	26	33	44	52	65	104	256	512	1280	2560
$minN_{sent}$	26	33	44	52	65	104	256	512	1280	2560
$t(sec)$	0.7	0.8	1.1	1.3	1.6	2.6	6.4	12.8	32.0	64.0

Table 2. Numerical results when $\alpha = 0.1$.

s	1	0.8	0.6	0.5	0.4	0.25	0.1	0.05	0.02	0.01
$minN_{drop}$	33	42	55	66	83	132	330	660	1650	3300
$minN_{sent}$	33	42	55	66	83	132	330	660	1650	3300
$t(sec)$	0.8	1.1	1.4	1.7	2.1	3.3	8.3	16.5	41.3	82.6

Table 3. Numerical results when $\alpha = 0.05$.

s	1	0.8	0.6	0.5	0.4	0.25	0.1	0.05	0.02	0.01
$minN_{drop}$	40	50	67	80	100	160	400	800	2000	4000
$minN_{sent}$	40	50	67	80	100	160	400	800	2000	4000
$t(sec)$	1.0	1.3	1.7	2.0	2.5	4.0	10.0	20.0	50.0	100.0

Table 4. Numerical results when $\alpha = 0.025$.

s	1	0.8	0.6	0.5	0.4	0.25	0.1	0.05	0.02	0.01
$minN_{drop}$	45	57	75	90	113	180	448	896	2240	4480
$minN_{sent}$	45	57	75	90	113	180	448	896	2240	4480
$t(sec)$	1.1	1.4	1.9	2.3	2.8	4.5	11.2	22.4	56.0	112.0

Table 5. Numerical results when $\alpha = 0.01$.

s	1	0.8	0.6	0.5	0.4	0.25	0.1	0.05	0.02	0.01
$minN_{drop}$	52	65	87	104	130	207	516	1032	2580	5160
$minN_{sent}$	52	65	87	104	130	207	516	1032	2580	5160
$t(sec)$	1.3	1.6	2.1	2.6	3.3	5.2	12.9	25.8	64.5	129.0

In our calculation, $r = 40$ packets/second, and $minN_{sent}$ ($minN_{drop}$) denotes the minimum number of packets need to be sent (dropped) to detect packet dropping.

The Originator and Recipient Collusion

From inequality (10), we get $N_{Br} \le \frac{w_r}{s \cdot \delta_0}$. So given a w_r and δ_0, the upper bound of N_{Br} can be calculated by this inequality. Suppose $\delta_0 = 1.3$, the relationship among s, w_r, and $maxN_{Br}$ are listed in the following table. Here is an example, when $w_r = 20$ and $s = 0.05$, we find $\frac{w_r}{s \cdot \delta_0} = 308$ at the intersection of the corresponding row and column. This means if a recipient gets 20 or more (much higher than 308×0.05) winning tickets within 308 packets, then the originator and recipient are suspected as colluding. The time needs to detect such attack can be calculated similarly as in equation (12).

Table 6. Numerical results when originator and recipient colluding.

w_r \ s	1/1.3	0.7	0.5	0.3	0.2	0.1	0.05	0.01
20	20	22	31	52	77	154	308	1539
40	40	44	62	104	154	308	616	3077
60	60	66	93	154	231	462	924	4616
80	80	88	124	206	308	616	1231	6154
100	100	110	154	257	385	770	1539	7693

Off-Line Karma: A Decentralized Currency for Peer-to-peer and Grid Applications

Flavio D. Garcia and Jaap-Henk Hoepman

Institute for Computing and Information Science,
Radboud University, Nijmegen, The Netherlands
{flaviog,jhh}@cs.ru.nl

Abstract. Peer-to-peer (P2P) and grid systems allow their users to exchange information and share resources, with little centralised or hierarchical control, instead relying on the fairness of the users to make roughly as much resources available as they use. To enforce this balance, some kind of currency or barter (called *karma*) is needed that must be exchanged for resources thus limiting abuse. We present a completely decentralised, off-line karma implementation for P2P and grid systems, that detects double-spending and other types of fraud under varying adversarial scenarios. The system is based on tracing the spending pattern of coins, and distributing the normally central role of a bank over a predetermined, but random, selection of nodes. The system is designed to allow nodes to join and leave the system at arbitrary times.

Keywords: Decentralised systems, micropayments, free-riding, security, grid, peer-to-peer.

1 Introduction

Peer-to-peer (aka. *P2P*) networks like BitTorrent [9], Gnutella [15] and Freenet [8], and grid systems like XGrid [1] are distributed systems without centralised control or hierarchical organisation. Given this flat structure, these systems scale very well when the number of nodes increases. Scalability is important, given the fact that the Internet is still growing exponentially and more people have permanent Internet connections.

Grid systems capitalise on the observation that computer resources are usually very badly distributed in both time and space, and that almost all of them are wasted most of the time. CPU cycles are maybe the best example of this. In an ideal grid system, the whole Internet constitutes a huge supercomputer with practically unlimited resources, that members can use as long as they contribute to it as well. Projects like seti@home, folding@home and distributed.net have shown that a large set of common desktop computers can provide a tremendous amount of computing power. Even though they receive no direct benefit, users participate in such projects because they associate themselves with the goals of the project. If such large scale computations are for an uncompelling cause, it is not easy to find people willing to donate their CPU time.

J. Ioannidis, A. Keromytis, and M.Yung (Eds.): ACNS 2005, LNCS 3531, pp. 364–377, 2005.

Also, many P2P networks suffer form the 'free-riders' problem where users only occasionally connect to the network to use the resources offered by it, but do not donate any resources themselves. Adar and Huberman [3] performed a traffic study on the Gnutella network revealing that 70% of the users share *no* files at all. To counter such problems, 'currencies' of some sort have been proposed to reward users contributing to the system and that can be used as payment when the resources of the network are used.

This paper extends our earlier work in this area [11, 12]. We refer to those papers for a more in depth discussion of the state of the art, and only briefly summarise it here. Several P2P systems use some kind of digital currency to enforce contribution and optimise resource distribution. All these systems use a central bank or broker to track each user's balance and transactions. Micropayment schemes [13, 19, 20] seem to be especially suitable for such a task. However, these schemes are centralised and the load of the central broker grows linearly with the number of transactions. It is clear that when scalability is of primary concern, a central bank or broker constitutes both a bottleneck as well as a single point of failure.

At the moment, the only distributed currency we are aware of that is fully decentralised is KARMA [23]. In that system, the bank for a user is distributed over a bank set of r users, that all need to be on-line, and that are all involved in all transactions between their "owners". This incurs a large overhead, especially in cases where the transaction rate is high.

Another interesting approach is PPay [24]. PPay is a lightweight micropayment scheme for P2P systems. In PPay the issuer of the coin is responsible for keeping track of it. With every transaction the issuer of the coin updates a pointer to the new owner, in a secure manner. The main drawback with PPay is that it uses a central server (called broker) when the issuer of a coin is off-line. Therefore, in certain situations PPay converges to a system with a centralised accounting bank.

1.1 Our Contribution

We present a completely decentralised, off-line karma implementation for *dynamic* P2P and grid systems, that detects double-spending and other types of fraud under varying adversarial scenarios. Previous work of us [11, 12] focused on the static case. The system is based on the tracing of the spending pattern of coins, and distributing the normally central role of a bank over a predetermined, but random, selection of nodes. Transactions between users do not require the cooperation of this distributed bank – this is more efficient, but as a result double spending cannot be prevented. Instead, karma coins need to be occasionally reminted to detect fraud. The system is designed to allow nodes to join and leave the system at arbitrary times.

We focus on the payment for CPU cycles as an application of our techniques, and show how a special minting technique allows us to initialise the system and provide its users with coins in a quite autonomous fashion. Coins correspond to CPU cycles, and the bag of coins owned by a user corresponds, in a sense, to a battery charged with CPU cycles. The battery is initially empty, and can be charged by minting coins. Minting takes quite a few CPU cycles. Alternatively, a coin can be obtained by performing roughly the same amount of work, but for another user. Extensions of our protocols to trade coins for other resources are certainly possible, and only involves initialising the system with a set of coins in a different manner.

We design our system on top of an arbitrary overlay network which provides certain services as described in Section 2.

The remainder of this paper is organised as follows. Section 2 discusses the model and notation used throughout the paper. We describe the system objectives and the capabilities of the adversary in Section 3. Then we present our karma implementation in Section 4, first for a static network and then the dynamic case. Finally, Section 5 discusses methods for early double-spending detection, and Section 6 presents our conclusions and directions for further research.

2   System Model

In the context of this paper we want to stay abstracted from the underlying overlay network. We are going to model common characteristics that apply to routing overlays like CAN [18], Chord [22], Pastry [21] and Tapestry [25] as in [5], were the reader can find also a nice and brief description of each system. In this abstract model, every node that joins the system is assigned a uniform random identifier u from the identifier space Π. We assume that the overlay network provides primitives for both user look-up and message routing. Furthermore, for each possible identifier u (whether u is part of the network or not) the overlay network can efficiently and reliably compute the *neighbour set* $\aleph_r(u)$, which consist of all on-line nodes *close* to u. The definition of *close* varies in each of the above mentioned systems, although it is always well-defined. We also assume that communication within this set is *efficient*, because nodes keep updated routing information of their neighbours. Given that the node identifiers are distributed randomly, any neighbour set represents a random sample of all participating nodes [5].

Off-line Karma requires every user to have his own public key pair (PK, SK) and a certificate that binds the public key with a node identifier. This may be provided by a trusted *Certification Authority* (aka. *CA*). We want to remark that the CA is only needed when a new user joins the system. After that communication with the CA is no longer needed.

Routing information in the overlay network is kept updated, in practise, by node join and node leave messages and periodic queries and fingers to detect when a node suddenly disconnects. This mechanism introduces propagation and update delays. This is, in fact, a discrete approximation of an ideal situation where any modification in the network topology is instantaneously detected by the overlay network. We assume such an ideal situation, and leave responsibility for emulating this ideal functionality in an efficient fashion to the overlay network. We also assume that node joins and leaves are atomic operations.

We also assume that the overlay network is capable of safely distributing a blacklist of banned users. Whenever a user detects fraud and has a proof of that, he can submit it to the overlay network which makes this information available to every user. How to implement the distribution of blacklist securely is beyond the scope of this paper.

2.1   Notation

We write $\{m\}_u$ for u's signature on message m, C_u for u's certificate, and `validSig`(m, u, C_u) for the function that checks u's certificate C_u, and if valid uses the key in C_u to verify a signed message m.

We also use a multisignature scheme. A multisignature scheme [16, 17] is a signature scheme where a set R of users sign a message. A multisignature $\{m\}_R$ for a message m has the same properties as if each user in R concatenates his own traditional public key signature to m, the only difference is that a multisignature is more efficient in size and in verification time (comparable to a single signer Schnorr's signature scheme). Unlike a threshold signature scheme however, it does not provide anonymity. We define $C_R = \{C_i : i \in R\}$ and `validSig`(m, R, C_R) is the function that checks the certificates and verifies the multisignature.

Security of our system is parameterised by a security parameter s. All cryptographic primitives we use satisfy the requirement that the advantage of the adversary breaking them is less than 2^{-s}. We show that the advantage breaking our karma system is at most that large too.

For describing protocols we adopt the notation $a \rightarrow b : m \rightarrow m'$ denote that Alice sends a message m to Bob which he receives as m'. Also $a : f$ means Alice computes f. If f is a predicate, Alice verifies $f \equiv true$ and aborts if not.

3   System Objectives and Threat Model

3.1   Threat Model

We consider a set of n users U of which at most t are under control of the adversary. In the context of P2P networks, there is an important difference in the difficulty for an adversary between adding new corrupted users to the system and getting control over chosen users. Therefore, we also define $0 \leq c \leq t$ to be the number of corrupt users chosen by the adversary after they joined the overlay network. Then, when $c = t$ we give the adversary full control over which nodes in the overlay get corrupted, while for $c = 0$ the adversary is only able to get a randomly chosen set of corrupted users of size t.

Furthermore, we assume that the adversary cannot make excessively many nodes join and leave the system, or let some nodes join and leave in a very high frequency (in attempts to mount sybil attacks, to use them as strawmen, or to overcome the random assignment of node identifiers). In fact, we do not allow the adversary any control over when nodes join the system. In practise, this could be achieved by requiring nodes to pay each time they register, or making node joins a time-intensive procedure (e.g., by requiring them to compute a moderately hard, memory bounded function [2, 10]).

3.2   System Objectives

We note that for any system offering off-line currency, double-spending *prevention* is generally speaking not possible, unless extra assumptions (e.g., special tamper proof hardware) are made. As we are designing an off-line system, we only require double spending detection. We do not consider issues like fair exchange or coin stripping. We focus on the payment itself and not on the exchange of coins for goods.

Then, the requirements on a usable, off-line and decentralised, karma system for P2P and grid applications are the following.

Scalability. Transaction cost should be independent of the size of the network.
No centralised control. The system should not rely on one or several central, special, nodes (e.g., banks or brokers) and should not require any predetermined hierarchy. We do allow a centralised registration procedure.
Load balance. The overhead of the protocol is, on average, evenly distributed over the peers.
Availability. Transactions among users can be processed uninterrupted even when users join or leave the system.
Double-spending detection. The system must detect double-spending, and for every double spent coin, a fraudulent user should be blacklisted.

4   The Off-Line Karma Protocol

4.1   Informal Description

To implement the CPU cycles battery metaphor presented in the introduction, a user can mint coins by finding collisions on a hash function (a la hashcash [4]). This rather expensive minting process is preferred over giving an initial amount of free coins to new users, as in that case the system becomes vulnerable to users changing their identities after spending those coins. A minted coin contains the name of the minting user as well as a sequence number (limiting the number of coins a single user can mint). User identity and sequence number together constitute the unique coin identity. Coins also contain a time stamp recording the time they were minted.

The coins are transferable [6]. A user can pay for resources by transferring a coin to another user. The sender signs the coin, and the receiver verifies this signature and stores the coin (with signature) for further use. With every transfer, a coin is extended with another signature. Thus, the sequence of signatures on a coin record the payment history of that coin. Double-spending is detected by comparing the history of two coins with the same coin identity, and the culprit (or his accomplice) will be found at the node where both histories fork. This check is performed whenever a coin is reminted. Fraudulent nodes are black-listed, together with a proof of their misbehaviour (namely two signatures of the fraudulent node over the same coin). This prevents unfair blacklisting.

Every once in a while (but at least before the coin expires), coins must be reminted. Reminting is used to detect double-spending, and at the same time to reduce the size of the coin by removing its history. In classical systems, reminting is done by a central bank. Here the function of the bank is distributed over a set of users on the network called the *reminters* for the coin. The set of reminters is constructed in such a way that

- at least one of the reminters is a non-corrupted node, and
- all honest reminters possess the history of previously reminted coins with the same identity.

We first describe the static case where we assume to have a set of n users which are always on-line and later, in Section 4.3 we describe the modifications needed for handling dynamic networks, where users join and leave at arbitrary times.

4.2 Off-Line Karma for Static Networks

Minting. Let $h_1 : A \to C$ and $h_2 : B \to C$ be hash functions, and suppose every user is allowed to mint 2^q karma coins. A user u has to spend some CPU time finding a collision y satisfying: $h_1(x) = h_2(y)$ and $x \neq y$, with

$$x = \underbrace{u || sn}_{coinId} || ts$$

where sn is the serial number $|sn| \leq q$ and ts is a time stamp. This is an expensive but feasible operation, for suitable functions h_1 and h_2. In analogy with the monetary system, imagine that the cost of the metal needed for minting a coin is greater than its nominal value. We define the new karma coin as

$$k_0 = \langle x, y \rangle$$

Spending. To spend a coin, a user u transfers ownership of it to the merchant m, by putting a signature over the coin together with the merchant identity m and a random challenge z it receives from the merchant. The random challenge is included to avoid uncertainty about who is the traitor in the case where a user spends the same coin twice at the same user. Otherwise, a fair user might look like the double-spender (unless he keeps a history of received coins forever). Concretely, suppose that the user s owns the coin k_i and wants to spend it at the user m. Then, the last one sends a random challenge z to the first one who computes:

$$k_{i+1} = \{k_i, z, m, C_u\}_u$$

and sends it to m.

Reminting. To prevent the coins to grow unreasonably large and to bound the amount of history that needs to be kept, coins must be reminted regularly, at least within the time to live T. This bank functionality is performed by a random but predefined set of users R_k. The selection of this set must be done in such a way that

- each user is responsible for reminting roughly the same amount of coins (load balance) and
- at least one honest user is a member of the remint set.

Whenever a user u has to remint a coin k, he sends it to each user in the remint set $R_k = \aleph_r(h(id(k)))$. Here the hash function is used as a consistent mapping from the coin identifier space to Π. Each user in R_k must verify the authenticity of k and store it in his local history database. If the verification succeeds, the reminters will create a multisignature

$$k_{new} = \{\mathtt{XY}(k), ts, R_k, C_{R_k}, u\}_{R_k}$$

for the new coin with the same coin identifier and owner, but with a new time stamp ($\mathtt{XY}()$ extracts the collision out of k). If the verification fails, either because the coin is invalid or because a coin with the same identifier and time stamp was already reminted, the reminters will audit the coin and trace back the cheater in the signature chain.

Protocol Description.

Minting. For a user u:
Initially: $K_u := \emptyset$; $sn_u := 0$
$sn_u := sn_u + 1$
$ts := \mathtt{now}()$
$x := u||sn_u||ts$
Find y satisfying: $h_1(x) = h_2(y)$
$k := \langle x, y \rangle$
$K_u := K_u \cup \{k\}$

Spending. User u spends a coin at merchant m:
m : pick nonce z
$m \to u : z$
u : select $k \in K_u$
$u \to m : \{k, z, m, C_u\}_u \to k'$
m : $\mathtt{check}(m, k', z)$
$u : K_u := K_u \backslash \{k\}$
$m : K_m := K_m \cup \{k\}$

where $\mathtt{now}()$ returns the current time and K_u is the bag of coins of user u

Reminting. User u remints a coin $k = \{\tilde{k}, z, u, C_s\}_s$:
$u : R = \aleph_r(h(id(k)))$
$u \to r_i : k, \mathtt{now}(), R \to k', t', R' \quad \forall i : r_i \in R$
$r_i : t' \approx \mathtt{now}()$
. $\quad R' = \aleph_r(h(id(k')))$
. $\quad \mathtt{check}(u, k', \perp)$
. $\quad \mathtt{verifyHistory}(k')$
. $\quad k_{new} = \{\mathtt{XY}(k'), t', R', C'_R, u\}$
$R \leftrightarrow u : \{k_{new}\}_R \to k_R \qquad$ (this is a three-round protocol)
$u : \mathtt{checkBase}(u, k_R)$

```
check(u, k, z) :
if isBase(k) then checkBase(u, k)
else {k', z', u', C_s}_s := k
    .       return (z' = z ∨ z = ⊥) ∧ u' = u
    .              ∧ validSig(k, s, C_s) ∧ check(s, k', ⊥)

checkBase(u, k):
if isReminted(k) then
    .       {k', newts, R', C_R, u'}_R := k
    .       return u' = u ∧ R' = R = ℵ_r(h(id(k')))
    .              ∧ newts ∈ [now() − T, now()]
    .              ∧ validSig(k, R, C_R)
else
    .       ⟨x, y⟩ := k
    .       u'||sn||ts := x
    .       return h_1(x) = h_2(y) ∧ u' = u
    .              ∧ ts ∈ [now() − T, now()]

audit(k, k'):
{... {k_0, z_1, u_1, C_0}_{u_0} ..., z_m, u_m, C_{m−1}}_{u_{m−1}} := k
{... {k'_0, z'_1, u'_1, C'_0}_{u'_0} ..., z'_{m'}, u'_{m'}, C'_{m'−1}}_{u'_{m'−1}} := k'
for(i = 1 to min(m, m')) do
    .       if(z_i ≠ z'_i ∨ u_i ≠ u'_i) then return u_{i−1}

verifyHistory(k):
Hcoin := {k' ∈ H| id(k) = id(k') ∧ ts(k) = ts(k')}
foreach k' ∈ Hcoin do
    .       B := B ∪ {audit(k, k')}
H := H ∪ {k}
return Hcoin = ∅
```

where B is the set containing all the blacklisted users and H is the set of all reminted coins.

Security Analysis. We will show that our protocol is secure by showing that for every double-spent coin, a corrupted node is blacklisted.

Lemma 1. *Let r be the size of the remint set R. If $r > \gamma s + c$, for some constant γ, then the probability that R contains no honest nodes is less than 2^{-s}.*

Proof. Since c nodes can be corrupted by the adversary at will, $r > c$. So we need to see how large the probability is that the remaining $r − c$ nodes happen to be taken form the remaining $t − c$ corrupted nodes when constructing the set R. We define a random variable X equal to the number of honest nodes in R, given that c nodes in R are already corrupted. We want

$$P(X = 0) < 2^{-s} \tag{1}$$

were s is our security parameter. As $t < n$ we have

$$P(X = 0) = \frac{\binom{t-c}{r-c}}{\binom{n-c}{r-c}} < \left(\frac{t-c}{n-c}\right)^{r-c}$$

and we want

$$\left(\frac{t-c}{n-c}\right)^{r-c} \quad < \quad 2^{-s}$$

$$\{\tfrac{t-c}{n-c} < 1\}$$

$$r - c \quad \geq \quad \log_{\frac{t-c}{n-c}} 2^{-s}$$

$$r \quad \geq \quad -s\left(\log_{\frac{t-c}{n-c}} 2\right) + c.$$

This completes the proof.   □

Lemma 2. *Given a coin k, $t = \mathtt{ts}(k)$, there is no relevant information in k after $t + T$.*

Proof. The proof is split in two cases.

- If k is never double-spent in the period $[t,t+T]$ then there is no relevant information at all.
- If k is double-spent first at time t' with $t < t' < t + T$ then:
  - If k is reminted before t' then the new coin $\hat{k}$ with $\mathtt{ts}(\hat{k}) > t$ contains the proof of double-spending and therefore there is no relevant information in k.
  - If k was not reminted before t' then both double-spent coins k_1 and k_2 must be reminted at least once before $t+T$(they would expire otherwise). Then any double-spending attested by k is detected before $t + T$.   □

Theorem 1. *Whenever a coin is double-spent, that coin expires or one corrupted node is identified.*

Proof. Whenever a coin is double-spent, both coins have the same identifier and time stamp. It is not possible for an adversary to change any of them: in case of a just minted coin they are protected by being part of the collision of the hash functions; and in the case of a re-minted coin it is not possible for an adversary to forge the multisignature, given that Lemma 1 ensures that there is always a fair user in every remint set. Then, coins with the same identifier must be sent to the same remint set before their expiration time, otherwise they expire and the condition of the theorem holds. Therefore, at least one fair user $\dot{u}$ must receive both coins before its expiration time. Let k_{i_1} and k_{i_2} be the first remint request of each version of the double-spent coin k_i, received by $\dot{u}$ after the double-spending. Then, $\dot{u}$ detects fraud and calls $\mathtt{audit}(k_{i_1}, k_{i_2})$. $\mathtt{audit}$ first checks whether the signatures are valid. It is clear that a user endorsing a coin with an invalid signature or that is improperly minted is faulty (he should have checked it). If that is not the case, then the coin is fairly minted and $id(k_{i_1}) = id(k_{i_2})$, at least the first user endorsing the coin is the same in k_{i_1} and k_{i_2}. Therefore, and given the fact that both coins are different, there must be one user in the signature chain that transferred the coin to two different users (or to the same user twice). In this case the userIds inside of the signature are different (or the nonces are different), which constitutes a proof of double-spending.   □

4.3   Handling Dynamic Networks

In a static network, the remint set R_k for a coin k never changes. That makes easy to verify that a given coin was fairly reminted at some point in the past, as verifying a remint set is as trivial as checking $R_k = \aleph_r(h(id(k)))$.

In a dynamic network, it is not possible to be so restrictive while defining a valid remint set. Otherwise every time a user $u_o \in R_k$ is off-line, the coin k cannot be reminted, and therefore may expire. On the other hand, the selection of the users in R should somehow be predefined in order to limit the influence of the adversary, and at least allow the validity of the remint set to be reliably determined at a later time (unless we require $r > t$, which trivially implies that at least one fair node is in the remint set).

As a solution we define a valid remint set for a coin k, as the closest r users to $h(id(k))$ in the identifier space, that are on-line at remint time. Then the verification of the fairness of a remint set is difficult, given that the verifier has no information about the state of the network at remint time. An adversary could try to unfairly construct a remint set with only nodes that are under his control, by claiming that all other (fair) users were off-line at remint time. We are going to prevent this kind of attack by taking the density of the set R as an indicator for the authenticity of the coin. We define the density as

$$d(R_k) = \max_{i \in R_k} |i - h(id(k))| \ .$$

Let us assume that the density of the overlay network does not change very fast. Meaning that it is very unlikely, in a worldwide network with a large amount of users, to have big fluctuations in the amount of users connected to it, in short periods of time. Let α be the maximal rate of change for the density of the overlay network, i.e. if T is the maximal time to live for a coin, and $d(t)$ is the density at time t, then for all t' between t and $t + T$, we have $\frac{1}{\alpha}d(t) \leq d(t') \leq \alpha d(t)$.

We call a remint set *acceptable* (for a coin) if it satisfies our constraints on the remint set, and does not contain members beyond the boundaries specified by the density. In such a scenario, an adversary does not have much freedom while selecting the users in R without drastically increasing $d(r)$.

Another issue that needs to be addressed in a dynamic network is the history transfer between users. The neighbourhood R_k for a coin k should keep as an invariant the history of any reminted coin within the period $[\mathtt{ts}(k), \mathtt{ts}(k) + T]$. Given that the history consists of signed coins, it is not possible for an adversary to forge it. Therefore, a joining user can just renew its history by querying its neighbours for it.

```
checkBase(u, k):
if isReminted(k) then
    .    {k', newts, R', C_R, u'}_R := k
    .    return u' = u ∧ R' = R
             ∧ newts ∈ [now() − T, now()]
             ∧ d(R) ≤ α d(now())
    .        ∧ validSig(k, R, C_R)
else
    .    ⟨x, y⟩ := k
    .    u'||sn||ts := x
    .    return h_1(x) = h_2(y)
             ∧ u' = u ∧ ts ∈ [now() − T, now()]
```

The only modification that remains, with respect to the static version, is the function checkBase, which now verifies the density of the remint set, instead of the equality with the neighbourhood.

Security Analysis. We analyse security of the dynamic protocol similar to the static case.

Proposition 1 (Hoeffding bound). *For a hyper-geometrically distributed random variable X, representing the number of successes among n draws, with probability p of success we have [7, 14]*

$$P(X \geq np + g) \leq e^{-2g^2/n}$$

Lemma 3. *Let $p = \frac{t-c}{n-c}$, fix β such that $c \leq \beta r$, and suppose $\beta + \alpha^2 p < 1$. If $r \in O\left(\frac{\alpha^2 s}{(1-\beta-p\alpha^2)^2}\right)$, then any acceptable remint set contains at least one honest node with probability $1 - 2^{-s}$.*

Proof. The remint set is fixed at remint time t. The adversary needs to pick r nodes for the remint set such that it does not violate the acceptability condition $d(R) \leq \alpha d(t')$, which is checked the next time the coin is reminted at time $t' \leq t + T$. At t', the density $d(t') \leq \alpha d(t)$ This means that at time t it can, at best, select r nodes from the first $\alpha^2 r$ nodes from the root of the coin and then take control over c of them. It is successful if among these $\alpha^2 r$ nodes there are $r - c$ faulty ones.

Let X be a random variable representing the number of faulty nodes in such a sample of $\alpha^2 r$ nodes from all n nodes ($t - c$ of which are faulty). Then the adversary is successful if $X \geq r - c$. X is distributed according to the hypergeometric distribution, with $p = \frac{t-c}{n-c}$, and we are interested in bounding

$$P(X \geq r - c) \leq P(X \geq r - \beta r) \qquad \{\beta + \alpha^2 p < 1\}$$
$$= P(X \geq p\alpha^2 r + (r - \beta r - p\alpha^2 r)) \qquad \{\text{Hoeffding bound}\}$$
$$\leq e^{-2(r-\beta r - p\alpha^2 r)^2/\alpha^2 r} = e^{-2r(1-\beta-p\alpha^2)^2/\alpha^2}$$

which we want to be less than 2^{-s}. Then, by taking logarithms

$$\log_2 e(-2r(1 - \beta - p\alpha^2)^2/\alpha^2) < -s$$

and hence

$$r \geq \frac{\alpha^2 s}{2(1 - \beta - p\alpha^2)^2 \log_2 e}$$

which completes the proof. ☐

Lemma 4. *In every remint set, fair nodes can always transmit their remint history to another fair node before leaving.*

Proof. As a corollary of Lemma 3 and given the assumption that node joins and leaves are atomic operations, at least two fair nodes must be in a valid remint set, whenever a fair node is going to leave it. This fact, together with the secure routing assumption over the overlay network, implies that fair users can always transmit their remint history to another fair node before leaving.

Theorem 2. *Whenever a coin is double-spent, that coin expires or one corrupted node is identified. (the proof in Theorem 1 also applies here)*

5   Early Double-Spending Detection

In some scenarios double-spending detection might not be good enough. This is the case when an adversary is able to add new corrupted nodes easily. It is possible for a corrupted user who owns a karma coin, to spend it many times and very quickly, especially when the coin is just minted (or reminted). Although those actions are eventually going to be detected, this is not going to happen until the first two remint-request of this coin are submitted. This user of course is going to be punished, but then the adversary might get another Id and repeat this operation. To counteract this kind of attacks, besides making it harder for an adversary to get new ids, it is possible to detect double-spending early. As a first line of defence, when a user receives a new coin, he performs a search over the coins he possess looking for duplicated identifiers. In case he succeeds, the double-spender is immediately blacklisted. The probability of finding a duplicated coin just like that is small, especially when the number of copies is not too big. To improve this, we introduce coin attractors to the system. An attractor is a user, whose hashed id is the closest to the hashed id of the coin. Then, when a user s wants to spend a coin at the merchant m, s searches over his coins for the one which has the minimum distance with the merchant's hashed id,

$$k_d = \min_{k \in K_s} |h(m) - h(id(k))| \,,$$

and pays with it. Even thought faulty nodes may avoid sending coin to attractors, eventually a good node will do so. At that point the attractor will detect the double spending.

6   Conclusions

We have presented a completely decentralised, off-line karma implementation for P2P and grid systems, that detects double-spending and other types of fraud under varying adversarial scenarios. This is, so far, the first system for truly off-line karma coins, which can be used in highly dynamic peer-to-peer networks and grid systems. Our system outperforms previously proposed system of similar characteristics, under certain scenarios. In particular, we are able to completely replace a central bank by a distributed remint set whose size is roughly proportional to the security parameter s.

Several interesting research questions remain. For instance, the length of a coin increases with every transaction, and involves several public-key cryptographic operations. This is quite heavyweight, in contrast with micropayment schemes that are usually associated with the kinds of value transfers we consider here. One open area of research is to investigate the use of micropayment techniques in off-line scenarios like karma. Another question is whether the use of trusted computing enabled nodes allows for more efficient implementations of karma.

References

1. Xgrid website. http://www.apple.com/acg/xgrid/.
2. M. Abadi, M. Burrows, M. Manasse, and T. Wobber. Moderately hard, memory-bound functions. In *Proceedings of the 10th NDSS*, pages 25–39, San Diego, CA, Feb. 2003. Internet Society.
3. E. Adar and B. A. Huberman. Free riding on gnutella. *First Monday*, 5(10), Oct 2000. http://firstmonday.org/issues/issue5_10/adar/index.html.
4. A. Back. Hashcash - a denial of service counter-measure. http://www.cypherspace.org/hashcash, Mar. 1997.
5. M. Castro, P. Druschel, A. J. Ganesh, A. I. T. Rowstron, and D. S. Wallach. Secure routing for structured Peer-to-Peer overlay networks. In *Proceedings of the 5th OSDI*, Operating Systems Review, pages 299–314, New York, Dec. 9–11 2002. ACM Press.
6. D. Chaum and T. P. Pedersen. Transferred cash grows in size. In R. A. Rueppel, editor, *Advances in Cryptology – EUROCRYPT 92*, volume 658 of *LNCS*, pages 390–407. Springer-Verlag, 1992.
7. V. Chvßtal. The tail of the hypergeometric distribution. *Discrete Mathematics*, 25(3):285–287, 1979.
8. I. Clarke, O. Sandberg, B. Wiley, and H. Hong. Freenet: a distributed anonymous information storage and retrieval system. In *International Workshop on Design Issues in Anonymity and Unobservability*, pages 311–320, 2000.
9. B. Cohen. Incentives build robustness in bittorrent. In *Proceedings of the Workshop on Economics of Peer-to-Peer Systems*, Berkeley, CA, USA, 2003.
10. C. Dwork, A. Goldberg, and M. Naor. On memory-bound functions for fighting spam. In D. Boneh, editor, *Advances in Cryptology – CRYPTO ' 2003*, volume 2729 of *LNCS*, pages 426–444. International Association for Cryptologic Research, Springer-Verlag, 2002.

11. F. D. Garcia and J.-H. Hoepman. Off-line karma: Towards a decentralized currency for peer-to-peer and grid applications (brief abstract). In *Workshop on Secure Multiparty Computations (SMP)*, Amsterdam, The Netherlands, Oct. 7–8 2004.

12. F. D. Garcia and J.-H. Hoepman. Off-line karma: A decentralized currency for static peer-to-peer and grid networks. In *5th Int. Networking Conf. (INC)*, 2005. (to appear).

13. S. Glassman, M. Manasse, M. Abadi, P. Gauthier, and P. Sobalvarro. The MilliCent protocol for inexpensive electronic commerce. In *Fourth International Conference on the World-Wide-Web*, pages 603–618, MIT, Boston, Dec. 1995. O'Reilly.

14. W. Hoeffding. Probability inequalities for sums of bounded random variables. *J. Amer. Statist. Assoc.*, 58:13–30, 1963.

15. P. Kirk. Gnutella. `http://rfc-gnutella.sourceforge.net`.

16. S. Micali, K. Ohta, and L. Reyzin. Accountable-subgroup multisignatures: extended abstract. In P. Samarati, editor, *Proceedings of the 8th CCS*, pages 245–254, Philadelphia, PA, USA, Nov. 2001. ACM Press.

17. K. Ohta and T. Okamoto. Multi-signature scheme secure against active insider attacks. In *IEICE Transactions on Fundamentals of Electronics Communications and Computer Sciences*, pages E82–A(1): 21–31, jan 1999.

18. S. Ratnasamy, P. Francis, M. Handley, R. Karp, and S. Shenker. A scalable Content-Addressable network. In R. Guerin, editor, *Proceedings of the ACM SIG-COMM 2001 Conference (SIGCOMM-01)*, volume 31, 4 of *Computer Communication Review*, pages 161–172, New York, Aug. 27–31 2001. ACM Press.

19. R. L. Rivest. Peppercoin micropayments. In A. Juels, editor, *Proceedings Financial Cryptography '04*, volume 3110 of *LNCS*, pages 2–8. Springer, Feb 2004.

20. R. L. Rivest and A. Shamir. PayWord and MicroMint: Two simple micropayment schemes. In M. Lomas, editor, *Proceedings 1996 International Workshop on Security Protocols*, volume 1189 of *LNCS*, pages 69–87, Cambridge, United Kingdom, Apr 1997. Springer-Verlag.

21. A. Rowstron and P. Druschel. Pastry: Scalable, distributed object location and routing for large-scale peer-to-peer systems. In *IFIP/ACM International Conference on Distributed Systems Platforms (Middleware)*, pages 329–350, Nov. 2001.

22. I. Stoica, R. Morris, D. Karger, M. F. Kaashoek, and H. Balakrishnan. Chord: A scalable peer-to-peer lookup service for internet applications. In *Proceedings of the 2001 conference on Applications, technologies, architectures, and protocols for computer communications*, pages 149–160. ACM Press, 2001.

23. V. Vishnumurthy, S. Chandrakumar, and E. G. Sirer. KARMA: a secure economic framework for peer-to-peer resource sharing. In *Proceedings of the Workshop on the Economics of Peer-to-Peer Systems*, Berkeley, California, 2003. Papers published on Website: `http://www.sims.berkeley.edu/research/conferences/p2pecon/index.html`.

24. B. Yang and H. Garcia-Molina. PPay: micropayments for peer-to-peer systems. In V. Atluri and P. Liu, editors, *Proceedings of the 10th ACM Conference on Computer and Communication Security (CCS-03)*, pages 300–310, New York, Oct. 27–30 2003. ACM Press.

25. B. Y. Zhao, L. Huang, S. C. Rhea, J. Stribling, A. D. Joseph, and J. D. Kubiatowicz. Tapestry: A global-scale overlay for rapid service deployment. *IEEE J-SAC*, 22(1):41–53, January 2004.

Building Reliable Mix Networks
with Fair Exchange

Michael K. Reiter[1], XiaoFeng Wang[2], and Matthew Wright[3]

[1] Carnegie Mellon University
reiter@cmu.edu
[2] Indiana University at Bloomington
xw7@indiana.edu
[3] University of Texas at Arlington
mwright@cse.uta.edu

Abstract. In this paper we present techniques by which each mix in a mix network can be paid for its services by message senders, in a way that ensures fairness and without sacrificing anonymity. We describe a payment mechanism for use in mix networks, and use this payment scheme in fair exchange mechanisms for both connection-based and message-based mix networks. In connection-based mix networks, our protocols achieve fairness in a weak sense: no player can benefit from stopping the exchange prematurely. In message-based mix networks, by taking advantage of each mix's next-hop neighbor as a rational third party, our exchange protocol guarantees strict fairness between initiators and mixes: either both parties successfully exchange payment and service or neither gains anything.

1 Introduction

Mixes are one of the most well-known and commonly-used privacy-preserving systems since their introduction by Chaum [9] over two decades ago. A *mix* is a server that accepts input messages, changes their form and outputs them to their destinations in a permuted order. This prevents an observer from linking inputs to the corresponding outputs. One can distribute trust in a mix system by transferring messages through a sequence of mixes (a *path*), each operated by a different entity. Whenever at least one mix in the path keeps the input/output relation secret, the privacy of the communication will be preserved. We consider both *message-based* mixes, in which each message is sent independently, and *connection-based* mixes, wherein each user maintains a path for a period of time and sends a stream of messages along that path.

The benefits of mixes depend on users trusting individual mixes. Any misbehavior, such as dropping messages or not correctly permuting messages, could jeopardize the credibility of the network of mixes, the *mix-net*, and thus drive away users. Previous research on reliability of mix networks has focused on how to *enforce* the proper operation of each mix. This has generally led to heavyweight solutions [1, 20, 22], or solutions without a rigorous foundation that cannot provide even weak guarantees of mix server behavior [14, 15].

J. Ioannidis, A. Keromytis, and M.Yung (Eds.): ACNS 2005, LNCS 3531, pp. 378–392, 2005.
© Springer-Verlag Berlin Heidelberg 2005

Most existing work assumes that individual mixes are either honest or malicious. The objective, then, is to identify these bad ones and separate them from the mix-net. However, recent research on the economics of anonymity systems [2] questions this assumption: instead of a black-and-white model, a mix server is better described as a *rational and self-interested* entity which strives to maximize its own profits. There are substantial costs involved in operating a server, keeping it running reliably, and providing bandwidth. A server operator, facing these costs and overheads, may drop connections to save bandwidth costs or perhaps simply neglect server performance as a low priority. Given sufficient economic incentives, the mixes can be *encouraged* to operate honestly. For example, a user can pay to use a mix-net, and tie the payments to good mix server performance. Such a scheme could motivate the mixes to properly relay messages, and thus increase the reliability of the mix-net.

Some incentive mechanisms [16, 18] have been proposed for anonymity protocols using digital cash. Unfortunately, they all miss a key issue: fairness in exchange of payment and service. Without proper handling of this problem, a self-interested mix may grab the payment without relaying users' messages, or a self-interested user may refuse to pay after having her messages transmitted. The rationale behind the incentive mechanism will collapse in these conditions.

Though fair exchange is a well-studied problem, a simplistic application of existing exchange mechanisms to anonymity systems might be problematic. The central concern here is how to preserve anonymity during the exchange process. In this paper, we address this problem and present the first design of a reliable mix network built upon fair exchange techniques. Specifically, we adopt the idea of *coin-ripping* for fair exchange to devise a protocol that encourages individual mixes to perform proper operations (in particular, to forward messages) under different scenarios, including connection-based mix-nets and message-based mix-nets.

The rest of the paper is organized as follows: Section 2 reviews related work. In Section 3, we model the fair exchange problem in mix-nets, explicate the assumptions we make in our research and describe our design of a coin-ripping protocol. Section 4 presents a fair exchange protocol for connection-based mix-nets. Section 5 describes a fair exchange protocol for message-based mix-nets. Section 6 analyzes privacy and fairness achieved by our protocols. Section 7 concludes the paper and proposes future research.

2   Related Work

This section reviews previous work related to this research. We first discuss the related concepts of reliability and *robustness* in mix networks and then discuss some of the relevant fair exchange mechanisms.

2.1   Reliability in Mix Networks

Significant attention in anonymity research has been focused on *robustness* in mix-nets. Robustness primarily refers to systems in which each mix is asked to provide a proof or strong evidence for its honest behavior [21]. Some robust mix-nets are also capable of successfully delivering messages even when $k < \ell$ out of the ℓ mixes on a user's path do not follow the protocol. Most of the proposed approaches have been built upon zero-knowledge proofs and secret sharing in re-encryption mix-nets. For example, Ogata et al. present a robust mix-net based on cut-and-choose methods [22]. Both Abe [1] and Jakobsson and Juels [20], propose more efficient zero-knowledge proofs which achieve *universal verifiability* [1]. This property allows a third-party to verify the proof of correct behavior.

In this paper, we focus on *reliability*, namely the property that individual mixes provide service according to the mix protocol. Instead of enforcing this by requiring a proof of service or another strong form of evidence, as with the approaches for robustness, *we intend to motivate each mix to voluntarily perform correct operations.* That is, our approach does not provide robustness guarantees against malicious service providers who seek to undermine the system. We assume that the service providers who run mixes are self-interested, rather than potentially malicious, and we provide a carefully designed mechanism that pays service providers for correct performance. This ensures reliability as long as service providers prefer to be paid rather than disrupt service.

Dingledine et al. [14] propose a different (though related) concept of reliability. They implement a reputation system to record the mixes' performance. This helps users to improve their long-term odds of choosing a reliable path and avoid failing nodes [14]. This works well when mixes are run by volunteers who receive no compensation for their service, but not for self-interested service providers. For example, in a mix cascade network, their protocol has participating mixes report the failures of message transmissions, which will lead to a decrease in the reporter's reputation. If mix server operators are paid based on reputation or usage statistics, as in our model, a self-interested mix will never take such an action. This kind of reasoning is justified by research on the economics of mix-nets [2], which argues that incentives play a central role in the practical deployment of anonymity systems.

Incentive mechanisms for mix-nets have been investigated by Franz, et al. [18] and Figueiredo et al. [16]. Both of them propose to use electronic payment to encourage mixes to behave honestly. The approach of Franz et al. divides electronic payment and messages into small chunks and allows mixes and users to do the exchange step-by-step. This approach is very inefficient. Moreover, it also gives the party that is second to act a small, undue advantage during the exchange. Such an advantage may exceed the cost of the exchange at some moment, causing the party to stop the exchange prematurely. For example, if the mix server goes second, it may receive the last payment and then fail to deliver the last part of the message. If this is the case, the sender would not even provide the last payment. Recursively, we can infer that the transaction completely falls apart – no rational sender will provide any payment and no rational mix will send any part of the message.

Figueiredo et al. propose to wrap an electronic coin in every layer of the onion – i.e., the message constructed by the user through layered encryption, in which each mix reveals the next hop on the path by decrypting the outermost layer – thus encouraging mixes to do decryption. However, the mixes have no incentive to forward the onion after obtaining the payment, and self-interested mixes can save bandwidth by simply dropping the packet. An improvement of the scheme encrypts the payment in each layer with a secret kept in the next layer of the onion. Unfortunately, this gives users a chance to replace payments with junk data and thus avoid payment. In fact, the very anonymity that the system provides means that users can cheat without their identity being exposed. On the surface, our scheme is similar to their approach, but we provide solutions to these problems.

2.2 Fair Exchange

The essential problem in the above mentioned incentive mechanisms is the fairness in exchange of service for payment. Fairness, in the strictest sense, means that either both parties get the items they want in exchange or none of them get any thing useful. A weaker sense of fairness is that no party will benefit from cheating.

The most straightforward way of doing fair exchange is through a *trusted third party* (TTP) [13, 30]. However, this does not work in mix-nets: not only does such an online TTP constitute a trust bottleneck, but it becomes a traffic bottleneck as well. A better alternative is the use of an *offline TTP* that gets involved only when something wrong happened during the exchange process [3, 6]. The problem is that the TTP might still have access to sender/receiver relationships once it participates, which is highly undesirable in an anonymity system. Previous research shows that without a TTP, fairness only can be achieved in a weak sense [6, 8, 26].

Jakobsson proposes *coin ripping* as an offline exchange protocol [19]. The idea is to split a digital coin, called a *rip coin*, into two halves. A customer may *rip spend* the coin by giving the vendor half of it before service is given. Once she receives the service, she gives the vendor the other half. Either half by itself carries no value – in this way, it is similar to using a bill of currency (e.g., a $100 bill) that's been ripped in half. Once the vendor gets the second half of the bill, she can tape the two halves together to form the original bill. However, unlike the bill, if one half has been spent, the other half may not be used as another "first-half" payment.

This idea works well for fair exchange in mix-nets, as we will demonstrate. In mix-nets one knows the mixes she is going to use up-front and is likely to stick to the same set of mixes for a period of time [28]. In the next section, we present a novel and efficient rip coin protocol by taking advantage of this property.

2.3 Cooperation

A related concept to fair exchange is cooperation. One of our approaches requires additional cooperation between mixes.

Evolutionary game theory [5] extensively studies the mechanisms to encourage self-interested players to cooperate. In particular, much of the work in this field uses a concept called *evolutionary stable strategies* (ESS). An ESS is a convention that, upon being established in a population, becomes an individual player's best response to others, even in the presence of single deviation. A famous ESS is the tit-for-tat (TFT) strategy, which offers incentives to rational players to behave cooperatively in the *repeated prisoner's dilemma* (RPD) game.

Simply put, the prisoner's dilemma problem can be modeled as a game played between two players, in which in any particular game, an individual will prefer to defect if she knows the other player is going to cooperate. However, if the game is played repeatedly between the two players (hence *repeated* prisoner's dilemma), each will be better off if they cooperate.

An extended version of TFT is used effectively in the BitTorrent peer-to-peer protocol to encourage file uploading [12]. BitTorrent has become the leading P2P file sharing system, making up 35% of all traffic on the Internet [23], so it appears that TFT works even in dynamic environments with little trust between players. Srinivasan et al. describe how to use generous TFT (GTFT) in ad-hoc networks to achieve the optimal throughput for each node. In GTFT, nodes sometimes cooperate with apparently uncooperative peers in order to keep temporary aberrations from halting cooperation in the long run. In Section 5, we show how to model a key part of our protocol for message-based mix-nets as an RPD and how to use GTFT to ensure cooperation between mixes.

3   Fair Exchange in Mix Networks

This section explicates the assumptions made in this research and the fair exchange problem in mix-nets, before presenting an efficient rip coin scheme for mix-nets.

3.1   Descriptions of Assumptions and Research Problem

In this paper, we propose to use electronic payment to encourage individual mixes to operate properly. The rationale of our approach is built upon following assumptions:

1. *All players (including users and mixes) are rational and self-interested.* A rational player seeks to maximize her own profits. Here we do not consider irrational players who just want to hurt others' interests regardless of their own interests. A mix could turn into an irrational player once being tampered with by an adversary. However, since this will also compromise the profits of the mix itself, we simply assume that the owner of the mix will take proper measures to prevent this from happening. In addition, we assume that every player in the mix-net behaves honestly when she is neutral between cooperation and defection.

2. *User payments exceed the cost of proper operation.* This assumption ensures that once a payment has been tied to the service, a rational mix's optimal strategy is to perform honestly.

Under the above assumptions, the reliability problem is converted into a fair exchange problem, i.e., how to achieve the fairness in exchange of service and electronic payment anonymously. Formally, given a user U communicating with a destination D via a path composed of mixes $N_1, \ldots, N_\ell$, the fair exchange problem here is described as:

1. If all parties are honest, then U receives *service* and $N_1, \ldots, N_\ell$ receive payments.
2. If U operates honestly, then each of $N_1, \ldots, N_\ell$ gains nothing unless it honestly completes the service for U.
3. If $N_1, \ldots, N_\ell$ operate honestly, then U gains nothing unless she spends the expected amount of payment for the communication.
4. Anonymity has been preserved in the course of the exchange: N_1 knows U but not D; N_i $(1 < i < \ell)$ knows neither U nor D; N_ℓ knows D but not U; an outside observer does not know the relationship between U and D.

In (1), the concept of *service* has different meanings in different settings: in a connection-based mix-net, service refers to the connection between U and D; in message-based mix-net, service means that D receives U's message and that $N_1, \ldots, N_\ell$ perform desired permutations on input messages. In (3), we do not specify whether mixes can get payment. If U can prevent mixes from getting payment after providing service (though doing so does not make U better off), we say that the fairness is *weak*. Otherwise, we say the fairness is *strict*.

In the next section, we present a design for electronic payment which helps build fair exchange protocols in a mix-net.

3.2 A Rip Coin for Mix Networks

For making electronic payments, we use a form of electronic cash (ecash). Ecash has the properties of anonymity and untraceability, which mesh well with mix-nets. In an off-line ecash system, the payment process does not need to go through the bank each time, and thereby is very efficient in communication. However, such an approach faces the threat of double-spending, that is, illegal use of the same coin multiple times. Existing solutions (e.g., [19]) to this problem typically construct a digital coin in such a way that double-spending will disclose the spender's identity. However, they tend to be more computationally intensive, involving multiple discrete exponentiations.

Double-spending can be more efficiently avoided with *vendor-specific coins*, each of which can be deposited by only a specific vendor; the vendor compares the current coin with the previous ones to ensure that it hasn't been used before [25]. However, as Rivest and Shamir point out [25], such coins are limited due to their inflexible nature: customers may not be able to predict which vendors they are going to patronize. In a mix-net, however, this is not a problem. Users of a mix-net must know ahead of time the path of mixes before constructing their onions. In our construction, the bank will not know which vendor the coin is for, so nothing is exposed by requesting vendor-specific coins. More importantly, previous research suggests that the users should stick to the same mix path to transmit their follow-up messages for a period of time, in order to prevent *passive logging attacks*, which allow an attacker to identify an initiator by logging observations over time [24, 28, 29]. This means that users should not need to interact with the bank very frequently.

Since users will know their vendors in advance and maintain their paths, we can design a very efficient vendor-specific rip coin for use in mix-nets. We describe the construction of this new coin, and the related protocols (withdrawing, spending, depositing) in the following paragraphs.

Rip coins: A rip coin for mix N is a pair $c_N = (c_{N,1}, c_{N,2})$, where $c_{N,1}$ is the first half and $c_{N,2}$ is the second half. $c_{N,1}$ consists of a string x_N and the bank B's signature σ on x_N. The string $x_N = N\|v_N$ is a concatenation of the mix's identity and a *verification string* v_N. $c_{N,2}$ is a random string. It is associated with $c_{N,1}$ through a public one-way function H, such that $v_N = H(c_{N,2})$.

Withdrawing coins: To withdraw a coin, user U has to obtain the bank's signature on the string x_N, known only to U. The bank B's signature must not be useful in producing a signature of another legal message. The signing technology implemented here is a *blind signature* [10], which makes sure that the bank cannot know which message was signed. For clarity of presentation, we do not present the details of the signature scheme here. Instead, we simply state that U holds a *blinding function* $f(.)$ and can unblind the signed message with another function $f^{-1}(.)$. In addition, we assume that every coin has the same publicly-known value. The process of user U withdrawing ℓ coins from bank B, at which U has a balance, proceeds as follows:

1. User U first generates a sequence of random strings $c_{1,2}, \ldots, c_{\ell,2}$ and then computes strings $v_1, \ldots, v_\ell$ such that $v_i = H(c_{i,2})$, $1 \leq i \leq \ell$. Then, U generates $x_1, \ldots, x_\ell$ where $x_i = N_i\|v_i$.
2. $U \longrightarrow B$: $f(x_1), \ldots, f(x_\ell)$.
3. $B \longrightarrow U$: $\sigma_1', \ldots, \sigma_\ell'$ where σ_i' is the bank's signature on $f(x_i)$. The bank will modify the balance of U's account accordingly.
4. The user U removes the blinding by performing $\sigma_i \leftarrow f^{-1}(\sigma_i')$, $1 \leq i \leq \ell$.

Spending a coin: User U can send the coin to N_i in whole or in parts. However, N_i obtains the coin only after receiving both halves. On receiving the first half $((N\|v), \sigma)$, N_i accepts it only if $N = N_i$ holds, v has never appeared before and σ is B's signature on $N\|v$. On receiving the second half u, N_i accepts it only if $v = H(u)$.

Depositing a coin:

1. $N_i \longrightarrow B$: a pair $((N\|v, \sigma), u)$.
2. The bank B verifies that $N = N_i$, v never appeared before in a coin for N_i, σ is a correct signature on $N\|v$, and $v = H(u)$. If so, B transfers the payment to N_i's account.

Note that in any known protocol that uses e-cash payments for anonymous communications, the bank is in a position to perform a weak intersection attack.

Coins spent and coins deposited will match services used over time. However, this attack can be mitigated by users withdrawing a number of coins in advance and by the digitial cash being used for other purposes and merchants besides anonymous communications servers.

In the following sections, we will show how to use this rip coin protocol to design a fair exchange mechanism in a mix-net.

4   A Fair Exchange Protocol for Connection-Based Mix-Nets

In a connection-based mix-net, user U can set up a connection with D by sending an onion though a sequence of mixes $N_1, \ldots, N_\ell$. Then, each mix $N_{i=1,\cdots,\ell}$ transmits data between U and D until finally U tears down the connection. In this section, we present a weak fair exchange protocol for connection-based mix-nets, assuming that user U neglects the communication costs of transmitting the second half coins.

Fair exchange in a connection-based mix-net can take advantage of the fact that the user knows whether the connection gets through. A simple approach proceeds as follows: user U pays each mix on its path the first half of a coin in the connection-setup phase; the mixes provide connection service to U; U issues the second halves when disconnecting. This protocol is incentive-compatible. U does have the incentive to pay the first halves, otherwise her connection won't get through. The mixes have an incentive to provide service honestly, otherwise they won't get paid. After paying the first halves, U has lost all these coins, and thereby would be willing to complete the payment if the costs of distributing second halves are negligible. This is especially true since U would likely need to make a special effort, e.g., modifying the client software or physically disconnecting the computer from the network, in order to disrupt payment. We call this protocol *direct anonymous exchange*. In the following paragraphs, we present the details of the protocol, especially how to achieve anonymity in the exchange process.

Connecting:

1. An user U who plans to connect to a responder D chooses a sequence of mixes $N_1, \ldots, N_\ell$ and withdraws from the bank a sequence of rip coins $c_1, \ldots, c_\ell$. Then U constructs an onion M_1 to wrap its connection message M. An onion $M_i, 1 \leq i \leq \ell - 1$ is constructed as follows, where $\{\cdot\}_{PK_i}$ denotes encryption under the public key PK_i of N_i:

$$M_i = \{N_{i+1}, c_{i,1}, M_{i+1}\}_{PK_i} \tag{1}$$
$$M_\ell = \{D, c_{\ell,1}, M\}_{PK_\ell}$$

In other words, U inserts a half coin at every layer of the onion constructed.
2. $U \longrightarrow N_1$: M_1.

3. $N_i \longrightarrow N_{i+1}$: M_{i+1}, where $1 \leq i \leq \ell-1$. In other words, each mix N_i decrypts M_i, takes off the half coin, records the connection state information (such as connection ID) and then forwards the rest of the onion (M_{i+1}) to the next hop.
4. $N_\ell \longrightarrow D$: M.
5. D and U complete the rest of connection procedure.

Communication: After establishing a connection, U and D exchange messages along the connection through $N_1, \ldots, N_\ell$.

Disconnecting:

1. After completing communication, U sends a message to D to tear down the connection. This message also signals to $N_1, \ldots, N_\ell$ that the connection is over, and final payment stage begins.
2. The user U sends a sequence of messages through the connection path (still to D) in the order $\rho_\ell, \rho_{\ell-1}, \ldots, \rho_1$, where ρ_i is the message containing half coin $c_{i,2}$.
3. Every mix N_i checks every message transmitting through the disconnecting connection: if a message ρ arrives, which includes u such that $v_i = H(u)$, N_i clears the connection state information and stops forwarding any message (including ρ) for this connection.

In Step 2, U distributes the second halves of the coins to mixes. U should send them out in a reversed order (from N_ℓ to N_1). This is because a rational mix will stop doing anything for the connection after receiving its payment. The central rationale of this protocol is that U would tend to neglect the overhead of a few more messages for completing the payment after accomplishing large amount of communication via the connection.

In the case that users do care about the overhead for sending second half-coin, an alternative is for the bank to periodically force users to submit, via a DC-net [11], the second half-coins. Here we briefly sketch the idea. Users form a neighbor-relationship graph in which one is represented as a vertex and shares a long secret key with each of her neighbors. The long key is divided into many slots, each the length of a second-half coin. To send her report, a user first XORs all her secret keys together to get a string (report), from which she randomly chooses several slots according to the number of coins being used to XOR the corresponding second halves onto. After collecting reports from all users, the bank XORs these reports together to obtain second halves[1]. This approach preserves full anonymity during the payment process, and permits the bank to detect if a user fails to submit second half-coins.

---

[1] Using reservation and trap technology [11], the bank can further detect and capture those who jam the communication by filling report with random bits.

5   A Fair Exchange Protocol for Message-Based Mix-Net

In this section, we describe a fair exchange protocol for message-based mix-nets, which can achieve strict fairness in exchange.

5.1   The Protocol

Previous research shows that without a trusted third party, strict fairness cannot be achieved in exchange [26]. In a message-based mix-net, the service a mix offers is to honestly process and forward a user's onion to the next hop. Therefore, we can use the next hop as a third party in the exchange of services and payment between the user and the mix. To implement this idea, we need to tackle two central issues. First, we expect a strict fair exchange. That is, either both parties get what they want or neither benefits. Therefore, the user should not give out her payment without ensuring that the mix will forward her message, and the mix will not forward the message without being assured that its successor can complete the payment for her. Second, the next hop itself is self-interested. We need an incentive mechanism to encourage it to follow the protocol.

We tackle the first issue as follows. The user U wraps inside each layer of her onion the second-half coin of the payment for the preceding hop, the first half of a coin for this hop, and an "envelope" that proves that the second-half coin for this hop is inside the next layer of the onion. This assures individual mixes that they will get the payment after forwarding the onion to the next hop. At the same time, it also assures U that her message will be forwarded. We further discuss a game theoretic strategy that provides a strict incentive to every player to help its preceding neighbor. For this construction, we assume that the destination D is a participant in the protocol. D is willing to follow the protocol because D is interested in the message contents. We will further discuss this assumption below.

The main protocol:

1. User U, who intends to send a message M to destination D, first chooses a sequence of mixes $N_1, \ldots, N_\ell$, prepares a sequence of coins $c_1, \ldots, c_\ell$ and then constructs an onion M_1. We describe the onion wrapped inside ith layer, $1 \le i \le \ell - 1$, as:

$$M_i = \{N_{i+1}, c_{i,1}, E_i, M_{i+1}\}_{PK_i} \qquad (2)$$
$$M_\ell = \{D, c_{\ell,1}, E_\ell, M_D\}_{PK_\ell}$$
$$M_D = \{M\}_{PK_D}$$

where E_i is an "envelope" that, intuitively, includes the second-half coin $c_{i,2}$ encrypted under PK_{i+1} in a way that N_i can verify this. How E_i is constructed is described in Section 5.2.

2. $U \longrightarrow N_1$: M_1.

3. $N_i \longrightarrow N_{i+1}$: E_i, M_{i+1}, $1 \le i < \ell$. Before making this move, N_i verifies the bank's signature on $c_{i,1}$ and the validity of E_i (see Section 5.2). If correct, N_i is convinced that U has completed her part of the payment and that N_{i+1} will be able to help her to obtain the rest of the coin.

4. $N_{i+1} \longrightarrow N_i$: $c_{i,2}$, which N_{i+1} extracts from E_i in a manner described in Section 5.2.

5. $N_\ell \longrightarrow D$: E_ℓ, M_D, after confirming the validity of E_ℓ.

6. $D \longrightarrow N_\ell$: $c_{\ell,2}$.

The above protocol guarantees that no mix profits without performing step 3. Therefore, the protocol is fair in a strict sense. The problem is how to ensure all players honestly perform step 4. Here we present a mechanism that achieves this goal in a self-enforcing way.

The cooperation problem in step 4 can be modeled as a RPD game, presuming that users create paths in such a way that for mixes N and N', N immediately follows N' in a path with the same probability with which it immediately precedes N' in a path. For example, suppose users randomly choose paths of length ℓ from a total of m mixes, without replacement. Then, the probability that mix N precedes N' is $\frac{\ell-1}{m(m-1)}$. This suggests that after receiving a message from mix N', N will be in the position of sending a message to N' within expected $\frac{m(m-1)}{\ell-1}$ transmissions. As such, two neighboring mixes repeatedly interact with each other, with the same probability of acting as the next-hop mix in Step 4 of the protocol. If both honestly execute Step 4, they are better off than if they both defect. Although one may enjoy "free riding" on the other's cooperation without reciprocation, according to our assumption 2 (see Section 3.1), the free-rider will lose more if the other does the same to it in the future.

"Tit-for-tat" (TFT) has been deemed as an effective means to encourage cooperation in a RPD game. We now describe how to implement it in mix-nets.

Incentive mechanism for Step 4:

1. N begins by cooperating, always performing Step 4.
2. If N' failed to send back a correct second-half coin in the last interaction (the message M was from N to N'), then N does not send to N' its coin in this interaction. Otherwise, N honestly follows the protocol.

Essentially, the above mechanism says that each mix always follows its neighbor's behavior in the last interaction, cooperation or defection. It retaliates against the mixes deviating from the protocol, thereby removing their economic incentives to defect in future moves. On the other hand, it also shows some forgiveness: after defectors return to cooperating, other mixes will cooperate with them.

Previous research shows that TFT satisfies evolutionary stability [5]: if all mixes play this strategy at the beginning, an individual mix's optimal strategy is to follow the strategy afterwards; even if a few mixes follow other strategies (e.g, they were temporally captured by adversaries), they will be attracted back to this strategy. An interesting property of this mechanism is that messages still get through the path even when some mixes are retaliating against each other.

A similar strategy also works for the responder, D. If mix N_ℓ has not received its coin from D in the last interaction, it will refuse to deliver the message in the current interaction but resume cooperation in the future. If D values reception of messages above processing overhead of Step 6, its optimal strategy is never defecting.

A default assumption for TFT strategy is that the communication channel is reliable: No message will be lost after transmission. On an unreliable channel, mix N may falsely retaliate against N' after the message in Step 4 is lost, which will further trigger N' to retaliate against N, and thus both parties will not cooperate afterwards. A simple solution is given by modifying GTFT: let individual mixes choose retaliation with a large probability. That is, instead of retaliating for every defection, a mix may completely forgive a defector with a small probability. This guarantees that once such a misunderstanding happens due to the lossy channel, the mixes will resume cooperation eventually.

5.2   Envelope Construction

Strict fairness requires that individual mixes know that the initiator has already *completed payment* before forwarding her messages. This is achieved in the protocol described in Section 5.1 through the construction of envelope E_i. A properly constructed envelope E_i consists of (i) a ciphertext encrypted under the public key PK_{i+1} of the next mix N_{i+1} and (ii) an accompanying noninteractive zero-knowledge proof Π that the corresponding plaintext is the second half-coin $c_{i,2}$ that matches the first half-coin $c_{i,1}$ (i.e., $H(c_{i,2}) = v$ where $c_{i,1} = ((N_i \| v), \sigma)$). Here we sketch one construction for E_i; others are possible, e.g., drawing from techniques for verifiable encryption of signatures (e.g., [4]).

For the encryption algorithm with which $c_{i,2}$ is encrypted under PK_{i+1}, a chosen-ciphertext-secure encryption is advisable since N_{i+1} acts as a decryption oracle for PK_{i+1} in the protocol of Section 5.1. Such cryptosystems were proposed by Shoup and Gennaro [27], for example, which are secure in the random oracle model assuming either the computational or decisional Diffie-Hellman assumption in a cyclic group $\mathcal{G}$. Rather than detail these encryption schemes here, we note that components of a ciphertext of a plaintext m using public key PK include elements of the form $\alpha = g^r$, and $\beta = m(PK)^r$ for public $g, PK \in \mathcal{G}$ (and secret r generated during encryption)[2].

The noninteractive zero-knowledge proof Π can thus be easily constructed for certain choices of the one-way function H. For example, suppose $\mathcal{G}$ is chosen such that computing square roots is intractible in $\mathcal{G}$, i.e., for any realistic adversary

---

[2] A ciphertext also includes an element $\bar{\alpha} = \bar{g}^r$ for a public $\bar{g} \in \mathcal{G}$, and a noninteractive zero-knowledge proof that $\log_g(\alpha) = \log_{\bar{g}}(\bar{\alpha})$. To further encourage N_i to deliver M_{i+1} to N_{i+1}, the sender could create the random challenge for this zero-knowledge proof by hashing over inputs that include M_{i+1}.

A, $\Pr[x \xleftarrow{R} \mathcal{G}; z \leftarrow A(x^2) : z^2 = y]$ is negligible[3]. For such a group, an appropriate choice for $H : \mathcal{G} \rightarrow \mathcal{G}$ is $H(x) = x^2$. In this case, Π can be constructed as non-interactive zero-knowledge proof of discrete logarithm equality, specifically that $\log_g(\alpha) = \log_{(PK)^2}(\beta^2 v^{-1})$. There exist such proofs in the random oracle model that are computationally as expensive as a digital signature, even if the order of $\mathcal{G}$ is unknown (e.g., [4, 17]).

6   Security Analysis

Here, we analyze anonymity and fairness achieved by the protocols presented in previous sections.

The exchange protocol presented in Section 4 fully preserves anonymity in connection-based mix-nets. In the protocol, the first-half coins are paid through the connection onion and the second-half coins are paid through the connection itself. Therefore, no extra information has been leaked to either mixes or external observers. This protocol also achieves fairness in a weak sense, given that users neglect the overheads of completing payment.

The exchange protocol presented in Section 5 is embedded in the original mix-net protocol. Therefore, no extra information is leaked out in either the forwarding process or the retaliation mechanism. The proposed protocol employs the successor of individual mixes as a third party in exchange of payment and service. An initiator U gives the first-half coin to the mix N_i via onion M_i, and encrypts the second-half coin in an envelope only accessible to the next hop mix N_{i+1}. On one hand, to collect the second-half coin, N_i has to honestly forward M_{i+1} (not a junk bit string) to the next hop. Otherwise, it will not get the right half coin from N_{i+1}. On the other hand, N_{i+1} also cannot steal N_i's coin because it does not have access to the first half-coin. The envelope in M_i also convinces N_i that U has completed the payment. Therefore, if N_{i+1} behaves rationally, strict fairness is achieved between the initiator and the mix. We take an evolutionary stable strategy called tit-for-tat to engineer third parties' incentive. Once established in the mix-net, this strategy becomes every player's optimal strategy towards the others. In other words, acting as an honest third party becomes every player's best choice. Implementation of this strategy also exhibits a very interesting property in mix cascade networks and mix networks: even in the presence of some defecting mixes, rational mixes still deliver initiators' onions as long as the responder behaved properly in previous interactions. This is because mixes retaliate against each other by not shipping the second-half coins, while the onions will still be forwarded.

---

[3] A suitable such group $\mathcal{G}$ is the subgroup of squares in $\mathbb{Z}_n^*$, where $n = pq$ and each of p, q, $\frac{p-1}{2}$ and $\frac{q-1}{2}$ are prime. The computational and decisional Diffie-Hellman problems are also believed to be hard in this group [7]. Though the Shoup-Gennaro cryptosystems [27] are specified for a prime-order group, they can be modified trivially to work over this group.

7   Conclusions

Reliability is a real problem in today's mix networks [14], and it is not likely to go away on its own. When we approach this problem, if we model nodes as either well-behaved or malicious, we end up with draconian, expensive solutions or heuristics that don't have strong properties. We believe that it is more useful to consider mixes and users as rational players who will act according to the incentives they can expect to obtain from their actions. Although we are not the first to consider a payment system in this model, we are the first to handle the crucial aspects of fair exchange in the payment process. Without fair exchange, incentives to provide service or provide payment will fail; rational agents do not enter agreements without fairness (unless they are the ones who can gain the unfair advantage).

Our constructions are not significantly more costly than existing protocols that do not have reliability, and are far more efficient than protocols with strong reliability guarantees. Furthermore, just as a business expecting income might spend money for cash registers and accountants, we expect that mix operators will be willing to do more work in a system that compensates them for the costs.

References

1. M. Abe. Universally verifiable MIX with verification work independent of the number of MIX servers. In *Proc. EUROCRYPT 1998*, 1998.
2. A. Acquisti, R. Dingledine, and P. Syverson. On the economics of anonymity. In *Proc. Financial Cryptography (FC '03)*, 2003.
3. N. Asokan, V. Shoup, and M. Waidner. Optimistic fair exchange of digital signatures. *IEEE Journal on Selected Areas in Communications*, 18(4):593–610, April 2000.
4. A. Ateniese. Efficient verifiable encryption (and fair exchange) of digital signatures. In *Proc. ACM Conference on Computer and Communications Security (CCS 1999)*, Nov. 1999.
5. R. Axelrod. *The Evolution of Cooperation*. Basic Books, 1984.
6. F. Bao, R. Deng, and W. Mao. Efficient and practical fair exchange protocols with off-line TTP. In *Proc. IEEE Symposium on Security and Privacy*, pages 77–85, 1998.
7. D. Boneh. The decision Diffie-Hellman problem. In *Proc. Third Algorithmic Number Theory Symposium*, volume 1423, pages 48–63, 1998.
8. L. Buttyan and J.P. Hubaux. Toward a formal model of fair exchange – a game theoretic approach. In *Proc. International Workshop on ecommerce*, 2000.
9. D. Chaum. Untraceable electronic mail, return addresses, and digital pseudonyms. *Communications of the ACM*, 24(2):84–88, February 1981.
10. D. Chaum. Blind signatures for untraceable payments. In *Proc. Crypto'82*, pages 199–203, 1982.
11. D. Chaum. The dining cryptographers problem: Unconditional sender and recipient untraceability. *Journal of Cryptography*, 1(1):65–75, 1988.
12. B. Cohen. Incentives build robustness in BitTorrent. In *Proc. Workshop on Economics of Peer-to-Peer Systems*, May 2003.

13. R. Deng, L. Gong, A. Lazar, and W. Wang. Practical protocols for certified electronic mail. *Journal of Network and Systems Management*, 4(3):279–297, 1996.
14. R. Dingledine, M. J. Freedman, D. Hopwood, and D. Molnar. A reputation system to increase MIX-net reliability. In *Proc. Financial Cryptography (FC '02)*. *SpringerVerlag, LNCS*, 2002.
15. R. Dingledine, N. Mathewson, and P. Syverson. Reliable MIX cascade networks through reputation. In *Proc. Financial Cryptography (FC '03)*, 2003.
16. D. R. Figueiredo, J. K. Shapiro, and D. Towsley. *Using Payments to Promote Cooperation in Anonymity Protocols*, 2003. Manuscript.
17. E. Fijisaki and T. Okamoto. Statistical zero-knowledge protocols to prove modular polynomial relations. In *Advances in Cryptology – CRYPTO '97 (LNCS 1294)*, pages 16–30, 1997.
18. E. Franz, A. Jerichow, and G. Wicke. A payment scheme for mixes providing anonymity. In *Proc. Trends in Distributed Systems for Electronic Commerce*, volume 1402, 1998.
19. M. Jakobsson. Ripping coins for a fair exchange. In *Proc. Advances in Cryptology – EUROCRYPT'95*, volume 921, pages 220–230, 1995.
20. M. Jakobsson and A. Juels. An optimally robust hybrid mix network (extended abstract). In *Proc. Principles of Distributed Computing - PODC '01*, 2001.
21. M. Jakobsson, A. Juels, and R. Rivest. Making mix nets robust for electronic voting by randomized partial checking. In *Proc. USENIX Security '02*, 2002.
22. W. Ogata, K. Kurosawa, K. Sako, and K. Takatani. Fault tolerant anonymous channel. In *Proc. Information and Communications Security – First International Conference*, volume 1334, pages 440–444, 1997.
23. A. Pasick. File-sharing network thrives beneath the radar. http://in.tech.yahoo.com/041103/137/2ho4i.html, November 2004.
24. M. K. Reiter and A. D. Rubin. Crowds: Anonymity for Web Transactions. *ACM Transactions on Information and System Security*, 1(1):66–92, November 1998.
25. R. L. Rivest and A. Shamir. PayWord and MicroMint – two simple micropayment schemes. *CryptoBytes*, 2(1):7–11, Spring 1996.
26. T. Sandholm and X. F. Wang. (Im)possibility of safe exchange mechanism design. In *Proc. National Conference on Artificial Intelligence*, 2002.
27. V. Shoup and R. Gennaro. Securing threshold cryptosystems against chosen ciphertext attack. *Journal of Cryptology*, 15:75–96, 2002.
28. M. Wright, M. Adler, B. Levine, and C. Shields. An analysis of the degradation of anonymous protocols. In *Proc. ISOC Symposium on Network and Distributed System Security (NDSS 2002)*, February 2002.
29. M. Wright, M. Adler, B. Levine, and C. Shields. Defending anonymous communication against passive logging attacks. In *Proc. 2003 IEEE Symposium on Security and Privacy*, May 2003.
30. J. Zhou and D. Gollmann. A fair nonrepudiation protocol. In *Proc. IEEE Symposium of Security and Privacy*, May 1996.

SCARE of the DES
(Side Channel Analysis for Reverse Engineering of the Data Encryption Standard)

Rémy Daudigny, Hervé Ledig,
Frédéric Muller, and Frédéric Valette

DCSSI Crypto Lab 51, Boulevard de Latour-Maubourg
75700 Paris 07 SP France
{Remy.Daudigny,Frederic.Muller,Frederic.Valette}@sgdn.pm.gouv.fr

Abstract. Side-Channel Analysis for Reverse Engineering (SCARE) is a new field of application for Side-Channel Attacks (SCA), that was recently introduced, following initial results on the GSM A3/A8 algorithm. The principle of SCARE is to use side-channel information (for instance, power consumption) as a tool to reverse-engineer some secret parts of a cryptographic implementation. SCARE has the advantage of being discrete and non-intrusive, so it appears to be a promising new direction of research.

In this paper, we apply the concepts of SCARE in the case of the block cipher DES. We measure the power consumption of a software DES executed on a target smart card and propose new methods to exploit this information. We manage to retrieve many details about the underlying device, including some constants used by the algorithm (*e.g.* permutation tables for the round function and for the key scheduling), but also interesting implementation choices (*e.g.* registers where subkeys are loaded). Of course some information was already known in our case, but situations can be envisaged where the designer would like to keep it secret.

An application of these methods is to reverse-engineer a proprietary algorithm, provided some information about its basic structure is know. Hence it illustrates the power of SCARE and demonstrates yet again the accuracy of Kerckhoff's principle. In addition, a better understanding of a cryptographic implementation can be a first step to mount more sophisticated Side Channel Attacks.

1 Introduction

Side-Channel Attacks (SCA) have been developed since 10 years to analyse the security of cryptographic functions in actual implementations. Compared to traditional attacks which exploit the standard input/output (*i.e.* plaintext and ciphertext) of a cipher to recover some secret data, SCA uses an auxiliary source of information to achieve the same goal. This side-channel information can originate from various types of leakage. The first example was due to Kocher [6] and was based on using timing information. Furthermore it was shown that the

J. Ioannidis, A. Keromytis, and M.Yung (Eds.): ACNS 2005, LNCS 3531, pp. 393–406, 2005.

power consumption of a cryptographic device could also reveal some useful information to an attacker [7]. Other attacks of the same vein use electro-magnetic radiations [3, 5] or fault injection [1, 2]. Many variations of these techniques have been studied in the recent years, and the general idea is always to recover some secret keys used by the cipher.

More recently it was proposed to exploit side-channel leakage for reverse engineering. This new idea consists in exploiting (for instance) the power consumption of a device to recover some secret or non-trivial details about the way cryptographic functions were implemented. This new technique is called SCARE (Side-Channel Analysis for Reverse-Engineering) and has initially been applied to the A3/A8 authentication and session key generation algorithm of the GSM standard. An initial attack was proposed by Novak [9] and was later extended by Clavier [4]. These results constitutes a new application of techniques developed for SCA.

In our opinion, SCARE is a very promising direction for future research. We believe it could be useful in two situations. First, there are cryptographic functions where some part of the specification is voluntarily kept secret by the designer. For instance, a proprietary cipher where the general structure is known, but some constants are kept secret. Secondly, think of the implementation itself: some information (although not of cryptographic nature) may need to remain secret. For instance, the techniques used by the developers, the order and the length of the instructions or even the registers in which the data are stored. This information is sensible because a company may want to protect its technology, but also because it can be useful for a side channel attack. In this last case, SCARE is just a preliminary step towards more sophisticated attacks. For instance, a thin understanding of the hardware is often useful to improve power attacks (by focusing on relevant portions of the power traces or by applying a dedicated attack depending on the hardware behaviour).

More generally, SCARE demonstrates once again the accuracy of Kerckhoffs' principle that the security of a cryptosystem should rely on the secrecy of the key and not the cryptosystem itself. It also demonstrates the difficulty to protect a cryptographic implementation in hostile environments. This new reverse-engineering method is expected to have a broad range of applications since it is efficient, discrete and non-intrusive. In the next section, we introduce some background about SCA against DES. Then we describe our algorithmic methods for SCARE, and describe the experimental results we obtained by analysing the behaviour of a target smart card. Finally, we discuss directions for further research.

2   Side-Channel Attacks and the DES

DES (Data Encryption Standard) is a well-known encryption standard adopted by the NBS in 1977 [10], and replaced since then by AES. DES is a 64-bit block cipher with 56-bits key based on a Feistel structure. We skip details about the algorithm specifications, which are very well known. The reader can refer to [10] to find more information.

Today DES is still widely used especially in cryptographic hardware devices thus it has been an important target for side-channel analysis, following the initial paper by Kocher [6]. Several attacks are known, the simplest of which is Simple Power Analysis (SPA), where the attacker observes directly one power trace of a DES execution to retrieve the value of manipulated data. Power consumption curves are typically not that easy to analyse, therefore advanced attacks are needed.

An interesting and famous technique is Differential Power Analysis (DPA) [7]. DPA is a statistical attack, requiring to analyse several messages with their corresponding power traces. More precisely, assume we obtain M power traces: $(T_1, \ldots, T_M)$ where the power consumption at time t is given by $T_i(t)$. We assume this consumption is correlated with the data manipulated at time t. For instance if a S-box is computed, $T_i(t)$ is correlated with the output of this S-box. However it is impossible to infer the data directly from one power trace, due to the noise in the measurement. A statistical attack is therefore necessary.

We consider a known-plaintext attacker. He targets the output of Sbox S_1 of round 1. We call this 4-bit output (a, b, c, d). It depends on 6 key bits and 6 plaintext bits. If the attacker guesses these 6 key bits, he can predict the value of a for each message. The corresponding power traces can thus be sorted in two groups G_0 and G_1 according to the predicted value of a. Group G_i corresponds to the value $a = i$. The "differential curve" is computed as

$$D(t) = \left| \frac{1}{|G_0|} \sum_{T_i \in G_0} T_i(t) - \frac{1}{|G_1|} \sum_{T_i \in G_1} T_i(t) \right|$$

This curve should present peaks, if we assumed the correct key bits and should be close to 0 otherwise. Indeed, for the instants t where the S-box S_1 is computed, the power consumption is correlated with a. Therefore, for the correct key, there is an important difference between the consumption of groups G_0 and G_1. Otherwise, there should be no significant difference between the two groups, hence the differential curve $D(t)$ should be close to 0. Of course, M needs to be large enough to eliminate the noise in the experiments.

To summarize, the attacker learns 6 key bits by statistical treatment of the power traces. There exists a similar attack that requires only knowledge of the ciphertext. In practice DPA is often more complicated: countermeasures can be implemented, so the analysis of power traces is rather subtle. Basically the attack can be improved if we know more about:

- which portions of the traces correspond to the computation of S_1. Then we can restrict the analysis to significant data.
- the electrical behaviour of the cryptographic device. There may be better ways to exploit the curves, assuming we understand well the correlation between internal data and power consumption.

Therefore it may be useful, before applying this attack to spend some time to understand better the target device. Then optimized versions of the attack can be applied. This is an important motivation for SCARE.

3   Methods and Goals of SCARE

3.1   Goals

In the context of SCARE, we no longer consider the point of view of an attacker but the one of a **reverse-engineer**. The primary goal of this new adversary is not to recover the secret key. He wants to know more about the implementation, which englobes several possible goals:

- **Learn secret constants**
  Sometimes, the general structure of an algorithm is known but some partial information is kept secret. For instance if a company develops a proprietary algorithm, it might prefer, for various reasons, to keep some constants secret. This situation has been encountered with the GSM authentication and session key generation algorithm A3/A8 [4, 9]. Some tables were kept secret, but it was later demonstrated that SCARE could be used to retrieve them.
- **Learn more about the algorithm**
  Consider a secret proprietary block cipher. Several reasonable assumptions about its general structure (Feistel cipher, SP network) can be made. A reverse-engineer expects to obtain more details using SCARE. For instance, how many S-boxes are used, what is the size of these S-boxes, . . .
- **Learn information about the implementation techniques**
  The way an algorithm was implemented can sometimes be considered as a secret by itself. It reveals secrets about the technology used by a company or methods used by the developers of its products.
- **Understand better the device**
  Knowing which instruction corresponds to which portion of the power trace improves the efficiency of many attacks (like DPA). Moreover, it is helpful to understand better the correlation between intermediate data and power consumption (for instance, what consumption model should be used).

3.2   Methods

In [4, 9], dedicated methods have been proposed in the case of the A3/A8 algorithm. They allowed to recover secret tables which were part of the algorithm specifications but kept secret. In this section, we propose and apply new methods to reverse-engineer a commercial smart card where a software DES implementation is available.

The first operation consists in monitoring the power consumption of a DES encryption. We mention that similar attacks could be envisaged if we monitor the electro-magnetic radiations. For each message, we obtain a trace which is represented by a collection of values, each of them associated with a certain time index t. The preliminary stage consists in synchronizing the curve in order for a given time index t to uniquely correspond to a given instruction. This pre-processing is usually done prior to most Side Channel Attacks. Afterwards, we denote by $T_i(t)$ the power consumption of the i-th trace at time index number t. Roughly, we can assume that each time index corresponds to one clock cycle.

Next, the goal of the reverse-engineer is to determine when each data is manipulated. If he knows nothing about the underlying algorithm, all he can do is detect when the algorithm inputs (such as the plaintext or the key) are manipulated. If he knows more, he can focus on any intermediate value, as long as no unknown material is needed to predict it. For instance, if we replace the DES permutation table by a random permutation, a reverse-engineer can predict intermediate values of the first round, until the new permutation is performed.

To determine when each data is manipulated, the reverse-engineer applies a statistical analysis to the power traces. For each intermediate bit he can predict, he tries to determine the time index t where it is manipulated. We call this result the **scheduling information** of the considered implementation. Afterwards, the reverse-engineer analyzes this information, hoping to learn the unknown material about the target algorithm. This second phase is detailed in Section 4.

Method to obtain scheduling information. Pick an intermediate bit a. The input consists in M messages and their corresponding power traces $(T_j)_{1 \leq j \leq M}$. We want to determine the clock cycles where a is manipulated. If no information about the cipher is initially known, we can start by choosing a to be a bit from the plaintext.

- Build two groups G_0 and G_1 according to the value of a in each encryption (G_i corresponds to $a = i$).
- For each clock cycle i compute the following value V_i

$$V_i = \frac{1}{|G_0|} \sum_{T_j \in G_0} T_j(i) - \frac{1}{|G_1|} \sum_{T_j \in G_1} T_j(i)$$

- If $|V_i| > \lambda$ for some appropriate threshold λ we decide that the bit a is manipulated at time i. In our experimental settings, we fixed the threshold afterwards, in order to keep only a short number of significant time index.

To summarize, the indicator V_i just measures how much the consumption at clock cycle i is affected by a. Hence large values of $|V_i|$ reveal when the bit a is manipulated.

An example. We present some experimental results obtained on our target smart card. Of course, we know the specification of DES. However, we first worked as if the algorithm was secret, hence all we know is the plaintext. Therefore we focused on obtaining the **scheduling information of the plaintext bits**. The initial permutation of DES only modifies the order in which plaintext bits are manipulated, so it does not really change the analysis.

We use $M = 1000$ power consumption traces. We pick a to be any plaintext bit, say the first input bit of the first S-box S_1 for instance. For each clock cycle i, we determine if a is manipulated or not by testing if $|V_i| > \lambda$. The unit of the V_i is arbitrary and has been normalized to range in the set $[0, 200]$. The threshold λ has been set to 10, so that only a small number of clock cycles i verify

$$|V_i| > \lambda$$

Table 1. A sample of experimental results.

Cycle i	Value V_i	Decision
1074	7	Bit NOT manipulated at clock cycle 1074
1075	14	Bit manipulated at clock cycle 1075
1076	50	Bit manipulated at clock cycle 1076
1077	24	Bit manipulated at clock cycle 1077
1078	−8	Bit NOT manipulated at clock cycle 1078
1079	14	Bit manipulated at clock cycle 1079
1080	76	Bit manipulated at clock cycle 1080
1081	41	Bit manipulated at clock cycle 1081
1082	8	Bit NOT manipulated at clock cycle 1082
1083	9	Bit NOT manipulated at clock cycle 1083

A significant portion of the results is represented in Table 1. For most of the other time indexes, the outcome is that the considered bit was not manipulated. Further analysis has revealed that the depicted interval corresponds to the computation of S-box S_1. A larger sample is represented in Appendix A. The sign of V_i may also reveal some partial information (for instance, a change of sign probably means that 1 was XORed to the manipulated bit), however we do not take into account this information.

4   Analysis of Our Results

In this section, we describe how to interpret the scheduling information obtained in Section 3.2. We first work as if the DES specifications were unknown, so we only exploit the scheduling information of the plaintext bits. This allows us to determine the expansion table of DES. Next, we demonstrate similar methods to retrieve other information about the algorithm.

4.1   Application to the Expansion Table

The round function of DES starts by expanding the input from 32 to 48 bits. The DES specification contains a table describing this expansion [10] (see Table 2). In this section, we show how to retrieve this table using SCARE. Of course a similar analysis could be applied to a cipher using a secret expansion table.

Table 2. The DES Expansion Table.

32	1	2	3	4	5
4	5	6	7	8	9
8	9	10	11	12	13
12	13	14	15	16	17
16	17	18	19	20	21
20	21	22	23	24	25
24	25	26	27	28	29
28	29	30	31	32	1

Let us focus on scheduling information corresponding to plaintext bits (this analysis can even be performed when nothing is initially known about the cipher). Scheduling information tells us when each single bit is manipulated. But we can also observe **the groups of bits which are manipulated together**. Such groups are likely to correspond to S-box inputs.

Table 3. Scheduling information of the first round input.

Cycle	First Round Input								
	Bit 1	Bit 2	Bit 3	Bit 4	Bit 5	Bit 6	...	Bit 31	Bit 32
1073	-	-	-	-	-	-		-	-
1074	-	-	-	-	-	-		-	-
1075	Y	-	-	-	Y	-		-	-
1076	Y	Y	Y	Y	Y	-		-	Y
1077	Y	Y	Y	Y	Y	-		-	Y
1078	-	Y	Y	Y	Y	-		-	Y
1079	Y	Y	Y	-	Y	-		-	Y
1080	Y	Y	Y	Y	Y	-		Y	Y
1081	Y	Y	Y	Y	Y	-		Y	-
1082	-	Y	Y	Y	Y	-		-	-
1083	-	Y	Y	Y	Y	-		-	-
1084	-	-	-	-	-	-		-	-
1085	-	-	-	-	-	-		-	-

As an illustration, Table 3 contains a relevant portion of the scheduling information. For sake of simplicity, the exact values of the indicator V_i are replaced by 'Y' (YES) when $|V_i|$ exceeds the threshold $\lambda = 10$ and '-' otherwise. In this sample, input bits number 1, 2, 3, 4, 5 and 32 are clearly manipulated together around clock cycles $1075, \ldots, 1082$. These 6 bits form the first line of the DES expansion table.

We observe that the bit number 31 is also manipulated at cycles 1080 and 1081. This phenomenon can be due to noise in the experiment. Another possible interpretation is that the bit 31 was stored in the same register than bit 32 and is manipulated, while bit 32 is loaded.

A similar property could be observed for input bits number 4, 5, 6, 7, 8 and 9 in the following clock cycles. This group forms exactly the second line of the DES expansion table. Similarly we can learn the rest of the expansion table.

More generally, the structure of the round function can be detected this way. Indeed SCARE reveals which plaintext bits are manipulated together. This reveals the S-box structure. For instance, an attacker knowing nothing about DES could suspect that it uses 8 S-boxes, each of them applied to 6 input bits.

4.2 Application to the S-Box Tables

We have not implemented any attack to recover the DES S-boxes. However it is likely that the methodology of SCARE could also be used here. It has already been verified experimentally in the case of the A3/A8 algorithm [4, 9]. Secret substitution tables have been recovered in the case, using the power traces of the cryptographic device.

4.3   Application to the S-Box Outputs

Now, we suppose that we know the expansion table and the DES S-box. Hence, we can predict the 32 output bits of the S-box layer and analyze the scheduling information concerning these bits. We observe several significant intervals, but focus first on a particular interval which was already analyzed in Table 3. We know it corresponds to the S-box computations. Other significant intervals are further investigated later in the paper.

Table 4. Scheduling information of the S-box outputs.

Cycle	First Round Output								
	Bit 1	Bit 2	Bit 3	Bit 4	Bit 5	Bit 6	Bit 7	Bit 8	...
1074	-	-	-	-	-	-	-	-	
1075	-	-	-	-	-	-	-	-	
1076	Y	Y	Y	Y	Y	-	Y	-	
1077	Y	Y	Y	Y	-	-	-	-	
1078	Y	Y	Y	Y	-	-	-	-	
1079	-	-	-	-	-	-	-	-	
1080	Y	Y	Y	Y	-	-	Y	-	
1081	Y	Y	Y	Y	-	-	-	-	
1082	Y	Y	Y	Y	-	-	-	-	
1083	-	-	-	-	-	-	-	-	
1084	-	-	-	-	-	-	-	-	
1085	Y	Y	Y	Y	-	-	-	-	
1086	Y	Y	Y	Y	-	-	-	-	
1087	Y	Y	Y	Y	-	-	-	-	
1088	Y	Y	Y	Y	-	-	-	-	
1089	Y	Y	Y	Y	-	-	-	-	
1090	Y	Y	Y	Y	-	-	-	-	
1091	Y	Y	Y	Y	-	-	-	-	
1092	-	-	-	-	-	-	-	-	
1093	-	-	-	-	-	-	-	-	

A sample of scheduling information is represented in Table 4. Focus on S-box S_1 (the corresponding output bits are indexed $1, 2, 3, 4$). The table confirms that S_1 is computed from clock cycle 1076 to 1091. Similarly S_2 is computed between clock cycle 1140 and 1160 (as indicated in Table 5). A surprising effect appears: at the moment S_2 is computed, the output bits of S_1 are manipulated again. This phenomenon occurs especially between clock cycles 1154 and 1160. We observe a similar behaviour for other pairs of S-box, (S_3, S_4), (S_5, S_6) and (S_7, S_8).

Table 5. Scheduling information of the S-box outputs.

Cycle	First Round Output								
	Bit 1	Bit 2	Bit 3	Bit 4	Bit 5	Bit 6	Bit 7	Bit 8	...
1138	-	-	-	-	-	-	-	-	
1139	-	-	-	-	-	-	-	-	
1140	Y	-	Y	Y	Y	Y	Y	Y	
1141	-	-	-	-	Y	Y	-	Y	
1142	-	-	-	-	Y	Y	Y	Y	
1143	-	-	-	-	-	-	-	-	
1144	-	-	-	-	-	Y	-	-	
1145	-	-	-	-	Y	Y	Y	Y	
1146	-	-	-	-	Y	Y	Y	Y	
1147	-	-	-	-	Y	Y	Y	Y	
1148	-	-	-	-	Y	Y	Y	Y	
1149	-	-	-	-	-	Y	-	-	
1150	-	-	-	-	-	Y	-	-	
1151	-	-	-	-	Y	Y	-	Y	
1152	-	-	-	-	Y	Y	Y	Y	
1153	-	-	-	-	Y	Y	Y	Y	
1154	Y	Y	Y	Y	Y	Y	Y	Y	
1155	Y	Y	Y	Y	Y	Y	Y	Y	
1156	Y	Y	Y	Y	Y	Y	Y	Y	
1157	Y	Y	Y	Y	Y	Y	Y	Y	
1158	Y	Y	Y	Y	Y	Y	Y	Y	
1159	Y	Y	Y	Y	Y	Y	Y	Y	
1160	Y	Y	Y	Y	Y	Y	Y	Y	
1161	-	-	-	-	-	-	-	-	
1162	-	-	-	-	-	-	-	-	

Our interpretation is that **the outputs of adjacent S-boxes are stored in the same register**. Therefore we are probably dealing with a 8-bit architecture and the implementation choice is to store the output of adjacent S-boxes in the same register.

4.4   Application to the Permutation Table

The last step of DES round function is a permutation of the 32 output bits. This permutation is also described by a table in the DES specification [10] (see Table 6).

The permutation of round 1 is computed just after the S-box layer. So we focus on this time interval and on the manipulation of S-box output bits (*i.e.* the input bits of the permutation). However the corresponding scheduling information is rather long. So we provide only a summary in Table 7. We focus on 8 among the 32 target bits which are manipulated first, and an interval is given where each of them is manipulated.

These 8 bits actually correspond to two lines (the 5-th and the 6-th) of the permutation table. Our interpretation is that the permutation is performed

Table 6. The DES Permutation Table.

16	7	20	21
29	12	28	17
1	15	23	26
5	18	31	10
2	8	24	14
32	27	3	9
19	13	30	6
22	11	4	25

Table 7. Summary of scheduling information for the permutation.

Output Bit number	Significant interval
2	$1814 - 1817$
3	$1886 - 1890$
8	$1826 - 1832$
9	$1888 - 1892$
14	$1850 - 1856$
24	$1838 - 1841$
27	$1874 - 1877$
32	$1862 - 1865$
$\dots$	$\dots$

in a byte-oriented way, *i.e.* the bits corresponding to two consecutive lines are extracted and stored in the same register. Moreover look at the order in which the bits of Table 7 are manipulated: 2 then 8, 24, 14, 32, 27, 3 and finally 9. This is exactly the order of the bits in the two corresponding lines of the DES permutation table. Our interpretation is that the corresponding byte is computed from the most to the least significant bit.

To summarize, SCARE can retrieve the content of a permutation table, as illustrated with the example of DES.

4.5   Application to the Key Scheduling

Inbetween rounds 1 and 2, there is a long time interval where the output bits of the first round function are apparently manipulated. This effect is surprising because these bits are not needed at this point. We think that **this time interval corresponds to the key scheduling** and that **power consumption is correlated with S-box output bits because the registers where they were previously stored are overridden by the round key**. Indeed it is well known that the power consumption is correlated with the new value written in a register, but also with its previous content.

In Table 8, we represent a summary of the scheduling information. The byte formed with bits $9, \dots, 16$ is manipulated starting from clock cycle 2698. Then its bits successively disappear from the scheduling information, *i.e.* they stop being manipulated. We believe it is because they are successively overridden

Table 8. Sample of scheduling information for the key scheduling.

Output Bit number	Significant interval
1	2718 − 2985
2	2718 − 2985
3	2718 − 2837
4	2718 − 2796
5	2718 − 2873
6	2718 − 2724
7	2718 − 2985
8	2718 − 2941
9	2698 − 2952
10	2698 − 2952
11	2698 − 2737
12	2698 − 2776
13	2698 − 2860
14	2698 − 2952
15	2698 − 2709
16	2698 − 2904
. . .	. . .

by round key bits. Let us look at the order in which this phenomenon occurs. This order is actually related to the permutated choice table PC-2 of DES (see Table 9). This table is used to extract the bits forming the round key.

Table 9. The DES Permutated Choice PC-2 Table.

14	17	11	24	1	5
3	28	16	6	21	10
23	19	12	4	26	8
16	7	27	20	13	2
41	52	31	37	47	55
30	40	51	45	33	48
44	49	39	56	34	53
46	42	50	36	29	32

In Table 8, the first bit to be overridden (in our target byte) is the bit 15, then 11, 12, 13, 16, 14, etc . . . .. This should be put into correspondence with the 3-rd line of PC-2 (see Table 10). The order in which the bits disappear corresponds to the order of extraction, assuming that high indexes are extracted first.

A similar behaviour is observed with 3 other lines from PC-2. Therefore we learn 4 lines of PC-2 by just looking at the order in which the previous data is overridden. Of course, this could be used to retrieve a secret extraction table. Moreover we learn that the round key bits are stored in registers where intermediate data were previously stored. This is an undesirable property and could be used in other power attacks.

Table 10. Correspondence between PC-2 and the Output bits.

Output bits	9	10	11	12	13	14	15	16
Order to disappear	-	-	2	3	4	6	1	5
3-rd line of PC2	-	-	23	19	12	4	26	8
Order of extraction	-	-	2	3	4	6	1	5

4.6   Application for Side Channel Attacks

All the information derived in previous sections allows the reverse-engineer to know precisely when each instruction is executed on the device. For a power attack, this is useful information. Indeed the data analysis can be restricted to significant portions of the traces. For instance, to apply DPA on the S-box S_1 of the first round, we can isolate a small significant time interval for the analysis. This has two advantages

- The size of the data to handle is smaller, which improves the speed of the analysis
- Meaningless portions of the curves are not taken into account, which reduces the underlying noise. So the probability of success of DPA improves, especially with a limited number of traces

As an example, from the previous analysis, we can deduce how DPA should be applied on this device. Since S-box S_2 outputs are combined with S-box S_1's outputs, basic DPA on S_2's outputs is likely to give noisy results. It should be more efficient to apply DPA to the S-box S_1 or to the permutation. This information may also be helpful to mount more sophisticated attacks, like the recently proposed Davies-Murphy Power Attack [8]. In this last case, we know that only the pairs of S-box (S_1, S_2), (S_3, S_4), (S_5, S_6) or (S_7, S_8) can be valid targets.

5   Conclusion

SCARE (Side Channel Analysis for Reverse Engineering) is a new field of application of Side Channel Attacks (SCA), where one tries to reverse-engineer an implementation, based only on the power consumption of the cryptographic device. We proposed new methods for SCARE and applied them to the famous block cipher DES.

We managed to retrieve experimentally many information about a target implementation, including constant tables used by the cipher, details of the architecture, registers where data are stored or the order of execution of the instructions. These results against DES suggest that it would be difficult to protect the secrecy of a proprietary algorithm regarding SCARE. We also consider this analysis to be an interesting preliminary step before applying power attacks to the device.

References

1. E. Biham and A. Shamir. Differential Fault Analysis of Secret Key Cryptosystems. In B. Kaliski, editor, *Advances in Cryptology – Crypto'97*, volume 1294 of *Lectures Notes in Computer Science*, pages 513–525. Springer, 1997.
2. D. Boneh, R. DeMillo, and R. Lipton. On the Importance of Checking Cryptographic Protocols for Faults (Extended Abstract). In W. Fumy, editor, *Advances in Cryptology – Eurocrypt'97*, volume 1233 of *Lectures Notes in Computer Science*, pages 37–51. Springer, 1997.
3. V. Carlier, H. Chabanne, E. Dottax, and H. Pelletier. Electromagnetic Side Channels of an FPGA Implementation of AES. Cryptology ePrint Archive, Report 2004/145, 2004. http://eprint.iacr.org/.
4. Christophe Clavier. Side Channel Analysis for Reverse Engineering (SCARE) - An Improved Attack Against a Secret A3/A8 GSM Algorithm. Cryptology ePrint Archive, Report 2004/049, 2004. http://eprint.iacr.org/.
5. K. Gandolfi, C. Mourtel, and F. Olivier. Electromagnetic Analysis: Concret Results. In Ç. Koç, D. Naccache, and C. Paar, editors, *Cryptographic Hardware and Embedded Systems (CHES) – 2001*, volume 2162 of *Lectures Notes in Computer Science*, pages 251–261. Springer, 2001.
6. P. Kocher. Timing Attacks on Implementations of Diffie-Hellman, RSA, DSS, and Others Systems. In N. Koblitz, editor, *Advances in Cryptology – Crypto'96*, volume 1109 of *Lectures Notes in Computer Science*, pages 104–113. Springer, 1996.
7. P. Kocher, J. Jaffe, and B. Jun. Differential Power Analysis. In M. Wiener, editor, *Advances in Cryptology – Crypto'99*, volume 1666 of *Lectures Notes in Computer Science*, pages 388–397. Springer, 1999.
8. S. Kunz-Jacques, F. Muller, and F. Valette. The Davies-Murphy Power Attack. In P.-J. Lee, editor, *Advances in Cryptology – Asiacrypt'04*, volume 3329 of *Lectures Notes in Computer Science*, pages 451–467. Springer, 2004.
9. R. Novak. Side-Channel Attacks on Substitution Blocks. In J. Zhou, M. Yung, and Y. Han, editors, *Applied Cryptography and Network Security (ACNS) 2003*, volume 2846 of *Lectures Notes in Computer Science*, pages 307–318. Springer, 2003.
10. National Institute of Standards and Technology (NIST). Data Encryption Standard (DES) FIPS Publication 46-3, October 1999. Available at http://csrc.nist.gov/publications/fips/fips46-3/fips46-3.pdf.

A   A Larger Sample of Experimental Results

The sample represented in Figure 1 illustrates the scheduling information we obtain in practice. It corresponds to the 32 input bits of the first round (*i.e.* 32 bits from the plaintext), and the corresponding information between clock cycles 1074 and 1116. We used coloured thresholds as a visual tool. Red corresponds to high values of the indicator V_i, and green to intermediate values. The content of Table 1 is actually extracted from this larger sample.

Large values in the tables correspond to clock cycles where plaintext bits are manipulated. One can observe that there are isolated signals probably corresponding to noise in the experiments. However some very significant portions clearly appear. For instance, bits number $1, 2, 3, 4, 5$ and 32 are clearly manipulated between clock cycles 1076 and 1081. This is likely to correspond to the computation of S_1.

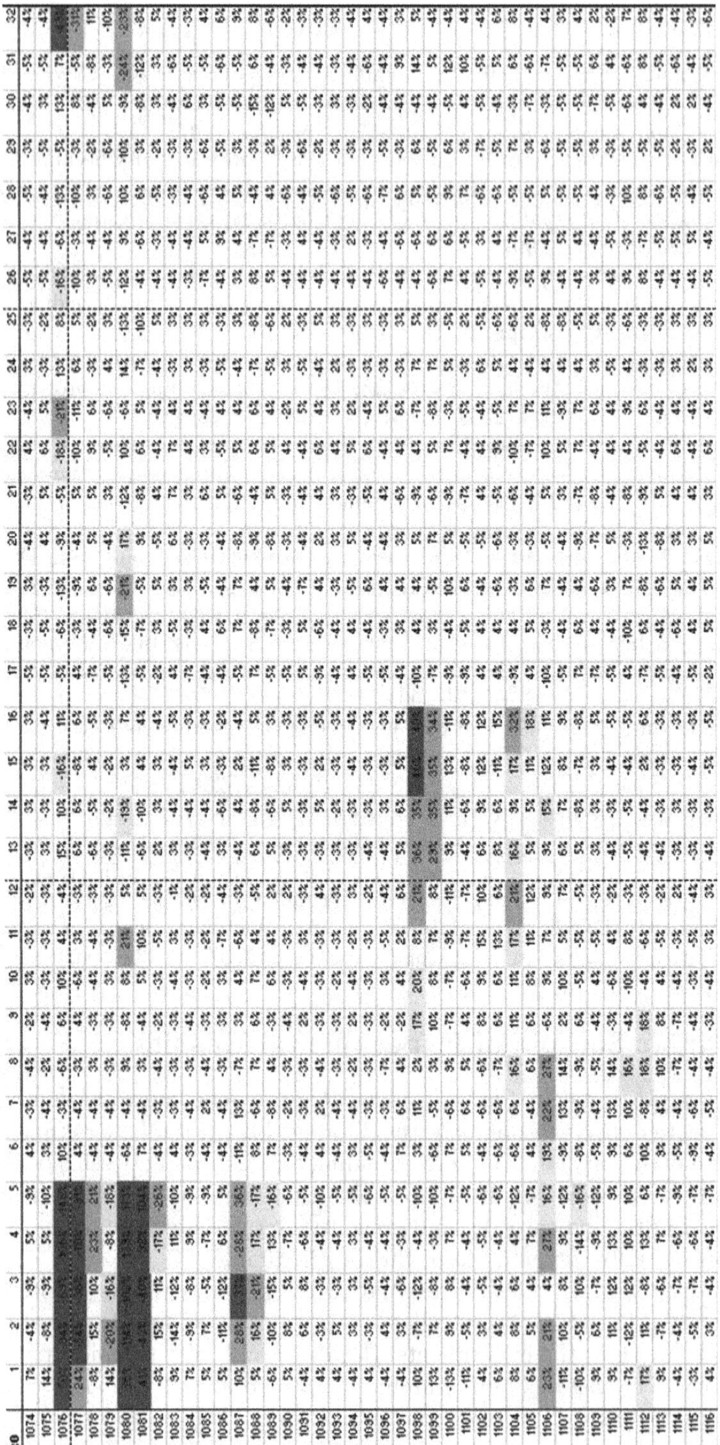

Fig. 1. A large sample of experimental results.

Robust Key Extraction
from Physical Uncloneable Functions

B. Škorić, P. Tuyls, and W. Ophey

Philips Research Laboratories
Prof. Holstlaan 4, 5656 AA Eindhoven, The Netherlands

Abstract. Physical Uncloneable Functions (PUFs) can be used as a cost-effective means to store key material in an uncloneable way. Due to the fact that the key material is obtained by performing measurements on a physical system, noise is inevitably present in each readout. In this paper we present a number of methods that improve the robustness of bit-string extraction from noisy PUF measurements in general, and in particular for optical PUFs. We describe a practical implementation in the case of optical PUFs and show experimental results.

Keywords: Physical Uncloneable Function, authentication, speckle pattern, Challenge-Response Pair, noise, error correction

1 Introduction

1.1 General Introduction to PUFs

A 'Physical Uncloneable Function' (PUF) is a function that is realized by a physical system, such that the function is easy to evaluate but the physical system is hard to characterize, model or reproduce.

Physical tokens were first used as identifiers in the 1980s in the context of strategic arms limitation treaty monitoring [1]. The concept was investigated for civilian purposes in the 1990s [2]. The tokens which were then studied are very hard to reproduce physically, but quite easy to read out completely, i.e. all the physical parameters necessary for successful identification are readily given up by the token. This makes these tokens suitable for systems where the verifier knows with certainty that an actual token is being probed and that the measuring device can be trusted. However, the tokens are not suitable for online identification protocols with an invisible party. An imposter can easily copy the data from someone's token, and then enter that data through a keyboard. The verifier cannot see the difference between the real token and the cloned data.

Truly uncloneable tokens (PUFs) were introduced by Pappu [3, 4]. These are so complex that it is infeasible to fully read out the data contained in a token or to make a computer model that predicts the outputs of a token [5]. This makes PUFs suitable for online protocols as well as verification involving physical probing by untrusted devices.

A PUF is a physical system designed such that it interacts in a complicated way with stimuli (*challenges*) and leads to unique but unpredictable *responses*. A

J. Ioannidis, A. Keromytis, and M.Yung (Eds.): ACNS 2005, LNCS 3531, pp. 407–422, 2005.

PUF challenge and the corresponding response are together called a *Challenge-Reponse-Pair* (CRP). A PUF behaves like a keyed hash function; The physical system consisting of many 'random' components is equivalent to the key. In order to be hard to characterize, the system should not allow efficient extraction of the relevant properties of its interacting components by measurements. Physical systems that are produced by an uncontrolled production process, e.g. random mixing of several substances, turn out to be good candidates for PUFs. Because of this randomness, it is hard to produce a physical copy of the PUF. Furthermore, if the physical function is based on many complex interactions, then mathematical modeling is also very hard. These two properties together are referred to as *Uncloneability*.

1.2   Applications

From a security perspective the uniqueness of the responses and uncloneability of the PUF are very useful properties. Because of these properties, PUFs can be used as unique identifiers, means of tamper-detection and/or as a cost-effective source for key generation (common randomness) between two parties. By embedding a PUF inseparably into a device, the device becomes uniquely identifiable and uncloneable. Here 'inseparable' means that any attempt to remove the PUF will with very high probability damage the PUF and destroy the key material it contains. A wide range of devices can be equipped with a PUF in this way, e.g. smart-cards, credit cards, RFID tags, value papers, optical discs (DRM), chips, security cameras, etc.

An identification scheme based on CRPs works as follows. First, one needs a detector for measuring the analog output of a PUF and an algorithm that extracts bit-strings from this output. The detector and the processor executing the algorithm can be located on the device with the embedded PUF, or inside a separate external reader device. The scheme consists of two phases: *enrollment* and *verification*. In the enrollment phase, the Verifier produces the PUF, embeds it in a device, and stores an initial set of CRPs securely in his database. Then the device is given to a user. The verification phase starts when the user presents his device to a terminal. The Verifier sends a randomly chosen PUF challenge from his database to the user. If the Verifier receives the correct answer[1] from the device, the device is identified. Furthermore, a secure authenticated channel can be set up between the verifier and the device, using a session key based on the PUF response.

A special class of applications becomes possible if so-called 'control' is introduced [6]. A *Controlled PUF* (CPUF) is a PUF that is bound to a processor which completely governs the input and output. The chip can prohibit frequent challenging of the PUF and forbid certain classes of challenge. It can scramble incoming challenges. Furthermore, it can hide the physical output of the PUF, revealing to the outside world only indirect information derived from the output,

---

[1]   In general, the 'answer' is the result of cryptographic operations involving the PUF response. For details on secure protocols we refer to [6, 7, 9].

e.g. an encryption or hash. This control layer substantially strengthens the security, since an attacker cannot probe the PUF at will and cannot interpret the responses. CPUFs allow for new applications such as 'certified execution' [6, 7] and 'certified measurement'.

1.3 Types of PUF / Physical Realizations

Several physical systems are known on which PUFs can be based. The main types are optical PUFs [3, 4], coating PUFs [7], silicon PUFs [8, 9] and acoustic PUFs [7]. In this paper we first discuss PUFs in general and then focus on optical PUFs.

Optical PUFs consist of a transparent material containing randomly distributed scattering particles. Their suitability as a carrier of secret key material derives from the uniqueness and unpredictability of speckle patterns that result from multiple scattering of laser light in a disordered optical medium [5]. The challenge can be e.g. the angle of incidence, focal distance or wavelength of the laser beam, a mask pattern blocking part of the laser light, or any other change in the wave front. The output is the speckle pattern. As the speckle pattern contains many randomly distributed bright and dark patches, a high-entropy bit-string can be extracted from it, using a modest amount of image analysis. Physical copying of optical PUFs is difficult for two reasons: (i) The light diffusion obscures the locations of the scatterers. At this moment the best physical techniques can probe diffusive materials up to a depth of approximately 10 scattering lengths [10]. (ii) Even if all scatterer locations are known, precise positioning of a large number of scatterers is very hard and expensive, and requires a production process different from the original randomized process. *Modeling*, on the other hand, is difficult due to the inherent complexity of multiple coherent scattering [11]. Even the 'forward' problem turns out to be hard. Given the details of all the scatterers, the fastest known computation method of a speckle pattern is the transfer-matrix method [12]. It requires in the order of $(A/\lambda^2)^3 d/\lambda$ operations (where A is the illuminated area, λ the wavelength and d the PUF thickness), which is larger than 10^{20} even if rather conservative values are chosen for A, λ and d.

1.4 The Robustness Problem

The main problem facing any non-digital data storage mechanism is reproducibility. Due to the inherent noisiness of physical measurements, a readout will never yield exactly the same result.

1. For uncontrolled PUFs the external reader that challenges the PUF and detects the response during the verification phase can be a different device than the one that was used in the enrollment phase. Alignment and sensitivity differences between readers give rise to noise, unless great pains are taken to enforce very small mechanical and/or electrical tolerances. However, the potential number of readers is enormous, making such a standardisation impractical and expensive. Hence, the inter-device deviations give an important contribution to the noise in the readout of uncontrolled PUFs.

2. Even repeated measurements with the same challenging and detection device do not give identical results. Time dependent external influences like temperature, moisture, vibrations, stray light, stray fields etc. can have an impact on the measurements.
3. The PUF itself is not immutable. It can accidentally get damaged. Another problem is spontaneous degradation. Most materials slowly change over time due to chemical reactions, friction and repeated thermal deformations. The rate of drifting determines the lifetime of the key material in the PUF.

Robustness can be achieved in two ways, which are best combined: (a) Reducing the noise at the source, and (b) Given a certain level of noise, extracting as much robust key material as possible by properly choosing an error correction algorithm. In Section 2 general measures are discussed to achieve both these goals. They apply to all types of PUF. The methods in Sections 2.3 and 2.4 are new. In Section 3 we present noise reduction methods for optical PUFs. In Section 4 we show experimental results on key extraction in the case of optical PUFs.

2 Key Extraction from Noisy Data

2.1 Shielding Functions

Generally speaking a key extraction algorithm is built on a Secret Extraction Code [13] or, equivalently, a Fuzzy Extractor[2] [14]. For the sake of simplicity we describe the algorithm in terms of a *shielding function* [16], which generates a special set of Secret Extraction Codes, while having all the necessary properties. We denote the analog PUF response to a challenge C during the enrollment phase by $R \in \mathbb{R}^n$ and during the verification phase by $R' \in \mathbb{R}^n$. A function $G : \mathbb{R}^n \times \mathcal{W} \to \{0,1\}^k$ is called δ-contracting if for all R there exists at least one element $W_C \in \mathcal{W}$ and $K \in \{0,1\}^k$ such that $G(R', W_C) = G(R, W_C) = K$ for all R' that lie within a sphere with radius δ around R (i.e. $||R' - R|| \leq \delta$). We use δ-contracting functions to extract keys $K = G(R, W_C)$ from noisy data R using *helper data* W_C.

The function $G(\cdot, \cdot)$ is called 'versatile' if the sets $S_G(R) = \{K \in \{0,1\}^k \mid \exists W_C$ such that $G(R, W_C) = K\}$ are sufficiently large for sufficiently many R.

A function $G : \mathbb{R}^n \times \mathcal{W} \to \{0,1\}^k$ is called ε-revealing if W_C leaks less than ε bits on K (in the information theoretic sense), i.e. $\mathbf{I}(W_C; K) \leq \varepsilon$. An (ε, δ)-shielding function $G : \mathbb{R}^n \times \mathcal{W} \to \{0,1\}^k$ is a function that is δ-contracting, versatile and ε-revealing. It is used to extract a secret of length k from the PUF response as follows.

– **Enrollment Phase:** The PUF is subjected to a challenge C and the analog response R is measured. Then a random key K is chosen from $\{0,1\}^k$ and helper data W_C is computed by solving $G(R, W_C) = K$ for W_C. The quadruplet $(\mathrm{ID}_{\mathrm{PUF}}, C, W_C, K)$ is then stored in a database.

[2] A special case of this construction was previously considered in [15] in the context of biometrics, where it was called a 'fuzzy commitment'.

- **Verification Phase:** When the PUF is inserted into the reader the PUF's identity is sent to the Verifier. The Verifier chooses a random challenge C from his database and sends it to the PUF together with the corresponding helper data W_C. Then the reader subjects the PUF to the challenge C and measures its response R'. The reader computes a key $K' = G(R', W_C)$.

It follows from the δ-contracting property of the function G that $K' = K$ if R' is sufficiently close to R.

In the case of analog outputs, $G(\cdot, \cdot)$ will typically comprise a quantisation procedure. If the strings obtained after quantisation are uniformly distributed, the distilled keys K can be used securely (the helper data leaks no information on K). However, if those strings are not uniformly distributed, a privacy amplification like step, e.g. based on universal hash functions, has to be applied to obtain a (shorter) key about which the adversary has only a negligible amount of information.

2.2   Example Algorithm

In order to illustrate the above definitions we present an example based on an Error Correcting Code $\mathcal{E}$. The algorithm makes use of so-called 'robust components', which are parts of the PUF response that are observed to be relatively insensitive to noise during enrollment. These are e.g. parts of the analog response R whose magnitude exceeds a certain threshold, or parts that do not strongly vary when the measurement is repeated a number of times. By A/D converting R, a 'raw' bit-string b is obtained. Substrings in b that correspond to robust components in R are referred to as 'robust bits'.

- **Enrollment Phase:** The PUF is subjected to a challenge C. The analog output is converted into a bit-string b. Robust components are determined, and a set $\mathcal{I}$ is constructed, consisting of indices pointing at the locations of the robust bits in b. The so-called *robust bit string* X is obtained by concatenating the robust bits. Then a *secret* key K is randomly generated and encoded to a code word $S_K \in \mathcal{E}$. The difference $W = X \oplus S_K$ is computed. The total set of helper data consists of the set $\mathcal{I}$ and the string W. The Verifier stores $(\text{ID}_{\text{PUF}}, C, \mathcal{I}, W, K)$.
- **Verification Phase:** When the PUF is inserted into the reader the PUF's identity is sent to the Verifier. The Verifier chooses a random challenge C from his database and sends it to the reader together with the corresponding helper data $\mathcal{I}, W$. The reader subjects the PUF to the challenge C and converts the analog response R' into a bit-string b'. It uses the helper data indices $\mathcal{I}$ to select bits from b', yielding a bit-string X'. It uses the second part of the helper data, W, to compute $S' = X' \oplus W = (X' \oplus X) \oplus S_K$. Finally, it employs $\mathcal{E}$ to correct any errors present in S'.

Clearly, if the number of errors is not too large ($X' \approx X$) then the error-correcting code will properly correct S' into S_K and yield K after decoding. Note that the δ-contracting property arises from the error correcting capacity of

$\mathcal{E}$, while the ε-revealing property follows from the fact that the secret S_K gets masked by the random variable X.

2.3 Calibration CRPs

In uncontrolled PUFs, the main source of noise is misalignment of the challenging apparatus. We describe a method to reduce this misalignment. A small number of CRPs is reserved for calibration purposes, and is never used for identification. The protocol works as follows.

- **Enrollment of Calibration CRPs:** In addition to the 'ordinary' enrollment, a number of *Calibration CRPs* $(C_{\text{cal}}, r_{\text{cal}})$ is measured and stored. (Here the notation r_{cal} stands for information about the response in general; r_{cal} does not have to be of the same type as the 'ordinary' response information that is stored for identification purposes). The Calibration CRPs have no challenges in common with the 'ordinary' CRPs. The Calibration CRPs are not secret and hence they can be stored in a publicly accessible way, e.g. next to the PUF.
- **Use of Calibration CRPs in the Verification Phase:** A PUF is inserted into a reader. The reader reads ID_{PUF} and acquires a Calibration CRP $(C_{\text{cal}}, r_{\text{cal}})$ corresponding to ID_{PUF}. (This CRP is obtained e.g. by reading it from the smart-card which contains the PUF, or the CRP is sent by the Verifier). The PUF is subjected to the challenge C_{cal}, and the response r'_{cal} is measured. Based on the difference between r'_{cal} and r_{cal}, the alignments of the reader are adjusted. The process of measuring the response to C_{cal} and adjustment is repeated until the difference between r'_{cal} and r_{cal} is reduced to an acceptable level. Only if this level is reached, the Verifier sends a challenge C intended for identification purposes, and the 'real' identification protocol as described in Section 1.2 starts running.

There are ways to improve this method. One option is to choose the calibration challenges such that identification challenges are never extremely far away from a calibration point. In this way the error introduced by moving away from a calibration point is reduced. Another option is to subdivide the process of looking for the correct settings into several stages: First a coarse search with low discriminating power, and then a finer search. In optical PUFs, the discriminating power can be adjusted by changing the laser beam diameter. The sensitivity to noise decreases with increasing beam diameter.

The search can be accelerated by storing additional 'perturbed' responses during enrollment. Pairs $\{\boldsymbol{\Delta}_i, R_{\text{cal}}(\boldsymbol{m} - \boldsymbol{\Delta}_i)\}$ are stored together with the CRP $(C_{\text{cal}}, R_{\text{cal}}(\boldsymbol{m}))$, where $\boldsymbol{m}$ denotes the correct settings of the reader, and $\boldsymbol{\Delta}$ a small perturbation. When, during the search, a response matches $R_{\text{cal}}(\boldsymbol{m} - \boldsymbol{\Delta}_i)$, the reader knows that its settings must be adjusted by an amount $\boldsymbol{\Delta}_i$.

2.4 Two-Way Use of Helper Data

In all schemes discussed so far, helper data is generated during enrollment and applied at the time of verification. However, the measuring device is capable of producing helper data also in the verification phase. Instead of discarding this extra information, one can use it to improve the robustness of the extracted keys. We present an interactive protocol in which the robust components obtained from enrollment and verification are combined using an 'AND' operation.

- **Enrollment:** The Verifier subjects the PUF to a challenge C and converts the analog response R to a bit-string $\boldsymbol{b}$. He determines robust components and constructs the helper data set $\mathcal{I}$ of pointers to the robust parts of $\boldsymbol{b}$. He stores $(\mathrm{ID}_{\mathrm{PUF}}, C, \mathcal{I}, \boldsymbol{b})$.
- **Verification:** The PUF is inserted into the reader and the reader sends $\mathrm{ID}_{\mathrm{PUF}}$ to the Verifier. The Verifier sends C and $\mathcal{I}$. The reader challenges the PUF with C and measures a response R', which it converts into a bit-string $\boldsymbol{b}'$. It determines the robust components of R' and constructs new helper data $\mathcal{I}'$. It sends $\mathcal{I}'$ to the Verifier. Both the reader and the Verifier now compute the *combined helper data* $\mathcal{J} = \mathcal{I} \cap \mathcal{I}'$. The Verifier computes $X = \boldsymbol{b}_{\mathcal{J}}$, while the reader computes $X' = \boldsymbol{b}'_{\mathcal{J}}$. (The notation $\boldsymbol{b}_{\mathcal{J}}$ indicates that only those bits are selected from $\boldsymbol{b}$ that are indicated in $\mathcal{J}$). Finally, X and X' are used for the construction of a secret key, e.g. using the algorithm described in Section 2.2.

An analysis of error probabilities and key lengths is presented in Appendix A. It turns out (see Eqs. 5,6) that the bit error probability in X' is drastically improved compared to the 'one way' case, where only the enrolled helper data is used ($X_{1\mathrm{way}} = \boldsymbol{b}_{\mathcal{I}}$; $X'_{1\mathrm{way}} = \boldsymbol{b}'_{\mathcal{I}}$). As a consequence, the amount of computational effort spent on the error correction using $\mathcal{E}$ is greatly reduced (linear in the number of correctible errors). Furthermore, it turns out that the extracted keys are longer because fewer redundancy bits are needed (see Eq. 8). For a reasonable choice of parameters, the improvement in bit error probability in X' can be as small as a factor 5 and as large as 50. The simultaneous improvement in key length varies between 20% and 70%. The difference between the two methods is most pronounced when the measurements are very noisy.

3   Noise Reduction for Optical PUFs

3.1   'Pyramid' Structure

In Fig. 1 we present an elegant way of detecting misalignments between an optical PUF and a camera. At the bottom of the PUF, a small pyramid-shaped volume is removed. When the laser beam enters the PUF, a fraction of the light reaches the bottom without being scattered by the random particles. There a certain fraction reflects off the pyramid structure and is divided into four sub-beams. These beams are partially transmitted through the PUF without scattering, and give rise to four bright spots on the camera. The spots are superimposed on the speckle pattern. Misalignments (translations and rotations in all directions) can be uniquely read off from the relative positions of the four spots (see Fig. 1 a–d). This allows the reader to adjust its settings.

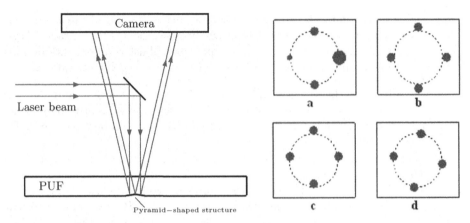

Fig. 1. Left: Light scattering from the pyramid structure. Right: Effects of misalignment. (a) Shift in x-direction. (b) Shift in z-direction. (c) Rotation around the x-axis. (d) Rotation around the z-axis.

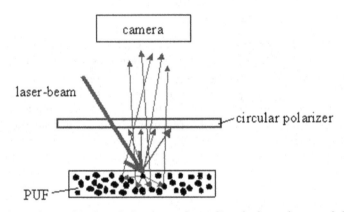

Fig. 2. Circular polariser blocking light that reflects directly from the top of the PUF.

3.2   Polarisation Selection

The noise due to scratches and dirt on the surface of an optical PUF can be reduced by making use of the fact that light changes its polarisation when it is reflected. The method works as follows. We assume a geometry as in Fig. 2. When the laser light is generated, it has *linear* polarisation. On its way to the PUF the beam passes through a *circular* polariser. Light that gets scattered from the top of the PUF, without entering it, will have reversed circular polarisation and hence will be absorbed when it meets the polariser again. Light that enters the PUF, however, is subjected to multiple scattering, which has a depolarising effect. Hence, a substantial fraction of the multiply scattered light will pass the polariser and reach the camera. In this way, direct reflection from scratches and dirt is eliminated. In order to improve the selectivity, one can add an additional quarter wave plate on top of the PUF; passing through it twice precisely negates the polarisation-reversing effect of a reflection.

4 Experimental Results for Optical PUFs

We show experimental results that demonstrate the effectiveness of helper data in the form of robust components. The algoritm of Section 2.2 was applied, without making use of the techniques decribed in Sections 2.3, 2.4 and 3. We used the following setup. The laser is a DBF laser with a wavelength of 785 nm (spectral width 1nm). The beam diameter is 1 mm. We have used five scattering samples with a thickness of 0.4 mm. Pictures of the reflected speckle pattern are taken with a 1024 by 768 pixel CCD camera with a pixel pitch of 6.25 mm. The bitmap has 256 gray levels. The distance between the laser and the sample is 10 cm, and the distance from the sample to the camera is 13 cm.

4.1 Binarized Gabor Coefficients

In order to extract bit strings from speckle images we have used the method of Gabor Transforms as proposed in [3]. Gabor Transforms are well suited since they are insensitive to small changes in an image and they reveal the locations as well as the orientations of structures at different spatial frequencies. They are used in a wide range of applications, such as iris recognition [17], texture analysis and image enhancement, coding and compression.

A two-dimensional Gabor basis function $\Gamma(s, \boldsymbol{k}, \boldsymbol{x}_0, \boldsymbol{x})$ is the product of a plane wave with wave vector $\boldsymbol{k}$ and a Gaussian centered on $\boldsymbol{x}_0$ with width s. ($\boldsymbol{x}$ denotes a location in the speckle image). We write the Gabor basis functions Γ and the Gabor coefficients G as follows.

$$G_{\text{IM}}(s, \boldsymbol{k}, \boldsymbol{x}_0) = \int d^2 x \; \Gamma_{\text{IM}}(s, \boldsymbol{k}, \boldsymbol{x}_0, \boldsymbol{x}) I(\boldsymbol{x}) \tag{1}$$

$$\Gamma_{\text{IM}}(s, \boldsymbol{k}, \boldsymbol{x}_0, \boldsymbol{x}) = \frac{1}{s\sqrt{2\pi}} \sin \boldsymbol{k} \cdot (\boldsymbol{x} - \boldsymbol{x}_0) \exp[-\frac{(\boldsymbol{x} - \boldsymbol{x}_0)^2}{4s^2}]. \tag{2}$$

Here I denotes the light intensity. We have selected the imaginary part of the transform, since it is invariant under spatially constant shifts of I. In the notation of Section 2, a bitmap image of a speckle pattern corresponds to the 'raw' bit-string $\boldsymbol{b}$. The 'robust' bit-string X is obtained as follows. Gabor coefficients G_{IM} are evaluated for a set of parameters s, $\boldsymbol{k}$, $\boldsymbol{x}_0$. Coefficients are discarded if they do not exceed a certain threshold T, i.e. one only keeps $|G_{\text{IM}}| > T$. Finally, the robust coefficients are binarized; positive values are mapped to '1' and negative to '0'.

Attention must be paid to the fact that Gabor coefficients can be strongly correlated. Ideally one should construct a bit-string from values that are almost independent. In general, correlations between $G_{\text{IM}}(s, \boldsymbol{k}, \boldsymbol{x}_0)$ and $G_{\text{IM}}(s', \boldsymbol{k}', \boldsymbol{x}_0')$ occur when their parameters do not differ much. Correlations also occur if $|\boldsymbol{x}_0' - \boldsymbol{x}_0|$ is smaller than the speckle size. An analysis of these correlations is presented in

Appendix B. For simplicity we have used the following parameters in our experiments: A single Gaussian width $s = 13$ pixels, a single length $|\mathbf{k}| = \pi/8$ pixels^{-1}, two directions of $\mathbf{k}$ (45° and 135°), and $\mathbf{x}_0$ positions in a square grid with a spacing of 8 pixels. This yields 2400 Gabor coefficients. There are very strong correlations (≈ 0.9) between diagonal neighbours on the $\mathbf{x}_0$-grid when $\mathbf{k} \parallel \mathbf{k}'$ and $(\mathbf{x}'_0 - \mathbf{x}_0) \perp \mathbf{k}$. Furthermore, there are strong anti-correlations (≈ -0.7) between diagonal neigbours when $\mathbf{k}$, $\mathbf{k}'$ and $(\mathbf{x}'_0 - \mathbf{x}_0)$ point in the same direction. Other correlations are zero or negligible. This explains the stripes in Fig. 3.

Fig. 3. Left: Example of a speckle pattern. **Middle:** Binarized Gabor coefficients at 45°. **Right:** Binarized Gabor coefficients at 135°.

The robustness threshold T was chosen such that in the enrollment phase there are always more than 1023 Gabor coefficients exceeding the threshold. We have used a BCH code with parameters (1023, 56, 191), i.e. 1023-bit code words, 56-bit message words (the actual key length), and correction of 191 errors. The high error-correcting capacity is necessary because the bit error rate (BER) in the robust bit-string X' is still high when no special measures are taken to reduce the noise. Without showing proof we mention that the Calibration CRP method reduces the BER to $< 5\%$, allowing for a BCH code with parameters (1023,553,52), i.e. robust 553-bit message words. Note, however, that the actual information content (entropy) is lower than 553 bits due to the strong correlations between the Gabor coefficients (see Appendix B).

The statistics of the Gabor coefficients is the subject of ongoing research.

4.2   Experimental Results

Fig. 3 shows a typical speckle pattern and the binarized Gabor coefficients. We studied the sensitivity of the binarized coefficients as well as the selected robust coefficients under small rotations and translations. All measurements were repeated ten times (re-inserting the samples each time) and averaged over these ten instances. As a direct measure of the difference between two speckle patterns B_1, B_2 we use the correlation $C_{\mathrm{bmp}} \in [-1, 1]$ between the bitmaps,

$$C_{\mathrm{bmp}} = \frac{\langle B_1(\mathbf{x}_i) B_2(\mathbf{x}_i)\rangle_i - \langle B_1(\mathbf{x}_i)\rangle_i \langle B_2(\mathbf{x}_i)\rangle_i}{\sigma_1 \sigma_2} \tag{3}$$

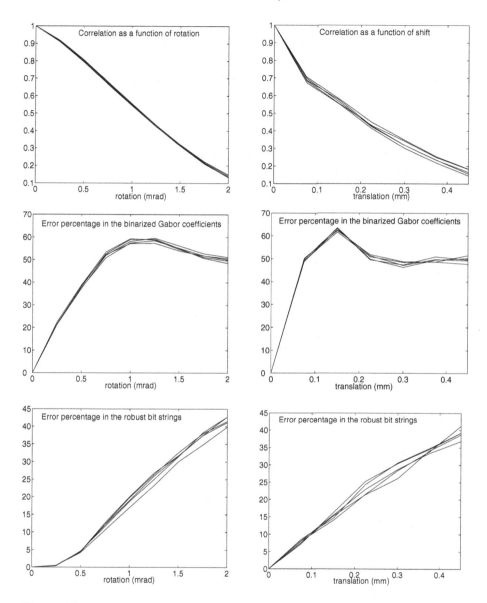

Fig. 4. Effects of misalignment. The five curves correspond to different samples. **Left:** Tilting of the laser beam. **Right:** Shift of the sample. **From top to bottom:** Correlation between original and perturbed speckle pattern; Error percentage in the binarized Gabor coefficients (2400-bit string); Error percentage in the selected robust bit-string (>1023 bits).

where $\langle \cdot \rangle_i$ denotes the spatial average and σ is the standard deviation in the gray level of the speckle pattern. The results of the measurements are shown in Fig. 4. The graphs show that for rotations larger than 0.7 mrad and shifts larger than

0.1 mm, the binarized coefficients look completely independent (50% errors). The robust bits, however, are significantly more resilient: There the BER level of 50% is reached only at rotations > 2mrad and shifts > 0.5mm. This demonstrates the usefulness of robust components as a form of helper data.

Acknowledgements

We thank Marten van Dijk, Vincent van der Leest, Sjoerd Stallinga and Ton Akkermans for useful discussions.

References

1. K.M. Tolk, *Reflective Particle Technology for Identification of Critical Components*, 33rd Annual Meeting Proceedings of the Institute of Nuclear Materials Management, July 1992.
2. Unicate BV's '3DAS' system, http://www.andreae.com/Unicate/Appendix%201.htm, 1999.
3. R. Pappu, *Physical One-Way Functions*, Ph.D. thesis, MIT 2001.
4. R. Pappu, B. Recht, J. Taylor, N. Gershenfeld, *Physical One-Way Functions*, Science Vol. 297, p.2026, Sept 2002.
5. P. Tuyls, B. Škorić, S. Stallinga, A.H.M. Akkermans, W. Ophey, *Information-Theoretic Security Analysis of Physical Uncloneable Functions*, Proc. Financial Cryptography and Data Security 2005.
6. B. Gassend, D. Clarke, M. van Dijk, S. Devadas, *Controlled Physical Random Functions*, Proc. 18th Annual Computer Security Applications Conf., Dec. 2002.
7. P. Tuyls, B. Škorić, *Secret Key Generation from Classical Physics*, Proceedings of the Hardware Technology Drivers for Ambient Intelligence Symposium, Philips Research Book Series, Kluwer, 2005.
8. B. Gassend, D. Clarke, M. van Dijk, S. Devadas *Silicon Physical Random Functions*, Proc. 9th ACM Conf. on Computer and Communications Security, 2002.
9. B. Gassend, *Physical Random Functions*, Master's Thesis, MIT 2003.
10. M. Magnor, P. Dorn, W. Rudolph, *Simulation of confocal microscopy through scattering media with and without time gating*, J.Opt.Soc.Am. B, Vol. 19, no. 11 (2001), 1695–1700.
11. J. F. de Boer, *Optical Fluctuations on the Transmission and Reflection of Mesoscopic Systems*, Ph.D. thesis, 1995, Amsterdam.
12. H. Furstenberg, *Noncommuting Random Matrices*, Trans. Am. Math. Soc. 108, 377, 1963.
13. P. Tuyls, J. Goseling, *Capacity and Examples of Template Protecting Biometric Authentication Systems*, Biometric Authentication Workshop (BioAW 2004), LNCS 3087, 158–170, Prague, 2004.
14. Y. Dodis, L. Reyzin, A. Smith, *Fuzzy Extractors: How to generate strong secret keys from biometrics and other noisy data*, in Advances in Cryptology – Eurocrypt'04, LNCS 3027, 523–540, 2004.
15. A. Juels, M. Wattenberg, *A Fuzzy Commitment Scheme*, in G. Tsudik, ed., Sixth ACM Conference on Computer and Communications Security, 28–36, ACM Press. 1999.

16. J.P. Linnartz, P. Tuyls, *New Shielding Functions to enhance Privacy and Prevent Misuse of Biometric Templates*, Proc. 4th International Conference on Audio and Video based Biometric Person Authentication, LNCS 2688, Guildford UK, June 9-11, 2003.
17. J. Daugman, *The importance of being random; statistical principles of iris recognition*, Pattern Recognition 36, 279–291, 2003.
18. J. W. Goodman, *Statistical properties of laser speckle patterns*, in Laser Speckle and Related Phenomena, 2nd ed., J. C. Dainty, Ed. New York: Springer-Verlag, 1984.

A   Two-Way Use of Helper Data

In this Appendix we use a simple model to analyse the effects of using the helper data that is generated during the verification phase as proposed in Section 2.4. We consider the measurement of n variables $x_1, \ldots, x_n$, representing the PUF response, which are independent and identically distributed according to a normal distribution with zero mean and standard deviation Σ_x. (This is sometimes called the 'inter-class' variation). The measurement error due to misalignment and external noise is assumed to be independently Gaussian distributed with standard deviation σ ('intra-class' variation). If the enrollment measurement yields a value f, with absolute value larger than some threshold T, the value is deemed 'robust'. We compute the probability P_{robust} of finding a robust value when a noisy measurement is done of a variable x_i, given that the 'noiseless' value of x_i is *unknown*. We have to take the inter-class variation into account and hence average over x_i,

$$P_{\text{robust}} = 1 - \int_{-T}^{T} \mathrm{d}f \int_{-\infty}^{\infty} \mathrm{d}x \, N_{0\Sigma_x}(x) N_{x\sigma}(f) = 1 - \mathrm{Erf} \frac{T}{\sqrt{2}\sqrt{\Sigma_x^2 + \sigma^2}}. \qquad (4)$$

Here the notation $N_{\mu s}$ stands for the normal distribution with mean μ and standard deviation s, and Erf denotes the Error Function. Given a robust measured f, the probability P_1 that a bit flip will occur in the second measurement, according to the one-way method, is equal to the probability that the second measurement yields a number F with sign opposite from f. Taking $f > 0$ without loss of generality, this probability is

$$P_1 = \int_{-\infty}^{\infty} \mathrm{d}x \, N_{f\sigma}(x) \int_{-\infty}^{0} \mathrm{d}F \, N_{x\sigma}(F) = \frac{1}{2} - \frac{1}{2}\mathrm{Erf} \frac{f}{2\sigma}. \qquad (5)$$

The first integral in (5) is an average over all the possibilities for the unknown 'true' value x. Given the fact that f was obtained in the first measurement, x is Gaussian-distributed around f, with standard deviation given by the noise strength σ.

On the other hand, if the two-way helper data method is used, the probability of a bit flip (P_2) is equal to the probability that F not only has opposite sign, but also has absolute value larger than the threshold T,

$$P_2 = \int_{-\infty}^{\infty} dx \, N_{f\sigma}(x) \int_{-\infty}^{-T} dF \, N_{x\sigma}(F) = \frac{1}{2} - \frac{1}{2} \text{Erf} \frac{f+T}{2\sigma}. \qquad (6)$$

The amount of computational effort that has to be spent on error-correcting codes is roughly linear in the expected number of errors. Hence we are interested in the expectation values $\langle P_1 \rangle$ and $\langle P_2 \rangle$, where the brackets denote averaging with respect to f (with $f \geq T$). Making a natural choice for the parameters, $\sigma < T < 2\sigma$ and $\Sigma_x > \sigma$, it turns out that the ratio $\langle P_1 \rangle / \langle P_2 \rangle$ lies in a range between approximately 5 and 50 (increasing with T/σ), indicating that the two-way method gives a huge reduction of the computational cost of using the error-correcting code $\mathcal{E}$.

One may worry that the two-way method yields shorter keys, as more bits are being discarded in the establishment of the robust bit-string X'. We show that, on the contrary, longer keys are extracted. In the one-way method, a variable x_i that has been found to be robust at enrollment ($f > T$) is always kept. In the two-way method there is a nonzero probability P_{discard} of discarding such a variable,

$$P_{\text{discard}} = \int_{-\infty}^{\infty} dx \, N_{f\sigma}(x) \int_{-T}^{T} dF \, N_{x\sigma}(F) = \frac{1}{2} \text{Erf} \frac{f+T}{2\sigma} - \frac{1}{2} \text{Erf} \frac{f-T}{2\sigma}. \qquad (7)$$

We denote the length of the robust string X' in the one-way method as $n_1 = n \cdot P_{\text{robust}}$. The corresponding length in the two-way case is $n_2 = n_1(1 - \langle P_{\text{discard}} \rangle)$, i.e. shorter than n_1. However, it is well known that the information capacity of a channel strongly depends on the error rate of the channel. Given an error rate p, the information content per transmitted bit is $1 - h(p)$, with $h(p) = -p \log p - (1-p) \log(1-p)$. The maximum entropy H of the derived key K in the two methods is given by

$$H_1 = n_1 [1 - h(\langle P_1 \rangle)] ; \qquad H_2 = n_2 [1 - h(\langle P_2 \rangle)]. \qquad (8)$$

For given signal to noise ratio Σ_x/σ, an optimal choice of T/σ exists (for each method separately) that yields the highest entropy. It turns out that the best H_2 is always larger than the best H_1. The difference between the two methods is most pronounced at small Σ_x/σ, i.e. noisy measurements.

B   Correlations Between Gabor Coefficients

In this Appendix we compute the correlation between the Gabor coefficients (1). We use the shorthand notation $G_{\text{IM}} = G_{\text{IM}}(s, k, x)$ and $G'_{\text{IM}} = G_{\text{IM}}(s', k', x')$. By σ_G and σ'_G we denote the standard deviation of G_{IM} and G'_{IM} respectively. We define the correlation $C_G \in [-1, 1]$ as

$$C_G := \frac{\langle G_{\text{IM}} G'_{\text{IM}} \rangle - \langle G_{\text{IM}} \rangle \langle G'_{\text{IM}} \rangle}{\sigma_G \sigma'_G} = \frac{\langle G_{\text{IM}} G'_{\text{IM}} \rangle}{\sqrt{\langle (G_{\text{IM}})^2 \rangle \langle (G'_{\text{IM}})^2 \rangle}}. \qquad (9)$$

The brackets denote averaging over speckle patterns. For the last equality we have used the fact that Γ_{IM} (2) is an odd function of x, which leads to $\langle G_{\text{IM}} \rangle = 0$

regardless of the choice of parameters. For the computation of the expectation values we use a result from [18],

$$R(\boldsymbol{x}_1, \boldsymbol{x}_2) := \langle I(\boldsymbol{x}_1)I(\boldsymbol{x}_2) \rangle = 4 \left[\frac{J_1(|\boldsymbol{x}_2 - \boldsymbol{x}_1|/M)}{|\boldsymbol{x}_2 - \boldsymbol{x}_1|/M} \right]^2 \tag{10}$$

where J_1 is a Bessel function and M is a constant proportional to the average speckle size, $M = \lambda z/(2\pi W)$, with λ the wavelength, z the distance between the exit plane of the PUF and the detector, and W the diameter of the illuminated area of the PUF. Substitution of (10) and (2) into (9) gives

$$\frac{\langle G_{\mathrm{IM}} G'_{\mathrm{IM}} \rangle}{\langle I \rangle^2} = \int \frac{d^2 x_1 d^2 x_2}{2\pi s s'} R \, e^{-\frac{(\boldsymbol{x}_1 - \boldsymbol{x})^2}{4s^2} - \frac{(\boldsymbol{x}_2 - \boldsymbol{x}')^2}{4s'^2}} \sin \boldsymbol{k} \cdot (\boldsymbol{x}_1 - \boldsymbol{x}) \sin \boldsymbol{k}' \cdot (\boldsymbol{x}_2 - \boldsymbol{x}'). \tag{11}$$

We introduce 'center of mass' coordinates as follows,

$$\begin{aligned}
\boldsymbol{x} &= \bar{\boldsymbol{x}} - \tfrac{1}{2}\boldsymbol{\Delta} & ; & \quad \boldsymbol{x}' &= \bar{\boldsymbol{x}} + \tfrac{1}{2}\boldsymbol{\Delta} \\
\boldsymbol{x}_1 &= \boldsymbol{m} - \tfrac{1}{2}\boldsymbol{\delta} & ; & \quad \boldsymbol{x}_2 &= \boldsymbol{m} + \tfrac{1}{2}\boldsymbol{\delta} \\
\boldsymbol{k} &= \boldsymbol{K} - \tfrac{1}{2}\boldsymbol{\zeta} & ; & \quad \boldsymbol{k}' &= \boldsymbol{K} + \tfrac{1}{2}\boldsymbol{\zeta} \\
1/s^2 &= p - \tfrac{1}{2}q & ; & \quad 1/s'^2 &= p + \tfrac{1}{2}q
\end{aligned} \tag{12}$$

In terms of these coordinates, the expectation value (11) can be expressed as

$$\langle G_{\mathrm{IM}} G'_{\mathrm{IM}} \rangle = \frac{\langle I \rangle^2}{\pi s s'} \int d^2 \delta \left[\frac{J_1(\delta/M)}{\delta/M} \right]^2 \exp[-\tfrac{p}{8}(\boldsymbol{\delta} - \boldsymbol{\Delta})^2] \tag{13}$$

$$\int d^2 m \, \exp[-\tfrac{p}{2}m^2 - \tfrac{q}{4}\boldsymbol{m} \cdot (\boldsymbol{\delta} - \boldsymbol{\Delta})]$$

$$\times \left\{ \cos[\boldsymbol{K} \cdot (\boldsymbol{\delta} - \boldsymbol{\Delta}) + \boldsymbol{\zeta} \cdot \boldsymbol{m}] - \cos[2\boldsymbol{K} \cdot \boldsymbol{m} + \tfrac{1}{2}\boldsymbol{\zeta} \cdot (\boldsymbol{\delta} - \boldsymbol{\Delta})] \right\}.$$

Here we have assumed, without loss of generality, that $\bar{\boldsymbol{x}} = \boldsymbol{0}$. The m-integral is readily evaluated, yielding

$$\langle G_{\mathrm{IM}} G'_{\mathrm{IM}} \rangle = \frac{2 \langle I \rangle^2}{p s s'} \int d^2 \delta \left[\frac{J_1(\delta/M)}{\delta/M} \right]^2 \exp[-(\tfrac{p}{8} - \tfrac{q^2}{32p})(\boldsymbol{\delta} - \boldsymbol{\Delta})^2] \tag{14}$$

$$\times \left\{ e^{-(1/2p)\zeta^2} \cos[(\boldsymbol{K} - \tfrac{q}{4p}\boldsymbol{\zeta}) \cdot (\boldsymbol{\delta} - \boldsymbol{\Delta})] \right.$$

$$\left. - e^{-(2/p)K^2} \cos[(\tfrac{1}{2}\boldsymbol{\zeta} - \tfrac{q}{2p}\boldsymbol{K}) \cdot (\boldsymbol{\delta} - \boldsymbol{\Delta})] \right\}.$$

The δ-integral cannot be evaluated analytically. Several trends can be observed, however. The integrand contains a rapidly decreasing function of $\boldsymbol{\delta}$ centered around $\boldsymbol{\delta} = 0$, with scale M, times another rapidly decreasing function of $\boldsymbol{\delta}$ centered around $\boldsymbol{\Delta}$, with scale $\approx s$. Hence, if $\boldsymbol{\Delta}$ is larger than $\min(M, s)$, then the expectation value (14) becomes very small. Furthermore, it can also be seen that the δ-integral becomes small when $\zeta^{-1} \ll \min(M, s)$, because then the oscillations cancel each other.

We make an approximation by writing $4[J_1(u)/u]^2 \approx \exp(-u^2/2\Sigma^2)$, with $\Sigma \approx 1.29$. This makes the δ-integral manageable and nicely captures the decay of the integrand between $u = 0$ and $u \approx 3.83$ where $J_1(u) = 0$, but the asymptotic behaviour at large u is misrepresented. Hence, the approximation is useful for small Δ. We present the result for $s' = s$:

$$C_{\mathrm{G}}(s' = s) \approx \exp\left[-\frac{1}{2} \cdot \frac{\Delta^2}{M^2\Sigma^2 + 4s^2}\right] \times \tag{15}$$

$$\frac{e^{\Gamma s^2 \boldsymbol{k}\cdot\boldsymbol{k}'} \cos\frac{\Gamma}{2}\boldsymbol{\Delta} \cdot (\boldsymbol{k}' + \boldsymbol{k}) - e^{-\Gamma s^2 \boldsymbol{k}\cdot\boldsymbol{k}'} \cos\frac{\Gamma}{2}\boldsymbol{\Delta} \cdot (\boldsymbol{k}' - \boldsymbol{k})}{2\sqrt{\sinh \Gamma s^2 k^2}\sqrt{\sinh \Gamma s^2 k'^2}}$$

where $\Gamma \in [0, 1]$ is defined as $\Gamma = [1 + M^2\Sigma^2/(4s^2)]^{-1}$.

Efficient Constructions
for One-Way Hash Chains

Yih-Chun Hu[1], Markus Jakobsson[2], and Adrian Perrig[3]

[1] UC Berkeley
[2] Indiana University at Bloomington
[3] Carnegie Mellon University

Abstract. One-way chains are an important cryptographic primitive in many security applications. As one-way chains are very efficient to verify, they recently became increasingly popular for designing security protocols for resource-constrained mobile devices and sensor networks, as their low-powered processors can compute a one-way function within milliseconds, but would require tens of seconds or up to minutes to generate or verify a traditional digital signature [6]. Recent sensor network security protocols thus extensively use one-way chains to design protocols that scale down to resource-constrained sensors [21, 29]. Recently, researchers also proposed a variety of improvements to one-way hash chains to make storage and access more efficient [9, 18, 33], or to make setup and verification more efficient [17, 21].

In this paper we present two new constructions for one-way hash chains, which significantly improve the efficiency of one-way chains. Our first construction, the Sandwich-chain, provides a smaller bandwidth overhead for one-way chain values, and enables efficient verification of one-way chain values if the trusted one-way chain value is far away. Our second construction, Comb Skipchain, features a new lower bound for one-way chains in terms of storage and traversal overhead. In fact previously, researchers [9] cite a lower bound of $\log^2(n)$ for the product of per-value traversal overhead and memory requirements for one-dimensional chains. We show that one can achieve a lower bound by considering multi-dimensional chains. In particular, our two-dimensional construction requires $O(\log(n))$ memory and $O(1)$ traversal overhead, thereby improving on the one-dimensional bound. In addition, the setup cost for the one-way chain is in contrast only $O(n/\log(n))$. Other benefits for both constructions include a faster verification step than the traditional hash chains provide; a verifier can "catch up" efficiently, after having missed some number of previously released hash values (for the Sandwich-chain); and resistance against DoS attacks on authentication values. Moreover, we describe fractal traversal schemes for our proposed structures, bringing down the traversal costs for our structure to the same as those of the simpler "traditional" hash chain.

Our new construction is orthogonal to most previously proposed techniques, and can be used in conjunction with techniques for efficient setup or verification of one-way chains.

Keywords: One-way hash chains, efficient constructions, broadcast authentication.

J. Ioannidis, A. Keromytis, and M.Yung (Eds.): ACNS 2005, LNCS 3531, pp. 423–441, 2005.
© Springer-Verlag Berlin Heidelberg 2005

1   Introduction

One-way chains are a widely deployed cryptographic primitive. Lamport first proposed to use one-way chains for efficient authentication of one-time passwords [20], which Haller later refined to the S/KEY standard [13]. Since Lamport's work, many researchers proposed to use one-way chains as a basic building block for a variety of applications, for example for digital cash [2, 15, 27, 31], for extending the lifetime of digital certificates [1, 25], for constructing one-time signatures [10, 23, 24, 32], for authenticating link-state routing updates [8, 14, 34], or for efficient packet authentication [28].

Despite the computational efficiency of one-way functions, one-way chains are still challenging to use in resource-constrained environments, such as on small mobile devices or sensor networks. Especially some of the proposed sensor networks have significant resource limitations, as they use minimal hardware to lower the energy consumption [19]. In these resource-challenged environments the setup, traversal, verification, and storage of long one-way chains is a major challenge.

Recently, researchers proposed a variety of improvements to one-way hash chains to make setup, traversal, and storage more efficient. A good metric for one-way chain efficiency is the product of the per-value traversal overhead and the memory requirements[1]. For example, simply storing each value of a one-way chain with length n would result in a cost of $O(n)$, as storage requires $O(n)$ memory and traversal is $O(1)$ (no computation necessary, the one-way chain values are simply stored in an array). Another straightforward approach is to only store the seed of the chain, and derive each value on the fly, with an $O(n)$ efficiency again, as storage costs are $O(1)$ and traversal costs $O(n)$. Jakobsson [18], Coppersmith and Jakobsson [9], and Sella [33] propose new techniques that make traversal and storage more efficient, and apply these techniques to traditional one-way chains. All of these techniques allow the computation of consecutive values in the hash chain at a cost of only $O(\log(n))$ one-way function computations (traversal cost), while also requiring $O(\log(n))$ storage, resulting in an efficiency of $O(\log^2(n))$. Given that the traversal techniques are applied to standard hash chains, the verification cost is not affected by the manner in which the values are represented and computed, making the verification cost $O(n)$. This is also the computational cost of the setup phase, in which the value at the endpoint is computed given a randomly selected seed; this computation may be performed by a powerful and trusted device, as opposed to the resource constrained device that performs the traversal.

Hu et al. propose a new structure for one-way chains, in which more than one level of chains are used [17]. The main benefit of their structure is that it allows for more efficient verification: a verifier would only have to compute the sequence of hash function evaluations corresponding to a small portion of the total number of traversed values. We review their approach in Section 4 and

---

[1] The traversal cost can be zero when the entire chain is stored, which would result that the product would be zero as well. We could deal with this by also accounting for memory accesses, or by adding 1 to the number of one-way function computations for the traversal cost. Both techniques result in a non-zero positive traversal cost.

refine their construction to design a new one-way chain that only requires $O(1)$ traversal overhead and $O(\log(n))$ storage. The resulting efficiency of $O(\log(n))$ is significantly better than previous bounds.

Liu and Ning propose a two-level one-way chain, where the chains of the second level are derived from values of the first level [21]. Their scheme provides a linear speedup for setup and verification, and thus still requires $O(n)$ setup, storage, and verification overhead.

Our approach is to design a new structure that allows for both rapid generation and verification of intermediary nodes, and without the increase in representation of approaches such as Merkle trees. Another interesting approach was recently taken by Fischlin [11], in which he shows how to augment the output from the hash chain traversal with a checksum in order to allow for faster verification of standard hash chain elements. Therein, security can be traded for efficiency by setting the appropriate parameter controlling the length of the checksum component. In contrast, we do not have to give up on security in order to achieve the increased efficiency of verification, but *do* have to augment the underlying graph structure. It appears likely that the methods can be combined, but we leave this as an open problem for future research

This paper makes the following contributions:

- **Framework.** We introduce a framework for comparing one-way chain techniques, considering setup, traversal, verification, storage, and communication overheads.
- **New two-dimensional chains.** We propose a new technique for authenticating chains below the first level of the hierarchy, producing three clear advantages in comparison to the related approach of [21]: First, it avoids jamming-based DoS attacks that focus on disrupting the transmission of the sensitive authentication values for secondary chains. Second, it allows users to store and forward the new authentication values for the benefit of other users, who did not receive them when first transmitted. This approach does not require users to trust one another. Note that we obtain this benefit without the use of digital signatures or other heavy-weight constructions; in fact, our approach has the same low computational demands as the approach taken in [21]. Third and finally, it allows a user who has missed some (potentially large) number of authentication values to "catch up" with a computational effort that is a fraction of number of transmitted authentication values missed by the user. This feature, which is not present in other proposals (whether those using traditional or hierarchical chains) may prove particularly beneficial in settings where nodes are mobile.
- **Light chains.** We propose the notion of *light one-way chains* to lower the communication overhead. These are relatively short hash chains whose values are shorter than what is normally needed to avoid attacks based on inverting or finding collisions; we show how to use these in a way that avoid attacks. Using known hash indexing techniques, we further make our proposal resistant against birthday attacks, that would otherwise reduce the security of the structure as its number of elements grows.

More specifically, we present two new one-way chain constructions: Sandwich-chain and Comb Skipchain. Sandwich-chain is a new hash chain structure with a fractal traversal algorithm requiring only $O(\log(n))$ computation and storage; a reduction of the bandwidth requirements; and a substantially reduced verification effort. The exact verification effort depends on parameter choices, and will be described in detail. Comb Skipchain is a new hash chain featuring only $O(n/\log(n))$ cost for setup, $O(\log(n))$ storage, and $O(1)$ cost for traversal. This construction is substantially more efficient than the lower bound for one-dimensional one-way chains. Like the new structures of [17, 21], our construction is not compatible with all previous uses of hash chains. However, and as will become evident, there are many common uses of traditional hash chains that can easily be adapted to use our structure.

The outline of the paper is as follows. Section 2 presents one-way chain basics and our evaluation framework. Section 3 introduces our Sandwich-chain, and Section 4 presents our Comb Skipchain construction. We describe the use of light chains in 5. Section 6 discusses different deployment scenarios and analyzes which one-way chain technique is most appropriate.

2   Background and Evaluation Framework

We present a framework for evaluating and comparing one-way chain proposals, comparing setup, traversal, verification, storage, and communication costs. Our constructions, like those of [21], are based on a hierarchy of chains, where values of some chains (which we refer to as *primary* chains) are used as roots for other chains (so-called *secondary* chains.)

One-Way Chain Setup. A one-way chain $(V_0 \ldots V_N)$ is a collection of values such that each value V_i (except the last value V_N) is a one-way function of the next value V_{i+1}. In particular, we have that $V_i = H(V_{i+1})$, for $0 \leq i < N$. Here, H is a one-way function, and is often selected as a cryptographic hash function, which is why the structure is often also called a *hash chain*. For *setup* of the one-way chain, the *generator* chooses at random the *root* or *seed* of the chain, i.e., the value V_N, and derives all previous values V_i by iteratively applying the hash function H as described above. The value V_0, which we refer to as the *end-value*, is normally made public, and potentially linked to the identity of the user possessing the corresponding root value. An example of a standard hash chain is shown in Figure 1.

Verification of One-Way Chain Values. We assume that the *verifier* knows an authentic value of the generator's one-way chain, usually the end-value V_0. To

Fig. 1. Standard one-level one-way chain.

verify an input value V_i of a chain, the verifier iteratively applies the one-way function H i times and compares the result to the trusted value V_0, i.e., verify that $H^i(V_i)$ equals V_0. If the computed and known values are equal, then the input value is said to be authentic. Note that if another value V_k, for $k < i$, is already known, then it suffices to iteratively apply the one-way function some $i - k$ times to the input value, and compare the result to this intermediate value.

One-Way Chain Traversal. When the generator discloses successive values of the one-way chain, we call this one-way chain *traversal*. In the introduction, we mentioned two simple traversal techniques: in one the generator stores all values of the one-way chain in memory, and in the other the generator recomputes each value from the seed value. In so-called *fractal* traversal techniques the set of values that is stored is modified over time in a manner that reduces the (storage-times-computation) complexity.

One-Way Chain Advantages and Disadvantages. Traditional one-way chains have many advantages. First of all, given only a trusted value V_i of the chain, it is intractable to find a value V_j, where $j > i$, such that $H^{j-i}(V_j) = V_i$ (assuming that H is a secure one-way function and that the output of H is sufficiently large, we further discuss the security of one-way chains below). However, it is easy to assess the validity of a value V_j, where $j > i$, by verifying that $H^{j-i}(V_j) = V_i$ (assuming that H provides weak collision resistance, also called second pre-image collision resistance).

A drawback of traditional one-way chains is that the verifier has to perform $j - i$ operations to validate V_j given V_i, which can be expensive if $j - i$ is large. Finally, the repeated disclosure of one-way chain values carries a cost related to the transmission of these values. The required bandwidth may be a burden to senders, especially in highly resource-constrained environments, such as in sensor networks.

Hierarchical One-Way Chains. A *hierarchical* one-way chain consists of two or more levels of chains, where values of a first-level ("primary") chain act as roots of a set of second-level ("secondary") chains. We refer to the secondary chain rooted in the ith value of the primary chain as the ith secondary chain. Here, all the values of the ith secondary chain are released before any of the values of the $i + 1$st chain is released; the primary chain value V_i is released in between. Figure 2 shows an example of such a structure.

As will be described later, different one-way functions may be used for primary and secondary chains, with the aim of lowering the communication costs.

To set up the hierarchical chain, the generator picks V_N at random and computes the primary chain $V_{N-1}, \ldots, V_0$. The generator computes the secondary chain on the fly. A clear advantage is the very efficient setup, as only N/K operations are needed to compute V_0, where K is the length of the secondary chain.

To use this one-way chain, the generator traverses all the secondary chains in sequence (e.g., $v_{00}, v_{01}, v_{02}, v_{20}, \ldots, v_{N0}, v_{N1}, v_{N2}$) and discloses the values of the primary one-way chain when possible.

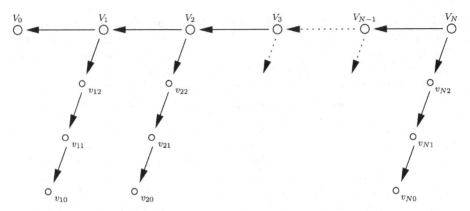

Fig. 2. Hierarchical one-way chain, where $V_N \ldots V_0$ are values on the one-way primary chain, and the values $v_{i0} \ldots v_{i2}$ are values of a secondary light chain. There is no subchain under V_0 since it serves as the verification value.

A disadvantage of the hierarchical chain is the authentication of end-values of secondary chain. This hierarchical chain was proposed by Liu and Ning [21]. Liu and Ning propose to use the TESLA authentication protocol [28] using the primary chain to authenticate the end-values of the secondary chain. This approach has the shortcoming that the hierarchical chain can only be used in conjunction with the TESLA authentication protocol, as they propose to authenticate the end-values of the secondary chain with the TESLA authentication protocol using the primary chain. The disadvantage of that approach is that the loss of the authentication message prevents the verifier to authenticate secondary chain values until the next value of the primary chain is disclosed[2]. Another shortcoming of their approach is that the authentication is staged, as the generator can only send authentication values at transitions of the primary chain. The tradeoff is clear, on one hand we would like to have infrequent transitions in the primary chain, but on the other hand we prefer a short authentication delay.

Note that the all end-values need to be authenticated – both that of the primary chain and those of all secondary chains. As we discuss above, the authentication mechanism by Liu and Ning has several shortcomings. To overcome these shortcomings, we propose the Sandwich-chain, enabling efficient authentication of the end-values of the secondary chain at any moment, without assuming any additional authentication protocols.

Light Chains. To lower the communication overhead, we introduce the notion of the *light chain*. This is a sequence of values derived from their respective predecessors by means of a one-way function that results in a relatively short output. In contrast, we may refer to standard one-way chains as *heavy chains*. This permits us to refer to a chain consisting of both light and heavy components plainly as a *one-way chain*, or more specifically, a *hash chain*. The way we combine light

---

[2] They propose to send redundant messages to achieve higher robustness against packet loss, however, this approach increases the communication overhead.

and heavy chains is to use a heavy chain as a primary chain, and let each value of the heavy chain be the root of a light secondary chain.

As described below, we select the hash function used for a particular light chain from a large family of potential functions, disclosing what function was used not long before the disclosure of values of the light chain begins – two different light chains would use two different functions. This way, we avoid the threat of pre-computation attacks, since an attacker would not be able to begin building an input-output dictionary until the selection of the function is disclosed. Still, it is clear that the shorter the values of the light chains are, the smaller the effort will be for an attacker to find collisions, or to invert the function. This presents us with a tradeoff between the savings in communication cost (related to the size of individual values of the light chain) and the time a particular light chain can be used. The latter, in turn, puts constraints on the maximum length of the light chain, given a known rate at which this is traversed and its values disclosed.

Choice of One-Way Functions. As mentioned before, different one-way functions may be used for the primary respectively secondary chains. (Moreover, different one-way functions may be used for different segments of the secondary chain, but for simplicity, we do not consider that option here.)

The basic security requirement for the generating function of a one-way chain is *one-wayness*, preventing an attacker from deriving the following value V_{i+1} of the chain when knowing V_i. In addition, the generating function also needs to provide second preimage collision resistance, which is also known as weak collision resistance. Weak collision resistance prevents an attacker from finding another V'_{i+1} after the generator disclosed V_{i+1}, which also satisfies $V_i = H(V'_{i+1})$ and $V_{i+1} \neq V'_{i+1}$. This would enable the attacker to forge one value of the one-way chain, and prevent the verifier from verifying subsequent values of the one-way chain, as almost certainly $V'_{i+1} \neq H(V_{i+2})$.

Candidate one-way functions are based on cryptographic hash functions, such as SHA-1 [26] or MD5 [30]. Here, the one-way function used to compute the values of the primary chain is denoted H, and the one-way function used to derive the values of the ith secondary chain is referred to as h_i. We derive the salts using a third one-way function, which we refer to as H_s. We let $H(\cdot) = H_s(\cdot) = hash(\cdot)$ and $h_i(\cdot) = trunc(hash(salt_i, \cdot))$, where $trunc$ denotes a function that truncates the input to the desired length.

Another construction that also provides the required security properties are pseudo-random functions (PRF) [12]. A PRF F has a key K and is often used in the following construction to provide one-wayness and weak collision resistance: $V_i = F_{V_{i+1}}(0)$, where 0 denotes a constant string of zero bits. Note that the value V_{i+1} is used as the key to the PRF. A commonly used instantiation of a PRF is to use a message authentication code (MAC), for example HMAC is a popular choice [4]. A pseudo-random permutation (PRP) (e.g., a block cipher) can also be used as a PRF, if the PRP is only used as many times as the birthday bound allows [3]. This construction though often has the disadvantage that the generator has to run key setup function for the block cipher for each one-way chain value, which is often inefficient.

Resistance Against Birthday Attacks. All previous proposals involving hash chains appear vulnerable to birthday attacks. More specifically, if an attacker selects a random seed and computes a hash chain from this, the chances for a collision between any one of the computed values and a value in an existing chain C increase with the length of C. This can be avoided by using a well-known technique[3] in which all hash functions used are indexed by their position in the chain. In other words, in order to compute the image V_i of a value V_{i+1}, one would compute the hash of $V_{i+1} \parallel i+1$ (where $\parallel$ denotes concatenation), as opposed to only the one-way chain value, as is commonly done. For simplicity of notation, we do not make this indexing explicit in the descriptions onwards. For a one-way chain value of m bits, the expected cost for an attacker to find a pre-image or even a second pre-image is 2^{m-1} one-way function computations.

Taxonomy of Hash Chain Usage. Though many proposed protocols use hash chains, we categorize these protocols into three categories: those which use every element (e.g. [13, 20]), those in which skipping elements is rare (e.g. [8, 14, 34]), and those in which skipping elements is common (e.g. [28]). In all protocols, fast traversal at the generator is desirable. In addition, when skipping elements is common, faster verification is desirable, especially when hash chain elements are used quickly. In some cases, such as wireless network protocols, network partitioning can force a node to perform a large number of hash functions to "catch up;" in these cases, faster verification can significantly improve protocol responsiveness.

Evaluation Metrics. We use the following five metrics to measure the efficiency of one-way chain techniques: setup, traversal, verification, storage, and communication cost. We describe each cost in more detail. The setup cost is measured by the number of hash function computations to derive the end-value of the one-way chain. The traversal cost is the average number of hash function computations that the generator performs to derive each one-way chain value, assuming that each chain value is consecutively disclosed. For real-time constrained environments, an upper bound on the traversal cost is desirable. The recently proposed efficient one-way chain schemes provide an upper bound of $O(\log(n))$ for the traversal cost [9, 18]. The verification cost is measured in the number of one-way function computations that the verifier performs to verify a one-way chain value. The verification cost is usually $O(1)$ if the verifier receives all one-way chain values, however, a more interesting metric is the verification overhead in case the verifier needs to "catch up" because it missed many one-way chain values or started receiving values late, i.e., the verifier may need to traverse a large part of the one-way chain to verify. Advanced one-way chains feature efficient mechanisms to "catch up". The storage cost is measured as the amount of memory that the generator needs to traverse the one-way chain. The communication cost measures the bandwidth overhead for distributing one-way chain values. We introduce the notion of light chains to lower the communication cost.

---

[3] This technique is attributed to Micali and Leighton, who in an unpublished manuscript propose the use of this technique to avoid birthday attacks in Merkle trees.

Requirements for Offline Verification. The chains we describe can be verified offline; that is, without communicating with the chain generator. However, this offline verification sometimes requires either reliable delivery or loose time synchronization. Of the chains we describe, the Sandwich-chain and light chains (Sections 3 and 5) require either reliable delivery or loose time synchronization to allow offline verification. On the other hand, Comb Skipchains (Section 4) do not have any special requirements for offline verification.

3   The Sandwich-Chain Construction

We previously mentioned why the primary and secondary chains (as Figure 2 shows) have a significant disadvantage over the simple one-way chain: if the commitment to the end-value of the secondary chain is lost, the verifier has to wait until the generating value of the secondary chain (i.e., the value of the primary chain) is disclosed.

We now describe the Sandwich-chain, a new construction which removes this drawback, and which has several nice properties. Figure 3 shows an example of a Sandwich-chain.

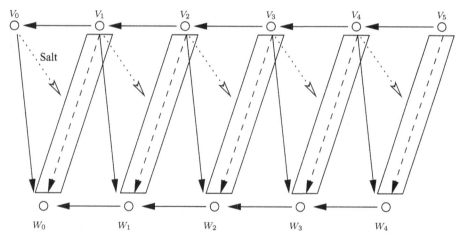

Fig. 3. A sandwich chain. The upper horizontal chain is the primary chain; the diagonal chains are secondary chains; and the lower horizontal chain is used for verification of end-points of secondary chains. The dotted arrows correspond to salt derivation, which is used in the computation of the diagonal chains only.

The Sandwich-chain is a combination of a hierarchical one-way chain and another one-way chain $W_N \ldots W_0$ used for verification of the end-values of the light chain. We now describe how the Sandwich-chain is generated, used, and how verifiers can authenticate values.

Sandwich-Chain Setup. The generator picks V_N and W_N at random and computes $V_{N-1}, \ldots, V_0$, where $V_i = H(V_{i+1})$. For each V_i, the generator derives the associated secondary chain $v_{i,K}, \ldots, v_{i,0}$ as follows: $v_{i,K} = h_s(V_i)$ (where V_{i-1} is used as the salt s), and $v_{i,j} = h_s(v_{i,j+1})$. Finally, the generator derives the W-value as follows: $W_{i-1} = H(W_i||v_{i,0}||V_{i-1})$. Figure 3 graphically represents these derivations.

Sandwich-Chain Traversal. Similar to the hierarchical chains described above, the generator uses the values of the light chains one after another, e.g.,

$$v_{1,0}, v_{1,1}, \ldots, v_{1,K}, v_{2,0}, \ldots, v_{N,0}, v_{N,1}, \ldots, v_{N,K}$$

. The V-values are disclosed after all the secondary chain values are published, for example after disclosing $v_{i,K}$, the generator can send V_i, which is needed for the salt of V_{i+1}'s secondary chain and also to authenticate W_i. W-values are disclosed as necessary, they are not secret, their use is only to authenticate the end-values of the secondary chain. The Sandwich-chain is traversed using fractal traversal [9, 18, 33].

Sandwich-chain Value Authentication. Initially, the verifier receives V_0 and W_0 over an authentic channel, and uses these values to authenticate all subsequent values. Using the trusted values V_0 and W_0, the verifier can easily authenticate the first value of the one-way chain $v_{1,0}$ by checking that $H(W_1||v_{1,0}||V_0)$ equals W_0 (this assumes that the verifier also received W_1).

We now describe how the verifier authenticates the end-value $v_{i,0}$ of a general secondary chain, assuming that the verifier always kept up with receiving and verifying the chain, thus trusting values V_{i-1} and W_{i-1}. (In Section 3.2, we describe an efficient verification technique if the receiver did not keep up with the verification.) In the light chain spanned by V_i, the verifier needs to know W_i to verify the end-value $v_{i,0}$. The verifier first computes $H(W_i||v_{i,0}||V_{i-1})$ and checks that it matches the stored W_{i-1}, in which case both W_i and $v_{i,0}$ are authentic. Since value W_i is not secret, the generator can retransmit it periodically. The value V_{i-1} is used as the salt in the secondary chain $v_{i,j}$, thus V_{i-1} also needs to be transmitted periodically, and can easily be authenticated. As additional measure to authenticate the secondary chain values, the verifier can also check that $v_{i,k} = h_s(V_i)$ after V_i is disclosed.

3.1   Efficient Authentication Using One-Way Functions

We describe a novel mechanism to authenticate arbitrary values, without using a MAC function. We assume a secure weak collision resistant one-way function F (to derive the one-way chain), and a secure one-way function G (to produce commitments). The generator then generates a one-way chain $V_N, \ldots, V_0$, where $V_i = F(V_{i+1})$. We assume that the generator and verifiers are loosely time synchronized, with a maximum synchronization error of T_Δ. The generator specifies a regular disclosure schedule for values of the the one-way chain, disclosing V_i at time $T_i = T_0 + i * T_d$, where T_d is the time delay between the disclosure of two values, and T_0 is the time of disclosure of value V_0. To authenticate a value r, the generator publishes $r' = H(V_j||r)$, where V_j is a value that will be disclosed in the future. When a verifier gets r, r', j at time t, it verifies that the generator did not yet disclose V_j by checking that $t + T_\Delta < T_j$. If this condition holds, it accepts r' and waits for the disclosure of V_j to authenticate r. The verifier first verifies the authenticity of V_j, by following the one-way chain to the last authentic value. If V_j is authentic then r is authentic if $r' = {}^{\cdot}H(V_j||r)$. This authentication is similar in nature to the TESLA authentication protocol, but it does not require a MAC computation.

3.2 Sandwich-Chain Using Our Efficient Authentication Technique

Our Sandwich-chain is especially constructed to also enable efficient authentication of the end-values of the light chain using the authentication technique described in Section 3.1. This has the advantage that a client who receives authentic values of the Sandwich-chain (i.e., V_0 and W_0), can efficiently authenticate secondary chain values in chain generated by V_i, without recomputing previous secondary chains. This approach thus substantially reduces the verification overhead for a new verifier that needs to "catch up" to current values of the chain.

We assume that the primary one-way chain $V_0, \ldots, V_N$ satisfies the requirements discussed in Section 3.1, i.e., the values V_i are disclosed after specific times T_i. A verifier can use the structure of the Sandwich-chain to authenticate the values of the W-chain without following it all the way back to the last authentic W value it trusts.

Consider a verifier that is time synchronized, who trusts value V_0, and who joins the transmission at time t_i, where $T_i < t_i < T_{i+1}$. The generator is thus currently traversing the values spanned by the secondary chain spanned by V_{i+1}, as V_i is already disclosed. At this point, the verifier cannot yet authenticate values $v_{i+1,j}$ it receives, as it may be computationally too expensive to recompute the Sandwich-chain all the way back to W_0. The generator periodically distributes W_{i+1}; as long as the verifier gets W_{i+1} before time $T_{i+1} - T_\Delta$, the verifier can later authenticate W_{i+1} after it receives V_{i+1}, W_{i+2}, and the value $v_{i+2,0}$. After successful authentication of value W_{i+1}, the verifier also knows that value W_{i+2} is authentic, and can use the values of the W-chain to immediately authenticate end-values of the following secondary chains.

Given loosely synchronized clocks, the Sandwich-chain thus enables computation-bound verifiers to very efficiently authenticate current one-way chain values (after waiting for a short time delay), without recomputing the majority of the Sandwich-chain.

4   The Comb Skipchain Construction

In [17], Hu et al. describe the skipchain mechanism. A skipchain is composed of a *signature chain* and a collection of secondary chains. A signature chain $(s_0 \ldots s_x)$ is a chain of one-time signatures. Each value s_i of the signature chain spans a one-time signature scheme, where the one-time signature values are again reduced to a single value s_{i-1}, thus resembling a one-way chain. The value s_i can be thought of the private key of the one-time signature, and the value s_{i-1} is the corresponding public (verifying) key. (Similarly, s_{i-1} and s_{i-2} form the next private/public key pair.) Hu et al. describe such a signature chain [17] and propose to use the Merkle-Winternitz signature [10, 23, 32] as the one-time signature scheme.

Each value s_i in the signature chain is used to derive a secondary chain $V_{i,0} \dots V_{i,y}$, where $V_{i,y} = H(s_i)$ and the other values are generated as we describe in Section 3. In the same vein as the hierarchical chain construction in Section 3, these light chains represent a single one-way chain of length $(x+1)(y+1)$, where the jth value is $V_{\lfloor \frac{j}{y+1} \rfloor, j \bmod y+1}$, and where y is the length of the secondary chain.

In this paper, we contribute a novel parameterization and traversal scheme that provides $O(1)$ computation, while retaining the $O(\log(n))$ storage requirement; a significant improvement over the previous $O(\log^2(n))$ bound [9].

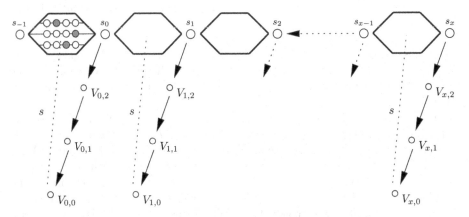

Fig. 4. Comb Skipchain, where $s_y \dots s_0$ are values on the signature chain, s_{-1} represents the initial verification value, and $V_{i,0} \dots V_{i,2}$ represent light chains. Each hexagon in the figure represents one instance of a Merkle-Winternitz signature (a simplified version of such a signature is shown inside the first hexagon). The s denotes that each s_i is used to sign each $V_{i,0}$.

Verification of Values of the Secondary Chain. Because values from the secondary chain cannot be verified through the repeated application of a one-way function, we must have a separate way of verifying them. Comb Skipchains use a one-time signature from each signature chain value to authenticate the end-value of each light chain. In particular, the ith one-time signature is used to sign $V_{i,0}$.

To verify this one-time signature, the verifier follows the signature chain all the way to a trusted value (in the same way as it follows a standard one-way chain). Note that the traversal of the primary chain makes previous one-time signatures redundant. In other words, while traversal in principle allows forgery of old one-time signatures, synchronization issues makes this a non-issue, just like knowledge of previously released chain values in general does not pose a security threat for the applications we consider.

Parameterization and Traversal. For a chain of length n, we choose $x = \frac{n}{\log(n)}$ and $y = \log(n)$. The important intuition that allows us to achieve $O(1)$ computation is that the fractal traversal of the signature chain already requires $O(\log(n))$ storage, so we can store an entire secondary chain of length $O(\log(n))$ with no penalty in the asymptotic storage cost. As a result, the traversal of the secondary chains can be achieved with constant computation; and the traversal cost of the signature chain $O(\log(n))$ can be amortized over an entire light chain (length $O(\log(n))$), thus resulting in a constant computation cost per emitted value. In particular, we perform efficient traversal on the primary (signature) chain (at cost $\log(x)$ memory, and $\log(x)$ computation per step), but to amortize the traversal over the y steps in the secondary chain, for $O(1)$ computation. In addition, we can traverse the secondary chain for $O(y)$ memory and $O(1)$ computation by storing the entire chain. Finally, we amortize the computation of the next light chain, which costs $O(y)$ memory and $O(1)$ computation. The total cost is then $O(\log(n))$ memory and $O(1)$ computation.

Initialization. We perform the initialization necessary for fractal traversal of the signature chain. We also compute and store the entire first secondary chain. Finally, we prepare for the initialization of the second secondary chain.

Main Routine. First, we perform a partial step in the signature chain. In particular, we follow the fractal traversal algorithm [9] until one hash operation is performed, for a cost of 1. After $\frac{1}{2}\log(n)$ steps are performed, the next signature chain value is ready. In particular, after $V_{i,\frac{y}{2}}$ is emitted, s_{i+1} becomes available.

Next, generate one more step of the next chain. In particular, when emitting $V_{i,j}$, we compute $V_{i-1,y-j}$.

Next, set the return value to the appropriate value previously computed. For example, when emitting $V_{i,j}$, we return the value computed when emitting $V_{i+1,y-j}$.

Analysis. In our first step, we perform only one hash operation, and a constant amount of work, so the first step requires $O(1)$ computation and $O(\log(n))$ memory. Our second step performs one hash operation, so it requires $O(1)$ computation and $O(\log(n))$ memory. Our third step consists of a single load, so it requires $O(1)$ computation and $O(\log(n))$ memory. In fact, the memory used by the second and third step can be combined so that together they require just $y+1$ hash values to be stored. The hash and signature are also constant time operations, and hence it also requires $O(1)$ computation. This represents a total cost of $O(1)$ computation and $O(\log(n))$ memory, for a memory-times-computation complexity of $O(\log(n))$. Our result substantially improves the previous result which provides memory-times-computation complexity of $O(\log^2(n))$, and establishes that as a lower bound.

Future Work. Comb Skipchains provide other efficiency improvements; for example, in our scheme, the setup time is $O(\frac{n}{\log(n)})$. In future work, we intend to examine the use of hierarchical Comb Skipchains, with multiple levels of signature chains, as a mechanism for improving setup times.

5   Light Chains

In resource-constrained environments (e.g., sensor networks), communication bandwidth is at a premium, as data sending and receiving is expensive in terms of battery energy. To reduce the communication overhead, we propose one-way chains with reduced value size, but we need to be careful not to introduce new security vulnerabilities.

A *light* one-way chain $(v_0 \ldots v_n)$ is a collection of values such that each value $v_i = h(v_{i+1})$, for $0 \le i < n$, where h is a one-way function with short output. That is, while the output of standard hash functions is typically 128 or 160 bits long, the output of h is much shorter, for example 64 bits long. Here, h is preferably a *salted* hash function (also referred to as a *keyed* hash function), whose output is truncated to some fixed length. Thus, each chain (or segment of a chain) has a salt s associated to it, which is appended to the input before the hash function evaluation. The effect of this is that the function h is selected from a family of functions, indexed by the salt.

Similar as for standard chains, v_0 is called the end-value, and v_n the root. The salt s of a chain (or chain segment) has to be selected before the chain is computed from the root value, but does not have to be released until a verifier needs it to verify the authenticity of a chain value.

Shorter sized values may introduce pre-computation attacks, such as the attack proposed by Hellman [16]. For a chain with m-bit values, the attacker performs 2^m operation to setup a graph of size $2^{2 \cdot m/3}$. Given the graph, the attacker performs $2^{2 \cdot m/3}$ operations to find a pre-image of a value. To thwart this attack, we use two countermeasures: salted hash functions, as described below; and indexed hash functions as described in Section 2 in the paragraph "Resistance against Birthday Attacks".

Use of Salts. We have that outputs of h_i may be substantially shorter than outputs of H. Thus, while inverting H will be assumed to be computationally intractable, it may be possible to invert, or find collisions for, h_i given sufficient time. Since we want it to be infeasible to invert h_i during the time period it is associated with, it is important that this time interval is shorter than a lower estimate of the time it takes to invert the h_i. Evidently, it is also crucial to prevent pre-computation attacks, which is where the salt comes in.

The effect of salting the hash function h_i is that of randomly selecting this function from a large family of such functions. Given sufficiently long salts, this effectively makes it infeasible to compute a table of all input-output pairs of h_i without knowledge of the salt. Since the salts are not made public until just before the time period their use is associated with, this prevents pre-computation attacks.

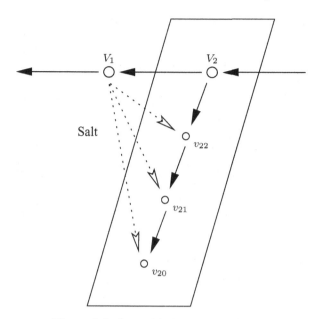

Fig. 5. Salt-derived light one-way chain.

6   Discussion

We give two examples of instances in which our constructions are useful. Table 1 summarizes these results. In our examples, we use light chains with 64 bits of security, and heavy chains with 80 bits of security. For the one-time signatures in Comb Skipchain, we use the Merkle-Winternitz construction [10, 23, 32] to sign the 64 bits of the end-value of the light chain. To sign 64 bits, we use 32 signature chains of length two, and three checksum chains of length two, and one checksum chain of length one. This construction requires 71 hash function computations to generate one signature, and on average 35 hash function computations to verify.

Our first application is a sensor network with resource-limited sensors. In the sensor network, the nodes use the TESLA protocol to broadcast authentic data over their lifetime, which we assume to be 10 years. To achieve a relatively low authentication delay, yet have short one-way chains, the sensors use one value of the one-way chain during one second, thus requiring a total of 315 million values over the lifetime of the sensor network. We first study the overhead if we use the Sandwich-chain. One of the main features of the Sandwich-chain is that it has a low communication overhead and enables fast verification of chain values in case a receiver was absent for some time or is newly deployed. To select the length of the secondary chain (the light chain), we say that a sensor should wait for at most 30 minutes to efficiently authenticate the chain values after deployment, thus the light chain has a length of $30 \cdot 60 = 1800$ values. The primary chain thus has a length of $315,360,000/1800 = 175,200$ values. The setup cost is $315,360,000 + 175,200 + 175,200 = 315,710,400$ hash function computations

Table 1. Performance of our structures as compared to a traditional hash chain. Storage is based on 3 hash computations per step in the reverse hash chain traversal. This results in prohibitive overhead for Sandwich-chains, which have competitive storage requirements when 5 computations can be performed in each step.

Construction	Storage	Worst-Case Verify	Network Overhead
Sensor Network (3.15×10^8 elements, 1ms per hash)			
Sandwich-chain	Very High	< 3 min	< 0.1 bits/value
Comb Skipchain	1188 bytes	7.71 days	1.43 bits/value
Hash Chain	5330 bytes	219 days	0
Micropayments (1.1×10^9 elements, $1\mu s$ per hash)			
Comb Skipchain	718–1246 bytes	36.8 sec	1.34 bits/value
Hash Chain	7310 bytes	18.5 min	0

to compute V_0 and W_0. Using fractal traversal [9, 18, 33], the traversal requires $O(\log(n))$ per-value computation and storage. The verification overhead is low, even if a sensor joins the network close to the end of its lifetime, it can verify the V-value in under three minutes, assuming that a hash function computation requires 1ms. In contrast, traditional one-way chains would take 1800 times longer. The communication cost is very low, as the light chain values are only 64 bits long, and only two heavy chain values of length 80 bits need to be disclosed after every 1800 values[4].

To lower the traversal and setup cost at the expense of a higher communication overhead, we can use the Comb Skipchain mechanism. In choosing the length of the light chains, we want a length that allows a the signature chain to be computed using a single hash operation per emitted element. Since each step in the signature chain requires 71 hash operations, and since each step in the signature chain requires a logarithmic number of applications of G, we need at least $71 \cdot \log_2(315,360,000) = 2004.5$ elements in the light chain. Since we use Sella's traversal [33], we can store ℓ elements from a chain of length $\frac{\ell(\ell+1)}{2}$ and provide reverse traversal with a single computation. As a result, we pick a minimum ℓ that allows us to traverse a chain of length at least 2005. In this case, $\ell = 63$, and each light chain is 2016 elements long. Our signature chains are of length $315,360,000/2016 = 156,429$, and initialization requires traversing one light chain (2016 hash functions) and the entire signature chain ($156,429 \cdot 71 = 11,106,459$ hash functions), for a total setup time of $11,108,475$. Traversal costs are 1 for each of the current light chain, the next light chain, and the signature chain, for a total of 3 applications. To perform these traversals, we require two sets of light chains to be stored simultaneously, for a storage cost of 63 values per chain. In addition, $\log_2(315,360,000/2016) < 18$ values are needed for the top chain, for a total of 144 values. By contrast, Sella's scheme requires 533 values to traverse the chain at a cost of three operations per el-

---

[4] For robustness against packet loss, the generator may periodically publish the latest V and W values required for authentication.

ement. The verification overhead is often lower than a traditional hash chain; for example, if a sensor joins the network close to the end of its lifetime, it can verify a chain element over 28 times faster than with a traditional hash chain. The added communication cost is fairly low; again, the light chain values are only 64 bits long, and a 360 byte signature needs to be disclosed every 2016 values (possibly more often for robustness). This represents roughly 1.43 additional bits per chain value.

Another example is for micropayments for Internet or peer-to-peer traffic. Such payments could be used, for example, to pay an ISP for dialup access, in open-access wireless hotspots, or to pay for content transfer from a peer-to-peer file sharing network. To estimate pricing for such services, we consider that cable modem pricing is around \$45 for a cap of 15 GB [7], and assume that the ISP requires revenue of \$45 for 5 GB of transfer. If a micropayment provider sold in increments of \$10, then each chain will be 1.1 billion elements long. When using Comb Skipchains, we compute the length of the light chains as above: $71 \cdot \log_2(1,111,111,111) = 2133.5$, so we choose $\ell = 65$ and a light chains length of 2145. As a result, our signature chains are of length $1,111,111,111/2145 = 518,001$. Initialization then requires $2145 + 518,001 \cdot 71 = 36,780,216$ hash functions. Again, traversal costs are 1 for each of the current light chain, the next light chain, and the signature chain, for a total of 3 applications. To perform these traversals, we require two sets of light chains to be stored simultaneously, at a cost of 65 hash values each (these can be stored together with just 66 values). In addition, $\log_2(1,111,111,111/2145) < 19$ hash values are stored for top chain, for a total of 149 hash values (85 if better optimized). By contrast, Sella's scheme requires storage of 731 values to traverse the chain at a cost of three operations per element. The verification overhead is higher than before; if a network node receives a micropayment close to the end of the chain, it may take 36 seconds to verify, assuming that a hash function computation requires $1\mu s$. The communication cost is fairly low; again, the light chain values are only 64 bits long, and a 360 byte signature needs to be disclosed every 2145 values (possibly more often for robustness). This represents roughly 1.34 additional bits per chain value.

7   Conclusion and Future Work

Our proposed constructions for one-way chains are useful in many settings, to speed up the current setup, traversal, and verification of one-way chains. Both constructions can be used as "drop-in" replacements for many current uses of one-way chains.

The Sandwich-chain is particularly useful in environments with low-bandwidth communication channels, and where the verifiers are computation constrained and may need to "catch up" (i.e., verify a chain value based on a distant trusted chain value).

The Comb Skipchain construction has a higher communication overhead than Sandwich-chain, but it provides a very efficient setup mechanism $(O(n/\log(n)))$ and a very efficient traversal $(O(1))$ with small storage overhead $(O(\log(n)))$. This construction beats the previously established lower bound for the product of memory overhead and traversal overhead, which was $O(\log^2(n))$. In contrast, our construction achieves a memory-times-computation complexity of $O(\log(n))$. This is possible (and does not contradict the previous lower bounds) given that we move from one-dimensional to two-dimensional (or hierarchical) chains.

Our future work includes investigating deeper hierarchies of our constructions, and to establish general bounds for the one-way chain costs.

References

1. William Aiello, Sachin Lodha, and Rafail Ostrovsky. Fast digital identity revocation. In Hugo Krawczyk, editor, *Advances in Cryptology – CRYPTO '98*, volume 1462 of *Lecture Notes in Computer Science*. International Association for Cryptologic Research, Springer-Verlag, Berlin Germany, 1998.
2. Ross Anderson, Harry Manifavas, and Chris Sutherland. A practical electronic cash system. personal communication, December 1995.
3. M. Bellare, J. Kilian, and P. Rogaway. The security of cipher block chaining. In *Advances in Cryptology - Crypto '94*, pages 341–358, 1994. Lecture Notes in Computer Science Volume 839.
4. Mihir Bellare, Ran Canetti, and Hugo Krawczyk. Keying hash functions for message authentication. In Neal Koblitz, editor, *Advances in Cryptology – CRYPTO '96*, volume 1109 of *Lecture Notes in Computer Science*, pages 1–15. International Association for Cryptologic Research, Springer-Verlag, Berlin Germany, 1996.
5. Giles Brassard, editor. *Advances in Cryptology – CRYPTO '89*, volume 435 of *Lecture Notes in Computer Science*, Santa Barbara, CA, USA, 1990. International Association for Cryptologic Research, Springer-Verlag, Berlin Germany.
6. M. Brown, D. Cheung, D. Hankerson, J. Hernandez, M. Kirkup, and A. Menezes. PGP in constrained wireless devices. In *Proceedings of the 9th USENIX Security Symposium*, pages 247–261. USENIX, August 2000.
7. Cable Datacom News. Time warner division implements consumption caps. Published at http://www.cabledatacomnews.com/may03/may03-7.html.
8. Steven Cheung. An efficient message authentication scheme for link state routing. In *13th Annual Computer Security Applications Conference*, pages 90–98, 1997.
9. D. Coppersmith and M. Jakobsson. Almost optimal hash sequence traversal. In *Proceedings of the Fourth Conference on Financial Cryptography (FC '02)*, Lecture Notes in Computer Science, 2002.
10. S. Even, O. Goldreich, and S. Micali. On-line/off-line digital signatures. In Brassard [5], pages 263–277.
11. M. Fischlin. Fast verification of hash chains. In *RSA Security Cryptographer's Track 2004*, pages 339–352. Springer Verlag, 2004. Lecture Notes in Computer Science, Volume 2964.
12. Oded Goldreich, Shafi Goldwasser, and Silvio Micali. How to construct random functions. *Journal of the ACM*, 33(4):792–807, October 1986.
13. Neil Haller. The S/KEY one-time password system. RFC 1760, February 1995.
14. Ralf Hauser, Antoni Przygienda, and Gene Tsudik. Reducing the cost of security in link state routing. In *Proceedings of the Symposium on Network and Distributed Systems Security (NDSS '97)*, pages 93–99, San Diego, California, February 1997. Internet Society.
15. Ralf Hauser, Michael Steiner, and Michael Waidner. Micro-payments based on iKP. In *14th Worldwide Congress on Computer and Communications Security Protection*, pages 67–82, C.N.I.T Paris-La Defense, France, June 1996.

16. Martin Hellman. A cryptanalytic time-memory trade-off. *IEEE Transactions on Information Theory*, 26(4):401–406, July 1980.
17. Yih-Chun Hu, Adrian Perrig, and David B. Johnson. Efficient security mechanisms for routing protocols. In *Network and Distributed System Security Symposium, NDSS '03*, pages 57–73, February 2003.
18. M. Jakobsson. Fractal hash sequence representation and traversal. In *Proceedings of the 2002 IEEE International Symposium on Information Theory (ISIT '02)*, pages 437–444, July 2002.
19. J. M. Kahn, R. H. Katz, and K. S. Pister. Mobile networking for smart dust. In *ACM/IEEE International Conference on Mobile Computing and Networking (MobiCom'99)*, Seattle, WA, August 1999.
20. Leslie Lamport. Password authentication with insecure communication. *Communications of the ACM*, 24(11):770–772, November 1981.
21. Donggang Liu and Peng Ning. Efficient distribution of key cahin commitments for broadcast authentication in distributed sensor networks. In *Network and Distributed System Security Symposium, NDSS '03*, pages 263–276, February 2003.
22. Mark Lomas, editor. *Security Protocols—International Workshop*, volume 1189 of *Lecture Notes in Computer Science*, Cambridge, United Kingdom, April 1997. Springer-Verlag, Berlin Germany.
23. Ralph C. Merkle. A digital signature based on a conventional encryption function. In Carl Pomerance, editor, *Advances in Cryptology – CRYPTO '87*, volume 293 of *Lecture Notes in Computer Science*, pages 369–378, Santa Barbara, CA, USA, 1988. International Association for Cryptologic Research, Springer-Verlag, Berlin Germany.
24. Ralph C. Merkle. A certified digital signature. In Brassard [5], pages 218–238.
25. Silvio Micali. Efficient certificate revocation. Technical Report MIT/LCS/TM-542b, Massachusetts Institute of Technology, Laboratory for Computer Science, March 1996. Technical memo.
26. National Institute of Standards and Technology (NIST). Secure hash standard, May 1993. Federal Information Processing Standards (FIPS) Publication 180-1.
27. Torben Pryds Pedersen. Electronic payments of small amounts. In Lomas [22], pages 59–68.
28. Adrian Perrig, Ran Canetti, J.D. Tygar, and Dawn Xiaodong Song. Efficient authentication and signing of multicast streams over lossy channels. In *IEEE Symposium on Security and Privacy*, May 2000.
29. Adrian Perrig, Robert Szewczyk, Victor Wen, David Culler, and J. D. Tygar. SPINS: Security protocols for sensor networks. *Wireless Networks*, 8(5):521–534, September 2002.
30. Ronald L. Rivest. The MD5 message-digest algorithm. Internet Request for Comment RFC 1321, Internet Engineering Task Force, April 1992.
31. Ronald L. Rivest and Adi Shamir. PayWord and MicroMint: Two simple micropayment schemes. In Lomas [22], pages 69 – 88.
32. Pankaj Rohatgi. A compact and fast hybrid signature scheme for multicast packet. In Gene Tsudik, editor, *Proceedings of the 6th ACM Conference on Computer and Communications Security*, pages 93–100, Singapore, November 1999. ACM Press.
33. Yaron Sella. On the computation-storage trade-offs of hash chain traversal. In *Proceedings of Financial Cryptography 2003 (FC 2003)*, 2003.
34. Kan Zhang. Efficient protocols for signing routing messages. In *Proceedings of the Symposium on Network and Distributed Systems Security (NDSS '98)*, San Diego, California, March 1998. Internet Society.

Privacy Preserving Keyword Searches
on Remote Encrypted Data

Yan-Cheng Chang and Michael Mitzenmacher

Division of Engineering and Applied Sciences,
Harvard University,
Cambridge, MA 02138, USA
{ycchang,michaelm}@eecs.harvard.edu

Abstract. We consider the following problem: a user $\mathcal{U}$ wants to store his files in an encrypted form on a remote file server $\mathcal{S}$. Later the user $\mathcal{U}$ wants to efficiently retrieve some of the encrypted files containing (or indexed by) specific keywords, keeping the keywords themselves secret and not jeopardizing the security of the remotely stored files. For example, a user may want to store old e-mail messages encrypted on a server managed by Yahoo or another large vendor, and later retrieve certain messages while travelling with a mobile device.

In this paper, we offer solutions for this problem under well-defined security requirements. Our schemes are efficient in the sense that no public-key cryptosystem is involved. Indeed, our approach is independent of the encryption method chosen for the remote files. They are also incremental, in that $\mathcal{U}$ can submit new files which are secure against previous queries but still searchable against future queries.

1   Introduction

We consider the following distributed file system: a user $\mathcal{U}$ pays a file server $\mathcal{S}$ for storage service, with the goal being that $\mathcal{U}$ can retrieve the stored files anytime and anywhere through Internet connections. For example, $\mathcal{U}$ may store files containing personal data that $\mathcal{U}$ may want to later access using his wireless PDA. A user might be willing to pay for such a service in order to have access to data without carrying devices with large amount of memory, and to have the data well-maintained by professionals. Such distributed file services already exist, such as the "Yahoo! Briefcase"[1]. We expect such services will grow with the expansion of mobile and pervasive computing.

In many cases $\mathcal{U}$ will not want to reveal the contents of his files to $\mathcal{S}$ in order to maintain security or privacy. It follows that the files will often be stored in encrypted form. Suppose, however, that later $\mathcal{U}$ wants to retrieve files based on a keyword search. That is, $\mathcal{U}$ wants to retrieve files containing (or indexed by) some keyword. If the files are encrypted, there is no straightforward way for $\mathcal{S}$ to do keyword search unless $\mathcal{U}$ is willing to leak the decryption key. A trivial solution that preserves the security of $\mathcal{U}$'s files is to have $\mathcal{S}$ send all the encrypted

---

[1] Emails are actually a typical example, as they are stored on remote servers [3, 11].

J. Ioannidis, A. Keromytis, and M.Yung (Eds.): ACNS 2005, LNCS 3531, pp. 442–455, 2005.
© Springer-Verlag Berlin Heidelberg 2005

files back to him. This may not be a feasible solution if $\mathcal{U}$ is using mobile devices with limited bandwidth and storage space. An additional complication is that $\mathcal{U}$ may naturally also want to keep secret the keyword that he is interested in as well.

We provide practical solutions to this problem with strong theoretical security guarantees that require only small amounts of overhead in terms of bandwidth and storage, as we describe more fully in the main text. Our solution utilizes the notion of a keyword index, which is created by $\mathcal{U}$. The keyword index associates each keyword with its associated files. We picture the keyword index being created offline, with a more powerful home machine, before the user wishes to access the files remotely with a mobile device. All keyword searches by $\mathcal{U}$ are based on this index; hence our scheme does not offer full pattern-matching generality with the actual text. In practice, this should be sufficient for most users. It is worth noting that in this framework $\mathcal{U}$ can have complete control over what words are keywords and which keywords are associated with which files, a power that can be useful for many applications.

We take care in defining a proper notion of security for this problem. Intuitively, after processing one of $\mathcal{U}$'s queries, $\mathcal{S}$ learns something: it learns that the encrypted files that $\mathcal{S}$ returns to $\mathcal{U}$ share some keyword. We want this to be all that $\mathcal{S}$ learns. We formalize this notion in cryptographic terms and prove that our schemes satisfies our formalization.

To set up our solution, we clarify further our methodology and our contributions. Our solutions are two-phased. In the first phase, we assume $\mathcal{U}$ is at home and is going to submit his files to $\mathcal{S}$, and assume that sufficient space is available to store a dictionary. In the second phase, we assume $\mathcal{U}$ becomes a mobile user and wants to retrieve some encrypted files from $\mathcal{S}$ by keyword searches. This is a very natural framework describing realistic distributed computing situations. We consider both the case that $\mathcal{U}$ can store a dictionary on his mobile device and the case that he cannot. The first case may be practical in some situations, where the mobile device has sufficient storage, and is useful for framing the solution to the second case, which is our main result.

Our main idea is the following: we let $\mathcal{U}$ use pseudo-random bits to mask a dictionary-based keyword index for each file and send it to $\mathcal{S}$ in such a way that later $\mathcal{U}$ can use the short seeds to help $\mathcal{S}$ recover selective parts of the index, while keeping the remaining parts pseudo-random. This requires some additional storage overhead on $\mathcal{S}$ as we clarify later.

No public-key cryptosystem is required in our schemes; only pseudo-random functions are used. We claim that this property significantly increases the practicability of our schemes, since in practice heuristic pseudo-random functions (that is, functions that appear pseudo-random enough for the specific application) can be implemented efficiently. Moreover, because our methodology is independent of the encryption method chosen for the remote files, our schemes have the advantage of working for different file formats (including compressed files, multimedia files, etc.), as long as a keyword index on the corresponding content can be built a priori.

Last but not least, we solve the update problem, which says how to ensure the security of the consequent submissions in presence of previous queries. Our solution enjoys very simply key management.

1.1   Related Works

In theory, the classical work of Goldreich and Ostrovsky [7] on oblivious RAMs can resolve the problem of doing (private) searches on (remote) encrypted data. Although their scheme is asymptotically efficient and nearly optimal, it does not appear to be efficient in practice as large constants are hidden in the big-O notation.

The question how to do *keyword* searches on encrypted data *efficiently* was raised in [11]. In that paper, they proposed a scheme which encrypts each word (or each pattern) of a document separately. Such an approach has the following disadvantages. First, it is not compatible with existing file encryption schemes. Instead, a specific encryption method must be used. Second, it cannot deal with compressed data, while we believe users will often want to save in storage costs by compressing their files, since generally the service fee is proportional to the storage space. Finally, as the authors themselves acknowledge, their scheme is not secure against statistical analysis across encrypted data (Section 5.5, [11]), in that their approach could leak the *locations* of the keyword in a document. Although some heuristic remedies (and an index construction alternative) were proposed, their security proof is at least not theoretically sound.

Recently, an alternative scheme aiming to solve this problem was proposed in [6]. The idea of that scheme is to build an index of keywords for each file using a Bloom filter [1], with pseudo-random functions used as hash functions. When $\mathcal{U}$ submits a document to $\mathcal{S}$, he also submits the corresponding Bloom filter. One inherent problem with this Bloom-filter-based approach is that Bloom filters can induce false positives, which would potentially cause mobile users to download extra files not containing the keyword. While sufficiently rare false positive might be acceptable in practice, we note that our scheme avoids this issue[2].

As further related work, the paper [3] studies the problem how to search on data encrypted by a public-key cryptosystem. In particular, they consider the problem of a user that wants to retrieve e-mails containing a certain keyword from his e-mail server, with the e-mails encrypted by the senders using his public key. The problem setting is related to but different from ours.

---

[2] We note that some care must be taken with this approach. For example, a preprint version of [6] did not take into account the following issue: because the number of 1 entries in a Bloom filter for a document is (roughly) proportional to the number of the distinct keywords in that document, some information is immediately leaked from the Bloom filters themselves. This problem can be avoided by padding the Bloom filters using arbitrary and otherwise meaningless keywords so that they all have the same number of elements; the latest version of [6] proposes an appropriate security model and a padding scheme to deal with this problem.

2   Preliminaries

We use the notation $a \leftarrow A$ to denote choosing an element a uniformly at random from the set A, and use *PPT* to denote *probabilistic polynomial time*. For a positive integer $n \in \mathbb{N}$, let $[n]$ denote the set $\{1, 2, \cdots, n\}$; for a string s, let $s[i]$ denote its i-th bit; for a function f, let $|f|$ denote its output length. We say a function is negligible in t if for any polynomial p there exists a t_0 such that for all $t > t_0$ we have $f(t) < 1/p(t)$. All logarithms in this paper have base 2.

2.1   Cryptographic Basics

For completeness we first define pseudo-random permutations and functions. Our definitions are standard; see, e.g., [5].

Definition 1. (Pseudo-random permutations) *We say a permutation family* $\{P_K : \{0,1\}^n \rightarrow \{0,1\}^n | K \in \{0,1\}^t\}$ *is* pseudo-random *if it satisfies the following:*

- *Given* $x \in \{0,1\}^n$ *and* $k \in \{0,1\}^t$, *there is a PPT algorithm to compute* $P_k(x)$.
- *For any PPT oracle algorithm A, the following value is negligible in t:*

$$|\mathbf{Pr}_{k \leftarrow \{0,1\}^t}[A^{P_k}(1^t) = 1] - \mathbf{Pr}_{p \leftarrow U_p}[A^{p}(1^t) = 1]|,$$

where U_p is the set of all the permutations on $\{0,1\}^n$.

Definition 2. (Pseudo-random functions) *We say a function family* $\{F_K : \{0,1\}^n \rightarrow \{0,1\}^m | K \in \{0,1\}^t\}$ *is* pseudo-random *if it satisfies the following:*

- *Given* $x \in \{0,1\}^n$ *and* $k \in \{0,1\}^t$, *there is a PPT algorithm to compute* $F_k(x)$.
- *For any PPT oracle algorithm A, the following value is negligible in t:*

$$|\mathbf{Pr}_{k \leftarrow \{0,1\}^t}[A^{F_k}(1^t) = 1] - \mathbf{Pr}_{f \leftarrow U_f}[A^{f}(1^t) = 1]|,$$

where U_f is the set of all the functions mapping $\{0,1\}^n$ to $\{0,1\}^m$.

For completeness, we include the following simple lemma, which says it is safe to feed pseudo-random functions with pseudo-random seeds instead of truly random seeds.

Lemma 1. *Consider two pseudo-random function families* $\{F_K : \{0,1\}^n \rightarrow \{0,1\}^m | K \in \{0,1\}^t\}$ *and* $\{G_K : \{0,1\}^\ell \rightarrow \{0,1\}^t | K \in \{0,1\}^t\}$. *For any PPT oracle algorithm A and any* $x \in \{0,1\}^\ell$, *the following value is negligible in t:*

$$|\mathbf{Pr}_{\sigma \leftarrow \{0,1\}^t, k = G_\sigma(x)}[A^{F_k}(1^t) = 1] - \mathbf{Pr}_{f \leftarrow U_f}[A^{f}(1^t) = 1]|,$$

where U_f is the set of all the functions mapping $\{0,1\}^n$ to $\{0,1\}^m$.

Proof. If (A, x) is a counterexample, then there is a construction of a *PPT* algorithm B using A, x, F_K such that the following value is not negligible in t:

$$|\mathbf{Pr}_{\sigma \leftarrow \{0,1\}^t}[B^{G_\sigma}(1^t) = 1] - \mathbf{Pr}_{g \leftarrow U_g}[B^g(1^t) = 1]|,$$

where U_g is the set of all the functions mapping $\{0,1\}^\ell$ to $\{0,1\}^t$. Clearly, it induces a contradiction.   □

In practice, we can use HMAC-SHA1 [2] to implement a pseudo-random function. Also, it is well known that a pseudo-random permutation can be constructed using a pseudo-random function in three rounds [8, 10].

2.2   Problem Setting

We define the problem of **P**rivacy **P**reserving **K**eyword **S**earches on Remote **E**ncrypted **D**ata (PPSED for short) in this section, and will hereafter use PPSED to denote this problem. Recall that we allow the user $\mathcal{U}$ to specify the relationship between files and keywords. That is, $\mathcal{U}$ can associate any collection of keywords with a file. Generally, when files are text files, keywords will be actual words of text. In order to formalize a clear definition, we only consider queries containing a single keyword. We emphasize that to deal with queries containing Boolean operations on multiple keywords in the security setting of PPSED remains a challenging open problem.

The formal definition of PPSED is as follows:

Definition 3. (PPSED) PPSED *is a multi-round protocol between a remote file server $\mathcal{S}$ and a user $\mathcal{U}$. The server $\mathcal{S}$ has a set of n encrypted files $\zeta = \{\mathcal{E}_1(m_1), \mathcal{E}_2(m_2), \cdots, \mathcal{E}_n(m_n)\}$ where for each $i \in [n]$, $\mathcal{E}_i$ is an encryption function and m_i is a file. The user $\mathcal{U}$ has decryption algorithms $\mathcal{D}_1, \mathcal{D}_2, \cdots, \mathcal{D}_n$ such that $\mathcal{D}_1(\mathcal{E}_1(m_1)) = m_1, \mathcal{D}_2(\mathcal{E}_2(m_2)) = m_2, \cdots, \mathcal{D}_n(\mathcal{E}_n(m_n)) = m_n$. Moreover, in each round $j \in \mathbb{N}$, $\mathcal{U}$ prepares a keyword $w_j \in \{0,1\}^*$. An implementation of PPSED with security parameter t must satisfy the following:*

1. *Correctness: In round j, for $i \in [n]$, if w_j is a keyword of m_i, $\mathcal{U}$ can obtain $\mathcal{E}_i(m_i)$.*
2. *Limits on the bandwidth and the storage space:*
   - *In round j, the number of bits sent from $\mathcal{S}$ to $\mathcal{U}$ is $\sum_{i \in \mathcal{I}_j} |\mathcal{E}_i(m_i)| + O(1)$,*
     where $\mathcal{I}_j = \{i|\ i \in [n], w_j \text{ is a keyword of } m_i\}$.
   - *The number of bits stored on $\mathcal{U}$ is $O(t)$.*
   - *The number of bits sent from $\mathcal{U}$ to $\mathcal{S}$ is $O(t)$ per keyword search.*
3. *Security requirement:*
   For $k \in \mathbb{N}$, let C_k be all the communications $\mathcal{S}$ receives from $\mathcal{U}$ before round k, and let $C_k^* = \{\zeta, Q_0 \equiv \emptyset, Q_1, \cdots, Q_{k-1}\}$, where for each $j \in [k-1]$, Q_j is an n-bit string such that for $i \in [n]$, $Q_j[i] = 1$ if and only if w_j is a keyword of m_i.

- *For $k \in \mathbb{N}$, for any PPT algorithm A, any $\Delta_k = \{m_1, \cdots, m_n, w_0 \equiv \emptyset, w_1, \cdots, w_{k-1}\}$, any function h, there is a PPT algorithm A^* such that the following value is negligible in t:*

$$|\mathbf{Pr}[A(C_k, 1^t) = h(\Delta_k)] - \mathbf{Pr}[A^*(C_k^*, 1^t) = h(\Delta_k)|.$$

(*Note the requirement captures the following: everything about Δ_k that can be computed given C_k can also be computed given C_k^*.*)

On the security requirement. Recall that our goal is the following: in round j, $\mathcal{S}$ can learn nothing more than "a keyword is shared by the sent encrypted files." To this end, consider an ideal case: $\mathcal{U}$ records in advance a set of linked lists such that each file index is associated with a list of all the keywords of the corresponding file. In this case, $\mathcal{U}$ knows for sure which files contain the keyword in round j, namely w_j, and hence it is enough for $\mathcal{U}$ to send $\mathcal{S}$ an n-bit string Q_j such that for $i \in [n]$, $Q_j[i] = 1$ if and only if w_j is a keyword of m_i (and $\mathcal{S}$ has to send $\mathcal{E}_i(m_i)$ back). Note C_k^* exactly consists of such communications from $\mathcal{U}$ before round k. To be sure that the security of an implementation P of PPSED is not worse than that of the ideal case, we ask all the communications from $\mathcal{U}$ before round k in the execution of P, namely C_k, cannot leak more information than C_k^*. Specifically, we ask everything about Δ_k that can be computed given C_k can also be computed given C_k^*. Notice that this ideal case is not a practical solution itself to the PPSED problem, since it would require $\mathcal{U}$ store these linked lists, which would be $\Omega(n)$ bits in total. (In particular, these lists would generally require significantly more storage than a dictionary.) It would also require potentially sending n bits from $\mathcal{U}$ to $\mathcal{S}$ for every query.

3 Efficient Schemes

In this section, we consider the following two cases separately: (1) a dictionary can be stored on $\mathcal{U}$'s mobile device, and (2) a dictionary cannot be stored on $\mathcal{U}$'s mobile device (ostensibly due to lack of space). We study the first case both for its own merit and to lead us to the solution of the second case. In either case, our scheme consists of two phases. In the first phase, we assume $\mathcal{U}$ is at home and is going to submit his files to $\mathcal{S}$, and assume a keyword dictionary is always available to $\mathcal{U}$. However, we do not exclude the possibility that $\mathcal{S}$ has a dictionary that is totally the same (i.e. the dictionary may be publicly accessible). In the second phase, $\mathcal{U}$ becomes a mobile user, and wants to retrieve certain files by keyword searches via his mobile device. The main idea behind our schemes is the following: $\mathcal{U}$ uses pseudo-random bits to mask a keyword index for each file and sends it to $\mathcal{S}$ so that later $\mathcal{U}$ can use the short seeds to help $\mathcal{S}$ recover selective parts of the index, while keeping the remaining parts pseudo-random.

3.1 When a Dictionary Can Be Stored on $\mathcal{U}$'s Mobile Device

We formalize the keyword dictionary as 2^d index-word pairs (i, w_i), with $i \in [2^d], w_i \in \{0,1\}^*$ for some constant d. Next, given the security parameter t, for

$K \in \{0,1\}^t$, let $P_K(x)$ be a family of pseudo-random permutations with domain $\{0,1\}^d$, let $F_K(x)$ be a family of pseudo-random functions mapping $\{0,1\}^d$ to $\{0,1\}^t$, and let $G_K(x)$ be a family of pseudo-random functions mapping $[n]$ to $\{0,1\}$. Here is our two-phase PPSED scheme.

| Scheme1 |

Noninteractive Setup at Home

- $\mathcal{U}$ chooses $s, r \in \{0,1\}^t$ uniformly at random and keeps them secret.
- Initially, for each file m_j, $1 \le j \le n$, $\mathcal{U}$ prepares a 2^d-bit index string I_j such that if m_j contains w_i, $\mathcal{U}$ sets $I_j[P_s(i)]$ to be 1, and otherwise $I_j[P_s(i)]$ is set to 0.
- Next, $\mathcal{U}$ computes $r_i = F_r(i)$ for $i \in [2^d]$, and for each file $m_{j,j\in[n]}$, computes a 2^d-bit *masked* index string M_j such that $M_j[i] = I_j[i] \oplus G_{r_i}(j)$.
- For $1 \le j \le n$, $\mathcal{U}$ submits $\mathcal{E}_j(m_j)$ to $\mathcal{S}$ along with the corresponding masked index string M_j.
- $\mathcal{U}$ copies the two secret keys s, r and the dictionary to his mobile device before leaving home.

1-round Mobile Retrieval

- To retrieve files with a keyword w_λ, $\mathcal{U}$ first retrieves the corresponding index λ from his dictionary, and then sends $p = P_s(\lambda)$ and $f = F_r(p)$ to $\mathcal{S}$.
- $\mathcal{S}$ then computes $I_j[p] = M_j[p] \oplus G_f(j)$ for $j \in [n]$. If $I_j[p] = 1$, $\mathcal{S}$ sends $\mathcal{E}_j(m_j)$ to $\mathcal{U}$.

Theorem 1. *Scheme1 is a correct implementation of* PPSED *where $\mathcal{S}$ sends* $\sum_{i\in\mathcal{I}_j} |\mathcal{E}_i(m_i)|$ *total bits, $\mathcal{U}$ stores $2t$ bits plus a dictionary of constant size, and $\mathcal{U}$ sends $(d+t)$ bits per keyword search.*

Proof. Because the correctness and the communication complexity of *Scheme1* can be easily verified, it suffices to prove $\mathcal{U}$'s security. W.l.o.g. we assume $\mathcal{U}$ does not make the same query twice, and hence the protocol consists of at most 2^d retrieval rounds.

In the following, by "the view of $\mathcal{S}$" we mean all the communications $\mathcal{S}$ receives from $\mathcal{U}$. Let ζ denote $\{\mathcal{E}_1(m_1), \mathcal{E}_2(m_2), \cdots, \mathcal{E}_n(m_n)\}$. Next, let

$$\mathcal{I}(a) = \{I_1[a], I_2[a], \cdots, I_n[a]\},$$
$$\mathcal{M}(a) = \{M_1[a], M_2[a], \cdots, M_n[a]\},$$
$$\mathcal{G}(a) = \{G_a(1), G_a(2), \cdots, G_a(n)\},$$

and let $\mathcal{M} = \{\mathcal{M}(1), \mathcal{M}(2), \cdots, \mathcal{M}(2^d)\}$. Moreover, let λ_v denote the dictionary index of the keyword in round v, and define $p_v = P_s(\lambda_v)$ and $f_v = F_r(p_v)$. In addition, let C_v denote the view of $\mathcal{S}$ before round v, so we have

$$C_1 = \{\zeta, \mathcal{M}\}, \quad C_2 = \{\zeta, \mathcal{M}, p_1, f_1\}, \quad C_3 = \{\zeta, \mathcal{M}, p_1, p_2, f_1, f_2\}, \quad \cdots.$$

Consider the ideal case which meets our security requirement perfectly: $\mathcal{U}$ records in advance a set of linked lists such that each file index is associated with a list of all the keywords of the corresponding file. In this case, the only message $\mathcal{U}$ needs to send in round v is the n-bit string Q_v such that for $j \in [n]$, $Q_v[j] = 1$ if and only if m_j contains the keyword in round v (and $\mathcal{S}$ has to send $\mathcal{E}_j(m_j)$ back). So if we let C_v^* denote the view of $\mathcal{S}$ before round v in the ideal case, we have

$$C_1^* = \{\zeta\}, \ C_2^* = \{\zeta, Q_1\}, \ C_3^* = \{\zeta, Q_1, Q_2\}, \ \cdots .$$

Observe that $Q_v = \mathcal{I}(p_v)$ for $v \in [2^d]$.

Our goal is to prove the following (for $k \in [2^d + 1]$): for any PPT algorithm A, any $\Delta_k = \{m_1, \cdots, m_n, w_0 \equiv \emptyset, w_1, \cdots, w_{k-1}\}$, any function h, there is a PPT algorithm A^* such that the following value is negligible in t:

$$\rho = |\mathbf{Pr}[A(C_k, 1^t) = h(\Delta_k)] - \mathbf{Pr}[A^*(C_k^*, 1^t) = h(\Delta_k)|.$$

Intuitively, suppose A^* on input C_k^* can generate a view C_k' that is indistinguishable from C_k. Then A^* can simulate running A with C_k' to give the desired result (that is, that ρ is negligible in t). We shall follow this intuition.

For $k = 1$, A^* just needs to choose $\mathcal{M}'$ from $\{0,1\}^{n2^d}$ uniformly at random, and feeds A with $\{\zeta, \mathcal{M}'\}$. We claim A^* is as desired as otherwise the pair (A, A^*) is a PPT distinguisher for pseudo-random bits and truly random bits. For $k > 1$, the strategy of A^* is as follows:

- A^* chooses $f_1', f_2', \cdots, f_{k-1}'$ uniformly at random from $\{0,1\}^t$, and chooses $s' = (p_1', p_2', \cdots, p_{k-1}')$ uniformly at random from $S = \{s \mid s \subset \{1, 2, \cdots, 2^d\}, |s| = k - 1\}$.
- A^* computes $\mathcal{M}' = \{\mathcal{M}'(1), \mathcal{M}'(2), \cdots, \mathcal{M}'(2^d)\}$ in the following way:
  • For $i \in [2^d], i \neq p_1', p_2', \cdots, p_{k-1}'$, choose $\mathcal{M}'(i)$ uniformly at random from $\{0,1\}^n$.
  • For $i \in [k-1]$, set $\mathcal{M}'(p_i') = Q_i \oplus \mathcal{G}(f_i')$.
- A^* feeds A with $C_k' = \{\zeta, \mathcal{M}', p_1', p_2', \cdots, p_{k-1}', f_1', f_2', \cdots, f_{k-1}'\}$.

We explain why this strategy works as follows. First, recall $Q_v = \mathcal{I}(p_v)$ for $v \in [k-1]$, and consider the following imaginary case: for each $i \in [2^d], i \neq p_1, p_2, \cdots, p_{k-1}$, $\mathcal{U}$ does not generate $\mathcal{M}(i)$ according to $Scheme1$; instead, $\mathcal{U}$ chooses $\mathcal{M}(i)$ from $\{0,1\}^n$ uniformly at random. Clearly, in this case, the only difference between the generation of C_k' and the generation of C_k comes from the employment of truly randomness in place of pseudo-randomness. Specifically, C_k' is generated using truly random p_j' and f_j' for $j \in [k-1]$, yet C_k is generated using pseudo-random p_j and f_j for $j \in [k-1]$. So we claim ρ must be negligible in t in this case as otherwise the pair (A, A^*) can be used to invalidate either P_K or F_K.

Next, consider the real case (that $\mathcal{U}$ does follow every step of $Scheme1$). An observation is for each $i \in [2^d], i \neq p_1, p_2, \cdots, p_{k-1}$, $\mathcal{M}(i)$ remains pseudo-random before round k. However, since this is the only difference between the real case and the imaginary case, we claim ρ must be negligible in t in the real case as otherwise the pair (A, A^*) can be used to invalidate G_K. In consequence, we have proven the desired security guarantee. □

Analysis. We examine the practicability of the above scheme with realistic parameters. First, if we set $d = 18$, the storage overhead on server is 32 kilobytes per file. Note the latest *Merriam-Webster's Collegiate Dictionary* contains only 225,000 definitions [9]. So even if $\mathcal{U}$ adds new words by himself, 2^{18} could be a reasonable upper-bound in practice for the number of all the distinct words in $\mathcal{U}$'s dictionary as well as in his documents. Second, notably only a few bits are sent from $\mathcal{U}$ per keyword search. If we set $t = 2030$, for example, only 256 bytes are required. Clearly, our scheme is independent of the encryption method chosen for the remote files, so it works for different file formats (including compressed files, multimedia files, etc.), as long as a keyword index on the corresponding content can be built. Moreover, only pseudo-random functions (and permutations) are used in the construction of our scheme. As mentioned earlier, these functions can be implemented efficiently by heuristic algorithms.

Although we assume the availability of a dictionary on $\mathcal{U}$'s mobile device, the assumption is not far-fetched as most of today's mobile devices are equipped with built-in electronic dictionaries (or can store one on a memory card). Actually, if we estimate the average length of a keyword by 2^3 ASCII characters, a dictionary only amounts to $(2^{18})(2^3)(8) = 2$ megabytes, which can be improved further using compression.

3.2 When a Dictionary Cannot Be Stored on $\mathcal{U}$'s Mobile Device

We now consider the same setting as the previous section, except that a dictionary cannot be stored on $\mathcal{U}$'s mobile device. Our new scheme is almost the same with *Scheme1*, with the pivotal difference being that $\mathcal{U}$ is asked to store an encrypted dictionary on $\mathcal{S}$.

Let w_{max} upper-bound the length of a word in $\mathcal{U}$'s local dictionary at home, let Φ be a family of pseudo-random permutations on $\{0,1\}^{w_{max}}$, and let $F_K^*(x)$ be a family of pseudo-random functions mapping $\{0,1\}^{d+w_{max}}$ to $\{0,1\}^t$. Here is our two-phased PPSED scheme.

⎡ *Scheme2* ⎤

Noninteractive setup at home
- $\mathcal{U}$ follows the first two steps of *Scheme1*, except he also chooses $\tau \in \{0,1\}^t$ uniformly at random and keeps it secret.
- $\mathcal{U}$ sends to $\mathcal{S}$ the following in order: $\varphi_1 = \Phi_\tau(w_{i_1}), \varphi_2 = \Phi_\tau(w_{i_2}), \cdots, \varphi_{2^d} = \Phi_\tau(w_{i_{2^d}})$ such that $P_s(i_j) = j$ for $j \in [2^d]$. ($\mathcal{S}$ then records (j, φ_j) for $j \in [2^d]$, following the order.)
- Next, $\mathcal{U}$ computes $r_i = F_\tau^*(i, \varphi_i)$ for $i \in [2^d]$, and for each file $m_{j,j\in[n]}$, computes a 2^d-bit *masked* index string M_j such that $M_j[i] = I_j[i] \oplus G_{r_i}(j)$.
- $\mathcal{U}$ follows the last two steps of *Scheme1*, except he copies τ, instead of the dictionary, to his mobile device before leaving home.

2-round mobile retrieval
- To retrieve files with keyword w_λ, $\mathcal{U}$ sends $\varphi = \Phi_\tau(w_\lambda)$ to $\mathcal{S}$.
- Let (p, φ_p) be such that $\varphi_p = \varphi$. $\mathcal{S}$ sends p to $\mathcal{U}$, who then sends $f = F_r^*(p, \varphi)$ to $\mathcal{S}$.
- $\mathcal{S}$ then computes $I_j[p] = M_j[p] \oplus G_f(j)$ for $j \in [n]$. If $I_j[p] = 1$, $\mathcal{S}$ sends $\mathcal{E}_j(m_j)$ to $\mathcal{U}$.

Theorem 2. *Scheme2 is a correct implementation of* PPSED *where* $\mathcal{S}$ *sends* $\sum_{i \in \mathcal{I}_j} |\mathcal{E}_i(m_i)| + d$ *total bits,* $\mathcal{U}$ *stores* $3t$ *bits, and* $\mathcal{U}$ *sends* $(w_{max} + t)$ *bits per keyword search.*

Proof. We first prove $\mathcal{U}$'s security, employing some of the notation in the proof of Theorem 1. Let $\tilde{C}_k$ denote the view of $\mathcal{S}$ before round k in *Scheme2*. It suffices to prove the following: for all k, for any PPT algorithm $\tilde{A}$, any $\Delta_k = \{m_1, \cdots, m_n, w_0 \equiv \emptyset, w_1, \cdots, w_{k-1}\}$, and any function h, there is a PPT algorithm A such that the following value is negligible in t:

$$|\mathbf{Pr}[\tilde{A}(\tilde{C}_k, 1^t) = h(\Delta_k)] - \mathbf{Pr}[A(C_k, 1^t) = h(\Delta_k)]|.$$

Recall C_k is the view of $\mathcal{S}$ before round k in *Scheme1*. In other words, we ask everything about Δ_k that can be computed given $\tilde{C}_k$ can also be computed given C_k. In other words, the information leakage of *Scheme2* is essentially no worse than that of *Scheme1*.

Since the retrieval phase is interactive, we know $\mathcal{U}$'s ongoing action depends on $\mathcal{S}$'s message, namely p. So we must consider the case that $\mathcal{S}$ might dishonestly send an arbitrary $p' \neq p$ to $\mathcal{U}$. However, let us start from the simplified case that $\mathcal{S}$ always sends the correct p to $\mathcal{U}$.

In the simplified case, we can assume w.l.o.g. that $\mathcal{U}$ always sends back p, along with f, to $\mathcal{S}$. Note this does not jeopardize $\mathcal{U}$'s security since $\mathcal{U}$ learns p from $\mathcal{S}$, while the difference between $\tilde{C}_k$ and C_k now comes from $\{\varphi_j\}_{j \in [2^d]} + \{\varphi = \varphi_p\}$ [3]. An observation is A can simulate each φ_j by flipping coins and can simulate φ by setting φ to be the simulated φ_p, in that each φ_j represents t pseudo-random bits and p is known to A (as $p \in C_k$ is part of the input to A). So all A needs to do is to feed $\tilde{A}$ with C_k and the simulated results.

Next, let us consider the case that $\mathcal{S}$ might be dishonest. Note if $\mathcal{S}$ sends $p' \neq p$ to $\mathcal{U}$, then the returning message from $\mathcal{U}$, namely $f' = F_r^*(p', \varphi)$, cannot be used for decryption and represents nothing more than t pseudo-random bits. Hence we can assume w.l.o.g. that $\mathcal{S}$ always simulate f' by flipping t coins and discarding f' from his view ($\tilde{C}_k$) in this case. Accordingly, it is enough to prove that for all k, for any PPT algorithm $\tilde{A}$, any $\Delta_k = \{m_1, \cdots, m_n, w_0 \equiv \emptyset, w_1, \cdots, w_{k-1}\}$, any function h, there is a PPT algorithm A such that the following value is negligible in t:

$$|\mathbf{Pr}[\tilde{A}(\tilde{C}_k, 1^t) = h(\Delta_k)] - \mathbf{Pr}[A(c_k, 1^t) = h(\Delta_k)]|,$$

---

[3] W.l.o.g. we can assume $F_K(j) \equiv F_K^*(j, \varphi_j)$ for all $j \in [2^d]$, i.e. $\{\varphi_j\}_{j \in [2^d]}$ is part of the description of F_K.

where $c_k \subset C_k$ is the *reduced* C_k defined as follows: c_k is constructed by mimicking S's dishonest behavior to discard the corresponding f from C_k. Clearly, A just needs to do the same simulations as in the simplified case and feeds $\hat{A}$ with c_k and the simulated results. Hence, we have finished the security proof by describing this PPT algorithm A.

There server S must send an additional d bits (namely p) beyond the files themselves. The on-mobile-device dictionary is replaced by a small storage overhead of t bits (namely the key to Φ_K). Moreover, we claim the correctness follows the fact that Φ_K is injective, and the user-side communication complexity can be easily verified. $\qquad\qquad\qquad\qquad\qquad\qquad\qquad\qquad\qquad\qquad\qquad\qquad\qquad$ $\square$

Analysis. If we estimate the maximal length of a word by 2^4 ASCII characters, we have $w_{max} = (2^4)(8) = 128$. Hence the encrypted dictionary amounts to $(2^{18})(128) = 4$ megabytes per user. The server-side storage overhead is the same with *Scheme1*. On the other hand, the communication complexity changes only slightly: S needs to send additional d bits per keyword search, while $\mathcal{U}$ now needs to send $(w_{max} + t)$ bits per keyword search.

4   Secure Update

In this section, we study how to securely submit new files to S. Basically $\mathcal{U}$ can follow all the steps in the first phase of either *Scheme1* or *Scheme2* to submit a new set of files, but some additional care is indispensable. First note if $\mathcal{U}$ treats the new files as a continuation of the old ones, or say, if $\mathcal{U}$ still uses the old pseudo-random seeds $\{r_i\}_{i \in [2^d]}$, then for any keyword that $\mathcal{U}$ has queried, S can learn (for free) whether the newly added files contain the (unknown) keyword or not as he already knows the corresponding pseudo-random seed. This says the newly submitted files suffer from a-prior information leakage before any query.

A solution is to choose independently a truly random seed r^θ to generate $\{r_i^\theta\}_{i \in [2^d]}$ for each file set ζ^θ, and to let S memorize the separating points amongst the asynchronous sets. When $\mathcal{U}$ makes a query, he should compute for each set ζ^θ a pseudo-random seed corresponding to the keyword index (using the truly random seed r^θ), and send all of them to S, who then decodes the encrypted index accordingly. In this way, the aforementioned a-priori information leakage can be avoided. However, this approach suffers from an increasing number of truly random seeds that have to be stored on the mobile device: it works well only when the updating process is not so frequent.

Fortunately, we can apply another pseudo-random function to generate each r^θ, which is thus not truly random anymore. But similarly to our previous approaches, we know it is safe to feed pseudo-random functions with pseudo-random seeds, and therefore we just need one truly random seed for the new pseudo-random function (and for all the sets). In consequence, we claim our schemes are incremental in the following sense: $\mathcal{U}$ can submit new files which are totally secure against previous queries but still searchable against future queries. Moreover, they both have very simple key management.

Remark. It is worth considering how to add new words to the dictionary too. Note though we use a real dictionary to estimate the storage overhead, $\mathcal{U}$ needs not to employ a real (fixed) dictionary in our schemes. This says which words to be included in the dictionary really depends on $\mathcal{U}$'s choice. Our *Scheme1* has the advantage that $\mathcal{U}$ can add new words to his dictionary freely (and directly), as long as the number of total words does not exceed some upper-bound. Our *Scheme2*, on the other hand, requires $\mathcal{U}$ should update the remote encrypted dictionary, and thus is less efficient.

5   Discussions

We discuss some security improvements and open problems in this section.

5.1   Security Improvements

It is worth taking into consideration a malicious $\mathcal{S}$, who may not follow the protocol at all. And it turns out both our schemes are capable of dealing with a malicious $\mathcal{S}$, with the help of some additional modules. Let us focus on *Scheme1* first. Note the first phase of *Scheme1* is non-interactive and the second phase is one-round. This basically says the only malicious action $\mathcal{S}$ can take is to send incorrect files (e.g. $\emptyset$) back to $\mathcal{U}$. However, since there is no way for $\mathcal{U}$ to stop $\mathcal{S}$ from doing this, the best $\mathcal{U}$ can do is to detect incorrect files when they are sent. And we claim $\mathcal{U}$ can always detect them using some cryptographic techniques. We outline the ideas below, and leave the details in the full version of this paper.

Note $\mathcal{U}$ only needs to check whether any of the returned files is counterfeit and whether the number of returned files is wrong, since w.l.o.g. we can assume $\mathcal{U}$ can always tell whether a genuine $\mathcal{E}_j(m_j)$ is associated with a given keyword or not by checking m_j. Here we employ a collision-resistant hash function h and a pseudo-random function $y : ([2^d], \{0, 1, \cdots, n\}) \rightarrow \{0,1\}^{t4}$; we also make use of some unforgeable signature scheme. The new modules are listed below:

- $\forall j \in [n]$, $\mathcal{U}$ computes $h_j = h(\mathcal{E}_j(m_j))$; $\mathcal{U}$ *signs* and stores each h_j on $\mathcal{S}$.
- $\forall i \in [2^d]$, $\mathcal{U}$ computes $y_i = y(i, num_i)$ using the secret random seed of y, where num_i is the number of files associated with the *permuted* keyword index i; $\mathcal{U}$ *signs* and stores each y_i on $\mathcal{S}$ [5].
- When $\mathcal{U}$ makes a query on i, $\mathcal{S}$ sends back the signed y_i and each signed h_j corresponding to the returned files so that $\mathcal{U}$ can first check the signatures and then verify the correctness. (Otherwise $\mathcal{U}$ refuses to trust in $\mathcal{S}$.)

Note the keys are (1) $\mathcal{U}$'s signature is unforgeable, (2) h_j is bound to $\mathcal{E}_j(m_j)$ because of collision resistance, and (3) y_i is bound to (i, num_i) because y should appear to be injective when t is large enough (as a truly random function does). Consequently, we claim that the above detection method works for *Scheme1*.

---

[4] Note we omit the secret random seed of y, which is known to $\mathcal{U}$ only, in the notation.

[5] Note it is important to keep num_i secret before $\mathcal{U}$ makes the corresponding query; this partially explains why we employ a pseudo-random function here.

As for *Scheme2*, recall its second phase contains two rounds and a dishonest $\mathcal{S}$ may send $p' \neq p$ back to $\mathcal{U}$ in the first round. So we have two cases:

- If $\mathcal{S}$ sends p, then the first round is correct and the above detection method can help $\mathcal{U}$ detect incorrect files in the second round.
- If $\mathcal{S}$ sends $p' \neq p$, then we have to let $\mathcal{U}$ detect that p' is incorrect. And the idea is to replace $y_i = y(i, num_i)$ by $y'_i = y'(w_{i^*}, i, num_i)$, where i^* should satisfy $P_s(i^*) = i$ (i.e. i^* is the *original* keyword index before permutation) and y' is a pseudo-random function similarly defined. By the same reasoning, we know y'_i is bound to (w_{i^*}, i, num_i) so that $\mathcal{U}$ can verify the mapping between w_{i^*} and i (which is secure against $\mathcal{S}$ by pseudo-randomness).

In consequence, we claim that *Scheme2* is also secure against a malicious $\mathcal{S}$.

Last, note it is unclear whether the related works [6, 11] can be modified to detect incorrect files without employing a similar approach to ours to record a keyword index, which can be associated with, say, the number of files containing a given keyword.

5.2   Open Problems

Dealing with queries containing Boolean operations on multiple keywords remains a significant and challenging open problem[6]. Similarly, allowing general pattern matching, instead of keyword matching, remains open. Solving these open questions would greatly enhance the utility of these schemes.

Our schemes can also deal with occurrence queries in a less efficient way. An occurrence query is a query like "I want to retrieve all the files containing more than 10 occurrences of PRIVACY." One simple solution coupled with our schemes is to also record each occurrence of a word in the encrypted index. Hence if the word PRIVACY appears 12 times in a document, each appearance would be labelled separately as PRIVACY1, PRIVACY2, ..., and a query could be done on PRIVACY10. This approach can dramatically increase the storage overhead on the sever-side; more efficient solutions would be desirable.

Finally, it seems that none of the existing schemes (including ours) can provide general secure update with *deletion*. Our schemes can ensure the security of newly submitted files against previous queries, but they cannot ensure the security of *previously* submitted files (which $\mathcal{U}$ now wants to delete) against *new* queries. The problem arises because $\mathcal{S}$ can always keep the old files and the corresponding keyword indices rather than delete them. This reasoning appears to apply to all existing schemes that we know of.

We believe these problems are of growing importance, as keyword searches on encrypted data might have a broad range of applications in distributed multi-user

---

[6] The paper [6] proposed a method to deal with Boolean queries such as $x \wedge y$ by letting $\mathcal{S}$ learn both which files contain x and which files contain y and then send the intersection set back to $\mathcal{U}$. This method can also be applied to our schemes; however, a stronger and clearly more suitable notion of security in this context is that $\mathcal{S}$ should only learn the set of files corresponding to the query $x \wedge y$, and not the set of files corresponding to x and y. This is the question that remains open.

settings. For example, [4] studies the problem how to efficiently share encrypted data on P2P networks. In similar settings, keyword searches on encrypted data are indispensable.

Acknowledgement

We would like to thank Benny Pinkas and anonymous referees for their comments.

References

1. B. Bloom, "Space/time trade-offs in hash coding with allowable errors," in *Communications of the ACM, Vol. 13(7)*, pp. 422–426, 1970.
2. M. Bellare, R. Canetti, and H. Krawczyk, "Keying hash functions for message authentication," in *Proceedings of CRYPTO'96*, Lecture Notes in Computer Science 1109, pp. 1–15.
3. D. Boneh, G. Crescenzo, R. Ostrovsky, and G. Persiano, "Public key encryption with keyword search," in *Proceedings of Eurocrypt 2004*, Lecture Notes in Computer Science 3027, pp. 506–522.
4. K. Bennett, C. Grothoff, T. Horozov, and I. Patrascu, "Efficient sharing of encrypted data," in *Proceedings of ACISP 2002*, Lecture Notes in Computer Science 2384, pp. 107–120.
5. O. Goldreich, *Foundations of Cryptography: Basic Tools*, Cambridge University Press, 2001.
6. E.-J. Goh, "Secure indexes," in Cryptology ePrint Archive: Report 2003/216 (http://eprint.iacr.org/2003/216/).
7. O. Goldreich and R. Ostrovsky, "Software protection and simulation on oblivious RAMs," in *Journal of ACM, Vol. 43(3)*, pp. 431–473, 1996.
8. M. Luby and C. Rackoff, "How to construct pseudo-random permutations from pseudo-random functions (abstract)," in *Proceedings of CRYPTO'85*, Lecture Notes in Computer Science 218, pp. 447.
9. F. Mish (editor in chief), *Merriam-Webster's Collegiate Dictionary, 11th edition*, Merriam-Webster, Inc., 2003.
10. M. Naor and O. Reingold, "On the construction of pseudo-random permutations: Luby-Rackoff revisited (extended abstract)," in *Proceedings of ACM STOC'97*, pp. 189–199.
11. D. Song, D. Wagner, and A. Perrig, "Practical techniques for searches on encrypted data," in *Proceedings of IEEE Symposium on Security and Privacy 2000*, pp. 44–55.

An Efficient Solution to the Millionaires' Problem Based on Homomorphic Encryption*

Hsiao-Ying Lin and Wen-Guey Tzeng

Department of Computer and Information Science
National Chiao Tung University
Hsinchu, Taiwan 30050
lrain.cis92g@nctu.edu.tw, tzeng@cis.nctu.edu.tw

Abstract. We proposed a two-round protocol for solving the Millionaires' Problem in the setting of semi-honest parties. Our protocol uses either multiplicative or additive homomorphic encryptions. Previously proposed protocols used additive or XOR homomorphic encryption schemes only. The computation and communication costs of our protocol are in the same asymptotic order as those of the other efficient protocols. Nevertheless, since multiplicative homomorphic encryption scheme is more efficient than an additive one practically, our construction saves computation time and communication bandwidth in practicality.

Keywords: secure computation, the greater than problem, the socialist millionaires' problem homomorphic encryption

1 Introduction

Yao's Millionaires' ("greater than" or "GT") problem is to determine who is richer between two parties such that no information about a party's amount of assets is leaked to the other party. Yao [Yao82] first proposed a solution for the problem. Thereafter, many other protocols with great improvement are proposed. Some protocols [BK04,IG03,Fis01] solve the problem directly by analyzing the special properties of the problem. Some others [ST04] solve it in the content of secure multiparty computation in which the problem is represented as secure evaluation of the "greater than" boolean circuit with encrypted inputs. The former solutions are more efficient, while the later ones are more general. The GT protocol has many applications, such as in private bidding [Cac99].

In this paper we analyze the special properties of the GT problem. We find that the GT problem can be reduced to the intersection problem of two sets by a special coding for the private inputs. We could tackle the set intersection problem by the method in [FNP04]. Nevertheless, the protocol for the GT problem by using the set intersection protocol in [FNP04] directly is less efficient in both computation and communication. We solve the GT problem by further probing the property of our coding method. Our protocol can be based

---

* Research supported in part by National Science Council grants NSC-93-2213-E-009-008 and NSC 93-2213-E-009-009.

J. Ioannidis, A. Keromytis, and M.Yung (Eds.): ACNS 2005, LNCS 3531, pp. 456–466, 2005.

on either an additive or a multiplicative homomorphic encryption scheme, while most previous protocols [BK04,Fis01] are based on additive or XOR encryption schemes only. The computation and communication costs of our protocol are in the same asymptotic order as those of the other efficient protocols. Nevertheless, since multiplicative homomorphic encryption scheme is more efficient than an additive one practically, our construction saves computation time in practicality.

1.1 Related Work

Secure multiparty computation (or secure function evaluation) is to compute a public function with each party's private inputs such that in the end only the evaluation result is known and the private inputs are not exposed except those derived from the result. Yao [Yao82] first proposed such a protocol for the GT problem, which is an instantiation of secure multiparty computation. Nevertheless, the cost of the protocol is exponential in both time and space. Later one, Yao [Yao86] and Goldreich, etc [GMW87] used the technique of scrambled circuits to solve the general multiparty computation problem. By applying this technique to the GT problem, the cost of the resulting protocol in computation and communication is linear. Recently, Schoenmakers and Tuyls [ST04] used threshold homomorphic encryption schemes as a tool to solve the multiparty computation problem. Applying to the concrete GT problem, it provides a threshold GT protocol, in which the private inputs are shared among a group of parties. The protocol takes $O(n)$ rounds.

On the other hand, protocols for solving the GT problem directly are more efficient. These protocols usually take a constant number of rounds. Ioannidis and Grama [IG03] used 1-out-of-2 oblivious transfer scheme to construct the GT protocol that runs n copies of the OT scheme in parallel, where n is the length of the private inputs. However, the length of the private inputs is restricted by the secure parameter of the based OT schemes. Fischlin [Fis01] used the Goldwasser-Micali encryption scheme (GM-encryption) to construct a two-round GT protocol. The GM encryption scheme has the XOR, NOT and re-randomization properties. They modified the scheme to get an AND property, which can be performed once only. The computation cost is $O(\lambda n)$ modular multiplication which is very efficient, where λ is the security parameter. Nevertheless, the communication cost is $O(\lambda n \log N)$ is less efficient, where N is the modulus. In [BK04], Blake and Kolesnikov used the additive homomorphic Paillier cryptosystem to construct a two-round GT protocol. The computation cost is $O(n \log N)$ and the communication cost is $O(n \log N)$.

2 Preliminaries and Definitions

The GT problem is a two-party secure computation problem of securely evaluating a predicate f such that $f(x, y) = 1$ if and only if $x > y$, where x is Alice's private input and y is Bob's private input. A solution protocol Π for the GT problem should meet the following requirements.

1. The involved parties Alice and Bob are both polynomial-time bounded probabilistic Turing machines. We assume that Alice and Bob are semi-honest. That is, they shall follow the protocol step by step, but try to get extra information by more computation.
2. Correctness: After execution of Π, Alice returns 1 if and only if $x > y$.
3. Alice's privacy: Holdings of x or x' ($x' \neq x$) are not computationally distinguishable by Bob. Let $View_B^\Pi$ be the real view of Bob when interacting with Alice with private input x. We say that Alice's privacy is guaranteed if there exists a simulator Sim_B such that for any x, $Sim_B(y)$ can generate a view indistinguishable from the view of Bob in the execution of the real protocol, that is,

$$Sim_B(y) \equiv^c VIEW_B^\Pi(A(x), y)$$

4. Bob's privacy: Alice cannot get extra information except those derived from x and $b = f(x, y)$. Bob's privacy is guaranteed if there exists a simulator Sim_A, such that for any y' with $f(x, y') = b$ and $f(x, y)$, $Sim_A(x, b)$ can generate a view indistinguishable from the view of Alice in the real execution, that is

$$Sim_A(x, f(x, y)) \equiv^c VIEW_A^\Pi(x, B(y'))$$

2.1   Homomorphic Encryption with Scalaring

We review multiplicative and additive homomorphic encryption schemes with the property of scalaring. Multiplicative homomorphic encryption schemes are usually more efficient than additive homomorphic encryption schemes,

An encryption scheme is *multiplicative homomorphic* if and only if

$$E(m_1) \odot E(m_2) = E(m_1 \times m_2),$$

where $\odot$ is an operator. An encryption scheme is *additive homomorphic* if and only if

$$E(m_1) \odot E(m_2) = E(m_1 + m_2).$$

An encryption is *scalarable* if $c = E(m)$ can be mapped randomly to a ciphertext $E(m^k)$ or $c' = E(km)$ for a random k.

The ElGamal encryption scheme is a multiplicative homomorphic encryption scheme with the scalaring property. For efficiency of computation, we modify the scheme so that each decryption takes 1 modular exponentiation. This modification does not affect the security of the scheme. Let $r \in_R S$ denote that r is chosen from S uniformly and independently.

- Key generation: Let $p = 2q + 1$, where p and q are both primes. Let G_q be the subgroup QR_p and g is a generator of G_q. The public key is $h = g^{-\alpha}$, where $\alpha \in Z_q$ is the corresponding private key.
- Encryption: The encryption of message $m \in G_q$ is a pair $E(m) = (a, b) = (g^r, mh^r)$, where $r \in_R Z_q$.
- Decryption: For a ciphertext $c = (a, b)$, the message is computed from $D(c) = b \times a^\alpha = m$.

- Scalaring: We can scalarize a ciphertext $c = E(m) = (a, b)$ by computing $c' = E(m^k) = (a^k, b^k)$ for $k \in_R Z_q$. If $m = 1$, the scalaring operation does not change the content of encryption. Scalaring makes c' indistinguishable from a random pair due to the DDH assumption (below).

The ElGamal encryption scheme is multiplicative homomorphic since

$$
\begin{aligned}
E(m_1) \odot E(m_2) &= (g^{r_1}, m_1 h^{r_1}) \odot (g^{r_2}, m_2 h^{r_2}) \\
&= (g^{r_1 + r_2}, (m_1 \times m_2) h^{r_1 + r_2}) \\
&= E(m_1 \times m_2)
\end{aligned}
$$

The security of ElGamal scheme is based on the DDH assumption, which states that it is computationally infeasible to distinguish the following two distribution ensembles:

- $D = (g^a, g^b, g^{ab})$, where $a, b \in_R Z_q$.
- $R = (g^a, g^b, g^c)$, where $a, b, c \in_R Z_q$.

If we only need an encryption of a random number, we need not choose a random number and encrypt it. This costs an encryption time. Instead, we choose a random pair $c = (a, b) \in_R G_q^2$, which is an encryption of some random number. By this technique, we save the encryption cost, which is crucial to the efficiency of our GT protocol.

The Paillier encryption scheme is additive homomorphic, which is as follows:

- Key generation: Let $N = pq$ be the RSA-modulus and g be an integer of order αN modulo N^2 for some integer α. The public key is (N, g) and the private key is $\lambda(N) = lcm((p-1), (q-1))$.
- Encryption: The encryption of message $m \in Z_N$ is $E(m) = g^m r^N$ mod $modN^2$, where $r \in_R Z_N^*$.
- Decryption: For ciphertext c, the message is computed from

$$
m = \frac{L(c^{\lambda(N)} \bmod N^2)}{L(g^{\lambda(N)} \bmod N^2)},
$$

where $L(u) = \frac{u-1}{N}$.
- Scalaring: For ciphertext $c = E(m)$, the scalaring is done by computing $c' = E(km) = c^k$ for $k \in Z_N^*$. If $m = 0$, the scalaring operation does not change the content of encryption.

The security of the scheme is based on the CRA (Composite Residuosity assumption, which states that it is computationally infeasible to distinguish whether an element $z \in Z_{N^2}^*$ is an n-residue or not.

The scheme is additive homomorphic since

$$
\begin{aligned}
E(m_1) \odot E(m_2) &= (g^{m_1} r_1^N) \cdot (g^{m_2} r_2^N) \\
&= g^{m_1 + m_2} (r_1 r_2)^N \\
&= E(m_1 + m_2).
\end{aligned}
$$

2.2   0-Encoding and 1-Encoding

The main idea of out construction is to reduce the GT problem to the set intersection problem. We use two special encodings, 0-encoding and 1-encoding.

Let $s = s_n s_{n-1} ... s_1 \in \{0,1\}^n$ be a binary string of length n. The *0-encoding* of s is the set S_s^0 of binary strings such that

$$S_s^0 = \{s_n s_{n-1} ... s_{i+1} 1 | s_i = 0, 1 \leq i \leq n\}$$

The *1-encoding* of s is the set S_s^1 of binary strings such that

$$S_s^1 = \{s_n s_{n-1} ... s_i | s_i = 1, 1 \leq i \leq n\}$$

Both S_s^1 and S_s^0 have at most n elements.

If we encode x into its 1-encoding S_x^1 and y into its 0-encoding S_y^0, we can see that

$$x > y \text{ if and only if } S_x^1 \text{ and } S_y^0 \text{ has a common element.}$$

We give an example. Let $x = 6 = 110_2$ and $y = 2 = 010_2$ of length 3 (we fill in the leading zeros.) We have $S_x^1 = \{1, 11\}$ and $S_y^0 = \{1, 011\}$. Since $S_x^1 \cap S_y^0 \neq \emptyset$, we have $x > y$ indeed. If $x = 2 = 010_2$ and $y = 6 = 110_2$, we have $S_x^1 = \{01\}$ and $S_y^0 = \{111\}$. Since $S_x^1 \cap S_y^0 = \emptyset$, we have $x \leq y$.

We note that the strings in S_x^1 have a prefix relation and the strings in S_y^0 also have a prefix relation when removing the last bit. Our protocol exploits this relation.

Theorem 1. *x is greater than y if and only if S_x^1 and S_y^0 have a common element.*

Proof. Let $x = x_n x_{n-1} ... x_1 \in \{0,1\}^n$ and $y = y_n y_{n-1} ... y_1 \in \{0,1\}^n$. For the forward direction, we can see that if $x > y$, there is a position i such that $x_i = 1$ and $y_i = 0$, and for all j, $n \geq j > i$, $x_j = y_j$. We have $x_n x_{n-1} ... x_i \in S_x^1$ by 1-encoding and $y_n y_{n-1} \cdots y_{i+1} 1 \in S_y^0$ by 0-encoding. Thus, S_x^1 and S_y^0 have a common element.

For the backward direction, let $t = t_n t_{n-1} ... t_i \in S_x^1 \cap S_y^0$ for some $t_i = 1$. Since $t \in S_x^1$, $x_n x_{n-1} ... x_i = t_n t_{n-1} ... t_i$, and since $t \in S_y^0$, $y_n y_{n-1} \cdots y_{i+1} \bar{y}_i = t_n t_{n-1} ... t_i$. We can see that $x > y$.

3   Our Protocols

If Alice and Bob compare the elements in S_x^1 and S_y^0 one by one, it would need $O(n^2)$ comparisons. Nevertheless, they can only compare the corresponding strings of the same length (if both of them exist) in S_x^1 and S_y^0. This reduces the number of comparison to $O(n)$.

Let (G, E, D) be a multiplicative homomorphic encryption scheme. Alice uses a $2 \times n$-table $T[i, j]$, $i \in \{0, 1\}$, $1 \leq j \leq n$, to denote its input $x = x_n x_{n-1} \cdots x_1$ with

$$T[x_j, j] = E(1) \text{ and } T[\bar{x}_j, j] = E(r) \text{ for some random } r \in G_q.$$

Since Alice need not know r (each entry uses a distinct r), she randomly selects $(a, b) \in G_q^2$ for $E(r)$. When Bob wants to compare a string $t = t_n t_{n-1} \cdots t_i$ in S_y^0 with the corresponding string of the same length in S_x^1, he computes

$$c_t = T[t_n, n] \odot T[t_{n-1}, n-1] \cdots \odot T[t_i, i].$$

We can see that c_t is an encryption of 1 if and only if $t \in S_x^1$ except with a negligible probability of incorrectness. Furthermore, since strings in S_y^0 have some sort of prefix relations, Bob can compute all c_t's in at most $2n$ homomorphic operations, instead of n^2 homomorphic operation.

Based on the previous discussion, our GT protocol is as follows:

1. Alice with private input $x = x_n x_{n-1} \cdots x_1$ does the following:
   - run G to choose a key pair (pk, sk) for (E, D).
   - prepare a $2 \times n$-table $T[i, j]$, $i \in \{0, 1\}$, $1 \leq j \leq n$, such that

   $$T[x_i, i] = E(1) \text{ and } T[\bar{x}_i, i] = E(r_i) \text{ for some random } r_i \in G_q$$

   - send T to Bob.
2. Bob with private input $y = y_n y_{n-1} \cdots y_1$ does the following:
   - for each $t = t_n t_{n-1} \cdots t_i \in S_y^0$, compute

   $$c_t = T[t_n, n] \odot T[t_{n-1}, n-1] \cdots \odot T[t_i, i].$$

   - prepare $l = n - |S_y^0|$ random encryptions $z_j = (a_j, b_j) \in G_q^2, 1 \leq j \leq l$.
   - scalarize c_t's and permutate c_t's and z_j's randomly as $c_1, c_2, \ldots, c_n$.
   - send $c_1, c_2, \ldots, c_n$ to Alice.
3. Alice decrypts $D(c_i) = m_i$, $1 \leq i \leq n$, and determine $x > y$ if and only if some $m_i = 1$.

When $x \leq y$, there is a negligible probability that our GT protocol returns a wrong answer due to randomization.

Our GT protocol can use additive homomorphic encryption. We only replace $E(1)$ by $E(0)$ in setting up the table T. In the end, Alice determines $x > y$ if and only if some $m_i = 0$.

3.1   Correctness and Security

Theorem 2. *The protocol constructed as above is a solution to the GT problem.*

Proof. We can verify correctness easily. The 1-encoding set of x is embedded into the table T. The 0-encoding set of y is computed by Bob directly. If there is a common element in both sets, some $c_i = E(1)$ by the previous discussion. Otherwise, no such $c_i = E(1)$ exists.

For Alice's privacy, we construct a simulator Sim_B which simulates the protocol by selecting randomly x' as input of Alice, and letting y as input of Bob. The view generated by Sim_B is $(y, T_{x'})$ and the view in the real execution is (y, T_x). Due to the security of the ElGamal encryption, T_x and T'_x are indistinguishable. Thus $Sim_B(y)$ and the real view $View_B^\Pi(A(x), y)$ are indistinguishable.

For Bob's privacy, we construct a simulator Sim_A to simulate the view of Alice without the private input of Bob. We need the view generated by Sim_A being indistinguishable from the view of Alice in the real execution. Sim_A simulates as follows. The input of Sim_A are the comparison result $b \in \{0, 1\}$ and Alice's private input x. Sim_A uses x to construct the table T for the first step. For the second step, Sim_A generates the sequence $c_1, c_2, \ldots, c_n$ according to the result value b. If $b = 1$, Sim_A generates $n - 1$ random encryptions and one encryption of 1, then Sim_B randomly permutates them as $c_1, c_2, \ldots, c_n$. If $b = 0$, Sim_A generates n random encryptions as $c_1, c_2, \ldots, c_n$. The view generated by Sim_A is $(x, T_x, c_1, c_2, \ldots, c_n, b)$.

Since T_x is constructed by using the value x, the distribution is identical to that in the real execution. For fixed output b, the sequence of the ciphertexts are computationally indistinguishable from the sequence in the real execution due to the scalaring property. Thus, Alice cannot compute Bob's private input y except knowing its relation with x.

3.2   Efficiency

In this analysis, the base encryption scheme is the ElGamal scheme. Let p be the modulus.

Computation Complexity. Let n be the length of the private inputs. We neglect the cost of choosing random numbers. The cost of choosing a public key pair for Alice is neglected also since this can be done in the setup stage. We don't count the cost of selecting keys in other protocols, either.

In Step 1, Alice encrypts n $1's$. In Step 2, Bob computes c_t, $t \in S_y^0$, by reusing intermediate values. This takes $(2n - 3)$ multiplications of ciphertexts at most. Step 2 uses n scalaring operations at most. In Step 3, Alice decrypts n ciphertexts.

To compare fairly, we convert all operations to the number of modular multiplications. For the ElGamal scheme, each encryption takes $2 \log p$ modular multiplications, each decryption takes $\log p$ modular multiplications, and each scalaring operation takes $2 \log p$ modular multiplications. Overall, our GT protocol needs $5n \log p + 4n - 6$ $(= n \times 2 \log p + 2 \times (2n - 3) + n \times 2 \log p + n \times \log p)$ modular multiplications.

Communication complexity. The size of exchanged messages between Alice and Bob is the size of T and $c_1, c_2, \ldots, c_n$, which is $6n \log p$ $(= 3n \times 2 \log p)$ bits.

3.3   Extensions

We can use the hash function to construct a simpler protocol. The protocol costs less communication bit.

The protocol is as follows: Let h be a public collision-free hash function.

1. Alice encodes x as S_x^1 and lets h_l be the hash value of the length-l string t in S_x^1 if t exists.
2. Alice encrypts h_l as c_l for existent h_l's and randomly selects $c_{l'}$ for missing $h_{l'}$, $1 \leq l' \leq n$.

3. Alice sends $c_1, c_2, \ldots, c_n$ to Bob.
4. Bob encodes y as S_y^0 and computes the hash value h_l' for the length-l string t in S_y^0 if t exists.
5. Bob computes $z_l = (a_l, b_l/h_l')$ for existent h_l' and $z_l = c_l$ for inexistent h_l', where $c_l = (a_l, b_l)$, $1 \le l \le n$.
6. Bob scalarizes and permutates $z_1, z_2, \ldots, z_n$ and sends them to Alice.
7. Alice decrypts $z_1, z_2, \ldots, z_l$ and outputs 1 if and only if some message is 1.

In the protocol, the computation of Bob for each value from Alice can be completed by inversion of the hash value, a multiplication and a scalaring of the ciphertext. Thus the computation cost in the protocol of Bob is $2n \log p + 2n$ modular multiplications. The computation cost of Alice is $3n \log p$ modular multiplications. The communication cost of the protocol is $4n \log p$ bits.

4 Other Protocols

For readability, we review the protocols in [BK04,Fis01].

Fischlin's GT Protocol. Fischlin's GT protocol [Fis01] uses the GM-encryption scheme and a modified GM-encryption. The GM-encryption scheme is as follows:

- Key generation: Let $N = pq$ be the RSA-modulus and z be a quadratic non-residue of Z_n^* with Jacobi symbol $+1$. The public key is (N, z) and the secret key is (p, q).
- Encryption: For a bit b, the encryption is $E(b) = z^b r^2 \mod N$, where $r \in_R Z_N^*$.
- Decryption: For a ciphertext c, its plaintext is 1 if and only if c is a quadratic non-residue. If c is a quadratic residue in Z_N, c is a quadratic residue in both Z_p^* and Z_q^*.
- xor-property: $E(b_1)E(b_2) = E(b_1 \oplus b_2)$
- not-property: $E(b) \times z = E(b \oplus 1) = E(\bar{b})$
- re-randomization: we can re-randomize a ciphertext c by multiplying an encrytion of 0.

Modified GM-encryption. To get the AND-homomorphic property, we need modify the GM encryption:

- Encryption: For encrypt a bit $b = 1$, $XE(b)$ is a sequence of quadratic residues. If $b = 0$, $XE(b)$ is a sequence of quadratic residues and non-residues. The length of the sequence is determined by a parameter λ.
- Decryption: For decrypting a ciphertext, we need check quadratic residusoity of all elements in the ciphertext.
- AND-property: For two ciphertext $XE(b_1)$ and $XE(b_2)$, their product $XE(b_1) \odot XE(b_2)$ is computed by multiplying elements pairwisely. The product of two ciphertexts is an encryption of b_1 AND b_2.

Protocol and Efficiency. The protocol in [Fis01] uses the properties of the GM- and modified-GM-encrytion schemes.

We use our notation to represent the (optimized) protocol in [Fis01] as follows:

1. Alice with private input $x = x_n x_{n-1} \cdots x_1$ does the following:
   - generate GM-instance N, z.
   - encrypt each bit of x and get $X_i = E(x_i)$ for $i = 1, \ldots, n$
   - send $N, z, X_1, \ldots, X_n$ to Bob
2. Bob with private input $y = y_n y_{n-1} \cdots y_1$ and messages $N, z, X_1, \cdots, X_n$ from Alice does the following:
   - encrypt y by the extended encryption and get the result $\boldsymbol{Y_i} = (Y_{i,1}, \ldots, Y_{i,\lambda}) = XE(y_i)$, where $Y_{i,j} = E(z^{1-y_i})$ or $E(0)$ randomly.
   - embed $[x_i = y_i] = [\neg(x_i \bigoplus y_i)]$ into extended encryption $\boldsymbol{E_i}$ for $i = 1, \ldots, n$. $\boldsymbol{E_i} = (E_{i,1}, \ldots, E_{i,\lambda}) = XE(\neg(x_i \bigoplus y_i))$, where $E_{i,j} = X_j \cdot z^{y_i} \bmod N$ or $1 \in QR_N$ randomly.
   - compute extended encryptions $\boldsymbol{P_i} = \boldsymbol{P_{i+1}} \cdot \boldsymbol{E_{i+1}} \bmod N = XE(p_i)$, where $\boldsymbol{P_n} = (1, \ldots, 1)$ and $p_i = \bigwedge_{j=i+1}^{n}[x_j = y_j]$ for $i = n-1, \ldots, 1$.
   - embed $\neg x_i$ into extended encryption $\bar{\boldsymbol{X}}_i$ for $i = 1, \ldots, n$. $\bar{\boldsymbol{X}}_i = (\bar{X}_{i,1}, \ldots, \bar{X}_{i,\lambda}) = XE(\neg x_i)$, where $\bar{X}_{i,j} = X_i$ or $1 \in QR_N$ randomly.
   - compute terms $t_i = y_i \wedge \bar{x}_i \bigwedge_{j=i+1}^{n}[x_j = y_j]$ in the extended encryption form: For $i = 1, \ldots, n$, $\boldsymbol{T_i} = \boldsymbol{Y_i} \cdot \bar{\boldsymbol{X}}_i \cdot \boldsymbol{P_i} \bmod N = XE(t_i)$.
   - randomly permute $\boldsymbol{T_1}, \ldots, \boldsymbol{T_n}$ and send to Alice
3. Alice receives n sequences of λ elements from Bob and does the following:
   - If there exists a sequence of λ quadratic residues then output $y > x$, else output $y \leq x$.

For computation, the protocol needs n GM-encryptions and n modified GM-decryptions in the client side (Alice in our protocol)[1]. The server side (Bob in our protocol) needs n modified GM-encryptions and $4n\lambda$ modular multiplications only.

The exchanged messages are n GM-ciphertexts and n modified GM-ciphertexts. Overall, the size is $(1 + \lambda)n \log N$ $(= n \log N + n\lambda \log N)$ bits.

4.1   Blake and Kolesnikov's GT Protocol

The GT protocol in [BK04] is based on the Paillier's encryption scheme. The additive homomorphic property is essential to their construction. Their protocol can be summarized as follows: Let $Enc(m)$ be the encryption of the message m.

1. Alice with private input $x = x_n x_{n-1} \cdots x_1$ does the following:
   (a) runs key generation phase
   (b) encrypts x bit-wise and sends $pk, Enc(x_n), \ldots, Enc(x_1)$ to Bob.
2. Bob with private input $y = y_n y_{n-1} \cdots y_1$ does the following for each $i = 1, \ldots, n$:
   (a) computes $Enc(d_i) = Enc(x_i - y_i)$
   (b) computes $Enc(f_i) = Enc(x_i - 2x_i y_i + y_i)$
   (c) computes $Enc(\gamma_i) = Enc(2\gamma_{i-1} + f_i)$ where $\gamma_0 = 0$

---

[1] In [Fis01], the computation cost of the client side is neglected.

(d) computes $Enc(\delta_i) = Enc(d_i + r_i(\gamma_i - 1))$ where $r_i \in_R Z_N$

(e) randomly permutates $Enc(\delta_i)$ and sends to Alice

3. Alice obtains $Enc(\delta_i)$ from Bob, then decrypts. If there exists a value $v \in \{+1, -1\}$ and output v.

In the protocol, if $x > y$, the output value $v = +1$; if $x < y$, $v = -1$.

For computation, the receiver (Alice) needs n encryptions and n decryptions. The sender (Bob) needs n modular multiplications in the $2a$ step, n modular multiplications and n inversions in the $2b$ step, $2n$ modular multiplications in the $2c$ step, and $(2 + \log N)n$ modular multiplications in the $2d$ step. Each inversion takes 1 modular multiplications. Overall, the protocol needs $4n$ modular exponentiations $(\mathrm{mod}\, N^2)$ and $7n$ modular multiplication $(\mathrm{mod}\, N^2)$

The communication cost is n ciphertexts for the receiver and n ciphertexts for the sender. The overall communication cost is $4n \log N$ bits

5 Comparison

Now, we compare our GT protocol with those in [Fis01,BK04] in computation and communication cost. We summarize the cost of operations for the protocols:

- Each GM-encryption needs 2 modular multiplications $(\mathrm{mod}\, N)$.
- Each modified GM-encryption needs 2λ modular multiplication $(\mathrm{mod}\, N)$ since each encryption contains λ GM-encryptions.
- Each modified GM-decryption needs λ modular multiplications $(\mathrm{mod}\, N)$, since there λ elements in a modified GM-ciphertext and quadratic residuosity can be checked in equivalent one modular mulltiplication.
- Each Paillier's encryption requires $2 \log N$ modular multiplications $(\mathrm{mod}\, N^2)$. In [BK04], they encrypt 0 or 1 only, the encryption for $m \in \{0,1\}$ needs $\log N$ modular multiplications $(\mathrm{mod}\, N^2)$.
- Each Paillier's decryption requires $2 \log N$ modular multiplications $(\mathrm{mod}\, N^2)$.
- Each Paillier's inversion requires one modular multiplications $(\mathrm{mod}\, N^2)$, where the inversion is done by the extended Euclidean algorithm.
- For Paillier's encryption, each modular multiplication $(\mathrm{mod}\, N^2)$ needs 4 modular multiplication $(\mathrm{mod}\, N)$.

Based on the above discussion, we summarize the comparison in Table 1. In the table, the modular multiplication for the protocols in [Fis01,BK04] is $\mathrm{mod}\, N$ and ours is $\mathrm{mod}\, p$.

6 Remarks

Our construction is secure in the semi-honest setting. In the malicious setting, each round requires additional messages to assure legality of the sent messages. The techniques are mostly based on non-interactive zero-knowledge proof of knowledge.

Table 1. Comparison in computation cost and communication cost.

	computation of Alice	computation of Bob	total computation	communication
Ours	$3n\log p$	$2n\log p + 4n - 6$	$5n\log p + 4n - 6$	$6n\log p$
Ours with hash	$3n\log p$	$2n\log p + 2n$	$5n\log p + 2n$	$4n\log p$
[Fis01]	$\lambda n + 2n$	$6n\lambda$	$7n\lambda + 2n$	$(1 + \lambda)n\log N$
[BK04]	$12n\log N$	$4n\log N + 28n$	$16n\log N + 28n$	$4n\log N$

*computation cost is measured in the number of modular multiplication
*communication cost is measured in bits
*Alice is called "receiver" in [BK04] and "client" in [Fis01].
*λ is set to $40 \sim 50$ in [Fis01]

References

[BK04]   Ian F. Blake and Vladimir Kolesnikov. Strong conditional oblivious transfer
            and computing on intervals. In *Proceedings of Advances in Cryptology -
            ASIACRYPT '04*, volume 3329 of *LNCS*, pages 515–529. Springer-Verlag,
            2004.

[Cac99]   Christian Cachin. Efficient private bidding and auctions with an oblivious
            third party. In *Proceedings of the 6th ACM conference on Computer and
            communications security - CCS '99*, pages 120–127. ACM Press, 1999.

[Fis01]   Marc Fischlin. A cost-effective pay-per-multiplication comparison method
            for millionaires. In *Proceedings of the 2001 Conference on Topics in Cryp-
            tology: The Cryptographer's Track at RSA*, volume 2020 of *LNCS*, pages
            457–472. Springer-Verlag, 2001.

[FNP04]   Michael J. Freedman, Kobbi Nissim, and Benny Pinkas. Efficient private
            matching and set intersection. In *Proceedings of Advances in Cryptology
            - EUROCRYPT '04*, volume 3027 of *LNCS*, pages 1–19. Springer-Verlag,
            2004.

[GMW87]   O. Goldreich, S. Micali, and A. Wigderson. How to play and mental game.
            In *Proceedings of the 16th Annual ACM Symposium on the Theory of Com-
            puting (STOC '87)*, pages 218–229. ACM, 1987.

[IG03]   Ioannis Ioannidis and Ananth Grama. An efficient protocol for yao's mil-
            lionaires' problem. In *Proceedings of the 36th Hawaii Internatinal Confer-
            ence on System Sciences 2003*, 2003.

[ST04]   Berry Schoenmakers and Pim Tuyls. Pratical two-party computation based
            on the conditional gate. In *Proceedings of Advances in Cryptology - ASI-
            ACRYPT '04*, volume 3329 of *LNCS*, pages 119–136. Springer-Verlag, 2004.

[Yao82]   A. C. Yao. Protocols for secure computations. In *Proceedings of 23th Annual
            Symposium on Foundations of Computer Science (FOCS '82)*, pages 160–
            164. IEEE, 1982.

[Yao86]   A. C. Yao. How to generate and exchange secrets. In *Proceedings of
            27th Annual Symposium on Foundations of Computer Science (FOCS '86)*,
            pages 162–167. IEEE, 1986.

Non-interactive Zero-Knowledge Arguments for Voting

Jens Groth*

Dept. of Computer Science, UCLA, USA
jg@cs.ucla.edu

Abstract. In voting based on homomorphic threshold encryption, the voter encrypts his vote and sends it in to the authorities that tally the votes. If voters can send in arbitrary plaintexts then they can cheat. It is therefore important that they attach an argument of knowledge of the plaintext being a correctly formed vote. Typically, these arguments are honest verifier zero-knowledge arguments that are made non-interactive using the Fiat-Shamir heuristic. Security is argued in the random oracle model.

The simplest case is where each voter has a single vote to cast. Practical solutions have already been suggested for the single vote case. However, as we shall see homomorphic threshold encryption can be used for a variety of elections, in particular there are many cases where voters can cast multiple votes at once. In these cases, it remains important to bring down the cost of the NIZK argument.

We improve on state of the art in the case of limited votes, where each voter can vote a small number of times. We also improve on the state of the art in shareholder elections, where each voter may have a large number of votes to spend. Moreover, we improve on the state of the art in Borda voting. Finally, we suggest a NIZK argument for correctness of an approval vote. To the best of our knowledge, approval voting has not been considered before in the cryptographic literature.

1 Introduction

Voting based on homomorphic encryption. A popular paradigm for constructing e-voting protocols is based on homomorphic threshold encryption. The homomorphic property is $E(m_1 + m_2; r_1 + r_2) = E(m_1; r_1)E(m_2; r_2)$. The authorities publish a public key and voters send in encrypted votes. Digital signatures or other means of authentication ensure that only eligible voters vote.

As an example consider an election where voters encode yes-votes as 1 and no-votes as 0. Holding encrypted votes $E(v_1), \ldots, E(v_m)$ the authorities can use the homomorphic property of the cryptosystem to compute $E(\sum_{i=1}^{m} v_i)$. They jointly decrypt this ciphertext to get out the number of yes-votes, $\sum_{i=1}^{m} v_i$. It is important that they have to cooperate to decrypt, if any single authority held the decryption key then the voters' privacy might be at risk.

More advanced encoding methods allow elections where voters have a wide range of options. In the paper, we treat the following possibilities:

---

* Part of the work done while at Cryptomathic, Denmark and BRICS, Dept. of Computer Science, University of Aarhus, Denmark.

J. Ioannidis, A. Keromytis, and M.Yung (Eds.): ACNS 2005, LNCS 3531, pp. 467–482, 2005.

- Limited vote: N out of L candidates.
- Approval vote: Any number out of L candidates.
- Divisible vote: A huge number of votes distributed among the candidates.
- Borda vote: A preference vote where the best candidate receives L votes, the second best $L - 1$ votes, etc.

The advantage of voting based on homomorphic encryption is that it combines efficiency with a reasonable amount of flexibility. In particular, in comparison with other voting paradigms such as mix-nets, it seems like a superior choice for divisible votes that occur quite frequently in shareholder elections.

Zero-knowledge arguments. We have to ensure that voters do not cheat. Consider for instance in the previous example a voter that sends in $E(-100)$. Effectively this voter is taking 100 yes-votes out of the ballot box. To avoid such attacks we let each voter submit a zero-knowledge argument of correctness of his vote.

In practice, we want to minimize interaction between voters and authorities when casting votes. The common approach is therefore to find an efficient honest verifier zero-knowledge argument for correctness of the vote and make it non-interactive using the Fiat-Shamir heuristic. This yields efficient non-interactive zero-knowledge (NIZK) arguments. Security is proved in the random oracle model[1].

Related work. The idea of using homomorphic encryption to construct voting protocols was suggested by Cohen and Fischer [CF85] and further developed in [BY86,Ben87]. Cramer, Gennaro and Schoenmakers [CGS97] suggested a reasonable efficient yes/no-voting scheme based on ElGamal encryption. Unfortunately, these schemes cannot handle large elections with many candidates.

Concurrently Baudron et al. [BFP+01] and Damgård and Jurik [DJ01][2] suggest voting schemes based on Paillier encryption [Pai99]. Their zero-knowledge arguments involve many encryptions and are therefore close to practical but still a little expensive.

Lipmaa, Asokan and Niemi [LAN02] propose the first practical zero-knowledge argument based on homomorphic integer commitments. Using integer commitments means that they can take advantage of integer properties such as unique prime factorization and get a practical zero-knowledge argument. Damgård, Groth and Salomonsen [DGS03] improve on this scheme and also propose a zero-knowledge argument for a limited vote.

Ishida, Matsuo and Ogata [IMO03] consider the case of shareholder elections and suggest a zero-knowledge argument for correctness of a divisible vote.

Wang and Leung [WfL04] investigate the case of Borda voting. They wish to construct a protocol that only reveals the winner, but not how many votes each candidate got. At a considerable efficiency cost, they proceed to construct such a multi-party computation protocol. Unlike them, we do not try to hide the number of votes candidates receive. Because of this difference, they are satisfied with letting each voter send a ciphertext for each candidate containing the number of votes on that candidate. Nonetheless, while not the focus of their paper they do need a NIZK argument for correctness

---

[1] See Section 2 for more details.

[2] Damgård, Jurik and Nielsen [DJN03] correct some flaws in this voting scheme.

of a Borda vote. They give a sketch of a NIZK argument for correctness of a Borda vote, however, it turns out the NIZK argument is not sound as it stands [Wan05]. The NIZK argument for correctness of a Borda vote we suggest in the paper can be adapted to their setting and solve their problem in a simple way.

We do not know of any work addressing approval voting in connection with homomorphic threshold encryption based voting schemes.

Our contributions. We observe that approval voting and Borda voting can be implemented efficiently using homomorphic threshold voting and offer corresponding NIZK arguments. We improve the NIZK argument for a limited vote of [DGS03] by simplifying the protocol. We suggest a NIZK argument for a divisible vote that is a factor $\log N$ more efficient, where N is the number of votes the shareholder can cast.

Table 1. Comparison of voting arguments.

Vote	Argument	Verification	Prior art	Argument	Verification
Limited	1	1	[DGS03]	1	1
	$6N + 4$	$3N + 3$		$8N + 2$	$7N + 2$
Approval	1	1	No prior work		
	$2L + 4$	$L + 3$			
Divisible	1	1	[IMO03]	$(5/2)L \log N$	$2L \log N$
	$10L + 4$	$5L + 2$			
Borda	1	1	[WfL04]	Not sound	
known shuffle [Gro03]	$4L + 2$	$2L + 3$			

For all arguments, the top line contains the number of encryptions, the bottom line the number of exponentiations to make commitments. For all verifications, the top line contains the number of encryptions and the number of exponentiations of ciphertexts (always identical numbers), the bottom line the number of exponentiations to verify the commitments.

In Table 1, we list computational complexities for each NIZK argument. Since a ciphertext containing a vote must remain secure also some time into the future, we often need a long security parameter for the cryptosystem. On the other hand, the NIZK arguments are usually verified by interested parties right after the election, and since they can be made statistical zero-knowledge we can use a much shorter security parameter for the commitment scheme. For the purpose of creating this table, we have assumed that to commit to n elements, one uses $n + 1$ exponentiations. In general, the expensive operations are those that involve ciphertexts.

One should be careful when using this table. For instance, the approval vote argument uses short exponents, while the limited vote argument may use longer exponents. The commitment exponentiations may therefore be cheaper for the approval vote argument in a setting with a similar number of voters and candidates. In the case of limited voting one should note that our NIZK argument unlike the [DGS03] NIZK argument is well suited for the use of multi-exponentiation techniques, so our gain is larger than what is indicated by Table 1. Finally, the verification process for most protocols may be sped up using batch verification techniques when verifying many votes at the same time.

Efficient range proof. Proving that a committed number x lies in some interval $[a, b]$ is useful in many protocols. Typically, we do that by proving that both $x - a$ and $b - x$ are non-negative. We can use either Boudot's method [Bou02] or prove that the number can be written as the sum of four squares [Lip03]. The two methods have comparable efficiency. In Section 5 we suggest a little trick to speed up the latter argument. Namely, to prove that y is non-negative we prove that $4y + 1$ is the sum of three squares. We highlight the trick here, since it may have independent interest.

2   Preliminaries

2.1   Voting Based on Homomorphic Encryption

Election parameters M, L, N. Throughout the paper, we assume that we have a group of voters that can choose between L candidates, which may include choices such as a blank vote or an invalid vote. A drawback of this type of election scheme is that the number of candidates is fixed; we do not allow write-in votes. We denote by M a strict upper bound on the number of votes any candidate can receive. In particular, if each voter has one vote then M is a strict upper bound on the number of voters. As will become apparent later, there is much to gain by selecting $M = p^2$, where p is a prime. A third parameter characterizing the elections is the number of votes the voter can cast, denoted by N.

Encoding votes. In the introduction, we sketched how to base voting protocols on homomorphic encryption. Let us offer some more details. The basic ingredient is a homomorphic threshold public-key cryptosystem. We will generate a public key for this cryptosystem, and the secret key is threshold secret shared amongst the authorities.

We assume that the message space is on the form $\mathbb{Z}_n$. We require that n does not have prime factors smaller than 2^{ℓ_e}, where ℓ_e is the length of the output of a suitable hash-function, and that $M^L \leq n$. We represent candidates with numbers $0, \ldots, L - 1$ and encode a vote on candidate i as M^i [3] Summing many such encodings gives us an M-addic representation of the result, $\sum_{i=0}^{L-1} v_i M^i$, where v_i is the number of votes on candidate i.

Representing votes this way, it is straightforward to encrypt a vote on candidate i as $E(M^i)$. Having received many such encrypted votes we may by the homomorphic property of the cryptosystem multiply all the ciphertexts and get a new ciphertext $C = E(\sum_{i=0}^{L-1} v_i M^i)$. We threshold decrypt this ciphertext and now it is straightforward to extract the result from the plaintext.

We shall see in the following sections that in a somewhat similar way it is possible to encode limited votes, approval votes, divisible votes and Borda votes, and therefore such types of elections can also be handled using this approach.

As mentioned in the introduction we need NIZK arguments for correctness of votes to avoid cheating and tampering with the result. In these NIZK arguments, we make use of homomorphic integer commitments. In the security proof of these NIZK arguments, we make use of a property of the integer commitment scheme and of the homomorphic

---

[3] As an alternative Lipmaa [Lip03] has suggested to encode votes as Lucas numbers.

cryptosystem known as root extraction. We also make use of the random oracle model. We will explain these concepts in the following.

2.2 Setup and Parameters

Throughout the paper, we make use of a semantically secure homomorphic threshold cryptosystem. We assume that the message space is $\mathbb{Z}_n$ for a suitable $n < M^L$ and the randomizer space is $\mathbb{Z}$. The latter assumption is purely out of notational convenience, there would be no problem in using a cryptosystem where the randomness is some finite group, for instance to use threshold Paillier encryption.

We also make use of a homomorphic integer commitment scheme. We always use randomizers from $\mathbb{Z}$. Again, there would be no problem to use other randomizer spaces but we do not yet know any such commitment scheme. The keys for both the cryptosystem and the commitment scheme are public and known to all parties.

We define the following parameters: $\ell_V = 2\lceil L(\log M)/2 \rceil$ is the maximal bit-length of a vote. We assume that the distribution of the randomizer space of the cryptosystem is to pick a random ℓ_R-bit randomizer. Similarly for integer commitments we pick a random ℓ_r-bit number as randomizer. Public keys are chosen with suitable security parameters. In large elections with many candidates, we may be forced to choose a large security parameter to accommodate this size of votes.

We need a couple of extra security parameters. We use a cryptographic hash-function that outputs an ℓ_e-bit number e. For instance, using SHA-256 we have $\ell_e = 256$. Furthermore, we need a security parameter ℓ_s, such that for any value a we have that $a + r_a$ and r_a are indistinguishable, where r_a is a random $|a| + \ell_s$-bit number. We suggest $\ell_s = 80$, this being large enough to ignore the off chance that $|a + r| > |a| + \ell_s$.

2.3 Homomorphic Integer Commitment and Homomorphic Cryptosystem

Integer commitment. We know only few homomorphic integer commitment schemes [FO97,DF02,Gro05], and they are all very similar in structure. As an example, we offer the following variant. We choose a modulus n as a product of two safe primes and random generators $g_1, \ldots, g_k, h$ of QR_n. To commit to integers $m_1, \ldots, m_k$ using randomness $r = (r_1, r_2) \in \{-1, 1\} \times \mathbb{Z}$ we compute $c = \text{com}(m_1, \ldots, m_k; (r_1, r_2)) = r_1 g_1^{m_1} \cdots g_k^{m_k} h^{r_2} \bmod n$. To open the commitment we reveal $(m_1, \ldots, m_k, r)$. A typical choice is $r_1 = 1, r_2 \leftarrow \{0, 1\}^{\ell_r}$, where $\ell_r = |n| + \ell_s$, which makes the commitment statistically hiding.

Root extraction property. When proving soundness and knowledge in our protocols we need the following root extraction property. If an adversary comes up with a commitment c, an opening $m_1, \ldots, m_k, r$ and $e \neq 0$, so $c^e = \text{com}(m_1, \ldots, m_k; r)$, then we must have $e|m_1, \ldots, e|m_k$ and be able to compute an opening $\mu_1, \ldots, \mu_k, \rho$ so $c = \text{com}(\mu_1, \ldots, \mu_k; \rho)$, where $\mu_i = m_i/e$.

Root extraction property of homomorphic cryptosystem. In the voting protocol, we use a semantically secure homomorphic threshold cryptosystem. Like the integer commitment scheme, it must have a root extraction property. If we create a ciphertext C

and $e \neq 0$ so $|e| < \ell_e$ and $C^e = E(M; R)$, then it must be possible to find μ, ρ so $M = e\mu, R = e\rho$ and $C = E(\mu; \rho)$.

ElGamal encryption [ElG84], Paillier encryption [Pai99] and several other homomorphic cryptosystems are semantically secure, have the root extraction property and admit threshold decryption.

2.4   NIZK Arguments and the Random Oracle Model

Consider a typical 3-move honest verifier zero-knowledge argument. The prover has some statement x that he wants to prove, and he knows a witness w. He sends an initial message a, receives a random challenge e and responds with an answer z. Given (x, a, e, z) the verifier can now choose whether to accept the argument or not.

Using Fiat-Shamir heuristic we let the prover compute the challenge e as a hash-function of x, a. I.e., the prover computes an argument (a, e, z), where $e = \text{hash}(x, a)$ [4]. This way we can make the argument non-interactive. Of course, the same methodology can be applied to arguments that use more than 3 moves.

As a heuristic argument of security of such protocols Bellare and Rogaway [BR93] suggest the random oracle model. The hash-function is modeled as a random function that pairs inputs (x, a) with a random output e. Furthermore, to argue zero-knowledge they allow the random oracle to be programmed. The simulator can choose inputs (x, a) and corresponding outputs e and the random oracle will on such an input return the corresponding output.

As a simple example, consider proving knowledge of the plaintext of a ciphertext C. We will present a well-known argument for this statement. Using the notation of [CS97] we write

$$\text{SPK}[(\mu, \rho) : C = E(\mu; \rho)].$$

We use Greek letters for the unknown variables we are proving something about and provide the statement that we are proving. This way we can quickly describe the goal of a NIZK argument without specifying the actual protocol. The following argument of plaintext knowledge is used as a subprotocol in most of our protocols.

Theorem 1. *In the random oracle model, the protocol in Figure 1 is a NIZK argument of plaintext knowledge.*

Proof. In the above argument, it is easy to see that we have completeness.

To argue zero-knowledge we pick e at random. We choose $\boxed{m} \leftarrow \{0,1\}^{|m|+\ell_e+\ell_s}$, $\boxed{R} \leftarrow \{0,1\}^{\ell_R+\ell_e+\ell_s}$. We set $C_R = E(\boxed{m}; \boxed{R})C^{-e}$. Finally, we program the random oracle to output e on input (C, C_R). We leave it to the reader to see that this is indeed a good simulation of an argument.

To argue knowledge we consider an adversary that has made a query (C, C_R) to the random oracle. If it is in a state where it has noticeable probability of using it in a valid argument, then we can upon seeing such an argument rewind it and feed it

---

[4] Sometimes some auxiliary information will be included in the hash-function. For instance, we might include the identity of the prover to avoid duplication of the proof. So we would write $e = \text{hash}(x, a, aux)$.

NIZK Argument for Plaintext Knowledge

Common input: Ciphertext C and public keys.
Prover's input: Message m and randomizer R so $C = E(m; R)$.

Argument: Choose $R_m \leftarrow \{0,1\}^{|m|+\ell_e+\ell_s}$ and $R_R \leftarrow \{0,1\}^{\ell_R+\ell_e+\ell_s}$. Set
$C_R = E(R_m; R_R)$.
Compute the challenge $e = \text{hash}(C, C_R)$.
Set $\boxed{m} = em + R_m$, $\boxed{R} = eR + R_R$.
The argument is $(C_R, \boxed{m}, \boxed{R})$.
Verification: Compute e as above. Verify $C^e C_R = E(\boxed{m}; \boxed{R})$.

Fig. 1. Plaintext Knowledge Argument.

with different random answers to the query. In expected polynomial time, we will get another acceptable argument. We now have two acceptable arguments $C_R, e, \boxed{m}, \boxed{R}$ and $C_R, e', \boxed{m}', \boxed{R}'$. With overwhelming probability, we have $e \neq e'$. From the verifying equations we have $C^e C_R = E(\boxed{m}; \boxed{R})$ and $C^{e'} C_R = E(\boxed{m}'; \boxed{R}')$. This means $C^{e-e'} = E(\boxed{m} - \boxed{m}'; \boxed{R} - \boxed{R}')$. From the root extraction property we can extract $\mu = (\boxed{m} - \boxed{m}')/(e - e')$ and ρ so $C = E(\mu; \rho)$. $\qquad\square$

Remark 1. We routinely use the notation $\boxed{a} = ea + r_a$ throughout the paper. As a reminder one can think of it as putting a in a box that hides a. As we shall see, the random factor e allows us to make computations with the hidden variable a. For instance, if an equation $\boxed{a}\boxed{b} = e\boxed{c}$ holds with non-negligible probability over e, then the secret variables a, b, c satisfy $c = ab$ with overwhelming probability. The box-notation is intended to show on one hand that the variable is hidden, one the other hand indicate that we can perform standard algebraic operations on the hidden variables and under the hood the expected results come out. We hope this notation can serve as a helping guide in complex zero-knowledge arguments using many hidden variables.

3   Limited Vote

In some elections, voters can vote multiple times, say, N times. It may be a requirement that they use all their votes on different candidates, or alternatively they may be permitted to spend several votes on the same candidates. We will present a protocol for the former case; it is easy to modify the protocol into one that admits multiple votes on the same candidate.

The voter encodes his vote as $V = \sum_{j=1}^{N} M^{i_j}$, where $0 \leq i_1 < \cdots < i_N < L$. He then encrypts the vote and has to form a NIZK argument that the plaintext is on the right form. In other words, we wish to make the following argument of knowledge

$$\text{SPK}[(v, \rho, \iota_1, \cdots, \iota_N) : C = E(v; \rho) \text{ and } v = \sum_{j=1}^{N} M^{\iota_j} \text{ and } 0 \leq \iota_1 < \cdots < \iota_N < L].$$

To make this argument of knowledge we actually use

$$\mathrm{SPK}[(v, \rho, \alpha_1, \ldots, \alpha_N, \beta_1, \ldots, \beta_N) :$$

$$C = E(v; \rho) \text{ and } v = \sum_{j=1}^{N} \alpha_j^2 \text{ and } \bigwedge_{j=1}^{N} \alpha_{j+1} = p\alpha_j\beta_j],$$

where p is a prime so $M = p^2$ and $\alpha_{N+1} = p^L$.

To see that the two arguments of knowledge are equivalent notice that $\bigwedge_{j=1}^{N} \alpha_{j+1} = p\alpha_j\beta_j$ implies $p\alpha_N|p^L, \ldots, p\alpha_1|\alpha_2$. I.e., we can write $\alpha_N = \pm p^{\iota_N}, \cdots, \alpha_1 = \pm p^{\iota_1}$, for some $0 \le \iota_1 < \cdots < \iota_N < L$. The second equation gives us

$$v = \sum_{j=1}^{N} \alpha_j^2 = \sum_{j=1}^{N} (\pm p^{\iota_j})^2 = \sum_{j=1}^{N} M^{\iota_j}.$$

The argument of knowledge is presented in Figure 2. In the protocol we argue knowledge of $\alpha_j, \rho_{a_j}, \beta_j, \rho_{b_j}, \Delta_j, \rho_{\Delta_j}$ so $\boxed{a_j} = e\alpha_j + \rho_{a_j}, \boxed{b_j} = e\beta_j + \rho_{b_j}, \boxed{\Delta_j} = e\Delta_j + \rho_{\Delta_j}$. We check that $\boxed{\Delta_j} = p\boxed{a_j}\boxed{b_j} - e\boxed{a_{j+1}}$, i.e.,

$$e\Delta_j + \rho_{\Delta_j} = e^2(p\alpha_j\beta_j - \alpha_{j+1}) + e(p\alpha_j\rho_{b_j} + p\beta_j\rho_{a_j} - \rho_{a_{j+1}}) + p\rho_{a_j}\rho_{b_j}.$$

The idea is that with overwhelming probability over e this equation can only hold if $p\alpha_j\beta_j - \alpha_{j+1} = 0$. Combine all these equalities to get $\bigwedge_{j=1}^{N} \alpha_{j+1} = p\alpha_j\beta_j$.

Included in the argument is an argument of plaintext knowledge of v, ρ_V so $\boxed{V} = ev + \rho_V$, as well as Δ, ρ_Δ so $\boxed{\Delta} = e\Delta + \rho_\Delta$. We check that $\boxed{\Delta} = \sum_{j=1}^{N} \boxed{a_j}^2 - e\boxed{V}$, giving us $e\Delta + \rho_\Delta = e^2(\sum_{j=1}^{N} \alpha_j^2 - v) + e(2\sum_{j=1}^{N} \alpha_j\rho_{a_j} - \rho_V) + \sum_{j=1}^{N} \rho_{a_j}^2$. With overwhelming probability over e this tells us that $v = \sum_{j=1}^{N} \alpha_j^2$. Finally, in the process we also argue knowledge of ρ so $C = E(v; \rho)$ in a similar way to the argument of plaintext knowledge in Section 2.4.

Theorem 2. *In the random oracle model, the protocol in Figure 2 is a NIZK argument of knowledge for C encrypting a correctly formed limited vote. If the commitment scheme is statistically hiding then the argument is statistical zero-knowledge.*

Proof. It is straightforward to verify that the protocol is complete. It remains to argue zero-knowledge and soundness and knowledge.

Zero-knowledge. To simulate an argument we pick a challenge $e \leftarrow \{0,1\}^{\ell_e}$ at random. Given the challenge e, we make a simulation like this. We pick $\boxed{V} \leftarrow \{0,1\}^{\ell_V + \ell_e + \ell_s}$ and $\boxed{R} \leftarrow \{0,1\}^{\ell_R + \ell_e + \ell_s}$. We pick $\boxed{a_1}, \boxed{b_1}, \ldots, \boxed{a_N}, \boxed{b_N} \leftarrow \{0,1\}^{\ell_V/2 + \ell_e + \ell_s}$ and $\boxed{r} \leftarrow \{0,1\}^{\ell_r + \ell_e + \ell_s}$. We set $\boxed{\Delta_j} = p\boxed{a_j}\boxed{b_j} - e\boxed{a_{j+1}}$, using $\boxed{a_{N+1}} = ep^L$. We set $\boxed{\Delta} = \sum_{j=1}^{N} \boxed{a_j}^2 - e\boxed{V}$. We set $C_R = E(\boxed{V}; \boxed{R})C^{-e}$. We set $c \leftarrow \mathrm{com}(0, \ldots, 0)$ and $c_r = \mathrm{com}(\boxed{a_1}, \boxed{b_1}, \boxed{\Delta_1}, \ldots, \boxed{a_N}, \boxed{b_N}, \boxed{\Delta_N}, \boxed{\Delta}; \boxed{r})c^{-e}$. Finally, we program the random oracle to return e when queried on (C, C_R, c, c_r).

Zero-Knowledge Argument for Correctness of a Limited Vote

Common input: Ciphertext C and public keys.
Prover's input: $0 \leq i_1 < \cdots < i_N < L$ and $R \in \{0,1\}^{\ell_R}$ such that
$C = E(\sum_{j=1}^{N} M^{i_j}; R)$.

Let $\alpha_{N+1} = p^L$. We prove correctness of the vote by producing

$$\mathrm{SPK}[(v, \rho, \alpha_1, \ldots, \alpha_N, \beta_1, \ldots, \beta_N) :$$

$$C = E(v; \rho) \text{ and } v = \sum_{j=1}^{N} \alpha_j^2 \text{ and } \bigwedge_{j=1}^{N} \alpha_{j+1} = p\alpha_j \beta_j].$$

Argument: Let $V = \sum_{j=1}^{N} M^{i_j}$, choose $R_V \leftarrow \{0,1\}^{\ell_V + \ell_e + \ell_s}$, $R_R \leftarrow \{0,1\}^{\ell_R + \ell_e + \ell_s}$ and set $C_R = E(R_V; R_R)$.
Let $a_j = p^{i_j}, b_j = p^{i_{j+1}-i_j-1}$, where $i_{N+1} = L$. Let $r_{a_{N+1}} = 0$ and choose $r_{a_1}, \ldots, r_{a_N}, r_{b_1}, \ldots, r_{b_N} \leftarrow \{0,1\}^{\ell_V/2 + \ell_e + \ell_s}$. Let $\Delta_j = pa_i r_{b_j} + pb_j r_{a_j} - r_{a_{j+1}}$ and $\Delta = 2\sum_{j=1}^{N} a_j r_{a_j} - R_V$. Set $c = \mathrm{com}(a_1, b_1, \Delta_1, \ldots, a_N, b_N, \Delta_N, \Delta; r)$. Set $c_r = \mathrm{com}(r_{a_1}, r_{b_1}, pr_{a_1} r_{b_1}, \ldots, r_{a_N}, r_{b_N}, pr_{a_N} r_{b_N}, \sum_{j=1}^{N} r_{a_j}^2; r_r)$.

Compute the challenge as $e \leftarrow \mathrm{hash}(C, C_R, c, c_r)$.

Set $\boxed{V} = eV + R_V = e\sum_{j=1}^{N} M^{i_j} + R_V$ and $\boxed{R} = eR + R_R$.
Set $\boxed{a_j} = ea_j + r_{a_j} = ep^{i_j} + r_{a_j}$, $\boxed{b_j} = eb_j + r_{b_j} = ep^{i_{j+1}-i_j-1} + r_{b_j}$ and $\boxed{r} = er + r_r$,

The argument is $(C_R, c, c_r, \boxed{V}, \boxed{R}, \boxed{a_1}, \boxed{b_1}, \ldots, \boxed{a_N}, \boxed{b_N}, \boxed{r})$.
Verification: Compute e as above. Let $\boxed{a_{N+1}} = ep^L$ and set
$\boxed{\Delta_j} = p\boxed{a_j}\boxed{b_j} - e\boxed{a_{j+1}}$ and $\boxed{\Delta} = \sum_{j=1}^{N}\boxed{a_j}^2 - e\boxed{V}$.
Verify that $C^e C_R = E(\boxed{V}; \boxed{R})$ and
$c^e c_r = \mathrm{com}(\boxed{a_1}, \boxed{b_1}, \boxed{\Delta_1}, \ldots, \boxed{a_N}, \boxed{b_N}, \boxed{\Delta}; \boxed{r})$.

Fig. 2. Limited Vote Argument.

To argue that the simulated argument is indistinguishable from a real argument, consider the following hybrid argument. Let $i_1, \ldots, i_N$ be the chosen candidates and define $i_{N+1} = L, a_j = p^{i_j}, b_j = p^{i_{j+1}-i_j-1}$. We proceed as in the simulation except when computing c. We set $R_V = \boxed{V} - e\sum_{j=1}^{N} M^{i_j}, r_{a_j} = \boxed{a_j} - ea_j, r_{b_j} = \boxed{b_j} - eb_j$. We let $a_{N+1} = p^L$ and $\Delta_j = pa_j r_{b_j} + pb_j r_{a_j} - a_{j+1}$. Compute $c \leftarrow \mathrm{com}(a_1, b_1, \Delta_1, \ldots, a_N, b_N, \Delta_N, 2\sum_{j=1}^{N} a_j r_{a_j} - R_V)$. The rest of the hybrid argument is carried out as in the simulation.

The hybrid argument is statistically indistinguishable from a real argument, all that is changed is the order in which we choose the elements. On the other hand, the only difference from a simulated argument is in the computation of the commitment c. The commitment scheme's hiding property shows that the hybrid argument is indistinguishable from a simulated argument of knowledge. Moreover, if the commitment scheme is statistically hiding then the hybrid argument is statistically indistinguishable from the simulated argument of knowledge.

Soundness and knowledge. Suppose an adversary produces a valid argument for ciphertext C containing a valid limited vote. We wish to extract a witness $(v, \rho, \iota_1, \ldots, \iota_N)$. To do so we rewind the adversary to the point where it queries the random oracle with C, C_R, c, c_r. We then give it random challenges until we get a new acceptable argument. This takes expected polynomial time. Let us call the two acceptable arguments $(C_R, c, c_r, e, \boxed{V}, \boxed{R}, \boxed{a_1}, \boxed{b_1}, \ldots, \boxed{a_N}, \boxed{b_N}, \boxed{r})$ and $(C_R, c, c_r, e', \boxed{V}', \boxed{R}',$ $\boxed{a_1}', \boxed{b_1}', \ldots, \boxed{a_N}', \boxed{b_N}', \boxed{r}')$. We compute the corresponding $\boxed{\Delta_1}, \ldots, \boxed{\Delta_N}$, $\boxed{\Delta}$ and $\boxed{\Delta_1}', \ldots, \boxed{\Delta_N}', \boxed{\Delta}'$ as in the verification.

Since the arguments are acceptable we have $C^e C_R = E(\boxed{V}; \boxed{R})$ and $C^{e'} C_R = E(\boxed{V}'; \boxed{R}')$. This gives us $C^{e-e'} = E(\boxed{V} - \boxed{V}'; \boxed{R} - \boxed{R}')$. With overwhelming probability we have $e \neq e'$ and using the root extraction property of the cryptosystem we can extract (v, ρ) so $C = E(v; \rho)$.

It remains to argue that v is a message on the form $\sum_{j=1}^{N} M^{\iota_j}$ for $0 \le \iota_1 < \cdots < \iota_N < L$. From $c^{e-e'} = \text{com}(\boxed{a_1} - \boxed{a_1}', \boxed{b_1} - \boxed{b_1}', \boxed{\Delta_1} - \boxed{\Delta_1}', \ldots, \boxed{a_N} - \boxed{a_N}', \boxed{b_N} - \boxed{b_N}', \boxed{\Delta_N} - \boxed{\Delta_N}', \boxed{\Delta} - \boxed{\Delta}'; \boxed{r} - \boxed{r}')$ we get an opening $(\alpha_1, \beta_1, \Delta_1, \ldots, \alpha_N, \beta_N, \Delta_N, \Delta, \rho_c)$ of c. From $c_r = \text{com}(\boxed{a_1}, \boxed{b_1}, \boxed{\Delta_1}, \ldots, \boxed{a_N}, \boxed{b_N}, \boxed{\Delta_N} \boxed{\Delta}; \boxed{r}) c^{-e}$ we then get an opening $(\rho_{a_1}, \rho_{b_1}, \rho_{\Delta_1}, \ldots, \rho_{a_N}, \rho_{b_N}, \rho_{\Delta_N}, \rho_{\Delta}, \rho_r)$ of c_r. Moreover, define $\rho_V = \boxed{V} - ev, \rho_R = \boxed{R} - e\rho$ and we have $C_R = E(R_V; \rho_R)$.

Consider now an adversary having noticeable probability of making an acceptable argument of knowledge using C, C_R, c, c_r. It must use $\boxed{a_j} = e\alpha_j + \rho_{a_j}, \boxed{b_j} = e\beta_j + \rho_{b_j}, \boxed{\Delta_j} = e\Delta_j + \rho_{\Delta_j}$. We have equations $\boxed{\Delta_j} = p\boxed{a_j}\boxed{b_j} - e\boxed{a_{j+1}}$, where by definition $\boxed{a_{N+1}} = e\alpha_{N+1} = ep^L$. This means $e^2(p\alpha_j\beta_j - \alpha_{j+1}) + e(p\alpha_j\rho_{b_j} + \beta_j\rho_{a_j} - \rho_{a_{j+1}} - \Delta_j) + p\rho_{a_j}\rho_{b_j} - \rho_{\Delta_j} = 0$. With overwhelming probability over the choice of e we then have $\bigwedge_{j=1}^{N} \alpha_{j+1} = p\alpha_j\beta_j$. This means $p\alpha_1|\alpha_2, \ldots, p\alpha_N|p^L$, so there exists $0 \le \iota_1 < \cdots < \iota_N < L$ so $\alpha_j = \pm p^{\iota_j}$.

Likewise, if the adversary has noticeable probability of making an acceptable argument of knowledge with C, C_R, c, c_r it must use $\boxed{\Delta} = e\Delta + \rho_\Delta$ and $\boxed{V} = ev + \rho_V$. We verify that $\boxed{\Delta} = \sum_{j=1}^{N} \boxed{a_j}^2 - e\boxed{V}$, i.e., $e^2(\sum_{j=1}^{N}\alpha_j^2 - v) + e(\sum_{j=1}^{N}\alpha_j\rho_{a_j} - \rho_V - \Delta) + \sum_{j=1}^{N}\rho_{a_j}^2 - \rho_\Delta = 0$. With overwhelming probability over e we must therefore have

$$v = \sum_{j=1}^{N} \alpha_j^2 = \sum_{j=1}^{N} (\pm p^{\iota_j})^2 = \sum_{j=1}^{N} M^{\iota_j}.$$

$\square$

4 Approval Vote

In approval voting the voter can vote for as many different candidates as he likes. The advantage of this kind of voting system is that the voter does not risk wasting votes by selecting his preferred candidate. Compare this to other voting systems where it may be foolish to cast a vote for a candidate who has little chance of winning. In this kind of election the number of votes cast by the voter may be anywhere between 0 and L.

Define $a_i = 1$ if the voter wishes to vote for candidate i and $a_i = 0$ if he does not. The plaintext vote is $V = \sum_{i=0}^{L-1} a_i M^i$. The voter encrypts this to get a ciphertext $C = E(\sum_{i=0}^{L-1} a_i M^i; R)$. He now needs to prove that indeed the plaintext is on the right form.

We commit to $a_0, \ldots, a_{L-1}$. In order to prove that the hidden $a_i \in \{0, 1\}$ we use the fact that $x^2 \geq x$ for any integer, obtaining only equality if $x = 0$ or $x = 1$. This means that if we can prove $\sum_{i=0}^{L-1}(a_i^2 - a_i) = 0$, then all a_i's belong to $\{0, 1\}$.

Using standard techniques, we get out hidden variables $\boxed{a_i} = ea_i + r_{a_i}$ as well as $\boxed{\Delta} = e\Delta + r_\Delta$, where Δ is a committed value. In the verification, we end up with an equation $\boxed{\Delta} = \sum_{i=0}^{L-1}(\boxed{a_i}^2 - e\boxed{a_i})$. The left hand side is a degree 1 polynomial in e and the right hand side is a degree 2 polynomial in e. With overwhelming probability over e, the equation implies $\sum_{i=0}^{L-1}(a_i^2 - a_i) = 0$ as we wanted.

The other parts of the NIZK argument are a proof of knowledge of the plaintext V, as well as an argument that this plaintext is constructed as described above using the a_i's that we committed to.

Theorem 3. *In the random oracle model, the protocol in Figure 3 is a NIZK argument of knowledge for C containing a correctly formed approval vote. If the commitment scheme is statistically hiding then the argument is statistical zero-knowledge.*

We prove Theorem 3 in the full paper.

Limited vote with large N. It is possible to modify the protocol into an NIZK argument of correctness of an approval vote with the additional condition that $\sum_{i=0}^{L-1} \alpha_i = N$ for some known N. The addition can be made at low computational cost. This variation can be used as an alternative to the limited vote argument from the previous section.

The $\boxed{a_i}$'s are of small size, while the limited vote argument may use very large exponents in large elections with many candidates. The limited vote argument is thus suitable when N is small in comparison with L, while for large N it is better to use the variation of the approval vote argument.

5   Divisible Vote

Consider a shareholder election where each share gives the right to cast one vote. It may be impractical for large shareholders to cast multiple single votes, or even to use the limited vote technique, since it forces them to make a huge number of encryptions. We prefer proving in a direct manner that the ciphertext contains a vote on the form $\sum_{i=0}^{L-1} v_i M^i$, where v_i is the number of votes on candidate i.

In [IMO03] they call this divisible voting and offer zero-knowledge arguments for correctness of a divisible vote. We suggest an alternative NIZK argument that takes full advantage of integer commitments. In comparison with [IMO03] we save a factor $\log N$ in complexity, where N is the number of votes the voter has, and we benefit from using integer commitments instead of encryptions.

Zero-Knowledge Argument for Correctness of an Approval Vote

Common input: Ciphertext C and public keys.
Private input: $a_0, \ldots, a_{L-1} \in \{0, 1\}$ and $R \in \{0, 1\}^{\ell_R}$ such that
$C = E(\sum_{i=0}^{L-1} a_i M^i; R)$.

We prove correctness of the vote by producing

$$\text{SPK}[(v, \rho, \alpha_0, \ldots, \alpha_{L-1}) : C = E(v; \rho) \text{ and } v = \sum_{i=0}^{L-1} \alpha_i M^i \text{ and } \sum_{i=0}^{L-1} (\alpha_i^2 - \alpha_i) = 0]$$

Argument: Choose $R_V \leftarrow \{0, 1\}^{\ell_V + \ell_e + \ell_s}$, $R_R \leftarrow \{0, 1\}^{\ell_R + \ell_e + \ell_s}$ and set
$C_R = E(R_V; R_R)$.
Choose $r_{a_0}, \ldots, r_{a_{L-1}} \leftarrow \{0, 1\}^{1 + \ell_e + \ell_s}$ and let $\Delta = \sum_{i=0}^{L-1} (2a_i - 1) r_{a_i}$. Choose
$r \leftarrow \{0, 1\}^{\ell_r}$ and set $c = \text{com}(a_0, \ldots, a_{L-1}, \Delta; r)$. Choose $r_r \leftarrow \{0, 1\}^{\ell_r + \ell_e + \ell_s}$
and set $c_r = \text{com}(r_{a_0}, \ldots, r_{a_{L-1}}, \sum_{i=0}^{L-1} r_{a_i}^2; r_r)$.

Compute a challenge $e \leftarrow \text{hash}(C, C_R, c, c_r)$.

Set $\boxed{R} = eR + R_R$. Set $\boxed{a_i} = ea_i + r_{a_i}$ and $\boxed{r} = er + r_r$.

The argument is $(C_R, c, c_r, \boxed{R}, \boxed{a_0}, \ldots, \boxed{a_{L-1}}, \boxed{r})$.

Verification: Compute e as above. Define $\boxed{V} = \sum_{i=0}^{L-1} \boxed{a_i} M^i$ and

$\boxed{\Delta} = \sum_{i=0}^{L-1} (\boxed{a_i}^2 - e\boxed{a_i})$.
Verify $C^e C_R = E(\boxed{V}; \boxed{R})$ and $c^e c_r = \text{com}(\boxed{a_0}, \ldots, \boxed{a_{L-1}}, \boxed{\Delta}; \boxed{r})$.

Fig. 3. Approval Vote Argument.

The idea is the following. We commit to $v_0, \ldots, v_{L-1}$. We prove that indeed the ciphertext contains $\sum_{i=0}^{L-1} v_i M^i$. We also prove that all these elements $v_0, \ldots, v_{L-1}$ are non-negative. Finally, we prove that their sum is N.

To prove that an element is positive we could use Boudot's argument [Bou02] or we could use [LAN02]'s argument where v_i is proven to be a sum of four squares. We offer a variation over the latter idea. It is a well-known fact from number theory that the only numbers that cannot be written as the sum of three squares are on the form $4^n(8k + 7)$. This means $4v_i + 1$ can be written as a sum of three squares. Obviously, writing $4v_i + 1$ as the sum of three squares implies that v_i is non-negative.

Rabin and Shallit [RS86] offer an efficient and simple algorithm for finding three such squares, for sufficiently large numbers. In our case, the numbers are relatively small though; in few elections do voters have more than a million votes. It is not hard to change their algorithm into something that is suitable for small numbers though, since for small numbers factorization is easy. We discuss in the full paper how to decompose $4v_i + 1$ into three squares.

Theorem 4. *In the random oracle model, the protocol in Figure 4 is a NIZK argument of knowledge for a ciphertext containing a specified number N votes. If the commitment scheme is statistically hiding then the argument is statistical zero-knowledge.*

We prove Theorem 4 in the full paper.

Zero-Knowledge Argument for Correctness of a Divisible Vote

Common input: Ciphertext C, a number of votes N and public keys.
Private input: $0 \leq v_0, \ldots, v_{L-1}$ and $R \in \{0,1\}^{\ell_R}$ such that $N = \sum_{i=0}^{L-1} v_i$ and $C = E(\sum_{i=0}^{L-1} v_i M^i; R)$.

We prove correctness of the vote by producing

$$\mathrm{SPK}[(v, \rho, v_0, \alpha_0, \beta_0, \delta_0, \ldots, v_{L-1}, \alpha_{L-1}, \beta_{L-1}, \delta_{L-1}) : C = E(v; \rho) \text{ and}$$

$$v = \sum_{i=0}^{L-1} v_i M^i \text{ and } \bigwedge_{i=0}^{L-1} 4v_i + 1 = \alpha_i^2 + \beta_i^2 + \delta_i^2 \text{ and } N = \sum_{i=0}^{L-1} v_i].$$

Argument: Find a_i, b_i, d_i such that $4v_i + 1 = a_i^2 + b_i^2 + d_i^2$. Choose $r_{v_i}, r_{a_i}, r_{b_i}, r_{d_i} \leftarrow \{0,1\}^{\log N + \ell_e + \ell_s}$. Let $\Delta_i = 4r_{v_i} - 2a_i r_{a_i} - 2b_i r_{b_i} - 2d_i r_{d_i}$. Choose $r \leftarrow \{0,1\}^{\ell_r}$ and set $c = \mathrm{com}(v_0, a_0, b_0, d_0, \Delta_0, \ldots, v_{L-1}, a_{L-1}, b_{L-1}, d_{L-1}, \Delta_{L-1}; r)$. Choose $r_r \leftarrow \{0,1\}^{\ell_r + \ell_e + \ell_s}$ and set $c_r = \mathrm{com}(r_{v_0}, r_{a_0}, r_{b_0}, r_{d_0}, -r_{a_0}^2 - r_{b_0}^2 - r_{d_0}^2, \ldots, r_{v_{L-1}}, r_{a_{L-1}}, r_{b_{L-1}}, r_{d_{L-1}}, -r_{a_{L-1}}^2 - r_{b_{L-1}}^2 - r_{d_{L-1}}^2; r_r)$. Let $R_V = \sum_{i=0}^{L-1} r_{v_i} M^i$ and choose $R_R \leftarrow \{0,1\}^{\ell_R + \ell_e + \ell_s}$. Set $C_R = E(R_V; R_R)$. Set $r_\Sigma = \sum_{i=0}^{L-1} r_{v_i}$.

Compute the challenge as $e \leftarrow \mathrm{hash}(C, C_R, c, c_r, r_\Sigma)$.

Let $\boxed{R} = eR + R_R$. Let $\boxed{v_i} = ev_i + r_{v_i}$, $\boxed{a_i} = ea_i + r_{a_i}$, $\boxed{b_i} = eb_i + r_{b_i}$, $\boxed{d_i} = ed_i + r_{d_i}$ and $\boxed{r} = er + r_r$.

The argument is
$(C_R, c, c_r, r_\Sigma, \boxed{R}, \boxed{v_0}, \boxed{a_0}, \boxed{b_0}, \boxed{d_0}, \ldots, \boxed{v_{L-1}}, \boxed{a_{L-1}}, \boxed{b_{L-1}}, \boxed{d_{L-1}}, \boxed{r})$.

Verification: Compute the challenge e as in the argument. Define
$\boxed{\Delta_i} = e(4\boxed{v_i} + e) - \boxed{a_i}^2 - \boxed{b_i}^2 - \boxed{d_i}^2$. Set $\boxed{V} = \sum_{i=0}^{L-1} \boxed{v_i} M^i$.
Verify $C^e C_R = E(\boxed{V}; \boxed{R})$, $c^e c_r = \mathrm{com}(\boxed{v_0}, \ldots, \boxed{\Delta_{L-1}}; \boxed{r})$ and $\sum_{i=0}^{L-1} \boxed{v_i} = eN + r_\Sigma$.

Fig. 4. Divisible Vote Argument.

6 Borda Vote

In Borda voting, voters cast weighted votes. The worst candidate gets 1 vote, the second worst 2 votes, and so forth. A valid vote is therefore on the form $\prod_{i=1}^{L} \pi(i) M^{i-1}$ for some permutation $\pi \in \Sigma_L$. We will suggest an efficient argument for correctness of such a vote[5].

---

[5] Interestingly, it turns out that in Borda voting we do not need an integer commitment scheme; we can use a commitment scheme based on a group of known order q. We just need to take care that q is large enough to avoid overflows, the $\boxed{a_i}$'s in the protocol should come out as unreduced integers.

480   Jens Groth

To prove correctness of a Borda vote corresponding to permutation π we form a commitment $c \leftarrow \text{com}(\pi(1), \ldots, \pi(L))$. Using the Fiat-Shamir heuristic on an argument for correctness of a shuffle [Gro03,Fur04a] we can demonstrate that c has been correctly formed. In [Gro03] there is a shuffle argument for known messages. This means we can take advantage of the fact that we know that the messages are known to be $1, \ldots, L$ to obtain greater efficiency. Once we have formed the commitment and demonstrated that the content is indeed a permutation of $1, \ldots, L$, then it is pretty straightforward to prove knowledge of the plaintext of the encrypted vote as well as show that the content is on the form described above.

Theorem 5. *In the random oracle model, the protocol in Figure 5 is a NIZK argument of knowledge of C containing a correctly formed Borda vote. If the commitment scheme is statistically hiding and the shuffle argument is statistical zero-knowledge then the argument is statistical zero-knowledge.*

We prove Theorem 5 in the full paper.

Zero-Knowledge Argument for Correctness of a Borda Vote

Common input: Ciphertext C and public keys.
Private input: $\pi \in \Sigma_L$ and $R \in \{0,1\}^{\ell_R}$ such that $C = E(\sum_{i=1}^{L} \pi(i) M^{i-1}; R)$.

We argue correctness of the vote by making the following signature of knowledge

$$\text{SPK}[(v, \rho, \pi \in \Sigma_L, \alpha_1, \ldots, \alpha_L):$$
$$C = E(v; \rho) \text{ and } v = \sum_{i=1}^{L} \alpha_i M^{i-1} \text{ and } \bigwedge_{i=1}^{L} \alpha_i = \pi(i)]$$

Argument: Define $a_i = \pi(i)$, choose $r \leftarrow \{0,1\}^{\ell_r}$ and set $c = \text{com}(a_1, \ldots, a_L; r)$.
In addition make a signature of knowledge of c being a commitment to a permutation of $1, \ldots, L$. I.e., set

$$p \leftarrow \text{SPK}[(\rho_c, \pi \in \Sigma_L) : c = \text{com}(\pi(1), \ldots, \pi(L); \rho_c)].$$

Choose $r_{a_1}, \ldots, r_{a_L} \leftarrow \{0,1\}^{\log L + \ell_e + \ell_s}$ and $r_r \leftarrow \{0,1\}^{\ell_r + \ell_e + \ell_s}$ and set $c_r = \text{com}(r_{a_1}, \ldots, r_{a_L}; r_r)$.
Define $R_V = \sum_{i=1}^{L} r_{a_i} M^{i-1}$. Choose $R_R \leftarrow \{0,1\}^{\ell_R + \ell_e + \ell_s}$ and set $C_R = E(R_V; R_R)$.

Compute a challenge as $e \leftarrow \text{hash}(C, C_R, c, c_r, p)$.

Set $\boxed{R} = eR + R_R$. Set $\boxed{a_i} = ea_i + r_{a_i} = e\pi(i) + r_{a_i}$ and $\boxed{r} = er + r_r$.

The argument is $(C_R, c, c_r, \boxed{R}, \boxed{a_1}, \ldots, \boxed{a_L}, \boxed{r}, p)$.
Verification: Verify the shuffle argument p. Compute e as in the argument. Set
$\boxed{V} = \sum_{i=1}^{L} \boxed{a_i} M^{i-1}$
Verify $C^e C_R = E(\boxed{V}; \boxed{R})$ and $c^e c_r = \text{com}(\boxed{a_1}, \ldots, \boxed{a_L}; \boxed{r})$.

Fig. 5. Borda Vote Argument.

Acknowledgment

Thanks to one of the referees for pointing us to [WfL04].

References

[Ben87]   Josh Cohen Benaloh. Verifiable secret ballot elections. Technical Report 561, Yale University, 1987. PhD thesis. x+123 pp.

[BFP⁺01]   Oliver Baudron, Pierre-Alain Fouque, David Pointcheval, Guillaume Poupard, and Jacques Stern. Practical multi-candidate election scheme. In *proceedings of PODC '01*, pages 274–283, 2001.

[Bou02]   Fabrice Boudot. Efficient proofs that a committed number lies in an interval. In *proceedings of EUROCRYPT '00, LNCS series, volume 1807*, pages 431–444, 2002.

[BR93]   Mihir Bellare and Phillip Rogaway. Random oracles are practical: A paradigm for designing efficient protocols. In *ACM CCS '93*, pages 62–73, 1993.

[BY86]   Josh Cohen Benaloh and Moti Yung. Distributing the power of a government to enhance the privacy of voters. In *proceedings of PODC '86*, pages 52–62, 1986.

[CF85]   Josh D. Cohen and Michael J. Fischer. A robust and verifiable cryptographically secure election scheme. In *proceedings of FOCS '85*, pages 372–382, 1985.

[CGS97]   Ronald Cramer, Rosario Gennaro, and Berry Schoenmakers. A secure and optimally eficient multi-authority election scheme. In *proceedings of EUROCRYPT '97, LNCS series, volume 1233*, pages 103–118, 1997.

[CS97]   Jan Camenisch and Markus Stadler. Efficient group signature schemes for large groups. In *proceedings of CRYPTO '97, LNCS series, volume 1294*, pages 410–424, 1997.

[DF02]   Ivan Damgård and Eiichiro Fujisaki. A statistically-hiding integer commitment scheme based on groups with hidden order. In *proceedings of ASIACRYPT '02, LNCS series, volume 2501*, pages 125–142, 2002.

[DGS03]   Ivan Damgård, Jens Groth, and Gorm Salomonsen. The theory and implementation of an electronic voting system. In D. Gritzalis, editor, *Secure Electronic Voting*, pages 77–100. Kluwer Academic Publishers, 2003.

[DJ01]   Ivan Damgård and Mads J. Jurik. A generalisation, a simplification and some applications of paillier's probabilistic public-key system. In *proceedings of PKC '01, LNCS series, volume 1992*, 2001.

[DJN03]   Ivan Damgård, Mads J. Jurik, and Jesper Buus Nielsen. A generalization of paillier's public-key system with applications to electronic voting. Manuscript, 2003. http://www.brics.dk/~ivan/GenPaillierfinaljour.ps.

[ElG84]   Taher ElGamal. A public key cryptosystem and a signature scheme based on discrete logarithms. In *proceedings of CRYPTO '84, LNCS series, volume 196*, pages 10–18, 1984.

[FO97]   Eiichiro Fujisaki and Tatsuaki Okamoto. Statistical zero knowledge protocols to prove modular polynomial relations. In *proceedings of CRYPTO '97, LNCS series, volume 1294*, pages 16–30, 1997.

[Fur04a]   Jun Furukawa. Efficient, verifiable shuffle decryption and its requirement of unlinkability. Manuscript, 2004. Full version of [Fur04b].

[Fur04b]   Jun Furukawa. Efficient, verifiable shuffle decryption and its requirement of unlinkability. In *proceedings of PKC '04, LNCS series, volume 2947*, pages 319–332, 2004.

[Gro03]   Jens Groth. A verifiable secret shuffle of homomorphic encryptions. In *proceedings of PKC '03, LNCS series, volume 2567*, pages 145–160, 2003.

[Gro05]   Jens Groth. Cryptography in subgroups of $\mathbb{Z}_n^*$. In *proceedings of TCC '05, LNCS series, volume 3378*, pages 50–65, 2005.

[IMO03]   Natsuki Ishida, Shin'ichiro Matsuo, and Wakaha Ogata. Divisible voting scheme. In *ISC '03, LNCS series, volume 2851*, pages 137–150, 2003.

[LAN02]   Helger Lipmaa, N. Asokan, and Valtteri Niemi. Secure vickrey auctions without threshold trust. In *proceedings of Financial Cryptography '02, LNCS series, volume 2357*, pages 87–101, 2002.

[Lip03]   Helger Lipmaa. On diophantine complexity and statistical zero-knowledge arguments. In *proceedings of ASIACRYPT '03, LNCS series, volume 2894*, pages 398–415, 2003.

[Pai99]   Pascal Paillier. Public-key cryptosystems based on composite residuosity classes. In *proceedings of EUROCRYPT '99, LNCS series, volume 1592*, pages 223–239, 1999.

[RS86]   Michael Rabin and Jeffrey Shallit. Randomized algorithms in number theory. *Commun. Pure and Appl. Math*, 39, suppl.:S240–S256, 1986.

[Wan05]   Changjie Wang. Personal communication, 2005.

[WfL04]   Changjie Wang and Ho fung Leung. A secure and fully private borda voting protocol with universal verifiability. In *proceedings of COMPSAC '04*, pages 224–229, 2004.

Short Signature and Universal Designated Verifier Signature Without Random Oracles

Rui Zhang[1], Jun Furukawa[2], and Hideki Imai[1]

[1] The University of Tokyo
zhang@imailab.iis.u-tokyo.ac.jp, imai@iis.u-tokyo.ac.jp
[2] NEC Corporation
j-furukawa@ay.jp.nec.com

Abstract. We propose the first universal designated verifier signature (UDVS) scheme whose security can be proven without random oracles, whereas the security of all previously known UDVS schemes are proven only when random oracles are assumed. To achieve our goal, we present a new short signature scheme without random oracles, which is a variant of BB04 scheme [4]. We also give new security definitions to UDVS. We note that our weakest security definitions are even stronger than any of previously known security definitions: We allow adversaries to behave more adaptively in oracle accessing and we also consider adaptive chosen public key attacks. The security of our UDVS scheme is then proven according to the new security definitions.

1 Introduction

SHORT SIGNATURES AND RELATED ASSUMPTIONS. Short signature was recently proposed by Boneh, Lynn and Shacham (BLS01) [5] with the good property that its size is only about half of DSA signatures with almost the same level of security. Security of BLS01 scheme was based on Gap Diffie-Hellman assumption in random oracle model [3, 8]. Later, Boneh and Boyen proposed another signature scheme (BB04) which is almost as short as DSA and the security of this scheme relies on Strong Diffie-Hellman (SDH) assumption [4, 14] over bilinear group pairs without random oracles. SDH assumption can be informally stated as follows: for $\mathbb{G}=<g>$ of large prime order p, given $g, g^x, g^{(x^2)}, ..., g^{(x^q)} \in \mathbb{G}$, there is no probabilistic polynomial time algorithm able to compute $(c, g^{1/(x+c)})$, for arbitrary $c \in Z_p^*$. The SDH assumption is analogous to the Strong RSA assumption, which has already been used to construct signature schemes existential unforgeable against chosen message attack without random oracles [7, 9].

UNIVERSAL DESIGNATED VERIFIER SIGNATURES. A normal digital signature has publicly verifiable property just as its real world counterpart. A verifier of a signature can convince any third party the fact by presenting a digital signature on a message. However, in the real world, sometimes it is desirable that a verifier should not present the signatures to other parties, such as certificates for hospital records, income summary, etc.

J. Ioannidis, A. Keromytis, and M.Yung (Eds.): ACNS 2005, LNCS 3531, pp. 483–498, 2005.
© Springer-Verlag Berlin Heidelberg 2005

Universal designated verifier signature (UDVS), introduced by Steinfeld et al [15, 16], is an important tool to protect the privacy of the signature holder from dissemination of signatures by verifiers. UDVS schemes are signature schemes with additional functionality where any holder of the signature alone can transform the signature to a non-interactive proof statement for a desired *designated verifier* using the knowledge of the signature, such that the designated verifier can verify the message is signed by the signer but cannot prove the same fact to a third party, since he can also produce such a proof statement using his secret key.

UDVS can be viewed as an application of general *designated verifier proofs*, introduced by Jakobsson, Sako and Impagliazzo [12], where a prover designates a non-interactive proof statement to a designated verifier, who can simulate this proof with his secret key thus cannot transfer it to a third party. We refer to [15, 16] for more related work and applications of UDVS.

The good properties of UDVS make it an important tool to prevent dissemination of digital signatures in user certification systems. It is thus desirable to have rigorous model and corresponding formal analysis regarding UDVS schemes. However, there is still no provably secure UDVS scheme ever reported yet, except those in the *random oracle* model [15, 16].

Random oracle model is a formal model in analyzing cryptographic schemes, where a hash function is considered as a black-box that contains a random function. However, many impossibility results, e.g. [6], have shown that security in the random oracle model does not imply the security in the real world in that a scheme can be secure in the random oracle model and yet be broken without violating any particular intractability assumption, and without breaking the underlying hash functions. Consequently, to design a provable secure UDVS based on standard intractability assumptions is both of theoretical and practical importance.

1.1   Our Contribution

SECURE SIGNATURE SCHEME WITHOUT RANDOM ORACLES. We present a new digital signature scheme which is a variant of BB04 scheme, and prove its security based on the Strong Diffie-Hellman assumption [4, 14]. This signature scheme does not resort to random oracles. We then construct our UDVS without random oracles using this new signature scheme.

REFINED SECURITY DEFINITIONS ON UDVS. Much work on modeling UDVS was previously done in the two papers of Steinfeld et al [15, 16], where two security definitions are introduced, namely, "DV-Unforgeability" and "PR-Privacy". However, the former requirement is weak in the sense that an adversary is not allowed to adaptively choose a designated verifier whom the adversary tries to forge DV-signatures with respect to. The latter requirement is weak in the sense that an adversary is not allowed to access designation oracle with respect to the message that the adversary chooses as a target before this target message is chosen. Hence, adversaries in the previous models are not allowed to fully-adaptively probe "weak" target verifier and "weak" target messages in their attacks.

In our refined security definitions, we give adversaries more freedom to select target verifiers and target messages. We also allow them to additionally access to key registration oracle and designation oracle. These abilities reflect those of real world adversaries. Moreover, we consider strong unforgeability (sEUF) in the sense of [1] for DV-signatures, though we also introduce a commonly-adopted weak version (wEUF), which suffices in many applications. We emphasize that our weak version of definition on DV-unforgeability is still strictly stronger than those given in [15, 16].

FIRST SECURE UDVS SCHEME WITHOUT RANDOM ORACLES. All previous known UDVS schemes are only secure in the random oracle model. We give the first provable secure construction of UDVS without random oracles. This also answers an open question raised in [15], where Steinfeld et al wondered how to construct UDVS schemes without random oracles. Furthermore, our scheme is analyzed in the new model, which is strictly stronger. The security of our UDVS is proven under both SDH and a natural extended version of the "KEA1" assumption [2, 11] in bilinear groups.

2   Preliminary

CONVENTIONS. Let $x \leftarrow X$ denote x is uniformly selected from distribution X. If X is an algorithm, $x \leftarrow X$ denotes x is set to the output of X. $x \leftarrow y$ denotes y is assigned to x. We say a function $f : \mathbb{N} \rightarrow \mathbb{R}$ is *negligible*, if for any $c > 0$, there exits $k_0 \in \mathbb{N}$, such that $|f(k)| < k^{-c}$ holds for any $k > k_0$, denoted as $\mathsf{negl}(k)$.

2.1   Signature Schemes

SYNTAX. A signature scheme consists of three algorithms: $SIG = (\mathsf{KG}, \mathsf{Sig}, \mathsf{Ver})$. $\mathsf{KG}(1^k)$ is the key generation algorithm, with internal random coin flipping, outputs a pair of keys (pk, sk), where pk is the public verification key and sk is the secret signing key. The signing algorithm S takes sk and a message m from the associated message space $\mathcal{M}$, with possible internal random coin flipping, outputs a signature s, denoted as $s \leftarrow \mathsf{Sig}_{sk}(m)$. Ver is the deterministic verification algorithm, takes pk, a message m, and s as input, outputs $\mathtt{acc}$ for "accepted" or $\mathtt{rej}$ for "rejected" as the verification result. The subscript of pk or sk may be omitted in clear contexts. We also require that $\mathsf{Ver}(m, \mathsf{Sig}(m)) = \mathtt{acc}$ for all $m \in \mathcal{M}$.

EXISTENTIAL UNFORGEABILITY. The widely-accepted security definition for digital signature is existential unforgeability against adaptive chosen message attack [10]. But we here consider a stronger version of it [1], called *strong existential unforgeability against adaptive chosen message attack* (sEUF-CMA).

Setup. KG is run, generates a public/secret key pair (pk, sk). pk is given to the adversary $\mathcal{A}$ and sk is given to a challenger.

Training. The adversary $\mathcal{A}$ requests signatures on at most q_s messages $m_1, m_2, ..., m_{q_s} \in \mathcal{M}$ chosen adaptively by itself. The challenger responds with the corresponding signature $s_i = \mathsf{Sig}(m_i)$, $i = 1, ..., q_s$.

Forge. Eventually, the adversary $\mathcal{A}$ outputs a pair (m, s) and wins the game if $(m, s) \notin \{(m_1, s_1), ..., (m_{q_s}, s_{q_s})\}$ and $\mathsf{Ver}(m, s) = \mathsf{acc}$.

For comparison, we also describe weak existentially unforgeability (wEUF-CMA), where the adversary is considered to win the game only if it can output $m \notin \{m_1, ..., m_{q_s}\}$ and $\mathsf{Ver}(m, s) = \mathsf{acc}$. However, we consider *only* strong existential unforgeability (sEUF) in the rest of the paper.

Let Adv be the probability that the adversary wins the above game, which is taken over the coin toss made by $\mathcal{A}$ and the Challenger.

Definition 1. *An adversary (q_s, t, ϵ)-breaks the signature scheme if $\mathcal{A}$ makes at most q_s signature queries, runs in time at most t and Adv is at least ϵ. A signature scheme is (q_s, t, ϵ)-strong existentially unforgeable if under an adaptive chosen message attack if no probabilistic polynomial time adversary (q_s, t, ϵ)-breaks it.*

2.2   Bilinear Groups

Let $\mathbb{G}_1$ and $\mathbb{G}_2$ be two cyclic groups of prime order p, where Computational Diffie-Hellman problem (CDH) is considered hard. Let g_1 be a generator of $\mathbb{G}_1$ and g_2 be a generator of $\mathbb{G}_2$. A bilinear map is a map $e : \mathbb{G}_1 \times \mathbb{G}_2 \to \mathbb{G}_T$ such that $|\mathbb{G}_1| = |\mathbb{G}_2| = |\mathbb{G}_T|$ with following properties:

1. Bilinear: for all $u \in \mathbb{G}_1$ and $v \in \mathbb{G}_2$ and $a, b \in \mathbb{Z}$, $e(u^a, v^b) = e(u, v)^{ab}$.
2. Non-degenerate: $e(g_1, g_2) \neq 1$.

Two groups $\mathbb{G}_1$ and $\mathbb{G}_2$ of prime order p are bilinear map group pair if there is an additional group $\mathbb{G}_T$ with $|\mathbb{G}_1| = |\mathbb{G}_2| = |\mathbb{G}_T|$, such that there exist a bilinear map and an efficiently computable isomorphism $\psi : \mathbb{G}_2 \to \mathbb{G}_1$. Especially e, ψ, and group operations in $\mathbb{G}_1$, $\mathbb{G}_2$ and $\mathbb{G}_T$ can be computed efficiently. Joux and Nguyen [13] showed that an efficiently computable bilinear map e provides an algorithm for solving the Decisional Diffie-Hellman problem (DDH) in $(\mathbb{G}_1, \mathbb{G}_2)$. One can set $\mathbb{G}_1 = \mathbb{G}_2$, however, above notations indicates more general cases where $\mathbb{G}_1 \neq \mathbb{G}_2$ so that certain families of elliptic curves can be used to obtain shorter representations for the group element of $\mathbb{G}_1$.

2.3   Strong Diffie-Hellman Assumption

Definition 2 $((q, t, \varepsilon)$-Strong Diffie-Hellman Assumption). *Let g_1 and g_2 be as above with $g_1 = \psi(g_2)$. We say a probabilistic polynomial time (PPT) adversary $\mathcal{A}$ (q, t, ε)-breaks the Strong Diffie Hellman problem in $(\mathbb{G}_1, \mathbb{G}_2)$ if after given q-tuples of $g_2^{(x^i)}$ with $1 \leq i \leq q$ and running time t, has the probability ε of* *outputting a pair $(c, g_1^{1/(x+c)})$ where $c \in Z_p^*$. Here the probability is taken over the random choice of generator g_2, the choice of $x \in Z_p^*$, and internal random coins of $\mathcal{A}$. The (q, t, ε)-Strong Diffie-Hellman assumption holds if no PPT algorithm solves the SDH problem. For simplicity, we sometimes write SDH assumption.*

3   Short Signature Scheme Without Random Oracles

3.1   The Proposed Scheme

There are many applications for digital signature schemes with small size [5]. Our new short signature scheme is a variant of BB04 scheme [4]. We highlight it here not only because this is an important building block for our UDVS scheme but also it may admit many other possible applications.

Let $(\mathbb{G}_1, \mathbb{G}_2)$ be bilinear groups where $|\mathbb{G}_1| = |\mathbb{G}_2| = p$ for some large prime p. m is the message to be signed and is encoded as an element of Z_p^*.

KG: Pick a random generator $g_2 \in \mathbb{G}_2$ and set $g_1 = \psi(g_2)$. Pick $x, y \leftarrow Z_p^*$, and compute $u \leftarrow g_2^x \in \mathbb{G}_2$ and $v \leftarrow g_2^y \in \mathbb{G}_2$. For fast verification, also compute $z \leftarrow e(g_1, g_2) \in \mathbb{G}_T$. The public key is (g_1, g_2, u, v, z) and the secret key is (x, y).

Sig: Given a secret key $(x, y) \in (Z_p^*)^2$ and a message $m \in Z_p^*$, pick $r \leftarrow Z_p^*$. If $x + r + ym = 0 \bmod p$, try again with a different random r. Compute $\sigma \leftarrow g_1^{1/(x+r+ym)} \in \mathbb{G}_1$. The signature is (σ, r).

Ver: Give the public key (g_1, g_2, u, v, z), a message $m \in Z_p^*$, and a signature (σ, r), verify if

$$e(\sigma, u \cdot g_2^r \cdot v^m) = z$$

Output acc if the equality holds; otherwise, rej.

The size of the signature is the same as that of the BB04 scheme and comparable to DSA. The key generation algorithm, the signing algorithm and the verification algorithm take exactly the same amount of time as those of BB04 scheme. One can also use pre-computation to speed up the online computation.

3.2   Security Analysis

The security of the short signature scheme in section 3.1 is guaranteed by following theorem:

Theorem 1. *If there exists a forging algorithm $\mathcal{F}$ that (q_s, t, ϵ)-breaks the strong existential unforgeability of the above signature scheme, one can build an algorithm that (q, t', ϵ')-breaks the SDH assumption, where $q_s < q$, $t' \leq (t - \Theta(q^2 T))$ and $\epsilon' \geq 2(\epsilon - q_s/p)$.*

The proof is given Appendix A.

Hash Variants. A standard argument shows that if a collision-free hash function is applied to m, whose output can be encoded as an element of Z_p^*, one can still prove the security against (sEUF-CMA) of the resulting signature scheme without random oracles. On the other hand, if we assume random oracles, we can have much efficient schemes.

4   Model of UDVS

SYNTAX OF UDVS. A universal designated verifier signature (UDVS) scheme $\mathcal{UDVS} = (\text{CPG}, \text{SKG}, \text{VKG}, \text{S}, \text{PV}, \text{DS}, \text{DV}, \text{P}_{\text{KR}})$.

1. **Common Parameter Generation** CPG – a probabilistic algorithm, given a security parameter k, outputs a string cp consisting of common scheme parameters (publicly shared by all users).
2. **Signer Key Generation** SKG – a probabilistic algorithm, on input a common parameter string cp, outputs a secret/public key-pair (sk_s, pk_s) for *Signer*.
3. **Verifier Key Generation** VKG – a probabilistic algorithm, on input a common parameter string cp, outputs a secret/public key-pair (sk_v, pk_v) for *Verifier*.
4. **Signing** S – possibly a probabilistic algorithm, on input Signer's secret key sk_s and a message m, outputs Signer's public verifiable (PV) signature s.
5. **Public Verification** PV – a deterministic algorithm, on input Signer's public key pk_s and message/PV-signature pair (m, s), outputs verification result $d \in (\text{acc}, \text{rej})$.
6. **Designation** DS – possibly a probabilistic algorithm, on input Signer's public key pk_s, Verifier's public key pk_v, and a message/PV-signature pair (m, s), outputs Designated-Verifier (DV) signature $\hat{s}$.
7. **Designated Verification** DV – a deterministic algorithm, on input Signer's public key pk_s, Verifier's secret key sk_v, and messge/DV-signature pair $(m, \hat{s})$, outputs verification decision acc or rej.
8. **Verifier Key-Registration** $\text{P}_{\text{KR}}(\text{KR}, \text{V})$ – a protocol between a Key Registration Authority KR and a Verifier V. The verifier registers a verifier's public key. On common input cp, KR and V interact with messages sent each other. At the end of the protocol, KR outputs a pair $(pk_v, Auth)$, where pk_v is the public key of V and $Auth \in \{\text{acc}, \text{rej}\}$ indicates whether or not the key-registration is successful.

Note that the key registration is necessary in practice because the signature receiver can easily convince a third party the validity of a signature by claiming he is the owner of the third party's public key and presents the UDVS to the third party.

4.1   Enhanced Security Notions

Strong DV-Unforgeability. Without designation, a UDVS scheme reduces to a normal signature scheme. There are two types of unforgeability to consider:

Public Verifiable signature unforgeability (PV-unforgeability), the security for the signer, which states that anyone should not be able to forge a PV-signature of the signer. Designated Verifier signature unforgeability (DV-unforgeability), the security for the designated verifier, which states that for any message, an adversary without a PV-signature should be unable to convince a designated verifier of holding such a PV-signature. DV-unforgeability always implies PV-unforgeability, because anyone able to forge a PV-signature can transform it into a DV-signature. Thus it is enough to consider only DV-unforgeability.

We consider strong form of existential unforgeability in the sense of [1]. In our model, a forger $\mathcal{F}$ succeeds in breaking the scheme if it can outputs a valid new pair of message/DV-signature, whereas in [16], a forger $\mathcal{F}$ is considered to succeed only if it is able to forge the DV-signature on a "new message".

We call this security definition *strong existential unforgeability for designated verifier against adaptive chosen public key and chosen message attack* (sEUF-DV-CPKMA). We define it via the following game:

Definition 3. *Let* $\mathcal{UDVS} = (\mathsf{CPG}, \mathsf{SKG}, \mathsf{VKG}, \mathsf{S}, \mathsf{PV}, \mathsf{DS}, \mathsf{DV}, \mathsf{P_{KR}})$ *be a UDVS scheme.* $\mathcal{F}$ *is a forger attacking the DV-unforgeability of* $\mathcal{UDVS}$ *that plays the following game with a challenger.*

Setup. *The key generation algorithms are run,* $cp \leftarrow \mathsf{CPG}(1^k)$, $(pk_s, sk_s) \leftarrow \mathsf{SKG}(cp)$, $(pk_{v_i}, sk_{v_i}) \leftarrow \mathsf{PKG}_i(cp)$ *for* $1 \leq i \leq n$. *All public keys are given to* $\mathcal{F}$ *and the challenger. All secret keys are given to the challenger. The challenger maintains two lists:* $\mathbf{M}$ *and* $\widehat{\mathbf{S}}$, *initially empty. The challenger additionally maintains a list* $\mathbf{L}$ *which consists of all the public keys* $\{pk_{v_i}\}$ *for* $1 \leq i \leq n$, *which are assumed to be already registered.*

Training. $\mathcal{F}$ *may adaptively issue* q_s *times signing queries,* q_d *times designation queries (see below),* q_v *times Designated Verification queries, and up to* $n - 1$ *times of key registration queries to the challenger. However, once* pk_{v_i} *is queried by* $\mathcal{F}$, *the challenger neglects further designated verification quires with respect to verifier* V_i *'s public key* pk_{v_i}.

- *On a Signing query by* $\mathcal{F}$ *on* m, *the challenger returns the corresponding signature* $s = \mathsf{S}(sk_s, m)$ *to* $\mathcal{F}$ *and adds* m *to* $\mathbf{M}$.
- *On Designation query by* $\mathcal{F}$ *on* m *and* pk_v, *the challenger first computes the corresponding PV-signature* $s = \mathsf{S}(sk_s, m)$, *compute the* $\widehat{s} = \mathsf{DS}(pk_s, pk_v, m, s)$. *The challenger then adds* $(m, \widehat{s})$ *to* $\widehat{\mathbf{S}}$, *and returns* $\widehat{s}$ *to* $\mathcal{F}$.
- *On a Designated Verification oracle query by* $\mathcal{F}$ *on* $(m, \widehat{s})$ *on* pk_{v_i}, *the challenger runs the designated verification algorithm* $\mathsf{DV}(pk_s, sk_{v_i}, m, \widehat{s})$ *and returns the corresponding verification result to* $\mathcal{F}$.
- *On a Key Registration query by* $\mathcal{F}$ *on* pk_v, *the challenger sends corresponding secret key* sk_v *to* $\mathcal{F}$, *and deletes* pk_v *from* $\mathbf{L}$.

Forge. *Denote* $\mathcal{F}$ *'s running time as* t. $\mathcal{F}$ *outputs* $(m^*, \widehat{s^*})$ *and wins the game if:* $\mathsf{DV}(pk_s, sk_{v^*}, m^*, \widehat{s^*}) = \mathtt{acc}$ *with* $(m^*, \widehat{s^*}) \notin \widehat{\mathbf{S}}$, *where* $pk_{v^*} \in \mathbf{L}$, $m^* \in \mathcal{M}$ *is a valid message from the message space.*

Suppose q_s, q_d, q_v and t are all polynomially bounded. A UDVS signature is secure against sEUF-DV-CPKMA *if no any probabilistic polynomial time $\mathcal{F}$, can win the above game with non-negligible probability. The probability is taken over coin toss of key generation algorithms, $\mathcal{F}$ and the challenger.*

An important refinement to [15, 16] is that we allow adversaries to adaptively corrupt designated verifiers and adaptively choose the target designated verifier, which reflects more essence of real world adversaries. Moreover, our DV-unforgeability is defined in the sense of strong unforgeability.

One can weaken this definition with minor changes on the requirement of the forgery: for $pk_{v^*} \in \mathbf{L}$, $\mathcal{F}$ wins the game if $\mathcal{F}$ outputs $\mathsf{DV}(pk_s, sk_{v^*}, m^*, \widehat{s^*}) = \mathsf{acc}$, with $m^* \notin \mathbf{M}$ and $(m^*, \cdot) \notin \widehat{\mathbf{S}}$. We call the resulting definition *weak existential unforgeability against chosen public key and chosen message attack* (wEUF-DV-CPKMA). We note that even this weaker definition guarantees stronger security than those considered in [15, 16].

Remark 1. We allow the adversary to make designation queries which captures the attack scenario where a real world adversary may obtain $(m, \widehat{s})$ without knowing corresponding PV-signature s. Though in previous models the adversary is not allowed to make designation queries, it turns out that previous model suffice in some sense when weak existential unforgeability of DV-signatures is considered, because given the signing oracle access, the adversary can simulate the designation oracle anyway. But we emphasize that our modeling approach is more general.

Non-transferability (Privacy Notion)

Definition 4. $\mathcal{A}$ *is an attacker that tries to brag about its interaction with the signature holder. $\mathcal{S}$ is a simulator that simulates the output of $\mathcal{A}$. $\mathcal{S}$ is able to access $\mathcal{A}$ as a black-box. $\mathcal{D}$ is a distinguisher that tries to distinguish whether a given output is of $\mathcal{A}$ or of $\mathcal{S}$. The run time of $\mathcal{S}$ does not include the run time of $\mathcal{A}$ that was black-box accessed by $\mathcal{S}$.*

Setup. $cp \leftarrow \mathsf{CPG}(1^k)$. $(pk_s, sk_s) \leftarrow \mathsf{SKG}(cp)$. KR *is a Key Registration oracle, who maintains a list of verifier's public keys, initially empty.*

Training. $\mathcal{A}$ *and $\mathcal{S}$ are allowed to have the following resources:*

- $\mathcal{A}$ *and $\mathcal{S}$ are allowed to access Signing oracle $\mathsf{S}(sk_s, \cdot)$ up to q_s times and q'_s times, respectively. However, after the challenge message m^* is output, they may not access to Signing oracle S with respect to this challenge message.*
- $\mathcal{S}$ *and $\mathcal{A}$ can output the challenge message m^* at arbitrary time but for only once.*
- $\mathcal{A}$ *and $\mathcal{S}$ are allowed to access* KR *up to q_k and q'_k times, respectively.*
- $\mathcal{A}$ *and $\mathcal{S}$ are allowed to access $\mathcal{D}$ up to q_c and q'_c times, respectively.*
- $\mathcal{A}$ *is allowed to access to designation oracles $\mathsf{DS}(pk_{v_i}, \cdot)$ up to q_d times as long as pk_{v_i} is correctly registered.*
- $\mathcal{S}$ *is NOT allowed to access* DS.

Guess. *Denote the running time of $\mathcal{A}$, $\mathcal{S}$ are t, t', respectively. Finally, $\mathcal{A}$ and $\mathcal{S}$ return to $\mathcal{D}$ their outputs with respect to m^*. $\mathcal{D}$ decides whether this output is of $\mathcal{A}$ or of $\mathcal{D}$.*

We say a UDVS scheme is unconditionally non-transferable against adaptive chosen public key attack and chosen message attack *(NT-CPKMA), if there exists $\mathcal{S}$ such that for every $\mathcal{A}$, every computationally unbounded $\mathcal{D}$ distinguishes outputs of $\mathcal{A}$ and $\mathcal{S}$ on any challenge message m^* with only probability $\mathsf{negl}(k)$, where the probability is taken over the coin toss of key generation algorithms, S, $\mathcal{A}$, $\mathcal{S}$ and $\mathcal{D}$.*

Our definition on non-transferability extends [16] in the sense that $\mathcal{A}$ is able to access to Designation oracle with respect to any message (including the challenge message) before the challenge message is determined. This helps the adversary adaptively choose the challenge message.

5   UDVS Without Random Oracles

5.1   The Proposed Scheme

We give our scheme below. For simplicity, we omit the verifier key registration protocol. As in practice this is needed to run only once and may be executed interactively using zero-knowledge proof of knowledge of his secret key to KR or let the verifier send his secret key to the KR directly.

1. **Common Parameter Generation** CPG: Choose a bilinear group pair which is denoted by a description string Str_D: $(\mathbb{G}_1, \mathbb{G}_2)$ of prime order $|\mathbb{G}_1| = |\mathbb{G}_2| = p$ with a bilinear map $e : \mathbb{G}_1 \times \mathbb{G}_2 \to \mathbb{G}_T$ and an isomorphism $\psi : \mathbb{G}_2 \to \mathbb{G}_1$. Choose a random generator $g_2 \in \mathbb{G}_2$ and compute $g_1 = \psi(g_2) \in \mathbb{G}_1$. Then the common parameter is $cp = (Str_D, g_1, g_2)$.
2. **Signer Key Generation** SKG: Given cp, pick random $x_1, y_1 \leftarrow Z_p^*$, compute $u_1 = g_2^{x_1}$ and $v_1 = g_2^{y_1}$. Specially, for speeding up the verification, one may also compute $z \leftarrow e(g_1, g_2) \in \mathbb{G}_T$. The public key is $pk_\mathsf{s} = (cp, u_1, v_1, z)$, the secret key is $sk_\mathsf{s} = (x_1, y_1)$.
3. **Verifier Key Generation** VKG: Given cp, pick random $x_3, y_3 \leftarrow Z_p^*$. Compute $u_3 = g_2^{x_3}$ and $v_3 = g_2^{y_3}$. The public key is $pk_\mathsf{v} = (cp, u_3, v_3)$ and the secret key is $sk_\mathsf{v} = (x_3, y_3)$.
4. **Signing** S: Given the signer's secret key (cp, x_1, y_1) and a message m, select $r \leftarrow Z_p^*$. If $x_1 + r + m y_1 = 0 \bmod p$, restart. Compute $\sigma = g_1^{1/(x_1 + r + m y_1)}$ and output $s = (\sigma, r)$ as the PV-signature.
5. **Public Verification** PV: Given the signer's public key (cp, u_1, v_1, z), and a message/PV-signature pair (m, s), output acc only if $e(\sigma, u_1 \cdot g_2^r \cdot v_1^m) = z$; otherwise output rej.
6. **Designation** DS: Given the signer's public key (cp, u_1, v_1), a verifier's public key (cp, u_3, v_3) and a message/PV-signature pair (m, s), where $s = (\sigma, r)$, let $h = g_2^r$ and compute $d = e(\psi(u_3), v_3^r) \in \mathbb{G}_T$. Then the DV-signature is $\hat{s} = (\sigma, h, d)$.

7. **Designated Verification** DV: Given a signer's public key (cp, u_1, v_1), a verifier's secret key (x_3, y_3), and message/DV-signature pair $(m, \widehat{s})$, output acc only if following two equations hold simultaneously:

$$z = e(\sigma, u_1 \cdot h \cdot v_1^m) \qquad \text{and} \qquad d = e(\psi(u_3), h^{y_3})$$

Otherwise, output rej.

Remark 2. In fact, the public key u_3 of the designated verifier can be replaced by any *certified* random generator of group $\mathbb{G}_1$. However, we consider scenarios where a designated verifier may become a signer himself, who in turn needs to have two public keys.

5.2   Security Analysis

The correctness of the scheme is obvious. The following two theorems guarantee that the proposed scheme are both strong existentially unforgeable against adaptive chosen public key attack and chose message attack for designated verifier and unconditionally non-transferable.

Theorem 2 (Strong Unforgeability). *Above UDVS scheme achieves* sEUF-CPKMA-*security, provided that SDH assumption and the following assumption hold in bilinear groups.*

Assumption 1 (Knowledge of Exponent Assumption [2, 11]) *Suppose that an adversary $\mathcal{A}$ is given a pair (g, h) which is randomly chosen from uniform distribution of $\mathbb{G}^2$ and that $\mathcal{A}$ is able to generate a pair $(x, y) \in \mathbb{G}^2$ where $\log_g h = \log_x y$, then there exists an extractor that extracts $\log_g h$ for $\mathcal{A}$.*

In fact, one can easily prove that an extended version of above assumption holds in generic bilinear groups, namely, for $(g, h) \in_R \mathbb{G}_2{}^2$ and $(f_1, f_2) \in_R \mathbb{G}_1 \times \mathbb{G}_2$, $\mathcal{A}$ generates $y \in \mathbb{G}_T$, such that $\log_g h = \log_{e(f_1, f_2)} y$, then there exists an extractor that extracts $\log_g h$ for $\mathcal{A}$.

Proof. Suppose that there exists an adversary $\mathcal{A}$ that breaks sEUF-CPKMA of the scheme and (σ, h, d) is the DV-signature that $\mathcal{A}$ forged. Then, from the knowledge of exponent assumption, there exists an extractor that is able to extract r from $\mathcal{A}$ such that $h = g_2^r$ holds and the resulting (σ, r) is a successful forgery of the proposed short signature scheme. Therefore, combined with Theorem 1, it is easy to see the proposed UDVS scheme achieves sEUF-CPKMA.

We have introduced two types of existential unforgeabilities, namely weak EUF and strong EUF, though usually it is considered wEUF is enough for most of the applications. We emphasize that even adopting a probabilistic signing algorithm, one can still achieve strong DV-unforgeability.

Theorem 3 (Non-transferability). *Above UDVS scheme achieves unconditional* NT-CPKMA-*security.*

Proof. $\mathcal{A}$ and $\mathcal{S}$ are able to access Key Registration oracle KR and Signing oracle S. $\mathcal{A}$ is able to additionally access Designation oracle and Designated Verification oracle. $\mathcal{S}$ is able to access $\mathcal{A}$ as a black-box.

The following is how $\mathcal{S}$ simulate an output of $\mathcal{A}$. $\mathcal{S}$ invokes $\mathcal{A}$ by feeding it a random tape.

1. Suppose that $\mathcal{A}$ accesses to KR for a public key u'_3, v'_3. Then $\mathcal{S}$ interacts, as KR, with $\mathcal{A}$. If $\mathcal{A}$, as KR, accepts Key Registration, $\mathcal{S}$ rewinds $\mathcal{A}$ and obtains its corresponding secret key x'_3, y'_3.
2. Suppose that $\mathcal{A}$ accesses to the Signing oracle with respect to u'_1, v'_1 for message m'. $\mathcal{S}$ access to the Signing oracle with respect to u'_1, v'_1 for message m' and obtains signature σ'. Then $\mathcal{S}$ sends this σ' to $\mathcal{A}$.
3. Suppose that $\mathcal{A}$ accesses to the Designation oracle with respect to u'_1, v'_1 for message m' as an designated verifier whose public key is (u'_3, v'_3). (u'_3, v'_3) is the public key that $\mathcal{A}$ has once registered to KR. Recall that $\mathcal{S}$ is not allowed to query S on m^*, However, $\mathcal{S}$ can still generate DV-signature as follows:

$$s \in_R Z_p^* \qquad \sigma = g_2^s$$
$$h = g_2^{1/s} u^{-1} v^{-m} \qquad d = e(g_1, h)^{x'_3 y'_3}$$

4. Suppose that $\mathcal{A}$ outputs its output to distinguisher $\mathcal{D}$, $\mathcal{S}$ outputs it to $\mathcal{D}$.

Since $\mathcal{S}$ has perfectly simulated Signing oracle, KR, Designation oracle to $\mathcal{A}$, $\mathcal{S}$ finally obtains the output that is perfectly indistinguishable from the output of $\mathcal{A}$. The simulation of $\mathcal{S}$ is perfect. This completes the proof.

References

1. J.H. An, Y. Dodis, and T. Rabin. On the security of joint signature and encryption. In *Eurocrypt'02*, volume 2332 of *LNCS*, pages 83–107, Springer-Verlag, 2002.
2. M. Bellare and A. Palacio. The Knowledge-of-Exponent Assumptions and 3-Round Zero-Knowledge Protocols. In *CRYPTO '04*, volume 3152. Springer-Verlag, 2004.
3. M. Bellare and P. Rogaway. Random Oracles are Practical: A Paradigm for Designing Efficient Protocols. In *ACM Conference on Computer and Communication Security*, volume 62-73, 1993.
4. D. Boneh and X. Boyen. Short Signatures Without Random Oracles. In *Eurocrypt'04*, volume 3027 of *LNCS*, pages 56–73. Springer-Verlag, 2004.
5. D. Boneh, B. Lynn, and H. Shacham. Short Signatures from the Weil Pairing. In *Asiacrypt'01*, volume 2248 of *LNCS*, pages 514–532. Springer-Verlag, 2001.
6. R. Canetti, O. Goldreich, and S. Halevi. The Random Oracle Methodology, Revisited. In *STOC'98*, pages 209–218. ACM Press, 1998.
7. R. Cramer and V. Shoup. Signature Schemes Based on the Strong RSA Assumption. *ACM Transactions on Information and System Security*, 3(3):161–185, 2000.
8. A. Fiat and A. Shamir. How to prove yourself: practical solutions to identification and signature problem. In *Crypto'86*, volume 263 of *LNCS*, pages 186–194. Springer-Verlag, 1987.

9. R. Gennaro, S. Halevi, and T. Rabin. Secure Hash-and-Sign Signatures without the Random Oracle. In *Eurocrypt'99*, volume 1592 of *LNCS*, pages 123–139. Springer-Verlag, 1999.

10. S. Goldwasser, S. Micali, and R.L. Rivest. A Digital Signature Scheme Secure Against Adaptive Chosen-Message Attacks. *SIAM J. Comput.*, 17(2):281–308, 1988.

11. S. Hada and T. Tanaka. On the Existence of 3-round Zero-Knowledge Protocols. In *CRYPTO '98*, LNCS, pages 408–423, 1998.

12. M. Jakobsson, K. Sako, and R. Impagliazzo. Designated Verifier Proofs and Their Applications. In *Eurocrypt'96*, volume 1070 of *LNCS*, pages 143–154. Springer-Verlag, 1996.

13. A. Joux and K. Nguyen. Separating Decisional Diffie-Hellman from Diffie-Hellman in Cryptographic Groups. Cryptology ePrint Archive, Report 2001/003, http://eprint.iacr.org/2001/003/, 2001.

14. S. Mitsunari, R. Sakai, and M. Kasahara. A New Trator Tracing. *IEICE Trans. Fundamentals*, E85A(2):481–484, 2002.

15. R. Steinfeld, L. Bull, H. Wang, and J. Pieprzyk. Universal designated-verifier signatures. In *Asiacrypt'03*, volume 2894 of *LNCS*, pages 523–542. Springer-Verlag, 2003.

16. R. Steinfeld, H. Wang, and J. Pieprzyk. Efficient Extension of Standard Schnorr/RSA Signatures into Universal Designated-Verifier Signatures. In *PKC'04*, volume 2947 of *LNCS*, pages 86–100. Springer-Verlag, 2004.

A   Proof of Theorem 1

Actually, we do be able to give another proof in the full version of this paper, however, we believe the proof adopted here is much easier to understand.

Theorem 1 is proved via following two lemmas. The first lemma, actually proves a basic scheme is existentially unforgeable against *weak chosen message attack*. The second lemma then shows the security of the basic scheme implies the full scheme.

Weak Chosen Message Attack (wCMA). First, the adversary outputs a list of queries q_s messages $m_1, ..., m_{q_s} \in \mathcal{M}$. Then KG is run, generating the public/secret key pair (pk, sk). pk is given to the adversary $\mathcal{F}$ and sk is given to the Challenger. The Challenger sends $\mathcal{A}$ signatures $s_i = \mathsf{Sig}(m_i)$ for $i = 1, ..., q_s$. At last, $\mathcal{A}$ outputs a pair (m^*, s^*), and wins the game if $m^* \notin \{m_1, ..., m_{q_s}\}$ and $\mathsf{Ver}(m^*, \sigma^*) = \mathsf{acc}$. Define $\mathsf{Adv}_{\mathcal{A}}$ to be the probability that $\mathcal{A}$ wins above game, taken over the coin toss of $\mathcal{A}$ and the Challenger. Then $\mathcal{A}$ (q_s, t, ϵ)-weakly breaks a signature scheme if $\mathcal{A}$ runs in time at most t, makes at most q_s Sig queries, and $\mathsf{Adv}_{\mathcal{A}}$ is at least ϵ. A signature scheme is (q_s, t, ϵ)-weakly existentially unforgeable under a weak chosen message attack if no PPT $\mathcal{A}$ (q_s, t, ϵ)-weakly breaks it.

BASIC SCHEME Let $(\mathbb{G}_1, \mathbb{G}_2)$ be bilinear group pair where $|\mathbb{G}_1| = |\mathbb{G}_2| = p$ for some prime p. m is encoded as an element of Z_p^*.

KG: Pick a random generator $g_2 \in \mathbb{G}_2$ and set $g_1 = \psi(g_2)$. Pick $x \leftarrow Z_p^*$, and compute $u \leftarrow g_2^x \in \mathbb{G}_2$. For fast verification, also compute $z \leftarrow e(g_1, g_2) \in \mathbb{G}_T$. The public key is (g_1, g_2, u, z).

Sig: Given a secret key $x \in Z_p^*$ and a message $m \in Z_p^*$, compute $\sigma \leftarrow g_1^{1/(x+m)} \in \mathbb{G}_1$. Here $1/(x+m)$ is computed modulo p. If $x + m = 0$, we set $\sigma \leftarrow 1$. The signature is σ.

Ver: Give the public key (g_1, g_2, u, z), a message $m \in Z_p^*$, and a signature σ, verify if $e(\sigma, u \cdot g_2^m) = z$. If the equality holds, output acc. If $\sigma = 1$ and $u \cdot g_2^m = 1$ also output acc. Otherwise, output rej.

Lemma 1. *Suppose (q, t', ϵ)-SDH assumption holds in $(\mathbb{G}_1, \mathbb{G}_2)$. The basic signature scheme above is (q_s, t, ϵ)-secure against existential forgery under a weak chosen message attack, where*

$$q_s < q \qquad and \qquad t \leq t' - \Theta(q^2 T)$$

Proof. Assume $\mathcal{A}$ is a forger that (q_s, t, ϵ)-breaks the signature scheme. We construct an algorithm $\mathcal{B}$ that, by interacting with $\mathcal{A}$, solves the SDH problem in time t' with advantage ϵ. Algorithm $\mathcal{B}$ is given a random instance $(g_1, g_2, A_1, ..., A_q)$ of the SDH problem, where $A_i = g^{(x^i)} \in \mathbb{G}_2$ for $i = 1, ..., q$ and for some unknown $x \in Z_p^*$. For convenience we set $A_0 = g_2$. Algorithm $\mathcal{B}$'s goal is to produce a pair $(c, g_1^{1/(x+c)})$ for some $c \in Z_p^*$. Algorithm $\mathcal{B}$ does so by interacting with the forger $\mathcal{A}$ as follows:

Query. Algorithm $\mathcal{A}$ outputs a list of distinct q_s messages $m_1, ..., m_{q_s} \in Z_p^*$, where $q_s < q$. Since $\mathcal{A}$ must reveal its queries up front, we may assume that $\mathcal{A}$ outputs exactly $q - 1$ messages to be signed (if the actual number is less, we can always virtually reduce the value of q so that $q = q_s + 1$).

Response. $\mathcal{B}$ must respond with a public key and signatures on the $q - 1$ messages from $\mathcal{A}$. Let $f(y)$ be the polynomial $f(y) = \prod_{i=1}^{q-1}(y + m_i)$. Expand $f(y)$ and write $f(y) = \sum_{i=0}^{q-1} \alpha_i y^i$ where $\alpha_0, ..., \alpha_{q-1} \in Z_p^*$ are the coefficients of the polynomial $f(y)$. Compute:

$$g_2' \leftarrow \prod_{i=0}^{q-1} A_i^{\alpha_i} = g_2^{f(x)} \qquad and \qquad h \leftarrow \prod_{i=1}^{q} A_i^{\alpha_{i-1}} = g_2^{xf(x)} = g_2'^{x}$$

Also, let $g_1' = \psi(g_2')$. and $z' = e(g_1', g_2')$. The public key given to $\mathcal{A}$ is (g_1', g_2', h, z'), which has the correct distribution. Next, for each $i = 1, ..., q-1$, Algorithm $\mathcal{B}$ must generate a signature σ_i on m_i. To do so, let $f_i(y)$ be the polynomial $f_i(y) = f(y)/(y + m_i) = \prod_{j=1, j\neq i}^{q-1}(y + m_j)$. As before, we expand f_i and write $f_i(y) = \sum_{j=0}^{q-2} \beta_j y_j$. Compute

$$S_i \leftarrow \prod_{j=0}^{q-2} A_j^{\beta_j} = g_2^{f_i(x)} = g_2'^{1/(x+m_i)} \in \mathbb{G}_2$$

Observe that $\sigma_i = \psi(S_i) \in \mathbb{G}_1$ is a valid signature on m under the public key (g_1', g_2', h, z'). Algorithm $\mathcal{B}$ gives $\mathcal{A}$ the $q - 1$ signatures $\sigma_1, ..., \sigma_{q-1}$.

Output. Algorithm $\mathcal{A}$ returns a forgery (σ^*, m^*) such that $\sigma^* \in \mathbb{G}_1$ is a valid signature on $m \in Z_p^*$ and $m^* \notin \{m_1, ..., m_{q-1}\}$ since there is only one valid signature per message. In other words, $e(\sigma^*, h \cdot g_2'^{m^*}) = e(g_1', g_2')$. Since $h = g_2'^x$ we have that $e(\sigma^*, g_2'^{x+m^*}) = e(g_1', g_2')$ and therefore

$$\sigma^* = g_1'^{1/(x+m^*)} = g_1'^{f(x)/(x+m^*)} \tag{1}$$

Using long division we write (1) the polynomial f as $f(y) = \gamma(y)(y+m^*) + \gamma_{-1}$ for some polynomial $\gamma(y) = \sum_{i=0}^{q-2} \gamma_i y^i$ and some $\gamma_{-1} \in Z_p^*$. Then the rational fraction $f(y)/(y+m^*)$ in the exponent on the right side of Equation (1) can be written as

$$f(y)/(y+m^*) = \frac{\gamma_{-1}}{y+m^*} + \sum_{i=0}^{q-2} \gamma_i y^i$$

hence

$$\sigma^* = g_1^{\frac{\gamma_{-1}}{y+m^*} + \sum_{i=0}^{q-2} \gamma_i y^i}.$$

Note that $\gamma_{-1} \neq 0$, since $f(y) = \prod_{i=1}^{q-1}(y+m_i)$ and $m^* \notin \{m_1, ..., m_{q-1}\}$, thus $(y+m^*)$ does not divide $f(y)$. Then algorithm $\mathcal{B}$ computes

$$w = \left(\sigma^* \cdot \prod_{i=0}^{q-2} \psi(A_i)^{-\gamma_i}\right)^{1/\gamma_{-1}} = g_1^{1/(x+m^*)}$$

and returns (m^*, w) as the solution to the SDH instance.

The claimed bounds are obvious by construction of the reduction.

Lemma 2. *Suppose the basic scheme of Lemma 1 is (q_s, t', ϵ)-weakly secure. The full signature scheme is (q_s, t, ϵ)-secure against existential forgery under a chosen message attack, where*

$$\epsilon \geq 2(\epsilon + q_s/p) \qquad and \qquad t \leq t' - \Theta(q_s T)$$

Proof. We explain informally our strategy. As mentioned above, for a forger $\mathcal{A}$ that breaks the full scheme, a forger $\mathcal{B}$ the basic scheme can be built as follows. $\mathcal{B}$ sends a list of randomly chosen message $M_1, ..., M_{q_s}$ and queries to its challenger, which returns the corresponding signatures $\sigma_1, ..., \sigma_{q_s}$. Then $\mathcal{B}$ is given the public key $u(= g_2^x)$ for some $x \in Z_p^*$. $\mathcal{B}$ chooses random secret key $y \in Z_p^*$, computes the public key $v = g_2^y$ and completes the public key for the full scheme with u and v. For q_s chosen message queried m_i by $\mathcal{A}$, $\mathcal{B}$ could compute an $r_i \in Z_p^*$ and such that $r_i + y m_i = M_i$. Then (σ_i, r_i) is a valid signature on m_i. Eventually, when $\mathcal{A}$ outputs a forgery (m^*, σ^*, r^*), $\mathcal{B}$ "switches" this forgery to $(M^* = r^* + y m^*, \sigma^*)$, which is a valid forgery for the full scheme. Next we give the detailed analysis and lower bound $\mathcal{B}$'s success probability. Denote two types of forger $\mathcal{A}$ as:

Type-1 Forger which either makes query for $m = -x$, or outputs a forgery where $m \notin \{M_1, ..., M_{q_s}\}$.

Type-2 Forger which both never makes query for message $m = -x$, and outputs a forgery where $r^* + ym^* \in \{M_1, ..., M_{q_s}\}$.

We describe $\mathcal{B}$ as follows:

Setup. $\mathcal{B}$ queries its challenger with a list of messages $M_1, ..., M_{q_s} \in Z_p^*$. The challenger responds with a valid public key (g_1, g_2, u, z) and signatures $\sigma_1, ..., \sigma_{q_s} \in \mathbb{G}_1$ on these messages, where $e(\sigma_i, g_2^{M_i} u) = e(g_1, g_2) = z$ for $i = 1, ..., q_s$. $\mathcal{B}$ chooses a random $y \in Z_p^*$ and chooses a bit $b \in \{1, 2\}$ randomly. If $b_{mode} = 1$, $\mathcal{B}$ gives $\mathcal{A}$ the public key $PK_1 = (g_1, g_2, u, g_2^y, z)$. If $b_{mode} = 2$, $\mathcal{B}$ gives $\mathcal{A}$ the public key $PK_2 = (g_1, g_2, g_2^y, u, z)$. In $\mathcal{A}$'s view, both PK_1 and PK_2 are valid public keys for the full scheme (g_1, g_2, U, V, z).

Signature Query. In order to respond, $\mathcal{B}$ maintains a H-list of three data entries: (m_i, r_i, W_i) and a counter l initiated to 0. If receiving a signature for m, it increases l by 1, and checks if $l > q_s$. If $l > q_s$, it neglects further queries by $\mathcal{A}$ and terminate $\mathcal{A}$. Otherwise, it checks whether $g_2^{-m} = u$. If so, the $\mathcal{B}$ just obtains the private key of its challenger. It can forge any number of signatures for its target. In this case, it terminates successfully.

Otherwise, if $b_{mode} = 1$, set $r_l = M_i - ym \in Z_p^*$. If $r_l = 0$, $\mathcal{B}$ reports failure and aborts. Otherwise, $\mathcal{B}$ returns (σ_l, r_l) as answer. This is a valid signature on m for PK_1 because r_l is uniform in Z_p^* and

$$e(\sigma_l, U \cdot g_2^{r_l} \cdot V^m) = e(\sigma_l, u \cdot g_2^{M_i - ym} \cdot g_2^{ym}) = e(\sigma_l, u \cdot g_2^{M_i}) = e(g_1, g_2) = z$$

if $b_{mode} = 2$, set $r_l = mM_l - y \in Z_p^*$. If $r_l = 0$, $\mathcal{B}$ reports failure and aborts. Otherwise, $\mathcal{B}$ returns $(\sigma_l^{1/m}, r_l)$ as answer. This is a valid signature on m for PK_2 because r_l is uniform in Z_p^* and

$$e(\sigma_l^{1/m}, U \cdot g_2^r \cdot V^m) = e(\sigma_l^{1/m}, g_2^y \cdot g_2^{mM_l - y} \cdot u^m) = e(\sigma_l, u \cdot g_2^{M_l}) = e(g_1, g_2)$$

$\mathcal{B}$ further saves tuple $(m, r_l, g_2^{r_l} \cdot V^m)$ to H-list.

Output. Eventually, $\mathcal{A}$ returns a valid forgery (m^*, σ^*, r^*). Note that by adding dummy queries, we may assume that $\mathcal{A}$ makes exactly q_s queries. Let $W^* \leftarrow g_2^{m^*} V^{r^*}$. Then according to two types of forger $\mathcal{A}$, we denote the following events as

F1. No tuple of the form $(\cdot, \cdot, W)$ appears on the H-list, or $\mathcal{A}$ has queried on m such that $u = g^{-m}$.

F2. The H-list contains at least one tuple (m_j, r_j, W_j) such that $W_j = W^*$.

Denote $E1$ to be the event $b_{mode} = 1$ and denote $E2$ to be the event $b_{mode} = 2$. We claim that $\mathcal{B}$ can succeed in breaking the basic scheme if $(E1 \wedge F1) \vee (E2 \wedge F2)$ happens.

- (Case $E1 \wedge F1$). If $u = g^{-m}$, then $\mathcal{B}$ has already recovered the secret key of its challenger, $\mathcal{B}$ can forge signature on any message of his choice. Let $M^* = r + ym^*$, then from the definition of $F1$, (M^*, σ^*) is a valid message/signature pair and it is not queried to $\mathcal{B}$'s challenger before.

- (Case $E2 \wedge F2$). Since $V = u$, then we know that there exists a pair $g_2^{r_j} u^{m_j} = g_2^{r^*} u^{m^*}$. Since $(m^*, r^*) \neq (m_j, r_j)$, otherwise it is not regarded as a forgery, $m^* \neq m_j$ and $r^* \neq r_j$. Write $u = g_2^\tau$, $\mathcal{B}$ can compute $\tau = (r_j - r^*)/(m^* - m_j)$ which also enables $\mathcal{B}$ to recover the secret key of its challenger.

Since $E1$ and $F1$ are independent with uniform distribution, $Pr[E1 \vee E2] = 1$ and $Pr[F1 \vee F2] = 1$, the probability that $\mathcal{B}$ succeeds is

$$Pr[E1 \wedge F1) \vee (E2 \wedge F2)] = 1/2$$

Then all left to do is lower-bounds $\mathcal{B}$'s abort probability. From above description of $\mathcal{B}$ we know that if $E1 \wedge F1$ happens, $\mathcal{B}$ aborts only if $r_l = 0$, i.e., $m_l = M_l$, this happens with probability at most q_s/p. If $E2 \wedge F2$ happens, $\mathcal{B}$ does not abort. Then $\mathcal{B}$ succeeds with probability at least $\epsilon/2 - q_s/p$. This completes the proof.

Efficient Identity Based Ring Signature*

Sherman S.M. Chow**, Siu-Ming Yiu, and Lucas C.K. Hui

Department of Computer Science
The University of Hong Kong
Pokfulam, Hong Kong
{smchow,smyiu,hui}@cs.hku.hk

Abstract. Identity-based (ID-based) cryptosystems eliminate the need for validity checking of the certificates and the need for registering for a certificate before getting the public key. These two features are desirable especially for the efficiency and the real spontaneity of ring signature, where a user can anonymously sign a message on behalf of a group of spontaneously conscripted users including the actual signer.

In this paper, we propose a novel construction of ID-based ring signature which only needs two pairing computations for any group size. The proposed scheme is proven to be existential unforgeable against adaptive chosen message-and-identity attack under the random oracle model, using the forking lemma for generic ring signature schemes. We also consider its extension to support the general access structure.

Keywords: Identity-based signature, ring signature, bilinear pairings, efficiency, real spontaneity, general access structure, anonymity

1 Introduction

Ring signature is a group-oriented signature with privacy concerns: a user can anonymously signs a message on behalf of a group of spontaneously conscripted users including the actual signer. Any verifier can be convinced that the message has been signed by one of the members in this group, but the actual signer remains unknown. However, the theory of ring signature faces two problems when it comes to reality.

In traditional public key infrastructure (PKI), the public key is usually a "random" string that is unrelated to the identity of the user, so there is a need for a trusted-by-all certificate authority (CA) to assure the relationship between the cryptographic keys and the user. As a result, any verifier of a signature must obtain a copy of the user's certificate and check the validity of the certificate

---

* This research is supported in part by the Areas of Excellence Scheme established under the University Grants Committee of the Hong Kong Special Administrative Region (HKSAR), China (Project No. AoE/E-01/99), two grants from the Research Grants Council of the HKSAR, China (Project No. HKU/7144/03E and HKU/7136/04E), and two grants from the Innovation and Technology Commission of the HKSAR, China (Project No. ITS/170/01 and UIM/145).
** Corresponding author.

J. Ioannidis, A. Keromytis, and M.Yung (Eds.): ACNS 2005, LNCS 3531, pp. 499–512, 2005.
© Springer-Verlag Berlin Heidelberg 2005

before checking the validity of the signature. In ring signature, not only the verifier must verify all the public keys of the group. The signer must do so as well or his/her anonymity is jeopardized (consider the extreme case that all certificates used are indeed invalid except the signer's one). The communication and the validation of a large number of public keys greatly affect the efficiency of the scheme. Moreover, real spontaneity is not always possible for ring signature under traditional PKI. The signer cannot spontaneously conscript users who have not registered for a certificate.

Identity-based (ID-based) ring signature solved these problems: the public key of each user is easily computable from a string corresponding to this user's identity (for example, an email address). This property avoids the necessity of certificates, and associates an implicit public key to each person over the world.

Unfortunately, the theory of ID-based ring signature still faces some obstacles in real application: ID-based ring signature schemes are usually derived from bilinear pairings, a powerful but computationally expensive primitive. The important properties of bilinear pairings and associated intractable problems are recalled in Section 3.

From the review in the next section, we know that the number of pairing computations of all existing ID-based ring signature from bilinear pairings grows linearly with the group size, which makes the efficiency of ID-based schemes over traditional schemes questionable. It is fair to say devising an ID-based ring signature using sublinear numbers of pairing computation remains an open question.

We close this open problem in this paper. An efficient ID-based ring signature is proposed in Section 5, which only takes two pairing operations for any group size, and the generation of the signature involves no pairing computations at all. The proposed scheme is proven to be existential unforgeable against adaptive chosen message-and-identity attack under the random oracle model. The framework and the security notion of ID-based ring signature are discussed in Section 4.

In the literature, 1-out-of-n-groups ring signature was also considered, which supports an ad-hoc access structure consisting of groups of different sizes. The verifier can be convinced that the signature is generated from all members of a certain group, but cannot know which group has indeed participated in the signing. We notice that an ID-based ring signature for the general access structure can be implemented by an 1-out-of-n-groups ring signature. Extension of the proposed scheme to support this general access structure is shown in Section 6.

2   Related Work

The first work on ID-based ring signature is in [13]. After that, [8] gave a more efficient construction, while [1] pointed out and fixed some small inconsistencies in [13] and [8]. Another ID-based ring signature scheme was proposed in [6]. An ID-based ring signature scheme for anonymous subsets (i.e. 1-out-of-n-groups instead of 1-out-of-n-individuals) was also considered in this work. The pairing operations in [6] can be executed in parallel, which is not possible in schemes like [1, 8, 13].

Threshold ring signature is the t-out-of-n threshold version of ring signature, where t or more entities can jointly generate a valid signature but $t - 1$ or fewer entities cannot. These schemes are applied in pervasive computing applications and mobile ad-hoc networks, where ad-hoc groups are very common. The first ID-based threshold ring signature scheme was proposed in [4]. It is robust and hence anyone can check whether the partial signature is valid for the construction of the final signature. Moreover, it supports trusted authority (TA) compatibility, which enables the signer to conscript non-participating signers under different TAs. The scheme's time and space complexity are up to the state-of-the-art of existing pairing-based ring signature and threshold ring signature, if not better. Actually, it was the most efficient (in terms of number of pairing operations required) ID-based ring signature scheme (when $t = 1$).

Taken into account the total computational costs of the signature generation and verification, existing solutions [1, 4, 6, 8, 13] need a number of pairing computations ranging from $n + 1$ to $4n - 1$ where n is the group size of the ring signature. Since pairing computation is usually the most expensive one among other computations in ID-based cryptosystems, this linear dependence with the group size is undesirable. We remark that this linear dependence also appears in non-ID-based ring signature schemes from bilinear pairings, for examples, [2, 9, 12, 14].

The efficiency gain in ring signature schemes is also beneficial to cryptographic schemes that are built on top of ring signature. Examples include multi-designated verifiers signature [7], non-interactive deniable ring authentication [10] and perfect concurrent signature [11].

In [5], an separable and anonymous ID-based key issuing protocol was proposed. The anonymity property assures that any eavesdropper cannot learn what is the identity associated with the private key being issued even though the key is not transmitted via a secure channel, which is an essential feature for ID-based ring signature. If the protocol reveals information about who has requested for his/her private key and who has not, the real spontaneity will be affected, as the actual signer cannot choose arbitrary any non-participating signer as other may know well that no one except the TA knows the corresponding private key.

3   Preliminaries

3.1   Bilinear Pairings and Related Complexity Assumptions

Bilinear pairing is an important primitive for many cryptographic schemes [1–14]. Here, we describe some of its key properties.

Let $(\mathbb{G}_1, +)$ and $(\mathbb{G}_2, \cdot)$ be two cyclic groups of prime order q. The bilinear pairing is given as $\hat{e} : \mathbb{G}_1 \times \mathbb{G}_1 \rightarrow \mathbb{G}_2$, which satisfies the following properties:

1. *Bilinearity:* For all $P, Q, R \in \mathbb{G}_1$, $\hat{e}(P+Q, R) = \hat{e}(P, R)\hat{e}(Q, R)$, and $\hat{e}(P, Q+R) = \hat{e}(P, Q)\hat{e}(P, R)$.

2. *Non-degeneracy*: There exists $P, Q \in \mathbb{G}_1$ such that $\hat{e}(P, Q) \neq 1$.
3. *Computability*: It is efficient to compute $\hat{e}(P, Q) \; \forall P, Q \in \mathbb{G}_1$.

Definition 1. *Given a generator P of a group $\mathbb{G}$ and a 3-tuple (aP, bP, cP), the Decisional Diffie-Hellman problem (DDHP) is to decide if $c = ab$.*

Definition 2. *Given a generator P of a group $\mathbb{G}$ and a 2-tuple (aP, bP), the Computational Diffie-Hellman problem (CDHP) is to compute abP.*

Definition 3. *We define $\mathbb{G}$ as a Gap Diffie-Hellman (GDH) group if $\mathbb{G}$ is a group such that DDHP can be solved in polynomial time but no algorithm can solve CDHP with non-negligible advantage within polynomial time.*

We assume the existence of a bilinear map $\hat{e} : \mathbb{G}_1 \times \mathbb{G}_1 \rightarrow \mathbb{G}_2$ that one can solve Decisional Diffie-Hellman Problem in polynomial time.

3.2   Forking Lemma for Ring Signature Schemes

The unforgeability of (ID-based) ring signature schemes can be proven with the help of the forking lemma for generic ring signature scheme [6]. Here we review the required conditions for a ring signature scheme to be considered as *generic*. Denote $H(\cdot)$ be a cryptographic hash function that outputs k bits, where k is the security parameter. Consider a group L of n members ($L = \{ID_1, ID_2, \cdots, ID_n\}$) and a message m, a generic ring signature scheme will produce ring signatures in the form of $\{L, m, R_1, R_2, \cdots, R_n, h_1, h_2, \cdots, h_n, \sigma\}$ where for $i \in \{1, 2, \cdots, n\}$, R_is are distinct and no R_i can appear in a signature with probability greater than $2/2^k$; $h_i = H(L, m, R_i)$ and σ is dependent on all of $\bigcup\{R_i\}, \bigcup\{h_i\}$ and m.

Theorem 1 *Consider a generic ring signature scheme using security parameter k. Let $\mathcal{A}$ be a probabilistic polynomial time algorithm which takes as the identity of each members in the group of L and the public parameters that can ask for at most Q queries to the random oracle; if $\mathcal{A}$ can produce a valid ring signature $\{L, m, R_1, \cdots, R_n, h_1, \cdots, h_n, \sigma\}$, for some $L^* \subset L$ of n users within time bound T and with non-negligible probability of success $\epsilon \geq \frac{7C_n^Q}{2^k}$, where C_n^Q is defined as the number of n-permutations of Q elements, i.e., $C_n^Q = Q \times (Q-1) \times \cdots \times (Q - n + 1)$. Then, within a time period of $2T$ and with probability greater than $\frac{\epsilon^2}{66 C_n^Q}$, we can use $\mathcal{A}$ to obtain two valid ring signatures $\{L, m, R_1, \cdots, R_n, h_1, \cdots, h_n, \sigma\}$ and $\{L, m, R_1, \cdots, R_n, h'_1, \cdots, h'_n, \sigma'\}$ such that $h_j \neq h'_j$, for some $j \in \{1, \cdots, n\}$ and $h_i = h'_i$ for all $i \in \{1, \cdots, n\} \backslash \{j\}$.*

In the practical implementation, we usually omit $\bigcup\{h_i\}$ in the ring signature as they can be correctly recovered during the verification process.

4   Framework of ID-Based Ring Signature Schemes

4.1   ID-Based Ring Signature

Framework. An ID-based ring signature scheme consists of the following four algorithms: `Setup`, `KeyGen`, `Sign`, and `Verify`.

- **Setup**: On an unary string input 1^k where k is a security parameter, it produces the master secret key s and the common public parameters *params*, which include a description of a finite signature space and a description of a finite message space.
- **KeyGen**: On an input of the signer's identity $ID \in \{0,1\}^*$ and the master secret key s, it outputs the signer's secret signing key S_{ID}. (The corresponding public verification key Q_{ID} can be computed easily by everyone.)
- **Sign**: On input of a message m, a group of n users' identities $\bigcup\{ID_i\}$, where $1 \le i \le n$, and the secret keys of one members S_{ID_s}, where $1 \le s \le n$; it outputs an ID-based ring signature σ on the message m.
- **Verify**: On a ring signature σ, a message m and the group of signers' identities $\bigcup\{ID_i\}$ as the input, it outputs $\top$ for "true" or $\bot$ for "false", depending on whether σ is a valid signature signed by a certain member in the group $\bigcup\{ID_i\}$ on a message m.

These algorithms must satisfy the standard consistency constraint of ID-based ring signature scheme, i.e. if $\sigma = \mathtt{Sign}(m, \bigcup\{ID_i\}, S_{ID_s})$, and $ID_s \in \bigcup\{ID_i\}$, we must have $\mathtt{Verify}(\sigma, \bigcup\{ID_i\}, m) = \top$.

A secure ID-based ring signature scheme should be unforgeability and signer-ambiguous.

Security Notions. The EUF-IDRS-CMIA2 game below formally defines the *existential unforgeability of ID-based ring signature under adaptive chosen-message-and-identity attack.*

EUF-IDRS-CMIA2 Game:

Setup: The challenger $\mathcal{C}$ takes a security parameter k and runs the **Setup** to generate common public parameters *params* and also the master secret key s. $\mathcal{C}$ sends *params* to $\mathcal{A}$.

Attack: The adversary $\mathcal{A}$ can perform a polynomially bounded number of queries described below in an adaptive manner (that is, each query may depend on the responses to the previous queries).

- Hash functions queries: $\mathcal{A}$ can ask for the values of the hash functions (e.g. $H(\cdot)$ and $H_0(\cdot)$ in our proposed scheme) for any input.
- **KeyGen**: $\mathcal{A}$ chooses an identity ID. $\mathcal{C}$ computes $\mathtt{KeyGen}(ID) = S_{ID}$ and sends the result to $\mathcal{A}$.
- **Sign**: $\mathcal{A}$ chooses a group of n users' identities $\bigcup\{ID_i\}$ where $1 \le i \le n$, and any message m. $\mathcal{C}$ outputs an ID-based ring signature σ.

Forgery: The adversary $\mathcal{A}$ outputs an ID-based ring signature σ and a group of n users' identities $\bigcup\{ID_i\}$ where $1 \le i \le n$. The only restriction is that $(m, \bigcup\{ID_i\})$ does not appear in the set of previous **Sign** queries and each of the secret keys in $\bigcup\{S_{ID_i}\}$ is never returned by any **KeyGen** query. i.e. no private keys in $\bigcup\{S_{ID_i}\}$ is known. It wins the game if $\mathtt{Verify}(\sigma, \bigcup\{ID_i\})$ is equal to $\top$. The advantage of $\mathcal{A}$ is defined as the probability that it wins.

Definition 4. *An ID-based ring signature scheme is said to satisfy the property of existential unforgeability against adaptive chosen-message-and-identity attacks (EUF-IDRS-CMIA2 secure) if no adversary has a non-negligible advantage in the EUF-IDRS-CMIA2 game.*

Definition 5. *An ID-based ring signature scheme is said to have the unconditional signer ambiguity if for any group of n users' identities $\bigcup\{ID_i\}$ where $1 \leq i \leq n$, any message m and any signature σ, where $\sigma = \mathtt{Sign}(m, \bigcup\{ID_i\})$; any verifier $\mathcal{A}$ even with unbounded computing resources, cannot identify the actual signer with probability better than a random guess. That is, $\mathcal{A}$ can only output the actual signer indexed by s with probability no better than $\frac{1}{n}$ ($\frac{1}{n-1}$ is $\mathcal{A}$ is in the signers group.*

4.2   ID-Based Ring Signature for General Access Structure

Framework. An ID-based ring signature scheme for the general access structure consists of the following four algorithms: $\mathtt{Setup}$, $\mathtt{KeyGen}$, $\mathtt{Sign}$, and $\mathtt{Verify}$.

- $\mathtt{Setup}$: Same as $\mathtt{Setup}$ of ID-based ring signature scheme.
- $\mathtt{KeyGen}$: Same as $\mathtt{KeyGen}$ of ID-based ring signature scheme.
- $\mathtt{Sign}$: On input of a message m, n groups of users' identities $\bigcup\{\mathcal{U}_i\}$, where $\mathcal{U}_i = \bigcup\{ID_{i_j}\}$ for $1 \leq i \leq n$, and the secret keys $\bigcup\{S_{ID_{s_j}}\}$ of each signer in one of the groups $\mathcal{U}_s$, where $1 \leq s \leq n$; it outputs an ID-based ring signature for access structure $\bigcup\{\mathcal{U}_i\}$ on the message m.
- $\mathtt{Verify}$: On input of a ring signature σ, a message m and n groups of users' identities $\bigcup\{\mathcal{U}_i\}$, where $\mathcal{U}_i = \bigcup\{ID_{i_j}\}$ for $1 \leq i \leq n$, it outputs $\top$ for "true" or $\bot$ for "false", depending on whether σ is a valid signature signed by all members of a certain group in $\bigcup\{\mathcal{U}_i\}$ on a message m.

These algorithms must satisfy the standard consistency constraint of ID-based ring signature scheme for the general access structure, i.e. if $\sigma = \mathtt{Sign}(m, \bigcup\{\mathcal{U}_i\}, \bigcup\{S_{ID_{s_j}}\})$ and $\bigcup\{ID_{s_j}\} \in \bigcup\{\mathcal{U}_i\}$ we must get "true" from the verification algorithm taking the signature, the message and the groups of identities as the input, i.e. $\mathtt{Verify}(\sigma, \bigcup\{\mathcal{U}_i\}, m) = \top$.

We say an ID-based ring signature scheme for the general access structure is secure if it satisfies unforgeability and signer ambiguity.

Security Notions. The following EUF-IDRSG-CMIA2 game formally defines the *existential unforgeability of ID-based ring signature under adaptive chosen-message-and-identity attack.*

EUF-IDRSG-CMIA2 Game:

Setup: The challenger $\mathcal{C}$ takes a security parameter k and runs the $\mathtt{Setup}$ to generate common public parameters *params* and also the master secret key s. $\mathcal{C}$ sends *params* to $\mathcal{A}$.

Attack: The adversary $\mathcal{A}$ can perform a polynomially bounded number of queries described below in an adaptive manner (that is, each query may depend on the responses to the previous queries).

- Hash functions queries: $\mathcal{A}$ can ask for the values of the hash functions (e.g. $H(\cdot)$ and $H_0(\cdot)$ in our proposed scheme) for any input.
- KeyGen: $\mathcal{A}$ chooses an identity ID. $\mathcal{C}$ computes $\mathtt{KeyGen}(ID) = S_{ID}$ and sends the result to $\mathcal{A}$.
- Sign: $\mathcal{A}$ chooses n groups of users' identities $\bigcup\{\mathcal{U}_i\}$, where $\mathcal{U}_i = \bigcup\{ID_{i_j}\}$ for $1 \le i \le n$, and any message m. $\mathcal{C}$ outputs an ID-based ring signature for the general access structure σ.

Forgery: The adversary $\mathcal{A}$ outputs an ID-based ring signature σ and n groups of users' identities $\bigcup\{\mathcal{U}_i\}$, where $\mathcal{U}_i = \bigcup\{ID_{i_j}\}$ for $1 \le i \le n$. The only restriction is that $(m, \bigcup\{\mathcal{U}_i\})$ does not appear in the set of previous Sign queries and for each group of identities $\bigcup\{\mathcal{U}_i\}$, at least one secret key in $\bigcup\{S_{ID_{i_j}}\}$ is never returned by any KeyGen query. It wins the game if $\mathtt{Verify}(\sigma, \bigcup\{\mathcal{U}_i\})$ is equal to $\top$. The advantage of $\mathcal{A}$ is defined as the probability that it wins.

Definition 6. *An ID-based ring signature scheme for the general access structure is existentially unforgeable against adaptive chosen-message-and-identity attacks (EUF-IDRSG-CMIA2 secure) if no adversary has a non-negligible advantage in the EUF-IDRSG-CMIA2 game.*

Definition 7. *An ID-based ring signature scheme for the general access structure is said to have the unconditional group of signers ambiguity if for any n groups of users' identities $\bigcup\{\mathcal{U}_i\}$, where $\mathcal{U}_i = \bigcup\{ID_{i_j}\}$ for $1 \le i \le n$, any message m and any signature σ, where $\sigma = \mathtt{Sign}(m, \bigcup\{\mathcal{U}_i\})$; any verifier $\mathcal{A}$ not from the actual signer group, even with unbounded computing resources, cannot identify the actual group of signers with probability better than a random guess. That is, $\mathcal{A}$ can only output the actual signers group indexed by s with probability no better than $\frac{1}{n}$.*

5   Efficient ID-Based Ring Signature

5.1   Construction

Define $\mathbb{G}_1, \mathbb{G}_2$, and $\hat{e}(\cdot, \cdot)$ as in the Section 3 where $\mathbb{G}_1$ is a GDH group. $H(\cdot)$ and $H_0(\cdot)$ are two cryptographic hash functions where $H : \{0,1\}^* \to \mathbb{G}_1$ and $H_0 : \{0,1\}^* \to \mathbb{Z}_q^*$.

Setup: The TA randomly chooses $x \in_R \mathbb{Z}_q^*$, keeps it as the master secret key and computes the corresponding public key $P_{pub} = xP$. The system parameters are: $\{\mathbb{G}_1, \mathbb{G}_2, \hat{e}(\cdot, \cdot), q, P, P_{pub}, H(\cdot), H_0(\cdot)\}$.

KeyGen: The signer with identity $ID \in \{0,1\}^*$ submits ID to TA. TA sets the signer's public key Q_{ID} to be $H(ID) \in \mathbb{G}_1$, computes the signer's private signing key S_{ID} by $S_{ID} = xQ_{ID}$. Then TA sends the private signing key to the signer via a secure channel, or using the secure and anonymous protocol proposed in [5].

Sign: Let $L = \{ID_1, ID_2, \cdots, ID_n\}$ be the set of all identities of n users. The actual signer, indexed by s (i.e. his/her public key is $Q_{ID_s} = H(ID_s)$), carries out the following steps to give an ID-based ring signature on behalf of the group L.

1. Choose $U_i \in_R \mathbb{G}_1$, compute $h_i = H_0(m||L||U_i) \; \forall i \in \{1, 2, \cdots, n\}\backslash\{s\}$.
2. Choose $r'_s \in_R \mathbb{Z}_q^*$, compute $U_s = r'_s Q_{ID_s} - \sum_{i \neq s}\{U_i + h_i Q_{ID_i}\}$.
3. Compute $h_s = H_0(m||L||U_s)$ and $V = (h_s + r'_s)S_{ID_s}$.
4. Output the signature on m as $\sigma = \{\bigcup_{i=1}^n\{U_i\}, V\}$.

Verify: A verifier can check the validity of a signature $\sigma = \{\bigcup_{i=1}^n\{U_i\}, V\}$ for the message m and a set of identities L as follows.

1. Compute $h_i = H_0(m||L||U_i) \; \forall i \in \{1, 2, \cdots, n\}$.
2. Checking whether $\hat{e}(P_{pub}, \sum_{i=1}^n (U_i + h_i Q_{ID_i})) = \hat{e}(P, V)$.
3. Accept the signature if it is true, reject otherwise.

5.2 Efficiency

We consider the costly operations which include point addition on $\mathbb{G}_1$ ($\mathbb{G}_1$ Add), point scalar multiplication on $\mathbb{G}_1$ ($\mathbb{G}_1$ Mul), multiplication on $\mathbb{G}_2$ or $\mathbb{Z}_q$ ($\mathbb{G}_2/\mathbb{Z}_q$ Mul), hashing into the group (Hash) and pairing operation (Pairing). We use the `MapToPoint` hash operation in BLS short signature scheme [3]. Before our proposal, the scheme that requires the least number of pairing operations is [4]. Table 1 shows a summary of the efficiency of our proposed scheme. Taken into account the total cost of the signature generation and verification, we can see that our proposed scheme is the only scheme using a constant number of pairing operations, and with the least total amount of other operations. Moreover, our scheme supports parallel operations for the computation about non-participating signers' parts like [4] and [6], which is not possible in schemes like [1, 8, 13].

Considering the signature size, we share the same order of space complexities as all other schemes we considered [1, 4, 6, 8, 13], we are not sacrificing the signature size for lowering time complexity. A final remark for the comparison is that all the schemes with formally proven security employ the forking technique like [6] in their proofs.

Table 1. Comparison of ID-based Ring Signature from Bilinear Pairings.

Schemes	$\mathbb{G}_1$ Add	$\mathbb{G}_1$ Mul	$\mathbb{G}_2/\mathbb{Z}_q$ Mul	Hash	Pairing	Parallelism	Proof
Zhang-Kim [13]	1	$2n$	$2n - 1$	$2n$	$4n - 1$	✗	✓
Lin-Wu [8]	$2n - 1$	$2n$	$3n$	0	$2n + 1$	✗	✗
Herranz-Sáez [6]	$3n - 1$	$2n$	n	0	$n + 3$	✓	✓
Awasthi-Lai [1]	$2n - 1$	$2n + 1$	$2n - 1$	0	$4n - 1$	✗	✗
Chow et al. [4] ($t = 1$)	$2n$	$4n$	$n - 1$	0	$n + 1$	✓	✓
Proposed Scheme	$4n - 3$	$2n + 1$	0	0	2	✓	✓

5.3   Existential Unforgeability and Signer Ambiguity

We summarize our proposed scheme's security in the following theorems.

Theorem 2 *In the random oracle model (the hash functions are modeled as random oracles), if there is an algorithm $\mathcal{A}$ that can win the EUF-IDRS-CMIA2 game with non-negligible probability by making a valid ring signature of group size n', in polynomial time with probability $\epsilon_\mathcal{A}$, asking at most q_S sign queries, q_H H_1 queries (including those implicitly asked by sign queries), q_E key generation queries and q_I identity hashing queries, CDHP can be solved with non-negligible probability in polynomial time.*

Theorem 3 *Our ID-based ring signature scheme has the unconditional signer ambiguity property.*

6   Extension

Now we show the extension to support an ad-hoc access structure consists of groups of different sizes. We employ the idea from [6], where the access structure $\mathcal{U}$ is defined as $\{\mathcal{U}_1, \mathcal{U}_2, \cdots \mathcal{U}_d\}$ (where $\mathcal{U}_i$ denotes a set of signers) and all the members of a particular set in $\mathcal{U}$ (says $\mathcal{U}_s$, where $1 \leq s \leq d$) participate in the signing. The signature can convince any one that all the members of a certain group in $\mathcal{U}$ have cooperated to give the signature, but does not know which group is signing.

6.1   Construction

The **Setup** and **Keygen** algorithm are the same as the basic scheme, except the security parameter in **Setup** should be chosen with the maximum number of subsets supported (n) in mind. Below are the descriptions of **Sign** and **Verify** algorithm.

Sign: Let $\mathcal{U}_s = \{ID_1, ID_2, \cdots, ID_{n_s}\}$ be the set of all identities of n_s users. They choose an access structure $\mathcal{U}$ is defined as $\{\mathcal{U}_1, \mathcal{U}_2, \cdots \mathcal{U}_d\}$ where $\mathcal{U}_s \in \mathcal{U}$. The ID-based ring signature for the access structure $\mathcal{U}$ can be generated as follows.

1. Compute $Y_i = \sum_{ID_j \in \mathcal{U}_i} (Q_{ID_j})$, $\forall i \in \{1, 2, \cdots, d\}$.
2. Choose $U_i \in_R \mathbb{G}_1$, compute $h_i = H_0(m||\mathcal{U}||U_i)$ $\forall i \in \{1, 2, \cdots, d\}\backslash\{s\}$.
3. Each signer $ID_{s_k} \in \mathcal{U}_s$ chooses $r'_{s_k} \in_R \mathbb{Z}_q^*$ and computes $U_{s_k} = r'_{s_k} Q_{ID_{s_k}}$, $\forall k \in \{1, 2, \cdots, n_s\}$.
4. Any particular signer who got the knowledge of $\bigcup_{s_k=1}^{n_s} \{U_{s_k}\}$ computes $U_s = \sum_{s_k=1}^{n_s} (U_{s_k}) - \sum_{i \neq s} \{U_i + h_i Y_i\}$ and $h_s = H_0(m||\mathcal{U}||U_s)$.
5. Each signer $ID_{s_k} \in \mathcal{U}_s$ computes $V_{s_k} = (h_s + r'_{s_k}) S_{ID_{s_k}}$.
6. Output the signature on m as $\sigma = \{\bigcup_{i=1}^{d} \{U_i\}, V = \sum_{ID_{s_k} \in \mathcal{U}_s} (V_{s_k})\}$.

Verify: A verifier can check the validity of a signature $\sigma = \{\bigcup_{i=1}^{d}\{U_i\}, V\}$ for the message m and the access structure $\mathcal{U}$ as follows.

1. Compute $h_i = H_0(m\|\mathcal{U}\|U_i)\ \forall i \in \{1, 2, \cdots, d\}$.
2. Checking whether $\hat{e}\{P_{pub}, \sum_{i=1}^{d}[U_i + h_i \sum_{ID_j \in \mathcal{U}_i}(Q_{ID_j})]\} = \hat{e}(P, V)$.
3. Accept the signature if it is true, reject otherwise.

6.2   Robustness

Robustness is often desirable in multi-party cryptographic protocols. If the scheme is not robust, the misbehavior of any participating signer cannot be detected, and the final signature will be invalid even there is only one misbehaving signer. In our scheme, the partial signature $\sigma_j = \{h_s, U_{s_k}, V_{s_k}\}$ generated by the signer ID_{s_k} can be verified easily by checking whether $\hat{e}(U_{s_k} + h_j Q_{ID_{s_k}}, P_{pub}) = \hat{e}(P, V_{s_k})$ holds.

6.3   Security

The scheme's signer ambiguity can be shown in a similar manner as the cases in our basic scheme. The proof of existential unforgeability is basically the same as that of our basic scheme. Due to page limit, we only highlight the differences here.

The first difference is concerned with the requirement on the forger's signature. For our basic scheme, the forger should not know all the private key associated with the signature, and this happens with probability $(1-\zeta)^{n'}$, where n' represents the total number of members associated with the forged signature. For our extended scheme, the forger must not know at least one private key for all group of signers, and the corresponding probability is $(1-\zeta^{n_1'})(1-\zeta^{n_2'})\cdots(1-\zeta^{n_d'})$ where n_i' is the group size of the i-th group of users. Suppose $N' = \sum_{i=1}^{d} n_i'$, this probability is greater than $(1-\zeta)^{n_1'}(1-\zeta)^{n_2'}\cdots(1-\zeta)^{n_d'} = (1-\zeta)^{N'}$. Hence the n' parameter in the proof can be replaced by N', which represents the total number of members in all d groups associated with the forged signature.

The second difference is about the solving of computational Diffie-Hellman problem. For our basic scheme, abP is computed by $y_s^{-1}(h_s - h_s')^{-1}(V - V')$. For our extended scheme, $(h_s - h_s')^{-1}(V - V')$ only gives the "private key" corresponding to $Y_s = \sum_{ID_j \in \mathcal{U}_s}(Q_{ID_j})$. To obtain abP, we should subtract other known private keys of this s-th group from this value. Suppose the unknown private key is indexed by s_k, we can compute abP by $y_{s_k}^{-1}\{(h_s - h_s')^{-1}(V - V') - \sum_{ID_j \in \mathcal{U}_s \setminus \{ID_{s_k}\}}[(y_j)(bP)]\}$, where y_js can be found by looking up the list L.

7   Conclusion

For ring signature schemes to be practical, we need to eliminate the need for validity checking of the certificates and the need for registering for a certificate before getting the public key. ID-based solutions can provide these two features. Nonetheless, all of the existing proposals of ID-based ring signature are computationally inefficient, since the number of pairing computations grows linearly with the group size. This paper closes the open problem of devising an ID-based ring signature using sublinear numbers of pairing computation. We construct an efficient ID-based ring signature which only needs two pairing computations for any group size. The proposed scheme is proven to be existential unforgeable against adaptive chosen message-and-identity attack under the random oracle model, using the forking lemma for generic ring signature schemes. We also consider its extension to support the general access structure. Future research direction include further improving the efficiency in the generation or the verification of an ID-based ring signature.

References

1. Amit K Awasthi and Sunder Lal. ID-based Ring Signature and Proxy Ring Signature Schemes from Bilinear Pairings. Cryptology ePrint Archive, Report 2004/184, 2004. Available at http://eprint.iacr.org.
2. Dan Boneh, Craig Gentry, Ben Lynn, and Hovav Shacham. Aggregate and Verifiably Encrypted Signatures from Bilinear Maps. In Eli Biham, editor, *Advances in Cryptology - EUROCRYPT 2003, International Conference on the Theory and Applications of Cryptographic Techniques, Warsaw, Poland, May 4-8, 2003, Proceedings*, volume 2656 of *Lecture Notes in Computer Science*, pages 416–432. Springer, 2003.
3. Dan Boneh, Ben Lynn, and Hovav Shacham. Short Signatures from the Weil Pairing. In Colin Boyd, editor, *Advances in Cryptology - ASIACRYPT 2001, 7th International Conference on the Theory and Application of Cryptology and Information Security, Gold Coast, Australia, December 9-13, 2001, Proceedings*, volume 2248 of *Lecture Notes in Computer Science*, pages 514–532. Springer, 2001.
4. Sherman S.M. Chow, Lucas C.K. Hui, and S.M. Yiu. Identity Based Threshold Ring Signature. In Choonsik Park and Seongtaek Chee, editors, *Information Security and Cryptology - ICISC 2004, 7th International Conference Seoul, Korea, December 2-3, 2004, Revised Papers*, volume 3506 of *Lecture Notes in Computer Science*, pages 218–232. Springer, 2004.
5. Ai fen Sui, Sherman S.M. Chow, Lucas C.K. Hui, S.M. Yiu, K.P. Chow, W.W. Tsang, C.F. Chong, K.H. Pun, and H.W. Chan. Separable and Anonymous Identity-Based Key Issuing. In *1st International Workshop on Security in Networks and Distributed Systems (SNDS 2005), in conjunction with 11th International Conference on Parallel and Distributed Systems (ICPADS 2005), July 20-22 2005, Fukuoka, Japan*. IEEE Computer Society, 2005.
6. Javier Herranz and Germán Sáez. New Identity-Based Ring Signature Schemes. In Javier Lopez, Sihan Qing, and Eiji Okamoto, editors, *Information and Communications Security, 6th International Conference, ICICS 2004, Malaga, Spain, October 27-29, 2004, Proceedings*, volume 3269 of *Lecture Notes in Computer Science*, pages 27–39, Malaga, Spain, October 2004. Springer-Verlag. Preliminary version available at Cryptology ePrint Archive, Report 2003/261.

7. Fabien Laguillaumie and Damien Vergnaud. Multi-designated Verifiers Signatures. In Javier Lopez, Sihan Qing, and Eiji Okamoto, editors, *Information and Communications Security, 6th International Conference, ICICS 2004, Malaga, Spain, October 27-29, 2004, Proceedings*, volume 3269 of *Lecture Notes in Computer Science*, pages 495–507, Malaga, Spain, October 2004. Springer-Verlag.

8. Chih-Yin Lin and Tzong-Chen Wu. An Identity-based Ring Signature Scheme from Bilinear Pairings. Cryptology ePrint Archive, Report 2003/117, 2003. Available at http://eprint.iacr.org.

9. Joseph K. Liu and Duncan S. Wong. On the Security Models of (Threshold) Ring Signature Schemes. In Choonsik Park and Seongtaek Chee, editors, *Information Security and Cryptology - ICISC 2004, 7th International Conference Seoul, Korea, December 2-3, 2004, Revised Papers*, volume 3506 of *Lecture Notes in Computer Science*. Springer, 2004.

10. Willy Susilo and Yi Mu. Non-Interactive Deniable Ring Authentication. In Jong In Lim and Dong Hoon Lee, editors, *Information Security and Cryptology - ICISC 2003, 6th International Conference Seoul, Korea, November 27-28, 2003, Revised Papers*, volume 2971 of *Lecture Notes in Computer Science*, pages 386–401, Seoul, Korea, 2004. Springer-Verlag.

11. Willy Susilo, Yi Mu, and Fangguo Zhang. Perfect Concurrent Signature Schemes. In Javier Lopez, Sihan Qing, and Eiji Okamoto, editors, *Information and Communications Security, 6th International Conference, ICICS 2004, Malaga, Spain, October 27-29, 2004, Proceedings*, volume 3269 of *Lecture Notes in Computer Science*, pages 14–26, Malaga, Spain, October 2004. Springer-Verlag.

12. Jing Xu, Zhenfeng Zhang, and Dengguo Feng. A Ring Signature Scheme Using Bilinear Pairings. In Chae Hoon Lim and Moti Yung, editors, *Information Security Applications, 5th International Workshop, WISA 2004, Revised Papers*, volume 3325 of *Lecture Notes in Computer Science*, pages 163–172, Jeju Island, Korea, August 2004. Springer-Verlag.

13. Fangguo Zhang and Kwangjo Kim. ID-Based Blind Signature and Ring Signature from Pairings. In Yuliang Zheng, editor, *Advances in Cryptology - ASIACRYPT 2002, 8th International Conference on the Theory and Application of Cryptology and Information Security, Queenstown, New Zealand, December 1-5, 2002, Proceedings*, volume 2501 of *Lecture Notes in Computer Science*, pages 533–547. Springer, 2002.

14. Fangguo Zhang, Reihaneh Safavi-Naini, and Willy Susilo. An Efficient Signature Scheme from Bilinear Pairings and Its Applications. In Feng Bao, Robert H. Deng, and Jianying Zhou, editors, *Public Key Cryptography - PKC 2004, 7th International Workshop on Theory and Practice in Public Key Cryptography, Singapore, March 1-4, 2004*, volume 2947 of *Lecture Notes in Computer Science*, pages 277–290. Springer, 2004.

Appendix

Proof of Theorem 2. Suppose the challenger $\mathcal{C}$ receives a random instance (P, aP, bP) of the CDHP and has to compute the value of abP. $\mathcal{C}$ will run $\mathcal{A}$ as a subroutine and act as $\mathcal{A}$'s challenger in the EUF-IDRS-CMIA2 game. During the game, $\mathcal{A}$ will consult $\mathcal{C}$ for answers to the random oracles H and H_0. Roughly speaking, these answers are randomly generated, but to maintain the consistency and to avoid collision, $\mathcal{C}$ keeps three lists to store the answers used. We assume $\mathcal{A}$ will ask for $H(ID)$ before ID is used in any other queries.

$\mathcal{C}$ gives $\mathcal{A}$ the system parameters with $P_{pub} = bP$. The value b is unknown to $\mathcal{C}$, which simulates the master key value for the TA.

H requests: We embed part of the challenge aP in the answer of many H queries. When $\mathcal{A}$ asks queries on the hash value of identity ID, $\mathcal{C}$ picks $y_i \in_R \mathbb{Z}_q^*$ and repeats the process until y_i is not in the list L_1. $\mathcal{C}$ then flips a coin $W \in \{0, 1\}$ that yields 0 with probability ζ and 1 with probability $1-\zeta$. (ζ will be determined later.) If $W = 0$ then the hash value $H(ID)$ is defined as y_iP; else if $W = 1$ then returns $H(ID) = y_i(aP)$. In either case, $\mathcal{C}$ stores (ID, y_i, W) in the list L.

Note that when $W = 0$, the associated private key is $y_i(bP)$ which $\mathcal{C}$ knows how to compute. But when $W = 1$, since both a and b are unknown to $\mathcal{C}$, a KeyGen request on this identity will make $\mathcal{C}$ fail.

H_0 requests: When $\mathcal{A}$ asks queries on these hash values, $\mathcal{C}$ checks the corresponding list L_2. If an entry for the query is found, the same answer will be given to $\mathcal{A}$; otherwise, a randomly generated value will be used as an answer to $\mathcal{A}$, the query and the answer will then be stored in the list.

Sign requests: $\mathcal{A}$ chooses a group of n users' identities $L = \bigcup\{ID_i\}$ where $1 \leq i \leq n$, and any message m. On input of (L, m), $\mathcal{C}$ outputs an ID-based ring signature σ as follows.

1. Choose an index $s \in_R \{1, 2, \cdots, n\}$.
2. Choose $U_i \in_R \mathbb{G}_1$, compute $h_i = H_0(m||L||U_i) \ \forall i \in \{1, 2, \cdots, n\}\backslash\{s\}$.
3. Choose $h'_s \in_R \mathbb{Z}_q^*$ and $z \in_R \mathbb{Z}_q^*$, compute $U_s = zP - h'_s Q_{ID_s} - \sum_{i \neq s}\{U_i + h_i Q_{ID_i}\}$.
4. Store the relationship $h_s = H_0(m||L||U_s)$ to the list L_2 and compute $V = z(bP)$, repeat Step 3 in case collision occurs.
5. Output the signature on m as $\sigma = \{\bigcup_{i=1}^{n}\{U_i\}, V\}$.

Finally, $\mathcal{A}$ outputs a forged signature $\sigma = \{\bigcup_{i=1}^{n}\{U_i\}, V\}$ that is signed by a certain member in the group $\bigcup\{ID_i\}$ where $Q_{ID_i} = H(ID_i) = y_i(aP) \ \forall i \in \{1, 2, \cdots, n\}$, i.e. $\mathcal{A}$ has not requested for any one of the private keys of members in the group.

Solving CDHP: It follows from the forking lemma for generic ring signature schemes [6] that if $\epsilon_{\mathcal{C}} \geq 7C_{n'}^{q_H}/2^k$, and $\mathcal{A}$ can give a valid forged signature within time $T_{\mathcal{A}}$ in the above interaction, then we can construct another algorithm $\mathcal{A}'$ that outputs within time $2T_{\mathcal{A}}$ two signed messages $\sigma = \{\bigcup_{i=1}^{n}\{U_i\}, V\}$ and $\sigma' = \{\bigcup_{i=1}^{n}\{U_i\}, V'\}$ and with at least $\epsilon_{\mathcal{C}}^2/66C_{n'}^{q_H}$ probability. Suppose $h_i = H_0(m||L||U_i)$ and $h'_i = H_0(m||L||U_i)$ for all $i \in \{1, 2, \cdots, n\}$, we have $h_i = h'_i$ for all $i \in \{1, 2, \cdots, n\}\backslash\{s\}$. Given $\mathcal{A}'$ derived from $\mathcal{A}$, we can solve the CDHP by computing $abP = y_s^{-1}(h_s - h'_s)^{-1}(V - V')$, where y_s can be found by looking for ID_s in the list L.

Probability of success: Now we determine the value of ζ. The probability that $\mathcal{C}$ does not fail in all the q_E private key extraction queries is ζ^{q_E}, and the probability that $\mathcal{A}$ forged a signature that $\mathcal{C}$ does not know all the corresponding private keys involved in the signature is $(1-\zeta)^{n'}$. So the combined probability is $\zeta^{q_E}(1-\zeta)^{n'}$. By simple differentiation, we find the value of ζ that maximize this probability is $\frac{q_E}{q_E+n'}$ and the maximized probability is $(1 - \frac{n'}{q_E+n'})^{q_E+n'}(\frac{n'}{q_E})^{n'}$.

The probability for $\mathcal{C}$ not to fail in all the q_S sign queries is $(1 - q_H\frac{2}{2^k})^{q_S}$, which is greater than $(1 - \frac{q_S q_H}{2^{k-1}})$. For very large q_E, the probability for $\mathcal{C}$ to succeed is $\epsilon_\mathcal{C} = \epsilon_\mathcal{A}(\frac{n'}{e q_E})^{n'}(1 - \frac{q_S q_H}{2^{k-1}})$. $\qquad\square$

Proof of Theorem 3. Since $\bigcup_{i\neq s}\{U_i\}$ and also r'_s are randomly generated, hence $\bigcup_{i=1}^{n}\{U_i\}$ are also uniformly distributed.

It remains to consider whether $V = (h_s + r'_s)S_{ID_s}$ leaks information about the actual signer. We focus on the value of $V - h_s S_{ID_s} = r'_s S_{ID_s}$ as h_s is publicly computable. Obviously, $r'_s S_{ID_s}$ is related to U_s. Any one can compute the value of $r'_s Q_{ID_s}$ by $U_s + \sum_{i\neq s}(U_i + h_i Q_{ID_i})$. Together with the fact that the bilinearity can relate $r'_s S_{ID_s}$ and $r'_s Q_{ID_s}$ by checking whether $\hat{e}(r'_s Q_{ID_s}, P) = \hat{e}(r'_s S_{ID_s}, P_{pub})$, one may be tempted to see if ID_j is the actual signer by checking whether the following equality holds: $\hat{e}(U_j + \sum_{i\neq j}(U_i + h_i Q_{ID_i}), P_{pub}) = \hat{e}(V, P)/\hat{e}(h_j Q_{ID_j}, P_{pub})$.

However, this method is of no use, as the above equality not only holds when $j = s$, but also $\forall j \in \{1, 2, \cdots, n\}\setminus\{s\}$. i.e. the signature is symmetric. Indeed, the above equality is just the same as the equality to be checked in the verification algorithm.

$$\hat{e}(U_j + \sum_{i\neq j}(U_i + h_i Q_{ID_i}), P_{pub})$$

$$= \hat{e}(\sum_{i\neq s} U_i + U_s + \sum_{i\neq j} h_i Q_{ID_i}, P_{pub})$$

$$= \hat{e}(\sum_{i\neq s} U_i + r'_s Q_{ID_s} - \sum_{i\neq s}\{U_i + h_i Q_{ID_i}\} + \sum_{i\neq j} h_i Q_{ID_i}, P_{pub})$$

$$= \hat{e}(r'_s Q_{ID_s} - \sum_{i\neq s} h_i Q_{ID_i} + \sum_{i\neq j} h_i Q_{ID_i}, P_{pub})$$

$$= \hat{e}(r'_s Q_{ID_s} + h_s Q_{ID_s} - h_j Q_{ID_j}, xP)$$

$$= \hat{e}(r'_s S_{ID_s} + h_s S_{ID_s} - h_j S_{ID_j}, P)$$

$$= \hat{e}(V - h_j S_{ID_j}, P) = \hat{e}(V, P)/\hat{e}(h_j S_{ID_j}, P) = \hat{e}(V, P)/\hat{e}(h_j Q_{ID_j}, P_{pub})$$

To conclude, for any fixed message m and fixed set of identities L, the distribution of $\{\bigcup_{i=1}^{n}\{U_i\}, V\}$ are independent and uniformly distributed no matter who is the actual signer. So we conclude that even an adversary with all the private keys corresponding to the set of identities L and unbounded computing resources has no advantage in identifying any one of the participating signers over random guessing. $\qquad\square$

New Signature Schemes with Coupons and Tight Reduction

Benoît Chevallier-Mames[1,2]

[1] Gemplus, Card Security Group,
Av. du Jujubier, ZI Athélia IV, F-13705 La Ciotat Cedex, France
[2] École Normale Supérieure, Département d'Informatique,
45 rue d'Ulm, F-75230 Paris 05, France
benoit.chevallier-mames@gemplus.com

Abstract. Amongst provably secure signature schemes, two distinct classes are of particular interest: the ones with tight reduction (*e.g.*, RSA-PSS), and those which support the use of coupons (*e.g.*, Schnorr signature).

This paper introduces a new generic signature scheme based on any zero-knowledge identification protocol $\mathcal{Z}$ and signature scheme $\mathcal{S}$ verifying basic security properties. The so-obtained signature scheme features provable security with tight reduction under the same complexity assumptions as the ones under which the basic zero-knowledge identification protocol and signature scheme are secure. In addition to that, interestingly, the combined scheme supports coupons.

We propose an application of our generic conversion scheme based on RSA. We note however that any computational problem $\mathcal{P}$ could be turned into such a tight signature scheme supporting coupons for any zero-knowledge identification protocol and signature scheme based on $\mathcal{P}$. Interestingly, our design technique provides an alternative to the RSA-PSS signature standard, as it enjoys an *equivalently* tight security while enabling the use of coupons for increased performances.

1 Introduction

Signatures are certainly the most extensively used functionality in public key cryptography. Most popular signature schemes include RSA [24] or Schnorr [25] but a lot of other signature schemes have been proposed through the years. However, one had to wait until 1995 to find adequate security analysis of these thanks to Bellare and Rogaway's random oracle model which provided the source of the first security proofs for practical signature schemes [1, 2]. The use of this model typically allows to give the attacker access to oracles simulating hash functions and signatures, resulting in the computational transformation of a forged signature into the solution of a problem taken as a reference and assumed to be hard to solve (*e.g.*, integer factorization, e-th root or discrete logarithm extraction).

Even though a few signature schemes exist that are proven secure in the standard model [9, 5], proofs in the random oracle model are still widely used today as they lead to better reductions than any other proof technique.

J. Ioannidis, A. Keromytis, and M.Yung (Eds.): ACNS 2005, LNCS 3531, pp. 513–528, 2005.
© Springer-Verlag Berlin Heidelberg 2005

Up to now, one of the most powerful reduction technique in the random oracle model is the Forking Lemma introduced by Pointcheval and Stern [19]. This technique is extremely general, and roughly consists in running the attacker repeatedly with different random oracles to get two distinct but related forged signatures. Most zero-knowledge signature schemes are such that, once applied, this technique allows one to recover the secret key.

The Forking Lemma is a powerful proof concept due to its generality: one only assumes the use of random oracles. Its major drawback, however, is that a loose reduction is obtained, *i.e.*, an attacker against the signature scheme can be used to break a supposedly intractable problem, but with a probability much smaller than the probability of a forgery. A consequence of that fact is that using a scheme proven secure with the Forking Lemma requires larger keys, resulting in a loss of efficiency. This constitutes a significant disadvantage in comparison with schemes such as RSA-PSS [2] for which there exists a proof turning a forger into a tight e-th root extractor [2, 4].

On the other hand, the Forking Lemma sometimes appears as the only way to come up with a proof that a given signature scheme is secure, particulary for those derived from zero-knowledge protocols via the Fiat-Shamir heuristic [8]. These last signature schemes have the appealing additional property that the signer can precompute a quantity of the signature independently from the message called a *coupon*, and use this precomputation later to generate the complete signature in a very fast way [8].

In [6], Goldreich and Micali proposed a method to convert signature schemes into schemes with coupons, with the restriction of using a one-time signature scheme. Later in [26], Shamir and Tauman proposed a different solution to achieve this goal relying on chameleon hash functions [15].

In this paper, we introduce a new technique to achieve the same goal, that combines a signature scheme with a zero knowledge identification protocol verifying properties discussed later in the paper. The obtained scheme can be simulated in the random oracle model in a very tight way; we show that the scheme is approximately as secure as the weakest of its constituents.

An attractive property of our scheme is that it is as fast as the third pass of the underlying zero knowledge identification protocol, as soon as the signer uses coupons while signing. We note that this is not possible with cryptosystems like RSA-PSS or RSA-FDH. Combining the properties of high computational performance and tight security reduction is especially desirable in constrained environments such as smart cards and shows the interest of our results for practitioners.

Our paper is divided into four parts. In the next section, we introduce zero-knowledge identification protocols, Σ-protocols and signature schemes. Section 3 describes our generic conversion and assesses its security in the random oracle model. We also compare our results with prior works [6, 26]. Finally, Section 4 provides a particularly interesting instantiation of our scheme based on the RSA problem.

2 Definitions and Related Work

2.1 Zero-Knowledge Identification Protocols

Zero-knowledge identification protocols were invented by Fiat and Shamir in [8] as an identification paradigm. They are often seen as a (usually three or four-pass) series of exchanges between a prover and a verifier. Zero-knowledge identification protocols are a way for the prover to convince that he knows a secret (thereby proving his identity) without revealing to the verifier any other information whatsoever about the secret itself. More precisely, a zero-knowledge identification protocol is referred to as a *proof of knowledge* that has in addition the zero-knowledge property captured by the notion of indistinguishable simulatability. We refer the reader to [17] for more about zero-knowledge protocols.

We consider in what follows a three-pass zero-knowledge identification protocol $\mathcal{Z}$ containing a key generator $\mathrm{Gen}_{\mathcal{Z}}$ which generates public parameters $\alpha \in \Lambda$ and private parameters $s \in S$. The protocol is also defined by some public functions $\mathcal{U} : R \mapsto X$, $\mathcal{V} : S \times R \times G \mapsto Y$ and $\mathcal{W} : \Lambda \times G \times Y \mapsto X$, and runs as shown on the following picture:

> - The prover picks a random $r \in R$, computes $x = \mathcal{U}(r)$ and sends x to the verifier.
> - The verifier verifies that $x \in X$ and sends a random challenge $g \in G$ to the prover.
> - The prover replies with $y = \mathcal{V}(s, r, g)$ and the verifier checks that $x = \mathcal{W}(\alpha, g, y)$ and $y \in Y$.

Fig. 1. A three-pass zero-knowledge identification protocol $\mathcal{Z}$.

2.2 Signature Schemes and Coupons

A signature scheme $\mathcal{S}$ is defined as a collection of probabilistic algorithms ($\mathrm{Gen}_{\mathcal{S}}$, $\mathrm{Sig}, \mathrm{Ver}$) used in the following way. During set up, a key pair is generated by running algorithm $\mathrm{Gen}_{\mathcal{S}}$, and the private key d is kept secret by the legitime user while the public key β is published. Given a message $m \in M$, the signer computes a signature $\sigma = \mathrm{Sig}(d, m)$. A verifier can ascertain that a signature is valid by checking that $\mathrm{Ver}(\beta, \sigma, m) = \mathrm{TRUE}$.

The well-known Fiat-Shamir heuristic allows to turn a zero-knowledge identification protocol into a signature scheme. Briefly, the Fiat-Shamir transform makes the protocol non interactive by replacing the verifier's challenge g by the result of hashing x and m with a secure hash function.

Signature schemes derived from identification protocols via the Fiat-Shamir transform are of particular interest as they allow the use of *coupons*: typically, the first step consisting in computing $x = \mathcal{U}(r)$ can be performed *before* receiving the message m. Later, the signature generation is completed with the computation of $g = \mathcal{G}(m, x)$ and $y = \mathcal{V}(s, r, g)$. This second, message-dependent computation stage happens to be much faster than the first step in most zero-knowledge identification protocols $\mathcal{Z}$.

2.3 Σ-Protocols and Forking Lemma

Σ-protocols are zero-knowledge protocols featuring an additional property: given any couple of correct transcriptions (x, g_1, y_1) and (x, g_2, y_1) with $g_1 \neq g_2$, it is computationally easy to recover the prover's secret key s and consequently solve the computational problem $\mathcal{P}_{\mathcal{Z}}$ underlying the identification protocol. This directly implies that a coupon must be used only once.

This property is fulfilled by many protocols and is in fact the cornerstone of the *Forking Lemma* introduced by Pointcheval and Stern in [19] to prove security in the random oracle model. The intuition is that an attacker capable of forging a signature with some probability ε can be transformed, in the random oracle model, into an algorithm that finds two valid signatures (x, g_1, y_1) and (x, g_2, y_1) with $g_1 \neq g_2$ under probability $\mathcal{O}\left(\varepsilon^2\right)$.

Briefly, the reduction technique runs the attacker over random definitions of the oracle $\mathcal{G}$ until a forgery (x, g_1, y_1) is output by the attacker. Then, in the *replay phase*, the attacker is rerun over partially modified oracle definitions with the hope to get a second forgery (x, g_2, y_2). In this second forgery, the answer g_2 is different from g_1 with overwhelming probability.

The Forking Lemma, however, provides *loose* security reductions as an attacker breaking the security of a Σ-protocol with probability ε is turned into an algorithm solving $\mathcal{P}_{\mathcal{Z}}$ with a significantly smaller probability.

Contrarily to loose security, there exist signature schemes admitting *tight* security reductions, meaning that an attacker breaking $\mathcal{S}$ with a certain probability can be used to solve the underlying computational problem with similar probability.

2.4   A Generic Construction for Tight Security with Coupons

Very few signature schemes feature both a tight security and coupons. There exists however a construction by Shamir and Tauman that achieves this twofold goal using chameleon hash functions [15]. The basic idea is to use a chameleon hash function $\mathcal{H}$ to compute $\sigma = \mathsf{Sig}(d, \mathcal{H}(m', r'))$ for randomly chosen $m' \in \mathcal{M}$ and $r' \in R$. Given the message m, the signer simply has to compute r so that $\mathcal{H}(m, r) = \mathcal{H}(m', r')$. The signature of $m \in \mathcal{M}$ is then (σ, r) and is easily verified by checking whether $\mathsf{Ver}(\beta, \sigma, \mathcal{H}(m, r)) = \mathrm{TRUE}$.

The construction described in this paper is different, and we compare it to Shamir and Tauman's approach later in the paper.

2.5   Known-Message and Chosen-Message Attacks

Several security notions have been defined for signature schemes and properly formalized in the seminal work of Goldwasser, Micali and Rivest [12, 13]. To quantify the security of a signature scheme, one has to define the adversary's *goal* and *ressources*.

A typical goal resides in *existential forgery*: the adversary tries to create a valid message-signature pair for a freely chosen message. The corresponding security property that a signature scheme fulfills to resist such an attack is called *existential unforgeability* (EUF).

Beyond the verification key which is public and hence known to the adversary, more information about the secret key may also be available. The strongest access to side information is captured by the scenario of *adaptive chosen-message attacks* (CMA), where the attacker may request the signer to sign any message of its choice in an adaptive way. In this paper, we also need a weaker type of attack called *known-message attacks* (KMA), where the attacker receives a number q_s of message-signature pairs (m_i, σ_i) she has no control on.

We say that a signature scheme is secure against adaptive chosen-message attacks if it resists existential forgeries under adaptive chosen-message attacks (EUF-CMA). A signature scheme is said to be secure against known-message attacks if no existential forgery is computationally feasible under any known-message attack (EUF-KMA).

Obviously, signature schemes that are EUF-CMA secure also are EUF-KMA secure. It is also known that there exist signatures that are EUF-KMA secure without being EUF-CMA secure, thereby showing that these two notions are distinct.

3   The Proposed Scheme

In this section, we introduce a novel conversion scheme which provides a way to build new signature schemes and discuss its features and security properties.

3.1   Our Construction

The first ingredient of our construction is a Σ-protocol $\mathcal{Z}$ which security relies on a problem $\mathcal{P_Z}$, defined as above by a key generator $\mathsf{Gen}_\mathcal{Z}$ generating public and private parameters $\alpha \in \Lambda$ and $s \in S$, and by some public functions $\mathcal{U} : R \mapsto X$, $\mathcal{V} : S \times R \times G \mapsto Y$ and $\mathcal{W} : \Lambda \times G \times Y \mapsto X$. This is as described on Fig. 1. Examples of such Σ-protocols are numerous, including Feige-Fiat-Shamir [7], Guillou-Quisquater [14], Schnorr [25], Poupard-Stern [21], Girault-Poupard-Stern [10, 20].

Our scheme also uses a EUF-KMA-secure signature scheme $\mathcal{S} : H \mapsto X$ based on a problem $\mathcal{P_S}$, defined as a triple $(\mathsf{Gen}_\mathcal{S}, \mathsf{Sig}, \mathsf{Ver})$. All known signature schemes that are EUF-KMA-secure in the random oracle model are such that there exists a probabilistic simulator Sim which outputs on demand the signature of q_s random messages in polynomial time $T_0 = \mathsf{poly}(q_s)$. We will make use of this simulator in our security proof. An example of such a simulator can be found in every known proof that FDH-RSA is EUF-KMA-secure. Finally, our scheme uses a collision-intractable hash function $\mathcal{G} : \mathcal{M} \times X \mapsto G$ and a full-domain-hash function $\mathcal{H} : X \mapsto H$.

Our signature scheme is as follows.

Key generation: A key is generated by running $\mathsf{Gen}_{\mathcal{Z}}$ and $\mathsf{Gen}_{\mathcal{S}}$. The private key of the scheme is (d, s) while the public key is (α, β).

Signature: To sign a message $m \in \mathcal{M}$, one randomly chooses $r \in R$ and computes $u = \mathcal{U}(r)$, $h = \mathcal{H}(u)$ and $x = \mathsf{Sig}(d, h)$. Upon receiving the message m, one computes $g = \mathcal{G}(m, x)$ and $y = \mathcal{V}(s, r, g)$. The signature on m is $\sigma = (x, y)$.

Verification: To verify a signature $\sigma = (x, y) \in X \times Y$, one computes $g' = \mathcal{G}(m, x)$, $u' = \mathcal{W}(\alpha, g', y)$ and $h' = \mathcal{H}(u')$. Finally, the signature σ is accepted iff $\mathsf{Ver}(\beta, x, h') = \mathrm{TRUE}$.

To simplify the description of the verification, we have supposed that $\mathcal{G}$ and $\mathcal{W}$ are only defined on their respective input sets, checking implicitly the fact that x and y are in the correct sets X and Y. When implementing these functions over larger sets, it is critical that these tests are added before computing $\mathcal{G}(m, x)$ and $\mathcal{W}(\alpha, g', y)$.

Note 1. Our scheme has basically three steps: computing a coupon of a zero-knowledge scheme, signing it with a signature scheme and, at the reception of the message, giving the response of the zero-knowledge scheme, corresponding to the hash of the message and the signature.

SIGNATURE SIZE. The size of the signature is $|X| + |Y|$. This differs slightly from the size of the original signature scheme derived from $\mathcal{Z}$ via Fiat-Shamir, as in this scheme, a technique due to Schnorr reduces the signature size to $|G| + |Y|$.

SIZE OF PUBLIC AND PRIVATE PARAMETERS. As a combination of two schemes $\mathcal{Z}$ and $\mathcal{S}$, our general scheme has a lot of parameters, public or private. But for particular scheme instantiations, some parameters could be shared between the signature scheme and the zero-knowledge identification protocol, thus reducing the number or size of the parameters. A concrete example is given in Section 4, with an instantiation of our scheme based on RSA.

PERFORMANCES OF SIGNATURE GENERATION. Used in a classical way, the execution time of our proposed signature is roughly the addition of the execution times of $\mathsf{Sig}, \mathcal{U}, \mathcal{H}, \mathcal{G}$ and $\mathcal{V}$. Using coupons, however, the off-line part (*i.e.*, pre-computing (x, r)) is carried out before the on-line part of the signature takes place. The on-line computation then requires computing a hash value and running $\mathcal{V}$ once. This, in most identification protocols, remains very fast. This is notably the case within Schnorr, Poupard-Stern and Girault-Poupard-Stern.

EASE OF IMPLEMENTATION. Our scheme relies on a few hash functions, an arbitrary EUF-KMA signature and a Σ-protocol that can be chosen among popular examples. Hence, the software development of new algorithms is unnecessary in order to implement our scheme, already existing software routines may be simply linked together as proposed. This is of particular interest for constrained devices such as smart cards, where the size of code memory is limited, and for which developments may take a long time. In this respect, clearly, the fact that our scheme reuses implemented and tested routines with *e.g.*, protections against side-channel and fault attacks is a strong advantage.

Furthermore, the management of the public key can be done within existing public key infrastructures (PKI) as soon as systems $\mathcal{S}$ and $\mathcal{Z}$ preexisted by themselves in the PKI.

COMPARISON WITH [6] AND [26]. The approach of [6] remains faster than the present work, but it suffers from imposing too large signatures. In this respect, the construction given in [26] is actually closer to our work, even if based on a totally different design. The same security level is achieved: [26] is tightly based on the problem of finding collisions in the chameleon hash function and of forging a signature with the EUF-CMA-secure signature scheme, while, as shown in the sequel, our construction is tightly related to the problem of recovering the secret key of the zero-knowledge scheme $\mathcal{Z}$ and of forging a signature of the EUF-KMA secure signature scheme $\mathcal{S}$.

SECURITY. Most interestingly, even against an EUF-CMA attacker, our scheme remains as secure as the weakest problem among $\mathcal{P_S}$ and $\mathcal{P_Z}$. This reduction is again tight, as shown in the next subsection. A natural construction is then to use a signature scheme $\mathcal{S}$ and a zero knowledge identification protocol $\mathcal{Z}$ that are based on the same problem, as proposed in Section 4.

3.2   Security of the Scheme

We will prove that our scheme is secure in the random oracle model even when the attacker is given access to the signature of q_s messages of her choice. The adversary may also invoke random oracles returning the hash value of q_h inputs (more precisely $q_\mathcal{H}$ and $q_\mathcal{G}$ queries to $\mathcal{H}$ and $\mathcal{G}$, respectively). We prove that an attacker against our signature scheme can be used to solve either $\mathcal{P_S}$ or $\mathcal{P_Z}$ with a probability approximately equal to the attacker's success probability. More formally, we state the following theorem:

Theorem 1. *Let $\mathcal{A}$ be an adversary producing with success probability ε and within time bound τ an existential forgery of the proposed scheme $(\mathcal{Z}, \mathcal{S})$ under a chosen-message attack. Then, there is an algorithm that solves either $\mathcal{P_Z}$ or $\mathcal{P_S}$ with probability ε' in time τ' where*

$$\varepsilon' \geq \varepsilon - \frac{(q_\mathcal{H} + q_s)^2}{|H|} - \frac{(q_\mathcal{G} + q_s)^2}{|G|} - \frac{(q_\mathcal{G} + q_s) \cdot q_s}{|X|}$$

and

$$\tau' \leq \tau + q_s T_W + T_0,$$

after $q_\mathcal{H}$ queries to $\mathcal{H}$, $q_\mathcal{G}$ queries to $\mathcal{G}$ and q_s queries to the signing oracle respectively, noting T_W the time of evaluating $\mathcal{W}$ and T_0 the time needed by the $\mathcal{S}$ oracle to compute and send q_s random message-signature pairs.

The formal proof of this theorem is given in Appendix A.

4   An Instantiation of the Proposed Scheme

In this section, we give a typical example of a scheme based on our generic construction. This example relies on the RSA problem, and uses FDH-RSA as the signature $\mathcal{S}$ and Poupard-Stern as the zero-knowledge identification protocol $\mathcal{Z}$.

4.1   Poupard-Stern: A Σ-Protocol Equivalent to Factoring

Poupard-Stern is a zero-knowledge identification protocol described in [21]. Its security relies on integer factorization. The scheme is described on Fig. 2.

Poupard-Stern uses as public key an RSA modulus n and a base a of maximal order modulo n, and the private key is $s = n - \varphi(n)$ of bitlength $\|s\| = \|n\|/2$.

- Prover P picks a random $r \in \{0, 2^\Gamma - 1\}$ and computes $x = a^r \bmod n$, which is sent to the verifier.
- The verifier verifies that $x \in \mathbb{Z}_n$ and sends a random $g \in \{0, 2^{\|g\|} - 1\}$ to the prover.
- The prover replies with $y = r + sg$, and the verifier verifies that $x = a^{y-ng} \bmod n$ and $0 \le y < 2^\Omega$.

Fig. 2. The Poupard-Stern Zero-Knowledge Identification Protocol.

The set Y is a critical part for the security of the scheme. Indeed, an attacker could try to use $\hat{y} = r + ng$ instead of the legitimate y that she can not forge. Because $s \ll n$, it is possible to thwart such a forge by maximizing the authorized y. Furthermore, an attacker should not use a y (or even a collection of y that could have been logged) to recover a part of the secret s. Hence, r must be large enough to ensure that s is totally hidden within y, with respect to a security parameter[1] $\kappa = 80$.

All of this can be done by using Y as the set of positive integers smaller than 2^Ω, and R as the sets of positive integers smaller than 2^Γ with $\Gamma = \|g\| + \frac{\|n\|}{2} + \kappa$ and $\Omega = \Gamma + 1$. We refer the reader to [21] for a more accurate analysis of the Poupard-Stern protocol.

SECURITY. Poupard-Stern is a Σ-protocol: being given $(g_1, y_1) \neq (g_2, y_2)$ so that $a^{y_1 - ng_1} = a^{y_2 - ng_2}$, one can deduce the factorization of n and thus s. Indeed, $y_1 - ng_1 = y_2 - ng_2 \bmod \lambda(n)$, and consequently $(y_1 - y_2) - n(g_1 - g_2)$ is a multiple of $\lambda(n)$. As $y_1 \ll n$ and $y_2 \ll n$, it is a non-zero multiple of $\lambda(n)$. Then, using Miller's algorithm [16], one can recover the factors of n in polynomial time.

4.2   A Signature Scheme with Coupons
and Tight Reduction to RSA

As explained earlier, coupons are not supported when using RSA and its numerous variants, including in this respect Guillou-Quisquater [14]. The scheme we

---

[1] *i.e.*, the legitimate y is statistically indistinguishable from a random of the same size, where the statistical distance is controlled by the security parameter κ.

now propose uses RSA and Poupard-Stern as instances of systems $\mathcal{S}$ and $\mathcal{Z}$ and fully supports coupons.

Our scheme makes use of an RSA modulus n of secret factorization which is common to the zero-knowledge scheme and the signature scheme. Like with RSA, the key pair contains a public and a private exponent e and d such that $ed = 1 \mod \lambda(n)$. The integer $s = n - \varphi(n)$ is kept secret as in Poupard-Stern.

This scheme is described as follows.

Key: The public key is (e, n, a) while the private key is (s, d).

Signature: To sign a message $m \in \mathcal{M}$, one randomly chooses $r \in \{0, 2^\Gamma - 1\}$ and computes $u = a^r \mod n$, $h = \mathcal{H}(u)$ and $x = h^d \mod n$. Upon receiving the message m, one computes $g = \mathcal{G}(m, x)$ and $y = r + sg$.
The signature on m is $\sigma = (x, y)$.

Verification: To verify a signature $\sigma = (x, y)$, one computes $g' = \mathcal{G}(m, x)$, $u' = a^{y - ng'} \mod n$ and $h' = \mathcal{H}(u')$. Finally, the signature σ is accepted iff $h' \overset{?}{=} x^e \mod n$ and $0 \le y < 2^\Omega$ and $0 \le x < n$.

As one can notice, we can not use directly the theorem of the previous section, as the $\mathcal{H}$ function of the general scheme and the full-domain hash function of the FDH-RSA signature have been combined. The complete proof of such a particular but interesting case is given in the full version of this paper [3]. The theorem stated there proves that in case of self-reducibility over the signature domain (as it is the case with FDH-RSA), one can combine the $\mathcal{H}$ function of the general scheme and the full-domain hash function of the FDH signature while keeping the security tightly equivalent to problems $\mathcal{P}_\mathcal{S}$ and $\mathcal{P}_\mathcal{Z}$.

In our case, $\mathcal{P}_\mathcal{S}$ is the RSA (*i.e.*, e-th root extraction) problem, while $\mathcal{P}_\mathcal{Z}$ is the factoring problem. As the RSA problem is easier than factoring, one can deduce that our proposed scheme is tightly equivalent to the RSA problem.

Hence, our scheme is as secure as RSA-PSS but also presents the practical advantage of allowing coupons. Using these, generating a complete signature is as fast as Poupard-Stern's second step: namely, we require to perform a multiplication, an addition and a hash computation, consequently resulting in a much faster procedure than carrying out a modular exponentiation with RSA-PSS. Again, this speed-up is not at the cost of a loose reduction, as it is the case with the non-interactive version of the original Poupard-Stern, which proof makes use of the Forking Lemma in a classical way.

A thorough comparison between RSA-PSS and our proposed scheme is provided in the following subsection.

4.3   Comparison of Our Scheme with RSA-PSS

RSA-PSS is described as a signature standard [18] and is extensively used worldwide, although not as fast as signature schemes with coupons. We compare our RSA-based scheme with RSA-PSS using a modulus of $\|n\| \ge 1024$ bits.

SIZE OF HASHES. Because of Th. 1, one can see that a hash function $\mathcal{G}$ with an output size of $\|G\| = 160$ bits is sufficient to resist an attacker allowed to make 2^{79} queries to the $\mathcal{G}$ oracle. Indeed, as $\mathcal{H}$ is by definition a full-domain hash, we have that $\|H\| = \|n\|$ and by construction, $\|X\| = \|n\|$.

SIZE OF PARAMETERS. In RSA-PSS, the public parameters are n and e (e is usually short), and the private key is d. In our proposed scheme, the public key is formed by a, e and n, while in the basic presentation of the scheme, the private key is d and s. However, one can see that we can take a small value for a (the only property we require is that a is of maximal order). Furthermore, d and s are redundant secrets, and one can easily compress them, if the size of the private key elements is more important than the execution time of the signature. Using d and $k_d = \frac{ed-1}{\varphi(n)}$ of bitsize $\|e\|$, one can recover $s = n - \frac{ed-1}{k_d}$ and then use it to sign.

Overall, the public keys have roughly the same size in RSA-PSS and in our scheme. The private key in our scheme is 50% longer than the private key in RSA-PSS, but one can compress this private key at the cost of an additional division by a small number during the generation of a coupon. In this last case, the size of both private keys are almost equivalent.

SIGNATURE SIZE. An RSA-PSS signature has $\|n\|$ bits while the size of our signature is $\|x\| + \|y\| = \|n\| + \|g\| = \|n\| + \|g\| + \frac{\|n\|}{2} + \kappa = \frac{3\|n\|}{2} + 240$. Hence, there is an advantage for RSA-PSS on this point, even if the proposed signature is in fact not quite twice as long as a RSA-PSS signature.

PERFORMANCES OF SIGNATURE GENERATION. Our scheme, very much like RSA-PSS, supports the Chinese Reminder Theorem [22] thereby allowing implementations with improved efficiency.

As mentioned earlier, our scheme is useful essentially if used with coupons. When this is the case, the comparison of execution times makes our scheme very appealing. RSA-PSS requires hash computations and a modular exponentiation of $\|n\|$ bits: using a modular exponentiation of complexity $2 \geq c \geq 1$, this requires $c\|n\|$ modular multiplications of $\|n\|$ bits if hash computations are neglected. On the other hand, our scheme with coupons is as fast as the last step in Poupard-Stern, i.e., one hash computation and one integer multiplication of $\|n\|$ bits times 160 bits. Clearly, our scheme (i.e., the online part of our signature) is more than $\|n\|$ times faster than RSA-PSS.

EASE OF IMPLEMENTATION. Most importantly, our scheme and RSA-PSS are similarly simple to implement, as they both make use of the same routines (modular exponentiation, hash functions). There is just an extra addition and integer multiplication in our scheme, and coding this remains a very simple operation.

SECURITY. On this point, both schemes are equivalent since equally tightly related to the RSA problem.

CONCLUSION. Hence, as far as the signature size is not a bottleneck, our scheme could be preferred over RSA-PSS as it allows a dramatic improvement in terms of performance for an equivalent security.

4.4   Other Signatures Based on Other Problems

As shown in the Section 3, our scheme is generic and the same technique can be applied to a large variety of signatures schemes and zero-knowledge identification protocols. The most interesting combinations seem however to be the ones where the underlying problems are the same in the two components, as in the example we proposed above where unforgeability is entirely based on the RSA problem.

There exist however other combinations that we do not explicit here, such as combining a signature scheme due to Goh and Jarecki [11], which is tightly equivalent to the Diffie-Hellman problem, with Schnorr's zero-knowledge protocol, which is a Σ-protocol proven secure under the discrete logarithm assumption. As the discrete log problem is at least as hard as the Diffie-Hellman problem, the combination of these systems gives a signature scheme tightly equivalent to the Diffie-Hellman problem, and that also supports coupons.

Another example is a combination of the Poupard-Stern Σ-protocol that we did already use in our RSA-based scheme and of the FDH-Rabin signature [23], which is a EUF-KMA signature scheme. Such a combination gives a scheme equivalent to integer factoring under a tight reduction which supports coupons as well.

We believe that other combinations of great interest are made possible with our construct.

5   Conclusion

In this paper, we proposed a new generic signature scheme constructed from a zero-knowledge identification protocol and a signature scheme. This new scheme features a tight provable security relatively to the problems which underly the security of its components. In addition to that, our scheme enjoys the appealing property of enabling the use of coupons. These two advantages were never before proposed together in a signature scheme. We also proposed an efficient application of our technique using the RSA problem which provides a high-speed alternative to RSA-PSS.

Acknowledgements

The author would like to thank his careful PhD advisor, David Pointcheval (ENS-CNRS), for teaching him so much about provable security. Many thanks also go to Marc Joye and Pascal Paillier for their attention and fruitful support in our research. Finally, the author thanks Jean-François Dhem, Philippe Proust and David Naccache.

References

1. M. Bellare and P. Rogaway. Random oracles are practical: A paradigm for designing efficient protocols. In *1st ACM Conference on Computer and Communications Security*, pp. 62–73. ACM Press, 1993.
2. M. Bellare and P. Rogaway. The exact security of digital signatures - How to sign with RSA and Rabin. In *Advances in Cryptology − EUROCRYPT '96*, vol. 1070 of *LNCS*, pp. 399–416. Springer-Verlag, 1996.

3. B. Chevallier-Mames. New signature schemes with coupons and tight reduction. Full version available from http://www.di.ens.fr/users/pointche/Chevallier-Mames.

4. J.-S. Coron. Optimal security proofs for PSS and other signature schemes. In *Advances in Cryptology − EUROCRYPT '02*, vol. 2332 of *LNCS*, pp. 272–287. Springer-Verlag, 2002.

5. R. Cramer and V. Shoup. Signature scheme based on the strong RSA assumption. Theory of Cryptography Library, 99-01, January 1999.

6. S. Even, O. Goldreich, and S. Micali. On-line/Off-line digital signatures. In *Advances in Cryptology − CRYPTO '89*, vol. 435 of *LNCS*, pp. 263–277. Springer-Verlag, 1990.

7. U. Feige, A. Fiat, and A. Shamir. Zero-knowledge proofs of identity. *Journal of Cryptology*, 1(2):77–94, 1988.

8. A. Fiat and A. Shamir. How to prove yourself: Practical solutions to identification and signature problems. In *Advances in Cryptology − Crypto '86*, vol. 263 of *LNCS*, pp. 186–194. Springer-Verlag, 1987.

9. R. Gennaro, S. Halevi, and T. Rabin. Secure hash-and-sign signatures without the random oracle. In *Advances in Cryptology − EUROCRYPT '99*, vol. 1592 of *LNCS*, pp. 123–139. Springer-Verlag, 1999.

10. M. Girault. An identity-based identification scheme based on discrete logarithms modulo a composite number. In *Advances in Cryptology − EUROCRYPT '90*, vol. 473 of *LNCS*, pp. 481–486. Springer-Verlag, 1991.

11. E.-J. Goh and S. Jarecki. A signature scheme as secure as the Diffie-Hellman problem. In *Advances in Cryptology − EUROCRYPT '03*, LNCS, pp. 401–415. Springer-Verlag, 2003.

12. S. Goldwasser, S. Micali, and R. Rivest. A "paradoxical" solution to the signature problem. In *Proceedings of the 25th FOCS*, pp. 441–448. IEEE, 1984.

13. S. Goldwasser, S. Micali, and R. Rivest. A digital signature scheme secure against adaptive chosen message attacks. *SIAM Journal of Computing*, 17(2):281–308, 1988.

14. L.C. Guillou and J.-J. Quisquater. A practical zero-knowledge protocol fitted to security processor minimizing both transmission and memory. In *Advances in Cryptology − EUROCRYPT '88*, vol. 330 of *LNCS*, pp. 123–128. Springer-Verlag, 1988.

15. H. Krawczyk and T. Rabin. Chameleon signatures. In *Symposium on Network and Distributed System Security − NDSS '00*, pp. 143–154. Internet Society, 2000.

16. G.L. Miller. Riemann's hypothesis and tests for primality. *Journal of Computer and System Sciences*, pp. 300–317, 1976.

17. A.J. Menezes, P.C. van Oorschot, and S.A. Vanstone. *Handbook of applied cryptography*. CRC Press, 1997.

18. PKCS #1 v2.1: RSA cryptography standard. RSA Laboratories, June 14, 2002.

19. D. Pointcheval and J. Stern. Security proofs for signature schemes. In *Advances in Cryptology − EUROCRYPT '96*, vol. 1070 of *LNCS*, pp. 387–398. Springer-Verlag, 1996.

20. G. Poupard and J. Stern. Security analysis of a practical "on the fly" authentication and signature generation. In *Advances in Cryptology − EUROCRYPT '98*, vol. 1403 of *LNCS*, pp. 422–436. Springer-Verlag, 1998.

21. G. Poupard and J. Stern. On the fly signatures based on factoring. *ACM Conference on Computer and Communications Security*, pp. 37–45, 1999.

22. J.-J. Quisquater and C. Couvreur. Fast decipherment algorithm for RSA public-key cryptosystem. *Electronics Letters*, 18:905–907, 1982.

23. M.O. Rabin. Digital signatures and public-key functions as intractable as factorization. Tech. Rep. MIT/LCS/TR-212, MIT Laboratory for Computer Science, 1979.

24. R.L. Rivest, A. Shamir, and L.M. Adleman. A method for obtaining digital signatures and public-key cryptosystems. *Communications of the ACM*, 21(2):120–126, 1978.

25. C.-P. Schnorr. Efficient signature generation by smart cards. *Journal of Cryptology*, 4(3):161–174, 1991.

26. A. Shamir and Y. Tauman. Improved online/offline signature schemes. In *Advances in Cryptology – CRYPTO '01*, vol. 2139 of *LNCS*, pp. 355–367. Springer-Verlag, 2001.

A   Proof of Theorem 1

Classically, we use the formalism of incremental games, starting with the real game $\mathbf{G}_0$ and ending up with $\mathbf{G}_6$. We are given a EUF-KMA-secure signature scheme $\mathcal{S}$ and a Σ-protocol $\mathcal{Z}$. The goal of our proof is to use an attacker against our scheme to solve one of the two problems $\mathcal{P}_\mathcal{Z}$ or $\mathcal{P}_\mathcal{S}$.

Game $\mathbf{G}_0$:   This is the real attack game, in the random oracle model, which includes the verification step. This means that the attack game consists in giving the public key to the adversary, as well as a full access to the signing oracle. If a forgery is output, it is checked for validity. Note that the adversary is authorized to ask q_s queries to the signing oracle, $q_\mathcal{H}$ queries to the hash oracle $\mathcal{H}$ and $q_\mathcal{G}$ queries to the hash oracle $\mathcal{G}$. We are interested in the event S_0 which occurs if the verification step succeeds (and the signature was never returned by the signing oracle).

$$\mathsf{Succ}^{\mathsf{euf-cma}}_{(\mathcal{Z},\mathcal{S})}(\mathcal{A}) = \Pr[\mathsf{S}_0]. \tag{1}$$

Game $\mathbf{G}_1$:   In this game, we simulate the hash oracle and the signing oracle, as well as the last verification step, as shown on Figure 3. From this simulation, we easily see that the game is perfectly indistinguishable from the real attack.

$$\Pr[\mathsf{S}_1] = \Pr[\mathsf{S}_0]. \tag{2}$$

Game $\mathbf{G}_2$:   In the next game, we use the $\mathcal{S}$ simulatability property. From the simulator $\mathcal{S}im$, we receive q_s pairs (r_i, σ_i) where the σ_i are valid signatures of r_i. This makes the game perfectly indistinguishable.

$$\Pr[\mathsf{S}_2] = \Pr[\mathsf{S}_1]. \tag{3}$$

Game $\mathbf{G}_3$:   In this new game, we perform the following step before running the attacker, and consequently before receiving any query from it. We generate q_s random pairs $(y_i, g_i) \in Y \times G$. Then, for each of them, we compute and store $u_i = \mathcal{W}(\alpha, g_i, y_i)$.

$\mathcal{H}$ oracle	For a hash-query $\mathcal{H}(q)$ such that $\exists h, (q,h) \in$ H-List, output h. Otherwise the output h is defined according to the following rule: ▶**Rule $\mathcal{H}^{(1)}$** Choose a random element $h \in H$. The record (q,h) is appended to H-List.
$\mathcal{G}$ oracle	For a hash-query $\mathcal{G}(q)$, such that $\exists g, (q,g) \in$ G-List, output g. Otherwise the output g is defined according to the following rule: ▶**Rule $\mathcal{G}^{(1)}$** Choose a random element $g \in G$. The record (q,g) is appended to G-List.
Sign oracle	For a sign-query $\mathbf{Sign}(m)$, we use the following rule: ▶**Rule Sign$^{(1)}$** One first generates a random $r \in R$, computes $u = \mathcal{U}(r)$ and $h = \mathcal{H}(u)$, and then computes $x = \mathrm{S}ig(d,h)$. A query to the simulation of the $\mathcal{G}$ oracle follows to obtain $g = \mathcal{G}(m,x)$. Finally one computes $y = \mathcal{V}(s,r,g)$. The output signature is then (x,y).
Verify oracle	The game ends with the verification of the output (x,y) of the adversary. One first asks to the oracle $g' = \mathcal{G}(m,x)$, then computes $u' = \mathcal{W}(\alpha, g', y)$ and $h' = \mathcal{H}(u')$. One then checks whether $\mathrm{Ver}(\beta, x, h') \overset{?}{=} \mathrm{TRUE}$, in which case the signature is a valid signature of m. Once again, it is supposed that $\mathcal{G}$ and $\mathcal{W}$ are only defined on their respective set, verifying implicitly the fact that $x \in X$ and $y \in Y$. Otherwise this test is added in the verification step.

Fig. 3. Simulation of the Attack Game.

Obviously, this maintains the game perfectly indistinguishable from the previous one:

$$\Pr[\mathsf{S}_3] = \Pr[\mathsf{S}_2]. \qquad (4)$$

Game G_4:   In this game, we change the way we simulate the $\mathcal{H}$ oracle.

▶**Rule $\mathcal{H}^{(4)}$**

  – if the query q is equal to one of the u_i, we set $h = r_i$
  – otherwise we choose a random element $h \in H \backslash \{r_i\}$ with some probability χ and $h \in \{r_i\}$ with probability $(1 - \chi)$.

  The record (q, h) is appended to H-List.

Parameter χ is chosen so that each element of H has an equal probability to be output. The evaluation of χ is not done here but trivially follows from simple considerations. As r_i are unknown to the attacker, this game is perfectly indistinguishable from the previous one.

$$\Pr[S_4] = \Pr[S_3]. \tag{5}$$

Game G_5:   In this game, we number the queries to the signature oracle with some index i. From now, we are able to sign any message, as follows:

▶**Rule Sign$^{(5)}$**

> For the i-th query, if $\mathcal{G}(m, \sigma_i)$ is already defined, the game stops. Otherwise, $((m, \sigma_i), g_i)$ is appended to G-List. Then the returned signature for message m is (σ_i, y_i).

As one may observe, the signature is valid: by definition, $\mathcal{G}(m, \sigma_i) = g_i$, $u_i = \mathcal{W}(\alpha, g_i, y_i)$, $\mathcal{H}(u_i) = r_i$ and σ_i is a valid signature of r_i.

This game is indistinguishable from the previous one, except that bad events may happen. More precisely, because σ_i can not be guessed by the attacker better than randomly (because it is the signature of a random element), the fact that $\mathcal{G}(m, \sigma_i)$ must not be defined introduces a factor $(1 - (q_\mathcal{G} + q_s)/|X|)^{q_s}$.

Hence, this game is such that:

$$\Pr[S_5] \geq \Pr[S_4] - \frac{(q_\mathcal{G} + q_s) \cdot q_s}{|X|}. \tag{6}$$

Game G_6:   This game is the final one, in which we use a forge output by the attacker. By definition, after q_h hash queries and q_s signature queries, the attacker $\mathcal{A}$ is able to output a signature $(\hat{x}, \hat{y})$ of some message $\hat{m}$ with probability ε and within time τ. If the attacker succeeds, we show how to use the forge to break one of the two computational problems. If no forge is output, the game is aborted.

First of all, we compute $\hat{g} = \mathcal{G}(\hat{m}, \hat{x})$ and $\hat{u} = \mathcal{W}(\alpha, \hat{g}, \hat{y})$. If one among these hash values was never queried by the attacker, the adequate oracles are solicited to recover its output. Using the same technique, we set $\hat{h} = \mathcal{H}(\hat{u})$. Then, we have three cases, as explained on Fig. 4.

Finally, in the three cases, this game can be used to solve one of the two supposedly intractable problems with probability

$$\Pr[S_6] \geq \Pr[S_5] - \frac{(q_\mathcal{H} + q_s)^2}{|H|} - \frac{(q_\mathcal{G} + q_s)^2}{|G|}; \cdot \tag{7}$$

Combining previous equations, one can see that

$$\varepsilon' \geq \varepsilon - \frac{(q_\mathcal{H} + q_s)^2}{|H|} - \frac{(q_\mathcal{G} + q_s)^2}{|G|} - \frac{(q_\mathcal{G} + q_s) \cdot q_s}{|X|}.$$

$\square$

Case One: In the first case, $\hat{h}$ is not an r_i. Then, $(\hat{h}, \hat{x})$ is a valid forgery against the signature scheme $\mathcal{S}$.

Case Two: In the second case, $\hat{h} = r_i$ and $\hat{x} \neq \sigma_i$ for some i. Then $(\hat{h}, \hat{x})$ is a valid forgery against the signature. Remark that this case can happen only if the signature is a probabilistic signature.

Case Three: In the last case, $\hat{h} = r_i$ and $\hat{x} = \sigma_i$ for some i. Then with overwhelming probability we have $\hat{u} = u_i$, otherwise a collision on $\mathcal{H}$ has been found. Hence, $\hat{u} = u_i$ with probability greater than $(1 - q_{\mathcal{H}}/|H|)^{q_{\mathcal{H}}}$.

By definition, we then have:

$$\hat{u} = u_i = \mathcal{W}(\alpha, g_i, y_i) = \mathcal{W}(\alpha, \hat{g}, \hat{y}) \ .$$

As one can see, we are now in the hypothesis of the Forking Lemma, *but without having to restart the attacker in any sense*, contrarily to what is usually done when using the Forking Lemma. Consequently, as $\mathcal{Z}$ is a Σ-protocol, we are able from this equality to recover the secret, as soon as $(g_i, y_i) \neq (\hat{g}, \hat{y})$.

As the forged signature is a *new* signature, we must have $(\sigma_i, m_i, y_i) \neq (\hat{x}, \hat{m}, \hat{y})$, which in this case means that $(m_i, y_i) \neq (\hat{m}, \hat{y})$.

- If $m_i = \hat{m}$, we immediately have $(g_i, y_i) \neq (\hat{g}, \hat{y})$.
- Otherwise, if $m_i \neq \hat{m}$, as $g_i = \mathcal{G}(m_i, x_i)$ and $\hat{g} = \mathcal{G}(\hat{m}, \hat{x})$, we have either $g_i \neq \hat{g}$ or a collision on $\mathcal{G}$ has been found by the attacker. This can not happen with a factor greater than $(1 - (q_{\mathcal{G}} + q_s)/|G|)^{q_{\mathcal{G}}+q_s}$.

Hence with probability $(1 - (q_{\mathcal{H}} + q_s)/|H|)^{q_{\mathcal{H}}+q_s} \cdot (1 - (q_{\mathcal{G}} + q_s)/|G|)^{q_{\mathcal{G}}+q_s}$, the second case of this final game allows to recover the secret s.

Fig. 4. Breaking problems $\mathcal{P}_{\mathcal{Z}}$ or $\mathcal{P}_{\mathcal{S}}$.

Author Index

Lecture Notes in Computer Science

For information about Vols. 1–3428

please contact your bookseller or Springer

Vol. 3486: T. Helleseth, D. Sarwate, H.-Y. Song, K. Yang (Eds.), Sequences and Their Applications - SETA 2004. XII, 451 pages. 2005.

Vol. 3483: O. Gervasi, M.L. Gavrilova, V. Kumar, A. Laganà, H.P. Lee, Y. Mun, D. Taniar, C.J.K. Tan (Eds.), Computational Science and Its Applications – ICCSA 2005, Part IV. XXVII, 1362 pages. 2005.

Vol. 3482: O. Gervasi, M.L. Gavrilova, V. Kumar, A. Laganà, H.P. Lee, Y. Mun, D. Taniar, C.J.K. Tan (Eds.), Computational Science and Its Applications – ICCSA 2005, Part III. LXVI, 1340 pages. 2005.

Vol. 3481: O. Gervasi, M.L. Gavrilova, V. Kumar, A. Laganà, H.P. Lee, Y. Mun, D. Taniar, C.J.K. Tan (Eds.), Computational Science and Its Applications – ICCSA 2005, Part II. LXIV, 1316 pages. 2005.

Vol. 3480: O. Gervasi, M.L. Gavrilova, V. Kumar, A. Laganà, H.P. Lee, Y. Mun, D. Taniar, C.J.K. Tan (Eds.), Computational Science and Its Applications – ICCSA 2005, Part I. LXV, 1234 pages. 2005.

Vol. 3479: T. Strang, C. Linnhoff-Popien (Eds.), Location- and Context-Awareness. XII, 378 pages. 2005.

Vol. 3478: C. Jermann, A. Neumaier, D. Sam (Eds.), Global Optimization and Constraint Satisfaction. XIII, 193 pages. 2005.

Vol. 3477: P. Herrmann, V. Issarny, S. Shiu (Eds.), Trust Management. XII, 426 pages. 2005.

Vol. 3475: N. Guelfi (Ed.), Rapid Integration of Software Engineering Techniques. X, 145 pages. 2005.

Vol. 3468: H.W. Gellersen, R. Want, A. Schmidt (Eds.), Pervasive Computing. XIII, 347 pages. 2005.

Vol. 3467: J. Giesl (Ed.), Term Rewriting and Applications. XIII, 517 pages. 2005.

Vol. 3465: M. Bernardo, A. Bogliolo (Eds.), Formal Methods for Mobile Computing. VII, 271 pages. 2005.

Vol. 3464: S.A. Brueckner, G.D.M. Serugendo, A. Karageorgos, R. Nagpal (Eds.), Engineering Self-Organising Systems. XIII, 299 pages. 2005. (Subseries LNAI).

Vol. 3463: M. Dal Cin, M. Kaâniche, A. Pataricza (Eds.), Dependable Computing - EDCC 2005. XVI, 472 pages. 2005.

Vol. 3462: R. Boutaba, K.C. Almeroth, R. Puigjaner, S. Shen, J.P. Black (Eds.), NETWORKING 2005. XXX, 1483 pages. 2005.

Vol. 3461: P. Urzyczyn (Ed.), Typed Lambda Calculi and Applications. XI, 433 pages. 2005.

Vol. 3460: Ö. Babaoglu, M. Jelasity, A. Montresor, C. Fetzer, S. Leonardi, A. van Moorsel, M. van Steen (Eds.), Self-star Properties in Complex Information Systems. IX, 447 pages. 2005.

Vol. 3459: R. Kimmel, N.A. Sochen, J. Weickert (Eds.), Scale Space and PDE Methods in Computer Vision. XI, 634 pages. 2005.

Vol. 3458: P. Herrero, M.S. Pérez, V. Robles (Eds.), Scientific Applications of Grid Computing. X, 208 pages. 2005.

Vol. 3456: H. Rust, Operational Semantics for Timed Systems. XII, 223 pages. 2005.

Vol. 3455: H. Treharne, S. King, M. Henson, S. Schneider (Eds.), ZB 2005: Formal Specification and Development in Z and B. XV, 493 pages. 2005.

Vol. 3454: J.-M. Jacquet, G.P. Picco (Eds.), Coordination Models and Languages. X, 299 pages. 2005.

Vol. 3453: L. Zhou, B.C. Ooi, X. Meng (Eds.), Database Systems for Advanced Applications. XXVII, 929 pages. 2005.

Vol. 3452: F. Baader, A. Voronkov (Eds.), Logic for Programming, Artificial Intelligence, and Reasoning. XI, 562 pages. 2005. (Subseries LNAI).

Vol. 3450: D. Hutter, M. Ullmann (Eds.), Security in Pervasive Computing. XI, 239 pages. 2005.

Vol. 3449: F. Rothlauf, J. Branke, S. Cagnoni, D.W. Corne, R. Drechsler, Y. Jin, P. Machado, E. Marchiori, J. Romero, G.D. Smith, G. Squillero (Eds.), Applications of Evolutionary Computing. XX, 631 pages. 2005.

Vol. 3448: G.R. Raidl, J. Gottlieb (Eds.), Evolutionary Computation in Combinatorial Optimization. XI, 271 pages. 2005.

Vol. 3447: M. Keijzer, A. Tettamanzi, P. Collet, J.v. Hemert, M. Tomassini (Eds.), Genetic Programming. XIII, 382 pages. 2005.

Vol. 3444: M. Sagiv (Ed.), Programming Languages and Systems. XIII, 439 pages. 2005.

Vol. 3443: R. Bodik (Ed.), Compiler Construction. XI, 305 pages. 2005.

Vol. 3442: M. Cerioli (Ed.), Fundamental Approaches to Software Engineering. XIII, 373 pages. 2005.

Vol. 3441: V. Sassone (Ed.), Foundations of Software Science and Computational Structures. XVIII, 521 pages. 2005.

Vol. 3440: N. Halbwachs, L.D. Zuck (Eds.), Tools and Algorithms for the Construction and Analysis of Systems. XVII, 588 pages. 2005.

Vol. 3439: R.H. Deng, F. Bao, H. Pang, J. Zhou (Eds.), Information Security Practice and Experience. XII, 424 pages. 2005.

Vol. 3438: H. Christiansen, P.R. Skadhauge, J. Villadsen (Eds.), Constraint Solving and Language Processing. VIII, 205 pages. 2005. (Subseries LNAI).

Vol. 3437: T. Gschwind, C. Mascolo (Eds.), Software Engineering and Middleware. X, 245 pages. 2005.

Vol. 3436: B. Bouyssounouse, J. Sifakis (Eds.), Embedded Systems Design. XV, 492 pages. 2005.

Vol. 3434: L. Brun, M. Vento (Eds.), Graph-Based Representations in Pattern Recognition. XII, 384 pages. 2005.

Vol. 3433: S. Bhalla (Ed.), Databases in Networked Information Systems. VII, 319 pages. 2005.

Vol. 3432: M. Beigl, P. Lukowicz (Eds.), Systems Aspects in Organic and Pervasive Computing - ARCS 2005. X, 265 pages. 2005.

Vol. 3431: C. Dovrolis (Ed.), Passive and Active Network Measurement. XII, 374 pages. 2005.

Vol. 3430: S. Tsumoto, T. Yamaguchi, M. Numao, H. Motoda (Eds.), Active Mining. XII, 349 pages. 2005. (Subseries LNAI).

Vol. 3429: E. Andres, G. Damiand, P. Lienhardt (Eds.), Discrete Geometry for Computer Imagery. X, 428 pages. 2005.